JUSTICE WITHOUT FRONTIERS: PROTECTING HUMAN RIGHTS IN THE AGE OF TECHNOLOGY

JUSTICE WITHOUT FRONTIERS:

PROTECTING HUMAN RIGHTS IN THE AGE OF TECHNOLOGY

VOLUME 2

C.G. Weeramantry

KLUWER LAW INTERNATIONAL
THE HAGUE / LONDON / BOSTON

A C.I.P. Catalogue record for this book is available from the Library of Congress.

ISBN 90-411-1098-4

Published by Kluwer Law International,
P.O. Box 85889, 2508 CN The Hague, The Netherlands.

Sold and distributed in North, Central and South America
by Kluwer Law International,
675 Massachusetts Avenue, Cambridge, MA 02139, U.S.A.

In all other countries, sold and distributed
by Kluwer Law International, Distribution Centre,
P.O. Box 322, 3300 AH Dordrecht, The Netherlands.

Printed on acid-free paper

Printed in the Netherlands

Table of Contents

Reflections

Sir Arthur C. Clarke, Kt, CBE

Lawyers, it has been said, belong to a profession that is older than Time – for who else could have created the Primeval Chaos out of which the universe emerged? Be that as it may, I was flattered when my friend, Vice-President Christopher Weeramantry of the International Court of Justice asked me to comment on Volume II of his *Justice Without Frontiers: Protecting Human Rights in the Age of Technology*.

This truly monumental work deserves a wide readership, because it is concerned with nothing less than the survival of humanity, and the necessity of making the right use of the awesome new powers that Science, and its (occasionally ugly) sister Technology have given us. Such a book is particularly appropriate now, when we are facing a danger which no earlier age could ever have imagined – the collapse of our simple-minded computers at midnight on 31st of December 1999!

The poet Robert Bridges in his *Testament of Beauty,* wrote that "Conduct lies in masterful administration of the unforeseen". Well, much of the future will always be unforeseen, but we can glimpse some of its possibilities, and by so doing, may be better prepared for them.

During the next century, our world will again be revolutionized by many technical developments. The harnessing of clean, and virtually infinite sources of energy is the most important, because it will mark the end of the Fossil Fuel Age. (Not necessarily a Good Thing – because we may *need* Global Warming! As Will Durant said many years ago, "Civilization is an interval between Ice Ages".)

The other device which will change society, perhaps out of recognition, is the 'Replicator', an inevitable development of nano-technology. This will multiply solid objects, just as the photocopier multiplies printed matter, and will thus make the production of all artefacts virtually costless.

And finally, there is the "Dream Machine" – the ultimate development of Virtual Reality. The most addictive of all inventions, this may lure millions into artificial worlds more enjoyable than the real one....

Yet I remain optimistic, if only for the reason that optimism can result in a self-fulfilling prophecy as *ditto* pessimism! So I am happy to see that Judge Weeramantry outlines many of the steps that must be taken, if we are not to follow the dinosaurs into oblivion.

The interrelationship between technology and law is one of the most important, yet most neglected facets of the impact of technology on society. This work seeks to examine this interrelationship in depth and is thus an important and constructive contribution to the better world we all desire.

Preface to Volume Two

The dangers posed to the rule of law by modern advances in science and technology are now universally perceived by lawyer and non-lawyer alike. There is indeed a feeling of deep concern that the new powers that science makes available, whether to scientists themselves, to corporate power or to the state, may well prove uncontrollable.

Since the 1970s, I have attempted to draw attention to the growing power of science and technology, and to the widening disparity between scientific power and legal controls. The addresses and writings collected in this volume, some of which date back to that period, are representative of these endeavours. They have been addressed to a variety of audiences — students, the general public, the legal profession, and various specialized groups of scientists. Some of the dangers they envisaged over twenty years ago have since materialized, sometimes in a more acute fashion than anyone might then have thought possible.

These essays are based on the general philosophy that the legal problems posed by advances in science and technology cannot be solved without more interdisciplinary interaction between the disciplines of law, philosophy, ethics, and sociology, on the one hand, and the sciences on the other. Medicine, microbiology, computer science, physics, chemistry, engineering, and the other sciences are all treading new legal and ethical ground by reason of their recent spectacular advances. If they are to serve society to their fullest capacity, they need a constant input from other disciplines. I have also pleaded for more interaction between lawyers, scientists and the general public.

The issues dealt with in this volume reach through to the core of human liberty under the rule of law, and affect every human right enshrined in international conventions and declarations.

As the trickle of legal writings upon the topic in the 1970s turns into a growing stream at the turn of the century, it is time to take stock of how far we have progressed, if at all, over the past decades, in bringing these vast new forces within the empire of the law. If humanity is to live under the rule of law in the next century, this problem needs to be urgently addressed.

I must thank Sir Arthur Clarke for the trouble he has taken to peruse this book and for his kind words regarding it. I particularly value his comments as his work has been a source of insight, inspiration and hope to all those — scientists and laymen alike — for whom the increasing dominance of technology over every facet of human life is a subject of interest and a cause of concern.

PART A

GENERAL PERSPECTIVES

1. The Tension between Scientific Power and Democratic Principles*

1. *Opening up the closed world of science*

Science has tended to become a closed enclave reserved for the experts. The expertise involved, as each branch of science increases in complexity, has made lay people willing participants in abdicating the field to the scientists — not merely the details, in respect of which they are obviously not competent, but also high policy matters involving the way of life of the community, the use of its resources and the direction of its development. These observations apply not only to science but to the technology that results from it. Together they dominate the world.

Since scientific[1] expertise is not a detached, academic specialization, but one which wields an ever-increasing volume of power over society, science tends thus to become an empire unto itself. The walls of expertise surrounding it render it a separate domain into which the lay person does not enter. Such a closed universe existing within the body politic — a universe into which the public writ does not run — raises grave issues regarding its consistency with democratic principle.

This is not often perceived by the public, and only marginally by the legal profession itself. The latter's duty of vigilance in the protection of the rule of law and of the liberties of the citizen obliges it to pay increasing attention to this significant area of erosion of the foundation of its discipline. Yet the voice of the law is scarcely heard in this all-important area.

This new dimension of power over the public is one of the most important legal and sociological phenomena of the modern age. This study will attempt very briefly to analyse its impact upon democratic principles in the light of some perspectives drawn from sociology, philosophy, and history.

* Based on a series of presentations to engineers and scientists at the Kirby Hall of Civil Rights, Lafayette College, Pennsylvania, 1985.

1 The words "science" and "scientific" are hereafter used compendiously in reference to both science and technology, unless the contrary is indicated.

We shall also observe, in the course of this inquiry, how the pursuit of science became progressively separated from the social and moral universe in which most other disciplines are grounded, thus helping it, on its onward course, towards becoming a self-contained discipline insulated from its social repercussions.

(A) A PERSPECTIVE FROM SOCIOLOGY

2. *Sociological Concerns with the Impact of Technology*

Sociology has shown more concern with the phenomenon of scientific power over society than the law. Yet in sociology itself the impact of science on society was not a systematic study until the 1930s. A major stimulus to this reawakening was the Second International Congress of the History of Science and Technology, held in London in 1931. This Congress brought into focus Marxist perspectives on the social determination and direction of knowledge. These perspectives influenced significant thinkers on the history of science and its impact on the community. Among them were an influential group of scientists at Cambridge University.[2] Some of the Cambridge scientists later helped in the 1960s to found the British Society for Social Responsibility in Science. The Society was founded rather late in the day, a generation after the notes of warning had been heard in the 1930s, and at a time when there was a general feeling that science, unrestrained by a sense of social responsibility, was careering on a course of its own, beyond the reach of moral restraint and social control.

The Congress helped to break through the insularities of the scientific establishment, showing its intimate connection with society, both in the process of formulation of apparently abstract science, and in the impact of that apparently abstract science on society. Often referred to in this context is Boris Hessen's paper at the Congress on "The Social and Economic Roots of Newton's Principia", which related even the abstractions of Newton's scientific formulations to their social and economic context.

Joseph Needham's epoch-making studies on science and technology in China provided a new perspective on the ways in which a society could live with science and technology without being mastered by it. Gunpowder, the magnetic compass and the art of printing, all of which were invented in China, and later found their way to the West, were picked out by Francis

[2] Among them were J.D. Bernal, Lancelot Hogben, and Joseph Needham.

Bacon as having "changed the appearance and state of the whole world".[3] Yet Needham showed that Chinese society and civilization could live at ease with those inventions for centuries, without being subjugated by them.[4] Chinese science had its counterparts of the West's outstanding figures in technology up to the 16th and 17th centuries, and Needham cites Chinese treatises from the 11th to the 17th centuries on such topics as horticulture, pharmacology, firearms, architecture, and horological engineering.[5] Yet all this was kept within the framework of traditional society and did not explode into an independent enterprise in its own right.

J.D. Bernal, who like Needham was influenced by the lines of thought emerging from the London Congress, made one of the first major studies of the impact of science on society and paved the way for other disciplines, including the law, to take note of this major area of social impact which was as yet unregulated by law.[6]

Mahatma Gandhi himself contributed from another perspective to the growing climate of concern about these issues. He brought into the debate the politico-philosophical considerations which loomed large in a colonial context where technology was perceived as an instrument of subjugation. Gandhi, in pronouncements which were not entirely lost on Western thinkers, predicted the ruin of civilizations depending on the values of an unbridled pursuit of science and technology.[7] Oswald Spengler argued that many of the forces now dominating the technological civilization of the West could lead to a precipitous decline of Western civilization.[8]

Among Western thinkers who were influenced by these lines of thought and pursued them further was Lewis Mumford who in several works dwelt

[3] Francis Bacon, *Novum Organum*, 1620, Book I, s. 129, E.P. Dutton & Co., 1987.

[4] See, generally, Joseph Needham, *Science and Civilization in China*, Cambridge University Press, 1954, Vols. 1–7. For a list of Chinese inventions and discoveries which entered the West and transformed Western society, see also Needham, "Science and China's Influence on the World", in Needham, *The Grand Titration*, London, Allen & Unwin, 1969, pp. 55–112. For a brief summary of Needham's conclusions, and for a comparison between Chinese and Western science, see Needham's "Mathematics and Science in China and the West", *Science and Society*, Vol. 20, 1956, pp. 320–343, reproduced in Barry Barnes (ed.), *Sociology of Science*, Penguin, 1972, pp. 21–44.

[5] Sociology of Science, op. cit., p. 28.

[6] J.D. Bernal, *The Social Function of Science*, George Routledge & Sons, London, 1939.

[7] M.K. Gandhi, *Hind Swaraj: or, Indian Home Rule*, Rev. new ed. reprinted, Navajivan, Ahmedabad, 1962; on Gandhi's debate with Nehru on this matter, see *The Collected Works of Mahatma Gandhi*, 1982, Vol. 35, pp. 469–70, and Nehru's *Selected Works*, Vol. 3, Orient Longman, 1972, pp. 13–14.

[8] Oswald Spengler, *The Decline of the West*, George Allen & Unwin, 1932.

upon the weaknesses of a culture and civilization based upon technology and the machine.[9] Ivan Illich, influenced by both Gandhi and Mumford, dealt in some depth with the ways in which industrial civilization could dehumanize society.[10] Books like Huxley's *Brave New World*[11] described a possible future where people could be tailor-made to perform different tasks in society. Around the 1960s, there was a great deal of thought about this ominous idea. It dovetailed also into theories of the regimentation of society by propaganda and other means, of which George Orwell's *1984* was one of the better known illustrations.

Despite all these perspectives, there was a continuing and conscious move to insulate science from the humanizing values. This tradition can, of course, be traced all the way back to its cardinal expositor, Francis Bacon, whose seminal works at the commencement of the seventeenth century provided the philosophical mould in which Western science has been cast ever since.[12] Yet it is significant that despite the new thinking that had emerged, it was possible as late as the 1960s for writers on science to assert, "Purpose, aesthetics, impulsiveness, ethics — these are outside the boundaries of science".[13]

Of cardinal importance to the philosophical concerns attendant on this debate is the work of Robert Merton. His work on the *Sociology of Science*[14] also links up with the Baconian perspectives just mentioned. Merton's work, which is intensely relevant to the subject of this chapter, premised an insulation of science from political life. Merton saw science as a social activity, but saw it as a process of production and accumulation of knowledge which was rational and disinterested. The scientist pursued his discipline without allegiances to one philosophy or another, one political interest or another. He lived in the world of his expertise and worked forward by a linear and inexorable process towards the advancement of knowledge in his sphere. The norms of science were critical evaluation, disinterestedness and universalism. Science was therefore value-free, objective and universalistic. The scientist pursued his work uninfluenced by external considerations. The

[9] Lewis Mumford, *The Myth of the Machine: The Pentagon of Power*, Harcourt Brace Jovanovich, New York, 1964.

[10] See I. Illich, *Deschooling Society*, Penguin, 1973.

[11] Aldous Huxley, *Brave New World*, The Vanguard Library, 1952 (1st ed. 1932).

[12] Bacon is referred to at greater length later in this Chapter.

[13] Magnus Pyke, *The Boundaries of Science*, Pelican, 1961, p. 201.

[14] R.K. Merton, *The Sociology of Science*, University of Chicago Press, Chicago, 1973. See also his article "Science and Democratic Social Structure", in R.K. Merton, *Social Theory and Social Structure* (rev. ed.), Free Press, 1967, pp. 550–561.

scientist felt justified by his achievements to such an extent as "to regard himself as independent of society and to consider science as a self-validating enterprise which was in society but not of it".[15] Merton's identification of the three important characteristics of science proved to be extremely influential.

T.S. Kuhn, however, asserted a contrary view that science is in fact an activity that is determined by factors external to itself.[16] Traditions, philosophies, historical models, all affect the work of the scientist. Questions of judgment come into play, and not merely of logic. Science is not a closed compartment within the universe of knowledge, but is part of a social whole.

The dramatic advance in the position and power of the scientist in recent years focuses attention on such discussions regarding the exclusiveness, objectivity and social detachment of science, and regarding the need to render more porous the walls which surround the scientific establishment. The scientific establishment is a vital part of society, and its work impacts heavily on society. There needs to be more interaction, more perception of social impacts, less disinterest in social and moral issues within the ranks of scientists. Without these, a so-called age of democracy would be undermined at its base, with scarcely an awareness of the resulting erosion of its central values.

This discussion will examine the expanded power and influence of the scientist and the conflict with democratic principles that results when such a source of power is insulated from interaction with the public who must play a participatory role in the policy-making processes of science.

3. *The expansion of scientific activity*

Since the end of World War II, there has been a momentous expansion, both in the amount of scientific activity and in the number of projects competing for public funds. Sir Solly Zuckerman, one of the outstanding scientific administrators of the early post-war period, pointed out in the 1960s that the scientific expenditure of Britain had increased from 1% of the Gross National Product to 2% between 1939, the year of the outbreak of war, and

[15] Merton, *Social Theory and Social Structure*, *op. cit.*, p. 551, cited also in Barry Barnes (ed.), Sociology of Science, op. cit., p. 66.

[16] T.S. Kuhn, *The Structure of Scientific Revolutions*, University of Chicago Press, Chicago, 1970.

1965, and in real terms from something like £7,000,000 to £750,000,000.[17] This scale of increase is reflected in all the major industrialized countries.

If that be the scale of the demands that are made by science for public money, the question at once poses itself: "Who is to decide between competing scientific projects in regard to the expenditure of these public funds?" In former times, the number of scientific projects competing for public attention was not so great as to denude the public resources. There were funds enough for them all. But today the number of projects has increased, the amount of money demanded by each of them has grown, and the overall total is such that not even the richest community in the world can bear that expense. It follows then that, where formerly science might have been permitted to take whatever direction it pleased, today the community must have a greater say in that expenditure. Consequently, whether one takes the view that society determines the course of science, or the opposite view, that science determines the course of society, we have reached a situation where it is quite clear that a selection must be made from among a vast number of scientific projects competing for attention. That choice belongs to the public, and viewed even from the financial angle alone, science can no longer be permitted to career uncontrolled.

Viewed in another way, we are reaching a situation which has a parallel in the world of commerce. In commerce too, the idea was prevalent in the age of *laissez-faire* that the trader could pursue the goals of expanding trade and increasing profits by any available means, without any interference by the law. Let no moral or social restraints stand in the trader's way. This prevailing philosophy of the last century could no longer hold unrestricted sway when the last frontiers were reached, when earth resources dwindled, when social iniquities commanded greater attention, and when, increasingly, the expanding enterprise could only expand at the social expense. There was no longer room for the unrestrained expansion of all, and free trade encountered a check in its hitherto unbridled career. It became necessary to recognize the community's right to place some kind of limitation upon the claim of the trader to trade without restraint. Law was slow to move to the defence of the public interest, but pressures piled up compelling it to do so.

I would submit that we have clearly reached a similar situation in science, and that its era of *laissez-faire* is spent. This necessitates an examination of the means by which the community can assert itself in this process of taking

[17] The Rickman Goodlee Lecture, delivered at University College, London — see Solly Zuckerman, *Scientists and War*, Hamish Hamilton, 1966, pp. 140, 145. In the 1990s this figure can only be assessed in tens of billions of pounds.

decisions upon scientific matters, seeing that it has no expertise whatsoever in the area of scientific speciality.

This is indeed one of the most important matters to which it becomes necessary from a practical point of view for us to address ourselves. This above all is an area where the need becomes evident for all three sections of the community — scientist, lawyer, and citizen — to act in collaboration and put their wisdom together. It is not the scientist alone who can take these decisions. The scientific vision, granted the utmost dedication to the public welfare, may still be insufficient by itself to guide the community. The lawyer cannot guide the community without the expertise of the scientist. The lawyer and the scientist together cannot guide the community, because they need feedback from the concerned citizen who is an expert in neither discipline. The nuclear debate in Austria, which I shall describe later, gives some indication of arrangements that can be made for a series of public debates involving scientists, lawyers, and lay people — a series of debates based upon the most careful examination of every aspect of the decision to be taken.

4. *Inability of Political Decision-makers to assess complex scientific questions*

Purely political decision-makers have often displayed their inability to assess complex scientific questions or to evaluate the scientific opinions involved. For example, in 1942, after a most successful year's work, the German scientists working on nuclear physics decided to hold a meeting at which to report their results, and formal invitations were sent to the highest party officials, including Göring, Himmler, Bormann, and Keitel. Still, the importance of nuclear research was so little understood by these personages that not one of them attended.[18] Likewise, on the allied side, despite the strongest opinion among the scientists that the bomb should not be used in populated areas, Sir Winston Churchill was able to write in after years:

> ... the decision whether or not to use the atomic bomb to compel the surrender of Japan was never even an issue. There was unanimous, automatic, unquestioned agreement around our table [at Potsdam]; nor did I ever hear the slightest suggestion that we should do otherwise.[19]

[18] R.W. Reid, *The Tongues of Conscience: War and the Scientist's Dilemma*, Constable, London, 1969, p. 101.

[19] W.S. Churchill, *The Second World War*, Cassell, London, 2nd ed., 1954, Vol. 6, p. 553.

Influential scientists were, however, quite concerned about this issue for a considerable time before the use of the weapon, but this message was apparently not reaching through to the highest levels of authority. These concerns have been recorded in minute detail by such writers as Robert Jungk.[20] Noted scientists such as Leo Szilard, James Franck, and Niels Bohr had been voicing these concerns. Niels Bohr, after an initial approach to President Roosevelt, did in fact have an audience with Churchill for half an hour[21], but the scientist and the statesman were apparently on different wavelengths and there was no real communication between them.

The Franck Committee on the social and political implications of the use of the bomb[22] had made the following urgent plea:

> ... the military advantages and the saving of American lives achieved by the sudden use of atomic bombs against Japan may be outweighed by the ensuing loss of confidence and by a wave of horror and repulsion sweeping over the rest of the world and perhaps even dividing public opinion at home.
>
> From this point of view, a demonstration of the new weapon might best be made, before the eyes of representatives of all the United Nations, on the desert or a barren island. The best possible atmosphere for the achievement of an international agreement could be achieved if America could say to the world, 'You see what sort of weapon we had but did not use. We are ready to renounce its use in the future if other nations join us in this renunciation and agree to the establishment of an efficient international control'.[23]

As late as 1959, Fred Hoyle, distinguished Cambridge astronomer, was able to voice the dissatisfaction of scientists with the scope afforded to them in the British political system, by making the hero of his novel, *The Black Cloud*, say:

[20] *Brighter than a Thousand Suns*, Penguin Books, 1958.

[21] Jungk, *ibid.*, p. 161.

[22] Named after James Franck, a Nobel prize-winner and one of the leading scientists who feared the use of the bomb, to whom the Pentagon recommendation that the bomb be used had been reported immediately after it took place on 31 May 1945.

[23] "A Report to the Secretary of War", in Morton Grodzins and Eugene Rabinowitch (eds.), *The Atomic Age: Scientists in National and World Affairs*, Basic Books, New York, 1963, p. 24.

> Politicians at the top, then the military, and the real brains at the bottom ... We're living in a society that contains a monstrous contradiction, modern in its technology, but archaic in its social organization ... We [scientists] do the thinking for an archaic crowd of nitwits and allow ourselves to be pushed around by 'em in the bargain.[24]

In so far as political decision-making involved the assessment of scientific data, there were thus gaping voids in the structures of power which needed to be filled.

5. *The movement of the scientist to the centre of executive power*

Into these voids in the structure of power have stepped the scientists, in their new role as decision-makers. Though their counsel may occasionally pass unheeded, their rise to this position has been so sudden and dramatic that those whose position has been taken over have not as yet grasped its full significance.

Power wielded by such figures as Lord Cherwell, who was Winston Churchill's adviser during World War II, or Sir Solly Zuckerman in later years, or of the many advisers to ministries of scientific affairs throughout the world[25] is an altogether new phenomenon in history. So, also, is the case with such figures as Professor Abdus Salaam of Imperial College, London, who was science adviser to the President of Pakistan, or India's leading nuclear scientist, Homi Bhaba, who lost his life in a plane crash in 1967. The latter was able during his lifetime, by reason of his closeness to Prime Minister Nehru, to brush aside phalanxes of New Delhi bureaucrats when he wanted to pursue a scientific project.

To appreciate this transformation in the scientist's status, it is useful to take a backward glance into history. It is true that individual scientists have at various times been close to the centre of power by reason of their special skills. Archimedes, for example, in the government of King Hiero of Syracuse, Aristotle in the time of Alexander the Great, Leonardo da Vinci in the court of Ludovico Sforza, or Tycho Brahe at the court of Holy Roman Emperor, Rudolph II, are a few examples. There were also exceptional cases of scientists like Benjamin Franklin and Thomas Jefferson being at the centre of power, but this was because they were statesmen in their own right, and not due to their connections with science. The position of the scientist in

24 *The Black Cloud*, New American Library, New York, 1959, p. 87.

25 See *Science and Society*, Stephen and Hilary Rose, Allen Lane, The Penguin Press, London, 1969, p. xii.

society down till well into the 20th century was basically one of non-recognition in political decision-making.

Science as a discipline was, likewise, insufficiently valued. When James Smithson, the British chemist, left the United States half a million dollars for founding a scientific institution, so little was its potential understood that Congress delayed sixteen years before creating the Smithsonian Institute.[26] Indeed, in England even the awarding of scientific degrees, as proposed many years earlier by the Royal Society, was retarded owing to objections raised by Oxford and Cambridge, and the systematic teaching of science did not commence until well into the nineteenth century. Socially, the scientist ranked so modestly that when a bishop was paid £10,000 a year, and a general £3,000 a year, Faraday's official salary at the Royal Institution was £200.[27]

The importance of the scientist as decision-maker is in fact a product of the World Wars, and up to the First World War, the value of the scientist was so little realized that both sides were guilty of a prolific waste of scientific talent in the trenches.

This is well revealed in a notable correspondence kept up across the line of battle between Rutherford in England and Geiger, then a brilliant young physicist serving in the German army. This correspondence[28] indicates the extent to which both sides committed their most promising scientific men to actual battle, regardless of the tremendous loss to science, and shows how many of these men in fact died in battle. In particular, the death at the Dardanelles on the British side of H.G.J. Moseley, one of the most talented and promising young British physicists, awakened both sides to the short-sightedness of such a waste of scientific manpower. Even toward the end of the First World War, scientists in England still felt that they had as yet not received sufficient recognition of their importance in society, and formed the

26 A. Hunter Dupree, *Science in the Federal Government*, Cambridge, Mass., 1957.

27 Rose and Rose, *Science and Society, supra*, p. 33. The same authors point out, on the basis of a 1961 London University research thesis by M. Pike, that when the income necessary to maintain a middle-class life was £200–£1,000 per annum, a chemist's starting salary was £25 per annum.

28 "I expect I shall be in the field again in about a fortnight. I think nearly everyone of my colleagues whom you know is in the field. Dr. Rumelin (also Reinganum and Glatzel) fell in one of the first months of the year. W.H. Schmidt is also dead; but from what I have heard, he must have been in a very bad and hopeless condition all last year and so it was perhaps the best for him. I sometimes hear from Professor Hahn who seems to stand the dangers of war very well and is apparently happy in his military position. Dr. Schrader is in the field artillery and is quite well up ..." [A.S. Eve, *Rutherford: Being the Life and Letters of the Rt. Hon. Lord Rutherford*, Cambridge University Press, 1939, p. 245. See *The Tongues of Conscience*, R.W. Reid, Constable, London, 1969, pp. 37–38.]

National Union of Scientific Workers (N.U.S.W.), urging that Science did not occupy its proper place in the national life because scientific workers did not exercise in the political and industrial world an influence commensurate with their importance.

A factor contributing powerfully to the rise in the influence of scientists was Germany's total inability to continue the war beyond the end of 1916 but for the work of two chemists. After supplies from Chile, the chief source of nitrate salts, had been cut off in 1914, through the annihilation of Admiral Graf von Spee's squadron at the Falkland Islands, an alternative method of supply was vital for national survival. The discovery by Fritz Haber of a method of ammonia synthesis, and by Wilhelm Ostwald of a method of conversion of ammonia to nitric acid, supplied Germany with the nitrating agents essential for the manufacture of explosives.

Events such as these brought home the truth that scientists were being placed in a singularly responsible position in society.

> It was also emerging that scientists could no longer expect to throw the responsibilities for the applications of their work on to politicians or on to soldiers, since such was the shape their work was taking, soon only they would be in a position to fully understand its significance and its practical consequences for mankind.[29]

This tendency was of course accentuated during the Second World War, and on both sides one sees scientific advances assuming such importance that decisions regarding their use required to be made at a level no less than that of the supreme authority in the State. The production of the V-weapons on the German side, and of the atomic bomb on the American, are among the more obvious illustrations.

It became patently clear at any rate by the conclusion of the war, that scientists must necessarily be drawn into the highest levels of decision-making, in cases where the problem involved was of a complex scientific nature and its likely impact on society was immense. The growing complexities of technology in the years succeeding the second World War only served to entrench the scientists' position.

To add to their strength, computers have become so important in the running of modern states that all government affairs of any importance came within their purview. They have acquired an expertise which those at the helm of affairs have perforce to depend on to such an extent that it could well be said, "The computer men have fingers literally on the buttons of

[29] R.W. Reid, *Tongues of Conscience, supra*, p. 45.

power. If they were sufficiently united among themselves, it would be very hard, in a highly computerized state, to keep them under control".[30]

B) A PERSPECTIVE FROM PHILOSOPHY

6. *The influence of Francis Bacon*

Prior to Francis Bacon, Western scientific inquiry often went hand in hand with religion and philosophy. For example, Albertus Magnus [*circa* 1200–1280], a key personality in the early history of Western science, was both a theologian and a scientist. Robert Grosseteste of Lincoln [1175–1253], an outstanding figure in the natural history of his time, Roger Bacon [1220–1292], a noted experimental scientist who antedated his more famous namesake Francis Bacon by three and a half centuries, Raymond Lully of Catalonia [1235–1316], the scientific school of Chartres, and many other instances can be quoted of the pursuit of scientific research within the framework of an overarching philosophical and religious vision of the place of nature and natural phenomena within the universal order. Experimental science and scholastic philosophy, with all its ethical concerns, were intertwined.

The later delinking of Western science from philosophy and the moral order unleashed it to pursue a highroad to power, unhindered by societal or scholastic restraint. That detachment, of which some early signs began to appear in the 14th century, was made definitive and was given its philosophical base by Francis Bacon [1561–1626].

The advent of science to its present position of power and its resulting conflicts with democratic principles can be traced conceptually through three important developments in the history of knowledge — the union of knowledge with power, the separation of power from ethics, and the unrestrained pursuit of power over man and nature. These are considered in the next succeeding sections and, significantly, a key figure in each of them was Francis Bacon.

Bacon, a lawyer, has probably exercised more influence over the rise to power of modern science than any scientist. A Lord Chancellor whose rectitude was much in question, he was yet a towering intellectual figure in the history of the organization of scientific knowledge. He could indeed be described as the philosopher *par excellence* of the resurgence of Western sci-

[30] Nigel Calder, *Technopolis: Social Control of the Uses of Science*, Simon & Schuster, New York, 1970, p. 313.

ence.[31] His *Novum Organum* has operated down the centuries as a sort of charter of scientific liberty, clearing the scientist's way of the debris of accumulated religious beliefs and philosophical restraints.[32]

Whether one examines the phenomenon of modern scientific power from the perspectives of Washington, Moscow or New Delhi, he stands out as a seminal figure, and the politics of modern science cannot be understood apart from him.

The universality of Bacon's thinking is dramatically portrayed by Nigel Calder in a striking passage:

> The ghost of Sir Francis Bacon must shiver o'nights, because he walks most frequently in Moscow. Sometimes, to be sure, he may be spotted on Pennsylvania Avenue, flitting into the Executive Office Building, or by his beloved Thames on Millbank, summoned there by some self-confident planner of discovery and invention. You may run into him, disconcertingly, among the bungalows of New Delhi, or glimpse his reflection in the lake at Canberra. But a bleak Moscow day, with the citizens queuing in their boots and the huge television tower swaying in the gale, is the easiest time to see him, if not near the Gorky Street science office, then out in the Academy territory along the Leninsky Prospekt. For Karl Marx, who was uncommonly hard to please, praised that Lord High Chancellor of England and a lot of people have never got over it.[33]

7. *The union of knowledge with power*

Bacon identified knowledge with power.

[31] On Bacon's work, generally, see Benjamin Farrington, *Francis Bacon: Philosopher of Industrial Science*, Macmillan, London, 1973. A concise and comprehensive recent account of Bacon's impact on modern science is Jatinder K. Bajaj's "Francis Bacon, the First Philosopher of Modern Science", in Ashis Nandy (ed.), *Science, Hegemony and Violence: A Requiem for Modernity*, UNU and OUP, 2nd ed., 1990, pp. 24–67.

[32] It is interesting to reflect that Bacon's devotion to the method of seeking truth through experimental research was such that he met his death by trying to perform such an experiment. Driving in his coach one winter's day, and seeing snow and ice all around him, he decided to check on freezing as a method for preservation of food for later use. He dismounted from his coach to conduct this experiment. Through his zeal for science, he unfortunately contracted a chill which brought about his death.

[33] Nigel Calder, *Technopolis, supra*, p. 68.

> There is a most intricate connection between the ways of human power and human knowledge ... and that which is most useful in practice is most correct in theory.[34]

Here is a most complete theoretical union of the three concepts of knowledge power and utility. Fairness or unfairness, good or evil, justice and injustice — all these idols had now been tossed out. The human intellect could zero in on the target of power and utility, unhindered by such cloudiness of thought. Since knowledge had been freed of ethics and knowledge had been identified with power, power also had been freed of ethics, and humanity was now free to pursue power and utility, liberated from the fetters that had held it back in many other civilizations. Chinese civilization, for example, had held back science when its destructive power, as in gunpowder, became self-evident.[35] Hindu civilization had held back science when its destructiveness exceeded the bounds of humanity,[36] even laying down rules of war which respected the integrity of the natural order and prohibited the use of hyperdestructive weapons which went beyond the purposes of war.[37] Islamic civilization, while encouraging the pursuit of knowledge,[38] had recognized that there were two routes to the acquisition of knowledge which could coexist in harmony with each other — the route of human inquiry and the route of divine revelation.

Islamic science, during the eighth and eleventh centuries, though far richer in its development than anything seen in Christian Europe at the time, always functioned within a world view based on the spiritual significance of nature, linked as it was with the sacred character of God's creation.[39]

[34] *Novum Organum*, II.4.

[35] See Joseph Needham, *Science and Civilization in China*, *supra*, Vol. 2, pp. 518–83 *et seq*.

[36] See Nagendra Singh, "The Distinguishable Characteristics of the Concept of the Law as it Developed in Ancient India", in *Liber Amicorum for the Right Honourable Lord Wilberforce*, 1987, p. 93.

[37] The relevant passage of *The Ramayana* is *Yuddha Kanda (Sloka)*, VIII.39. See, also, *Mahabharatha*, *Udyog Parva*, 194.12, cited in Nagendra Singh, "The Distinguishable Characteristics of the Concept of Law as it Developed in Ancient India", *op. cit.*, p. 93.

[38] See the author's *Islamic Jurisprudence: Some International Perspectives*, Macmillan, London, and St. Martin's Press, New York, 1988, pp. 94 *et seq*.

[39] For a more recent comparison between Islamic science and Western science, see Seyyed Hossein Nasr, "Islamic Science, Western Science: Common Heritage, Diverse Destinies", in Ziauddin Sardar (ed.), *The Revenge of Athena: Science, Exploitation and the Third World*, Mansell Publishing Ltd., London and New York, 1988, p. 239. See, also, this author's *Islamic Jurisprudence: Some International Perspectives, supra*.

Bacon thus cleared the way for a science based on power rather than contemplative wisdom, and propelled the advance of Western science to its present freedom from the restraints imposed by spiritual or philosophical concerns.

8. *The separation of power from ethics*

In his *Novum Organum*, Bacon derided the "corruption" of mixing natural philosophy with faith and religion.[40] Natural phenomena had to be observed and studied for what they were. The method for doing so was also laid down in the *Novum Organum*. Orderly arrangement of data as obtained by observation and experimentation was the first step.[41] Axioms were to be derived from this data, which were to be kept under further observation and experimentation. This was the proper scientific method.

Religion and faith and morals had nothing to do with this process. Bacon scoffed at "cobwebs of learning, admirable indeed for the fineness of thread, but of no substance or profit".[42] There must be no extraneous interference in the orderly movement from the particular to the general. Religion, faith, and morals all tend to be obstructions along this road, interfering with the methodical transition which was the essence of the new prescription which he was forging. Philosophers like Aristotle had gone along the road of empirical observation before, but he accused even Aristotle of an inclination to introduce metaphysical considerations into the process of pure observation.

There is a wide array of false beliefs and unproved assumptions that obstruct this path. They must all be dismissed. They comprise a vast number of influences upon the process of judgment which he categorizes under the picturesque heads of Idols of the Tribe, Idols of the Den, Idols of the Market, and Idols of the Theatre. The first group in this famous categorization are frailties of perception inherent in human nature and the human race. These frailties, like uneven mirrors, distort the reflection of reality.[43] Idols of the Den derive *inter alia* from each individual's peculiarities of mind and body, education and habit and accident.[44] Idols of the Market result from intercourse with others, with all the interferences "which have entwined themselves round the understanding from the associations of words".[45] Idols of

40 I.65.

41 *Ibid.*, I.100–7.

42 *Advancement of Learning*, Bk. I, Preface, p. 45.

43 *Novum Organum*, I, 41.

44 *Ibid.*, I, 53.

45 *Ibid.*, I, 59.

the Theatre "have crept into men's minds from the various dogmas of peculiar systems of philosophy". As in plays, these have created fictions and theatrical worlds of make-believe.[46]

Thus is the pursuit of human knowledge obstructed, and his philosophy was aimed at clearing the road. In the result, he bequeathed to future scientific inquiry the principle, which has now become a tradition, of brushing aside ethical considerations in the pursuit of knowledge.

9. *The unrestrained pursuit of power over man and nature*

One of the basic postulates of the Baconian approach to science was that science should generate power. It should be useful. In this respect it was an early antecedent of utilitarianism — the measure of its worth was its utility, free of the cloudiness of moralistic philosophizing.

Since knowledge is power and power must not be useless, but must be put to service, his *Advancement of Learning* offered a blueprint for the organization of knowledge in the service of power. He invoked the precedent of Alexander placing vast resources at the service of his friend Aristotle, for the organization of his scientific research. The wielders of power in the State should take control of the new knowledge and put its power to their service. Science, freed of superstition, morality, theology and philosophy was thus to become an instrument in the hands of power — a frightening anticipation of the anti-democratic potentialities of science against which we need to protect ourselves.

The new power that science was to acquire under Baconian philosophy was envisaged as an increased power over nature — a sentiment in direct opposition to the Chinese philosophy of respect for nature and of going along with nature rather than attempting to tame or subdue it. But every species of power over nature becomes also a species of power over human beings, and Bacon was too much of a pragmatist not to have realized this. Indeed, his answer to the malevolent use of scientific power was that the same could be said of every worldly good, talent or strength. It needed to be regulated in its possessor by right reason and (strangely enough) by true religion.[47]

This Baconian philosophy and defence against the misuse of power are the very arguments which defenders of the integrity of today's scientific establishment advance against all attempts at external interference and control.

[46] *Ibid.*, I, 44.
[47] *Ibid.*, I, 129.

Bacon consolidated his vision of science as a new source of power in the hands of the sovereign and, through him, of the people, in his *New Atlantis*, which paints a picture of the new Utopia for the age of science. The scientific fraternity, a privileged group of elite, was to bring their powers over nature to the service of the State.[48] The assumption was that this power would not be misused. The concept of checks and balances, so fundamental to democratic thought, was totally absent. Modern science has followed this track ever since. It is time to wrench it out of this Baconian mould.

While Bacon was the seminal figure in the divorce of science from morality, there were various other movements and individuals which contributed to the final result.

The mechanistic view of the universe, which pictured it as functioning rigidly like clockwork on the basis of set physical rules, resulted from the work of Galileo [1564–1642], and continued through the eighteenth century philosophers of the Enlightenment, to the work of Newton and Descartes. The certainty of Newton's laws gave strength to the mechanistic view of a master builder who, having set the universe in motion, allowed the physical laws He had ordained to govern it with the minimum of intervention on the part of the author. Descartes' sharp separation of mind from matter supported a dualistic world view in which the material world and the world of thought and emotion functioned in watertight compartments.

Various superstructures and embellishments were thus added by various thinkers to the independent structure of modern science, but the philosophical foundations on which its absolutism is based were firmly laid by Francis Bacon.

10. *The linkage between scientific positivism and legal positivism*

These thoughts regarding the isolation of science and the scientific community from their social context prompt a thought regarding a possible interlinkage between the disciplines of law and science. In a work dealing with law and science, it would not be proper to pass it by, as it can be of immense significance.

The concentration of modern science upon its objective methodology and its divorce from all subjective elements has resulted in what an eminent observer of the scientific scene, Edmund Husserl, has described as "The

[48] In this scientific Utopia, Bacon did indeed lay down a code of ethical and social responsibility for scientists, but this was within the overall context of science being used to advance the interests of the State.

Crisis of European Sciences".[49] Husserl argues that by adopting the objectivist-positivist attitude, science considers as irrelevant to its pursuit of objective truth such questions as the "reason" or the "meaning" of the world. This results in what he describes as a feeling of "distress" in all the sciences regarding their meaning. Hence the crisis in European sciences which have virtually lost their way.

A parallel in the field of law is the philosophy of extreme positivism which pursues an objectivist analysis of law as it is stated in the books, divorced from its social context and from the law as it operates in the field. In fact extreme legal positivism models itself on the objectivist-positivist approach of modern science, from which it derives no little inspiration. Such extreme positivism in law stimulated the emergence, as a corrective, of a sociological school of jurisprudence which aimed at relating law to its social context in much the same manner as the philosophers of science were stimulated into relating scientific endeavour to its social context.

This is possibly an important point of interlinkage between the philosophy of science and the philosophy of law. Especially in 19th century Europe, law tended to pursue the goals of certainty and precision on the model of scientific certainty and precision. That approach was *de rigueur* in the field of exact scholarship. In fact, philosophers of law were fond of speaking of legal studies as the *science* of law. With all the striking achievements of scientific method as proof of its virtues, the methods of Western science commended themselves to philosophers, teachers and practitioners of law. It is fascinating to think of positivist philosophers of law such as John Austin, and the generations of Western lawyers who were influenced by his philosophy, as direct lineal successors of Francis Bacon — not Francis Bacon the Lord Chancellor, but Francis Bacon the philosopher of science, the philosopher who set this discipline on a course of its own, detached from the social milieu of which it formed a part.

According to some philosophers, Western law is in crisis by reason of its disrelation to social realities.[50] The causes discerned by Husserl for the Crisis of European Sciences may well have relevance to the context of legal "science" as well.

[49] Edmund Husserl, *The Crisis of European Sciences and Transcendental Phenomenology*, David Carr (tr.), Evanston, North Western University, 1970.

[50] See, also, on this aspect this author's *The Law in Crisis: Bridges of Understanding*, Capemoss, London, 1975.

C) A PERSPECTIVE FROM HISTORY

11. *The conflict between science and authority*

Control and restraint there must then be, but at what point and in what manner and to what degree? It would be useful at this point to take a brief look at this historic conflict.

It is possible to trace the conflict through distinct stages, in which authority triumphed, a compromise was reached and, finally authority capitulated and left the field to science. It is in this last stage we find ourselves now.

(a) Phase I — The triumph of authority

In the earliest stage of this conflict, the clergy saw in science a threat to the hold they had on people's minds. The doctrine of revealed truth and scientific knowledge were uneasy bedfellows, and since the doctrine of revealed truth had powerful sanctions to back it, it became a potent instrument for placing a curb on science. The clergy could pour ridicule on scientists,[51] or otherwise use their vast resources to bring them into disrepute.

Another method used was social ostracism. The mystic sanctions of religion were invoked to place scientific knowledge within the category of the black arts and, in the result, the borderline between science, on the one hand, and witchcraft and magic, on the other, became extremely blurred.

One has only to read any historical novel cast in times prior to the fourteenth century to see how deep was the social ostracism to which scientists were subjected. Alchemy, astronomy, astrology, witchcraft, sorcery, were all tarred with the same brush, and their exponents received no quarter from either Church or State. The fact that most scientific knowledge filtered

[51] Lactantius, one of the prominent early writers of the Church, discoursed in this fashion on the question of gravity: "Is it possible that man can be so absurd as to believe that there are crops and trees on the other side of the earth, that hang downward and that men have their feet higher than their heads? If you ask them how they defend these monstrosities, why things do not fall away from the earth on that side, they reply that the nature of things is such that heavy bodies tend toward the centre like the spokes of a wheel, while light bodies, as clouds, smoke and fire, tend from the centre to the heavens on all sides. Now I am really at a loss what to say of those who, when they have once gone wrong, steadily persevere in their folly and defend one absurd opinion by another." (John M. Zane, *The Story of Law*, Gaunt, 1996 (1927), p. 202.)

through from heathen Spain, whither science had arrived with the great waves of Mohammedan conquest, helped also to keep up this antagonism.[52]

The extent of the authoritarian reaction against scientific inquiry is well illustrated by Bertrand Russell when he compares the reactions of their respective societies to the work of Aristarchus of Samos and of Copernicus.[53] Aristarchus of Samos, as early as the third century, had propounded a theory very similar to that formulated by Copernicus, and had worked out a theoretically correct method of estimating the distances of the sun and the moon. He suffered neither prosecution nor persecution. By the sixteenth century, however, when Copernicus propounded the same theories as Aristarchus, the impact of his ideas on society was too great to be disregarded, and a tremendous commotion resulted.

In this first stage, then, the contest between authority and science was thus an unequal one and the day was with authority.

(b) Phase II — the reconciliation between science and authority

In due time, however, the Renaissance, with its broadened vision, induced a more enlightened attitude towards scientific knowledge and reduced to some extent the antagonism that had prevailed between authority and science. Following hard on its heels was Francis Bacon, whose influence we have examined.

An important philosophical breakthrough which helped phenomenally in liberating science from the stranglehold of religion was the earlier work of Ibn Rushd (Averroes) [1126–1198], the philosopher of Islamic Spain, which was adopted by the Averroists at the University of Paris and later found its way into the mainstream of European thought through the thinking of Thomas Aquinas and others. The Arabian philosopher had found the same problem in relation to knowledge revealed by human reason as his Christian counterparts, for in both religions the view had long prevailed that divine revelation was the only route to legitimate truth. Averroes taught that just as truth was revealed to humans through revelation, it could also be revealed through human reason. This doctrine of "double truth" sought to eliminate conflicts between theological truth and scientific truth on the basis that knowledge could not be at war with itself, since scientific knowledge was,

[52] The Universities of Cordoba, Seville, and other Spanish centres were to a large extent the source whence mediaeval Europe drew its little knowledge of chemistry, physics, and medicine; and, indeed, it was through Muslim Spain and through Arabic translations that even the works of Aristotle first reached the Western Christian world. See Julius Stone, *Human Law and Human Justice*, Stanford University Press, Stanford, California, 1965, pp. 46–51.

[53] Bertrand Russell, *Human Knowledge: Its Scope and Limits*, 1948, p. 25.

like theological knowledge, but a sub-department of knowledge in its totality. In Christian terms, one could render unto Caesar the things that were Caesar's without affecting the performance of one's duties to God. So, also, a loyalty to scientific truth could co-exist with a loyalty to theological truth, without any clash of loyalties. This attitude helped greatly to free science from the taint of association with the powers of darkness, with necromancy, and a possible pact with the devil. The Faust legend still persisted but science could now come into the open without the fear that it was arousing any conflict between itself and the revealed beliefs of humanity.

Moreover, on all hands the spirit of enquiry began to unearth new facts so stubborn that no dogmas could prevail against them. The mariner's compass, the invention of gunpowder, the establishment of the printing press — these were no academic matters, but had the profoundest impact upon society. The discovery of America was a fact to be accepted, though it upset the settled ideas of the time. Science was no longer a matter of individual interest, but was of social concern.

The forces of tradition nevertheless did not give up the struggle without a rear guard action. The trial of Galileo for heresy was only three centuries ago, and it rather shocks us that the leading scientist of the day should, so long after the New Learning was abroad, have been threatened with torture by a Church court until he recanted his proposition that the earth moves around the sun and not the sun around the earth. But still, the intellectual climate had changed. Scientists were able to claim and demonstrate that the truths they discovered need in no way unsettle the fundamental beliefs of Christianity.

It was at this stage that a powerful impetus was given to the progress of science by the work of Bacon, through whose teaching science could make out that its goal was the maximization of power over nature. Hence science could lead to wealth and abundance for the community, or to use his words, "the relief of man's estate". It was no longer an ally of the powers of darkness.

By the close of the seventeenth century, the new attitude was well established, and science progressed apace, meeting with only slender impediments to its progress. It appeared indeed that the old controversy was now at rest.

(c) Phase III — The triumph of science

The third phase opens with Darwin's *Origin of Species*,[54] which set off an explosion and once more drove science and religion into a head-on clash with each other. No doubt, by this time religion was not synonymous with authority, as it had been some centuries earlier, but established religion was still a very live force, with which authority aligned itself.

The controversy sparked off by Darwin's work re-echoed through the fields of the human intellect, until a working arrangement was restored again, largely through the realization that the word of Scripture did not necessarily have to be understood in a literal sense. It took time for people to adjust themselves to this attitude, and to adopt as a truism the view that the world did not commence in 4004 BC. The conflict, once resolved, died down and science began a forward march which has been unimpeded and unrestricted since.

There are, of course, notable exceptions in times much nearer our own. The Nazi discouragement of the teachings of Jewish scientists such as Freud and Einstein, and the burning on 10 May 1933 of 25,000 volumes of Jewish authors at the University of Berlin is one example. A quaint American example was the prosecution in 1925 of a Tennessee teacher named John Thomas Scopes for violation of a statute making it unlawful to teach any theory denying the method of divine creation as taught in the Bible.[55] Apart from such atrocities and aberrations, however, it was quite undeniable that the barriers were down, as far as science was concerned.

It has since marched into the territories even of the liberal disciplines annexing large spheres of influence in the process. Of history, for example, Toynbee says, that:

> Science had set itself to annex, with varying degrees of success, sundry provinces of the domain originally left to the historians — such provinces as, for example, those of anthropology, economics, sociology, and psychology. In the dwindling remainder of their territory, on which an ever-advancing Science had not yet set foot, the historians continued to pursue their 'fact-finding' activities undisturbed.[56]

[54] Charles Darwin, *The Origin of Species by Means of Natural Selection, or the Preservation of the Favoured Races in the Struggle for Life*, 1859, (Arden, 1982).

[55] See Jerry R. Tompkins (ed.), *D-Days at Dayton: Reflections on the Scopes Trial*, Louisiana State University Press, Baton Rouge, 1965.

[56] Arnold J. Toynbee, *A Study of History*, Abridgement of Vols. VII–X, by D.C. Somerville, Oxford University Press, 1960, pp. 265–266.

What Toynbee says of history, applies to other disciplines as well, and the sphere of law is indeed no exception.

It seems indeed that science will, unless the law takes note, now meet with no further checks or restraints. The scientist is thus well on the way to being the master of the world, and all legal and authoritarian restraints in the way of this triumphal progress seem to be ineffectual.

12. *The unpredictability of scientific progress*

It is no argument against planning that scientific progress has been unpredictable in the past. We all know how there has been a tremendous unpredictable spin-off of hundreds of inventions, useful in daily life, from the work of scientists engaged in space and atomic research.[57] We all know that research upon electricity can for example yield unexpected results in the field of cancer research, and that the laser, invented by physicists, was taken over by eye surgeons to detach retinas. There is also the unforeseeable element of chance, as when Sir Alexander Fleming, although he had been at work for twenty years searching for an antibiotic substance, may well have ended without success if he had not left his window open to a penicillium spore which floated on to his bacterial preparation. It is true also that no one, not even the scientists, can forecast the direction research will take ten, twenty, or thirty years from now. Rutherford, whose basic work helped produce the atom bomb, was so off the mark in relation to the results of his work as to believe in 1933 that "anyone who looks for a source of power in the transformation of atoms is talking moonshine".[58]

[57] Professor H.H. Bolotin of Melbourne University, reporting on the Nuclear and Particle Physics Conference held at the University on May 14–18, 1973 (*The Age*, 4/6/1973), observed that "esoteric ivory tower" research has led, and continues to lead, to a flood of revolutionary developments in other fields, and to a succession of new dramatic breakthroughs in areas of important down-to-earth practical benefits to our everyday lives.

"A listener, hearing these many spin-offs from nuclear physics research discussed, could now very well associate a conference of nuclear and particle physicists with the latest developments in such areas as the diagnosis and treatment of cancer, nutrition, the possible start of a new 'green revolution', the age of the Earth and the Moon, methods for the discovery of valuable ore deposits, establishing new forms of criminal evidence, research in air and water pollution, the production of better welding rods for industry, fundamental studies of the mechanism of tooth decay, glaciology, early diagnosis of certain diseases, blood deficiencies, pacemakers for regulating damaged hearts, discovery of art forgeries, and a host of other analytical tools and methods of great importance in industry, health, the environment, etc., etc.

The list is so long as to be considered limitless."

[58] Stephen and Hilary Rose, *Science and Society, supra*, p. 3.

Granted all this unpredictability, we must still recognize that we are past the stage when the argument of possible unforeseen benefits could be used to stifle scientific planning. The world can no longer afford the luxury of unplanned science merely in the expectation of surprise dividends. Whether we accept the traditional view that science progresses inexorably in an orderly way irrespective of social trends, or the Marxist view of science and society which asserts that society determines the trend of scientific development,[59] it is clear that science is now advancing upon so many fronts that we cannot afford the sheer cost of an unplanned advance in all directions.

Moreover, having regard to the speed of advancement of science, there is great urgency about this work. Indeed, the very unpredictability of scientific progress is a reason for taking stock of the situation now, as the French Government did by setting up a "Commission de 1985", and the American Academy of Arts and Sciences by creating its "Commission on the Year 2000".[60] President Kennedy, in speaking to the National Academy of Sciences in 1963, recalled in this connection the story of the famous French Marshal Lyautey, who said to his gardener, "Plant a tree tomorrow". The gardener said, "It won't bear fruit for a hundred years". "In that case", said Lyautey, "plant it this afternoon". "That is how I feel about your work," said Kennedy to the scientists.

The same considerations apply to the need to take stock of the direction of science in our age.

D) SCIENTIFIC POWER AND DEMOCRATIC PRINCIPLES

13. *The undermining of basic assumptions of democratic government*

Two basic assumptions underlying traditional democratic government — the intelligibility of problems to people of average ability and the competence of

[59] As, for example, when the industrial revolution necessitated improvements in the generation and conservation of power, and in effect pressed technology to advance in this field, or when the Egyptians, in building their pyramids, produced such mathematical advances in mensuration as the discovery by an unknown Egyptian of about 1850 B.C. of a correct formula for the volume of a frustum of a truncated square pyramid, or when the Babylonians, for the needs of their religion, developed astronomy so as to predict the movement of heavenly bodies.

[60] Erich Jantsch, in a report to the Organisation for Economic Co-operation and Development (OECD) in 1967, estimated that American industry was spending 60–65 million dollars a year on technological forecasting. Erich Jantsch, *Technological Forecasting in Perspective: A Framework for Technological Forecasting, its Technique and Organization* (1967).

legislative processes to handle them — are both endangered by the rise to power of science and the scientist.[61] Democracy functions on the assumption that the people or their representatives have the information and the understanding necessary to form a judgment on the matter. Further, such understanding and theoretical competence are totally unavailing unless the will of the people, as expressed through the legislature, can be enforced over all sections of the community, however powerful. In the sphere of scientific power, both these assumptions are eroded.

> The scientific revolution is undermining the first of these assumptions by posing problems too technical for laymen to fathom. It is undermining the second by making it impossible for legislatures to lay the foundation for the future. The result is already evident: we either have to invent new procedures for handling science policy or be ruled by technology.[62]

It is evident that the particular choice of a scientific or technological project may well determine the pattern of a country's economic and social developments for many years. The decision therefore carries important political implications, but the people's representatives may in practice be shut out from the decision-making by reason of sheer lack of expertise.

Where formerly science and technology could follow any course they pleased, and the necessary social and economic re-structuring of society followed, it is clear then that in the future the process may well need to be reversed.

> We must decide *first* what society wants and needs — then tailor our technology to help where it can. We cannot any longer let technology run rampant and structure our social environment because of a planning vacuum.[63]

We have already referred to some of the literature which drew attention to the dangers to society of science careering unchecked, such as Aldous Huxley's *Brave New World*, George Orwell's *1984*, and Oswald Spengler's *Decline of the West*. There were, on the other hand, certain optimistic estimates

61 See Harvey Wheeler, "Bringing Science under Law", (1971) *Dialogue*, Vol. IV, No. 1, 104, at 106. See also the author's *Law: The Threatened Peripheries*, Lake House, 1984, pp. 111–113.

62 *Ibid.*

63 Congressman Emilio K. Daddario, Chairman of the U.S. Congress Sub-committee on Science Research Development, of the House Committee on Science and Aeronautics, in "Technology Assessment — A Legislative View", (1967–68) 36 *George Washington Law Review*, 1044.

such as Kahn and Wiener's *The Year 2000*[64] which provided an extremely hopeful framework for speculation for the next thirty years.

However the notes of warning came in thick and fast in the 1970s as more detailed studies were undertaken. In particular the Club of Rome study, *The Limits to Growth*,[65] predicted a dire future for humanity if the present rate of scientific damage to the environment proceeded without controls. It was based upon a mass of scientific data carefully collected and meticulously analysed. From other angles, Paul Ehrlich's *The Population Bomb*[66] and Forester's *World Dynamics*[67] painted frightening scenarios of what might be lying in store for humanity at current rates of progress, fuelled by advances in technology.

All of this reinforced the dire prediction of Bertrand Russell made on his ninetieth birthday in May 1962, to the effect that unless something drastic was done, under the leadership or through the inspiration of the scientific world, the human race would rush to its destruction, like the Gadarene swine, in blind ignorance of the fate which scientific skill had prepared for it.

A scientific establishment wielding its power without the restraints that democracy attaches to power was being increasingly perceived as one of the major dangers threatening civilization.

14. *A closed empire of power within the body politic*

Sufficient has been said already to show that the scientific establishment represents a vast empire of power. Bacon's adage that knowledge is power highlights the creation of a centre of power within the body politic, influencing the lives of citizens in every way. Yet it is closed to the public, not by legal decree but by the walls of its expertise. For the reason that it has not been formally closed, the closure escapes detection and protest. Little has been said or done to draw attention to it.

The traditional arms of state power — legislature, executive and judiciary — tend to leave it alone. The public likewise — the ultimate source of power — tend to pass it by. It tends thus to flourish, free of the controls which democracy has devised to restrain all other varieties of power.

64 Herman Kahn and Anthony J. Wiener, *The Year 2000*, Macmillan, New York, 1967.

65 D.H. Meadows *et al*, *The Limits to Growth*, Signet Books, 1972, pp. 92–93.

66 Paul R. Ehrlich, *The Population Bomb*, Ballantine Books, New York, 1968.

67 Jay W. Forester, *World Dynamics*, Wright-Allen Press, Cambridge, Mass., 2nd ed., 1973.

Notwithstanding the fact that in many jurisdictions there are attempts today to render scientific activity accountable to the public, there is a tendency for other principles to reign within the scientific establishment.

Within this closed empire, other principles reign than those which are axiomatic in democratic theory. Among these are the following:

(a) there is a total absence of accountability to the public who are affected to the last detail of their lives by the activities and decisions taken in the realm of science;

(b) the obligation to disclose relevant information does not exist. The channels of information are closed;

(c) the moral restraints that normally accompany the use of power, and which democratic processes can assert in a variety of ways, are unknown;

(d) alliances are made with other power centres such as corporate might, with no consultation whatever with those who are most affected;

(e) although knowledge is power and modern science is a vast source of power, this knowledge is treated as private property, thus making power over the body politic a matter of private property;

(f) in alliance with corporate might, further screens of invisibility are imposed between the power wielders and those most affected, for multiple corporate registrations often render impossible the location of the actual author of an act damaging the public interest which emanates from the corporation. Individual accountability is thus negated;

(g) with the alliance with corporate might, control of a particular technology can pass out of the power of a country where it is applied, to another country, the capital of the corporation concerned. From that centre, the strings of scientific power are controlled, without the possibility of control from within the country where the technology is applied;

(h) the entrenchment of knowledge as private property through the registration of patents creates a climate of opinion which regards intellectual property as sacrosanct. Not only its use, but also its abuse, then comes to be regarded as free of public control;

(i) with special reference to the developing world, scientific power becomes in practice free of control, for technology, in combination with corporate power, lays down its terms from a position of unassailable strength. The country desperately needing the technology has no alternative but to accept it on the terms offered, however undemocratic or contrary to human rights. Some of these aspects are discussed elsewhere in this book. This has become a significant cause of tension between the developed and developing worlds.

15. Legislative incompetence in the face of scientific complexity

It is an axiom of democracy that a legislature, representative of the people's will, should have the competence and the ability to prescribe the contours for the exercise of power within the state. We have seen that the power that flows from scientific knowledge is so large as to affect the lives of every individual in the community. In accordance with basic democratic principle, such knowledge would require to be controlled by the representatives of the people. But the new technology is so complex as to place it beyond the reach of the legislators and the legislator's traditional advisers.

Moreover, in practice, most legislators and administrators tend to be persons with liberal, rather than scientific, backgrounds. For example, in 1965, when the British press, after the general election of that year, hailed the advent to Parliament of a large number of intellectual young men, it was found that only one of them, a physicist from Manchester, was a scientific research worker.[68] Little wonder that governments feel the weakening grip of the legislature over matters of science and technology, and that President Eisenhower found it necessary in 1961 to issue his famous warning, "that public policy could itself become the captive of a scientific-technological elite".[69] The more relatively incompetent will legislators be, the more technology grows in complexity. And the growth rate of technology is an unending source of wonder[70].

[68] Nigel Calder, *Technopolis, supra*, p. 7

[69] Farewell Radio and Television Address to the American People, *Pub. Papers*, 1039 (Jan. 17, 1961).

[70] The growth rate of scientific information is so rapid as to provoke some bizarre statistics. It has been estimated that the present rate of increase of publications, if maintained, will mean that in a hundred years the combined weight of scientific journals will exceed that of the earth! [See Rose and Rose, *Science and Society*, Allen Lane, The Penguin Press, London, 1969, p. xv.] So, also, the numbers of active scientists have been doubling every 10–20 years over the last 300 years, a growth rate which, if maintained, will exceed the population of the earth in a hundred years! [See D.J. de Solla Price, *Discovery*, Vol. 17, 1956.] The growth rate of the physical power produced by science has likewise been estimated to increase in geometrical progression as science grows more abstract. [See Henry Adams, *The Degradation of the Democratic Dogma*, Putnam, 1958 (1919).]

Since actual power is passing out of the hands of those who have traditionally wielded power into the hands of the scientists themselves, they are being transformed from experts confined to their skills in laboratories into decision-makers. The decisions requiring to be made include, firstly, the allocation of funds between research and other state needs and secondly, a decision between competing research projects. Each of these decisions involves the expenditure of millions of dollars of public money, and when the scientist enters the discussion, there is none that can parley with him on equal terms. Nor, when the choice is once made and money committed to it, can the reins be held back if the adverse results to society begin to manifest themselves.

Indeed, the scientists' control over such decisions is so complete that they seem able to push them through even in the face of objections that seem compelling. Nearly a billion dollars were spent in America in developing a nuclear powered aircraft, despite the absence of means to prevent the contamination of the countryside in the event of a crash. Expenditure exceeding a hundred million dollars was nearly incurred on the famous Mohole project (to sink a hole into the mantle of the earth, right through the earth's crust), because "earth scientists" sought to steal a little of the thunder of space scientists by pressing for investigation of the earth's "backyard" before probing into outer space. The immense and unknown pressures such an operation might release did not apparently stand in the way of the plan.

16. *Judicial inadequacies in the face of scientific complexity*

This aspect is dealt with in greater detail in Chapter 2.

17. *Disproof of the belief that science and democratic values are invariably complementary*

There was another and more disturbing lesson emerging from the Second World War. Time was when it was believed that science could only flourish in an atmosphere of intellectual freedom and therefore only in a liberal democracy. Indeed, there was a belief that science and democracy complemented each other. Each concept was believed to depend on the free exchange of thoughts and views, and the one no less than the other was assumed to have as its objective the good of society. The notion implicit in works like George Orwell's *1984*, that science did not necessarily tend to complement democracy, but might be the instrument of its very negation, had scarcely penetrated the popular consciousness.

The authoritative disproof of the belief that science needed an atmosphere of freedom if it were to flourish was furnished by the macabre happenings in the Nazi concentration camps. Here was an awful demonstration that the most acute scientific research was possible under conditions of complete regimentation. The Nuremberg Trials revealed the use of living human beings as guinea pigs for scientific experiments, and a total disregard by the scientists of an enlightened country for all those values of human personality which had taken centuries to develop. As the concentration camps yielded up their dark secrets after the war, the world was shaken to know of the facility with which scientists lent themselves to a callous book-keeping system in which human beings were no more than ciphers, and the object of the exercise was to wipe out rather than increase the balance in hand.

More disturbing still was the realization that the perpetrators of the crimes in the concentration camps included persons belonging to the medical profession — the one branch of science which professed an ethical code to which its members were sworn.[71] What dangers might there be where the scientist in question was not already subject to an ethical code, and where he professed no loyalties to values other than the pursuit of science itself? Could not chemists defoliate the countryside, poison the rivers and pollute the seas, physicists cause irreversible chain reactions, and engineers perfect ever more excruciating weapons of death? Problems posed by socially harmful activities of this nature could well present themselves even outside a framework of regimentation and compulsion.

The very Utopias of modern science fiction seem permeated with what even a Marxist scientist like J.D. Bernal describes as "a lack of freedom consequent on perfect organization".[72] Likewise, Max Weber, one of the most outstanding figures in sociology, foresaw that the rationalization of the world implicit in modern science would lead to a "disenchantment of the world",[73] and to an impersonal and inhuman bureaucracy.

[71] "Under the Nazi regime in Germany, nearly 200 doctors, some of them eminent in the world of medicine, took part in experiments on Jews and Russians and Polish prisoners. Thousands of other physicians knew of these experiments, some of which were the subject of lectures at medical academies. Yet the records show that the doctors sat through medical reports of the infliction of horrible injuries on these 'lesser races' and then proceeded to discuss the medical lessons to be learned from them without anyone making even a mild protest about the nature of the experiments." (Peter Singer, *Animal Liberation*, Random House, N.Y., 1975, pp. 29–30.

[72] J.D. Bernal, *The Social Function of Science*, *supra*, p. 381.

[73] H.H. Gerth and C.W. Mills, *From Max Weber*, Routledge & Kegan Paul West, London, 1948, pp. 129 ff.

Science, formerly the ally and handmaiden of democracy, was now appearing in the malefic guise of an ally and henchman of tyranny.

E) THE HEIGHTENING OF PARTICIPATION

18. *Impracticability of existing methods of public participation*

What attempts there have been to draw the public directly into the decision-making process have only illustrated the impracticability of existing methods of direct participation. This is well illustrated by the "Torrey Canyon" affair in England and the fluoridization question in the United States.

After the grounding of the "Torrey Canyon", the whole coastal area of Cornwall and Brittany was polluted with floating oil. When a special cabinet sub-committee, chaired by Sir Solly Zuckerman, announced that it would receive suggestions from the public, the Committee was snowed under with so many solutions that they could scarcely all be considered. An interesting footnote to the episode was that, with all this multiplicity of advisers, the eventual decision — to spray the oil with detergent with a view to sinking it — is thought to have killed more marine life than the oil itself would have done. The introduction of fluoride into water to prevent tooth decay was heavily resisted in the United States by large numbers of persons on the basis that the daily ingestion of fluoride, which in practice would thus become compulsory, would result in health hazards, the full extent of which was not yet known. This apparently simple question required several hundred referenda in the United States since 1950[74] and still opinion was inconclusive.

The illustrations we have mentioned are two instances in which the public has become emotionally involved in a scientific issue. In the majority of scientific decisions, however, it is not possible to generate such a degree of interest, and we are not likely to have the degree of public involvement manifested in great issues of the past such as slavery and free trade, which had a direct relationship to the life and emotions of the individual citizen.[75] Meaning much to citizens in personal terms, they permitted individuals to identify themselves passionately with these issues. The arguments for and against were intelligible, and the individual could approve or disapprove of the reasoning adduced in support of either view.

[74] There were over 900 up to 1966 — U.S. Public Health Service, Fluoridation Census 342, 3rd ed., 1966.

[75] See Hans Morgenthau, "Modern Science and Political Power", (1964) 64 *Colum. L.Rev.*, 1386 at 1404.

Most scientific decision-making, though as important to the individual's life, does not however induce in him or her any sense of involvement, and the arguments one way or another are in general uninteresting to the lay public. In scientific decisions, moreover, far from the reasons being made available, a great degree of secrecy generally accompanies decision. So much is such decision-making a closed-door operation, that the scientists of one government department may even preserve secrecy from those of another, upon a matter which interests them both. Morgenthau[76] relates how, when in 1957 the Army and Air Force competed in the development of ballistic missiles, each service withheld information from the other. When Air Force General Schriever visited the Army installations, he was, apparently, not allowed to be accompanied by the head of the Air Force program. Far less is the average citizen permitted any awareness of what goes on.

In the result, he or she is not only unwilling, but unable to participate in the great decisions of our time.

19. *Stepping up the level of citizen participation*

It would be useful to illustrate possible methods of generating a lay input into scientific discussion by recounting some particulars concerning the Austrian nuclear debate. Whereas in 1971 there was hardly any opposition to the first nuclear power station, by the Spring of 1975, 60,000 signatures had been collected against the construction of further plants. At that stage the Government decided to halt all further commitments till it knew more about the positions of the scientists, the lawyers and the public, and planned a campaign in three phases. The first, Part A, was a stage where an inter-ministerial committee went into all the relevant materials and produced a catalogue of 91 questions with liberty to add more. Once these crucial questions were determined, 10 working groups of experts were set up with six or seven scientists in each, chosen to represent both points of view. These committees balanced the arguments and prepared a report. The last stage of that first phase provided for public debates in halls seating 600 to 1,200 people, and with extensive media coverage. A concluding report was then produced setting out the questions on which a consensus had been reached, and questions on which debate must continue. The second phase began when the clarified issues were presented at extensive public debates which were again covered by the media, and a report was then made of all the important conclusions of that debate. The third stage was the stage of parliamentary debate. All this had been conceived on the basis that it was

[76] *Ibid.*, at 1397.

essential that there be more democracy in decisions affecting technology, and a greater transparency in regard to the way in which those decisions were reached.[77]

With such models before us, there are indeed several steps that may be conceived towards increasing lay interaction with scientific activity.

One of these is to give increased strength to citizens' committees, which are already an active instrumentality attempting to restrain some damaging activities of scientists and technologists. In the first place, it is essential that they should be invested with a recognized legal status which will enable them to pursue a matter of public interest in their own right.[78] Committees which have demonstrated their interest in social issues should qualify for such recognition and should, moreover, be given positive incentives towards building up their strength. Subsidies from the State in regard to such activities, income tax relief, and campaigns to build up membership and educate the public on particular issues are other means by which they can be assisted. A party playing the devil's advocate must have both a recognized status and a well prepared brief.

It is also essential to their discharge of such a function that more information should be made available to an interested and enlightened public. The Freedom of Information Act in America[79] seems to point to a means by which the present tendency to withhold information from the public can be curbed.[80] Likewise, scientists and other specialists working on projects likely to have important effects upon the community need to be encouraged to publicize the results of their research. Where alternative means of reaching the desired result are available, the public would thus become aware of the alternatives, whereas under present procedures it often becomes aware of possible alternatives only after the decision has been taken.

Though such committees have in recent years had impressive records, particularly in such fields as pollution and consumer protection, they lack funds, personnel and continuity of action, for citizen activity often tends to be sporadic. Moreover, there is often a lack of co-ordination between different societies pursuing the same ends. To add to all this, their activities gener-

[77] For these details, see *Austria Today, A Quarterly Review of Trends and Events*, Vol. II, Autumn/Winter, 1976, p. 19.

[78] See the reference in the next chapter ("The Tension between Scientific Power and the Law") to the Sierra Club's failure before the courts to establish its status regarding a move to halt a commercial development in the Yosemite National Park.

[79] 5 U.S.C. 552.

[80] Even in this field, however, there are obstacles despite the Act, as was evidenced in *Soucie* v. *Doubridge*, 448 F. 2d. 1067 (D.C. Cir. 1971), where the report to the President of the Office of Science and Technology on the S.S.T. was withheld from conservationists.

ally commence at a stage when heavy commitments to a given project have already taken place, in the shape of manpower and expenditure. Such societies should aim at taking action before the project is too firmly established to be easily dislodged, and this means that greater opportunities should be made available to them to receive information from official sources about lines of research which are in hand, even before the research reaches the stage of technology.

It is to be remembered that citizens' groups campaigning in relation to some major project are often pitted against deeply entrenched and well organized vested interests. The resources and staying power of the latter are far greater than those of the citizens' groups. Active encouragement of those groups should therefore be considered a matter of public policy.

Before a scientific idea reaches society in practical form, it must progress through three stages of development. It must progress, broadly speaking, from basic principles to applied science, from applied science to technological development, and from technological development to production and practical use. Any system of control, if it is to be effective, must be capable of applying pressure at all or any of these points. It is essential therefore that these committees should be kept sufficiently informed of scientific research to be able to prevent harmful technology, at the stage of transformation of science into technology, or at the earlier stage when pure science moves on into applied science.

Other bodies to which society can turn are public agencies such as Environmental Protection Councils, which are vested by the State itself with power and responsibility in this technical sphere. These agencies must cease to be a series of disparate bodies, as they are now, lacking overall policies to guide them. They must also enjoy complete independence from political or economic controls if their decisions are to be completely free of extraneous pressure.

20. *Stepping up the level of expert participation*

One of their prime weaknesses is that the experts, on whose opinions the lay public relies, are probably persons already deeply involved in the type of scientific activity in question; and a detached and independent decision, which might even call a halt to the type of activity from which their careers have grown, may be too much to expect from them.[81] In any event, their

[81] See Michael S. Baram, "Social Control of Science and Technology", in 172 *Science, the Journal of the American Association for the Advancement of Sciences* (1971) No. 3983, 535 at 537.

concentration on the technical aspects of their work may probably cloud their vision of the social perspectives against which the problem must be viewed. It is necessary that the experts whose advice is sought should have sufficient protections to be able to grow out of the feeling that their continued employment depends upon the nature of their advice.

A greater reliance by public interest bodies on what may be described as "the trained amateur" is also to be desired. This group would consist of advisers who are not scientists, but persons whose training has equipped them with a more refined ability than the average layman possesses, of discrimination between alternative lines of scientific policy and direction. The key to this is inter-disciplinary education which must become more generally available at tertiary institutions.

Another aspect worth pursuing is to build up a participatory system of decision-making in which decisions are taken jointly by the experts, who know the facts, and the people, on whom ultimately the decision will operate. To attain this, decisions likely to affect the community should, it is suggested, be the subject of public debate in which the technical knowledge of the expert and the values of the community would equally enter into the discussion. The debate could well be carried over public media such as television.

21. *Stepping up the level of bureaucratic interaction with science*

It is important to reinforce the top ranks of governmental administration with a quota of scientific experts who will give the necessary expert advice to those charged with policy making and the implementation of decisions. Their effectiveness will of course be limited by the presence of many other factors, essentially economic and political, which might underlie decisions that have to be made. Nevertheless, such advisers can serve a most useful purpose if their functions do not end with mere advice, but involve the setting out of arguments for and against a proposed decision. This document should be made public, with copies available from the office in question to any citizen who seeks it.

Yet again, the creation of an arm of government, invested with the responsibility of co-ordinating scientific research and policy, would have the advantage that research upon morally indefensible lines may be questioned or subjected to the necessary scrutiny. The difficulty inherent in such a scheme is the lack of technical skill of the bureaucrat. The problems involved are of such a complex nature that the bureaucrats of any government would find themselves out of their depth in attempting to regulate the scientists in their respective technical fields. Far less would this task be within the competence of the legislators or elected ministers. This is another pointer to the need for inter-disciplinary education which we have referred to earlier.

A science-oriented committee of high-ranking bureaucrats who have sufficient personal interest in this area could also be assembled. Meeting regularly and on a voluntary basis, they could routinely survey scientific activities in their ministries, examining them for their moral and ethical implications, and issuing reports on these matters, for further consideration by the appropriate authorities.

22. *Legislative Restructuring*

Much of the legislation of the future will be science-oriented, or at least have some interface area with technology. Most legislatures of the world, as presently structured, do not have a built-in scientific resource for consultation regarding legislation which involves the use of technology in a manner which may have social implications. Nor do most legislators have the necessary background of scientific expertise to comprehend fully the implications of science-related legislation.

In the result, many legislators tend to be overly susceptible to the influence of lobbyists, who give them a scientific perspective from the standpoint of those who wish to promote the legislation, or those who wish to oppose it. Lobby groups are very powerful and have great resources at their command which can rarely be matched by the expertise available to individual legislators.

An in-house repository of scientific expertise could be useful in this regard, so that legislators would be able to obtain a disinterested opinion in relation to proposed legislation before the lobbyists get to work. Also, it may be possible for lawmakers with a scientific training to pool their resources and give the House the benefit of their own expertise, when such matters come up for discussion.

Even more importantly, impact-assessment boards should be set up to which legislation can be referred which will make an impact upon society and upon human rights. Such impact-assessment boards or technology-assessment boards, as they are commonly called, would need to be interdisciplinary, and it would help legislators if a given piece of legislation is cleared with this board before it passes into law.

Another source of guidance on these matters would be provided by the creation of centres in each country for the study of scientific policy. Each country would know its particular technological needs and the likely impact of a given technology upon its society and environment. It would help greatly if such studies could be made prior to the passing of legislation, rather than to delay them until legislation has passed into law and then becomes difficult to alter.

23. *Continuing education programmes*[82]

Taking this idea into the realm of continuing education, it will be important to give thought to the organization of a series of workshops where lawyers and scientists interact on these issues. In the biomedical field, this is already happening, but there is not much evidence of similar movements in regard to other fields of science.

The idea should also be considered of the establishment of institutions for the study of humanistic science,[83] with an emphasis on those branches of science pertaining to life and the life sciences. A prototype of this kind of institution is the Mitsubishi Kasei Institute of Life Sciences in Tokyo, which emphasizes the humanistic aspects of science and promotes cross-disciplinary and public understanding of the interrelationship between science and society. Major technological enterprises, as also governments, could take the initiative in this regard.

Another important step is the orientation of lawyers towards the problem of the impact of technology on human rights. It would be useful if organizations of lawyers, who traditionally set up sub-committees dealing with different aspects of their activities, should be alerted to the need to set up a special committee of the bar of each country to review the ongoing relationship between technology and human rights in that country, and to alert the community of any possible dangers. The American Bar Association's Standing Committee on Law and Technology, and its quarterly journal, *The Jurimetrics Journal*, could be used as a prototype for such efforts.

If a serious effort is to be mounted to preserve communities from the adverse effects of technology upon their human rights, it is a vital need that technology and human rights education should go hand in hand. Training young people in technology is by itself insufficient. Along with that training, there must also be a requisite input of human rights education, enabling them to see the interrelationship between technology and human rights, with particular reference to their own societies.

It is important that, at the vocational colleges, institutes of technology and universities, courses on technology should be supplemented with the relevant human rights perspectives. Most courses in the sciences do not currently contain a segment on human rights.

[82] See further Chapter 4 below on "Legal Education for the Age of Technology".

[83] See Chapter 24 below.

Human rights are important, not merely from the standpoint of attuning the minds of decision-makers to the human rights nuances of their decisions on science and technology. Human rights become relevant also in the sense of the right of access to information that bears upon this technology. Very often, the technical information essential to a proper decision regarding the use of a product is not easily available. This is sometimes so even in regard to the decision-maker himself, because a wall of secrecy relating to the impact of that technology comes between the decision-maker and his decision. A classic instance of the withholding of technical information relating to a given product is the withholding of scientific information relating to the adverse impact of tobacco smoking. This scientific information was kept away from consumers for many years. This illustration will indicate how important it is, in connection with science and technology, that there be a well recognized right of access to the relevant information.

If decision-makers are often kept away from relevant information, it is quite evident how easily the actual consumer can be denied the relevant scientific information relating to the product he or she is invited to use. It is vital that those in charge of decisions relating to science and technology should insist on a free flow of the requisite technological information to the prospective users of the product, be they industrialists or the humble farmer in the field. It is only through such a free flow of information that the community would eventually have a guarantee that the proper decision has been made in regard to the acceptance or otherwise of a given technology.

24. *An Ombudsman for Science*

Another desirable improvement is that every worker engaged in scientific research should have access to some central authority, should there be any manner of complaint in regard to the research he or she is called upon by his or her employers to perform. A worker suffering from qualms of conscience at his or her work assignment should be at liberty to make representations setting out the substance of this complaint or inquiring to what overall purpose the work is to be directed. A mechanism to this end is an ombudsman functioning as an agency geared and empowered to receive and review complaints against the acts of officialdom. So, likewise, should there be an ombudsman in the realm of science, geared and empowered to receive and review complaints against the wielders of scientific power.[84]

[84] See Harvey Wheeler, "Bringing Science under Law", (1971) 4 *Dialogue*, No. 1, at p. 112.

The right of scientists who object on moral grounds to a project or to the work they are called upon to do requires also the formulation of a code by this authority. This Code would embody not only a set of ethical principles, but also provisions relating to the rights of scientists, to raise matters of conscience, and the procedures by which they could do so. The Code would also have provisions relating to enforcement. All of this is part of the new Jurisprudence for Science which may well emerge, comparable to that which has been developed for administrative law, and comparable to what the Press Council is developing to guide the conduct of the press.

25. *Technical Hazards Boards*

Even with legislative machinery as it stands at present, a step urgently needing to be taken is the formation of what has been described as a Technical Hazards Board which may appear before the legislature as a lobbyist against schemes involving potential risks.[85] Public servants with the requisite scientific background would be employed as full-time researchers into these problems, and would make their expertise available to the legislature. Such a body must not base its activities upon the mere submission of a report to the legislature, but should have a right of audience to press its views. It is too well known that reports, however carefully prepared, are often not even read by members of the legislatures who eventually take decisions upon them.

At a higher level, it is necessary also that concern for these issues should seep into the highest legislatures and emerge as statutes laying down guidelines for planners and administrative agencies, such as has occurred in America in the National Environment Policy Act.[86]

Among the immediate advantages resulting from such statutory measures are the habits of inter-disciplinary consultations which the new legislation

[85] See Michael Wollen, "Controlling the Hazards: Technology Assessment and the Law", 36 *Geo. Wash. L. Rev.*, 1105, 1136 (1968).

[86] 42 U.S.C. 4531 *et seq.* See review by R.C. Peterson of Yale Law School, Title I of National Environment Policy Act of 1969, available from the Environmental Law Institute, 1346 Connecticut Ave, N.W., Washington, D.C. Among the directives so laid down are that federal agencies in their policies, recommendations, and other major actions affecting environmental quality should include a detailed statement on (i) the environmental impact of the proposed action, (ii) any adverse environmental effect which cannot be avoided, should the proposal be implemented, (iii) alternatives to the proposed action, (iv) the relationship between ... short-term uses ... and long-term productivity, and (v) any irreversible and irretrievable commitments of resources which would be involved. They are also required to study, develop and describe appropriate alternatives.

will inculcate and the generation of information which, in association with the Freedom of Information Act, will then be available to the public.[87]

All these suggestions, useful in themselves, do not however provide a complete answer.

What seems to be required above all is an authority vested with supervisory and advisory functions covering the whole field of scientific research.

Indeed, it has been suggested that an organization on the pattern of a bicameral legislature could be set up for this purpose, the two houses being composed of scientists and laymen respectively.[88]

The mechanisms of representation upon this controlling body can of course be worked out in greater detail once suggestions for this purpose take shape, but if the civilian authority of the law loses its grip upon the problem at this vital stage, it may be lost for ever. Failing such awareness and remedial action, it would before long be true to say that mankind no longer lives under the rule of law, but under the rule of science — a dismal prospect more than one great jurist has foreshadowed.

The need for such a two-tiered representative authority is underlined by the fact that there is need for a pooling of resources in both the scientific and the non-scientific aspects of decision-making.

26. *A Supra-national Advisory Board*

In its ultimate stage since all such regulation by one country may well be defeated by the uncontrolled activities of another in the same field, it becomes desirable that the international community should combine in a supranational organization which will, in matters of great importance, lay down policy guidelines, transcending narrow national boundaries. It will make evaluations of major technology, having regard to the welfare of the world community and of future generations. It will draw attention to moral considerations as and when they arise. It will liaise with the United Nations with which it will have consultative status.

Those who are inclined to the view that supra-national controls are unworkable should remind themselves of the fact that organizations such as the World Health Organisation have been able to girdle the globe with a network of regulations which operate effectively from Dar-es-Salaam to Rio de Janeiro.

[87] See Baram, *supra*, p. 538.

[88] See Harvey Wheeler, "Bringing Science under Law", *supra*, pp. 112–3.

27. *Conclusion*

The matters discussed in this chapter and the suggestions made are but a representative sampling from the enormous slate of issues which demand discussion. Every community needs to be alerted to the intricate interrelationship between advancing technology and human rights. Decision-makers and professionals, in particular, need to be sensitized to this problem and to have it very much in mind when called upon to make decisions, directly or indirectly, involving a technological element. All too often decisions are made with a complete lack of awareness of the interlinkages which are the subject of this chapter.

This discussion will have shown that science is an important source of power affecting the public and that it would be contrary to basic democratic assumptions that such a source of power should function in isolation from the public. It will have shown the importance of lay participation in major matters involving the impact of science on society, and indicated some ways in which this can be achieved.

There are indeed other concentrations of power in modern society which are not amenable to the ordinary processes of democratic control. Major corporate conglomerates are one, and the media are another. Moreover, there is an element of interdependence between the scientific establishment and each of these sources of power. However, the presence of such other sources of violation of democratic principle does not justify an unquestioning acceptance of another.

Society and lifestyles are altering fast and we are moving into a science-dominated age. It is essential that we no longer sweep under the carpet, especially in the academic world, the problems outlined in this discussion. They need to be addressed by all who are concerned with justice. This makes it the very special concern of the legal profession and of those who are now in training to join that profession.

As we move into the next century, every citizen will live increasingly under the dominance of science. Unless these problems are addressed now, they may well be uncontrollable, and technology would reign uncontrolled even in areas where it nullifies important human rights. The price of freedom, it is said, is eternal vigilance. Here is an area where special vigilance is demanded, for the threats it poses are often unseen. They must be detected and addressed in time, and will not be so addressed except by communities alerted to the presence of dangers surpassing in power and pervasiveness any that have been encountered in the long annals of the law.

2. The Tension between Scientific Power and Law*

The previous chapter examined some incompatibilities between the present state of the scientific enterprise and the principles of democracy. This chapter will examine some of the incompatibilities between the present state of the scientific enterprise and the law itself.

In the context of accelerating progress in all the sciences, we shall look at the inadequacies of traditional legal concepts, structures and techniques in handling the scientific revolution which is dominating our age. To what extent do time-honoured legal principles have to yield in the face of new technology? I shall submit that it is particularly important that there should be an increasing interchange of ideas between the scientific community and the legal community, for it seems impossible that problems of this magnitude can be handled by either of those groups alone.

Whatever views I may express are not intended in any way to derogate from the lustre of the scientific achievement. While we must necessarily regard with immense admiration the dedication, skill, and expertise of the scientific profession, it seems self-evident that the whole scientific enterprise does not exist out of, nor is it exempt from, the society of which it forms a part. As a constituent part of society, it is subject to the laws governing that society. If it seems to be racing beyond the reach of those laws, that is a matter for urgent consideration by the community of lawyers.

1. NEW WINE IN OLD BOTTLES: ADVANCING SCIENCE AND OUTMODED LAW

Technology is a new source of power. It gives to those who command it a means of control over other members of society, which is in many ways more fundamental and far-reaching than any known before in the long history of humanity. It gives more control over the human environment, human

* Several of the issues discussed in this chapter were addressed in a public lecture titled "Will Law Retreat before Science?", delivered by the author at the Indian Law Institute, New Delhi, in January 1978, and published thereafter in *Law: The Threatened Peripheries*, *op. cit.*, pp. 109–132.

society, the human body and the human mind than was possible to the most powerful potentates of the past. It follows that this new dimension of power, like all other dimensions of power, must be subject to law. However, so fast has been the progress of technology that law and lawyers have been late in responding to the new challenge, by which time the new technologies had already raced ahead, well nigh out of legal control. When at last the lawyers got down to the task, it was only to find that legal structures, legal procedures and legal concepts were scarcely geared to face the new challenges thus confronting the law. All of these had been fashioned to meet the needs of a time when power meant largely physical power, when trespass meant largely physical trespass, when assault meant largely physical assault. Science had undermined such basic assumptions, but the apparatus of the law remained anchored to its ancient framework.

Parallel to this growth of technology has been the growth of the corporate empires which own them. Since sophisticated technology is expensive and needs great wealth to generate and control it, the vast business corporations of today tend to become its proprietors. Those corporations, whose financial power in many instances exceeds that of many a nation State, give technology an added dimension of power — the combination of technological and economic strength. Together they represent a phalanx of power which is well beyond the ability of the individual to resist.

Yet another dimension to this phalanx of power is the alliance that has been forged between technology, economic power and the military establishment. Technology, at its highest levels, becomes invaluable for purposes of war and, consequently, strikes an alliance with the military establishment in many countries. Each helps and sustains the other, for the military need the improved weapons that technology can devise and the technologists need the political and economic support that come from the military establishment. In the result, we are faced with the phenomenon of the military-industrial complex, regarding whose growing power over society President Eisenhower warned the American people, in his farewell speech.[1] The world is facing globally the dangers that Eisenhower spoke of in a domestic context.

Law is the community's bastion of protection against power. Its moral strength lies in its availability and competence to control and handle the most powerful forces in any society. The scientific revolution, by creating a force of hitherto unparalleled power within civil society which the law may be unable to control, is undermining the basic authority of the law.

1 Farewell Radio and Television Address to the American People, *Pub. Papers*, 1039 (Jan. 17, 1961).

The situation of danger is upon us and we still do not give adequate thought to preventive measures. Long before these dangers were apparent, however, some thinkers foresaw them with remarkable prescience and warned against them. Outstanding among them was the historian Henry Adams whose famous *Letter to American Teachers of History*, published in 1910, should have been an epoch-making document, but left his contemporaries quite unshaken.[2] In an earlier letter, in 1905, Adams wrote that:

> it is quite sure according to my score of ratios and curves that, at the accelerated rate of progress since 1600, it will not need another century or half century to turn that [the prevailing ratios of power] upside down. *Law in that case would disappear as theory or* a priori *principle and give place to force. ... Explosives would reach cosmic violence.* Disintegration would overcome integration.[3]

Adams' prediction of the malefic turn that would be taken by the progress of an apparently beneficent science has been confirmed by events. His other prediction, that of the human debacle that is to follow unless there is a profound reorganization and reorientation, remains before us as a constant warning.

2. INADEQUACIES OF DOMESTIC LAW

Cases involving complex technology surface in increasing numbers before domestic courts. They often relate to disputes which have implications reaching far beyond the two immediate parties involved. Enormously complex technological issues may have to be determined by scientifically unqualified judges and jurors before whom conflicting opinions of highly qualified technical experts are placed. They must make a considered determination on matters concerning which the experts themselves are divided. What is more, their decision on the questions involved reaches far beyond the immediate parties, to affect the rights of society as a whole. The rights of the public often turn on such decisions, as where they relate to environmental concerns, or human experimentation, or technological monopolies of one form or another.

[2] Henry Adams, *A Letter to American Teachers of History* (1910). In that letter, Adams suggested that teachers of history should address themselves to understanding the forces then at work and by pooling their resources devise the institutional changes necessary to turn them to human advantage since, if uncontrolled, "bombs of cosmic violence" might bring civilization itself to an end.

[3] Quoted in Lewis Mumford, *The Pentagon of Power*, Secker and Warburg, 1964, p. 232.

The inadequacies of national legal systems to deal with the problems of modern technology may conveniently be considered under the heads of legal structures, legal procedures and legal concepts.

A) *Legal Structures*

(i) Judicial inability to forecast social impact

Courts, as presently structured, are equipped to give their rulings only after the event. An event occurs, the damage follows, the matter thereafter comes to court, and the judge then tries to work out responsibility. But the judiciary, by the very nature of its task, is not a planning agency. The judge looks at the event only after the damage is done, and seeks to resolve the dispute only after the parties have joined issue on their rights. It is then too late, at any rate so far as concerns the parties, to lay down the rule by which they should have governed their conduct. Secondly, the judge only decides the matter that is before the court and cannot make a general policy. Judicial law-making is therefore done in bits and pieces. The judge does not make law out of whole cloth, but adds just a thread here and a thread there which are thus woven singly into the legal system. The judicial approach lacks the ability to lay down guidelines in advance for a given problem. Other institutions exist in democracies, which are charged with this responsibility, but a consideration of future social impact, though often important in the decision of specific cases, is not what the judge is equipped or expected to do.

Occasionally the citizen might be able to obtain an injunction when the damage or the danger is practically upon him, but the preventive procedures of the courts are tailored largely for *ad hoc* determinations and not for general prohibitions. Without extensive refashioning, current injunction procedures are unable to protect the community as a whole. The courts need to be aided in this aspect of their jurisdiction by a technology assessment board.

The task of making projections into the future calls for a degree of informed skill in prediction and judgment which is beyond the traditional expertise of courts which have hitherto concentrated on areas of known injury and on techniques of dispute resolution. Social planning, on the other hand, functions in the area of the foreseen rather than the known, and concerns itself not only with redress of injury, but also with the fashioning of preventive structures. An excessive reliance upon technical and procedural objections, on rules of evidence, pleadings, laches and so forth, which have no relevance whatsoever to the urgent and massive sociological problems involved, also seems to add to the disqualifications of the courts in handling matters of social planning and technological control.

A monograph on the subject observes:

> It seems clear that we cannot rely on the courts alone to protect society against fast-moving technological development. Judge-made rules of law always come after, and usually long after, the potential for injury has been demonstrated.[4]

Consequently, other agencies are sought after to determine these matters on behalf of the community. Suggestions have been made to this end from time to time, such as human rights committees, watchdog agencies of the public to monitor new technologies, administrative agencies, citizens' societies, legislative committees, scientific groups, technical impact assessment boards, and interdisciplinary committees. They lack co-ordination, are differently motivated and achieve only a patchwork control. Moreover, what little work they can do seems to be hindered by existing legal procedures.

All of these must be studied for their usefulness in this regard. It should, in short, be realized that the traditional reliance on judicial mechanisms for the protection of the public against the invasion of their rights by modern technology is becoming increasingly inadequate. Since their traditional structures and procedures are not geared to the assessment of scientific material or its impact upon the community, the courts, as presently structured, are ill-equipped to be watchdogs of human rights in this regard.

(ii) Lack of expertise of courts

The inadequacy of legal structures is illustrated from time to time in trials before domestic courts where scientific complexities are placed before judges and juries who do not necessarily enjoy the benefit of a scientific training. Reams of expert scientific evidence are tendered before judges and juries who often find themselves quite out of their depth, but are yet required to render a decision. The right to a fair trial may sometimes be jeopardized by the extreme sophistication of scientific evidence today. Moreover, the judicial function is such that the judge or jury *must* render a decision. The judge cannot walk away from the problem on the basis that it is too difficult to decide.[5] Nor can the judge pass it over to another state agency as many other functionaries can, for the parties would say to the judge that it was after exhausting all other resources that they had come to the court.

4 H. Green, "The New Technological Era: A View from the Law", Monograph I, Program of Policy Studies, George Washington University, Washington, D.C., 1967.

5 Except, within limits, in the very exceptional situation of *non liquet*.

Indeed, science and the law now speak in such different languages that it is sometimes difficult to find a meeting ground between them, far less for the latter to control the former. In a fairly obvious sphere, the law can hardly understand the language of computers, but needs to control them.

This is not to be wondered at, seeing that even the scientists themselves are narrowing down their specialities to the point where multitudes of little cultures have grown up within the scientific establishment itself, and communication between these mini-cultures has become a problem.

Although the lay observer may have the impression that a lawyer cross-examining an expert knows more about the subject than the expert himself, this is a delusion. The lawyer has made a study of a microscopic area of the science in question, and can succeed in creating a false impression of competence in this limited field. But science is becoming increasingly inaccessible to the lawyer.

> A lawyer of scientific interests can still, if he works hard at it, achieve an amateur's beginning of an understanding of the essentials of contemporary physiology, where observation and laws proceeding directly from observation are relatively central, but he is lost in the world of contemporary physics, where the scientist speaks the Pythagorean language and seems to roam in a world far removed from the world of ordinary sense experience ... the admission fee to the mysterious precincts of science is far more than the mastery of the second law of thermodynamics. I know because I have done my own homework on Lord Kelvin, with the hope that this might give me a Rosetta stone, but the literature of contemporary physics remains as opaque to me as it was when I thought a Carnot cycle was some kind of velocipede.

So wrote Professor Harry W. Jones, Cardozo Professor of Jurisprudence at Columbia University, after a serious effort to come to terms with the language of modern science,[6] and no lawyer, who is not a mathematician or physicist, can seriously contend that he or she feels at home in the rarefied world of tensor calculus and quantum mechanics. The same difficulties confront the judge or juror who is called upon to make a determination involving some complex scientific question, involving masses of highly complicated data and statistics.[7]

[6] Harry W. Jones, "Legal Inquiry and Methods of Science", in *Law and the Social Role of Science*, Harry W. Jones (ed.), Rockefeller University Press, N.Y., 1966, p. 120.

[7] The point here made was graphically illustrated by an Australian case which attracted world attention in 1982. In the Chamberlain murder trial, the mother of a nine and a half-week old baby, Azaria, was charged with its murder. The body was never found and the defence

(iii) Consequent loss of judicial authority

A simple illustration of authority consequently slipping away from legal hands may be drawn from the sphere of patent law, where the increasing lack of competence of judicial tribunals to handle the scientific matters involved is leading to a demand for the withdrawal of this jurisdiction from the courts of law and to its committal to a competent scientific body. To take another example of a sort which will occur increasingly in the future, the adjudicatory function in regard to the licensing of nuclear reactors has, in the United States, been entrusted by statute to a three-man board, of whom two are technically qualified and the third need not even be a lawyer.[8] Their decisions would take into account statutory and regulatory requirements as well as the application of legal precedents.

We must indeed become wary when this feeling of dissatisfaction with the courts reaches proportions even bordering on contempt. Thus the sociologist, Jacques Ellul, in a well known analysis of technical civilization, has observed:

> The judicial regime is simply not adapted to technical civilization, and this is one of the causes of its inefficiency and of the ever greater contempt felt towards it.[9]

claimed that the baby had been carried away and devoured by a dingo, a species of Australian wild dog found in the Ayers Rock area, where the baby disappeared. The circumstantial evidence led by the prosecution depended heavily on the most advanced developments in immunology and protein chemistry. A key question in the case was whether the bloodstains detected in a car came from Azaria or from some other person, in particular, an injured passenger transported in the car to hospital on an earlier occasion. The distinction between adult haemoglobin and foetal haemoglobin was vital for this purpose, as babies' blood, until the age of six months, contains about 25% foetal and 75% adult haemoglobin. Immunology offered a means of investigating the blood samples through the use of antisera. Protein chemistry offered a means of further individual identification of the blood by using a genetic marker not unlike those employed in paternity suits for matching the blood of offspring and father. The required identification could only be made by the most sophisticated and advanced biotechnology, such as isoelectric focusing, the results of which were actually led in evidence in the case. Clearly, the scientific evidence involved was of a degree of sophistication well beyond the ability of average lay people to grasp fully. The tests discussed and used in this case take us to the frontiers of scientific knowledge in these fields. The professors concerned had to explain to a lay jury in a limited time many scientific intricacies which would have required several lectures even for scientists to understand. The accused was convicted upon a jury finding, but a Royal Commission of Inquiry found new evidence and, by executive act, the accused was freed.

8 42 U.S.C. s.2241(a) (1964).

9 Jacques Ellul, *The Technological Society*, Random House, N.Y., 1964, p. 251.

Such strong expressions of dissatisfaction cannot leave unmoved all those who cherish human rights and the rule of law, for if the courts lose respect the last bastion of protection is gone.

(iv) Tacit abdications of judicial authority

There is also a tacit abdication of judicial authority in another great area. Where technology involves hazards to the general public, as with radiation, sonic booms, or the spraying of pesticides, a technically qualified board determines the tolerable level, having made a decision as to the level which, in its view, is desirable or undesirable. The courts would thereafter be reluctant to impose liability where the hazard is within the limits thus pre-set by government authority, and this is therefore the level which the public will then have to tolerate. Cases of alleged radiation injuries, where the exposure was within these limits, bring home this point, for the courts have been disinclined to grant relief.[10] In the result, the degree of danger which falls short of negligence and which the public must tolerate in their daily living depends on the views of administrators rather than of the courts.

Similar considerations also apply to machine evidence which is increasingly tendered in courts of law. From simple matters such as the speed of motor cars and blood alcohol levels, to complex computerized models coordinating vast masses of data, which the court and the parties are out of their depth in checking, machine evidence is often the basis of judicial decision. It passes unquestioned on the supposition that it must be correct, though the error factor cannot be eliminated.

(v) Inadequacies of the legislature

If the courts are not equal to the task, the question may be asked why society's accepted mechanism for law-making — the legislature — cannot rise to the occasion. However, parliaments in most countries have a crowded roll of legislative business, and it is only certain selected items that can be the subject of full debate. Secondly, the parliamentarians, like the judges, are not scientific experts. They will be advised by scientists, provided the scientists can reach them. Thirdly, where there is some new science that some interest desires to push, there will be an interest group presenting to parliamentarians a rather one-sided picture, and that interest group has great power, through lobbying and other ways, over members of parliament. Fourthly, when there is some project or piece of legislation involving much use of technology, it

[10] See *Garner* v. *Hecla Mining Co.*, 19 Utah 2d 364, 431, p. 2d, 792 (1967); *Employers Mutual Liability Ins. Co.* v. *Parker*, 418 S.W. 2d 570 (Tex. Civ. App. 1967); *Mahoney* v. *United States*, 220 F. Supp. 823 (E.D. Tenn. 1962).

tends all too often to be passed through Parliament before an adequate and comprehensive technology assessment review has been undertaken of the impact of that legislation. All of these factors, in combination, prevent our legislative mechanisms from being any more effective than the judicial.

(vi) Proposals for judicial restructuring

In former times, as special fields of law developed, special courts or divisions, such as probate, divorce and admiralty jurisdictions, emerged with special experience in that field. The increasing frequency with which science-related matters will surface before the courts has led to suggestions that judicial bodies should similarly comprise special divisions of judges with a scientific background who would be better equipped to handle sophisticated scientific evidence. This is still not even discernible on the horizon.

Since the courts, as presently structured, are not equipped for such aspects as technology assessment and environmental impact evaluation which will be important areas of litigation in the future, some thought needs to be given towards assisting the judicial process in this respect. The Supreme Court of Japan has a judicial research arm with specialists in different areas of law available to prepare a detailed dossier for judges. Some scientifically trained lawyers could perhaps be recruited for such a task. The Supreme Court of India has machinery for enabling the social impact of a given piece of legislation to be reported on for the benefit of the Court. Some adaptations of those ideas could, with profit, be considered in so far as concerns matters of a highly technical scientific nature.

(vii) The tardiness of the courts

The delay involved in court proceedings is incompatible with the urgency often required in the investigation of a fast-moving technological source of harm. Even urgent injunction procedure could take several days, if not weeks. The substantive issues would take up to a year or two for determination in the original courts, with an appellate process which may require a similar length of time.

It is true, emergency injunction procedures, in the form of interim relief, are theoretically available in situations of extreme urgency, but the machinery is not within everyone's reach. The formality attendant on all court proceedings can deter many persons deserving of relief, but unable to reach it. Perhaps some more informed dispute resolution structures, such as those available under the Civil Liberties Commissioners scheme in Japan, might be an answer.[11] An instance that comes to mind is the noise pollution created by industrial activity, which may take years to determine in a formal court of law,[12] but yet can be amicably and more speedily solved by other procedures.

(viii) Outmoded attitudes in regard to questions of standing

The inadequacies of current legal structures are shown also in questions of the status of concerned bodies to take legal action in pursuit of their objectives. When in America the Sierra Club sought to take action against the granting of approval or issuance permits for commercial exploitation of a national game refuge adjacent to Sequoia National Park, the US Supreme Court, affirming the judgment of the US Court of Appeals for the Ninth Circuit, held that the club lacked standing to maintain the suit because it failed to allege that it or its members were adversely affected by the proposed action — despite the fact that the club had alleged that it had a "special interest in the conservation and sound maintenance of the national parks, game refuges and forests of the country".[13] Justice Douglas, in his dissenting judgment, pointed out that inanimate objects such as ships are sometimes parties to litigation and that a corporation is likewise invested with legal personality. He argued that "So it should be as respects valleys, alpine meadows, rivers, lakes, estuaries, beaches, ridges, groves of trees ..." that feel "the destructive pressures of modern technology and modern life".[14] The position is improving. Class actions fill the gap to some extent. Unofficial organizations of various sorts are receiving increasing recognition. Yet the traditional character of a lawsuit, as being a contest between two parties having a direct monetary interest in the subject matter, dies hard.

B) *Legal Procedures*

(i) Lack of precise standards of proof

Although the judge (or jury) must make a decision, there is a total lack of precision as to the decisional standards that should be employed. Should it be proof "beyond reasonable doubt", or proof "by a balance of probability"? These two much-used expressions concerning judicial proof are totally divorced from standards of scientific proof. As any lawyer would admit, these

[11] See Chapter 7, *Justice without Frontiers*, Vol. I.

[12] *Ibid.*, p. 147.

[13] *Sierra Club* v. *Morton* 405 US 727.

[14] 405 US 743 (1972); see, also, Christopher D. Stone, "Should Trees Have Standing? Towards Legal Rights for Natural Objects", 45 *S. Cal. L. Rev.* 450 (1972), which was cited by Justice Douglas in his dissent.

are extremely vague standards whose precise implication is obscure even to lawyers and judges.

(ii) Balance of probabilities not the best method of ascertaining scientific truth

Judicial procedures are largely adversarial and in the common law world almost entirely so. Two parties present opposing viewpoints to the court and the court decides, upon a balance of probabilities, which of the two contending parties should win the day. This is not the best method to determine the social or human rights impact of a new piece of technology. Existing judicial structures are therefore not the appropriate agencies for making such determinations. In addition, they are hampered by sometimes archaic and often formalistic rules of procedure which require evidence to be produced in a certain manner and which penalize a party not following the rules, by shutting out the evidence that party proposes to tender. Evidence vital to the ascertainment of truth may thus be excluded on the ground that a party has not complied with the formal rules of evidence. Moreover, current procedures are expensive and dilatory.

Many of the rules of evidence in the common law jurisdictions are based on principles of fairness as between the litigating parties. If a certain state of affairs has not been duly pleaded or has not been supported by legally admissible evidence, it will not be taken into account by the court, however truly it may exist in reality. This is not the best method for the ascertainment of factual truth.

(iii) Limited nature of the judicial perspective

In adversarial procedure, there are two parties, each advancing a point of view before the judge, while the judge sits like a dignified sort of umpire, and says which of the two parties should win. The result is an award which may, of course, be an unimpeachable award, as between the two players.

Legal systems based on the civil law approach this question rather differently, with the judge playing the role more of the inquirer rather than of the umpire. Yet, under both systems there are certain rules which must be complied with, and the task of deciding who wins according to the rules is a totally different undertaking from the pursuit of scientific truth.

Furthermore, judges are rather reluctant to innovate because they feel they have no mandate from the people in the same way that parliament has. So the judge tends to be extremely conservative and will think hard before venturing out into new ground. Procedures perfectly appropriate for determining, between two competing parties, which party deserves success are not appropriate for determining questions of community welfare.

For example, adversary rules of procedure would say, if John Smith has a case against Joe Brown, and Smith wants to produce a document which is in Brown's custody, that Smith must notice Brown to produce that document. If Smith fails to serve notice on Brown, to produce that document, Smith cannot produce the copy that is with him. Well and good, because as between Smith and Brown, if Smith has not followed the rules of the game, Smith must be penalized. But suppose what we have to find out is the level of radiation which the community can be expected to tolerate, or whether a scientific experiment involving a brink situation has to be halted. In such a case, even though Smith be the complainant and Brown the party to be restrained, the issues concern the whole community and not merely Smith and Brown. If Smith has been negligent in following rules of procedure, it helps little in assessing the true danger to the community that Smith should be penalized, and not be able to produce a document that would assist the court in ascertaining the truth.

(iv) Estoppel

Another illustration comes from the rules of estoppel. If a person has made a representation on the basis of which another has acted and suffered prejudice, the former cannot thereafter go back upon that statement. Well and good, provided these two are the only two parties. But if it is a matter of the ascertainment of scientific truth, that rule falls to the ground. It ceases to be effective because it does not enable the court to ascertain what is the true scientific result. It may well be that a party who has behaved in a negligent or inconsiderate fashion is still the party asserting a scientific truth. While that party deserves to be penalized, the community, on whom the judgment will inevitably make an impact, should not be affected in its rights owing to the conduct of a negligent litigant who, after all, is only an individual, though he or she may be litigating on a matter which has considerable importance for the community.

In consequence the community would suffer if the adversary system does not alter its procedures to meet the new threats that are posed by a scientific age, which demands from judges and lawyers an expertise which they probably do not have and which, certainly they do not have a procedure for using.

(v) Courtcraft and Advocacy

While it is true that many cases decide themselves on the basis of their own merits, it is also true that the adversarial system enables those who can command the necessary legal expertise to enjoy an edge over their opponents which can turn the scales in their favour. The experienced advocate is always at an advantage over the inexperienced one, despite the efforts of the best of judges to redress the imbalance. This is scarcely the appropriate process for fact finding in scientific matters. For this reason, the adversarial method has been strongly condemned as unsuitable for technologically-oriented cases. In this context, it has been criticized for its unscientific method, under which the ascertainment of fact is made to depend upon a system which "places a premium on tactical advocacy".[15]

(vi) Precedent cannot be the basis of scientific truth

The methods of courts are not suited to the evaluation of scientific material because the constant progress of science calls for more flexible methods for the use and assessment of that knowledge. The law generally functions on the basis of precedent. Yesterday's authority is today's law. But in science, "yesterday's truth is today's error".[16] And if we proceed on the basis that we must follow the decisions that were given before, we may well be heading along a path that has been proved to be wrong. As has been so well observed:

> ... scientific material is always provisional and is constantly becoming out-of-date, so that yesterday's truth is today's error. Unfortunately, however, in the law yesterday's belief, when embodied in a binding precedent, becomes authority for today. Hence courts may, with the best of intentions, find themselves unwittingly perpetuating what the world of science now regards as error.[17]

(vii) Evidentiary method

Moreover, the methods used by courts for the reconstruction of past transactions are still based upon a common law theory of witnesses as passive observers and recallers of what they perceived. They are tested by processes of cross-examination which may sometimes intimidate the honest witness and give a premium to the artful dissimulator. The scholar, accustomed to the quietness of the study or laboratory, may falter or wilt under the pressure and fail to sustain the impression of coherence and reliability. Scientific predictions and informed forecasts of likely effects were not within the contemplation of this system when it was structured.

* * *

[15] Peter Brett, "Implications of Science for the Law", 18 *McGill Law Journal*, 170, 191 (1972).

[16] *Ibid.*, p. 184.

[17] *Ibid.*, pp 184–5.

There hence results a feeling of dissatisfaction with the courts and with the traditional framework of a legal system which was not designed to face the problems now posed by science.

The failure of the courts to deal adequately with these problems results also in a greater share of the responsibility being thrust upon the administration. The latter can cope more adequately with the technical problems involved and, in the result, is constantly enlarging its authority by making inroads upon the judicial sphere, "which remains centred on vanishing problems such as codicils, community reversions, and the like".[18]

In an earlier age, the Luddites, who felt that the Industrial Revolution was upsetting their world, attempted to destroy the technology that was ruining them by smashing up the stocking frames of the industrialists. Technology is too complex today for even the most naive to believe that it can ever be smashed up. Failure of the courts, the one authority that might be expected to control it, may well result, in this field at any rate, in society displaying towards that authority a corresponding attitude of frustration.

(C) Legal Concepts

As with legal structures and procedures, so also with legal concepts. They have been tailored by generations of lawyers to meet the needs of formalistic and individually based legal systems. They need considerable modification if they are to deal adequately with the age of technology. A few examples follow from many which could be selected.

(i) Absolute ownership

The concept of absolute ownership of property can be very damaging to human rights, for it enables owners of property to use the full armoury of modern technology to extract from land the maximum benefit it can yield — even to the extent of mining it down to an empty shell which thereafter serves no practical purpose. The concept enables the use of land as the owner's private preserve without regard to the social obligations which ownership imposes. In treating absolute ownership as conferring on the owner a bundle of rights to be enjoyed by the owner at will, the law generally treats land no differently from an article of movable property — which the owner can damage or destroy it at will. To apply these concepts to immovable property is to invite the owner of land to lose sight of its central importance to the continuing life of the community.

[18] Jacques Ellul, *The Technological Society*, *supra*, p. 251.

Such attitudes have resulted in the environmental devastation we see all around us. Deforestation of tropical rainforests by the logging industry is another example. Traditional notions of absolute rights of private property need reconsideration under the pressures of modern technology. They can prove to be totally inconsistent with the notion of environmental rights, the social use of property, and the concept of intergenerational fairness, which is a human rights concept only now beginning to emerge.

(ii) Intellectual property

The concept of private property carries over into technologies that can be of vital importance to the community. A vast amount of the technology — probably more than 95% of it — which is needed for development purposes in the developing world is controlled by owners — mainly multinationals — in the developed world. They are of course entitled to rights in this knowledge, rights which they have bought from the inventors. Indeed some of this knowledge has been acquired in their own research laboratories. Yet these are not absolute rights to be used in a manner that negatives basic human rights. A proper balance must be struck between the owner's rights and the needs of those who desperately require that technology. The law is not as yet sufficiently geared to a recognition of this need.

The problem comes out in one of its acutest forms in the seed industry and in regard to genetic resources in plant stock. This has been the subject of concerned debate at the Food and Agriculture Organization (FAO). Agricultural ministries in developing countries often watch helplessly while the owners of new seedstock refuse to share breeding information, on the basis of concepts of absolute ownership of the intellectual property involved, and demand high prices for it. Seed supply has become a high technology genetics industry.

The question has indeed been raised as to whether plant germplasm is not the world's common heritage rather than the exclusive preserve of a few.

This is only an example. Numerous others could be cited in such fields as the patenting of hybrids, pharmaceuticals, pesticides, and the foods industry.

Patents in new varieties of seedstock, vital to the developing world, permit the corporate interests owning them to raise prices even to an extent which may be unconscionable. The right of ownership would in such instances be standing in the way of the right to food. A solution in between needs to be found. In the hypothetical case of an invention of a sure fire cancer cure, the inventor, in the exercise of his right of private property, can scarcely be permitted to fix the price of his remedy at $10,000 a pill. The inventor or discoverer is entitled to the advantages of a vital invention or discovery, but not on a basis which conflicts with basic human rights such as the right to health.

(iii) The monogenerational perspective

Current legal systems are geared to think only in terms of the present generation. This is a concept, traditional to Western legal systems, which stands urgently in need of review in the light of the power of science and technology to cause damage on a scale affecting even a thousand generations to come. Modern technology presents this problem fairly and squarely to legal systems, and they have not responded appropriately at the conceptual level. Concepts such as those of intergenerational rights or trusteeship for future generations are still a long way off from recognition in legal systems, and furnish telling examples of the inadequacy of legal concepts to handle the age of technology.

(iv) The lack of a common heritage concept

While technology forces on us a recognition of a common planetary home, with finite resources which must be carefully husbanded, legal systems still remain as they were tailored to an age which imagined that the planet's resources were boundless. The sea, the atmosphere, the land were seen as infinite resources, with an abundance in which all comers could share. There was no need for conservation as there was enough to go round, however many might be the claimants. Those assumptions are in tatters owing to the reach and power of modern technology. The legal concepts tailored to fit that world view are very much intact.

(v) Freedom of contract

Similar considerations apply to the concept of absolute freedom of contract, which needs to be adapted to the requirements of the technological age. Modern technology gives vast power to global conglomerates who make commercial bargains in all parts of the world for the sale and use of their technology. The bargains are between parties of vastly unequal bargaining power, with one party desperately needing the technology which only the other can offer. The result can sometimes be very damaging to human rights. There is a fierce free-for-all in the global marketplace, where the weak cannot parley on equal terms with the strong.

It is indeed a strange anomaly that while this is very much the case in international trade dealings, domestic legal systems have adjusted to the notion of the unfairness of unbridled freedom of contract, and have to a large extent adjusted their contractual concepts so as to grant some protection to the weaker contracting party. Yet, internationally, in the vast commodity contracts on which the subsistence of hundreds of millions of the world's population depends, there has been no adjustment. Thus the technologically strong country can trade its technology on the strongest possible terms to the weak developing country, on a basis which accords an ever-diminishing real return to the latter. The industrial product, such as a truck, which cost the equivalent of x bags of cereal ten years ago now costs the equivalent of 2x or 3x bags of the same cereal. Yet there is no legal concept of fair trade to protect the weaker party. Modern technology, unless restrained by appropriate legal concepts, can drive that party to the wall.

3. INADEQUACIES OF INTERNATIONAL LAW

Just as the rapid progress of technology poses grave new problems for domestic law, it poses new problems also for international law.

(i) Tardiness of the mechanisms of international law

The problem here is of a somewhat different kind, for, despite all its limitations, domestic law can *legislate* to meet a new need, and can impose the will of the legislature upon its subjects. International law is not equipped with such a direct mechanism for formulating a binding rule of law. Operating as it does through treaties, customary law, general principles of international law, decisions of tribunals and the writings of jurists, it is difficult for international law to lay down specific rules on such matters. The closest approach it can make to laying down rules after the manner of domestic legislation is an international treaty, but an international treaty needs the consent of every state that is to be bound, and takes a great deal of negotiation to achieve.

Technology at an international level develops at an ever-increasing speed. Yet, international law is even slower than domestic law to respond to the threats posed by technology to human rights. Further, states that have a vested interest in the particular technology that is under discussion will tend to oppose any international attempt to regulate it. A treaty binding that country will therefore be difficult to obtain.

However, international lawyers are conscious of the need for haste in the formulation of new rules of international law and are sometimes able to achieve these with remarkable speed — as in the case of the new rules of international law which were rapidly created for the handling of matters relating to outer space.

(ii) Non-binding nature of resolutions and declarations

It may be possible to build up a sufficient body of international opposition to the development or extension of a new technology through international conferences which evolve a kind of consensus in condemning a particularly damaging kind of technology. It is often through such international conferences that a feeling emerges in the international community that a particular technology needs to be controlled. Discussions may then take place in the General Assembly of the United Nations and a Declaration can emerge. But Declarations are by their nature non-binding and are often more honoured in the breach than in the observance.

Whether such a General Assembly declaration has the status of customary international law is a question that international lawyers have long debated. Some hold that it has no legal force whatever, but others view such widely accepted declarations as soft law which in due time receives recognition as a rule of customary international law.

This brief discussion will show how difficult it is to regulate internationally such technology-related dangers as threats to the ozone layer, atmospheric and marine pollution, and threats to endangered species. The fact that hundreds of bird and mammal species and tens of thousands of plant life species are threatened with extinction does not seem to be sufficient to overcome these barriers to the formulation of new principles of international law.[19]

Also, international law has gone some way towards regulating many areas of technological danger — as, for example, in regard to nuclear technology or computer privacy. International lawyers are constantly discussing ways in which the formulation of rules of customary international law can be speeded up to meet such challenges.

(iii) Lack of mechanisms for surveillance and enforcement

Unlike domestic legal systems which are equipped with the necessary mechanisms for harnessing the might of the state to enforce the law, the international system lacks the necessary mechanisms to enforce its will upon a state that refuses to submit to its rules. Many a treaty has in-built surveil-

[19] There have recently been a large number of treaties on matters concerning the environment — the 1976 Boundary Waters Convention, the 1992 Rio Biodiversity Convention, the 1989 Economic Commission for Europe Charter on Groundwater Management, the 1979 Berne Convention on the Conservation of European Wildlife and Natural Habitats, and the 1971 Ramsar Convention on Wetlands of International Importance. An important recent treaty with far-reaching environmental consequences is the Chemical Weapons Treaty which came into force in 1997.

lance mechanisms and, indeed, international sanctions can theoretically be brought to bear upon a defaulting nation, but such action is exceptional and difficult to invoke. One of the best examples of well organized surveillance mechanisms is the Atomic Energy Agency's nuclear inspectorate which does conduct inspections and must be accorded facilities for this purpose. Yet various question marks hang over the international community's ability to enforce its wishes in this regard.

* * *

All of these factors leave the law and its institutions in grave danger. The need to take stock comes through with clarity in assessments such as the following:

> Law is conceived as a function of a traditional society. It has not registered the essential transformation of the times. Its content is exactly what it was three centuries ago. It has experienced only a few fragmentary transformations (such as the corporation) — no other attempts at modernization have been made. Nor have form and methods varied any more than content. Judicial technique has been little affected by the techniques that surround us today; had it been, it might have gained much in speed and flexibility.[20]

Against this background, we find ourselves increasingly asking the question whether the law as the traditional medium of social control will be left standing helpless while the juggernaut moves on.

4. CONCERNS OF THE DEVELOPING WORLD

Modern technology is largely the product of the developed world. It is also an instrument of power. The developing world, which is largely the passive recipient of this technology, hence feels a sense of deep concern in regard to the possible misuse of technology. Since the current legal order seems unable to protect it, that feeling of unease is heightened.

The deep concern felt by the developing world in regard to the misuse of science and technology is reflected in a growing volume of literature.[21] Areas

[20] Jacques Ellul, *The Technological Society*, *supra*, p. 251.

[21] For a recent volume collating several of these studies, see *The Revenge of Athena: Science, Exploitation and the Third World*, Ziauddin Sirdar (ed.), Mansell Publishing Ltd., London and N.Y., 1988. See, also, Susantha Goonatilake, *Crippled Minds: An Exploration into Colonial Culture*, Vikas Publishing House, 1982; *Science, Hegemony and Violence: A Requiem for Modernity*, Ashis Nandy (ed.), United Nations University Press, Tokyo and Oxford University Press, Delhi, 1988.

of dissatisfaction include the neglect and obsolescence of time-honoured technologies and crafts adapted to the needs of the region concerned, the control of plant genetic resources and the impact of new seed technologies, the dumping of sub-standard industrial goods and of industrial waste, the concentration of scientific manpower on the needs of the armaments industry rather than on the needs of development,[22] the testing of pharmaceuticals and medical procedures on populations of developing countries, the difficulties in the way of the transfer of appropriate technologies, and the concentration in the developed countries of knowledge concerning the developing countries. This literature also deals with the ways in which, in the era of colonialism, technology was used as an instrument of domination rather than a means of social upliftment.

This dissatisfaction has also been reflected at various international conferences, commencing in the 1970s. Some of these have been referred to in Chapter 4 above, including the "Poona Indictment" which is one of the best known. This Declaration was adopted at a meeting of the World Order Models Project held in Poona, India in July 1978. The Declaration, titled "The Perversion of Science and Technology: An Indictment",[23] recited that it was "an indictment of the way in which science and technology had become instruments of a global structure of inequity, exploitation and oppression". It referred, *inter alia*, to drug testing among poor populations, and the employment of 50 per cent of all research scientists in the world in military research and development. Among specific areas referred to were the indiscriminate fishing methods used by mechanized trawlers, deforestation resulting in flooding of land and silting of rivers, and the drive to sell the products of modern technology, regardless of whether they served a real social need. The Declaration stressed the need to direct scientific enterprise towards the needs, skills and knowledge of the majority of the underprivileged peoples of the world and discussed the lack of inclination among scientific elites in the developed and developing worlds to discuss the critical issues mentioned in the declaration.

Such statements, indicative of the deep concern felt in the developing world at the direction of growth of science and technology have far-reaching human rights implications. True, some of the concerns thus expressed in the 1970s have attracted a measure of attention from the scientific community, but many of them still remain unaddressed.

[22] Estimated at a ratio of 51% to 1% by the Brandt Commission — see *North-South: A Programme for Survival*, Pan Books, 1980, p. 197.

[23] Burns H. Weston *et al*, *Basic Documents in International Law and World Order*, 1980, p. 421.

Since the Poona Indictment, there have been many international conferences dealing with such global issues as desertification, pollution and the dumping of shoddy goods and industrial waste, but the competing interests involved in furthering these technologies, and in containing them, pose a continuing problem.

5. THE ENTRY OF SCIENCE INTO A LEGAL ALSATIA

We have discussed at the commencement of this chapter the inadequacies of the law in handling science, even in territory which is within the known empire of the law. Science has, however, run beyond these boundaries into a no-man's land where the writ of the law has never run. Its control in such territory becomes doubly difficult.

It is within the scientist's power, for example, to melt the polar ice-caps and submerge the world's major centres of population under swollen seas, to divert the course of a hurricane and devastate millions of acres, to raise the level of radioactivity in the atmosphere to the point of danger to all life. In Colorado the disposal of radioactive waste by the Government apparently raised fears of the possibility of a serious earthquake in the city of Denver in the near future.[24]

Even more worrying results flow from the progress in biological sciences which, after the dominance of physics and chemistry for three centuries, are now coming to the fore. Short of concerted international action and the emergence of effective moral codes among the ranks of scientists themselves, such activities are likely to defy all attempts at regulation.

In this field, scientists are attempting to meddle with the processes of life itself. They have broken the genetic code and can create mutations and determine thereby the pattern of growth of living organisms.[25] The possibility of directing the evolution of special characteristics by the process of genetic selection has indeed progressed so far that it has been suggested recently by the French physicist, Pierre Auger, that it may even be possible for the molecular biologist to recall into life some of the forms of creatures which have existed in antiquity but are now extinct.[26]

[24] In Utah, 6,000 sheep were killed in circumstances strongly suggestive of their death having been caused in consequence of chemical warfare tests conducted by the Army. [Michael Wollan, "Controlling the Hazards of Government-Sponsored Technology", 36 *George Washington Law Review*, 1105, at 1134–5 (1968), (citing *New York Times*, March 27, 1968, at 46).]

[25] See Chapters 14, 17 and 20, *infra*.

[26] A prophecy that has since been vividly brought home to the world's imagination by the film *Jurassic Park*.

At a time by no means distant from the present, they will no doubt attempt to tinker with the genetic code concerning the human body itself. Recent researches on DNA seem to throw open all sorts of possibilities, for the genes which determine the qualities of the individual can be drastically interfered with in the embryo and it is anyone's guess what may result.

The babies bred in bottles that Aldous Huxley wrote of in *Brave New World*[27] in 1932, are fast becoming a reality of life and possibilities are opening up which even Huxley did not contemplate. Science looks today even beyond sperm banks to the possibility of preparing a fertilized egg which will grow in a host medium, not necessarily the woman's, feeding itself on the trophoblast it produces in its medium. Not even the apparent mother would then be the true parent of a child and the choice may be open to the prospective parents to choose parentage from any one of a series of donor fathers and donor mothers. Can scientists be permitted to do this without check or restraint merely on the basis that they are pursuing pure science? Can a biologist, unrestrained by the ethical scruples which trouble a doctor, be permitted to produce by mutation a grotesque deformity? Would not the argument always be available that these horrible things are being done for the advancement of knowledge?

Despite the obvious dangers of genetic research, the fact is that it is progressing at an alarming rate. At a meeting of the Australian College of Medical Administrators, 1969, a speaker observed that a scientist at Oxford had transferred nuclei from the skin of a male toad to the unfertilized egg of a female toad, thus producing an exact replica of the original male toad — an experiment showing that the creation in laboratories of hundreds of thousands of identical toads was no longer beyond the realm of possibility. The scientist who referred to this phenomenon, while appreciating that its extension to human beings still lay in the distant future, observed that "there is no fundamental reason why this could not happen with human beings". Alvin Toffler, in his *Future Shock*, refers to the very real possibility of mass production of human beings with identical characteristics.[28]

The legal consequences that would result if such a thing should ever become reality need the most careful attention now, before we awaken one day to find it a reality. If this experiment be extended to the human being, what is the position in regard to all the human rights that have been evolved for several generations upon the basis of identity, integrity, and individuality of the human personality? If, as some believe, the cloning of humans is only

27 Aldous Huxley, *Brave New World*, Harper & Row, 1969 (1932).

28 Alvin Toffler, *Future Shock*, Bantam Books, N.Y., 1971, pp. 197 *et seq.* See further Ch. 17, *infra*.

five or ten years away, the time has surely come for legislators, the public and lawyers (who have a particular role to play in such matters) to consider whether means of control over such activities should not be urgently devised.[29]

The problem becomes more grotesque when we read today of possibilities of brain transplants which have indeed been successfully achieved for short terms with animals at Cleveland and other centres. What of the attendant complications involving problems of human personality, for it may well be that the donee in such event carries forward the personality of the donor?

Similar dangers lurk in other fields.

We have already noted the weaknesses of legal structures, procedures and concepts. When we contrast this weakness with the enormous power of science, there is cause for deep concern as to whether this enormous power is passing beyond the pale of legal regulation. A specific instance from a small department of science will illustrate this aspect.

6. TECHNOLOGY'S ABILITY TO KEEP A STEP AHEAD OF LEGAL REGULATION

It is possible to make a case-study, in relation to almost any field of research, of the ways in which that research tends invariably to be a step ahead of legal controls. Computer technology is demonstrating this in one of the latest fields of scientific research. But so it has been throughout the history of science. Perhaps we could use pharmacology as an historical illustration of the way in which legal controls tend to trail behind scientific advance.

Ever since arsenic made its way into Europe after its discovery by the Arab, Al Jabir, in the 12th century, science, in discovering new poisons, has been a step ahead of the ability of the law to track down its abuse. The white odourless powder was easy to administer and difficult to trace in a dead body, thereby affording a convenient new weapon to the murderer. It left in

[29] In February 1997, the successful cloning of a sheep ("Dolly") by scientists in Edinburgh opened the way to the cloning of all mammals and led to great fears that the technique could be used with humans. *The New York Times* of February 24 quoted a bio-ethicist from the University of Missouri as saying that, "the technology is not, in principle, policeable" (Gina Kolata, "With Cloning of a Sheep, Ethical Ground Shifts", *N.Y. Times*, Feb. 24, 1997 at A 1). President Clinton expressed his deep concern about these experiments and asked a federal bio-ethics advisory commission to examine the ethical implications of the new technique (Todd S. Purdum, "President Asks for Advice on New Reality of Cloning", *N.Y. Times*, Feb. 25, 1997, at A 15). He also barred the use of federal funds for research on the cloning of human beings. There have been many calls for a voluntary moratorium on research in this area.

its wake a trail of unavenged death right up to the 19th century, and its frequent use to enable the unscrupulous to help themselves to rich inheritances caused it to be known as "inheritance powder". The great case of Madame Lefarge in France in the last century was one of those which attracted attention to the inability of the law to handle a simple case of arsenic poisoning.

The prosecutor later acquired the ability to track down this form of poisoning when Orfila, the father of toxicology, developed a method for obtaining precipitates of arsenic in the form of yellow flakes, by treatment of portions of the dead body. James Marsh, in 1836, made a further breakthrough by finding a process so sensitive that a thousandth of a milligram would show up in the form of a deposit.

By this time, however, other chemicals had appeared which eluded the prosecutor. There first came the vegetable poisons, more difficult to detect. Unlike mineral and metallic substances, which remained when the body tissues were destroyed, these left no traces upon analysis, for they were themselves destroyed in the course of analysis of a specimen of body tissue. Famous trials, such as those of Esme Castaing (morphia), Gustave Fournies (nicotine), de Pauco (digitalin), focused public opinion on the dangers of vegetable poisoning. Unceasing effort was then required till reagents were discovered which reacted in typical ways when mixed with certain alkaloids. In this way, morphia, heroin, codeine, atrophine, digitalin, nicotine, and many others were conquered.

But another round was then to begin. With the synthesis of barbituric acid by Adolph von Baeyer (1835–1917) in the late 19th century came the barbiturates, appearing so fast that the law cannot keep pace with them. The enormous expansion of the pharmaceutical industry today places new poisons in the hands of the unscrupulous and they appear under a variety of names. Their appearance races ahead of the availability of methods to track them down in the event of their abuse.[30]

So it is with nearly every branch of science. As soon as one form of activity is nailed down and brought within the sphere of legal regulation, another appears which escapes the net of controls and safeguards. Evasion is always a step ahead of regulation, and an ever advancing body of science and technology places tools in the hands of the unscrupulous which the best legal systems cannot reach.

[30] See Jurgen Thorwald, *Proof of Poison*, Thames & Hudson, London, 1966.

7. LOOPHOLES FOR EVASION OF THE LAW AND HUMAN RIGHTS

The mechanisms that existed in traditional societies for the absorption of science into the social system, and subjecting it to social controls and checks and balances, have somewhere along the way been lost in Western societies.[31] There are many checks and balances in all societies and, in traditional societies, there are very strong checks and balances outside the legal system proper — moral prohibitions, taboos, and the like. Modern societies, however, resort mainly to the law, for the other social checks and balances have largely disappeared. When the law is itself inadequate to handle a matter, the community's control over the activity in question is lost.

Dangerous science has many screens and loopholes through which it can evade scrutiny while in fact denigrating law and human rights. For example, under cover of medical treatment, numerous invasions of human personality can be practised in a manner difficult for a legal agency to police. Modern experience with drugs and narcotics has shown to what extent the human mind itself may be influenced by such means. Some of these are indeed today so potent that they may even change an individual's personality. Under their influence a person may suffer the loss of a sense of discrimination between right and wrong and become virtually an automaton, prepared to act at the behest of an unscrupulous mind.

A person may indeed be conditioned, not only by drugs, but in a multitude of other ways only too familiar to our age, and these can take place, under cover of medical treatment, in places of confinement such as mental institutions and prisons which, furthermore, are often beyond the reach of legal surveillance. Electrical stimulation of pre-selected areas of the brain can produce changes in behavioural patterns and even gases might be used to produce a false feeling of happiness and satisfaction with one's environment, or even of forgetfulness of some episode deemed inconvenient by those who administer it. With all the equipment of modern science at their disposal, what considerations are there to prevent persons being used in this fashion to further the unscrupulous ends of others?[32] All this may well take place under cover of alleged medical treatment, and any scientist not restrained by the traditional codes of ethics of the medical profession would enjoy increasing areas of power and dominion over the wills of others.

Under cover of pure academic research, a chemist may produce a deadly gas, a physicist a lethal ray, a psychologist a brainwashing technique. Com-

[31] See Chapter 1, *supra*.

[32] See Chapters 10, 14, 17 and 20, *infra*.

munity controls do not exist and no legal restraints stand in the way. Once developed, these threats would be with us for all time, raising the further problem of the near impossibility of perpetually policing this new danger. These may well be weapons so powerful as to enable their possessors to hold the rest of the community to ransom. A single demented person now has power, unthinkable a generation ago, to inflict upon society damage which can be measured in thousands, if not millions, of human lives.[33]

Nor can all dangerous science or dangerous materials be inventorized. An interesting illustration of the alarming possibilities resulting from the impossibility of accurate accounting of fissile material was the appearance in London, as early as October 1972, of a leaflet entitled "Towards a People's Bomb". This purported to describe how plutonium could be spirited away from nuclear plants and a crude nuclear weapon could be made by agencies other than governments. Although this claim was naturally viewed with the greatest scepticism, investigations conducted in consequence of the alarm it raised revealed many interesting facts concerning the dangers of nuclear material falling into unauthorized hands. It appeared also that every year about one percent of the plutonium processed throughout the world "disappears" and that the loss is put down to natural wastage. The possibility of an employee stealing minute quantities of atomic fuel pellets and stockpiling them over a period of time without an alarm being raised, cannot also be discounted.

About 200 distinguished scientists who met at Oxford in 1972 at the Pugwash Conference on World Affairs, raised an alarm about the possibility of nuclear weapons being used by tomorrow's terrorists. It would appear that shipments of spent fuel from Britain's eleven power stations were taken to Cumberland by lorry and train. This spent fuel contained plutonium which was extracted at the British Nuclear Fuels' plant at Windscale. Twenty pounds of plutonium would suffice to make an atomic bomb capable of devastating a large city. From Windscale, the almost pure plutonium was sent out by road, rail and air. Some of these routes traversed lonely country areas. Some shipments may have been sent by air. If hijacking of such a consignment should result in sufficient quantities of plutonium entering the hands of terrorists, it would enable them, with powerful aid from business or State sources, to hold the rest of the world to ransom. The Pugwash Conference emphasized the need for national and international action for safeguards against such possibilities, seeing that "there is a danger that, to some degree,

[33] See Harold P. Green, *The New Technological Era: A View from the Law*, Monograph No. 1, George Washington University Program of Policy Studies in Science and Technology, Jan. 1968, at 2.

fissile products (such as plutonium) may fall into the hands of irresponsible and even criminal groups". Fears of such terrorist activity have by no means abated over the years, and news items from various parts of the world relating to the transport of spent fuel continue to cause concern.

The problems faced by Britain in this respect could well be duplicated in every country where atomic power stations discharge spent fuel.[34] Moreover, such plants may be located in desolate regions where the possibility of hijacking a consignment is not easily ruled out. In an age in which the hijacking of planes, the mass murder of international athletes, and other atrocities in pursuit of a cause are possible occurrences, it is wise to realize that forces are at work which will stop at nothing, however serious, if only the means were available to them.

The truth is that existing biological, physical, and chemical means, any one of them potent enough to wreck the entire world, are being constantly perfected and new ones are being constantly discovered. A cloak of protection or of secrecy hides these activities. There are loopholes through which science and technology project themselves well out of the range of legal controls. All of them offer illustrations of the importance of grappling with the problem of bringing science within the dominion of the law.

8. THE COLLAPSE OF THE PHYSICAL ASSUMPTIONS UNDERLYING TRADITIONAL LEGAL CONCEPTS

Most legal concepts are based upon certain assumptions of possibility and impossibility. On this basis, which has been true since the beginnings of all forms of social control, the social controls embodied by the law have evolved. Trespass presupposed physical invasions of territory, theft presupposed physical removal of property, assault presupposed physical contact, invasions of privacy presupposed physical surveillance. All legal concepts were structured on certain physical assumptions. Many of those assumptions have collapsed, but the concepts live on.

Long after modern technology renders possible that which was impossible from the beginning of time, and renders the resulting legal concept ineffective, the concept tends to be retained unaltered despite the change.

As elsewhere, many legal concepts can be used as illustrations. Merely as an illustrative example, which can be duplicated in almost any field, we shall here discuss an anecdote related by Winston Churchill in his autobiography,

[34] In March 1997 mass protests were staged in Germany against the movement of nuclear waste by road and rail. These protests attracted much international attention.

when describing his service in the Boer War. X-ray photography had just been invented.

> There was a song called 'The New Photographee' about some shocking invention which had just been made, enabling photographs to be taken through a screen or other opaque obstruction.

It appeared that there might soon be an end to all privacy, and popular reaction was summed up in the soldiers' song:

> The inside of everything you see
> A terrible thing, an 'orrible thing
> Is the new photographee.[35]

This was a light-hearted expression of a fear that this scientific device might enable persons so minded, including even the public authorities, to trespass upon a person's privacy in defiance of the principle that "every man's home is his castle". Privacy law, framed on the assumption that I must set foot in your territory if I am to intrude on your privacy, lingered on, continuing to rest on old assumptions.

The humour has long passed out of the situation. There is an unending array of devices today available to the public authorities, if not to one's enemies and rivals, to probe into the innermost secrets of one's affairs. Wire tapping, by which telephone conversations can be heard and recorded, or the electronic eye by which the contents of any confidential postal package can be scanned, or the "bug" by which any office or hotel room may be wired for sound without the victim's knowledge, are among the simplest of these devices. In the not too distant future, it may conceivably be possible to train a scientific device from a distance upon a closed room and pick up the scenes and conversations enacted within it, without any awareness by the victims that they are under observation. The inventions are piling up at a rate which far outpaces the possibilities of legal control. The law is not ready with the appropriate armoury of new concepts to challenge these new weapons of intrusion. The law is devising them still. But even as the law fashions new concepts and remedies, new technologies render these new remedies outmoded even before they see the light of day.

Moreover, even when legislatures decide to move in the matter, they often meet with a variety of obstacles. Thus a series of bills was introduced in the United Kingdom to protect various aspects of privacy in the 1960s, but they all ran into difficulties and had to be abandoned. However, a bill put forward by Brian Walden, MP, resulted in an undertaking by the Home Sec-

[35] Winston Churchill, *My Early Life, 1874–1908*, Fontana, 1969, (1930), p. 130.

retary to appoint a committee to inquire into the protection of privacy, if the Bill was withdrawn.[36] The Committee, chaired by the Rt. Hon. Kenneth Younger, reported in 1972.[37] The Report is commonly referred to as the Younger Report. However, even this high-level Committee was confined by its terms of reference to invasions of privacy in the private sector and could not inquire into intrusions by the State.

When, in the United Kingdom, the Younger Committee on Privacy received evidence on technical surveillance devices available, one firm of private detectives provided it with copies of its sales catalogue in which some of the microphones available were illustrated disguised as a box of matches, a fountain pen, and a lapel badge.[38] Among the devices listed by the Commission[39] were a needle thin flashlight used as a scanner to read the contents of envelopes, the proverbial "bug" which could be used in a cocktail olive or a tie pin (the practical transmission range of this device is about a quarter of a mile), a microphone about the size of a match head which would pick up a whisper at 20 feet, tap-on devices to tap telephone lines at any point, drawing an undetectable amount of electricity from the telephone wire and giving no betraying noises, and numerous others.[40]

Even more chilling evidence was outlined in a 1973 Report of the Secretary-General to the United Nations[41] — such as special bulbs in overhead fixtures or lamps which flood a dark room with infra red light for clear snapshots and films (para. 106), substances which give the appearance of solid wall panels which do not permit the passage of regular light, but do transmit infra red light (para. 107), passing "infra red energy" through sealed envelopes to take pictures (para. 108), "optical fibres" that can bend light around corners (para. 103), fluorescent powders or dyes applied secretly to a person's hands or clothing, or hair tonic which a person applies regularly (para. 111), an aerial hovering device which can take pictures and listen to activity a mile away from a person's property (para. 113), and a "bug" installed in a victim's telephone which enables an eavesdropper, even thousands of miles away, to listen to any conversation taking place within earshot of the victim's telephone (para. 93). The list is endless. It needs little imagi-

36 See James Michael, *Privacy and Human Rights*, UNESCO, 1994, pp. 100–101.

37 Report of the Committee on Privacy, Cmnd. 5012 (London, HMSO, 1972).

38 Younger Report, para. 509.

39 See Table attached to § 505.

40 *Ibid.* One can well imagine the further refinements that have taken place in the quarter century that has elapsed since then.

41 "Respect for the privacy of individuals and the integrity and sovereignty of nations in the light of advances in recording and other techniques", E/CN.4/1116 of 23 January 1973.

nation to visualize how the intervening quarter century has immensely improved upon these methods.

Forty years ago these dangers were visualized by Justice Douglas of the United States Supreme Court:

> conversation within the home and the office could be recorded without tapping any wire. The intimacies of private life can be made public without a key being turned or a window being raised, and those who listen in may be private detectives and blackmailers, as well as law enforcement officials.[42]

Sixty years ago, Justice Brandeis saw the problem stretching even into the sphere of the psychic sciences. He said:

> The advances in science — discovery and invention — have made it possible for the government to effect disclosure in court of 'what is whispered in the closet' — by means far more effective than stretching the defendant upon the rack. By means of television, radium and photography, there may some day be developed ways by which the Government could, without removing papers from secret drawers, reproduce them in court and lay before the jury the most intimate occurrences of the home. It is conceivable, also, that advances in the psychic and related sciences may afford means of exploring a man's unexpressed beliefs, thoughts and emotions.[43]

Legal systems in many countries have over the years realized their inadequacy in the face of the manifold threats to privacy posed by these devices and have taken steps to protect the citizen against them.[44] In France, a new article (Article 9) was introduced into the French Civil Code by a Law of 17 July 1970, declaring that "Everyone has the right to respect for his private life".[45] On the same day, certain new articles were introduced into the Penal Code, creating new offences which included private spying by audio-visual devices. In West Germany, attempts to embody the right in a statute failed in

[42] Justice Douglas, *The Right of the People*, 1957, p. 98.

[43] From a Memorandum of Feb. 16, 1928 on his dissent in *Olmstead* v. *United States*, 277 U.S. 438, at 473–4 (1928). Cited in Julius Stone, *Social Dimensions of Law and Justice*, Maitland Publications (Sydney), 1966, p. 215.

[44] It is noteworthy that some States indeed look upon wire tapping as being so grave a menace as to embody a clause in their Constitution against this practice. The Constitution of Puerto Rico, for example, provides that "wire tapping is prohibited" (art. 1, § 10).

[45] In France the notion goes all the way back to 1858 when the courts began to build up a *droit personnalité* through an interpretation of general tortious liability as contained in Article 1382 of the Civil Code.

1958 and 1959, but a strong body of case law has been built up establishing a right to privacy. In The Netherlands, the Criminal Code was amended by an Act of 7 April 1971 making it an offence to listen in to a conversation carried on in a dwelling or private premises by means of a technical device, other than on the instructions of a participant in that conversation. In England, the Younger Committee on Privacy, to which we have already referred, submitted a detailed report containing proposals for the improvement of the law.

The Committee observed, "Leaving aside the law's various protections, such as they are, against the unauthorized use of personal information once it has been obtained without authority, *there is little in either the civil or criminal law to control technical surveillance devices*". The Committee pointed out[46] that the only parts of the criminal law directed specifically at some of the technical devices were the Wireless Telegraphy Acts of 1949 and 1967.[47]

Amendments to the Swiss Penal Code in 1969 aimed at protecting the individual's privacy against invasion by technical devices. In all legal systems, new torts and new crimes of unlawful surveillance by technological devices are needed.

The Nordic Conference of Jurists in May 1967 analysed the right to privacy as meaning the individual's right to lead his own life protected against interference with private or mental integrity or moral or intellectual freedom; attacks on honour or reputation; being placed in a false light; the disclosure of irrelevant, embarrassing facts relating to private life; the use of name, identity or likeness; spying, prying, watching and besetting; interference with correspondence; misuse of private communications, written or oral; and disclosure of information given or received by a person in circumstances of professional confidence.[48]

Technology makes nearly all of these types of interference easy.

The Standing Committee on Law and Technology of the Union Internationale des Avocats suggested an approach to privacy based upon a view of it as an essential possession to be interfered with only for the best of reasons and as sparingly as possible.

46 § 520 and 521, the Younger Report, *supra*; emphasis added.

47 A Draft Right of Privacy Bill, prepared by the National Council of Civil Liberties (see Appendix F to the Younger Report), defined the right of privacy as including the right of a person to be protected from intrusion by spying, prying, watching, or besetting, unauthorized recording of spoken words, unauthorized making of visual images, and a variety of other means.

48 See, generally, Louise Doswald-Beck, "The Meaning of the 'Right to Respect for Private Life' under the European Convention of Human Rights", 4 *Hum. Rts. L.J.* 283 (1983).

There has been much debate on whether this right is a general right, like a right of property, or whether it is a right protecting the individual against interference by the state. The Nordic Conference favoured the former view; the Legal Committee of the Consultative Assembly of the Council of Europe favoured the latter.[49]

Thus, though with some delay, the prescient warnings of Brandeis and Douglas have struck an answering chord in a concerned international response over the past quarter century, and the momentum of this response is being steadily increased under the impact of ever more sophisticated technological advances.

Practical solutions, however, keep receding even as the law advances, for increasingly sophisticated devices are steadily becoming more difficult to detect and are keeping the law at bay. Consequently, though rights to privacy may be defined by the law and sanctioned by heavy penalties, they tend in practice to be ineffective. In the result, serious encroachments have been made on the individual's freedom and privacy without adequate countermeasures by the law.

Privacy cannot however be an absolute and unfettered right. Some surrender of privacy will be needed in the interests of society. The Nordic Conference of Jurists phrased the limitations well when it observed:

> In modern society, the right to privacy, as any other human right, can never be without limitations except in the sense that nothing can justify measures which are inconsistent with the physical, mental, intellectual or moral dignity of the human person.

As with all areas of technology, the need is thus manifest for close study and the careful formulation of principles and exceptions.[50]

The complexities thus attendant on privacy law can be duplicated in almost any area of new technology one may care to name.

We have commenced this discussion with problems of individual privacy, because they readily come to mind as areas of intrusion by science into the life of the individual. However, they are not by any means the gravest of the problems posed by the progress of science.

As everyone knows, the influence of scientific advance spills over from the laboratory into every aspect of human life, sparing neither the patterns of government, nor the routines of the home. The technology of the future will

[49] See, e.g., Council of Europe, Draft Convention for the Protection of Individuals with Regard to Automatic Processing of Personal Data, 19 *I.L.M.* 284 (1980).

[50] Media intrusion into the lives of famous personalities have highlighted this conflict in the late 'nineties.

wield immensely greater influence, enabling those who enjoy it to exercise dominion over people's thoughts and lives as never before.

9. INADEQUACY OF COURTS AS AN INSTRUMENT OF SOCIAL PROTECTION

For such reasons, then, the existing legal machinery needs to be reviewed to heighten its adequacy to deal with the problems of the age of science. We must ask whether we are content to have a highly technical matter involving the health and welfare of the entire community decided by a judge who has no expertise for the task, using tools which were not fashioned for it. We must examine how we can infuse a greater expertise into the judge's training, and a greater suitability into the tools he uses. We must study the possibility of improving the situation through steps towards inter-disciplinary education in the law schools, through similar steps in the schools of science, and through seminars which will bring in the layman. As already suggested, we could even take the idea a step further by setting up a special scientific section of the courts to consider the ever increasing number of matters of a scientific nature that demand decision from time to time. Throughout history those legal systems have tended to flourish which have been sufficiently resilient to adapt themselves to meet new situations and new challenges, developing areas of special expertise for this purpose, as in the field of commercial law. Living as we do in an age dominated by technology and science, might it not be appropriate to consider whether we should not set up some tribunals better equipped to handle this kind of technological matter?

10. INABILITY OF THE LAW TO CALL A HALT WHEN "BRINK SITUATIONS" ARE REACHED

One other danger to the rule of law and to democracy as we understand it today remains to be mentioned. It is indeed even more portentous than any we have mentioned thus far.

Science has reached a point at which it takes civilization to the brink, in a sense different from that of physical annihilation. Science has reached a stage where its further advance in certain directions may confront humanity with what Professor Julius Stone has described as "catastrophic choices between achieving the impossible and suffering the insufferable".[51] This brings us to what has been described as the "brink situation". Many jurists

[51] Julius Stone, "Knowledge and the Human Predicament", 1 *The Medical Journal of Australia*, 787 at 789 (1970).

have written on this in recent years — notably Professor Julius Stone[52] — and they have used the term "brink situation" or "limit situation" to describe the stage reached where two or three steps more may take all mankind over the brink, into a universal and irreversible catastrophe. In those brink situations it will soon be too late to attempt to impose controls or to slow down the rate of research.

What is here referred to is the fact that in many fields of scientific research, science is on the brink of reaching knowledge which, once attained, cannot be contained. There is no known way of preventing such knowledge from reaching the hands of those who will use it without scruples in order to dominate the rest of the community. Human nature being what it is, it is impossible to hope for the happy state in which those who can use that knowledge to perpetuate their tenure of power will voluntarily refrain from doing so.

Of this kind of activity, the discovery of nuclear weapons is but one aspect. Another aspect is the development of techniques of mass indoctrination, through which it is possible to manipulate the thought processes of vast numbers of people; and of social destruction by techniques of mass propagation of forms of human life unwilling or unable to defy the authority of those who bring them into being. "Compared with this prospect, our present subjection to the 'hidden persuaders' of Madison Avenue, the public relations professions and the mass media, is a state of political bliss."[53]

Nobel laureate, Sir MacFarlane Burnet, has observed that the human implications of work on tissue-cultured cells, bacteria and viruses is "at best dubious, and at worst frankly terrifying".[54]

Then again there is the possibility of manipulation of the human brain.[55] In this field there seems to be a whole array of devices available to modern science for interfering with functions basic to individuality — surgical treatment, electrical treatment, drug treatment, behavioural treatment. A number of methods already exist through which people can be made to act differently from the manner in which they might have acted under their own volition. The extent to which these possibilities might in the future make procedures available to the unscrupulous for compelling people to act at their

[52] See Julius Stone, "Knowledge, Survival and the Duties of Science", 23 *American University Law Review*, 231 (1973).

[53] Stone, "Knowledge and the Human Predicament", *supra*, p. 788.

[54] MacFarlane Burnet, "Men and Molecules, a Tilt at Molecular Biology", 1 *The Lancet* 37 (1966).

[55] See Chapter 17 below ("Some Orwellian Scenarios").

behest is surely deserving of consideration here and now. What happens then to notions of legal responsibility? What happens to the criminal law?

If we should face a brink situation in the environmental field, how would we cope with it? We are being told a great deal about the release of fluorocarbons. Five hundred thousand tons have apparently been released into the atmosphere and we do not know how much the ozone layer can take. Twenty billion tons of carbon dioxide are being discharged every year. Lead is discharged at a growth rate of 3.4 per cent per year. The Club of Rome says we do not know how much punishment the atmosphere can take and at what stage precisely we will reach a state of breakdown, when the life support systems of the earth collapse with frightening suddenness. We do not know these things. No doubt the scientists know them better than laymen, but among the scientists themselves there seem to be differences of opinion.

It is well beyond the competence of laymen to make assessments of the precise results that will flow from the advancement of knowledge in fields such as this. It is clear however that these advances are posing problems at least as serious to the future of mankind as were posed by the invention of nuclear weapons, and that we are reaching what may be described as a limit-situation in scientific knowledge.

Once this knowledge is achieved, it will be too late to devise methods of control. It will carry with it the implications of the destruction of society as we know it. How then are the limitations to be placed upon the pursuit of knowledge for its own sake where that knowledge takes society to the brink of destruction? Does the old argument, that the pursuit of knowledge for the sake of knowledge cannot justifiably be hindered, still obtain in such field? Or rather has not the situation changed so considerably that some limitation must be placed upon this age-old principle? We were inclined to think at one stage that the resources of the world were so large and that the sea and the atmosphere were so vast that waste or pollution could not materially deplete the former or affect the latter. We reached a limit-situation far sooner than we expected. In the pursuit of scientific knowledge, we are fast reaching similar limit-situations and it would be a problem for serious consideration by humanity, whether some controls ought to be imposed, and if so, by whom.

Professor Stone summarizes the problem by posing the question:

> As scientists seek and find drugs and psychological techniques for manipulating the human will and the human brain, or for controlling human heredity through growing knowledge of the gene-bearing substance DNA, may they too not be bringing about situations in which social and political life is put wholly at the mercy of a handful of manipulators?[56]

Law and lawyers cannot stand away from this problem, for if any solution is possible, they are among the best equipped to suggest it. The duty to alert the public as well as to suggest means for regulation lies upon them.

The point that emerges is this: If we are uncertain of the effect of any further progress in certain particular danger areas, is it not wise to apply the brakes, halt for a while, assess our progress, and make sure in what direction these dangerous activities are leading us?

When Sir MacFarlane Burnet suggested such a moratorium in the 1960s, he was practically a lone voice, but in the 1970s there has been a powerful support for his point of view. The American Academy of Sciences has accepted the notion of voluntary moratoria in regard to molecular genetics, or in certain areas of it at least. The British Medical Association has also taken up the idea, and voluntary moratoria have been imposed in respect of certain kinds of scientific activity, as, for example, in regard to recombinant DNA experimentation.[57]

11. RE-LINKING SCIENCE AND SOCIETY

(i) *An Ethic for Scientists*

The scientific enterprise has functioned hitherto on the basis that truthfulness of scientific reporting is the prime value. The primary principle that governs the scientific ethic is the principle of loyalty to truth. The emphasis on this ethical aspect has tended to cloud the importance of other ethical issues.

The medical profession has been an exception in this regard, for the Hippocratic oath has from very early times set before the medical practitioner certain ethical standards which he or she is expected to observe over and above the mere standard of scientific loyalty to truth. However, the Hippocratic code is a very rudimentary ethical code, totally inadequate to the vast new problems which today raise issues of an ethical nature. Even more im-

[56] Stone, "Knowledge and the Human Predicament", *supra*, 790.

[57] See, generally, British Medical Association, *Our Genetic Future: The Science and Ethics of Genetic Technology* (1992). In the context of the cloning of sheep in 1997, the question of a scientific moratorium on this sort of experimentation has been revived.

portantly, it is to be noted that most other bodies of scientists do not owe loyalty to any formulated ethical code. The computer scientist, the engineer, the microbiologist, the physicist, the chemist — all of these, despite the vast social implications of their research, do not have an ethical code which binds them to the observance of certain ethical values.

It is true that today an awareness of the need for such ethical codes is growing, and that such bodies as associations of engineers, or computer workers, are working out some basic ethical codes which practitioners of the relevant disciplines are expected to observe. These codes are still largely rudimentary and, by and large, not obligatory in their nature. Consequently a researcher engaged on some research which may well be damaging to human rights is not required to take this factor into consideration in deciding whether or not to pursue that kind of activity. Consequently, scientists engaged in work which can be very damaging to the environment, or weapon scientists engaged in the perfection of some new lethal weapon, are not obliged under the present dispensation to consider the human rights implications of their work.

Notable exceptions do of course exist, as where scientists engaged on recombinant DNA experimentation imposed a moratorium on their own research in the fear that a newly synthesized microbe could be created of unknown lethal potential which could decimate the human race. In such notable instances, which are indeed exceptional, ethical principles have indeed been translated into practical restraints on scientific research.

The human rights implications of damaging technology are however so great as to make it an urgent problem that the importance of an ethical code for scientists should be brought home to the practitioners of all branches of science. It is no longer adequate for the scientist to say that he or she is a concerned human being like everyone else and can be depended upon to bear in mind any possible damage to society resulting from the work in hand. It has not worked out thus in the past and it will not in the future. One recalls contemporaneous accounts of the jubilation shown by the scientists at Los Alamos when news was brought to them of the successful detonation at Hiroshima of the nuclear weapon they had created.[58]

A view heavily stressed in the 1960s was that the purpose to which science was applied was outside the boundaries of science itself. As observed in a well-known book of that period on the scientific enterprise, "Purpose, aesthetics, ... ethics — these are outside the boundaries of science".[59] Whatever

[58] R.W. Reid, *The Tongues of Conscience: War and the Scientist's Dilemma*, Constable, 1969, pp. 103–104.

[59] Magnus Pyke, *The Boundaries of Science*, Pelican Books, 1963, p. 201.

be the correctness of this observation within the purely scientific operations involved, it should not cloud the vision of the scientist regarding the purpose of his or her research. It is essential for the scientist to bear in mind that it is the same set of technical rules that would be used, whether for the construction of a hospital or for a torture chamber. It will not do for the scientist to give of his or her expertise, without regard to the end result for which that expertise is used.

(ii) *Some problems of self-regulation*

Before we pass on to the problem of external regulation of this titanic power, it becomes necessary to examine whether internal regulation from within the ranks of scientists themselves is possible. This raises the question of the need for an ethical code in science, seeing that at present no ethic or code of conduct exists to regulate scientific activity. The only ethic so far recognized (apart, that is, from the ethical code of the medical profession) is loyalty to truth, for the scientist has been taught that he or she must on no account distort the truth in an attempt to prove a hypothesis. In science, misreporting of experiments is the gravest of crimes, but there is no prohibition upon the lending of one's expertise for the most nefarious purposes.

Moreover, the participant in a limited scientific experiment directed by a superior authority may have no knowledge that the small part he plays is meant to fit, together with the efforts of others similarly placed, into the pattern of a project which in its totality he would condemn. The individual scientist thus engaged upon a small component part of a large project, would find also that the resources made available for such research are ampler by far than any that would be available to pursue an individual line of interest independently of the greater scheme, and this constitutes a strong inducement to stay on.

The vast resources and power of the modern State or transnational corporation make it a distinct possibility that hundreds of scientists are thus employed in research to which they would not lend themselves had they a bird's eye view of it. Such employers may well take special pains to screen the individual scientist from a view of the overall picture and, in the result, the best scientific brains could be used as innocent tools in a project cutting across the moral fibre of the entire community. Especially in those vastly complex commercial organizations which are a feature of modern life, the same considerations apply, for their left hand may not know what their right hand does, and can far less discern what goes on in their controlling minds.

The frightening overall picture of such research presents itself only when it is too late for the scientist to retract from the venture or withdraw the knowledge he or she has contributed. Thus those whose scientific skill went into the making of the first atomic bomb were not all aware of the end to which their overall research was directed. Wernher Von Braun, the father of rocketry, has written:

> With the tight press censorship imposed by Hitler, the abuses of his regime were not nearly as visible to the average German as they were to an outsider who had free access to the international news media. For this reason, I must say, more by way of a statement than as an apology, that I never realized the depth of the abyss of Hitler's regime until very late and particularly after the war, when all those terrible abuses were first published.[60]

Moreover, when the pangs of conscience strike, they may strike too late. One recalls the deeply moving observation of Oppenheimer, the atomic scientist who helped create the atom bomb. When it was too late to retrace his steps, he used the words of the Hindu classic, *The Bhagavad Gita*, to confess to a feeling that, "I am become Death, the destroyer of worlds".

The same applies no doubt to other lethal creations as, for example, weapons used in germ warfare, where the biologist, the medical expert, the pathologist and others, may each be employed to work on different aspects of the enterprise, without any one of them realizing the lethal overall purpose for which the individual's work is required.

In considering an ethic for scientists, a distinction may have to be drawn between pure research (if indeed there is such a thing) and its practical applications. The former may conceivably be free of objection on the basis that it is the pursuit of knowledge for its sake; but unforeseen ethical implications may begin to take shape at the stage of its practical application outside the laboratory. Once the pure scientist has obtained the necessary knowledge and perfected the process in question, such a scientist may have no control over its practical application, which is often a matter for other hands and other minds. At what stage, then, is the ethic, if any, to be imposed? Could Einstein, a man of peace, have prevented the application of the knowledge he had found to the creation of the atomic bomb? If not, should or could any restraint have been applied at an earlier stage? But at the earlier stage his research was perfectly compatible with its peaceful use. The illustration is perhaps not the aptest, but it shows the two stages of the scientific process in a manner which commands ready understanding. Foreseeability of danger might well be the test, for if a scientist foresees that his or her research can lead to consequences dangerous to humanity, the scientist is conceivably

[60] R.W. Reid, *The Tongues of Conscience*, *supra*, p. 105 (letter to author).

under a duty to sound a note of warning and seek clearance for such research, not merely from fellow-scientists, but from the community. The latter, acting through its representatives, will need the scientist's guidance, and at this point the highest ethical duties of complete disclosure and impartial advice would lie upon the scientist concerned. The scientist's conscience will at this stage be his or her guide and it will probably be by this yardstick that the scientist's responsibility will eventually be judged. The concept of the scientist's responsibility for the foreseeable effects of his or her research is growing, and I venture to think we are not far from the day when it will be a recognized axiom not only of morality, but also of jurisprudence.[61]

(iii) *The concept of social responsibility in science*

The idea of an ethic for science goes back to the Hippocratic oath, but has not developed outside the area of medical science and, even in medical science, has not developed far from its Hippocratic origin.

A hopeful sign in the direction of further development was the formation in America of a Society for Social Responsibility in Science, followed in 1969 by the creation of a similar society in Britain. An interesting assertion by scientists of their right to protest against the uses to which their research was being put was a strike in March 1969 by faculty members of the Massachusetts Institute of Technology and other American Universities for a token day against the abuse of science for war. Again, a Hippocratic oath has been proposed for the engineer of the future.[62]

The formulation of a complete ethical code which will say what is "right" and "wrong" from the point of research is, of course, too much to hope for, but it is not too much to expect a set of *ad hoc* rulings from time to time by a body like the Press Council of England, which will in time produce an acceptable set of ethical principles.

It is unlikely however that the self-restraints or the necessary effectiveness will be forthcoming from the scientists concerned, for narrow disciplinary backgrounds, self-interest, and the lack of ethical values in existing

[61] See Julius Stone, "Knowledge, Survival and the Duties of Science", 23 *American University Law Review*, 231 (1973).

[62] *Journal of the Royal Society of Arts*, April 1966. The suggested oath reads: "On becoming a Chartered Engineer, I vow to use my best endeavours to consider how my engineering skill may contribute towards the happiness of mankind."

schemes of professional training (apart, that is, from the medical profession) contribute to render such self-restraint unlikely.[63]

Scientists of the utmost intelligence and integrity are often carried away by their devotion to the work they have in hand. When the A4 rockets launched from Peenemünde on 3 October 1942[64] proved to be a success, a celebration party was held at Peenemünde that evening. When the news of the successful explosion of the atomic bomb on Hiroshima was received at Los Alamos laboratory, where so much work was done upon it, there was apparently such jubilation that scientists could be seen rushing to the telephone to order celebration dinners at nearby restaurants[65]. The degree of their immersion in their work was apparently such that the thought did not strike them in either case that what they were celebrating involved the painful death and suffering of many thousands.

One recalls with a feeling of helplessness an appeal issued by Bertrand Russell and Albert Einstein two days before the latter's death (in what has come to be known as the Russell-Einstein Manifesto of July 1955), outlining the risks of thermonuclear war and concluding:

> We appeal, as human beings to human beings; remember your humanity and forget the rest. If you do so, the way lies open to a new Paradise; if you cannot, there lies before you the risk of universal death.[66]

It seems axiomatic also that one cannot, speaking in practical terms, expect the employer of the scientist to restrain itself by respect for an ethical code.

Scientists employed by business interests will be working to promote the interests of the business, and ethical considerations scarcely come into play. Business concerns itself largely with questions of marketability and overcoming sales resistance and governmental objections, but does not devote anything like the same degree of thought to the question of the good or ill effects upon society of a proposed innovation. This even applies to University-sponsored research, for the Universities themselves sometimes permit their position and resources to be exploited by commerce and State. The pressures of State or financial power can on occasion prove too powerful for them to resist, and research is all too often undertaken for no better reason

[63] See H. Morgenthau, "Modern Science and Political Power", (1964) 64 *Col. L. Rev.*, 1386.

[64] R.W. Reid, *Tongues of Conscience, supra.*, p. 103.

[65] *Ibid.*, p. 214.

[66] This led to the Pugwash movement, by which Cyrus Eaton, Cleveland industrialist, financed meetings of leading scientists at Pugwash, his birthplace, and afforded a forum and means of expression for scientists in the cause of peace.

than that funds are made available for it. Research should not be available on tap merely because an external source produces the funds and the University has the talent.

The mechanisms for setting up such controlling bodies are already taking shape in the US and elsewhere. Technology assessment boards, at both the national and international level, are urgently required, with a combination of technical and inter-disciplinary talent as well as public representation. Guidelines for research in particular fields (such as the 200-page book of guidelines for genetic research issued by the National Institute of Health in America) need to be issued. Legislative, executive, and judicial restructuring needs to be undertaken. The legal profession, the Universities, the media, the education authorities, all have a part to play. New principles need recognition regarding science and scientific research. But above all a great reawakening is required from within the ranks of the scientific community itself.

(iv) *The need for interdisciplinary interaction*

This necessitates the building up of a programme of inter-disciplinary education at institutions of higher learning. Such programmes will provide personnel, not only for purposes such as those envisaged in the preceding paragraph, but will also furnish leadership for the crusading movements of the future.

Attempts have already been made in this direction as, for example, at Boston University Law School which has established a new Center for Law and Health Sciences. At this Center, law students meet and work with graduate students from other disciplines and earn academic credits for this work. In a summer pilot programme, 15 graduates from Boston, Brandeis, Harvard and Massachusetts Institute of Technology were divided into four inter-disciplinary teams, each of which grappled with a complex problem such as genetic counselling. Faculty members representing the necessary expertise stood by for consultation.[67] So, also, as early as 1965, the Rockefeller University held a conference on Law and the Social Role of Science, under the joint auspices of the University and the Walter E. Meyer Research Institute of Law.

It is thought by workers in this field that such training is one of the most important tasks at hand for schools of law, science and engineering in the future, and that such projects are in need of intensive public support.[68]

[67] See Michael S. Baram, "Social Control of Science and Technology", 172 *Science*, 538, 538–9 (1971).

[68] On legal education for the age of technology, see Chapter 4, *infra*.

Such an inter-disciplinary education will also be important for the training of the bureaucracy of the future. It does not have to be a training in the minutiae of any particular scientific discipline, but an inter-disciplinary education ranging across fields of physics, chemistry, electronics, psychology, literature, civilization, and history, in much the same way as a lawyer's general training ranges across the numerous fields of family law, industrial law, criminal law, administrative law, and so on. The bureaucrat must know sufficient to enable him or her to approach a problem correctly when there is a science-oriented problem in hand. Since knowledge has now grown so extensive that the details in any field must be left to experts, the educated citizen of the future and, more importantly, the competent bureaucrat, must be one who is not deterred from assessing the broad aspects of a matter merely because it occurs in a discipline which is not home ground to the person concerned. The bridge between the cultures must be broad and strong, and there should be constant traffic upon it.

Another aspect of inter-disciplinary education which is perhaps essential for the future is the widening of outlook of the future scientist through an exposure to other disciplines. Just as the old criticism that lawyers tended to be narrow in their outlook was met by exposing law students to compulsory courses in other disciplines, so also must the outlook of the young scientist be enlarged. A compulsory year of sociology and of special courses alerting students to the social responsibilities of scientists must certainly leave an impact on their minds which will help to temper their activities throughout their careers. Students are particularly receptive to these ideas today, and will certainly appreciate a course helping them to make a greater contribution to society. Such a course will help also when they mature into active scientists, to generate in them a respect for ethical values which, when generally shared by scientists, can result in a climate of opinion among them, which can act as a most effective check against unethical or antisocial activity.

12. A NEW JURISPRUDENCE FOR THE SCIENTIFIC AGE

As we move on towards the close of this century, and the commencement of the next, and as the centre of gravity of society shifts inexorably in the direction of the scientists, new principles, traditions and rules relating to matters we have discussed may well occupy, in the foreseeable future, as important a place in the scheme of public affairs as constitutional law occupies today. There may well be a whole department of jurisprudence specially evolved by an age of science to deal with the problems that result from science. While the total body of scientific knowledge in the world appears to be doubling every seven to ten years, the quantum of non-scientific knowledge and skill remains approximately the same. The relative disparity which now exists between scientific and non-scientific skill is thus but a fraction of what it will be in the foreseeable future. The law would be out of tune with the needs and temper of that future if it does not equip itself now to prepare for that future.

Outworn concepts must be discarded, new procedures fashioned, new principles of conduct moulded. Law would fail society in discharging its role of guardian of its rights and obligations if it set about its task on the basis of attitudes that have outlived their context, and procedures that have outlasted their utility.[69]

The new methods and structures for the age of science are now in the process of being evolved. It is vital that, in their formative stage, concerted attention be given to them by lawyer and layman alike, for else they will soon settle firmly into moulds whose shape it may be too late to alter. In that form, they will govern the lives of people for generations to come.

Clemenceau once said of war that it is too serious a business to be left to the generals. So, also, is science too serious a business to be left to the scientists.

[69] For some suggestions see Ch. 25, *infra*.

3. The Tension between Scientific Power and Human Rights*

The areas of intrusion into basic rights, where the law lags behind its duties of protection, could be conveniently grouped under the categories of the human body, human society, and the human environment.

(i) *The Human Body*

The preamble to the Universal Declaration of Human Rights commences with a reference to the inherent dignity of all members of the human family and provides more specifically that all human beings are born free and equal in dignity and rights (Art. 1); that no one shall be subjected to torture or to cruel, inhuman or degrading treatment or punishment (Art. 5); and that everyone has the right to recognition everywhere as a person before the law (Art. 6). Article 29(1) recognizes the importance of the free and full development of human personality.

What are the technologies that erode this high recognition of human dignity through their impact upon the human body?

A vast range of biotechnological developments comes immediately to mind — human experimentation, foetal experimentation, sale and hire of organs, torture techniques, psychosurgery, personality tests, the use of untested drugs, genetic engineering, selective breeding, pre-selection of sex are some of these. Sperm and ova banks, *in vitro* fertilization, embryo transplantation, foetus farms — all of these raise important ethical and human rights issues.

The problem here is that research on the human body for therapeutic and preventive purposes must always go ahead. On the other hand, as more knowledge is acquired, new possibilities open up of the use of that knowl-

* The tables at the end of this Chapter are extracted from the author's *The Slumbering Sentinels: Law and Human Rights in the Wake of Technology*, Penguin, 1983, pp. 14–25, and the text is a summary of Chapters 4, 5 and 6. This chapter serves as an introduction to the fuller discussion of many of these topics in later chapters of this book.

edge for unethical purposes, or for purposes whose ethical value is debatable.

The author's personal experience of speaking on these matters since the mid-1970s to medical audiences led him to sense, at the time, that the intrusion of non-medical personnel such as lawyers into the arena of medical activity was unwelcome. The point of view was expressed that doctors, no less than other human beings are concerned members of society and could be trusted to use their expert knowledge in the best interests of society. The area they were in charge of was a specialist area and they were the best judges of how their particular expertise could be ethically used.

In the past fifteen or twenty years, that attitude has changed remarkably, with a growing awareness that the problems posed by scientific developments are so complex that they cannot be solved within the confines of any one discipline. Today, discussion of ethical issues in the medical field by non-medical persons, such as lawyers, ethicists and theologians is welcomed. Major hospitals have set up inter-disciplinary committees involving such personnel, to function alongside of doctors in order to assist them in reaching decisions on difficult issues. Universities have set up ethics committees to exercise control over such areas as medical experimentation and psychological research.

In short, constant vigilance is required to ensure that new advances in medical technology are kept within ethical guidelines[1].

Advances in medical technology, as in biotechnology, can spill over from the realm of pure science to the realm of commerce, and at that stage, the areas of possible abuse multiply. Human experimentation with new pharmaceutical products, in developing countries, is an example often cited. Organ transplants, extremely valuable as a new scientific technique, can become the subject of commercial exploitation. The sale of organs is sometimes organized on a commercial basis, with intermediaries and advertisements luring persons from the poor world into the rich world to donate organs such as a kidney for a price that seems attractive to the poor person concerned. The donor can indeed live without a kidney, and is prepared to undergo the resulting inconvenience for the affluence that this brings him in his own society. Worse abuses are now taking place, as has been alleged recently in regard to destitute street children being rounded up in big cities for the alleged purpose of using their organs.

Examples such as these show that the problems become of urgent concern, both nationally and internationally.

[1] See Chapter 19 below for a fuller discussion of medical ethics.

Likewise, in regard to the human mind, invasive techniques such as psychosurgery have been the subject of much abuse until, comparatively recently, professional controls in this regard were somewhat tightened. Instances of unwanted brain surgery in the United States for example have proliferated to the point of becoming a matter of grave national concern.

The possible invasions of human dignity and of the integrity of the human body are too varied and unforeseeable to catalogue in any single study.

(ii) *Human Society*

Brick-and-mortar concepts of deprivation of liberty, on which the law's protections are largely based, now convey only a small part of the picture. Stone walls and iron bars which came primarily to mind as the means of extinguishing liberty[2] are no longer the principal means of extinguishing a person's liberty. This can be done electronically.

Concern about the damaging impacts of information technology upon society dates back to the early 1970s. Senator Sam J. Ervin, Jr., Chairman of the United States Senate Subcommittee on Constitutional Rights, in writing a Foreword, in 1970, to a well known work on the assault on privacy resulting from computers, data banks, and dossiers, observed that the book "should bestir all Americans to claim their constitutional legacy of personal privacy and industrial rights and to demand an end to abuses of computer technology before the light of liberty is extinguished in our land".[3]

During the period that has elapsed since this warning, computer power has grown exponentially.

With the trend towards centralization, there is a tendency for a merger of various databanks in which such information is held. A pooling of data contained in income tax records, customs records, police records, health records, credit records, motor registration records and the like can give any government a vast dossier of information about each individual citizen. In addition, there are records held by public authorities such as universities or national insurance schemes, which can add to the information available, providing many details which the individual concerned may prefer to keep private. Moreover, the growth of commercial organizations operating multinationally means that their thousands of employees and customers also run the risk of a pooling of data concerning themselves in a central databank which is often beyond the control of national laws of the individual employee or customer.

2 "Stone walls do not a prison make, Nor iron bars a cage".

3 Foreword to Arthur R. Miller, *The Assault on Privacy: Computers, Data Banks and Dossiers*, Signet Books, 1971.

In the result, major problems arise of protection of the citizen against the abuse of this information, for information is power, and whoever holds a complete dossier of information about every facet of a person's life has power over that person.

Moreover, there is the problem of transborder data flow, that is, the flow of data concerning citizens of a country which escapes beyond national borders and thereafter remains free of the control of the country to which that individual belongs. Transborder data flow has attracted much attention, particularly from the OECD countries which have adopted strict guidelines regarding the control of such personal data.

The lack of the necessary controls, in regard to the vast bulk of the world's citizens, poses grave human rights problems, sometimes summarized in the term "the new information tyranny". Both governments and corporate establishments can be the entities that may abuse such information power.

The preceding paragraphs deal with tyranny through information concerning a citizen. There is also the growing danger of the monopolization of the means of mass information by governments or media groups. This constitutes another aspect of tyranny through information, for it enables the controllers of the media to determine what information shall reach the average citizen and what shall not. They are thus able to mould public opinion, for the public can only form its opinions on the basis of the information it receives. A newly emergent human right is the right to information.[4] Citizens are entitled to a full and free flow of information (subject, of course, to certain obvious safeguards in the public interest), concerning matters of importance in the running of their daily lives. Selective, incomplete or distorted information can be a real threat to the exercise of all the other human rights which a citizen enjoys in a free society — including even the right to vote, for this presupposes the right to proper information. The right to health can be similarly damaged by incomplete information regarding food, drugs or environmental dangers.

Yet another form of tyranny, which modern technology is rendering easier to achieve than ever before, is through the perfection of methods of psychological and physical torture. Many governments across the world have been documented as resorting to torture as an instrument of government. New techniques are being perfected and new forms of psychological and physical torture, strange to say, are still being devised. Amnesty International has considered this problem at great length and has referred to it as an "epidemic of torture" practices that is sweeping the world. Among the new instruments of torture are drugs, which induce certain psychological reactions

4 On this right, see Vol. 1, *Furthering Human Rights*, 1997, Chapter 12.

such as horror or fear or disorientation, and finely graded electrical shock. There is also pharmacological torture, where the victim does not know which drugs, of a range of drugs causing predictable unpleasant symptoms such as temporary paralysis, will be administered to him. Psychological tortures used for interrogation in-depth are other developments.

All of these impose a heavy responsibility on the medical profession (especially those connected with prisons and the army) to refuse to be party to the use of such techniques, and to report them when they do occur.[5]

Another aspect of high technology which has adverse social implications is the way in which technological secrets are jealously guarded. While the possessor of technology is entitled to protect the intellectual property associated with it, there is often a shrouding of the research results and the impact assessments of that technology, thereby preventing the public from being able to assess its usefulness or otherwise.

In a related area, problems can arise regarding patent rights in new discoveries or inventions, with implications for basic human rights. Let us take, for example, the right to health and, as a perhaps fanciful illustration, the creation of a drug which cures cancer. To what extent does the creator of the drug have the right to fix exorbitant price levels, placing the drug beyond the reach of the global public? Likewise, problems can arise regarding patent rights in agricultural products such as "miracle grains", disease resistant species of essential crops and newly created hybrids.

In all of these, the inventor or the creator or the owner of the patent has rights which must be respected. At the same time, one cannot ignore the interest of the community in the product. A proper balance needs to be struck, but the principles and mechanisms for achieving such a balance need further study.

In regard to the impact of technology on society, another trend to be noted is the spread of sophisticated technology to various terrorist movements, both domestic and international. The devices available to terrorist organizations keep increasing in sophistication and some organizations even maintain their own research laboratories for furthering and refining their weapons of attack. Terrorist organizations are sometimes in communication with each other, thereby enabling a pooling or exchange of the technical knowledge in their possession.

These are all problems awaiting concerned domestic and international attention.

5 On relevant principles of international law, see Chapter 19 below.

(iii) *The Human Environment*

It is not necessary to delve in depth into this area which has been the subject of much popular attention. The depletion of the ozone layer, the extinction of fauna and flora, the felling of rainforests, desertification, the pollution of the atmosphere, of lakes, rivers and seas — all these are proceeding apace. Major international conferences, such as the 1992 Rio Conference on the Environment,[6] bring together all the member states of the United Nations community for the purpose of addressing these problems.[7] They make some progress but, by and large, the solutions, if any, are only partial and the problems grow in intensity from year to year.[8]

Oil spills, discharges into the ocean of radioactive and other toxic wastes, unregulated depletion of marine species from plankton to whales, destruction of coral reefs — all of these cumulatively can affect the global food chain, apart from their damaging effects upon the right to a pure and healthful environment.

New technologies make massive deforestation a much easier operation than ever before. The loss of tree cover caused by uncontrolled felling of forests has an impact in several major ways. In the first place, it raises the carbon dioxide levels of the atmosphere which otherwise the forests might have absorbed. Secondly, it erodes the valuable topsoil on which agriculture depends. Deforestation exposes humus-covered soil, the richness of which is rapidly washed away. Studies reveal that tens of thousands of millions of tons of topsoil have been irreversibly lost in this fashion. Thirdly, it raises the water table, for the deep roots of trees no longer suck out the water and pump it into the atmosphere, with the result that the water table rises, carrying its salt layer to the surface and turning green belts into arid wastes. Fourthly, land once covered by luscious vegetation can become converted into dust bowls.

Similar analyses could be made of the ill-effects of many other activities connected with science and technology. Mining, for example, converts once attractive landscapes into barren moonscapes, totally devoid of life-

6 The Rio Conference was held in Rio de Janeiro, Brazil in 1992. One of the primary documents resulting from that conference is the Rio Declaration on Environment and Development, U.N. Doc. A/Conf. 151/26, *reprinted in* 31 I.L.M. 874 (June 13, 1992).

7 See Geoffrey Palmer, "The Earth Summit: What Went Wrong at Rio", in Geoffrey Palmer, *Environment: The International Challenge*, Victoria University Press, 1995, pp. 112–144.

8 For recent surveys of two other important Conventions, see Fiona McConnell, *The Biodiversity Convention: A Negotiating History*, Kluwer, 1996; and Joyeeta Gupta, *The Climate Change Convention and Developing Countries: From Conflict to Consensus?*, Kluwer Academic Publishers, 1997.

sustaining topsoil. The land is rendered useless unless a special effort is made to restore the land to a usable condition — which, again, is not always possible. Fortunately, in several countries, modern legislation requires the miner to restore land to a usable condition after mining. Dumping of industrial waste defaces and pollutes the land in many countries; and many a developing country becomes a dumping ground for the developed world's industrial machine.

Nuclear reactors raise the question of the dumping of nuclear waste. Across the world and its oceans, nuclear waste, capable of polluting the environment for 20,000 years and more, is dumped in containers which may or may not last for that period of time. When anyone of those containers will spring a leak and damage the environment for a thousand generations is anyone's guess.[9]

Reference should also be made to the vast increase in the manufacture and use of new chemicals. Nearly one thousand new chemicals, many of them untried, come on the market each year, swelling the ranks of the nearly 100,000 chemicals already in use. The World Health Organization estimates that nearly 75–85% of cancers are triggered by environmental agents such as industrial chemicals.[10] Herbicides such as Agent Orange are thought to have caused cancer, sterility and deformities.[11]

Thermal pollution, acid rain, depletion of the ozone layer and the greenhouse effect are all manifestations of the problems which the present generation is bequeathing to succeeding generations.

With massive industrialization of cities, large proportions of the rural population migrate to the cities, producing urban squalor and pollution on a scale unknown before. Industrial accidents can release toxic chemicals and fumes with great resulting danger to the right to health.[12]

9 In 1986 Chernobyl proved to the world the dangers resulting from one malfunctioning nuclear reactor. With hundreds dotted across the surface of the globe, the possibility that another may malfunction is too real to be treated lightly.

10 United States Office of Technology Assessment, *Assessment of Technologies for Determining Cancer Risks in the Environment* (1981); see also Rebecca Head, "Health-Based Standards: What Role in Environmental Justice", in *Environmental Justice: Issues, Policies, and Solutions*, Bunyan Bryant ed., (1995); United States Environmental Protection Agency, "Proposed Guidelines for Carcinogen Risk Assessment", 61 Fed. Reg. 17960 (1996).

11 John Harte *et al*, *Toxics A to Z*, California U.P., 1991.

12 The Bhopal disaster spelt death and suffering on such a scale that it attracted worldwide attention to the dangers attendant on the handling of hazardous material by modern industry.

Modern international law and human rights are developing the notion of intergenerational rights owed by one generation to its successors. Those other generations, not yet being in existence, are not yet recognized by most legal systems as bearers of rights and, consequently, their interests tend to be totally neglected. The recognition of this new human rights concept can reduce the damage caused to future generations by the self-centred orientation of current legal systems.

* * *

This Chapter is not an attempt to question the enormous benefits science and technology have so far conferred on humanity. Nor does it attempt to question its undoubted potential for leading humanity to the world of plenty which has long been its dream. The question is, rather, whether society is sufficiently alert to the dangers in the path of scientific and technological advancement, and whether lawyers have been properly vigilant. Are legal concepts adequate to take the thrust of these new directions in science, and are human rights adequately protected against the abuse of scientific knowledge?

In reconciling conflicting interests in this technological age, the law has a basic duty to protect every individual's personality, health, freedom, and dignity, and to be sensitive to current human rights thinking on these issues. It must monitor the new technology against abuse. It must work out legal responses to the novel conflicts of interests that will arise.

Irreversibility of a course, once taken, is one of the law's cardinal difficulties in its confrontation with science. Modern technology's effects are often for ever. It threatens the environment with irreversible pollution, brings within human reach the power of structuring people, makes nuclear terrorism a reality for all time, and produces drugs which can paralyze the world. Nothing this or future generations can do can take this knowledge away from mankind. Like nuclear wastes, which will be with us for at least 20,000 years, this information will be with us forever.

We are privileged to live in the one remaining age when something can be done. In our children's time, it will be too late, if it is not too late already. If the present slide towards uncontrollability should continue for another decade, technology will have mastered us.

Every invention that has given us power over our environment, has also given us power over people. Fire, the wheel, gunpowder, the ship, the internal combustion engine, the telephone, telegraphy, the radio, are all powerful conquests, both *by* us and *of* us. All of them, excellent servants but callous masters, have required us to alter our way of life. We have not always been able to hold them on a leash. Each one of them in its own way has transformed society and required us to recast our lifestyles to take account of them.

The technologies now unfolding before us will raise technology to a new level of dominance over people, unless society becomes intensely conscious of the need to control them. To this end, the collective strength of the international community will be needed. Yet, even this collective will can achieve little unless law and lawyers are sufficiently stimulated to move into action. Otherwise we would be back where we started, for in attempting to improve the quality of life through technology, we would have debased it. The longer we delay, the more stringent will be the necessary measures.

It is now a truism that never before has man been able to physically destroy the environment or the life-support systems, or the species itself. Never before was it possible to reduce man to the level of an object, or human society to the level of a systems programmer's blueprint.

We live in an age when old moral guidelines have broken down. A new course must be set.[13] There are three groups of people whose knowledge, views and wishes are essential to the charting of our new course: the scientist, the lawyer and judge, and lay people. Without any of these participants, the dialogue breaks down. Of our judges, a recent writer in the *British Medical Journal* has said:

> These are busy times for our black-robed Judges as they toil in their chambers, poring over dusty volumes and burning the midnight oil to solve the problems of a perplexing world ... Increasingly it is the Judges — not the elected representatives of the people — who decide who shall be terminated, compensated, reinstated, executed or resuscitated, vivisected or desegregated, dialysed, certified or involuntarily medicated, mercy killed, educated ...[14]

But it is not even the judges who will be deciding the great issues of life and death, health and ill-health, and free will and regimentation, in the technological age that is engulfing us. It is often the scientist, in the privacy and protection of the laboratory, functioning away from the glare of publicity and the reach of social controls. It is they who will decide on the refinements of new methods of mind conditioning or psychological torture, and whether to grow a foetus *in vitro*, or blend the genes of humans and animals. They will evolve new surveillance devices, new personality tests, new methods of cultural indoctrination, new techniques for structuring the human body and

[13] See Lord Radcliffe, *The Law and its Compass*, Northwestern University Press, 1960.

[14] G. Dunea, "Hyperactive Judges", *British Medical Journal*, Vol. 281, 4 October 1980, p. 926.

conditioning the human mind. These activities may never come before the judges for scrutiny.

The most important member of this trinity, the citizen, remains strangely silent, although he or she is the party most concerned and the legitimate source of authority for all socially-oriented decision-making.

Technology has the potential to clash with nearly every human right one can think of.

In order to convey some idea of the various human rights which may thus be affected, it would be useful to consider some of the more important human rights in relation to the technologies that might denigrate them. The following tabular statement, listing only a fraction of the technologies that might be cited, will perhaps convey some idea of the all-pervading nature of the problem. A similar list of technologies could be compiled in regard to every one of the human rights contained in the Universal Declaration, as well as the other major human rights documents, such as the International Covenant on Social, Economic and Cultural Rights, and the International Covenant on Civil and Political Rights.

Human Dignity

Provisions

Preamble to the Universal Declaration (recognition of the inherent dignity of all members of the human family is the foundation of freedom, justice and peace in the world.

Article I — All human beings are born free and equal in dignity and rights…

Article 5 — No one shall be subjected to … degrading treatment.

Article 6 — Everyone has the right to recognition everywhere as a person before the law.

Article 29(l) — 'Free and full development of … personality' is a basic value.

Sources of Possible Denigration

Foetal experimentation
Human experimentation
Embryo transplantation
In vitro fertilization
Foetus farms
Sperm and ova banks
Combinations of human and other genetic material
Selective breeding
Genetic structuring of humans
Preselection of sex
Societal breeding
Unwanted surgery
Organ transplants
Enzyme engineering
Sale of human tissue
Screening procedures
Psychosurgery
Behaviour therapy
Electroconvulsive therapy
Personality tests
Torture techniques
Use of drugs in interrogation
Surveillance devices
Euthanasia techniques
Machine decision-making
Computerized regimentation of society
Data bank infringements of privacy

Freedom of Thought

Provisions

Article 18 — Everyone has the right to freedom of thought, conscience and religion.

Article 19 — Everyone has the right to freedom of opinion ... this right includes freedom to hold opinions without interference.

Sources of Possible Denigration

Psychosurgery
Chemical controls of the mind
Data banks
Use of drugs in interrogation
Psychotherapy
Personality tests
Behaviour therapy
Electroconvulsive therapy
Mind conditioning through media technologies, e.g. subliminal advertising, advertising directed at children
Surveillance devices

Right to Life

Provisions

Article 3 — Everyone has the right to life...

Sources of Possible Denigration

Abortion
In vitro fertilization
Embryo transplantation
Human experimentation
Foetal experimentation
Organ transplants
Unwanted surgery
Euthanasia techniques
Technological terrorism, e.g. nuclear
Torture techniques
Military technology, e.g. chemical, germ, nuclear.

Right to Bodily Security

Provisions

Article 3 — Everyone has a right to … security of person.

Article 5 — No one shall be subjected to torture or to cruel, inhuman or degrading treatment or punishment.

Sources of Possible Denigration

Torture techniques
Organ transplants
Sale and hire of organs
Sale of human tissue
Euthanasia techniques
Unwanted surgery
Human experimentation
Foetal experimentation
Abortion
Military technology
Nuclear terrorism

Right to Health

Provisions

Article 25(1) — Everyone has the right to a standard of living adequate for the health and well-being of himself and of his family ... including ... medical care.

Article 23(1) — Everyone has the right to ... favourable conditions of work.

Sources of Possible Denigration

Recombinant DNA experimentation
Military technology
Chemical hazards in industry
Euthanasia
Human experimentation
Organ transplants
Unwanted surgery
Untested drugs, e.g. thalidomide
Genetic engineering
In vitro fertilization
Psychosurgery
Behaviour therapy
Torture techniques
Depletion of the ozone layer
Atmospheric pollution through discharge of industrial waste
Heat pollution
Noise pollution
Chemical pollution
Nuclear pollution
Chemical controls of the mind
Chemical and biological weapons
Nuclear weapons

Privacy

Provisions

Article 12 — No one shall be subject to arbitrary interference with his or her privacy.

Sources of Possible Denigration

Computer technology
The technology of computer crime
Surveillance devices
Media technology
Human experimentation
Use of drugs in interrogation
Artificial insemination
Cloning
Sperm and ova banks
Screening procedures
Personality tests
Mind manipulation
Psychotherapy
Psychosurgery
Chemical controls of the mind
Behaviour therapy

Rights of Marriage and Procreation

Provisions

Article 16(i) — Men and women of full age, without any limitation due to race, nationality or religion, have the right to marry and to found a family.

Sources of Possible Denigration

Sperm and ova banks
In vitro fertilization
Embryo transplantation
AID procedures
Genetic engineering
Screening procedures
Sale of organs
Nuclear Power
Nuclear Weapons
Organ transplants, e.g. testes, Fallopian tubes
Nuclear pollution
Untested chemicals in industry
Radiation hazards
Pesticides

Protection of Motherhood and Childhood

Provisions

Article 25(2) — Motherhood and childhood are entitled to special care and assistance.

Sources of Possible Denigration

Foetal experimentation
Foetus farms
In vitro fertilization
Embryo transplantation
Artificial Insemination procedures
Genetic engineering
Amniocentesis and foetoscopy
Abortion
Preselection of foetal sex
Nuclear Power
Nuclear weapons

Right to Cultural Life

Provisions

Article 27.1 — Everyone has the right freely to participate in the cultural life of the community, to enjoy the arts and to share in scientific advancement and its benefits.

Sources of Possible Denigration

Media technologies for cultural indoctrination and saturation
Monopolies and intellectual property in scientific knowledge
Scientific secrecy
Computerized regimentation of society
Surveillance devices
Invasions of privacy

Right to Work

Provisions

Article 23.1 — Everyone has the right to work, to free choice of employment, to just and favourable conditions of work and to protection against unemployment.

Sources of Possible Denigration

Personality tests
Data banks
Screening procedures
Computerization of industry

4. Legal Education for the Age of Technology: A Plea for an Interdisciplinary Perspective*

INTRODUCTION

In a tribute to one who has in our time so signally pushed forward the frontiers of jurisprudence, it is appropriate that a vital field into which he has helped to bring the jurisprudential plough — the impact of technology on law and human rights — should be the subject of some comment. The deep concern for every facet of the human endeavour which permeates the attitudes and work of Julius Stone took him into this field at a time when lawyerly intrusions upon it tended to be decried as officious. As early as 1946 Stone had warned, in *The Province and Function of Law*:[1]

> The point has been repeatedly made, without losing any of its force, that the contemporary social order must collapse if man's understanding and control of his human relations do not keep pace with technological development, that is, with his control of external nature.

The addition of Stone's influential voice to the all too few that had been heard on this topic in the early post-war years powerfully reinforced the call for greater concern among lawyers, scientists and laymen.

More than twenty years later Stone was still repeating his warning, now in more pointed form, in the context of pharmaceutical, psychological and biomedical research:

* This essay, a tribute to Professor Julius Stone, legal philosopher and international lawyer, appeared in the volume *Legal Change: Essays in Honour of Julius Stone*, A.R. Blackshield (ed.), Butterworths, 1983. Stone was one of the earliest jurists to visualize and warn against the danger to legal systems of the neglect to consider the legal implications of science and technology.

1 Stone, *Province and Function of Law*, Maitland Publications, Sydney, 1950, 479.

> As scientists seek and find drugs and psychological techniques for manipulating the human will and the human brain, or for controlling human heredity through growing knowledge of the gene-bearing substance DNA, may they too not be bringing about situations in which social and political life is put wholly at the mercy of a handful of manipulators?[2]

The obligations placed upon lawyers by modern developments in science and technology are urgent, and unparalleled in the many centuries of the legal profession. The reason is, or ought to be, self-evident; for the pitfalls strewing our way in this age of technology are of a nature and magnitude such as no prior system of jurisprudence has ever been called upon to face. The unprecedented nature of the challenge was underlined by Stone when he spoke in one of his addresses of the 'limit situations' to which science has taken mankind on many fronts: in these proliferating 'situations' one further step in the unravelling of fresh knowledge may, unless we are structurally and conceptually armed to meet it, take mankind irreversibly over the brink.[3] Nuclear physics once provided the example *par excellence*. More recent examples are genetic engineering and techniques of mind manipulation.

Where now do we stand in this all-important phase of an increasing subjugation by a particular discipline (to wit, science and technology) of the thoughts, the habits, the lives and the futures of contemporary mankind? Do we watch impotent from the sidelines while the chariot moves on inexorably, or does jurisprudence have any insights to offer us wherewith to face this strange new chapter in human history? Each new advance in technology spawns new social and legal problems for which the answer is not to be found in technology. Society looks to the law for answers. The law cannot run away from the problems, nor from the technology that begets them. If the law is to face them realistically, the requisite concern and sensitivity need to be systematically inculcated at the stage of the training of lawyers, rather than left to the hope that fortuitous events in a lawyer's career will kindle the requisite interest.

More than once before, mankind has faced the challenge of being torn away from its ancient intellectual moorings, to be cast adrift upon uncharted waters. Each time the challenge has been met by the devising of new intellectual tools. The Greeks, hauling down the gods from Mount Olympus and placing man at the centre of the stage of affairs, devised a man-based philo-

[2] J. Stone, 'Knowledge and the human predicament' [1970] 1 *Medical J of Australia* 787, 789.

[3] J. Stone, 'Knowledge, survival and the duties of science' (1973) 23 *American ULR* 231, 240; substantially repeated in J. Stone, *Of Law and Nations*, William S. Hein & Co., Buffalo, 1974, Ch. 15, 383.

sophical approach to replace the god-based one they had long considered irreplaceable. Renaissance and Reformation tore contemporary Europe asunder and, dethroning the ancient authority of Pope and Emperor, caused new philosophical attitudes to emerge as guides for the secular nation state which was launching upon its tempestuous career. The student of history will offer, from the history of each civilization, other examples of watershed eras wherein the past ceased to offer relevant guidance, and new approaches were devised to meet the problems of the day.

Yet, as Stone reminds us,[4] in none of these eras was the human future so heavily imperilled that a single false step might mean destruction of the species and its environment. In none of them was man's power over man so increased as to reduce man to a man-made object. In none of them were physical and intellectual and economic power so inextricably fused as to present a front of unassailable might against which current legal orderings might be no more than flappings in the void.

That some lawyers at least are making a concerted effort to meet these problems is due in no small measure to the vision of jurists like Stone. Had jurisprudence continued within its traditional niche, we might yet be labouring under the complacent belief that these were problems exclusively meant for other hands and other minds. Late though the lawyerly concern has surfaced, it is not too late to take stock of our deficiencies and construct adequate programmes to meet this future which past experience cannot illuminate.

If law is to continue to be a leading social and humanistic discipline, it needs also to take note that one major result of the technological revolution is that it increases the range of choices and options open to mankind. We can pick and choose our social goals, and pick and choose among different methods of achieving those goals, as never before. These choices involve value judgments which science and technology cannot furnish. If the law fails to make its contribution to their determination, with due regard for ensuring the ideals of human freedom to which it is committed, what other discipline can? And will not the law have failed the people in a crucial era where a false choice is often irreversible and all generations may be committed to living with it?

Among the many deficiencies we lawyers must acknowledge, not the least must lie in the manner of our preparation of the lawyers of the future. What legal education neglects, the law in its turn will neglect; and we thereby delay by a generation the legal response to one of the most sensitive and urgent issues of our time.

4 J. Stone, *American ULR* 240; Stone, *Of Law and Nations*, 383.

Knowing as we do that today's law students will live out their lawyerly vocations in a technology-oriented world, we still proceed as though we were training them for a world as far removed from technology as that of the Greeks and Romans. True, we have in recent years added some socially-oriented subjects, generally as avoidable options in an overcrowded curriculum. Stone's broad perspectives have helped law teachers to realize that much of life which was considered to be extraneous to the law must be taken within the net of legal education. Yet, for some inexplicable reason, technology stands out. Many law schools do not yet offer a course in 'Law, Science and Technology' or in 'Technology and Human Rights'. In nearly all of them the curriculum contains no compulsory component to provide a bridge of any sort between law and technology. One reason for this hiatus is probably that many lawyers and law teachers have not themselves realized the extent of the technological threat to their traditional methodology. Another is that they lack the materials, as well as the knowledge and interest, to make this a viable course component.

We have only to take the most cursory look at the current legal apparatus — concepts, structures, methodology and personnel — to realize the urgency of the need; for we will see that, at many points, the assumptions of two thousand years are being undermined by science and technology. If those assumptions become invalid, there collapses with them the superstructure which generations of legal learning have constructed upon them.

CONCEPTS

Examples may be multiplied; but a few chosen at random will illustrate the point.

Privacy

The common law threw up no such general concept. Its limited perception of the rights of individuals to exclude others from interference with their property took the form of territorial protection. Every man's home was his castle. Let no man set foot within this preserve. Technology makes nonsense of territorially based privacy, for laser beams bounced off a window pane can reflect conversations carried on within a room, long distance scanners can pry within it, a man's innermost thoughts can be probed by modern psychiatry, his feelings can be controlled by drugs and surgery, his life history can be stored on computer tapes and flashed on a screen at the press of a button. To locate a solution to these new challenges in the case law of the past is no better than the attempt to trap the proverbial moonbeam.

Life, Death, Freewill and the Integrity of the Human Body

Current medical and biological research has cut the ground from under the accepted connotations of these terms. Organ transplantation, *in vitro* fertilization, sperm and ova banks, enzyme engineering, preselection of sex, recombinant DNA experimentation, genetic engineering, psychosurgery — these are but a few in a long catalogue of current developments which destroy the traditional legal assumptions on which rules of criminal and civil law relating to the human personality have been based. New concepts and approaches can certainly be devised, but not by law and lawyers alone. In the mix of skills necessary to face these problems, science and technology play a most important role.

Corporate Power

Technology has made possible concentrations of economic and corporate power of a magnitude impossible before. These are new power centres which affect the rights of the individual no less than did the public instrumentalities which were power centres before. These 'private governments' may often wield more influence over the individual than the public governments to which he or she is subject. New legal concepts are necessary to deal with this unprecedented situation, for which the traditional conceptual framework will be inadequate. The protection of the individual, caught up in an age of giantism, stripped of his or her personality and reduced to the level of a book entry, will be one of the great legal problems of the future.

Constitutional Change

Few indeed are the lawyers who perceive today that political institutions themselves will need restructuring in the light of scientific advance. While one need not go all the way with those who observe that the advent of the techno-corporate state is the most profound constitutional change that has occurred in the history of the advanced industrial nations,[5] it is reasonably clear that constitutional change of a most far-reaching character will be a natural result of the penetration of society by science.

Electronic referenda, for example, might mean the availability of an instant direct public reaction to new developments, and might undermine the party system which delegates the voter's authority to a representative elected

[5] See A.S. Miller, 'The rise of the techno-corporate state in America' (1969) 25 *Bulletin of the Atomic Scientists 14*.

some years earlier upon a slate of issues with all of which the voter did not necessarily agree. Parliamentary procedures may have to be revamped, and constitutional conventions regarding action consequent upon the defeat of a Prime Minister reviewed. The wired city, newsprint and electronic technology, the technologies put to use in torture and terrorism, the neuro-stabilized state which makes massive use of modern psychiatric techniques — all these have a social and constitutional impact which current constitutional orderings may be unable to handle. Especially dangerous are the technologies which will assist those in authority to regiment their subjects and to entrench themselves in authority indefinitely, binding down, with securer fastenings than have been known before, those who are subject to their rule.

Planning Law

One aid towards the mass society and to regimentation, which is fraught with dangers not as yet fully recognized, is the systems programming made possible by the computer. Science enables man to undertake schemes of a magnitude never before dreamed possible. Formerly man's plans needed to fit in with his environment. Today his planning ability is such that he can restructure his environment to suit his plans. Such massive reordering necessitates that each individual fit docilely into the requirements of the master plan, which will brook no deviation from its preplanned blueprint. It has been too expensive to set it in motion for it to be reversible. Thus the individual gives way to the plan, the servant becomes the master, the plan and its devisors hold the citizen in a straitjacket of steel. New legal concepts must be fashioned to meet this new situation.

METHODOLOGY

The Concept of Stare Decisis

Yesterday's clarification illuminates the path to tomorrow. Such is the supposition on which this legal methodology rests. Science does not act on this assumption. Yesterday's determination is often today's error. Tomorrow will prove today to be wrong. Theories, like waves, will rise, swell and subside — with an average life span of four to six years. The rate of their acceptance and rejection is far too swift for the leisurely processes of precedent. A legal decision involving a scientific matter will be outmoded in the scientific journals while the law journals still surround it with every aura of validity.[6]

The Adversary System

When determining scientific truth for the purposes of a case we cannot act the umpire, awarding the laurel wreath to the party that wins according to the rules of the game. We cannot apply formal rules of evidence, excluding this document for want of formality and including that because it satisfies the rules of evidence. Scientific truth is often to be found somewhere between the formal lines of evidentiary rules or statutes — the surreptitious copy made, by an employee, of the log book of a nuclear reactor, the unconfirmed 'hunch' of the dedicated researcher, the vital recollection of the hearsay witness. To exclude these may be to hamper the search for truth.

The Advent of the Machine

The machine as decision-maker will play an increasing role in the judicial process of the future. Computerization has already entered many spheres of the administration of justice, though of course it will never entirely replace the human judge.[7] It already performs routine tasks of standardization of sentences and orders and researching decisions and statutes, and is progressively undertaking tasks of increasing sophistication. Yet large numbers of lawyers and judges continue to function in relative ignorance of computer methodology.

The Marshalling of Facts

Within limits, a party to an adversarial proceeding tends to keep away from court such evidence or witnesses as may not favour his cause. The court is largely content with the parties' choice of witnesses, rarely calling them of its own motion, and often knowing little of the available evidence which has not been placed before it. Few methodologies can be further from the needs of scientific fact-finding.

[6] See generally P. Brett, 'Implications of science for the law' (1972) 18 *McGill LJ* 170.

[7] See J. Stone, 'Man and machine in the search for justice' (1964) 16 *Stanford LR 515*; *Law and the Social Sciences in the Second Half-Century*, Minnesota UP, Minneapolis, 1966; *Social Dimensions,* 687–96.

Delay

Technical rules of procedure do not assist us in determining whether injunctions should be issued urgently to halt some dangerous activity such as the release of an untried chemical, or some experiment involving the possible escape of dangerous viruses into the biosphere, or some drug whose carcinogenic effects have not been adequately tested. By the time the technicalities have been argued and the legal i's and t's dotted and crossed, there will often not be much purpose in the exercise.

Levels of Proof

The scientific fact-finder demands a high level of certainty and accuracy for his conclusions. The nature of the judicial process is such that courts have traditionally been content with such low-level formulae of certainty and accuracy as proof 'on the balance of probabilities' in civil litigation, and proof 'beyond a reasonable doubt' in criminal cases. For scientific fact-finding this is totally inadequate. Further, for the resolution of questions involving science and society, the judge often lacks the social data essential for his or her decision. In this field, too, the data will be presented to the court within the framework of the adversarial format. The technique of preparing a 'Brandeis brief' is not yet accepted as an ordinary incident of common law methodology. Not all courts have the ability, in any event, to muster such data unless they have a social research arm and a wealth of assistance — such as, for example, the Supreme Court of Japan might enjoy through its prestigious Judicial Research Division. Certainly such investigation forms no part of the regular common law judicial process.

Estoppel

Another large category of rules, the rules of estoppel, prevent a party from making assertions contrary to earlier assertions by the same party, on the faith of which the other party has acted to its detriment. A party who has earlier taken up a certain position is thus held bound to that position whether it is true or false. Such a method employed in the field of scientific fact-finding can obviously be quite disastrous.

PERSONNEL

Training

As long as our courts of law are manned by judges and lawyers trained exclusively in 'black letter law', they will become increasingly irrelevant to an age dominated by science and technology. Jacques Ellul gave strong expression to his fears in this regard when he observed: 'The judicial regime is simply not adapted to technical civilisation, and this is one of the causes of its inefficiency and of the ever greater contempt felt towards it'.[8] Some lawyers and judges have had the benefit of a training that is not merely unidisciplinary. Some indeed might even have a degree in science, and hence be quite familiar with scientific methodology. These, however, are a small minority, and are not necessarily the only ones who will be called on to act and adjudicate in science-related fields.

Specialization

Just as an evolving common law, recognizing the need for a division of forensic and judicial labour, worked in divisions devoted to equity, matrimonial law or admiralty law, our age will soon call for specialist legal handling of matters of a scientific nature going far beyond the narrow specialization that now exists in such fields as patent law. Lawyers and judges equipped with the necessary scientific background will be required for work in these areas. A scientific division of the judicial arm, manned by such interdisciplinary personnel, may be one answer. Proposals for a 'science court' are not new, and can take a variety of forms.[9] All of them underline the inadequacy of our existing judicial structures.

Participation

If lawyers are to make a worthwhile contribution to the resolution of society's science-related problems, they must equip themselves for serving on those numerous other science-related decision-making agencies to which society will look for guidance in the future. The alternative is that these agencies will be dominated by other elements, without legal training, with resultant damage to the fabric of liberty and the rule of law.

[8] J. Ellul, *The Technological Society*, tr. J. Wilkinson, Knopf, NY, 1964, 251.

[9] See J.N. Martin, 'Procedures for decision-making under conditions of scientific uncertainty: the science court proposal' (1979) 16 *Harvard J Legislation* 443.

As Stone has cogently pointed out,[10] scientists will in the future need counselling and support in making decisions which may involve considerations of moral and political rightness as well as more specialized expertise. Such responsible decision-making needs to be 'properly illuminated by the relevant resources and wisdoms in the community'. We have no legal personnel trained to discharge this role.

The Law School Curriculum

If we face these problems realistically, it is submitted that we must admit that there is no substitute for the incorporation, in the basic legal education of the entire profession, of a course which brings the two disciplines together in an organized manner, and sensitizes the lawyers and judges of the future to their interaction.

STRUCTURES

Courts of law by their very nature are not the best instrumentalities for making science-related decisions. From a vast array of reasons, a few of the more apparent are listed below.

The Inability of Courts to Make Value Choices

Disputes involving a scientific component come increasingly before the courts, and a great proportion of these depend for their eventual determination upon a value choice that needs to be made. Chief Judge David L Bazelon of the United States Court of Appeals for the District of Columbia Circuit, writing in the *Cornell Law Review* in 1977,[11] noted that some two-thirds of the caseload in that Circuit now involved reviews of action by federal administrative agencies, and that more and more of such cases involved matters on the frontiers of technology. He enumerated some of the questions coming before his Court for decision. They involved such problems as: What are the ecological effects of building a pipeline to carry oil across the Alaskan tundra? How can society manage radioactive wastes from nuclear reactors, which remain toxic for two hundred centuries or more? Shall we ban DDT? Or Concorde supersonic transport? Or lead in gasoline?

[10] Stone, *American ULR*, 254; Stone, *Of Law and Nations*, 396.

[11] D.L. Bazelon, 'Coping with technology through the legal process' (1977) 62 *Cornell LR* 817.

Each of these questions involves a value choice, a system of priorities, an order of resource allocation. The ecological preservation of the tundra needs to be balanced against society's need for oil; the hazards of radioactivity to future generations against the urgent energy needs of the present; the economic advantages of a pesticide against its medical disadvantages; the advantages of speed against the disadvantages of the sonic boom; the advantage of a smoother fuel against the disadvantage of atmospheric pollution.

When cases of this nature come before the courts, they impose upon them a burden which the courts were not structured to handle.[12] As Judge Bazelon points out,[13] the courts may have an appropriate function in scrutinising and monitoring the decision-making process of the agencies which take these decisions, thus ensuring that the process is thorough, complete and rational; but this needs a growing consciousness of the limitations of the judicial process. Value choices, resource allocations and community priorities in matters of this nature are scarcely the questions which the courts as presently equipped have the mandate, the competence or the machinery to handle.

Preoccupation with Redress rather than Prevention

One of the foremost questions bearing on the competence of the courts to handle scientific questions is whether the courts afford the means to check a potentially harmful development in technology before it inflicts irreparable harm on society.

Thoughtful observers are not sanguine. 'It seems clear', writes Harold Green in a monograph on the subject, 'that we cannot rely on the courts alone to protect society against fast-moving technological development. Judge-made rules of law always come after, and usually long after, the potential for injury has been demonstrated.'[14]

The courts as presently structured are scarcely competent to assess the long-range effects of a particular scientific or technological idea whose possible harmfulness is under review. The task calls for a degree of informed skill in prediction and judgment which is beyond the traditional expertise of

[12] *Cf.* A.R. Blackshield, 'Legal responses to cultural change', paper presented to annual conference of Australasian University Law Schools Association, Hobart, mimeo, 15 August 1972, 41–2, commenting on *Committee for Nuclear Responsibility, Inc* v. *Schlesinger ('The Amchitka Island Case')*, 404 US 917 (1971).

[13] Bazelon, *Cornell LR,* 823.

[14] H.P. Green, *The New Technological Era: A View from the Law* (Program of Policy Studies in Science and Technology, Monograph No 1), George Washington University, Washington, 1968, 2.

courts, which have hitherto concentrated on areas of known injury and on techniques of dispute resolution. Social planning, on the other hand, functions in the area of the foreseen rather than the known, and concerns itself with the fashioning of benefits rather than the redress of injury. Its technique is not the resolution of disputes after they occur, but the formulation of procedures to prevent their occurrence. An excessive reliance upon technical and procedural objections, on rules of evidence, pleadings, laches and the like, which have no relevance whatsoever to the urgent and massive sociological problems involved, seems also to add to the disqualifications of the courts in handling matters of technological control.

The Obscuring of Public Interest Considerations

Another facet of the inability of current legal procedures to assist the community with preventive action was well illustrated in the thalidomide case. An extensive research report on this matter could only be published in the London *Sunday Times* in June 1976 after legal procedures had kept it away from the public by means of court injunction for as long as four years. If the effect of the law is to keep away from the public a knowledge of matters which so intimately concern it, the law needs to be reformed by allowing priority to the public over the private interest.

As the *Sunday Times* said in an editorial on the subject: 'For 14 years, thanks initially to the extraordinary failure to order a public inquiry, this disaster has languished under a system of legal censorship that is archaically against the public interest'.[15] Indeed, the courts held that even if the defendants' documents disclosed negligence, they could still be suppressed on grounds of confidence.[16] The editorial went on to comment: 'A legal disaster such as we analyse on these pages might, for all we know, be happening again somewhere now'.

The Abdication of Judicial Authority

The inability of the courts to deal adequately with these problems results also in the responsibility for their solution being thrust in ever-increasing measure upon the administration, without even such safeguards as the courts

[15] *The Sunday Times* (London). 27 June 1976, 15; and see *The Times* (London), 24 June 1976, 17.

[16] *A-G* v. *Times Newspapers Ltd.* [1974] AC 273; but see *Sunday Times* v. *United Kingdom* [1979] 2 European Human Rights Reports 245. And see now *Schering Chemicals Ltd.* v. *Falkman Ltd.* [1981] 2 WLR 848.

can competently and legitimately impose. By exercising its authority without the necessary judicial checks, the administration is constantly enlarging its authority.

The Undermining of Democratic Government

Two of the basic assumptions underlying democratic government are the competence of the community or its representatives to handle the matters that come up for decision and their ability to implement those decisions once made. In other words, there must be both the *ability* to understand these matters and the *power* to handle them.[17] Increasingly, science is posing problems too technical for the layman to understand, and giving scientists power too great for the layman to handle. As scientific decision-making increases in volume, and its subject-matter represents a greater share of the community's total economic enterprise, two of the bases of democratic government are steadily undermined. This fear was reflected in President Eisenhower's warning as early as 1961 'that public policy could itself become the captive of a scientific-technological elite'.[18]

The Waste of Potential for the Public Benefit

The enormous potential of science as a force for the public benefit remains largely untapped for lack of appropriate structures to assess and handle it. These structures, whether 'Technology Assessment Boards', 'Science Commissions', or 'Committees for Alternative Futures', need a heavy input of lawyers' skills.

THE CUMULATION OF CHALLENGES: EXPONENTIAL GROWTH

These preliminary observations will suffice to highlight the importance to the future lawyer of an understanding of the technological impact upon society and upon all social mechanisms, including the law.

Especially is this so in an age of proliferating sub-departments within the boundaries of knowledge. An age when a Chief Justice of England could write scientific papers well in keeping with the most advanced scientific knowledge of his time — as Sir Matthew Hale did when in 1673 he wrote 'An Essay Touching the Gravitation of Fluid Bodies' — functioned on the

17 H. Wheeler, 'Bringing science under law' (1971) 4 *Dialogue* No 1 (quarterly journal of opinion, US Information Service, Washington), 104, 106.

18 *The New York Times,* 18 January 1961, 22.

basis of the unity and interrelatedness of all human knowledge. Our age seems to do the reverse. What is more significant is that it is sprouting subcultures with specializations so intense that an expert in one department of biology or mathematics may not understand the language or research of an expert in another department of the same science.

When the growth rate of scientific knowledge is exponential, while that in the humanities is negligible by comparison, this must swing the centre of gravity of the intellectual enterprise in the direction of science. Law and lawyers, unable to provide the necessary insights for guiding society through that new age, will fall by the wayside, pressed into little compartments of increasingly irrelevant expertise.

CURRICULUM DEVELOPMENT: THE OBSTACLES

One must necessarily be acutely aware of the many practical difficulties standing in the way of any proposal for the introduction of a science-related component into the current structure of legal education. Among these are:

1. The pressure exerted by professional bodies, as well as by students, for expertise in 'black letter' subjects which tend to squeeze out interdisciplinary or 'perspective' approaches.
2. The wide disparities in scientific background among students — varying from the PhD or honours graduate in science, to the student who does not even have the benefit of an elementary fourth form exposure to physics, chemistry or biology. The task of devising a course against this background is a daunting one.
3. The lack of personnel qualified to undertake this pioneering and difficult task.
4. The difficulty of structuring within the confines of a single subject or unit a sufficient exposure to science and its implications to render the course worthwhile or significant.
5. The traditional isolation of law schools from the other disciplines.
6. The self-satisfied belief that legal education inculcates a methodology so all-embracing as to be adequate to handle all questions, however technical, which come in contact with the law.
7. Resistance by law school teachers to areas outside their training, and by law school students to subjects outside their core curriculum.
8. In an age of financial stringency, the difficulty of obtaining the funding necessary for such a programme.
9. An insufficient awareness, on the part of the community, of the immediate and future importance of the law-science interface, with resulting lack of social pressure for such courses.

10. The lack of media for communication between the two disciplines, whether through journals or seminars or symposia.
11. Fear of a lack of depth or usefulness in any course thus devised.
12. Lack of teaching materials.

SOME POSSIBLE COURSES OF ACTION

There are many possible approaches to the problems raised in this essay. Some of them relate to training prior to commencement of the law course, some to training at law school itself, and some to 'continuing education'. They will be discussed in that order.

Prior to Law School

(a) Law schools invariably prescribe a pass in certain specified subjects at Higher School Certificate or other appropriate level as a prerequisite to entry. A pass at this level in any science subject, or in mathematics, if prescribed as a prerequisite, would ensure that entrants to law school would not be total strangers to the discipline and methodology of science, as is not infrequently the case under the present dispensation.

(b) Efforts need to be made to contradict the impression — which often prevails among students at the secondary school level — that law is a discipline which stands by itself and can be learnt in isolation from other fields of knowledge such as the technological. In other words the interrelatedness between legal and other studies needs to be stressed.

(c) If students do not have any knowledge of science at Higher School Certificate level, thought must be given to devising a preliminary course, covering the essentials of scientific methodology, which the student would be required to complete at some time prior to graduation. This course in methodology should include the methodology of handling quantitative scientific data. Lawyers faced with such data, as in environmental litigation, are often completely at a loss as to how to handle them, and tend to be led blindly by the experts.

(d) Courses in basic physics, chemistry and biology need to be made available, from among which law students could make a choicc either prior to or even at law school. For example, a lawyer studying environmental law will quickly find himself out of his depth without sufficient chemistry to understand pollutants, sufficient physics to understand the ionosphere, and sufficient biology to understand ecological structures. He will come upon such concepts as biogeochemical cycles, energy flow in ecological systems, ionizing radiation, the effects of irradiation on species diversity, nutrient cycles and energy fixation. Where is he or she to turn when confronted with such concepts if the law school, in concert with its scientific counterparts, does not make available some basic instruction in these otherwise mystical areas?

At Law School

Within this category there are again three basic approaches.

(a) The first is a program making use of scientific training which the student has already received. Such a course would not aim at inculcating scientific knowledge, but would work upon students who already have some scientific background. It would therefore suffer from the drawback of being unavailable to those without such a background; it would turn out a select group of students with a law/science background, while many students would graduate with as little knowledge in this field as they had before entry into law school. Since the proportion of students with non-science orientations is quite considerable, it is submitted that such a solution by itself would be unacceptable. The law schools would still be discharging into a science-oriented age too many lawyers without the relevant intellectual equipment or sensitivity which society is entitled to expect.

On the other hand, if such a course could be offered *in addition to* courses catering for students without special scientific knowledge, it would have the advantage of providing training of a specially intensive nature, available for selection by those who see themselves as likely to be working in technology-related areas.

(b) The second approach is to add a law/science/technology course to the traditional law school offerings. Among the possibilities are the following:

  (i) The introduction of a compulsory course on science and society — for example, 'The Social Responsibilities of Science and Scientists'.

  (ii) The inclusion in law school curricula of a variety of units dealing with the interrelationship of science and law — such as 'Science, Technology and the Law'; 'Science, Technology and Human Rights'; 'The Social Responsibilities of Scientists'; 'The Impact of Science on Constitutional Structures'; 'The Inadequacy of Current Legal Procedures for Technological Decision-Making'; 'Medical Negligence'; 'Environmental Assessment'; 'Energy, Society and the Law'; 'Techniques of Impact Assessment'; and so on. From such a slate of alternatives, students could be required to select one unit as a compulsory component of the Bachelor of Laws degree.

(iii) The introduction of a course which may be described as one in basic scientific literacy, equipping the student with knowledge of basic chemistry, physics and biology along the lines already discussed for possible offerings prior to law school.

(iv) The addition of a course on science and social responsibility to existing jurisprudence courses, especially those already based on the sociological school. Discussion of materials with a sociological orientation lends itself readily to the introduction of scientific and technological perspectives, which can quite easily be expanded into a course in itself. Where jurisprudence is taught by offering the student a choice among several units, a science-related unit could be added to the existing alternatives.

(v) Universities need to inaugurate centres integrating law and science studies such as the programme in Science, Technology and Law at the Cornell Law School, the Science and Technology program at George Washington University Law School, and the Center for Science, Technology and Public Policy at the University of Virginia. Such centres will be sources from which the necessary materials and ideas will flow out to those conducting particular courses in a law/science/technology area.

(vi) One of the obstacles standing in the way of law/science/technology courses is the absence of readily available teaching materials. It is hoped that academics interested in this field, who are now producing a significant volume of literature upon various aspects of the law/science confrontation, will spare some time to produce primers and collections of readings for use in such courses. These would be valuable not only for teachers, but also for lawyers and scientists.

(vii) Some law faculties have already begun appointing non-lawyers such as economists and historians to the academic staff, to gain access to areas of expertise which are relevant to the teaching of law but which lawyers themselves are unable to produce. Having regard to the importance of science, it is suggested that law faculties should give some thought to the appointment to the staff, of a scientist able to communicate broad perspectives relating to scientific methodology and the scientific enterprise. Having such a person available as a faculty member would greatly stimulate the attention that other faculty members would devote to this neglected area.

(viii) In line with the suggestion above, it is suggested also that when deciding on visitors' programmes, law faculties should give consideration to inviting scientists who can meet the specifications outlined above.

(ix) The research programmes which law students are called upon to undertake throughout their years at law school could readily be structured so as to include the requirement that at least one of the pieces of research and writing to be done by them should be in the law/science/technology area. This research would require the students to go out into the field and collect their data, thus coming into direct contact with law/science/technology problems as they operate in society.

(x) Many university faculties so conduct their affairs that the university may be described as a collection of different colleges, united only by the fact that they are housed on a common campus. Faculty members' tendencies to congregate together, even on social occasions or at faculty clubs, often result in an intellectual isolation which inhibits cross-disciplinary contact. A consistent effort needs to be mounted to break down this isolation. The incentive for such a movement must come from general university policy: building up interdisciplinary activity needs affirmative action, perhaps with a special functionary charged with this specific responsibility and appointed for this specific purpose. In building bridges between the faculties, such a functionary would actively examine all possibilities for interdisciplinary courses or lectures.

(xi) As an adjunct to the programme just outlined, a university could designate a special year when each faculty would put on display its interdisciplinary activities, inviting all other faculties with which it can build intellectual bridges to participate in its activities, and reaching out actively in return to participate in theirs. Alternatively, years could be designated for particular co-operation between specified faculties — a law/science year or an economics/education year — when both faculties would attempt to reach out towards each other. Such a principle, once established, might result in a proliferation of interdisciplinary activities which would make universities truer to their name, and to their mission of integrating rather than separating knowledge.

(xii) An important exercise which faculty members should engage in is an identification of the obstacles to co-operation between law and science, and an effort to eliminate them. A preliminary list of such obstacles appears earlier in this essay; but it needs extensive elaboration.

(xiii) One of the principal reasons for the failure of any significant law/science dialogue has been the lack of media for communication between the two disciplines. Lawyers write for lawyers and scientists for scientists. It would be an interesting and rewarding activity for faculty members in either discipline to commence a journal in which the members of the two disciplines could cross-publish for each other, each in language which the other could understand. Popular science magazines attempt this with some degree of success in the scientific field; but in the legal field such activities are singularly lacking. At the very least lawyers should write in scientific and medical journals, as Stone has done, and scientists should write in legal journals.

(xiv) Scientific methodology being so important to an understanding of any scientific problem presented in a legal forum, this subject could be offered as a compulsory unit.

(xv) Given that many law faculties already require some non-legal subjects to be studied as part of the normal requirements for the Bachelor of Laws degree, it would be an easy matter to vary this arrangement by stipulating a compulsory choice of at least one subject from the field of science.

(xvi) There are already in existence numerous institutions which examine and disseminate society-related scientific knowledge. The program of Policy Studies in Science and Technology at the George Washington University in Washington, DC, is one example. The Scientists' Institute for Public Information was founded for this purpose in the United States as early as 1963. Australia has the Scientific Policy Studies Section of the Department of Science and the Environment in the national capital. The Human Rights Division of the United Nations organizes regular seminars, and issues a wealth of literature, on relevant developments and problems. Law faculties could help their programs greatly by building up contacts with such bodies.

(c) The third approach is to launch a basically interdisciplinary program, involving co-operation between faculties of law and science.[19] This approach involves sophisticated preparation across disciplinary bounda-

[19] See to this effect T.G. Field, Jr., 'Science, law and public policy: meeting the need in legal education' (1977) 13 *New England LR* 214, 223.

ries. It is much more than a combination of a law degree and a science degree; it requires the coherent structuring of a series of subjects approached from an interdisciplinary angle. It would inevitably be in the nature of a specialized course, and might not fit in easily with existing curricular structures. Nor would it be fair to require all students to participate in it. It is suggested that while there is great value in courses of this sort, they should be reserved for postgraduate studies or diplomas, to be undertaken by students with a special desire for more intensive study in this area.

After Law School

The field of 'continuing education' offers many avenues through which a constructive initiative could quickly show positive results.

(a) Needless to say, there is a great need for interdisciplinary seminars, to be attended by lawyers, scientists, ethicists, members of the public and others, in which attention would be drawn to problem areas and the main issues would be exposed for discussion.

(b) Bar associations which have not already done so need to set up law/science/technology committees charged with examining areas of current importance and promoting the study of these areas by members of the bar. A regular report by such a committee on the principal law/science/technology issues arising in the course of each year would be a welcome measure.

(c) National judicial colleges, where they exist, should pay special attention to educating judges on the issues that arise. Institutions like the National Judicial College in the United States, which already offer a wide variety of courses bringing the judges up to date in different fields, would be well able to add a number of law/science areas to their offerings. Where judicial colleges do not exist, this task needs to be undertaken by faculties of law.

(d) Law faculties or bar associations should offer, for the benefit of scientists, basic courses on the rules of legal process and their special applicability to the science/technology area.

(e) Workshops can be organized on the cross-education of lawyers and scientists — as the American Bar Association has done on more than one occasion.[20]

[20] See W.A. Thomas, 'A report from the workshop on cross-education of lawyers and scientists' (1978) 19 *Jurimetrics J* 92.

(f) Interprofessional associations such as medico-legal associations can actively foster study in the interdisciplinary area.
(g) Centres of continuing education in universities should look upon this area as one of their major responsibilities.

THE CONTENT OF LAW/SCIENCE/TECHNOLOGY COURSES

Some comment is necessary on the content of any general law/science/technology courses of the kind envisaged above. Such courses, it is submitted, should aim at achieving some at least of the following (among other) objectives:

1. Acquainting the future lawyer with the use of scientific terminology in context.
2. Sharpening skills in identifying the scientific issues involved in a legal problem and the legal issues involved in a scientific problem.
3. Increasing awareness of the literature of science, with sufficient knowledge to track down with particularity the latest literature on any specific subject.
4. Informing the student of the organizations and sources from which he or she can obtain more particular scientific knowledge for the purposes of a problem in hand.
5. Familiarizing the student with the essentials of scientific methodology.
6. Sensitizing the student to the social responsibilities of science and scientists, and to the responsibilities of the legal profession in a science-oriented age.
7. Exploring the nexus between science and law in the light of the growing literature upon the subject.[21]
8. Improving communication skills between lawyers and the scientific fraternity.
9. Assisting in the evaluation of technology from the standpoint of moral and social considerations.
10. Examining critically the interdisciplinary structures and procedures presently available between law and science, and investigating possibilities for their improvement.
11. Analysing the adequacy of basic legal concepts and structures in the light of the needs of science and technology.
12. Studying the evolving international regulatory system in selected fields of science and technology.

[21] See the proposal by Lee Loevinger in W.A. Thomas (ed.), *Scientists in the Legal System*, Ann Arbor Science Publishers, Ann Arbor, Michigan, 1974. 7, 15–6.

13. Investigating the ways in which a practising lawyer can use scientific/technological knowledge to achieve a specific result, in the context of particular cases, or of his practice in general.

CONCLUSION

It is hoped that these few observations will be of some assistance in directing legal education into a channel which the work of Julius Stone has foreshadowed, and which the events of every passing year invest with an added and compelling urgency. Lawyers and law teachers will not be able to delay shouldering this responsibility much longer without leaving themselves open to the charge of insensitivity to one of the deepest currents coursing through society in our time.

5. International Controls on Technology: The Gathering Momentum*

THE INSECURITY OF ORTHODOX ASSUMPTIONS

Sixty years ago the philosopher-scientist, Alfred North Whitehead, delivering the Lowell lectures, observed that a characteristic of the present epoch was that so many complexities had developed with regard to material, space, time and energy, that the simple security of the old orthodox assumptions had vanished.

> The new situation in the thought of today arises from the fact that scientific theory is outrunning common sense. The settlement as inherited by the eighteenth century was a triumph of organized common sense. It had got rid of medieval phantasies.... The eighteenth century opened with the quiet confidence that at last nonsense had been got rid of. Today we are at the opposite pole of thought. Heaven knows what seeming nonsense may not tomorrow be demonstrated truth.[1]

Concepts of law, dating back many centuries, and even concepts of human rights going back to the aftermath of World War II, have needed to be constantly reviewed. The impossibility of yesterday having become the reality of today, yesterday's method of handling real-life situations becomes outmoded and often irrelevant. We do not know what quantum leaps into the future science and technology hold in store for us. They have already unveiled some of their marvels in the fields of microbiology, space exploration, cybernetics, deep sea mining, nuclear physics, medicine, and surgery. Concepts based on old assumptions regarding the limits of the possible have signally failed to protect the human environment, human society and even

* Published in *India International Centre Quarterly*, Vol. 13, Nos. 3 & 4, December 1986, in the special issue titled "The Right to be Human".

1 A.N. Whitehead, *Science and the Modern World*, Mentor Books, 1925, pp. 115–116.

the human body[2] from denigrations of their integrity, which were earlier dismissed as fanciful, if indeed they received any consideration at all.

Science fiction, transmuting itself into reality, has empowered us to tamper with the molecules which are the building blocks of life, transplant living organs, enable the dead to father children, record conversations within a room by bouncing laser beams off a window pane, pollute the entire ocean for twenty thousand years, and destroy all life on an entire continent with the missiles housed on board a single submarine. The potential of science and technology for good and for evil appears boundless. The good needs to be encouraged, the evil to be curbed. Neither can be achieved by outmoded concepts or continued complacency.

The future of human rights in an age of aggressively burgeoning science and technology is therefore extremely problematic, unless we accept the need for the most constant surveillance of the continuing impact of science and technology upon human rights. This article outlines the rather slow international progress towards an awareness of the dangers, and it foreshadows some means of handling this continuing problem in the future.

Even in the post-war years, the old assumption that science and technology moved in step with human freedom died hard. It is true it had been rudely disturbed by the misuse of technology in the concentration camps, and by the nuclear bomb. Yet, perhaps owing to the power and the prestige of the scientific establishment, international opinion and action moved at a snail's pace. However, although the realization of possible damage to human rights through science and technology has been slow, it has been gathering momentum in recent years. The need has been widely acknowledged for monitoring science and technology for their damaging impacts, and for attracting to the problem the attention of the international community, national governments, and the public in general.

THE PROCLAMATION OF TEHRAN

How slow this realization has been can be gauged from the fact that it was not until the Proclamation of Tehran of 1968 that the problem received explicit consideration from the international community. The Universal Declaration of Human Rights in 1948 had indeed referred to the impact of scientific advancement on human rights, but only in terms of its benefits. Article 27(1) provided that everyone "has the right ... to share in scientific

[2] See *supra* Chapter 3.

advancement and its benefits". Its possible dangers and the need to guard against them were not considered by the draftsmen[3].

The International Conference on Human Rights, which was held in Tehran in 1968 to mark the International Year for Human Rights, resolved that "while recent scientific discoveries and technological advances have opened vast prospects for economic, social and cultural progress, such developments may nevertheless endanger the rights and freedoms of individuals and will require continuing attention".[4]

The Conference recommended to the organizations of the United Nations family that they undertake studies in regard to:

1. Respect for privacy in view of recording techniques.
2. Protection of the human personality and its physical and intellectual integrity in view of the progress in biology, medicine and biochemistry.
3. The uses of electronics which may affect the rights of the person and the limits which should be placed on its uses in a democratic society.
4. More generally, the balance which should be established between scientific and technological progress and the intellectual, spiritual, cultural and moral advancement of humanity[5].

There were many reasons for the late awakening of the United Nations system to this danger. Not the least of these was a lack of immediacy as compared with other and seemingly more urgent issues confronting the newly independent states that were emerging from colonial rule. Interest was triggered off, however, by the widely shared view that extremely sensitive political issues could arise in this area,[6] as, for example, with possible uses of scientific and technological development for purposes of state control.

Once the United Nations system began to interest itself in this field, it went on to concern itself with a varied range of the threats from new technology, and both the Secretary-General and various specialized agencies

[3] Article 27(2) provided protection for the author in respect of "the moral and material interests resulting from any scientific ... production". Patent rights in new technology have become a global human rights issue today. This aspect was not even contemplated at the time of the Universal Declaration.

[4] United Nations, Final Act of the International Conference on Human Rights, Tehran, 22 April to 13 May 1968, p. 5.

[5] *Ibid.*, p. 12.

[6] See Sadako Ogata, "Introduction: United Nations Approaches to Human Rights and Scientific and Technological Development", in *Human Rights and Scientific and Technological Development*, C.G. Weeramantry (ed.), UNU Press, 1990, p. 3.

prepared a series of reports upon the subject. Among the subjects studied were computerized data systems and electronic communications techniques which might affect rights of privacy; biochemical and medical advances such as artificial insemination and psychotropic drugs; the harmful effects of automation and mechanization of production.

The problems under consideration were not of course without their continuing political overtones. For example, just as it could be argued that it was necessary to protect the individual against intrusions or controls by the State, based upon the new technology, so also it could be argued that science and technology could be used by powerful states for violating the integrity of weaker states, interfering with national liberation movements and exploiting their natural resources. In fact, such a political shift to the debate, switching the emphasis from individual domestic protections, to supranational state obligations occurred when the Soviet Union, in 1974, in association with the German Democratic Republic, Hungary and Poland and others, brought to the General Assembly a draft declaration on the use of scientific and technological progress in the interests of peace and for the benefit of mankind.

Even by 1966, when the International Covenant on Economic, Social and Cultural Rights was adopted, the problem of the adverse effects of technology was still very much in the background. Article 15*(b)* of the Covenant recognized the right of everyone to "enjoy the benefits of scientific progress and its applications". It was almost as if the underlying assumption was the need for more and more technology. If it also entailed dangers, that was scarcely a matter for specific articulation. It was a risk which was so outweighed by the benefits, that it had to be unquestioningly accepted. The Bhopal-type implications were furthest from the thoughts of the draftsmen.

For these reasons, the Proclamation of Tehran represented a milestone. Paragraph 18 expressed the view that:

> While recent scientific discoveries and technological advances have opened vast prospects for economic, social and cultural progress, such developments *may nevertheless endanger the rights and freedoms of individuals and will require continuing attention*. (Emphasis added.)

The Conference recommended, in resolution XI, that the various organizations of the United Nations "should undertake a study of the problems with respect to human rights arising from developments in science and technology".

The specific reference to the dangers posed by technology was only one of nineteen paragraphs of the Tehran Declaration, which dealt with a variety of subjects bearing upon human rights. Still, this was the first affirmative step towards the study of the relation between human rights and science and technology.

REACTIONS OF THE GENERAL ASSEMBLY TO THE TEHRAN DECLARATION

The Tehran recommendations were taken up by the General Assembly later in the same year and, on 19 December 1968, the General Assembly also invited the Secretary-General[7] to undertake a study of the problems in connection with human rights arising from developments in science and technology. The study was to be undertaken with the assistance, *inter alia*, of the Advisory Committee on the Application of Science and Technology to Development, and in co-operation with the executive heads of the competent specialized agencies. The particular areas specially recommended for study were:

(1) respect for the privacy of individuals and the integrity and sovereignty of nations, in the light of advances in recording and other techniques;

(2) protection of the human personality and its physical and intellectual integrity, in the light of advances in biology, medicine, and biochemistry;

(3) uses of electronics which may affect the rights of the person and the limits which should be placed on such uses in a democratic society; and

(4) more generally, the balance which should be established between scientific and technological progress and the intellectual, spiritual, cultural, and moral advancement of humanity.

The scope of the recommendations appears somewhat narrow by today's standards: we now take a far broader view of the possible areas of denigration of human rights by technology. Today we also concentrate heavily on the interlinkages between economic and technological forces in causing a deprivation of human rights — the technology of the armaments industries, deep sea mining, agricultural patents owned by multinational agri-business, dumping of shoddy goods, problems of sharing and withholding technology. In 1968, the concentration was on the denigrations then becoming increasingly visible owing to dramatic developments in electronics and biology. Significantly, this area could infringe on privacy and encourage totalitarian rule through an information tyranny, based on computer and other forms of

[7] By resolution 2450 (XXIII) (1968).

surveillance. The latter threatens to undermine the essential dignities associated with the human personality.

THE SECOND UNITED NATIONS DEVELOPMENT DECADE

The Secretary-General was commissioned to prepare a summary of studies made in the enumerated fields, and to prepare a draft programme of work to be undertaken in fields "in which subsequent surveys would be necessary for the attainment of the objectives ... of the resolution". This report[8] was placed before the Human Rights Commission at its twenty-sixth session in 1970, and it led to resolution 10(XXVII) of 18 March 1971, in which the Commission related the problem to the needs of the Second United Nations Development Decade.

In this resolution, we find an increasing recognition of the economic impact of modern technology in such areas as the right to work, in conditions of automation and mechanization of production. Technology appropriate for a developed industrial nation may not be appropriate for a non-industrialized nation. The resolution stressed the protection of human rights "in accordance with the structure and resources of States and the scientific and technological level they have reached", and related these problems to the mechanization of industry. Development in the Third World did not necessarily mean the use of tractors in its fields and of robots in its factories. Labour needed to be used in the manner most suitable to the economies of these countries, and methods that were "backward" from the standpoint of advanced technology might be the methods best suited to the satisfaction of human rights where technology was less advanced. The human rights so affected include the rights to employment, food and shelter. The divergences between the roads to technological advance and to the assurance of basic human rights in Third World countries were becoming apparent, and they received due recognition from the Human Rights Commission.

Other matters referred to in the resolution were the affirmative use of scientific and technological developments to foster respect for human rights, and the prevention of the use of scientific and technological achievements to restrain fundamental democratic rights and freedoms.

International attention to these problems was now gathering momentum. Between 1971 and 1976, a series of reports reached the Commission on Human Rights and the General Assembly, from both the Secretary-General and the specialized agencies. The prime concerns were:

[8] E/CN.4/1028.

(i) the invasion by surveillance technologies on human freedoms,[9] covering such areas as auditory and visual surveillance, "personality tests", lie detectors, narco-analysis, and blood, breath and other bodily tests for non-medical purposes;

(ii) the biological, medical and biochemical denigrations of personality[10] dealing, *inter alia*, with artificial insemination, prenatal diagnostic procedures, psychotropic drugs, and food additives;

(iii) the automation and mechanization of the means of production;[11]

(iv) the deterioration of the environment;[12]

(v) the destructive effects of modern weaponry and atomic radiation;[13]

(vi) the preservation of the basic human rights to food, clothing, just remuneration, housing, leisure, and social security;[14]

(vii) the impact of computers on democratic society and the limits to be placed on them;[15]

(viii) the preservation of cultural values and the achievement of a balance between scientific and technological progress, on the one hand, and the intellectual, spiritual, cultural and moral values of humanity on the other.[16]

DECLARATION ON THE USE OF SCIENTIFIC AND TECHNOLOGICAL PROGRESS, 1975

International consciousness of these problems, thus alerted by this spate of activity, moved forward to another milestone — the *Declaration on the Use of Scientific and Technological Progress in the Interests of Peace and for the Benefit of Mankind*.[17] Some non-industrialized countries, such as Bangladesh and Mauritius, were among those responsible for bringing this resolution before the General Assembly. The Soviet Union had presented a draft decla-

9 E/CN.4/1116.
10 E/CN.4/1172.
11 A/10146.
12 *Ibid.*
13 *Ibid.*
14 E/CN.4/1084; E/CN.4/1115; E/CN.4/1141; E/CN.4/1198.
15 E/CN.4.1142.
16 E/CN.4/199.
17 Resolution 3384(XXX) of 10 November 1975.

ration on this subject at the twenty-ninth General Assembly in 1974, along with some Eastern European countries.

The Declaration called on all states to prevent the use of scientific and technological developments to limit or interfere with human rights and basic freedoms.

One of the articles of this Declaration noted the responsibilities of states:

> to extend the benefits of science and technology to all strata of the population and to protect them from possible harmful effects of the misuse of scientific and technological developments.

The Western countries abstained from voting on the Declaration. All states were required, in terms of this Declaration, to:

> refrain from any acts involving the use of scientific and technological achievements for the purposes of violating the sovereignty and territorial integrity of other states, interfering in their internal affairs, waging aggressive wars, suppressing national liberation movements or pursuing a policy of racial discrimination.[18]

These political overtones did not however obscure the importance of the problem. They rather highlighted its gravity and urgency, for they made it evident how far-reaching and many-faceted the impact of technology could be.

The Declaration noted, as the prior documents had already done, that while scientific and technological developments could better the human condition, they could also threaten fundamental human rights and freedoms. Having done so, it went on to pronounce specifically upon a series of duties that devolve upon states in view of the damaging potential of technology. The problem was now moving upwards to the level of state duty, rather than mere general concern. The nine provisions of the Declaration were, significantly, cast in terms of mandatory state obligation, and can thus well form the basis for an eventual recognition of these duties as part of customary international law. It is true that the recognition of this duty appears in a Declaration and not a multilateral treaty, but one can see in it a clear recognition of a growing international sentiment that these norms should, by agreement of the international community, form the basis of state action. It is true also that, assuming such an obligation exists, it is binding primarily on states and not on those industrial-corporate-technological complexes which tend to be the most frequent violators of these norms. Yet, the last three principles in the Declaration are worthy of note in this respect, for they speak in

[18] GA resolution 3384(XXX) (1975).

terms not merely of the duties of states to order their own conduct, but also to take legislative measures to ensure the achievement of the Declaration's objectives.

Thus, Principle 8 requires states to take "effective measures, *including legislative measures*, to prevent and preclude the utilization of scientific and technological achievements to the detriment of human rights and fundamental freedoms and the dignity of the human person". Nor does the duty end there. Principle 10 requires all states, whenever necessary, to "take action to ensure compliance with legislation guaranteeing human rights and freedoms in the conditions of scientific and technological developments".

The Declaration at various points stresses the necessity for using technology for the purpose of the economic and social development of peoples, thus bringing the economic dimension prominently into focus.[19]

The General Assembly pursued this matter (in resolution 31/128 of 16 December 1976), by calling upon the member states to take account of the Declaration of 1974, thus enhancing the status of that document. Specialized agencies were also requested to take the provisions of the Declaration fully into account in their programmes and activities, while the Commission on Human Rights was required to give special attention to the implementation of the Declaration.

RESPONSES OF THE COMMISSION ON HUMAN RIGHTS

The Declaration received further recognition when the Commission on Human Rights (resolution 108(XXXIII) of 11 March 1977) welcomed the adoption of the Declaration by the General Assembly. Among the matters on which the Commission focused attention were the formulation of guidelines to protect persons, detained on grounds of mental ill-health, against treatment that might adversely affect the human personality and its physical and intellectual integrity, and a study of guidelines in relation to computerized personal files.

A strong case can thus be made that the terms of the Declaration, and with it the obligations it imposed upon states, are now built into the current body of human rights norms. Among the studies subsequently undertaken in 1981, in terms of the General Assembly Declaration, were "the right to work" and "the right to development".

The Commission continued its interest in this matter and, in 1983, invited all member states and relevant international organizations to submit their views "on the most effective ways and means of using the results of scien-

[19] See Principles 1 and 5.

tific and technological developments for the promotion and realization of human rights and fundamental freedoms".[20] This was followed by an invitation to the United Nations University and other interested academic and research institutions to examine the positive and negative aspects of scientific and technological progress.

THE LINKAGE OF SCIENTIFIC AND TECHNOLOGICAL PROGRESS WITH PEACE

One could continue with a list of further items of international responses to this growing interest in the impacts of science and technology on human welfare.[21] It will suffice for the present purpose to refer to two further resolutions of the General Assembly (resolutions 37/189A and 37/189B, both of 18 December 1982). The first exhorted all member states, appropriate organs of the United Nations, specialized agencies, inter-governmental and non-governmental organizations to take the necessary measures to ensure that scientific and technological progress was used *exclusively (i)* in the interests of international peace; *(ii)* for the benefit of mankind; and *(iii)* for promoting and encouraging respect for human rights and the fundamental freedoms, without distinction as to race, sex, language or religion. The second resolution called upon all states to make every effort to use the achievements of science and technology in order to promote peaceful social, economic and cultural development and progress. At the highest level, therefore, of international organization, the safeguarding of human rights in an age of burgeoning technology is an on-going activity, attracting a substantial degree of attention.[22]

THE ROLE OF SPECIALIZED AGENCIES

Unesco has taken the lead in directing attention to the human and cultural implications of scientific and technological advances. The focusing of public attention on the marvels of technology has tended to draw it away from a

20 Commission on Human Rights, Res. 1983/41.

21 For a fuller account of the international responses, see Hiroko Yamane, "Impacts of Technological Progress on Human Rights: Normative Response of the International Community", in C.G. Weeramantry (ed.), *Human Rights and Scientific and Technological Development*, United Nations University Press, 1990, pp. 91–104.

22 At subsidiary levels, likewise, sufficient momentum has been generated to maintain an appropriate level of activity independent of pressures from the General Assembly. In particular, three areas of activity need to be mentioned: the work of Unesco, of WHO and of independent gatherings and groups of concerned individuals.

consideration of the damaging effects of technology on the social and cultural environment. A report on this subject by the Director General of Unesco (A/9227) led to a General Assembly resolution in 1973[23] on the need for

(i) intensified efforts to prevent the misuse or abuse of scientific developments which endangered the distinctive character of all cultures; and

(ii) necessary steps being taken towards the preservation, enrichment and further development of national cultures and ways of life.

A specific manifestation of this concern, in the context of a particular cultural region, was the Dakar resolution of 1974 of the Ministers of African States Responsible for the Application of Science and Technology. At a conference sponsored by Unesco, these ministers drew attention to the necessity for the "safeguarding of African cultural values". A similar meeting of Ministers of Arab States in 1976 at Rabat considered what they described as "the overall cost of technology" and stressed the need to assess this in the context of possible damage to traditional cultural values.

The need to study the impacts of a technology before deciding to implement it received attention also at Nairobi in 1976. We are at a stage in the spread of technology where various new developments automatically tend to be received into countries of the Third World without an assessment of their "overall cost" to the society concerned, including the cost in terms of their cultural values. Computer technology, for example, or satellite transmission of television programmes — not to speak of techniques of artificial insemination or *in vitro* fertilization, or tractor farming, or nuclear power plants — can all make their entry into these societies almost as a matter of course, on the assumption that they represent "progress" or help the economy. A more sophisticated cost-benefit analysis, in which intangible cultural values are also thrown into the balance, is called for. Unesco has consistently stressed this aspect.

The World Health Organization (WHO) likewise has an important role to play in numerous human rights fields, ranging from torture practices to bottle-feeding.

Torture is one of those negations of human rights which has flourished under the influence of modern science and technology. New torture techniques, making use of the most sophisticated psychological and medical information, are being steadily perfected. The Council for International Or-

[23] Resolution 3148(XXVIII) of 14 December 1973.

ganizations of Medical Sciences responded to a request by WHO for a Code of Ethics relating to the duties of medical personnel in protecting persons against torture practices by formulating a set of Principles of Medical Ethics. This Code was endorsed by WHO in January 1979, and will prove valuable in the important task of guiding medical personnel in protecting persons against cruel, inhuman or degrading treatment or punishment. Medical personnel are called upon for such purposes as certifying the fitness of a person for interrogation or physical punishment, as well as attending to such persons after they have been subjected to such treatment.

Such matters as human experimentation and genetic engineering also call for guidelines. So, also, does externally funded medical research in Third World countries, for advantage can be taken of easier opportunities for conducting research on human subjects in those countries. WHO has been active in these fields. A conference in Mexico in 1980 on medical ethics and medical education, and another in Manila in 1981 on human experimentation and medical ethics, are examples of such WHO-sponsored work.

Perhaps the best known example of an acute human rights problem arising from the attempts of the modern technological-industrial complex to market its products in the Third World is the advertising of milk food formulas for infants. All the relevant research indicated a sharp rise in infant mortality when bottle-feeding was substituted for breast-feeding, but the advertising campaign continued to be pushed by the milk food manufacturers in the Third World. The World Health Assembly deplored this campaign in 1974 by resolution,[24] but the campaigns continued. A long struggle ensued, and eventually a Code restraining such advertising was adopted in May 1981, as a Recommendation under the Constitution of WHO by 118 votes to 1. The single vote cast against a Code directed at reducing infant mortality in the Third World was justified by the voter, the United States, as being necessitated on constitutional and legal grounds associated with freedom of speech. Restraints on advertising allegedly infringed on this right.[25] This case is a useful warning of the fact that basic human rights such as the right to food and the right to health are sometimes met by claims of alleged adherence to other basic human rights — such as the right to freedom of speech and of advertisement. In the field of science and technology, a

[24] Resolution WHA 27.43 of May 1974. See WHO Handbook of Resolutions and Decisions of the World Health Assembly and the Executive Board, Vol. 11, 3rd ed., 1973–1978. Other resolutions will be found in 4th ed., 1981.

[25] Press statement by Assistant Secretary of State Abrams, 15 May 1981, Department of State Bulletin, Vol. 81, No. 2062, July 1981, p. 54.

common conflict of freedoms is that between social interest considerations and freedom of research and inquiry.

The milk foods case is an excellent example of the need for a reconciliation to be effected with due regard for common sense. Free speech cannot prevail against the human rights to food and health, where it is clearly demonstrable that it leads to mortality on a scale of tens of thousands. In the future there will be many instances of such a clash of human rights that will need to be resolved, and we must be on our guard against pursuing an abstract right to the limits of its logic without regard to realities.[26]

We have thus far examined in some detail the activities of the United Nations and its associated bodies in bringing into focus the possible conflicts between technology and human rights. We must also make note of extensive unofficial activity directed towards the same end.

UNOFFICIAL ACTIVITY

One of the strongest statements in this field is the "Poona Indictment". The Fourteenth meeting of the World Order Models Project, held in Poona, India in July 1978, passed a resolution entitled "The Perversion of Science and Technology: An Indictment",[27] condemning "the way in which science and technology have become instruments of a global structure of inequity, exploitation and oppression".

Among the human rights violations dealt with by the resolution are drug testing among poor populations of the Third World; the misuse of the concept of "appropriate technology" by transnational corporations; the employment, for armaments manufacture, of 50 per cent of all research scientists in the world; the drive to sell products made possible by modern technology, regardless of whether they serve any real social need; and the undermining of Third World resources to feed the demands of the machines of the industrial nations. Scientific inquiry should lead, in the words of the declaration, to "technologies which liberate the many rather than facilitate control by the few". The declaration also draws attention to an important facet of the relationship between science, technology and human rights — that "The scientific enterprise must henceforth be directed especially towards the needs,

[26] On this episode, see generally A. Eide *et al* (eds.), *Food as a Human Right*, United Nations University Press, Tokyo, 1984, Ch. 18, "WHO and the Right to Food: Infant Nutrition Policy as a Test Case".

[27] Reprinted in (1979) 4 *Alternatives — A Journal of World Policy*, p. 413. The declaration is also reproduced in Weston, Falk and D'Amato, *Basic Documents in International Law and World Order*, West Publishing Co., 1980, p. 421.

skills and knowledge of the majority of the underprivileged peoples of the world, especially those in the Third World". This is a factor often overlooked in a world that devotes less than one per cent of its scientific skills to the needs of the poor world, but 50 per cent or more to the manufacture of weapons of death.

This last sentiment re-echoes the Cocoyoc Declaration of October 1974,[28] adopted by the participants in the UNEP/UNCTAD Symposium on Patterns of Resource Use, Environment and Development Strategies. Adopted at Cocoyoc, Mexico, this Declaration called upon universities, other institutions of higher learning, research organizations, and scientific associations all over the world to reconsider their priorities. Research needed to be focused more on the satisfaction of fundamental needs.

> A rejuvenated United Nations System should be used to strengthen the local capabilities for research and technology assessment in the developing countries; ... and to support research in a better and more imaginative utilization of potentially abundant resources for the satisfaction of the fundamental needs of mankind.

Two other important declarations, foreshadowing the role of technology in the future, call for mention: the Dai Dong Declaration on the Environment and the Oi Committee Declaration.

The Dai Dong Declaration of 1972 was adopted by the participants in the Dai Dong Independent Conference on the Environment, held in Sweden a week before the Conference that led to the more well known Stockholm Declaration on the Human Environment.[29] Among its conclusions were:

(i) We cannot reject technology *per se*, because economic development of any kind will require technology. Rather, we must restructure and re-orient it. We need ecologically sound technologies, complemented by a technology review and surveillance system.

(ii) The culture of the industrial nations reflects their political and economic ideology, and is based, among other things, upon an uncritical reliance on technology to solve humanity's problems. The ethical element is a forgotten dimension in this ideology and must be restored.

[28] See (1974) 1 *Alternatives — A Journal of World Policy*, p. 396; Weston, *et al*, *supra*, p. 415.

[29] For the Dai Dong Declaration, see (1975) 1 *Alternatives — A Journal of World Policy*, p. 406; Weston *et al*, *supra*, p. 424.

(iii) Military technology, being such a large part of industrial activity, particularly in economically developed countries, is a major cause of global pollution and resource depletion.

(iv) The basic right of peoples to control their own resources is affected, *inter alia*, by the technological practices of the industrial states operating in the developing countries. These practices must be curbed and altered in the interests of the world's people in this and future generations.

With this may be compared the Stockholm Declaration[30] which was adopted the following week. In that Declaration, of 16 June 1972, the United Nations Conference on the Human Environment stressed (in Principle 18) that science and technology, as part of their contribution to economic and social development, must be applied to the identification, avoidance and control of environmental risks, the solution of environmental problems, and the common good of mankind. Principle 20 recognized the need for properly oriented science and technology, by encouraging its promotion in all countries, especially the developing countries. In this connection, the free flow of up-to-date scientific information and transfer of experience must be supported and assisted.

The last document to which I shall refer is the aptly termed Oi Committee Declaration. The Oi Committee International, an International Committee of Young Scientists and Scholars for a Critical Holistic Approach to Development and the Human Environment, was so named from the initial letters of a Swahili proverb, "*Ote iwapo!*", meaning "All that is, must be considered".[31]

The Declaration not only dwelt at length on specific problems, such as environmental development, agricultural development, public health, population, rural development and urbanization, and the arms race, but also made some valuable general observations on the humanizing of technology and the social responsibility of science. On the former point, it stressed the need for a reorientation of technology towards more egalitarian goals, and for a "more humane technology" for the Third World. On the latter aspect, it stressed the need for a new technology based upon a new concept of science, intended only for the social well-being of peoples. "Scientists and other workers alike have the responsibility to participate in the economic and social development of all people and in the struggle for liberation of mankind as a whole."[32] The concept of "neutrality of science" was explicitly rejected.

30 (1972) 11 I.L.M. 1416; see Weston *et al*, *supra*, p. 343.

31 For the Oi Declaration, see Weston *et al*, *supra.*, p. 427.

32 *Ibid.*, p. 431.

FUTURE DIRECTION

What comes from all this survey of the current international awakening to this rather overwhelming problem of the impact of science and technology on human rights? What directions will human rights take under the heavy influence of technology in a future that will inevitably be dominated by these forces?

Certain essential principles stand out: there is scope here only to enumerate some of the more important, rather than to comment on them.

(1) Science and scientists, like technology and technologists, cannot pursue their expertise in disregard of social obligations.

(2) A more caring, humane attitude towards humanity and its environment is required of scientists than has been the case in the past.

(3) The scientist must accept moral responsibility for his or her work and its foreseeable consequences.

(4) Ethical codes need to be urgently formulated for the different areas of scientific development, relating scientific obligation to the needs of humanity.

(5) International adoption of such ethical codes by appropriate bodies of scientists is required, as purely national ethical codes can have no operative value.

(6) Along with international ethical codes there will be an increasing need for international regulatory mechanisms in many areas of science and technology.

(7) Science and technology must break their habit of subservience to the needs of corporate industrial might, through the growth of a professional scientific ethic which enables scientists to see themselves as skilled professionals, loyal to a professional code, rather than as employees bound by the dictates of those who pay them.

(8) The process of technology assessment, both national and international, needs to be stepped up, so that the human rights and social implications of technology are assessed, as far as possible, before the technology is released upon the public.

(9) In the process of such assessment, due weight should be given to the preservation of spiritual, cultural and moral values.

(10) Interdisciplinary education for scientists and technologists must be stressed, with particular emphasis on the social implications of science and technology.

(11) Legal education should step up its emphasis on understanding technology and its human rights impact.[33]

(12) An International Code of Conduct on the Transfer of Technology needs to be evolved, based on the proposition that technology is part of the common human heritage.

(13) The law of intellectual property must make more accommodation for the concept that in appropriate instances the public interest can prevail over proprietary interests in knowledge.

(14) Civil liberties committees and human rights commissions must step up their vigilance in respect of scientific and technological invasions of human rights.

(15) Institutions need to be set up for the study of humanistic science.

(16) Steps should be taken towards evolving a code of conduct for scientists involved in the armaments industry, emphasizing the moral responsibilities involved in their work.

(17) The needs and problems of the Third World should figure far more prominently on national and international agenda for scientific and technological activity, so as to divert more scientific and technological expertise towards their resolution.

(18) Such rights as freedom of inquiry, freedom of speech, freedom of advertisement, and freedom of trade can conflict with many fundamental human rights, notably the rights to food and health, and cultural rights. In such conflicts it should be more readily recognized that the former rights cannot be treated as absolute.

(19) Far greater stress needs to be placed upon the development of scientific and technological skill in the developing countries.

(20) There needs to be more stress on research aimed at a better and more imaginative utilization of potentially abundant resources for the fundamental needs of mankind.

[33] See *supra*, Chapter 4.

(21) The use of technology, in such a manner as to interfere, directly or indirectly, with the rights of nations to control their own resources, must be the subject of greater national and international vigilance.

(22) Universities and other institutions of higher learning, research organizations and scientific associations should give a lead in reconsidering their priorities for scientific and technological research.

(23) A new concept of science should be recognized, based on the social well-being of peoples rather than the blind pursuit of knowledge.

(24) The notion of the neutrality of science should be rejected.

These are just a few of the directions which need to be taken in the myriad interactions that will occur between science, technology and human rights. Failure to give attention to these aspects will inevitably lead to a continuing denigration of human rights. Legal inattention to pressing social problems has in the past been largely capable of correction through belated action. In the area of science and technology it cannot be too strongly stressed that much of the damage that can be caused will be totally irreversible.

6. The Problem of Appropriate Technology*

In 1986 the General Assembly in its Declaration on the Right to Development (GA Res 41/128 of 4 December 1986) formulated the right to development in terms that:

> The right to development is an inalienable human right by virtue of which every human person and all peoples are entitled to participate in, contribute to, and enjoy economic, social, cultural, and political development, in which all human rights and fundamental freedoms can be fully realized.[1]

The Declaration is particularly significant because it linked development and human rights, and specifically recognized the right to development as a human right. There had long been a tendency to decry the right to development as being only an aspiration which was far from reaching the level of a human right. The Declaration was thus a welcome and long overdue recognition by the international community that it was in fact a right which was both conceptually powerful and practically useful.[2]

Since the date of that Declaration, the recognition of the concept has progressed enormously. Treaties, state practice, and academic writing have accorded it increasing recognition and it is today a right whose international acceptance into the corpus of international law can scarcely be denied.

It is not proposed in this chapter to enter into jurisprudential discussions on the question of the status of this right in terms of international law or rigorous legal analysis. It is sufficient for our purposes if we recognize its existence. At the least, it is an evolving norm of international law.

* Adapted from the author's chapter on "Human Rights, Technology, and Development", in C.G. Weeramantry (ed.), *Human Rights and Scientific and Technological Development*, United Nations University Press, Tokyo, 1990, pp. 151–184.

1 This text was drafted between 1981 and 1984 by a Working Group of Governmental Experts. It was passed by 146 votes in favour. Only one State voted against — the United States.

2 *Cf.* Upendra Baxi: "The easy-minded cynicism towards the right to development has to be displaced; its practical uses demonstrated; its scope concretized through *praxis*". ("The Development of the Right to Development", in E.S. Venkataramiah (ed.), *Human Rights in the Changing World*, ILA, Regional Branch (India), 1988, p. 10.)

Nor is it proposed to attempt definitions of the concept of development, except to observe that development will not be taken as being confined to economic or material advancement, but is conceived of rather as "the upward movement of the entire social system and in conditions which afford individual members of the society the opportunity to benefit personally from the upward movement."[3]

To what extent, then, can technology (I use the term here as a shorthand expression for "science and technology," especially as it is the practical applications of science that concern us most in relation to the developing world) be used to promote the objectives encapsulated in the General Assembly's definition of the right to development?

It will be seen that there are three principal elements involved, namely:

(1) participation in decision-making regarding the introduction of a new technology:

(2) contribution to the creation of the technology in question; and

(3) enjoyment of the development resulting from technology.

The development itself could be economic, social, cultural, or political.

A. PARTICIPATION

1. *Factors excluding Participation*

Where technology is of a sophisticated nature, the stages of participation and contribution tend to be long delayed. There is also a greater tendency for the creators and the owners of the technology to keep to themselves the decision-making process regarding their product and its adaptations. They tend to delay even more resolutely the process of scientific input into the technology itself. Thus, far from there being a spontaneous spread of technology and industrialization as some theorists once expected (*cf.* theories of the spontaneous spread of capitalism), the events especially of the past half century have shown that technology which is of monetary value tends to become concentrated in the hands of those who create or own it, thus confining it largely to the developed world. This is despite theories of freedom of scientific knowledge. Although there is a desperate need for that technology in the developing world, the latter seems unable to draw the technology

[3] *The Right to Development at the International Level*, Hague Academy of International Law/UN University, Sijthoff & Noordhoff, 1980, p. 94.

to itself and absorb it into its own social and cultural milieu. If it comes in, it does so with strings attached, which can be manipulated from afar. It assumes a place in developing societies very much like that of a foreign body in a biological system, which never integrates fully with its host.

Contrary, therefore, to the theory that knowledge is universal, technological knowledge seems to belong — and to retain the semblance of belonging — to the developed world, wherever it may be actually applied. A principal reason for this is the lack of third-world participation and contribution, as outlined above. Through such lack of participation, attitudes have evolved in many countries of viewing modern technology as a distant and foreign thing.

2. *The Resulting Alienation from Western Science*

This sentiment often manifests itself in a plan for the total rejection of Western science, such as was voiced by some delegates at the recent conference on "Crisis in Modern Science" held at Penang, Malaysia in 1987 and hosted by the Third World Network and the Consumers' Association of Penang.[4] Some advocates of Islamic and Hindu science, pointing to the undoubted fact that science had made considerable independent and pioneering progress under these systems, sought to detach science from its existing international base and build it up anew on their own cultural base.[5]

Short of calls for total rejection, there has for long been a call for the diversion of science from its present course of being used as an instrument for the denial of human rights

Reference may here be made to the well-known 1978 Poona Declaration on Scientific Responsibility, adopted by the participants at the 14th Meeting of the World Order Models Project, held in Poona, India, in July 1978.[6] Describing itself as an indictment on the perversion of science and technology, this Declaration spells out in quite explicit terms some of the human rights problems caused by technology. Among the items mentioned are biological farming in the Third World by pharmaceutical transnationals, the banishment of a growing number of First World poor from productive activity through increasingly capital-intensive technology, and the employment of 50% of all

[4] On the crippling effect of Western science on the scientific creativity of developing societies, see Susantha Goonatilake, *Aborted Discovery: Science and Creativity in the Third World*, Zed Books, 1984, esp. Chs. 3 and 5.

[5] K. Sharma, "In Search of an Alternative Science," *Development and Co-operation*, No. 4 (1987), 26 at 27.

[6] "The Perversion of Science and Technology: An Indictment," in R. Falk, S. Kim, and S. Mendlovitz (eds.), *Towards a Just World Order*, Westview Press, 1984, p. 359. See also the reference to this Declaration in Ch. 5, *supra*.

research scientists in the world in military research and development. The resolution urged serious reflection and a vigorous debate on the need for an active search for alternative perspectives on science and technology which related to both the pursuit of truth and the process of human liberation.[7]

The universalism of science must be respected, even in countries which see themselves as its exploited victims. It is by participation and contribution that such attitudes of alienation can be averted and full use made of the beneficial potential of science and technology for every society. Everything traditional can sometimes be romanticized at too high a cost. An effort is therefore required to accelerate the ability of developing countries to participate in and contribute to such technology.

3. *Transforming passive receivers into active deciders*

This brings us to an issue which lies very much at the heart of the problem — the way in which it tends to be assumed that the developing world's role is that of passive receiver of technology, rather than of active determinant of the particular technology it will receive. It is true there are many situations where the freedom to choose is circumscribed, but at the same time the range of choices available is often much larger than is commonly supposed.

A conscious choice on the part of the recipient country must determine what technology it will accept or reject. That choice is not purely a scientific one, but depends upon social and economic factors and the expertise of many disciplines. This becomes all the more important when we realize that science is essentially a social product. Its development in Europe reflected a particular socio-economic context and, as it developed, it interacted in that socio-economic context to create a new set of needs which it began to serve. Technology has an even more intimate interaction on society than pure science. All of this interaction, heavily influenced by Western needs and norms, can well render a particular technology ill suited for a totally different third-world context — hence the importance of participation in determining the technology.

A prime factor in this process of determination is the principle that technological choice should turn in the direction of technologies which liberate the many rather than strengthen the few. Unfortunately, the choice of technology in the developing world is often in the hands of those who would like it to be an instrument in the furtherance of their own power — the power of

[7] For some of the extensive literature that has grown up around this theme, see Ch. 2, above, fn. 21.

the controlling elite.[8] Unfortunately also, there are many technologies, particularly in the information area, which facilitate processes of social and political control.

The bending of technology to service rather than oppression necessitates a preliminary examination of the routes through which a new technology finds its way into developing countries. We shall therefore look at some ways in which the developing world's participation in the decision-making process can be strengthened.

B. ROUTES OF ENTRY OF TECHNOLOGY INTO THE DEVELOPING WORLD

A new technology finds its way into a developing country either:

(a) by the country's own decision, uninfluenced by external factors;

(b) under the pressure of external factors which for one reason or another it is unable to resist; or

(c) through a combination of internal and external factors.

It is the author's view, which needs to be empirically tested, that the technologies introduced to the developing world under head *(b)* are more numerous and extensive than is commonly acknowledged, and that they tend to be the dominant technologies in nearly every developing country.

I shall deal briefly with each of these in turn.

(a) Internal Decisions Uninfluenced by External Factors

A developing country may take a decision to import a new technology because its government:

(i) genuinely believes that that technology is truly essential to the well-being or development of the country;

(ii) believes that there will be a political advantage to it in importing such technology, e.g., that computerization of the governmental process will give it greater control over its citizens; or that some extensive project, e.g., an irrigation project, will gain it political mileage;

[8] See Saneh Chamarik, "Technological Self-reliance and Cultural Freedom", in Weeramantry (ed.), *Human Rights and Scientific and Technological Development*, United Nations University Press, Tokyo, 1990.

(iii) is under pressure from internal vested interests to import such technology. Such pressures may come from economic interests it needs to cultivate for political reasons or from powerful individuals who will develop a vested interest in the new technology;

(iv) has corrupt reasons, in the sense that individual members of the government or their associates may see private profit in it for themselves;

(v) sees advantages in the offer of a technology highly attractive to the dominant classes in the target country, though not directly of benefit to the masses. Such an elitist class and its demands are often psychologically linked to those of the consumer society of the West.[9] As Marc Nerfin, the President of the International Foundation for Development Alternatives, so cogently observed at a UNU Workshop in Indonesia in 1986, "there is a fracturing into two of every society, much worse than the traditional East-West and North-South rifts: the two Indias, the two Chiles, the two USAs, the two worlds".[10]

The list is not exhaustive. It becomes important to gather information regarding the factors preceding the decisional process. If there are circumstances pointing to the existence of such factors as are listed in *(ii)*, *(iii)* and *(iv)* above, they need analysis and exposure. This is not always easy, for we are here on sensitive ground. It is better, however, that the reality be recognized and be taken into consideration than that we should continue paying obeisance to the myth that the problem disappears when the decision is a purely autonomous one.

(b) *Pressure of External Factors*

The government may be powerless to resist a new technology or product for many reasons. For example:

(i) It may be tied to an aid package and must therefore be taken along with it.

(ii) It may be a technology sought to be introduced by a multinational corporation which is so influential in the country concerned that

9 For a reference to such a class in Africa and Asia and its links with multinational corporations, see Louis Turner, *Multinational Corporations and the Third World*, Allen Lane, 1973, p. 67.

10 "Neither Prince Nor Merchant: Citizen", *Development Dialogue*, Vol. I (1987), p. 170.

the government cannot afford to displease it and has no option but to permit its introduction.

(iii) It may be associated with a military or economic alliance or grouping and the country concerned is hence not in a position to resist it.

(iv) The country concerned may have adopted an open-door economic policy and feels it may damage its image as a free investment country by denying entry to a technology which is heavily pushed by powerful overseas financial interests.

(v) The technology emanates from a country which is the most powerful trading partner of the developing country concerned. Any refusal to permit the importation of the technology could have severely damaging effects upon the trading relationship, to the grave detriment of the country concerned.

(vi) The technology emanates from a country to which the country concerned is heavily in debt. Similar factors operate as in *(v)* above.

(vii) The technology may be one associated with the arms trade. The armaments industry, already in a relationship with the government of the country concerned, presses it and the country cannot resist.

(viii) Massive advertising campaigns launched with all the powerful economic resources of the developed world may create a captive market in the target country, which exercises compelling pressures upon the government to permit admission of the project.

(ix) The technology concerned may be made available apparently free of charge, but the strings attached are that the providing country becomes the sole market for the apparatus that needs to be purchased for implementing the technology, e.g., television infrastructure or a high-technology hospital.

(c) *Mixed Internal and External Factors*

There could be a blend of one or more of the factors enumerated above, in numerous permutations and combinations.

The decisional process prior to the creation or importation of the new technology must take account of all these possibilities, each in its own way a very real factor, finally resulting in the entry of unsuitable or oppressive technologies. The factors outlined above have serious implications, not only in regard to the prevention of harmful technology, but also as inhibiting factors preventing access to technology which could foster and promote human rights, as well as free choice of such technologies. Compulsion to choose a given technology in a limited economic situation often means compulsion to forgo another more beneficial or more desired technology.

Indeed, the matter does not end here, but these influences continue after the introduction of the technology. It brings more unsuitable technologies in its train as the original technology, once entrenched, becomes too expensive to dislodge.

It is vital to the connection between technology and the right to development that there be a clearer understanding of these decisional processes and of the complex of factors that contribute to them. This is an important area of analysis in any study. It will be a useful research project to analyse, in the context of two or three countries, the decisional routes of entry into them of perhaps five selected technologies.

Such enhanced understanding is an important means of introducing more real participation in the decision-making that introduces technology into developing countries. Often these factors convert an apparent freedom to decide into a situation of non-freedom — a situation where the vast bulk of a developing country's population has the decision thrust upon them, that they will receive an unsuitable or exploitative technology.

Such considerations lead logically to the need for the more widespread diffusion of information in those communities, regarding not only the alternative technologies available, but also, the inhibiting decisional factors outlined above. This involves an educational process which will produce results in the long term, but in the short term it necessitates the setting up of multidisciplinary committees charged with the task of assessing the new technologies in the light of the country's economic, social, and cultural needs. Purely scientific committees are inadequate to cope with these decisions, as has now been well accepted for several years.[11] A greater awareness of the technological alternatives is important to the work of these groups.

In other words, there has to be a break from the deterministic theory regarding technology, which holds that technology runs an inevitable course and that it cannot be resisted, as it has a motive force of its own.

[11] See, generally, C. Cooper "Science, Technology, and Production in the Underdeveloped Countries: An Introduction", *Journal of Development Studies*, Vol. 9, No. I (1972); F. Stewart, *Technology and Underdevelopment*, 2nd ed., Macmillan. 1982, p. 278.

TECHNOLOGY SURVEILLANCE

In an examination of the means by which the developing world's participation in decision-making can be heightened, it is important to note that technology has a way of taking control over the areas to which it applies. Once a sophisticated technology is introduced — be it in the field of information, engineering or agriculture — it tends to dictate its own requirements and make all else subservient to its own needs. Often the very problem itself, which the technology was intended to serve, becomes subordinate to the servicing of the technology. The intended servant becomes the master.

It is necessary, especially in developing societies, to keep constantly in view the principle that technology is there to serve the people and not to be served by them. There should be control over it at every point. This means among other things a continual process of review by committees or groups, of which citizens form an important element. The experts are no doubt necessary, but there needs to be constant questioning as to whether the technology is serving its purpose, or creating new problems or being in fact counterproductive from the standpoint of the needs of any particular country.

A matter to be considered is whether, in relation to developing countries, mechanisms ought not to be devised which will achieve this purpose.

Just as developing countries all too often exhibit an attitude of resignation to the inevitability of technology, they also entertain a feeling of futility in regard to any attempt to control it. It is both too complex and too powerful to admit of lay attempts at control. That attitude needs re-examination.[12]

It is necessary to create a trend in developing countries towards setting up institutional structures for the constant surveillance of technology. Such structures need to be set up as a matter of course. The habit of technology surveillance does not exist in most developing societies and it must be stimulated to emerge.

The techniques of technology assessment, well developed and entrenched in the affluent world, can afford useful guidelines. We have here an ironic situation. New technologies are evolved largely in the developed world and are hence suited for the developed world. They are scrutinized in the developed world by technological assessment committees. Yet before their introduction to the developing world, for which they are far more likely to be unsuitable, they are not scrutinized by comparable boards or committees. Indeed, the need for such scrutiny in the developing world is even greater, for another reason. The developed world has already felt the impact of most

[12] See, generally, C.G. Weeramantry, *The Slumbering Sentinels: Law and Human Rights in the Wake of Technology*, Penguin Books, 1983.

of these technologies and adjusted to it, while the developing world has yet to feel the first impact of many of them. That impact must be assessed before the technology is foisted on them, for it can disrupt many factors essential to the stability of those societies; one example might be a labour-saving technology such as robotization for which that country is not yet ready.

A large segment of the industrial production of the third world is directly or indirectly affected by new technologies — e. g., microchips and the creation and use of new materials. Even seemingly remote technologies such as organ transplants can assume human rights dimensions in the developing world, as for example, when they generate a traffic in organ donation between the rich and the poor worlds. Vigilance is required at all points of possible contact between new technologies and the developing world.

Often a correct choice cannot be made for lack of knowledge of the new technologies on the part of local decision-makers. It is essential therefore that decision-makers in third-world situations be better informed of the entire concept of technology assessment.

We cannot, of course, leave this topic without referring to the Bhopal disaster and the surveillance systems resulting from it. The chemical hazard control programme launched by India is a very ambitious one. It includes identification, analysis, and control of all industrial activities involving potentially hazardous chemicals and processes. It also involves a census of India's estimated 5,000 chemical production units and a wide range of safety measures, including a greatly strengthened factory inspectorate. Unless developing countries think in these terms they are more than likely to be dumping grounds for careless or untested technology, with consequent damage to human rights.[13] If, on the other hand, they are prepared to think in these terms it will make possible a great enhancement of the enjoyment of technology.

EARLY RECOGNITION AND ALERT SYSTEMS

When a new technology is introduced, there should be early recognition and alert systems in regard to its impact. With this end in view, workshops have already been organized, such as the International Workshop on Advanced Technology Alert Systems: Towards Exchange of Experiences and Promotion of International Co-operation in Technology Assessment, which was organized by the German Foundation for International Development (DSE), in West Berlin in December 1985. The deliberations of that committee

[13] Thomas Land, "India Tightens Chemical Hazard Control", *Development and Co-operation*, No. 6 (1987), p. 18.

brought out the fact that technology assessment, linked with technology management and technology transfer policy, is indispensable. Professor Rohatgi from India, one of the participants in this workshop, declared:

> We feel this application of formal and quantitative techniques of technology forecasting assessment and alert systems could lead to a vastly improved and comprehensive identification of opportunities and emerging technologies for developing countries well in advance.

Private corporations in India have recently begun to conduct forecasting studies relevant to their own research and production codes. The general use of such methods by administrators is, however, still far away.

The Advanced Technology Alert System (ATAS) offered by the United Nations Committee on Science and Technology for Development is also making a substantial contribution to the early recognition of possible applications of new technologies. Other international organizations, like ILO and UNIDO, offer international monitoring and warning systems, especially in the fields of microelectronics, genetic engineering and biotechnology. It would indeed be true to say that the new technologies can, before their full impact is sufficiently realized, make a great dent in the cultural and social progress of third-world countries unless thought is given in advance to their impact upon the social systems concerned.

Pursuing these notions further, technology assessment *prior* to the creation of the product, can lead to the fashioning of a product more suitable to the recipient's needs and social and economic conditions. This is an important feature of the rights of protection against the harmful effects of scientific and technological developments. It is a vital part of the informational process preceding the evolution of an appropriate product. It is also an important way in which developing societies can make a greater *active contribution* to the development of technology, as suggested in the General Assembly's Resolution on the right to development.

With more participation by developing countries, they will have a greater ability to resist deterministic beliefs about the inevitability of technological change. As an Australian study advocated for Australia, itself often a receiver of technology:

> Technological change is not inevitable and predetermined. We must resist deterministic talk about inexorable change ... There is and must be choice. We can, and must, influence choices made in technological decision-making.[14]

C. CONTRIBUTION

1. *Involvement at the stage of evolution*

We have dealt thus far with participation in decision-making about the introduction of new technology. If developing-world scientists and decision-makers are involved at the stage of evolution of a new technology, there can be an even more substantial attempt to turn technology to the service of development.

A writer on the subject has observed:

> Techniques do not exist in heaven, in Platonic caves or in entrepreneurs' imagination, ready to be plucked from the air and incorporated into use. Techniques, whether they be methods of administration or machines to produce consumer goods, have to be invented, developed, introduced, modified, etc. The development of techniques is essentially a historical process in which one technique with one set of characteristics replaces another in the light of the historical and economic circumstances of the time. The historical nature of technological development means that the time and circumstances in which any particular technique is developed heavily influence its characteristics.[15]

At the same time we must be conscious of practical restraints, such as the fact that a multinational can rely on expertise from all over the world to develop a project, while a local operator, who comes to the project for the first time, will have to make all the mistakes the multinational has already made and still not possess a fraction of the latter's experience.[16]
We shall look at some facets of these problems.

[14] A.W. Goldsworthy, *et al*, *Technological Change: Impact of Information Technology*, Australian Government Publishing Service, 1981, p. 56.

[15] F. Stewart, *Technology and Underdevelopment*, Note 11, *supra*, p. 3.

[16] Louis Turner, *Multinational Corporations and the Third World*, Note 9; *supra*, p. 70.

2. *Participation in Product Designing*

The needs of the country concerned, together with the dangers and the advantages, should wherever possible be part of the input into the *designing* of the technology. This avoids the unsatisfactory situation of the developing country being presented with a completed technology or technological product which it must either accept or reject. Every country has its own requirements and is entitled to products tailored to those requirements. This may not always be feasible, but in many cases where it is in fact feasible the unsuitable product tends to be designed without adequate participation from the recipient country.

An important guideline for the export of technology should be that where a particular developing-world market is sought, representatives from the recipient country should wherever possible be brought into the designing stage prior to the final completion of the product. It is true that the forces of the market-place sometimes bring about that result, but the formulation of such guidelines will assist in making this a routine procedure wherever possible.

3. *Joint Venture Enterprises*

Where a technology is involved which is too sophisticated for the developing country to produce by itself, joint venture enterprises would be essential. The developing world would have a substantial share in these and hence be able to contribute its own expertise to the process of production.

Research in international trade law aimed at giving more strength to the local component of joint venture enterprises can establish more ways in which that local component can assert itself. At present the foreign participant often enjoys dominance by virtue of being the owner of the technology.

Research would need to cover the basic transfer modes of technology, such as licensing or franchising, subcontracting, and supply of equipment, materials, or technology. Much technology comes in the form of total package transfer, including such components as market survey, product mix, design, production plan, quality control, and manufacturing processes and procedures. Also involved are the foreign exchange component and managing and marketing skills.[17] Selected aspects of this package can be scrutinized with a view to increasing the local input. Indeed, there should be the capability of untying the whole package in order to scrutinize its different component elements with a view to maximizing the local input in conso-

[17] Turner, *supra*, pp. 70–71.

nance with local needs. Tied packages of conditions which must be taken or rejected as a whole often enable very exploitative conditions to be foisted upon recipients. There is an important field of work here for the lawyers and international consultants of the developing world. Currently the legal expertise available in most parts of the developing world cannot match the expertise that can be commanded by the joint venture partners of the developed world. Perhaps the United Nations University or the Human Rights Commission could assist in this respect by organizing seminars or training courses for developing world lawyers and administrators in this field.

Where there is a process of subcontracting, the relationship between the large or parent enterprise and the subcontractor needs to move away from the "parent-child" type of relationship to one of equal partnership. Local legislation can provide additional strengths to the local partner, making the bargaining relationship closer to one of equality.

Where the transfer is through a supply of equipment, material, and basic technology, there will be considerable room for adaptation to local needs. This will also generate technological skills in the recipient countries.

In every one of these types of operation the importance of the generation of local skills cannot be over-emphasized.

4. *Restrictive Trade Practices*

An important area of legal research involved in all of these types of technology transfer is in the area of restrictive trade practices. Inherent in many of them are restrictions which severely inhibit local input and the spread of local expertise. For the socio-economic development of a nation, the latter is particularly important and cannot be left to the chance forces of the marketplace. It requires deliberate policy measures by the government of the recipient country. Indeed, government agencies, such as the Council of Science and Industrial Research set up by the Government of India, or Institutes of Small-scale Industries or National Science Development Boards, can help in co-ordination and in giving advice on some of the technical aspects involved in such policies. Non-governmental organizations, such as trade associations and industrial co-operatives, can also provide these services.[18]

The process of technology transfer to developing countries often comes up against a problem sometimes described as "the double economic structure." By this is meant the fact that in many of these countries there is, in and around the large cities, a prosperous and sophisticated consumer group, often

[18] See generally *Intra-national Transfer of Technology*, Asian Productivity Organization, Tokyo, 1976, chap. 2.

with Western-oriented tastes, while in the other areas there is a large population with a different background and tastes. Both are potential groups of customers. To which groups does one cater?[19]

There are heavy human rights overtones in the decision to be made. The chances are that the economically and often politically more powerful urban group would be the target of the introduced technology. The decision-makers invariably come from this group. Their needs tend to be supplied, while the needs of the rest, however urgent, pass unheeded. Sophisticated cookers for the urban elite would for example gain priority over the development of a simple solar cooker for the rural population. Instances could be multiplied.

Governments need to develop scales of priorities based on human rights, of which the most relevant for our purpose are the rights to food, health, shelter, and a decent standard of living. These must take priority over the sophisticated technologies demanded by the elite. The competing claims to technology of these two groups are often lost sight of when technology is received or accepted by developing countries. It is important that the human rights aspect be given a higher profile, so that decision-makers in receiving technology will bear in mind this dichotomy of demands within the same system.

THE COMPUTER AS THE GENERATOR OF NEW PRODUCTS

To all this must be added the fact that the actual processing of information, as well as the dissemination of information — not to speak of the storing of information — requires intensive investments in computerization. These again are largely within the control of one sector of the world's economy and it is that sector which thus acquires increasing control over the product and the information embodied within it.

The computer is no longer merely an assembler of information. It is today extensively used to generate new products and tailor them for particular purposes and specific markets. This resource, extremely expensive and beyond the reach of most developing societies, gives the developed world an irreversible lead in the ability to design a product for the markets of the developing world, so that there can in fact be little real competition.

It is to be remembered in this connection that the developing world's superiority lies not merely in the computer technology with which to process information. It lies also in its superior access to the information itself. There is many times more information regarding the developing world in the data banks of the developed world than in all the data banks of the developing

[19] See Turner, *supra*, p. 67.

world. The developed world thus has a double lead over the developing world in the sphere of information — superiority in basic information, as well as superiority in the means of assessing and processing it. This imbalance acts as a powerful inhibitor of participation of developing countries and is more fully dealt with in the next chapter of this book.

The future will see the further spread of new computer techniques, including that of robot technology, which can have severe repercussions on the labour forces of developing countries. Such technology could thus in effect deprive a developing economy of the use of its labour, which is one of its most important economic resources. Important policy decisions are called for in this area, in order to increase the ability of developing countries to make an input at the designing stage into the new technology.

D. PARTICIPATION

1. *The link between contribution in fashioning the product and participation in the enjoyment of it*

A steady policy aim of generating increasing technological skills in the local population is an important part of any policy aimed at turning technology to the service of human rights. Scientists and technologists from the country itself are likely to be far more aware of pressing local needs and demands than those from abroad. With more such skills available locally, there will also be a greater trend towards fashioning a product more in keeping with the needs and the way of life of the people, and towards analysing a complex technological package so as to rid it of elements that are unsuitable for the recipient country.

2. *Education for Participation*

A change of attitude is required here in the entire educational structure — a change that will accept technology not as a foreign graft but as an integral part of the local culture. Marrying traditional local technology to the new, will have important psychological overtones for this process. The dichotomy between the traditional way and the technological way, which leads to the us/them syndrome regarding technology in developing countries, needs to be broken down. We are one world, and technology is the common inheritance of this one world, without which no part of it can survive. Just as Japanese culture integrated Western technology into its way of life, to the extent that there is now nothing "foreign" about it, so also all developing countries must integrate technology into their way of life.

The educational process must aim not merely at producing scientists and technologists who can actively participate. It must aim also at the general population, with the intention of making them more receptive to the technologies that will assist them.

3. *Targeting Publications at the Grass Roots*

Any process of educating the community must take note of the current deficiencies in the technological communications network.

Even within the UN system, despite its enormous output of publications, there is an insufficient targeting of "grass-roots" audiences. For example, a recent survey found that of WHO's list of approximately 1,300 titles, only 11 titles were suitable for primary health workers.[20] Although there were 1,800 publications (including periodicals) issued within the UN system in 1981, the average print run was only 2,000 copies per publication, despite the fact that the seemingly large number of 3.6 million volumes and journals was thus produced.[21] Of this limited output around 80% went to the industrialized countries. For WHO the figure was 80%, for ILO 78%, and for the UN itself 91%.

4. *Use of the Media*

The problem is important enough to warrant a national effort with governmental support at using the media — print, radio and television — to bring home to the population that the new technologies are in their country for their own participation and enjoyment, and not as tokens of domination by foreign interests. As more of the public are drawn into the resulting discussions, the feeling of alienation and lack of interest will dissipate and there will be a greater willingness to reap the advantages of a given technology and, in doing so, to help in fashioning it to the needs of the country.

[20] Christopher Zielenski, "Reaching the Grassroots: Publishing Methodologies for Development Organizations," *Development Dialogue*, Vol. I (1987), p. 196.

[21] See *Publications Policy and Practice in the United Nations System*, Joint Inspection Unit, Geneva, 1984 (Doc. no. JIU/REP/84/5).

5. *Practical methods*

Such figures underline the necessity for new concepts and methods relating to publishing for the grass roots. It is to be remembered that publication is not the only route by which the grass roots can be reached. Other alternatives that have been satisfactorily employed are:

> *(i) Demonstrations*
> This is especially useful with small-scale technology. Nothing succeeds like the demonstration of a good example.
>
> *(ii) Prototypes*
> It is useful to start a prototype of a new scheme at the grass roots and monitor its progress. Material can then be put out showing how the prototype can be replicated, drawing on the experiences in that very community.
>
> *(iii) Promotion of the idea and of adaptations*
> This is a process that must be actively undertaken at all levels of community interaction.

Academic publications, while they have their own merits, are no substitute for revitalized attempts to take technology to the grass roots.

6. *Increasing the Stress on Appropriate Technology*

This is a topic that has generated a vast literature. Schumacher's *Small is Beautiful*[22] is perhaps still the outstanding work in this genre, which has now grown to thousands of titles and a flood of articles, reports, and symposia. Since appropriate technology aims at adaptation of technology to the needs of the recipient country, the local input into the actual technology is considerable. This has the additional advantage of preventing a sense of alienation. Mahatma Gandhi's approach was not against machines but against man becoming mechanized. With appropriate technology, which is adapted to the service of the receiving community, there is little chance of man becoming the servant of the technology.

Appropriate technology does not necessarily mean that it should be entirely the adaptation of the receiving country. Some developed countries have active programmes for contribution towards the evolution of appropriate technology, as for example the German Appropriate Technology Ex-

[22] E.F. Schumacher, *Small is Beautiful: A Study of Economics as if People Mattered*, Abacus, London, 1978.

change (GATE) under which various German agencies joined in developing a service package for developing countries. It concerns itself with the planning and implementation of technical co-operation projects dealing with the development, adaptation, transfer, and propagation of appropriate technologies. Developed countries can assist considerably in this way. Schumacher's vision of a new method of production, rooted in what may be described as Buddhist economics, which should be simple, non-violent, kind to the environment and not aimed at the stimulation and satisfaction of superfluous material needs, has many ideas within itself which can assist in turning technology to the furtherance of human rights.

In the midst of all this discussion we must not lose sight of the fact that education is a major lever for development. There must therefore be a plan to spread among each community an understanding of the way in which technology can be of assistance to them in their day-to-day problems. It is true, there are already rather loose organizations aimed at spreading this sort of knowledge among the populations of Third World countries. There needs to be some co-ordinated effort, the guidelines for which may perhaps be formulated by the Human Rights Commission, in relation to the way in which each government could maximize the communication system concerning the technology which would be appropriate for those local communities.

7. *Widening the Circle of Beneficial Users*

The purpose of all the decisional and participatory processes thus far considered is of course the enjoyment of the technology by the maximum number of citizens of the country concerned. While the technology benefits society generally, it must also be capable of individual enjoyment. It must not, in other words, be a technology which only the privileged can enjoy.

In deciding which of various sectors of a country's population should have priority in a given area of technology, perhaps a computation on the lines of a Benthamite calculus of utility could be employed. The technology must be capable of enjoyment by the largest possible sector of the population.

This is perhaps the most important of the trilogy of requisites comprised within the General Assembly's definition, and we need to examine the serious obstructions impeding the movement of science and technology from the point of its creation, to the point of its delivery to the individual member of society who is to enjoy it.

In this section I propose to examine some of these major obstacles. They include current attitudes of the scientific establishment, the tendency of the information technology to concentrate and entrench the technological dominance of the Western world, the armaments trade, the politics of food, and the inadequacies of the law in keeping pace with technology. The list is by no means exhaustive, and I have selected only a few major areas. I shall consider each of these in turn.

It will be noted that some of them have relevance also to the earlier topics of participation and contribution.

8. *Changing Scientific Priorities*

If we are to turn technology to affirmative service in the cause of human rights, we cannot even hope to achieve this result unless we can enlist the co-operation of the scientific establishment. Indeed, if we can, half the battle is won.

The Brandt Report, which stated that while 51% of the developed world's scientific expenditure was devoted to the manufacture of weapons, less than 1% was devoted to researching the needs of the developing world,[23] makes imperative the diffusion of such knowledge. One begins to wonder whether there is not a responsibility lying on the appropriate international bodies to suggest some scale of priorities in relation to technological research. It is true there can be no enforcing mechanism in relation to priorities, but guidelines in this area would be of great value.

A disproportionate amount of resources is sometimes devoted to an area of research which benefits extremely few and may not contribute at all to a vast segment of the human race. Elaborate and expensive procedures for organ transplants or *in vitro* fertilization may prolong individual human life or result in the possibility of the creation of life in laboratory conditions. Such technology benefits the few, and involves immense resources, thus leading us to the vital question of priorities in a world of shortages.

We need to work towards securing an acknowledgement, from prestigious scientific organizations, of the need to step up the amount of scientific endeavour spent on researching the technical needs of the developing world.

The universal eradication of malaria could be achieved at a cost far less than the rate of expenditure for one hour on the global armaments race. Common sense would dictate which one of these is the priority, but we tend to continue pouring money into the technological processes dictated by the needs of corporate, industrial, and military might.

[23] *North-South: A Programme for Survival*, Report of the Independent Commission on International Development Issues, Pan Books, 1980, pp. 197–198.

9. *Heightening the Social Responsibilities of Scientists*

Unfortunately there has not been a sufficiently sustained effort to bring home to scientists the human rights implications of their work. Scientists as individuals are as well intentioned as any other members of society, but their work has immense potential for the destruction of human rights.[24] All too often, however, the scientist, engrossed in his or her own particular research, does not see the social consequence of that work.

It is vital that a heightened consciousness of these social implications be fostered in scientists. This may be done through social responsibility courses introduced into all tertiary science curricula, where today they are singularly lacking, or by the introduction of ethical codes which different disciplines of scientists, e.g., engineers, would adopt. It could also be achieved through a wider diffusion of relevant information among scientists, of the social consequences of their work, which international organizations such as UNEP (the United Nations Environmental Programme), Unesco, or UNDP could stimulate. Indeed, there is room here for an international journal on the Current Social Consequences of Science, which one such organization, or even UNU, could undertake.

This leads in turn to a consideration of the responsibilities of the scientific community who, after all, are in the vanguard of this process of diverting earth resources and human resources into wasteful expenditure. Scientists and technologists tend to give their expertise to the highest bidder. There can be no quarrel with this, but when the overall result is one which produces a degree of iniquity as great as that embodied in the 51% versus 1% differential referred to in the Brandt Report, one begins to wonder whether the scientific community ought not to be devoting some effort to evolving a code of social responsibilities.

This is a much neglected area and, except for the very rudimentary code of medical ethics centring around the Hippocratic oath, and some extremely rudimentary codes of the engineering profession or in the computer field, the vast profession of science is completely unregulated by ethical codes such as exist among lawyers and accountants. Consequently many of the world's most talented scientists devote their expert talent and skill to perfecting weapons of destruction, with no apparent mental qualms resulting from the perception that a fraction of their talents, directed into different channels, could save tens of thousands from starvation or malnutrition. In short, the scientific conscience needs to be stimulated.

24 See C.G. Weeramantry, *The Slumbering Sentinels*, *supra*.

The attention of future scientists should be particularly drawn to the imbalance in scientific effort already mentioned. They need to be shown how this may result in tensions so severe as to create dangers to world peace in the future. With the virtual monopoly of expensive scientific technology currently enjoyed by one sector of the world economy, the imbalance in the relative economic positions of the different sectors of the world is heightened to acute proportions, and may result by the turn of the century in the bitterest conflicts — conflicts that will unsettle the rich and poor world alike.

We should perhaps be considering also the inauguration of centres where international co-operation between scientists can be generated by drawing together scientists from different sections of the world for a discussion of these socially-oriented problems.

10. *Remedying the Informational Imbalance*

Another great roadblock on the way to the bending of science and technology to greater human service, is the way in which information technology is helping in the polarization of developed and developing worlds. Although one would expect that the explosive growth of information technologies in recent years would enure to the benefit of the average citizen in the developing world, by making a knowledge of science and technology more freely available in quarters that it would not otherwise have reached, the information revolution has thrown up yet another obstacle to the delivery of appropriate technology to the developing world.

It is to be remembered also that whereas earlier technology, dating back to steam and electricity, greatly magnified physical power, modern information technology greatly enhances man's intellectual power,[25] and therefore greatly magnifies its possessor's powers of domination.[26]

11. *The Role of the State*

It is clear that the state has an important role to play in achieving the maximum enjoyment of technology by its citizens. One of the most important problems faced by developing countries is the nature and extent of this state role.

It would be of assistance to examine in this connection a pioneering Sri Lankan project, the Million Houses Programme (MHP). This programme

[25] See *Technological Change: Impact of Information Technology*, Australian Government Publishing Service, 1981, p. 50.

[26] On this aspect, see further Ch. 7 *infra*.

offers both an interesting philosophical base and a practical example in fulfilling the basic human right to shelter of a large segment of the population. At the thirty-fifth General Assembly of the UN in 1980, Sri Lanka proposed the concept of a selected year to focus on shelter, which resulted in the UN's International Year of Shelter for the Homeless, 1987. The rationale behind the proposal, as stated by Prime Minister Premadasa to the UN (12 October 1987) was that great industrial and agricultural visions tended to by-pass the centre of human development — the home.

The programme, which has already achieved the construction of half a million houses, rests upon a support-based paradigm (S-BP) rather than the traditional provider-based paradigm (P-BP). This means that it is poor families and poor communities that both *decide* and *do*, the role of the government being to support and complement their initiatives. Under this philosophy all technology issues are individually and locally determined by the micro-context rather than determined from above in conformity with a macro-scheme. In making known the technologies available, the government has an important role to play, as it has in providing credit, basic services, training, and technological assistance. Housing options and loan packages (HOLPs) facilitate choice of technology and materials. Yet the underlying philosophy is that the state participates in the people's process rather than the people in the process of the state. State support is maximal; its intervention is minimal. Technology choices are for the people and individuals of the area. Their range of information is considerably magnified by the services provided by the state.

We refer later in this chapter to the importance of self-help. It may well be that there are principles of global significance in this regard in the Sri Lankan experience.

E. BARRIERS BETWEEN MODERN TECHNOLOGY AND ITS MOST APPROPRIATE USE

1. *The Armaments Trade*

Another dimension of the problem under review is the interconnection between disarmament and development. Although the intertwining of disarmament and global development is well acknowledged in theory, very little has been done in practice to achieve the desired result of diverting some portion of world resources currently wasted on armaments, into the field of development. This is an area involving superpower and regional politics, but also one to which the Human Rights Commission may have some worthwhile contribution to make. Indeed, the Commission would perhaps fail in its duty to consider the overall picture if it did not give some attention to this vital aspect of the development dialogue.

There have been insufficient analytical studies of the ways in which the arms trade conflicts with nearly every canon of the current universally accepted body of human rights.[27] This can be written on *in extenso*, but it is not within the scope of the present study.

However, an important area of the arms trade which needs continuing in-depth research is the question of diverting the productivity of the armaments industry into products of a peaceful nature. Conversion of swords into ploughshares is perhaps the most important and urgent of the studies that need to be undertaken. Considerations of space prevent a more detailed study of this area, which is rapidly becoming a major area of research.

2. *The Politics of Food*

A major obstacle to the enjoyment of modern technology by a vast segment of the world's population in a vital arena is the fact that food is treated as just another commercial commodity, by a political-economic-technological complex that works its equations of profit ratios, far from the starvation and malnutrition produced by the maldistribution of food. These human problems are seen almost as an academic exercise, far from the scene of the problems themselves. The resources of computer technology and satellite scanning are used to manipulate the futures market in grain, and the ledgers recording these transactions show only the number of dollars gained rather than the number of human lives lost.

Thus, although through the aid of technology world cereal production has steadily outstripped world population growth, and although the world produces more food per head of population than ever before in human history (in 1985 it produced nearly 500 kilograms per head of cereals and root crops),[28] more than 730 million people did not, amidst this plenty, eat enough to lead fully productive lives.[29]

This increase in food production is of course the result of improved technology, some of it of the most sophisticated kind. Satellite imagery, micro-

[27] See, on this aspect, Ch. 11 of Vol. 1.

[28] *Our Common Future*, Report of the World Commission on Environment and Development, Oxford University Press, 1987, p. 118, based on data from *FAO Production Yearbook 1985*, Rome, 1986.

[29] See World Bank, *Poverty and Hunger Issues and Options for Food Security in Developing Countries*, Washington, D. C., 1986.

electronics, computer sciences, biotechnology, tissue culture techniques, and other frontier technologies help produce this result. These technologies are, however, under the control of the affluent world. Its grain traders can put together a forecast of the world's crops by using satellite infra-red scanning procedures for forecasting a bad wheat crop — e. g. in the Soviet Union — thus assisting in the manipulation of futures markets. Its politicians can use the supply or withholding of grain as political weapons and can decide when its farm production of surplus grain is to be curtailed or stocks are to be destroyed to bolster up prices. Its industrial-technological complex can offer or withhold a new grain production technology to a third-world government or ruling elite.

In the decisions that are taken, the interests served are of course not those of the bulk of the world's population, but the financial and political interests of the owners of the technology. Else we would not see, for example, vast stocks of food being burned or cattle being slaughtered. Nor would we see massive cutbacks in agricultural production made mandatory by law in great grain-producing countries such as the US or Australia.

The fact that food production and technology go hand in hand in the 1980s points to the need for food technology to be harnessed in the service of that greatest of human rights — the right to life. Food, adequate to the maintenance of a life of dignity, is a human right, and technology needs to be harnessed in the cause of food security.

All of the technologies we have mentioned and many more must be tapped to meet the needs of the developing world, but the obstacles caused by commercial attitudes of profit-making, scientific and technological lack of concern, and feelings of futility and resignation on the part of third-world leaders and scientists must be overcome.

The solution lies clearly not in the handing out of food bonanzas to the developing world on a regular basis, but in their greater participation in such technology. To this end we need revised attitudes of the ruling elites, greater scientific and social awareness, and international norms which regard food as a public resource rather than a purely private right.

The following areas are suggested as needing increased attention:

1. The development of norms of national and international law in the field of intellectual property, seeking to build up within the universal domain a pool of scientific and technological knowledge. By way of example, private companies seeking property rights to improved seed varieties tend often to fail to recognize the rights of the countries from which the plant matter was obtained. As the World Commission on Environment and Development pointed out (p. 139), such practices

could discourage countries rich in genetic resources from making these internationally available, thus reducing the options for seed development in all countries. Norms of international co-operation can also be built up in these areas, just as such norms have been built up in the field of environmental law.

2. International organizations such as FAO already hold an unrivalled bank of agricultural statistics and inventories of the world's physical resources. Such organizations can draw in the most sophisticated modern technology to help the Third World. An outstanding example is FAO's satellite-based alert system, backed by scientific establishments in the Federal Republic of Germany, which is used to give early warning of drought, crop failures, and insect plagues in Africa, thus enabling preparation for major food shortages before they occur.[30] Databases are being built up covering agro-climatological statistics, day-to-day vegetation indexes, and an analysis of potential locust habitats in Africa, the Middle East and South-West Asia.

3. Within the developing countries there must be a greater readiness to set up and finance research institutions that can help in channelling the new technologies towards the needs of the country in question. Many third-world countries, knowing their weakness in research, tend to take this situation for granted. This further increases the technological gap with the developed world instead of providing the technological bridge we need.

4. More specific international guidelines and national laws are required for regulating food technology that is introduced into a developing country.

5. International lending institutions such as the World Bank and the Asian Development Bank can lay down firmer guidelines requiring the development of local technological skills in relation to agriculture and fisheries.

6. The world community, through its resources and encouragement, must seek to divert towards food technology an increasing segment of the world's scientific skill — far more than the 1% which is currently devoted to the needs of the developing world. The vast bulk of scientific research on agriculture still concentrates on the needs of the developed world, whose resource-rich conditions and ample water

30 *Development and Co-operation*, No. 2, (1988), p. 24.

supplies contrast with many areas in Africa and Asia which suffer from unreliable rainfall and poorer soils. These call for new and specialized technologies suited to each particular area, which would represent a combination of the modern and the traditional.

7. The food problem is linked with the land problem, and research is required to free the maximum amount of land for food production. Land law reforms would often have to be effected to meet this need. The necessary studies would include the disciplines of law and economics, having regard, in particular, to the fact that much of the most serviceable food-producing land in the developing world grows produce for the developed world, rather than food for its own population.

8. Freeing more land for food production involves environmental concerns as well, such as rehabilitation of mined-out land. Many new technologies are available for this, and they need to be harnessed, while, at the same time, the principles of environmental law need to be developed.

9. Human resources need development through educational processes, leading to a greater receptivity to modern technology — e.g., hydroponic cultivation, biomass generation of energy, use of wind power for irrigation, solar energy for such simple purposes as cooking, compost production in place of imported fertilizers, crystal distribution techniques for enhancing the water retention capabilities of soil. Many of these technologies, often thought of as remote and sophisticated, are well within the reach of the average third world peasant. Many new products such as fertilizers and pesticides are misused for lack of necessary technical knowledge. In short, a wider spread of technological knowledge, both at the level of the research institute and the average farmer, is required, if the politics of food as an exploitative weapon is to be blunted, and the technology of food production is to be brought into the affirmative service of promoting human rights.

10. A number of matters concerning the ethical aspects of the right to development were stressed in the 1978 UN Study on development as a human right.[31] Since science and technology are a major component of the concept of development, every one of these propositions would apply to science and technology and the sharing of such knowledge,

[31] E/CN/4/1334, paras. 39–54.

which is universal in its nature. There is thus a firm ethical base, soundly grounded in international law and its evolving norms, for the proposition that the shrinking world in which we live needs to be protected, for our common benefit, by treating science and technology not as a private preserve but as a universal inheritance.

3. *Inadequacies of the Law*[32]

Even in the affluent world, the dynamic growth of science and technology has outstripped the ability of the law to control it. Both legal procedures and legal concepts have proved unequal to the challenge. In the developing world, where the power ratios of science and technology to public authority are weighted much more heavily towards the former, the imbalance is considerably greater.

Any study of legal inadequacies would have to concentrate on four important aspects — structures, concepts, procedures, and personnel. Quite often all of these, even in post-colonial contexts, still bear the stamp of their colonial origins and orientations.

A formalized legal structure, with formal and expensive procedures and legal concepts tailored to the needs of the individualist, property-oriented colonial society of the past, are hardly adequate for guarding against technology's potential for damaging human rights or for assisting in the transference of appropriate technology to the Third World. This is an important roadblock on the way to turning technology to the affirmative service of human rights in those societies.

Even in Western societies courts are recognized as not being suitable agents for the monitoring of technology or for determining in advance whether a given technology is suitable. Yet such questions tend often to come before the courts. Other agencies are required for this, as, in general, a court looks back at a past event rather than forward to the future. Value judgments, resource allocations, and community priorities are not appropriate matters for courts. Moreover, judges are not trained in science and technology, and therefore lack the expertise with which to judge the increasing proportion of technology-related disputes which come before them.[33]

Against this background, the inadequacy of formal court structures and procedures to meet Third-World conditions becomes even more apparent. Adversarial litigation does not provide for representation of the public inter-

[32] For a fuller discussion, see the author's *The Slumbering Sentinels, supra*, Chap. 3, "The Inadequacies of the Law".

[33] On these aspects, see Ch. 2, *supra*.

est but only for that of the two contending parties. It produces a finding which is effective only between the two parties and is not necessarily related to social needs. It aims at finding which of two parties should win by the rules of the game, rather than at ascertaining the truth. Its procedures are expensive and dilatory, whereas technology often requires quick perception and action. Evidentiary rules are often archaic and exclude, for formal reasons, many considerations which could be of real value in fact-finding. The thalidomide case provided an excellent example of the inadequacy of old procedures to deal with a great social issue resulting from technology. A decision of the British House of Lords had to be departed from by the European Court of Human Rights, in order to enable publication, in the public interest, of material which the British courts had shut out on grounds of legal procedure and privilege.

Old concepts of the law are likewise proving inadequate. Concepts of privacy and physical trespass were worked out before the days of surveillance devices, "bugging," and computers. Laissez-faire principles in scientific research are still accepted without limitation, despite the public interest in science and technological matters. Concepts of unrestricted private property are still unthinkingly applied by courts and judges.

Many Third World societies still believe that their courts and legal systems can carry burdens in the scientific and technological age which they were never designed to bear. In this belief they refrain from constructing the new structures and instrumentalities which are needed to monitor technology and make it harmonize with the needs of people. The existence of this obstacle must be more widely realized if science and technology are to serve human rights more affirmatively in Third World societies.

It will be necessary for a special study to be made, identifying legal obstacles that stand in the way of the realization of these objectives. Work has already been done in relation to development, by such centres as the International Centre for Law and Development, to identify legal obstacles to the realization of alternative development strategies. This work has studied the ways in which those who desire to preserve the *status quo* on the developmental and technological fronts, use law as a means of obstructing change.

The problem is both a national and an international one, and the study undertaken will thus have to be in the context of both domestic law and international law. There will also need to be a study of the ways in which cooperation can be achieved among domestic legal systems, in eliminating these obstacles. More specifically, studies will be needed of ways of building into legal structures in developing countries, a greater control over production and the processing of information. Other areas where greater legal control will be required will be in relation to control of trading relations and control of prices.

In the last section of this chapter we consider the reorientation of lawyers' attitudes that will be necessary for this purpose.

F. SOME DESIDERATA

1. *The Human Factor*

In a programme on human rights and development, we cannot afford to lose sight also of the central fact that, in all development processes, one of the most important aspects is the human factor. In the words of the Declaration: "the human person is the central subject of development" and therefore "an active participant and beneficiary of development" (Art. 2), and this has indeed been described as the *leitmotif* of the Declaration.[34] The human factor has sometimes been described as the missing factor in development because it tends so easily to be overlooked. This human resource consists of the basic skills of the workforce, the administrative skills, the social structure of the rural sector, and the expertise already contained within the scientific and technological communities, however small, in these countries. It is important that all these resources should be marshalled as part of the general effort towards making these societies receptive to the better impacts of the new technologies.

It is to be remembered also that, although in Western countries, with a tradition of three or four centuries of industrial development, there has been built up over the centuries an appropriate infrastructure for the spread of technology, in the developing world, this long process is now being compressed within a very short time-frame. If the beneficial effects of the new technologies do not reach those who can best benefit from them, this is a principal cause. Much of the effort that we shall be putting into the use of new technologies will be dissipated in the absence of due attention to the human-resources aspect of development.

Traditional technology, rich especially in relation to agricultural activity, embodies the wisdom of generations. The tendency to cast it aside without due examination for modern technologies, such as high-level fertilizers and Western machinery, should be resisted. This is a rich human resource which needs to be taken into consideration and adequately used.

[34] Upendra Baxi, *op. cit.*, p. 4.

As the Brandt Commission observed, after a wide-ranging survey of the concept of development:

> This Commission did not try to redefine development, but we agreed (among other things) that the focus has to be not on machines or institutions but on people. A refusal to accept alien models unquestioningly is in fact a second phase of decolonization. We must not surrender to the idea that the whole world should copy the models of highly industrialized countries.[35]

2. *Raising the Political Priority of Development*

Another aspect to which the Human Rights Commission could give its attention is the means of raising the political priority of development, both in the developed world and in the developing world. In the developed world there is a strong feeling that the assistance given for the process of development finds its way into the wrong hands and that much of it is frittered away. Consequently, there is a perception that money spent on such forms of assistance is not money that truly filters into the process of development. In the developing countries themselves there is a growing impression that assistance given in this way is in fact a means of increasing economic and political control over the recipient country.

An effort needs to be mounted to ensure that both these criticisms will be met by appropriate corrective action. This can assist in countering the increasing resistance now discernible in the developed countries, both in government and in public attitudes, towards the giving of assistance which does not really reach its target beneficiaries. Moreover, if assistance in relation to technology comes without economic or political strings, its acceptability and impact in the developing world will be all the stronger. Studies of the extent to which development assistance is frittered away or made contingent on benefits to the donors will be useful pointers to the way in which these abuses can be minimized in the future. With a reduction of these abuses the political priority of development will rise.

At the same time the communication apparatus which is now growing up in the developing countries can also be used to spread, not only among political leaders but also among the people of those countries, the need for development aid to be received in an independent fashion, without political or economic strings attached to it.

35 *North-South: A Programme for Survival, op. cit.*, p. 23.

3. *Self-help*

Self-help groups need also to be generated, not only in local areas but also in relation to particular industries. The communication technology available already in developing countries has not been used sufficiently for the purpose of generating the necessary concern and interest, which would result in viable self-help groups. There is a feeling that nothing one can do will halt the inevitable, and the resulting frustration needs to be countered. Demonstrations of the ways in which new technology can be used and new products generated need also to be taken to the rural areas, as well as to the workplace. A new work ethic and a new self-confidence must emerge.

4. *Training of Personnel*

The training of personnel for development purposes is an important facet which needs attention. This may seem too obvious to stress, but one criticism that can be made of many of these programmes is that they tend to be European- or American-centred. It takes time for a selected trainee to acclimatize himself or herself to the social and linguistic milieu in which he or she is to receive training. One area that needs to be explored is the way in which training courses can be planned within the region concerned. This will not only have the advantage of making the trainees feel more at home but will also give the instructors more insights into local conditions and ways of thought. It will keep both instructors and trainees closer to the immediate problem and enable an exchange of experiences with local populations. The tendency to depend on foreign expertise dies hard.

5. *Law Reform*

It is important that the services of lawyers in developing countries be enlisted to serve the aim of turning technology towards the furtherance of human rights. There is much that needs to be restructured in the fields of legal concepts, procedures and structures. Moreover, the attitudes of lawyers themselves need to be reoriented, for their thinking is often cast in a predominantly Western mould by reason of the Western-oriented training they have received.

All this is vitally important to development, as one of the principal roadblocks on the way to development is presented by outmoded legal concepts, structures and procedures.

In other words, a new Third World jurisprudence must be developed. Hopeful steps in this direction have already been taken. In the words of Professor Marasinghe, one of the editors of a study on this subject:

> It is arguable that one of the roles of law in development should be seen as the integrator of ecological, cultural, social, economic, institutional and political dimensions of a given society, so that the diverse trends and aspirations in each of these fields could be synthesized in a way that society as a whole could evolve into a cohesive social unit.[36]

A distinguished former President of the International Court of Justice, in his Foreword to that volume, observed that the lawyer will have many roles to play:

> All these considerations lead us to envisage the possible role of law and the lawyer in this great task ahead of the nation. Is the lawyer, on whom the burden will likely devolve, to be just a utilitarian in search of the greatest happiness of the greatest number, an analytical jurist primarily concerned with concepts, a social engineer preoccupied with how law affects man's social interests, a functionalist anxious to ascertain the functioning of legal rules, a realist sold on the idea that psychology is of the essence in the judicial process, a Pericles engaged as a policy-maker wisely dispensing laws, or a plumber skilled only as a technocrat whose main interest is in 'lawyers' law'?[37]

It is idle to speak of developing human rights unless we enlist the co-operation of the legal profession in each country, for they can be profound helpers, just as they can be great obstructionists, in such a cause.

6. *Case-Study Projects*

I would like to conclude this paper by referring to a very practical problem, in which I have been involved, which clearly illustrates the importance of using modern technology for the purpose of promoting human rights. In the island of Nauru, phosphate lands have been mined out by various occupying powers from the beginning of this century, leaving large portions of the island with nothing more than bare coral pinnacles, very much resembling a moonscape. A large portion of the area of that little island is now unfit for human occupation, and unfit for any other purpose, and the inhabitants of the

[36] M. L. Marasinghe and W. E. Conklin, *Essays on Third World Perspectives in Jurisprudence, Malaysian Law Journal*, 1984, p. 4.

[37] Judge T.O. Elias, *ibid.*, p. v.

island do not enjoy the basic human right of enjoyment of their natural environment.

This is eminently a situation where science and technology can be affirmatively used for the furtherance of human rights. Article 13 of the Charter of Economic Rights and Duties of States of December 1974 clearly states that every State has the right to benefit from the advances and developments in science and technology for the acceleration of its economic and social development. Article 9 of the same document points out that all States have the responsibility to co-operate in the economic, social, cultural, scientific and technological fields for the promotion of the economic and social progress throughout the world, especially that of the developing countries.

The situation in which the island of Nauru is now placed requires, then, that a co-operative effort be made by all nations to assist in bringing to its aid all the resources that modern technology can offer, not merely because it is an environmental problem involving the human rights of the people of Nauru, but also because it is an environmental problem which affects the people of the world generally — the sort of problem that could well exist or be duplicated in other societies.

It may be worthwhile to consider cases of this nature as specific case-study projects with a view to seeing in what way the immense benefits of technology can be harnessed towards the solution of a problem of great consequence to human rights. In addressing a problem such as this, we may well find answers not only to the specific problem, but also answers which can be used for the solution of others.

* * *

The preceding discussion covers some of the ideas which may be pertinent to the task of turning technology to the service of the people. It would be too ambitious to undertake an examination of them all, but it may be that some at least of these ideas will be considered important enough to warrant further research. Attention to these problems will certainly assist in improving the total benefit that developing countries will receive from the vast movements of science and technology that are now taking place. The smoother and more harmonious international relations that will emerge will be a potent factor in staving off dangerous polarities and antagonisms between North and South. These could well develop if the current trend towards the technological domination of the developing world by the developed world continues unabated. The resulting contribution to global peace and harmony will amply reward developing world and developed world alike.

7. The Problem of the Flow of Technological Information*

Article 6(3) of the Declaration on the Right to Development, 1986, calls upon States to take steps to eliminate all "obstacles to development" which arise from the failure to respect rights and freedoms, civil, political, economic, social and cultural. One of the principal obstacles to the proper enjoyment of these rights is the lack of a free flow of information. The more powerful the impact on society of the influence under consideration, the more important it is that these obstacles be removed. Having regard to the immense power of technology upon society today, it is therefore vitally important that the obstacles in the way of its proper service to society should be considered. Since the Declaration elevates the duty to remove obstacles to the level of a State obligation, the consideration of this matter is all the more vital.

As early as 1972, the Stockholm Declaration on the Human Environment identified the need for the flow of technological information to the developing countries. In Principle 20, it observed that scientific research and development in the context of environmental problems must be promoted in all countries, especially the developing countries. In that connection, "the free flow of up-to-date scientific information and transfer of experience must be supported and assisted". It observed also that environmental technologies should be made available to developing countries on terms which would encourage their wide dissemination.

The Brandt Report, likewise, identified this need for a free flow of information. It observed:

* Adapted from a presentation by the author at a session of the United Nations University's Committee on Human Rights and Scientific and Technological Development, Tokyo, 1989.

> It is essential, in the first place, that information about technology should flow more freely both between and within nations. Many international organizations, including FAO, UNIDO, UNEP, UNESCO, ILO, WHO and UNCTNC, now operate systems which collect, store and make available information on the technological possibilities of interest to developing countries; private commercial systems are also becoming a valuable source. But the potential users are at a loss to know where to go for what.[1]

The Report recommended that the existing channels for the transmission of technology need to be enlarged and rendered more effective.

This paper approaches the question of the interrelationship between science, technology and human rights from the standpoint of the generation, processing, and transmission of information which results in the creation of new products. Many studies thus far have concentrated on the product and its effects upon society subsequent to its creation and release. However, it is equally vital to trace back the process that precedes its creation, because the violation of human rights can be better prevented, and the promotion of human rights better assisted, through a knowledge and monitoring of those early stages which are dominated by the informational aspect. Such an information-based approach will also give us a better understanding of the points of contact between the new technologies and the development process.

In relation to the developing world, such a study will afford us an opportunity of gathering more information on the three categories of human rights which are related to scientific and technological development, namely:

(a) The right of *protection* against possible harmful effects of scientific and technological developments;

(b) The right of *access* to scientific and technological information that is essential to development and welfare (both at the individual and collective levels);

(c) The right of *choice*, or the freedom to assess and choose the preferred path of scientific and technological development.

Every one of these three facets — protection, access and choice — is heavily dependent on the free flow of information. Indeed, their achievement becomes totally impossible when the flow of information is as restricted as it

[1] International Law Commission Report of the Independent Commission on Information Development Issues, *North-South: A Programme for Survival*, Pan Books, 1980, p. 197.

now is, and when it suffers from such an imbalance as now prevails between the supplier of the technology and the consumer of that technology.

THE CONCENTRATION OF INFORMATION IN THE DEVELOPED WORLD

The generation of information, which is the prelude to the creation of a new scientific product, often takes place through the availability of information-related resources in the developed world, which few developing countries possess. These resources consist of trained researchers, as well as an expensive apparatus for the collection of data.

80% of the information about Africa is held outside Africa.

While at the economic level there was a ratio of 12:1 between the developed and the developing world, in the knowledge industry the imbalance is thought to be of the order of 30:1.[2]

Although the collection of this raw data takes place in all parts of the world, it is often processed in the developed world, at centres far separated from the actual venues wherein the information is collected. This is the first stage in the surrender of control by the developing world, of knowledge concerning itself, to assist in the creation of a future product for use in its own territory.

Much of this information bears upon the increasingly recognized human right to regulate transborder data flow, which international agencies are striving to protect. If knowledge is power, knowledge of local conditions, needs, strengths, and shortcomings is power over the society in question. Such data, once it travels beyond the boundaries of the country where it is collected, ceases to be under its control. The first stage in the fashioning or introduction of a new technology for a given territory is thus placed beyond the control of the recipient territory. It is vital that this question be addressed, bearing in mind also the proposition that knowledge is free and that research should be unfettered. There is here an important dilemma to which we should address ourselves.

The scarcity in the developing world of the two resources earlier mentioned, namely, the human resource of the skilled researcher and the information gathering apparatus, is one of the root problems creating this

[2] Scc M. Pecujlic, *et al.*, (eds.), *The Transformation of the World: Science and Technology*, UNU/Macmillan Press, 1982, p. 34. The statistic that around 80% of the information, even about Africa itself, is held outside Africa does not take into account other technical information concerning products used in Africa, which is held almost exclusively outside the African countries where they are used.

dilemma. It is possible that it could be addressed by devising an appropriate combination of resources from the two countries mentioned — the giver and the recipient of the technology — rather than that there be a total surrender of control at this early stage to the giver. In other words, it should be possible to introduce a scheme of participation in the project, and sharing in the resulting information.

Even before manufacture of the product which results from the information thus generated, it thus already embodies property (in the form of raw or processed information) which belongs to the developed world, although its eventual target is the developing world. When the technological input takes place, the totality of the product becomes the property of the developed world and, under current concepts of property and free trade, it can do with it what it pleases, and sell it on terms which it alone determines. However much it might be needed in the developing country, barriers then arise between the product and the place in which it is to be used.

These barriers take the form of protection of intellectual property, protection of financial investments in the generation of the new product, and political barriers which need to be penetrated before the product can really serve the people for whom it is intended. These political barriers take the important form of levers of social, political and economic control which are manipulated almost exclusively from the developed world.

Various aspects of human rights become relevant to a consideration of the resulting problems.

INDIVIDUAL RIGHTS OF INTELLECTUAL PROPERTY *VERSUS* THE SOCIAL RIGHT TO FREEDOM OF TECHNOLOGICAL INFORMATION

In theory, there should be a free and unimpeded flow of technological information from producer to consumer. In fact and in law, there can be many barriers. Some of these pose problems of clashes of human rights principles.

One example comes from the field of intellectual property. The creator of a product has a recognized right to property in his or her ideas. They are just as much their owner's property as a material object is the subject of ownership. The proprietor of that knowledge can prevent all others from using it, because the inventor is entitled to turn it to his or her private profit.

The concept of the right of the inventor to profit from his or her own inventions and to protect them is unimpeachable, but at the same time some weightage has to be given to the social interest. Just as the owner would thus enjoy individual rights of property, so also there is, on the other hand, a general principle that science and technology are primarily intended for the use of humanity and that information is free. The matter can be illustrated by a contemporary example. It has been advertised recently that a medical product which prolongs the life of an AIDS sufferer will shortly be on the market at a cost of approximately $20,000 a year for each user. This may well be beyond the financial reach of a person who desperately needs this drug. We can think in similar context of a hypothetical cancer cure which is marketed at $1,000 a pill.

Such examples highlight the clash between two human rights, each of which is valuable in its own context, but which, when posed in opposition to each other, necessarily result in the subordination of the right which in the circumstances seems to be the less compelling.

There are overtones here of the heavy protections of the right of property under the Western jurisprudential tradition, while considerations of social interest and of humanity occupy a much lower priority in the hierarchy of values. The limitations that must be placed upon the absoluteness of ownership principles tend therefore to be blunted.

Such conflicts are not easy to resolve, but there are some trends in human rights jurisprudence that can be called in aid. One of these is the growing emphasis upon the concept of universalization of human rights norms. Concepts of absolute rights of property in the interests of the individual find it increasingly difficult to maintain their regime unimpaired, when confronted universally by rival human rights traditions that emphasize the social interest, and do not accord this sacrosanct importance to the concept of individual rights of property, when in conflict with the social interest.

All of this is rooted in the individual civil and political rights which form the kernel of the Western human rights tradition. Social, economic and cultural rights which are rooted in other traditions are, however, increasingly coming to the fore. In the sphere of technological information, we shall probably see in the future the need to strike a mean between these two traditions.

All of these result in the progressive attrition of property rights in the interests of social welfare.

THE RIGHT TO FREEDOM OF EXPRESSION *VERSUS* THE RIGHT TO AN UNBIASED FLOW OF INFORMATION

Another example that comes to mind in this connection is the clash between the right to advertise, which is based on freedom of speech and expression, and the right of the consumer to have a balanced and unvarnished view of the facts concerning a given product. Modern advertising is a powerful force with many weapons at its disposal, including mass advertising campaigns, and heavy television coverage. Advertisement of a product can be misleading, as with cigarette advertising which identifies smoking with the great outdoors and hence with health. So also in product advertising, the facts brought to the notice of the consumer tend to be selective.

Sometimes the products concerned are harmless, but some of these goods may well relate even to such matters as health and the right to life. In recent years much attention was focused on the advertising of infant milk food products which, according to all the scientific research that had been done on them, were generating a considerably higher rate of infant mortality than was the case with breast-feeding. This provided a textbook example of a clash between two human rights — the human right to freedom of speech and the press (including advertising) which producers of the milk food contended for, and the human right to life which was advanced as a reason for curbing advertising of these milk foods. The universal medical view, as stated at the WHO Convention which considered this matter, was that marketing of these milk foods with unrestrained advertising would step up the infant mortality rate in poor countries. Despite the fact that this vital human right was involved, the marketers of the product were still insisting on their right to free advertising as being an essential right, and one which did not admit of curtailment.

The dissemination of products in the developing world is often based upon advertising. Heavy advertising campaigns precede the introduction of a product; and rival products, especially those produced in the developing world, often lack the resources to match this campaign. Consequently, there is in most instances a one-way information flow regarding the product in question.

The right to know, which is unimpeachable,[3] is of course based upon the premiss that the knowledge thus disseminated is not selective knowledge, but rather the whole truth as known. This is precisely what many advertisers do not do. It is only a selected bundle of facts concerning the advantages of the product, that are disseminated. Moreover, the versions offered regarding the properties of rival products tend, likewise, to be based upon selected facts which exhibit that product in a disadvantageous light.

Where human health is involved, as in the milk foods example, we have an instance of a rather strange confrontation between two human rights, where there would be no doubt as to which way a reasoned or reasonable decision should fall. Nevertheless, financial interests involved do not always see things with the degree of objectivity which seems in this instance to be dictated by common sense. In consequence, there could be a rather unjustified pressure for the adoption of the lesser right in preference to the greater.

[3] See Chapter 12, Volume I.

Such illustrations underscore the need for a study of the clashes of different human rights that occur when information regarding a particular technology is being relied upon. Many more examples could be cited and a worthy object of study may be to make a classification, in relation to the different areas involved, of the particular clashes of human rights resulting in that given conflict situation. In this way it may be possible to construct a tabular statement of the human rights involved, which could point more clearly to a decision as to priorities in the event of such conflict.

Such examples draw attention to the dilemma that constantly faces the international community, both in relation to expensive technologies which the developing world needs desperately, but which can only be obtained at a price beyond their reach, and in regard to technologies which it does not really need, but which are forced upon it by advertising and other means. In the former case, while we must have due regard to the expense, risk and expenditure of human resources involved in the generation of the product, there is room for the argument that the product, once achieved, belongs to all mankind, subject to a reasonable compensation to the generator of the product for the effort and expense involved. In the latter case, the human right to health must prevail over such rights as the "right" of the advertiser to disseminate selective information.

SCALES OF PRIORITIES OF HUMAN RIGHTS

The clash of principles, outlined above, points to the need for various international principles and regulatory processes to be evolved and brought into play, so as to achieve a workable reconciliation between the two principles.

For example, it may be possible to define a set of guidelines under which products which are vital to life, once generated, become universal property, subject to a right of compensation at a level deemed appropriate by an international authority set up for this purpose. The funds for such payments may not be available for those who need the product, and it may be necessary to build up a buffer fund which can in such instances make good to the producer a fair reward for the initiative, effort and expenditure that have gone into the product.

This is not to say that every product thus generated will become the subject of such free transfer. The principles outlined above will apply in exceptional instances, such as are defined by the appropriate authority, and the justification for this would be that the right to health and life stand above all other rights.

The writer is conscious, of course, that such a principle can operate as an inhibitor of research. It may well be that research organizations, particularly pharmaceutical companies, may not invest, in potential products, the effort they are currently prepared to devote to them, if there was a possibility of the assimilation of the resulting knowledge into the universal domain. On the other hand, it is only in exceptional cases that the principles outlined would be brought into operation and, in any event, there will be a reasonable costing of the effort and expense involved, so that loss will be averted and there will be a reasonable profit for the outlay.

Another consideration to be borne in mind is that the profits currently made through such technologies are often well in advance of what may be described as reasonable remuneration. Pharmaceutical companies not infrequently retain for themselves very substantial profits, far exceeding what is considered a reasonable remuneration, even in the competitive financial world, for the outlay of resources. It may well be that similar principles apply in regard to new technologies that generate agricultural products.

The point made in this presentation is that resources are needed for the collection and processing of information, which are an essential prelude to the creation of a product. The task involved is not merely one of the collection and classification of facts. There must also be an analysis and comparison of the applicable principles under which those facts are evaluated. Seeing that the informational dimension prior to the creation of the product will be the basis of scientific and technological development for the foreseeable future, the problem we are confronted with will become more acute and intense with the passing years unless we can address it now.

COMPUTERIZATION

To all this must be added the fact that the actual processing of information as well as the dissemination of information — not to speak of the storing of information — all require intensive investment in computerization. These again are largely within the control of one sector of the world's economy and it is that sector which thus acquires increasing control over the product and the information embodied within it.

The computer is no longer merely an assembler of information. It is today extensively used to generate new products and tailor them for particular purposes and specific markets. This resource, extremely expensive and beyond the reach of most developing societies, gives the developed world an irreversible lead in the ability to design a product for the markets of the developing world, so that there can in fact be little real competition.

The future will see the further spread of new computer techniques, including that of robot technology, which can have severe repercussions. Such technology could thus deprive a developing economy of the use of its labour, which is one of its most important economic resources.

ONE-WAY INFORMATION FLOW

Another area of marked imbalance in the current world order is the imbalance between the resources of the developing and the developed worlds in relation to news flow. This may not at first sight be seen as a means of perpetuating technology differentials, but it is, in fact — especially when one considers that the entire global communications network, as currently organized, presents a largely one-sided information flow. Raw information may come in from the developing to the developed world, but the processed information travels out in a one-way stream of traffic from the developed to the developing world, while nothing that can match it flows in the reverse direction. The developing world has striven hard to achieve what has been described as a new world information order, but little success has been achieved in reversing the one-way information flow. In the result, many basic human rights of a vast sector of the world's population are adversely affected.

The lack of availability of such a system means that the human rights of this vast group are impaired, for the entire world receives its news, and forms its views, on the basis of the one-way flow of information generated in the developed world. This is not merely in regard to information which we call "news", but in regard to all species of information, on the basis of which needs are perceived, policies are made, and products are designed. In the result, the problems of the developing world are not seen by the world public in the real way in which they should be seen, that is, in their overall context. The assessment in the developed world of a Third World problem or need tends often to be distorted, not for lack of good will, but for lack of information.

This means that in the resulting technologically-related decisions, or in the resulting economic transactions, the legitimate human rights of such developing world populations would tend to be negated or whittled down to an extent not permissible under current universal perceptions of human rights. UNESCO at one stage considered this imbalance in detail in the context of news. We need also to consider the imbalance in the light of technologically-related information. The impact of technology on development and developing societies cannot be considered adequately without due reference to this aspect, and it forms an important segment of human rights research that awaits the scholars of the developing world.

ANALYSIS OF THE NETWORK OF PRIOR INFLUENCES

Having regard to the fact that information constitutes one of the bases of this session, it is necessary to give thought to planning methods of making the network of influences leading to the project clear and traceable. The continuing threads of influence of the product upon society should likewise be clear and traceable. One of our objectives will need to be the setting up of mechanisms which will underline these aspects as an important part of the planning method.

In the previous chapter, we have dealt with the routes by which a new technology finds its way into a developing country:

(1) by the country's own decision, uninfluenced by external factors; or

(2) under the pressure of external factors which for one reason or another it is unable to resist; or

(3) through a combination of internal and external factors, where there is an element of volition in each.[4]

Information is necessary at each of these points, if the rights of the recipient country are to be safeguarded.

DUMPING OF GOODS

Lack of information regarding the prior history of technological products leads also to another area of infringement of human rights such as the right to health and the right to a pure environment. This is caused by the dumping of shoddy goods on developing countries, who are not provided with the prior history of such goods. These goods, which fail to satisfy the health requisites of the developed world — including even foodstuffs exposed to radiation — are often received without sufficient knowledge of their antecedents.

Human rights violations are also involved in the schemes currently used by some owners of high technology for the release of inferior goods to Third World countries, under the guise of "appropriate technology". The Third World thus becomes a dumping ground for products which are either untested or not good enough for use in the developed world. Here, again, there is a need for guidelines on dumping and for more active implementation of international agreements in relation to the dumping of shoddy goods.

[4] See *supra*, Chapter 6.

All too often, especially in the field of pharmaceuticals and consumer goods, the developing countries lack the necessary avenues of information. Policing of standards is likewise difficult. In the result, the Third World often becomes a testing ground for human experimentation. Products, whose effects may not be capable of being evaluated until 10 or 15 years have passed, may be used on such populations, where the high standards prescribed by monitoring bodies in thc developed world would not have tolerated them.

A network of information exchange between quality control and standards bureaux of all countries needs to be established, in a co-operative spirit, to avoid such abuses.

TECHNICAL CO-OPERATION AMONG DEVELOPING COUNTRIES

In the midst of all these discussions, we must not lose sight of the fact that there are great informational resources within the developing world itself. Much of this has evolved with special reference to the needs of the developing world. It is true that it comprises only a small percentage of the totality of global scientific and technological knowledge. It is nevertheless sufficiently significant for a concerted effort to be made to share this around, among the developing countries themselves. They can do this with less expense to themselves, and the efforts that have so far been made for technical co-operation amongst developing countries (TCDC) need to be stepped up. TCDC is an idea which has already produced considerable results. The problem relates again to the question of information flow which we discussed earlier. There needs to be a network of communication among scientists of the developing world, and it could well be that the United Nations University can step up the global effort to promote such an exchange of information as well as of personnel.

Attention needs therefore to be given to the mediums by which such information can be disseminated, and among these will be the publication of appropriate scientific journals containing extracts of articles, books, and reports dealing with various technologies of special significance to the Third World. Solar energy is one such field. Tropical health and diseases, agricultural procedures, low cost housing, and cottage industries, are other areas where technological information can well be exchanged among Third World countries. It would be helpful if the journals in question also carry a list of experts in those fields, along with their addresses. Such a network of information is already evolving in the form of ASSET (Abstracts of Selected Solar Energy Technology), and the work that has been done in the ASSET field could well be duplicated in other fields. Attention needs therefore to be given to linking together technologists and scientists in particular areas of expertise from various developing countries.

The programme of action on the establishment of a new international economic order urges developing countries to promote and establish effective instruments of co-operation in the fields of science and technology, transport, shipping and mass communication of media. This can only be given effect to, if proper vehicles of communication can be devised. One of the means towards this end is an exchange of scientists and technologists, and an exchange fellowship scheme needs perhaps to be considered in this context.

In December 1972 the United Nations General Assembly passed a Resolution which authorized the United Nations Development Programme (UNDP) to convene a special working group to examine ways for developing countries "to share their capacities and experiences with one another with a view to increasing and improving development assistance"; and one of the several factors which were identified as tending to inhibit technical co-operation among developing countries was the lack of a communication and information system in relation to the capacities and requirements of developing countries. There was also a reference to an "attitudinal barrier" which favoured the use of experts, consultant firms and equipment from developed countries. Efforts must be made to overcome that attitudinal barrier.

COMMUNITY EDUCATION FOR TECHNOLOGY

In the midst of all this discussion, we must not lose sight of the fact that education is a major lever for development. There must therefore be a plan to spread among each community an understanding of the way in which technology can be of assistance to them in their day to day problems. It is true there are already rather loose organizations aimed at spreading this sort of knowledge among the populations of Third World countries. There needs to be some co-ordinated effort, the guidelines for which may perhaps be formulated by this conference, in relation to the way in which each government could maximize the communication system, in a manner which would be appropriate for those local communities.

TECHNOLOGY ASSESSMENT

Another area of importance in relation to Third World development is technology assessment. Technology assessment depends heavily on a free flow of information. Although developed countries are now devoting a considerable amount of time and effort to it, technology assessment has not yet become a routine procedure in the developing world. This is despite the fact that the impact of many of these technologies upon the developing world is even greater than it is upon the developed world. The developed world has already felt the impact of most of these technologies and adjusted to it, while the developing world has yet to feel the first impact of many of them.

It has been estimated that about 65% of the industrial production in the Third World is directly or indirectly affected by the new technologies — microchips, the use of new materials, the consequences of genetic engineering and so forth. It is important to the Third World that there should be a correct choice of macro-economic and entrepreneurial policies, but such a correct choice cannot often be made for lack of knowledge of the new technologies on the part of local decision-makers.

Consequently, it is essential that decision-makers in Third World situations be better informed of the entire concept of technology assessment.

INTERNATIONAL EXCHANGES OF TECHNOLOGICAL ASSESSMENT

A network of information exchange between quality control and standards bureaux of all countries needs to be established in a co-operative spirit. This committee can perhaps contribute substantially to the evolution of such a network by studying ways and means for the co-ordination and exchange of such information and by making facilities available for the exchange of policing and investigating services, information and rules.

The Dag Hammarskjöld Seminar for Alternative Development Strategies in the Southern African Region, 1985, suggested a regional weekly newsletter linked to local, district and national papers for the exchange of technological information pertinent to the region.[5]

THE HUMAN FACTOR

In a programme on human rights and development, we cannot afford to lose sight also of the central fact that, in all development processes, one of the most important factors is the human factor. In fact this has sometimes been described as the missing factor in development, because it tends so easily to be overlooked. This human resource, which we tend so often to overlook, consists of the basic skills of the workforce, the administrative skills, the

[5] *Another Development for SADCC*, Report of a Seminar of November 1985, in Lesotho, Dag Hammarskjöld Foundation, 1987, p. 164.

social structure of the rural sector, and the expertise already contained within the scientific and technological communities, however small, in these countries. A free flow of technological information at appropriate levels of understanding is essential to the creation and sustenance of this base.

In Western countries, with a tradition of three or four centuries of industrial development, there has been built up, over the centuries, a higher degree of social awareness of the available resources and the likely effects of various technologies. There is in a sense a built-in infrastructure for the spread of knowledge concerning technology. In the developing world, all this long period of development is now sought to be concentrated within a very short space of time. This is one of the reasons for the failure of the beneficial effects of the new technologies to reach those who can best benefit from them, and much of the effort that we shall be putting into the use of new technologies will be dissipated unless the human resources aspect of development receives sufficient attention.

Another aspect of this same proposition is that tradition, which is very often rich in relation to particular types of activity, ought not to be neglected. This applies with special emphasis in relation to agricultural activity where the wisdom of generations tends sometimes to be cast aside under the impact of modern technologies. This is a rich information resource which needs to be marshalled and appropriately disseminated.

DISARMAMENT AND DEVELOPMENT

Another dimension of the problem under review is the interconnection between disarmament and development. Although the intertwining of disarmament and global development is well acknowledged in theory, very little has been done in practice to achieve the desired result of some portion of world resources currently wasted on armaments being diverted into the field of development. This is an area involving super power relations but, at the same time, it is an area in relation to which the community can make a worthwhile contribution if it has more information.

There have been insufficient analytical studies of the ways in which the arms trade conflicts with nearly every canon of the current universally accepted body of human rights. This can be written on *in extenso*, but there is no scope for it within the present study. From the point of view of information, two aspects need special mention. One is the fact that the interconnection between armaments technology and human rights, though well known academically, is insufficiently known by the general public. More communication is wanted on this matter between the academic world and the public, if public opinion, especially in the developed world, is to become sufficiently aware of this. Secondly, specific information is required of the manner in which particular earth resources and raw materials needed for development are used up by the arms trade, resulting in an escalation of the prices the developing nations pay for them.

Forecasts for the foreseeable future are also required, of the ways in which the continuing expansion of the arms trade will further damage basic human rights, especially the rights to food and health. The results of such a study may well be so alarming as to jolt the world public into a realization that some urgent action is essential to avoid catastrophe on a global scale — not through nuclear war, but by a sheer run on essential resources.

COMMODITY PRICES

Another factor which creates a linkage between human rights, technology and development, is that most of the poorer countries will find it increasingly difficult to order their affairs on the basis of a dependence on raw materials. The collapse of the Tin Agreement in 1985 was an important signal pointing to the fact that raw materials cannot possibly maintain a stable price level relative to the products of the developed world. All forecasts seem to indicate that the value of raw materials will continue to fall relatively, so that countries that have traditionally been dependent upon raw materials will need to reorientate their attitudes in order to provide a greater place in their overall financial framework for industrial products. This of course links with technology, and this committee will need to give its close attention to ways in which technology can be used, in different developing countries, to remedy the increasing imbalance in their economies that will be caused by what has been called the raw materials trap. Among the aspects to be considered, is the employment of technology to devise new means of using those raw materials in the developing countries themselves, rather than their still being content to have them exported to the developed world for processing.

Whether one is speaking in terms of agricultural produce or minerals, the same principle holds good. The dictation of prices for these occurs in circumstances over which developing countries have no control. The London Metal Exchange fixes the prices for Third World minerals and the producing countries have little opportunity to make their impact felt. Likewise, the international grain and commodities markets are regulated from a distance, so far as the producing countries are concerned. All of these organizations are fed by a vast network of information which places them in a position of enormous advantage in matters of price fixing. This inescapable fact leading to bargaining inequality needs to be the subject of concentrated studies, aimed at redressing the imbalance; and it is quite clear that the interrelationship between technological information and basic human rights will increase in importance as the bargaining power of raw materials declines.

THE PROBLEM OF INEQUALITY OF BARGAINING POWER

I approach this matter from the standpoint of the law of contract. There is no lawyer in any national jurisdiction today who would maintain that the principle of free contract, as understood in the 19th century, ought to apply within the national boundaries of a country. There is a general realization that free contract, unrestrained by legislative or judicial intervention, results in the possibility of the strong driving the weak to the wall, and the rich being able to take advantage of the poor. Consequently, in the course of this century, various legislative and judicial initiatives in many jurisdictions have resulted in a weightage in favour of the weak. There is a general acceptance of the proposition that the fierce competition of the Hobbesian market place would result in a progressive diminution of the powers of resistance of the poorer contracting party to the point where it becomes a victim of severe exploitation.

Unfortunately, however, as far as the international market place is concerned, no such principle has emerged. The same lawyers who, within their national context, would admit without any reservation that there has to be a principle of compensation operating through the legislature or the courts, would insist on the international market place being free of controls. It is in consequence of this factor that the constant imbalance between the relative prices of the developed and the developing world results in a growing inability on the part of the producing countries to satisfy their basic economic needs. They produce more, they invest more on the purchase of fertilizer and farm apparatus, but still the resulting product takes them no further than in the days when their production was less. We have the situation of resources being poured into the production of these commodities without any corresponding advantage to the producing country. This of course affects basic human rights, because it relates to basic human needs and, in the last analysis, can lead to famine and starvation.

Information technology can be used to assist in the consideration of this problem in many ways. One method is through the diffusion of information on these matters, especially to the public of the developing world. Another is by the careful compiling of statistical information regarding the growing disparities in the returns the developing world receives from its primary produce, as compared to what it pays to the developed world for its products. The same number of bags of sisal or rice would purchase diminishing fractions of a single turbine or railway engine as the years go by. A wide variety of statistics on such matters could be compiled. Computer projections into the future could possibly demonstrate that a continuation of the trend requiring 500 bags of a product for the purchase of what 250 bags purchased 5 years ago, would result in the total impoverishment of many Third World countries, and a destruction of their agricultural base. If the figures are compelling enough, there is a possibility that some response would emerge from the industrialized nations and that international law itself could see the emergence of some fair trade principles to counter inequality of bargaining power, on much the same basis that domestic law has recently evolved such principles. With such information in more readily available form, the assistance of human rights and legal experts can be called in aid to seek ways and means of introducing into the international marketplace some basic principles of fair trade that are accepted without question within most domestic markets.

CONTRACTS FOR THE SALE OF TECHNOLOGY OR TECHNOLOGICAL PRODUCTS

Ever so often, contracts are entered into between major industrial enterprises and the governments of developing countries, relating to some major venture involving high technology. Such contracts may range from the installation of a nuclear energy facility to the construction of a major irrigation or hydropower scheme. It may also cover a range of factories or industrial installations in which goods are processed.

There is often an imbalance here in regard to the information available to the two contracting parties. The advisers of one party have available to them an enormous range of technological information that is not necessarily available to the other. In the absence of equality of information, the resulting contract tends to be weighted against the developing country, for even the technical advisers of the latter may not have access to some of the information that is vital to a proper decision.

With a wider dissemination of information, and better and more up to date technological training within the recipient nation, the chances of a fairer contract would be considerably enhanced.

FOOD AS A HUMAN RIGHT: COLLECTING THE NECESSARY DATA TO ADDRESS THE PROBLEM OF HUNGER

Of necessity, a great deal of the technology devoted to the developing world needs to concentrate on food production, which is one of the greatest challenges we face in our time. Since the right to food is now recognized as one of the basic human rights, and since a large percentage of the global population suffers from a dire need of this basic resource, modern technology needs to home in on this problem through every possible route. Approaches to the problem of hunger have taken many forms.

Earlier approaches tended to view the problem as one of increasing the production and supply of food. Improving the technology of food production was seen as the answer. However, it is being increasingly realized today that, while technology is a prime requirement for this task, technology cannot function alone. It needs the assistance of many other disciplines, especially those of the social sciences — sociology, political science, law and human rights, cultural anthropology, to mention a few. This means the collection of data from a variety of sources.

One could approach the informational problems involved along many avenues. One recent study has suggested five approaches — from the points of view of health, ecology, econometrics, social structures and group action.[6]

(a) *Health*

There have been many statistical analyses of the diseases resulting from malnutrition. These medical studies have not been adequately correlated with the social sciences in determining the causes of malnutrition to which attention should be directed if the problem is to be solved. Treating the disease is only a social "band-aid" unless we identify the social causes. Until recently, this was a much-neglected field. Information on this topic began to flow in the 1970s.[7] We need information on the social obstacles to nutrition programmes, such as servicing the wrong groups, and the enrichment of corrupt officials. Also, food aid sometimes acts negatively by crippling markets for local foods through a distortion of prices and the creation of an artificial demand for imported food.[8]

(b) *Ecology*

What is the raw data regarding the various forms of environmental degradation in a country? What are the statistics regarding the pollution of its lakes and streams, its atmosphere, its topsoil? What are the causes of these? How

[6] Thomas J. Marchione, "Approaches to the Hunger Problem: A Critical Overview", in *Food as a Human Right*, Asbjorn Eide *et al* (eds.), United Nations University Press, Tokyo, 1984, pp. 117–118.

[7] B. Winikoff (ed.), *Nutrition and National Policy*, MIT Press, Cambridge, Mass., 1978.

[8] F.M. Lappé (ed.), *Aid as Obstacle*, Institute for Food and Development Policy, 1980.

many tons or gallons of effluents, pesticides, industrial wastes have been discharged into the environment and by whom? How many of these sources are local and how many foreign? Under what pressures did these occur? How much topsoil has been lost, how many species of fauna and flora have been endangered, how much deforestation has taken place? What is the nett result of all of this on food productivity?

There has been an interest from the 1960s in the overall question whether the world's food supply can keep pace with expanding population. The neo-Malthusian negative view on this subject has come under challenge by those who point out that there is food enough to feed all the world's population, except that it is not properly distributed.[9] Statistics of production and obstacles to distribution need wider dissemination. Social structures may be to blame and also exploitation by powerful interests.[10]

(c) *Econometrics*

Does the solution of hunger lie along the road of increasing economic growth? With more overall prosperity will there be a trickle-down effect to reach all sectors of the population.

Such theories were, in the 1950s and 1960s, based upon free market models, and did not at first adequately consider the information that was emerging from a study of social indicators, rather than market indicators. A reliance on market indicators produces, as Galbraith and other economists have demonstrated, distortions in social priorities, private affluence and public squalor.[11] Market indicators might suggest that there was a great need for a particular product, and that product would in fact be absorbed by the market. Yet, it did not benefit those at the bottom end of the social scale. A means had to be found to assess their needs independently of market indicators, and to feed this information into the determining process. This has been pointed out in studies, urging that social indicators must be evolved.[12]

[9] Lappé, *ibid.*, pp. 13–46; Cheryl Christensen, *The Right to Food: How to Guarantee*, World Order Model Project, Working Paper No. 6, 1978.

[10] See Lester Brown, *Food or Fuel: New Competition for the World's Cropland*, World Watch Paper No. 35, 1980; see, also, this author's *Nauru: Environmental Damage under International Trusteeship*, Oxford University Press, 1992.

[11] See Louis Turner, *Multinational Companies and the Third World*, Allen Lane, 1973, pp. 67–68. See, also, at p. 67 a description of the affluent in the developing world who create a demand for luxury goods while squalor prevails in their countries.

[12] For example, M. Haq, *The Poverty Curtain — Choices for the Third World*, Columbia University Press, New York, 1976, p. 43.

Econometric approaches now take into account social indicators and basic needs approaches, rather than rely purely on market indicators and market forces. This requires considerable work in collecting data in the field — among the poverty-stricken, the slum dwellers, the economically most deprived. They are far removed from the sophisticated technological product which may find a ready sale among the comparatively affluent upper third of a community, and give the false impression that the country in question has a need of that product.

(d) *Social Structures*

There has been "... a recognition by some food researchers, planners and advocates that most widespread nutritional deficiency problems are imbedded in the social fabric of the communities, national societies, and global systems in which they are found".[13]

This approach aims at examining the role of basic social structures in perpetuating and intensifying want. There is much injustice embodied in existing social structures — public institutional structures, as well as non-formalized social structures as they really operate in a given society. Structural analyses see as a major cause of malnutrition and starvation, not merely the lack of food, but also the structures of exploitation and oppression which can result in these human rights denials even despite the availability of food.[14] Malnutrition is the result of poverty and poverty is often the result of social structures.

Planning food aid strategies in the absence of structural data can be a futile operation.

(e) *Group Action*

Attention is here centred on certain conflicts of interest and resulting antagonisms between groups such as the producer and the consumer, the multinational actor and the local citizen, the industrialist and the wage earner.

This requires the collection of information, not otherwise readily available, regarding immoral, unjust or sharp trading practices in relation to the pricing, the purchase, the distribution, and the marketing of food. All of

[13] Marchione, *op. cit.*, p. 117.

[14] See S. George, *How the Other Half Dies*, Penguin Books, London, 1976; *The Hunger Problematique and a Critique of Research*, United Nations University Press, Tokyo, 1980; P. Alston, *Development and the Rule of Law: Prevention versus Cure as a Human Rights Strategy*, International Commission of Jurists, Geneva, 1981.

these have their effects upon the availability of food and consequently on problems of hunger and malnutrition. A wide range of organizations and of individual activists has emerged to perform this function — consumer unions and church groups among others.

This is a potent factor redressing the imbalance of information which had operated uninterruptedly for several decades. Yet it only partially fills the information gap between producer and customer, as it can fill the information gap only on an *ad hoc* basis.

A correlation of all these species of information can immeasurably strengthen the thrust for human rights in the developing world.

THE PROMOTION OF HUMANISTIC SCIENCE

In the generation or selection of technology for the use of the developing world, one cannot ignore the human aspects of science and technology. This is a needed corrective to the compartmentalization of science, which has seen scientific expertise and information in this generation fragmenting into ever narrower specialities and sub-specialities. The deeper one delves into a narrow area of science, the narrower becomes one's outlook. The perspectives that ought constantly to be before the scientist tend to be shut out. A needed corrective to this informational imbalance is to see science in an overall or holistic content. Apart from the injection of social perspectives into existing science curricula, there is a need for the establishment of centres devoted to this holistic approach.

Such a holistic approach would necessarily involve interdisciplinary studies, and would bring together sociology, economics, the humanities, philosophy, jurisprudence, and many other areas of human knowledge which can make a direct contribution to fostering in scientists and in the scientific product a greater regard for humanity and the environment, which, in the last resort, scientists and science are intended to serve. Many of the problems concerning the impact of science on society and, in particular, on Third World societies are the result of failure to have this broader dimension prominently placed before the scientific enterprise.[15]

The informational aspects that go into the creation of new science and technology need this orientation, and it is most important that these perspectives be fed in, prior to the generation of the product — hence the importance of the humanistic approach at the prior stage before the technology actually is created. The impact of such a new attitude will be felt also in the field of scientific method, where results are currently determined by experi-

[15] On humanistic science, see *infra*, Ch. 24.

ments tightly controlled within their own narrow framework, without regard to the broader social dimension. Results that fit in with the postulates of the narrow frame of reference are not results that will necessarily fit within the postulates of a broader frame. The framework of scientific research must, in other words, be considerably broadened to take on a humanistic dimension.

IDENTIFICATION OF LEGAL OBSTACLES

Many of the concepts referred to in the preceding sections are difficult to achieve in consequence of existing legal principles, structures and practices. It will be necessary for a special study to be made, identifying legal obstacles that stand in the way of the realization of these objectives. Work has already been done by such centres as the International Center for Law and Development, to identify legal obstacles to the realization of alternative development strategies. These have studied the ways in which those who desire to preserve the *status quo* on the developmental and technological fronts use law as a means of obstructing change.

The problem is both a national and an international one, and the study undertaken will thus have to be in the forums of domestic law as well as international law. There will also need to be a study of the ways in which co-operation can be achieved among domestic legal systems in eliminating these obstacles. Among the matters that will be studied under this head will be the changes in legal systems and principles that will be necessary in order to give to developing countries a greater share in the control of the process of production, and the processing of information which precedes production. Other areas where greater control will be required will be in relation to control of trading relations and control of prices.

In working out this elimination or reduction of legal obstacles, there will need to be considerable North/South dialogue as well as South/South co-operation.

***

The foregoing discussion represents some of the ideas which may perhaps be pertinent to the task of harnessing information technology in the cause of development. Such an approach could eliminate some of the roadblocks on the way to development. It would be too ambitious to undertake an examination of all of them, but it may be that some at least of these ideas will be considered important enough to pursue. Attention to these problems will certainly assist in improving the total benefit that developing countries will receive from the vast movements in science and technology that are now taking place, in which they are to a large extent passive spectators rather than active participants.

8. Some Cross-cultural Perspectives on Technology and the Environment*

In this age of advanced technology, there are many insights regarding environmental protection which we can derive from traditional systems of law. Conscious attention to the protection of the environment has been a very real concern in many civilizations from a period antedating the crystallization of our modern ideas regarding environmental protection.

As modern legal systems, both domestic and international, begin very belatedly to address these problems, they can benefit greatly from a closer familiarity with the wisdom and the foresight enshrined in these traditional systems.

It is appropriate also, in this decade of international law which the United Nations has proclaimed, that we should address this practical problem to as wide an audience as possible, seeking to show the linkages between modern international law and traditional global wisdom.

THREE BASIC CONSIDERATIONS

I would like to preface this discussion with a reference to a few broad considerations that envelop our topic.

(i) *the environment knows no national frontiers*

First, the global environment knows no national frontiers. What we are considering is not a matter of concern to any one country. It is a matter of concern to the whole world. What environmental concerns are demonstrating today is that no one country, however powerful, has the capacity to deal unaided with environmental problems, even within its own boundaries. It is impossible to regulate global warming or nuclear contamination, ozone de-

* Based upon an address delivered at the Peace Palace, The Hague, on 8 November 1996, at a meeting organized by the Dutch Association for the United Nations in celebration of the International Court's 50th Anniversary.

pletion or the extinction of species, by unilateral action within any country, however supposedly sufficient unto itself. Environmental concerns do not stop at national boundaries, but overflow beyond them to affect all other countries in the tightly-knit and interdependent global community of today. We must therefore work towards some kind of global regulation of these affairs.

(ii) *we are in the realm of future generations*

The second important aspect we have to bear in mind is that when we are in the realm of environmental matters, we are also in the realm of future generations, because our power to damage the environment is now so strong that we can damage it for generations to come — not merely for a few generations, but even for thousands of years. The strange anomaly about dealing with the rights of future generations is that, although we do in fact deal with them and pretend to have the right to deal with them, we do so without hearing them, or anyone arguing on their behalf, and indeed do so without even giving thought to them. In the self-centred and short-sighted satisfaction that our legal systems are just, we often perpetuate gross iniquities upon generations yet unborn. Since they have no spokesmen, it is for the law to try to remedy this lacuna, and it should take special pains to consider the rights of future generations. This is the least we owe to those who are not here to tell us their views, and whose health, wealth and welfare we are gravely damaging by the kind of pollution we impose upon the planet which will be their legitimate inheritance as it was ours. Such attitudes offend one of the most basic legal principles lying at the foundation of all civilized[1] legal systems — that a trustee must not consume the resources over which he stands as protector and guardian.

In a recent case before the Court — *Request for an Examination of the Situation of the Nuclear Tests (New Zealand* v. *France)* — one of the lawyers, addressing the Court, observed that if Stone Age man had caused the sort of damage that might be caused by nuclear contamination today, that damage would be with us still. And we, as the generation that came tens of thousands of years after Stone Age man, would be grappling with a problem which we had no hand in creating, a sentence imposed upon us which we did not deserve. We would probably be heaping blame upon a generation we saw as insensitive, unjust, and self-centred. Fortunately, that is not the case be-

[1] The term is not used in any pejorative sense, but is the phrase which appears in Article 38(1)*(c)* of the Statute of the International Court, listing the sources of international law, one of which is stated to be "the general principles of law recognized by civilized nations".

cause they left to us a clean and unpolluted planet. But it is likewise our responsibility to think in terms of the future. Generations as far remote from us as Stone Age man, and all the generations in between, would accuse us of immoral conduct if we do not look after the planet in a manner that shows respect and responsibility towards them in respect of the environment, which is theirs as much as ours.

(iii) *the scale of environmental damage is ever increasing*

The third broad consideration is that many of the violations of justice with which we come in contact when we consider these matters are both facilitated and sharpened by the reach and power of modern technology. Modern technology is a tool available, on a scale never known before, for the denudation of the countryside, the pollution of the atmosphere and the poisoning of the seas. It can erode the land, extinguish living species, unsettle the ecological balance, and generate noxious wastes — all on an unprecedented scale. Moreover, modern technology has in its evolution shaken itself free of moral restraints. Legal restraints likewise are few, and technology thus tends to function to the very limits of its power, regardless of its impacts upon land, sky or sea. Legal controls over technology lag far behind the latter's progressive ability to increase the scale of environmental damage.

(iv) *we are in the realm of active international co-operation rather than mere passive co-existence*

The scale of environmental damage which modern technology can cause forces us to move into another dimension in international relations, for no one state can, of its own resources, handle the new environmental problems in all their vastness. The international law of the pre-World War II period was based on the passive co-existence of states. The international law of the future will be based on the active co-operation of states, without which humanity cannot survive. Of no department of international law is this truer than in regard to the international law of the environment.[2]

(v) *environmental considerations transcend the realm of individual rights*

In environmental matters we cannot afford to concentrate on the rights and duties of one individual towards another. Rather, we are in the realm of the

2 On this aspect, see W. Paul Gormley, *Human Rights and the Environment: The Need for International Co-operation*, A.W. Sijthoff, Leiden (1976), esp. pp. 32–48.

duties of each individual towards the entire community. Our traditional ideas of justice and legal procedure have been fashioned *erga singulum*, i.e., against an individual or individuals. Notions of environmental justice go far beyond this notion and are based on obligations *erga omnes*, i.e., towards the whole world. Traditional legal procedures and concepts will need to be recast in the light of this reality, so far as environmental matters are concerned.

(vi) *we are in an area where traditional wisdom has much to offer us*

Environmental law is a fast developing area of law. There is a certain urgency attaching to it, for the magnitude of the damage that can be caused is such that it may even touch the very survival of humanity. Yet, strangely enough, this is one of the least developed areas of international law.

When we consider the thousands of years in which traditional legal systems of one sort or another have held sway over various parts of the world, we tend to wonder whether they have all shown an insensitivity to the future such as we show now. Is there not any inspiration, any set of guiding principles, which we of this generation can derive from generations past? They may not have formulated their concepts in terms of environmental law, but they nevertheless displayed a wisdom we have lost, in their linkage of rights and obligations which bind the generations and ensure the survival of the race. We have no right to starve the developing body of international environmental law of the nourishment it can derive from those insights which encapsulated some of the timeless wisdom of humanity since first our race carved out for itself a special place upon this planet.

(vii) *the appearance of a series of emerging norms*

The fledgling discipline of international environmental law is now actively nurturing many principles to which traditional legal systems have much to contribute. Principles such as that of the trusteeship of earth resources, rights *erga omnes* (i.e., towards all the world), duties *erga omnes*, intergenerational rights, the common heritage of humanity, the prohibition of conduct which causes damage to neighbouring states, the protection of the environment in time of war, are only now being worked into the corpus of international law. These principles are not new. They have been known for thousands of years to a variety of legal systems. If international law is to develop into a truly international and multicultural system, as it ought to, we cannot leave these traditions aside and treat them as if they do not exist. Modern international law far too often seeks to develop itself as though it is a monocultural system. That tendency must be resisted, international law must be properly fertilized, and the ancient wisdom of humanity must be tapped in this area in which it has developed and functioned so richly for millennia.

We have therefore a great need to look into the past of the human family, not merely for a century or two centuries, but to take a much longer view of how humanity has in the past adjusted its rules of conduct to the needs of the future. A great repository of untapped wisdom awaits us if we only took the trouble to contemplate ways in which various races inhabiting the planet — some of them superciliously regarded as not being of a very high level of civilization — embodied in their customs and ways of life an immense amount of perennial planet-related wisdom.

ABORIGINAL ATTITUDES TO THE ENVIRONMENT

To give you an obvious example, let us consider the Aborigines of Australia. The Aborigines of Australia are said by historians to have an unmatched achievement to their credit: that they have preserved a stable lifestyle for at least 50,000 years[3] on the world's most inhospitable and driest continent. How did they do it? When you look at their traditions you find that they are teeming with respect for the environment, teeming with ways in which man and the environment can harmonize without damage to the interests of the one or the other. Their art forms depict humanity as linked by an umbilical cord to mother earth, the source of nourishment and sustenance of every human being. Mother earth is to be treated with respect and reverence. Land had a vitality of its own and was not to be denuded. Conservation of resources was deeply ingrained in their culture, as evidenced by the traditional "walkabout" of the Aboriginal people. They would use the resources of an area and then move on to other areas, allowing the first area sufficient time to regenerate. Had they failed to do this, land which afforded them sustenance for 50,000 years may well have been turned into deserts.

There are many other important ecological lessons to be learnt from the Aborigines, which are only slowly being uncovered by modern investigation and scholarship — as, for example, extracting the maximum value to man from the hundreds of individual species of plant, animal and insect life which other cultures treat as valueless. There is a great deal of environmental wisdom of that sort we can derive from many other traditions as well.

[3] In the Kimberley region in Western Australia, Australian researchers have recently found specimens of rock art 116,000 to 176,000 years old, and four sculpted boulders 75,000 years old.

Nor must it be thought that the Aboriginal people were without their own technology or their schemes of development.[4] What is important is that in their culture the protection of the environment was central to their activities.

THE ENDLESS VARIETY OF ENVIRONMENTAL PROBLEMS

Environmental problems may come before the Court in a variety of ways in the future. The problems are legion and, if one sought to name them, there would be no end — deforestation, desertification, devastation of the mining areas, pesticides, oil spills, erosion, holes in the ozone layer, thermal pollution, acid rain, the "greenhouse" effect, extinction of species, unrestrained fishing and whaling, toxic chemicals, nuclear waste, space debris, marine pollution, melting of the polar icecaps. The unrestrained use of modern technology is at the root of most of these problems. Any one item on this unending list has the potential to create or generate a situation that seriously jeopardizes the future of our planetary home. We must concern ourselves with these problems, for they may eventually end in an international arbitration, or perhaps at the doors of the International Court itself.

To take just one of these, the melting of the polar icecaps has been a cause of much concern for some time. In the Pacific countries particularly, this is a matter of very real fear because many of those little Pacific islands are at sea level. If the sea level should rise by even three or four feet, entire nations in the Pacific could be submerged. One reads sometimes of this

[4] To quote a modern Australian text on engineering:

"There were remarkable Aboriginal water control schemes at Lake Condah, Toolondo and Mount William in south-western Victoria. These were major engineering feats, each involving several kilometres of stone channels connecting swamp and watercourses.

At Lake Condah, thousands of years before Leonardo da Vinci studied the hydrology of the northern Italian lakes, the original inhabitants of Australia perfectly understood the hydrology of the site. A sophisticated network of traps, weirs and sluices were designed to take advantage of rising and falling waters, allowing eels to be caught throughout the year. The traps were built at different levels so that as the water rose and fell, different traps progressively came into operation." (Stephen Johnson *et al*, *Engineering and Society: An Australian Perspective*, Harper Educational, 1995, p. 35.)

"At Toolondo an elaborate system of water control was developed ... The system was designed to retain water during droughts and to cope with excess water during floods ... The chairperson of the Aboriginal Culture Centre ... believes that fish traps on the Barwon River could be one of the oldest man-made structures on Earth. The traps are believed to have stretched over 400 metres of rapids, and were set at different levels to suit varying river heights." *Ibid.*, p. 37, citing Josephine Flood, *Archaeology of the Dreamtime*, Collins, 1983, p. 208.

brand new concept of "environmental refugees" — people fleeing not from the violence of humanity towards itself, but from the violence of humanity towards the planet. The wicked intent of chasing them away from their homes is not directly present, but the culpable mental state is present of thoughtlessness in pursuing a wasteful and unthinking lifestyle. Holland, which is perhaps the world's expert on keeping the sea at bay, has a particular interest in this problem, for it lives on the edge of the environmental problem of the encroaching sea. By sheer skill and determination, it has been able to co-exist with the elements that surround it. These are problems of very great interest and urgent concern to the Pacific countries. This country, whose skills have done so much to develop international law, may then have to contribute a different sort of skill towards saving the world from the consequences of the violation of a basic rule of international law — that we must not cause harm to others.

ROUTES OF ENTRY OF TRADITIONAL LAW INTO MODERN ENVIRONMENTAL LAW

It could perhaps be asked whether, having regard to the way in which modern international law is structured, there is any methodology available for drawing this body of wisdom into the corpus of modern law. By what mechanism can we, in the International Court or anywhere else, make use of this kind of traditional wisdom that we should be exploring? For the benefit of the non-lawyers in the audience, I should state that Article 38 of the Statute of the Court affords us a means to do so. It enables us to draw upon international conventions, international custom, general principles of law recognized by civilized nations (that is the archaic phraseology of the Statute), the writings of jurists and judicial decisions. This gives us plenty of room, under the head of international custom or general principles of law, to benefit from the wisdom of traditional systems. That is part and parcel of our common inheritance, which we are entitled to draw upon for the purpose of building environmental law. Jurists are also becoming increasingly conscious of this problem and there are various solutions that jurists have propounded in their juristic writings. We can use all those ideas. Traditional law can be accommodated within many of these sources of international law.

Another channel through which we can develop environmental concepts is human rights, which is now an important part of international law. Human rights guarantees mean nothing if they do not also include such rights as the right to health. Article 21 of the Universal Declaration states that everyone has the right to a standard of living adequate for the health and well being of himself and his family. We obviously cannot have a right to health if our environment is so polluted that it is leading us to ill health and premature death.

There is also the provision regarding human dignity in the Universal Declaration. If you have a squalid planet, a planet that is thoroughly polluted, you cannot lead a life of human dignity.

There is, again, the right to life which is guaranteed in Article 3. Everyone has the right to life, and we all know how incidents like Chernobyl, for example, have deprived people of the right to life and the right to health.

The right to marriage and procreation offers another opening. Everyone has the right to marriage and to found a family. There is also the protection of motherhood and childhood. We know that many modern forms of environmental pollution cause damage even to the unborn child, and that is a clear contravention of the rights that are guaranteed to everybody under modern human rights discourse.

In the result, a wide a variety of routes is open to the international law of the future from which to draw into its body of learning some basic principles which may help us to live in greater harmony with our environment.

Another concept we can draw upon heavily is the concept of equity, which is part of customary international law and part of the "general principles of law". From this we derive the principle of the equitable use of the resources of the planet — not a selfish appropriation thereof by any one group or generation. The concept of the equitable use of earth resources is now well ingrained within international law. Here, again, traditional systems can help us, for one of their areas of wisdom is the emphasis they place on the principle of equity in all our relationships, including our relationship with future generations.

Those are various ways in which it is open to the Court to draw upon traditional wisdom in enriching its jurisprudence in relation to environmental rights. As you know, the Court can be resorted to not only for contentious cases, but also for advisory opinions. Quite recently two advisory opinions were requested by the World Health Organization and the General Assembly on various aspects of the legality of nuclear weapons. Important environmental matters could thus come before the Court in the form of an abstract legal question being referred to it for an opinion and, in dealing with that, the Court could use all these sources that I have mentioned to you. I should also point out that there are well over 300 treaties which specify that, in the event of a dispute regarding the interpretation or application of the treaty, the matter shall be settled by the International Court. There are several environmentally related treaties among this number. Even such a sophisticated area of regulation as the Convention on Climate Change has a provision in relation to the settlement of disputes by the International Court.

There are thus numerous situations which can offer the Court opportunities for the development of the principles of environmental law. In doing so, it would be grave neglect on the part of international law if it did not look at these traditional systems.

THE IMPACT OF COLONIALISM

I have referred to civilizations that have flourished for thousands of years. In the nineteenth century particularly, many of these civilizations were interfered with by colonialism. Colonialism took over a large part of the world, and started altering the traditional lifestyles of those regions. In many of these countries, there had been an economy suited to the needs of the people, fashioned to that end over the centuries, if not over the millennia — which enabled those people to live in harmony with their environment. Those ways of life were often linked to land; and principles relating to the use of land were heavily based upon the traditional wisdom which placed humanity in its environmental setting.

Humanity was not seen as an entity existing separately from the environmental order, and attempting to tame and subjugate it. It was widely realized that if humanity clashed with nature, it was humanity that would perish. At every stage, therefore, ritual and lifestyle decreed homage to nature — at springtime, at harvest, drought, or flood, oblations of one kind or another were made to nature, betokening an understanding that there was a relationship of permanent dependence. Land and its sustaining qualities lay very close to the centre of the social order.

When colonialism took over, those territories were subjected to an economic system which was largely fashioned to suit the needs of the colonial rulers. That system was a cash economy in which every component element of the lifestyle — land included — became subordinate to the needs of that economy. Moreover, the dominant idea of colonialism was the use of the colonies to strengthen the economy of the metropolitan power — not that of the subject territory.

In many of these colonial territories, the new rulers concentrated intensively upon the production of some particular type of commodity, for the production of which that colony was particularly suited. This benefited the colonial power which was thus able to procure the raw materials it needed at a privileged price. It also benefited the cash economy of the colony, and therefore gave the appearance of being a desirable policy to pursue. But its unnoticed effect was that, in trying to develop that particular product, the lifestyle that had prevailed in that territory for generations was disrupted. Rice-producing communities were turned into specialized producers of coffee or cotton, tea or rubber, copper or tin. Handicrafts and traditional skills attuned to the materials found in the region languished and often disappeared. The entire economy centred on the new industries, to the neglect of all the traditional activities which had sustained those societies in the past. Such technologies as were evolved were those which were necessary to service the new economy (such as the technology related to railways, harbours and mines) — not the technologies that were necessary to revive and service the old.[5] Instead, such technology as there was for these purposes tended to die out.

For the moment, the new orientation seemed fine, and generated cash for the colony and industrial and financial strength for the mother country. What was not seen was that this was at the cost of the traditional harmony between the people and their environment. Ancient irrigation systems which had nourished the people for centuries fell into disrepair. The small peasantry was dispossessed and vast plantations took over their smallholdings.

One of the best examples of this comes from the Sri Lankan context. For upwards of twenty centuries, there had been an environmentally friendly lifestyle based upon an agricultural system nourished by an interconnected network of man-made reservoirs and canals. There were major reservoirs enclosing several square kilometres of water, and thousands of smaller reservoirs, interconnected by a system of irrigation channels.[6] So sophisticated was this system that Arthur Clarke, the noted futurist, has described this system in the following terms:

> Of all Ceylon's archaeological wonders, however, the most remarkable — and certainly the most useful — is the enormous irrigation system which, for over two thousand years has brought prosperity to the rice farmers in the regions where it may not rain for six months at a time. Frequently ruined, abandoned, and rebuilt, this legacy of the ancient engineers is one of the island's most precious possessions. Some of its artificial lakes are ten or twenty kilometres in circumference, and abound with birds and wildlife.[7]

5 See Susantha Goonatilake, *Crippled Minds: An Exploration into Colonial Culture*, Vikas Publishing House, New Delhi (1982), p. 95.

6 D.L.O. Mendis, "Lessons from Traditional Irrigation and Eco-systems", in Ziauddin Sardar (ed.), *The Revenge of Athena: Science, Exploitation and the Third World*, Mansell Publishing Ltd., London and New York (1988), pp. 316 ff.

7 Arthur C. Clarke, *The View from Serendip*, Victor Gollancz Ltd. (1978), p. 121.

It is noteworthy that some of these colossal reservoirs, built more than two thousand years ago, are still in service — so well did they harmonize with their environment.[8]

It is noteworthy also that these stupendous technological achievements, were always linked to the needs of the environment by a conscious and articulated philosophy of respect for the environment.[9]

With colonialism, there came an emphasis on the production of tea and rubber. With that concentration, the old irrigation systems fell into disrepair. Vast extents of land were acquired, much of it from smallholders and much of it from forest reserves that had been preserved in their pristine condition for ecological reasons. The plantations and their needs assumed priority in the national economy.

All this made for efficiency of production, so long as the infrastructure provided by colonialism lasted. Even though the traditional lifestyles had made the whole country a granary, rice could now be cheaply imported to feed the population. The plantations were the prime concern and their needs had priority. The imperial economy could be likened to a large department store, with several departments, specializing in different products — one specializing in cameras, another specializing in confectionery, and another in clothes. The department store functions with great efficiency because there is the background organization to provide all those departments with their necessary infrastructure. But if the separate departments are released to manage their affairs on their own, the camera department, the confectionery department, the tailoring department, and others, would all have to build their infrastructure afresh. They cannot function as independent entities because their sole function thus far is the sale of one product.

So it was when colonialism was lifted. Each of those territories was released into the world community to fend for itself, with an imbalance in its economy, a traditional lifestyle which had been damaged, and a total lack of support services such as an independent nation would require. Infrastructures and attitudes towards the environment which had taken centuries to generate could not be reproduced overnight. With the felling of forests, the liquidation

8 More details regarding this remarkable system will be found in the author's Separate Opinion in *Gabčíkovo-Nagymaros Project (Hungary/Slovakia), I.C.J. Reports 1997*. Joseph Needham, in his survey of science and civilization in China, makes several references to it when discussing contemporaneous technological civilizations — e.g., *Science and Civilization in China*, Vol. 4, *Physics and Physical Technology*, 1971, p. 372.

9 Among the principles so articulated in the ancient literature were the principle of trusteeship of earth resources, the principle that natural resources such as water should not be wasted, the principle of protected forests, and the principle that wild life should be protected.

of smallholdings, the neglect of agriculture, and the ignoring of traditional ecological wisdom, the scene had been set for further divergences between the people and their environment.

The contrast with pre-colonial agriculture which had a sturdier recipe for survival is striking. As observed in a study dealing with the vexed question of the patenting of new varieties of seed:

> Subsistence farmers in the Third World have been cultivating major food crops for over ten thousand years. By observing the natural process of mutation and by careful seed selection over the centuries, these farmers have developed an astonishing range of crop variability. This diversity has been necessary for survival. No one wheat or rice variety can provide adequate protection against monsoon failures, pests, rust or blights.[10]

With the neglect of agriculture, this rich variety disappeared,[11] breeding a dependence on just a few varieties.

Colonialism had no truck with the traditional conception of land as a dynamic entity which lived and grew with the community, and did not permit it to be treated as a passive object. Such traditional attitudes stood in the way of the extraction from it of the maximum of wealth it could give, without regard to the future, and represented a philosophy directly antithetical to the objects of colonialism. There is a human rights element as well which is involved in this, for as one writer has pointed out:

> It was the available gold and stones which led to the martyrdom of the Inca Indians; it was the raw rubber of the virgin forests of Africa which led to the enslavement of the natives in French and Belgian Congo. It was the scintillating gleam of gold in the rock strewn ground of Matabeleland that forced Sir Starr Jameson's hand and compelled him to invade the Matabele ...[12]

Moreover, land itself had become an object of common merchandise to be bought by or sold to the highest bidder, regardless of the honoured place which it had held under traditional systems.

[10] Pat R. Mooney, *Seeds of the Earth: A Private or Public Resource?*, International Coalition for Development Action, London (1969).

[11] Lawrence Surendra, "Plant Genetic Resources and the Impact of New Seed Technologies", in Ziauddin Sardar (ed.), *The Revenge of Athena: Science, Exploitation and the Third World*, *supra*, pp. 157 ff.

[12] John H. Harris, *Slavery or "Sacred Trust"?*, Williams and Norgate, London, 1926, p. 68.

NINETEENTH-CENTURY LEGAL ATTITUDES TOWARDS TRADITIONAL LEGAL SYSTEMS

At this point, I should say a word about the attitude of modern law towards traditional law. Nineteenth century legal attitudes were heavily influenced by the school of legal thought known as positivism. John Austin in England and many other European scholars had the idea that if a legal system was to deserve the name of a legal system, and if a legal principle was to deserve the name of a legal principle, it had to be written and it had to be specific. It had to deal with a particular matter, and it had to proceed from the central organization in the State — that is, from the command of the sovereign. Anything that fell short of those standards was belittled, and was looked upon as unworthy of the name of law. It was not a serious enough manifestation of law to be considered to be a law properly so-called. Just as such rules of conduct were removed from the concerns of the serious lawyer, the philosophy behind those rules was even further removed.

This view was so deeply entrenched that it was difficult to dislodge. It provided the pattern for the colonial legal administration which sought to organize itself on principles of clear and succinct legal formulations of the law which the courts would enforce. Other traditionally binding norms tended to fall into desuetude, including those relating to the manner of use of land.

This juristic attitude was to come under scrutiny in the twentieth century under the influence of new schools of legal thought. Bronislaw Malinowski, who studied the problems and the practices of the Pacific countries in particular, made a great dent in the belief that the only legal systems worthy of the name proceeded from a sovereign's will, by demonstrating that, even though a principle of traditional ordering of society might not measure up to the Austinian standards of positive law, it was still firm and binding law, for the community it regulated.[13] Malinowski's researches broke through that theoretical framework which denied full recognition to customary systems.

Looking at the customs of the Trobriand Islanders, then supposed to be very primitive people, Malinowski pointed out that there was a well understood concept among them of the duties and entitlements of every member of the tribe. Every member was well aware of the laws and the traditions of the community. He knew precisely what was expected of him. He knew precisely the ways in which he should protect the environment, and the common fishing grounds. Such was the precision of this system that every member knew precisely even his place in the boat, his share of the catch, the

[13] B. Malinowski, *Crime and Custom in Savage Society*, Kegan Paul (1926).

permitted fishing grounds, and the permitted fishing practices. Malinowski discovered that the unwritten traditions of a customary society were in some respects ahead of developed societies, in being able to bring home to every member of the community their particular duties. An important object of these rules was the survival of the tribe as a group, and the preservation of the common environment which was the group's source of sustenance. Modern legal scholarship, following in the wake of Malinowski and others, has demonstrated to us that we must look at traditional systems with much more respect than we did in the past because, among other reasons, there is a great deal of environmental wisdom enshrined in them.

Scholars like M. Gluckman,[14] who have studied African customary law, Karl Llewellyn,[15] who researched the customs of the American Indians, and E. A. Hoebel,[16] who studied the Australian Aborigines, have likewise revealed the existence of a large number of principles which will be of very great importance when we consider how we must enrich the environmental law of the future. Their results are indeed dramatic, for they show that the legal systems of these peoples were elaborated, circumscribed and protected by checks and balances in a manner which Western jurisprudence has been unable to achieve. Indeed, these communities had achieved some of the most prized values of Western jurisprudence which Western legal systems have been unable to achieve, such as:

- that a law should be known to those it governs;
- that it should be immediate and not remote;
- that legal institutions should not lose touch with the people;
- that laws should be honoured in the observance rather than the breach;
- that they should not depend for observance on a formal policing apparatus;
- that rules of conduct should be definite;

[14] M. Gluckman, *African Traditional Law in Historical Perspective*, Oxford University Press, 1974; *The Ideas in Barotse Jurisprudence*, 2nd ed., Yale University Press, 1972, and *The Judicial Process among the Barotse*, Manchester University Press, 1955; A.L. Epstein, *Juridical Techniques and the Judicial Process: A Study in African Customary Law*, Manchester University Press, 1954.

[15] Karl Llewellyn and E.A. Hoebel, *The Cheyenne Way*, University of Oklahoma Press, 1941.

[16] E.A. Hoebel, *The Law of Primitive Man*, Harvard University Press, 1964; see, also, E.M. Eggleston, *Fear, Favour or Affection*, Australian National University Press, 1976.

- that their enforcement should not be rigid, but tempered with equity and a consideration of the individual factors involved;
- that there should be near-total participation of all members of the community in the legal system;
- that law is not an instrument of repression but a means for harmonious co-existence and advancement;
- that informal but totally acceptable dispute-resolution mechanisms should be freely available;
- that justice is impartial, inexpensive and not delayed;
- that the wrongdoer's punishment does not alienate him or her from society;
- that society should be structured on basically egalitarian lines.

MAJOR DIFFERENCES BETWEEN MODERN AND TRADITIONAL LEGAL SYSTEMS

(i) *The Group Concept*

One of the reasons for the rapid environmental degradation we see all around us is the elevation of individual rights to the extent that they are protected by the law, even where they operate in clear conflict with the interests of the group or of society. Traditional law attached great importance to the group concept. Land and other communal resources exist for the benefit of the group. Individual rights there are within the group, but subservient always to the rights of the group. So strong was this tradition in India that Mahatma Gandhi sought even to have the concept of group rights entrenched in the Constitution. He was unsuccessful, but Article 39 of the Indian Constitution captures something of the idea of restraint of individual exploitation of the environment by providing that:

> The State shall, in particular, direct its policy towards securing … that the ownership and control of the material resources of the community are so distributed as best to subserve the common good.

Modern law tends very often to expand the rights of the individual to the point where they clash with the rights of the group. Modern environmental concerns are highlighting the importance of the group concept, and the important protective purposes it served in all traditional systems. Indeed, even in the European situation, the group concept was of cardinal importance until about the time of the French Revolution, because society functioned on the basis of group organization such as the guild, the manor, and the parish. There was a wide variety of group organizations to which each individual belonged. The French Revolution destroyed this group structure and wiped the slate clean, so to speak, leaving the individual to protect himself or herself unaided. The strong individual prospered at the expense of others, where formerly the group would have protected the latter. The weak individual was crushed as never before by many forces abroad in society, from an overweening neighbour to the all-powerful State. The collective strength of the group was no longer a source of protection. With the group structure destroyed, individual self-interest began to be pursued, without regard to communal or group needs. It mattered little that the individual was profiting out of resources that an earlier age would have instinctively regarded as communal resources.

Here is an important reason why environmental concerns are causing so much worry today. Individual exploitation of the communal environment proceeds in developed economies in a manner which would not have been permissible in traditional societies. With the emergence of the individual in modern law, as contrasted with the strength of the group in traditional law, a major cause of environmental damage was unleashed from the many restraining factors which had held it back in all the prior centuries of human existence.

(ii) *The Concept of Duties*

Traditional law was based upon an underlying concept of duties. It was the individual duty that was emphasized rather than the individual right. Modern law, in contrast, emphasizes rights rather than duties. In those traditional societies, a dominant social idea was that, with the proper performance of one's duties, one's rights automatically fall into place. The performance of duty, not the assertion of rights, was the cement of society.

Growing individualism tended to lead to the neglect of duties, with a resulting imbalance in social relations. A corollary to the assertion of individualism was the assertion of individual rights, without a feeling of responsibility for discharging the correlative duty. It followed inexorably that individual rights were asserted to the point of causing damage to the rights of the group.

A major theme of discussion in modern human rights discourse is a criticism of the stress it lays on human *rights*, rather than human *duties*. We are constantly reminded of the need to attach greater weight to human duties. It is said that there should be a universal declaration of human duties alongside of a universal declaration of human rights. For example, we have a human right to health. Have we not a human duty to look after the environment which gives us that health? In that way, the idea that these old communities stressed, of duty rather than right, is now reviving. In the context of the future of environmental law, we will need to consider very seriously the extent to which we can inject more life into the concept of duties.

(iii) *The Intergenerational Perspective*

Let us take as an example traditional African law. Traditional African law views the human community as three-fold — those who are alive here and now like ourselves, those who went before us, and those who are yet to come. All three together form the human community, not one alone. But we concentrate on ourselves. We gloss over the rights of future generations and, in our concentration upon the present, tend to deride the traditions of the past. With the focus exclusively upon the present, we overlook the needs of the future. In the result, we deprive future generations of their rights as members of the human community, in the sense underlined by the African tradition, which has a time dimension to its thinking which seems lacking in modern law. That culture sees past, present and future stretched out in a vast panoramic view of humanity and its endeavours. Modern legal systems have a circumscribed vision, enlightened though we consider them to be.

(iv) *Living Things as Bearers of Rights*

Our modern law tells us that only human beings have rights. Traditional systems tell us that other living creatures have rights. I shall give you some examples as we go along. If living creatures also have a place on this planet, that place ought to be recognized in a more substantive form than in the remote peripheral recognition we give it, if we give it any recognition at all. Their wanton destruction for profit or for pleasure has placed them in a legal category little different from inanimate objects, whereas they are a living part of our environment, placed there for greater purposes than we have understood thus far — purposes which are constantly unfolding to our limited vision as modern science increases our understanding of the environment. Those common inhabitants of our planet have a right not to be wantonly destroyed, a right to life however conditional, which our legal systems need to accord to them. They cannot speak for themselves, but one of the functions of a developed legal system is to protect the rights of those who are voiceless, or have no advocates to present their cause.

Modern jurisprudence is beginning to show a sensitivity to these issues which traditional legal systems viewed as central, for their vision of the time horizon was far more sweeping than ours. It is not surprising therefore to find articles appearing in law journals on such subjects as "Do Trees Have Standing?".[17] Likewise, there are schools of thinkers who expound the rights of animals, basing themselves on a great deal of philosophical tradition drawn from different cultures.[18]

Traditional systems went even further than the recognition of living things such as animals and trees as bearers of rights. Many systems — Amerindian and Aboriginal systems, for example — invested the sky, the lakes, the rivers, and the mountains with personality, and consequently with attributes of the right to existence and protection.

(v) *The Subjects of Property Rights*

Our modern concepts of property treat every material object, other than human beings, as the subject of property rights. It is somebody's property; and a characteristic of property rights, as understood in our modern legal traditions, is that the owner can do what he or she pleases with the property which is the subject of ownership. It can even be destroyed at will. No distinction is drawn between the animate and the inanimate, between the socially useful and the socially useless, between the movable and the immovable. Such an attitude is anathema to societies which show a traditional reverence for land and the living things associated with it. Indeed, in some societies, as in the Pacific, land is regarded as a living, breathing thing, which lives with the community, sharing a common life with it. If the land prospers, the community prospers. If the land withers, the community withers with it. If you abuse the land, you destroy yourself with it.

It must not be thought that such a notion is entirely alien to modern juristic thought. I refer in this context to the dissenting opinion of Justice Douglas of the United States Supreme Court in the case of *Sierra Club* v. *Morton*,[19] to the effect that parts of our natural surroundings such as rivers, beaches and trees should have standing before the courts in the protection of

[17] See, for example, Christopher D. Stone, "Do Trees Have Standing?", 45 *Southern California Law Review*, 1972, p. 450. See also the dissenting judgment of Justice Douglas in *Sierra Club* v. *Morton*, p. 54, *supra*.

[18] See Peter Singer, *Animal Liberation: A New Ethics for our Treatment of Animals*, Cape, 1976.

[19] 405 US 727 (1972).

their interests.[20] That learned judge was so moved by this concept that he observed:

> The river, for example, is the living symbol of all the life it sustains or nourishes — fish, aquatic insects, water ouzels, otter, fisher, deer, elk, bear, and all other animals, including man, who are dependent on it or who enjoy it for its sight, its sound, or its life. The river as plaintiff speaks for the ecological unit of life that is part of it. Those people who have a meaningful relation to that body of water — whether it be a fisherman, a canoeist, a zoologist, or a logger — must be able to speak for the values which the river represents and which are threatened with destruction.[21]

(vi) *Subordination of the Environment to the Concept of Development*

Modern legal systems, and the economic philosophy underlying them, tend to subordinate many traditional values, even of Western societies, to the notion of development. The priority accorded to development means, *inter alia*, that all natural resources lie at the service of development, however treasured they might be. Most traditional societies refused to recognize this subordination of their environmental heritage to any commercial values, whatever the economic advantage.

These are a few of the major differences between modern and traditional attitudes.

I would wish at this point to expand a little on traditional concepts relating to land.

CONCEPTS RELATING TO LAND

By way of contrast to ancient tradition, modern law tells us that ownership gives us absolute rights over land. If I own this table, I can do with it whatever I please. It is nobody else's business. Why? Because ownership gives me absolute rights over this table. A grave mistake of modern law, both common law and civil law, is to extend this concept unduly. Thus, if I have ownership of a stack of corn, I can do with it what I will. I can burn it in the face of my starving neighbour whom I am angry with, merely to spite him — because that is my property. I can do so for the basest of motives — as to show him my power — for the law rarely concerns itself with motives. Since

20 See *supra* Chapter 2, p. 54.

21 405 US 727 (1972), at 743.

modern law tells me that I can do what I will with my property, nobody can interfere with my handling of it. That is contrary to the attitudes of traditional systems which stressed the existence of a social duty in regard to the ownership of property.

This lack of concern for the higher issues reaches its highest point in relation to the ownership of land, for modern law tells me that if I am the owner of land, I can even reduce it to the barrenness of a lunar landscape. That is the opposite of attitudes which viewed land as one with the people, in consequence of which the people merged into the land, and the land merged into the people.

Some years ago, I had the privilege of chairing the Commission of Inquiry that was investigating international responsibility for the exploitation of Nauru. The environmental problems of Nauru were caused by mining for phosphates, since that little island contained some of the richest deposits of phosphates in the world. Modern mining technology had rendered possible the exploitation of the land with much more "efficiency" than had been possible before. Phosphates had been mined out of Nauru to such an extent that the greater part of the island had been left like a picture we see of the moon. There was not even a half-inch of topsoil left in the mined-out areas, and they were absolutely unfit for human use or occupation. In the course of that inquiry, we had to examine the environmental customs of the various Pacific countries and we noticed that there had been a Land Inquiry Commission in the Solomon Islands, at which one of the Solomon Islanders had told the Commission:

> Land is for us not like a six-sided box, not like an article of merchandise, which I can buy and you can sell. Once I buy it from you, I can do with it what I will. It is part of our tradition, it is part of our culture, it is part of our people. And therefore land is not an article of merchandise.[22]

This statement emphasizes rather dramatically how modern law treats land very much like an article of merchandise. The owner can cut it up into pieces, sell it in little parcels, fell primeval forest, defoliate it, or denude it of topsoil. All this is nobody's concern but his.

By way of contrast, many traditional societies viewed land as being very much like a part of one's own body. In fact, some African traditions consider that selling a piece of land is like chopping off a part of one's body. The land

[22] See P. Sack, *Land between Two Laws*, ANU Press, Canberra, 1973, p. 33. See, also, this author's *Nauru: Environmental Damage under International Trusteeship*, Oxford University Press, 1992, p. 164.

is one and integral, and it is an entire entity of which we are but a part.[23] We cannot make it a subject of merchandise by selling it in little brown paper parcels, so to speak.

Since this idea of modern law, that property confers absolute rights, is flatly in contradiction of traditional law, we need to see to what extent we can benefit from that basic assumption of traditional law.

An episode comes to my mind which will illustrate this attitude. I once spent a few months as a Visiting Professor at the University of Papua New Guinea. Port Moresby, the capital, is a developing city with high-rise buildings, and the land on which it is situated — the traditional land of certain groups — is very valuable. In between the developed areas, there still remain some pockets of undeveloped land. Those pockets of undeveloped land belong to various communities, tribes and families that have held them from time immemorial. There was a young law lecturer in the Faculty who happened to be a member of a family that owned one of these areas of undeveloped land. There were many foreign visitors to the Law Faculty, and I remember in the common room one day one of those visitors said to him, "You are sitting on a gold mine, aren't you, because that block of land belonging to your family is immensely valuable. Has it ever occurred to you to sell it? You could make a packet if you did." That provoked a tirade from the young man who said, "Do you not understand our customs? How can I sell that land? That land came to me from my forefathers, and it belongs to my posterity. How can you even suggest that I can sell it?"

That observation reflected that country's attitude to land — an attitude oriented towards the needs of future generations. That attitude would not permit land to be looked upon as a dead object for exploitation, but rather saw it as a living resource. It did not see land as a thing from which *existing* wealth could be extracted on a once-and-for-all basis, but rather as a living resource which would actively generate wealth and continue to do so indefinitely. Land can be killed and rendered useless through a false idea of "development", or it could be sustained as a continuing source of benefit to the

[23] For an American judgment reflecting a similar approach, see *Matter of Application of Christenson* 417 NW 2d 607 (1987), a decision of the Supreme Court of Minnesota denying the owner of a wetland a permit to drain it. The wetland served as a habitat for a wide variety of animal and bird life. The Supreme Court observed: "Over ten years ago this court cited the conservationist Aldo Leopold for his espousal of a 'land ethic' which envisions a community of independent parts. 'The land ethic simply enlarges the boundaries of the community to include soils, waters, plants, and animals or collectively the land' *County of Freeborn* v. *Bryson* 243 NW 2d at 332, citing Sand County Almanac (1949) p. 203. We reaffirm our statement that the state's environmental legislation had given this land ethic the force of law ..."

community. Such attitudes encapsulated the modern notion of "sustainable development". Modern attitudes leave little room for a bond between the people and their land — the key to the approach of most traditional systems.

CONCEPTS RELATING TO CONTRACT

Another concept of modern law which bears upon the misuse of technology is the concept of freedom of contract. This has been discussed in Chapter 2 above. Freedom of contract, regardless of the social results of such a doctrine, is carried to lengths today which the group-oriented societies of the past would find strange. The idea of individual rights — for example, under a mining contract — being relentlessly asserted whatever the damage to the environment, would not accord with communal-based attitudes or with the traditional respect for land that was characteristic of those societies. The combination of modern concepts relating to land and modern concepts relating to contract has been devastating to the environment. The individual or corporation enjoying power under contract to deal with land is able to do so with scarcely any restraint.

CONCEPTS GAINING RECOGNITION IN MODERN ENVIRONMENTAL LAW

Modern law, rather late in the day, is awakening to these anomalies between its concepts and the fundamentals of traditional wisdom, and is evolving important new concepts. Rights *erga omnes*, that is, rights towards all of humanity, as opposed to rights as against a person, are gaining recognition and validity. Correspondingly, there are duties *erga omnes* towards everybody. In relation to environmental matters, duties that are owed to everybody acquire special significance.

The new notion of intergenerational rights is coming into modern international law and gathering momentum. Other new notions are the notion of trusteeship of earth resources; the notion of the common heritage of mankind; the notion of group rights; the notion of social use of property; and the notion of the precautionary principle. All of these received recognition in one form or another in traditional societies.

Before I cause any damage to the environment, or to my own land, I am now required to consider, somewhat more than a generation ago, the environmental consequences that might ensue. I am reminded here of a principle followed by the Native American people which required that, before they carried out any project which had a lasting effect on their land, they should consider its impact for seven generations. Seven generations, probably as far as the mind of man could perceive, were probably symbolic of all future time, and this rule embodied a desire that the land and its usefulness should be preserved in perpetuity.

Belatedly, modern law is awakening to these ideas and is producing concepts that look enormously advanced. In reality, they are concepts that ancient and traditional systems knew well and respected deeply — concepts that they had observed from time immemorial. Since we are now developing those concepts, it may well be that we can derive immense practical guidance and wisdom from these traditional systems.

AN ILLUSTRATIVE TRADITIONAL SYSTEM FROM THE PACIFIC

Let me illustrate from a traditional legal system I have had occasion to study in some detail — that of Nauru. In Nauru, traditional law was able to regulate effectively the use of the sea as well as the land. As far as the sea was concerned, there were portions of sea allocated to each tribe for fishing, with very strict rules about preservation of the fish stock they carried. Very strict rules were laid down prohibiting fishing at certain times, or at certain periods, or in certain areas if the fish stocks were running down. Likewise, a taboo could be placed upon a reef for the preservation of certain kinds of fish. It became illegal to fish in those reefs if the fish supplies were running down.[24]

Similar concern was shown for the protection of trees. It is a very small country and there were certain areas where almost every tree was marked. In time of drought or shortage, there would be a taboo placed upon the use of certain trees. No nuts could be plucked from certain trees and that taboo or that prohibition was effective throughout the community. That was a method of conservation. In time of adversity there were traditions and rules in relation to the sharing of water from the wells. Of course, land was not a commodity to be bought or sold. To this day, the idea of sale of land is anathema to the people of that country. They say that it is as absurd as to try to sell a portion of a river or even a portion of the sun. It is a notion that is quite alien to their customs. All these rules and concepts were well known to all members of the community and were faithfully observed.

In all these respects, one is reminded of the pioneering studies conducted by Professor Bronislaw Malinowski in regard to the Trobriand islands, to which we have already referred. By revealing to the world of modern legal scholarship the power, the detail and the effectiveness of traditional systems of law, he highlighted many principles of juristic organization which our

[24] See *Nauru: Environmental Damage under International Trusteeship*, *op. cit.*, p. 161.

modern systems of law see as desirable, but unattainable owing to our legal formalism.

HINDUISM

Let me take you to another part of the world, the sub-continental region of India , where a four thousand year old tradition is recorded in the Hindu scriptures, the *Vedas*. The Hindu traditions, embodied in the *Vedas*, spoke of all nature as being a manifestation of the Divine. There was something in every living thing that was part of the divinity. There was a unifying concept behind all creation because everything is interlocked. *A fortiori*, all living things are interlocked.

There was in that tradition a profound respect for the environment. Let me recount an episode in the *Ramayana*, which is a great classic of India. It recounts in photographic detail the story of a great war. The Indian prince, Rama, was engaged in a mortal conflict with Ravana, the ruler of Sri Lanka. At one stage in this prolonged encounter, Rama was informed of the existence of a hyperdestructive weapon which could destroy and ravage the entire countryside of his enemy. He was advised, in accordance with the traditions of his time, that he should not use it without first consulting the sages of the law. Rama consulted the jurists of his age, and was advised that the weapon went far beyond the purposes of war and, as such, was not a legitimate weapon of war. The purpose of war is to subjugate one's enemy, not to ravage his countryside, or to destroy entire communities. Therefore Hindu tradition, as reflected in the sacred law, banned the use of the weapon, and Rama refrained from using it. This is just a part of the wealth of environmentally related wisdom which one finds in the *Vedas*. Deep respect for the integrity of the environment thus translated itself into even a principle of the laws of war — a ruling anticipating by millennia the belated acknowledgement in the modern laws of war that parties engaged in military conflict should not ravage the environment.

BUDDHISM

Buddhism goes even further, with its tradition of compassion (*karuna*), which extends to *all* living things. They all have a place on the planet, the common home of all. Asoka, the great Buddhist Emperor of India, even established a hospital for animals, and proclaimed the necessity for the protection of all living things. In Sri Lankan tradition, the sermon preached to the King of Sri Lanka which converted the King to Buddhism, included the first principle of environmental law — the principle of trusteeship of earth resources. It also included the concept that fauna and flora were entitled to protection. Here is a part of that sermon:

> O great King, the birds of the air and the beasts have as much right to live and move about in any part of your dominions as you. Land belongs to all people and all living beings. You are only a guardian of it.[25]

The King was on a hunting trip at the time the sermon was preached to him, and this very circumstance highlighted the importance of the message of respect for all life which was powerfully preached on that occasion. So great was the impact of this notion on Sri Lankan history that legislation for the protection of fauna and flora, based on this Buddhist principle, extended till well into the 18th century[26] when the country fell into the grip of colonialism. Buddhism pursues this idea of an ingrained respect for all life even further into its juristic connotations. In modern human rights law, the notion of the right to life is developed into the concept that everyone is entitled to the right to freedom from fear. That is considered a modern notion which advances respect for the integrity of the human personality. It is interesting to note that the Buddhist literature specifically teaches that the right to freedom from fear should extend to birds and beasts as well.[27]

Buddhism emphasizes the idea of the interrelatedness of all living things. This leads to the notion that one cannot divide the observed world into separate and distinct compartments and treat each of them as an entity in itself, because they all intermingle. They all have their impact one upon the other. The phenomenon of life is an interrelated network, and to interfere with any part of that network is to damage oneself.

These Buddhist ideas of compassion (*karuna*) have been very greatly developed in a manner that is relevant to the environmental field. Schumacher's well-known work, *Small is Beautiful*, conveys a glimpse of Buddhist economics, the Buddhist idea of shifting emphasis away from the pursuit of profits, progress and giant operations back to human beings and human values, and the small organizational unit. That is all an aspect of the richness of Buddhist thought, which is related to the environmental problems of today, and affords us an insight into possible solutions.

[25] See the reference to this famous sermon, in the context of Sri Lankan environmental attitudes, in Arthur C. Clarke, *1984: Spring*, Del Rey Books, N.Y., (1984), pp. 236–238, republishing his article in *National Geographic*, August 1983.

[26] See K.N. Jayatilleke, "The Principles of International Law in Buddhist Doctrine", (1967–I) 120 *Recueil des cours*, p. 588.

[27] *Digha Nikaya*, III, Pali Text Society, p. 850.

All this was manifested in Sri Lanka in various state policies. For example, after the sermon just referred to, the King established sanctuaries for the beasts and the birds, and those sanctuaries continued in force for several centuries. They were amongst the earliest sanctuaries in the world for the protection of wild life.

Likewise in regard to crown forests. Crown forests were deemed to be immune from felling and the reason for that, as we now discover, was the wisdom of the ancients that immense tracts of crown forest attracted the rain which fed the rivers, which in turn fed the fields. If those crown forests were destroyed, the ancients knew that the entire agricultural system would be destroyed. So there was a ban placed upon the felling of large areas of crown forest. In ancient Sinhalese law, they were known as *thahanam kalay* (protected forests).

Likewise there was the philosophy of the ancient kings that no drop of water should pass from a river into the sea without first irrigating the fields. The best known pronouncement on this matter was by the great king Parakrama Bahu I (1153–1186 A.D.). That king brought to its highest point the ancient irrigation system of Sri Lanka which had been built up from the 5th century, B.C., an irrigation system which consisted of several dozen enormous reservoirs, each containing thousands of acres of water surface, and 25,000 to 35,000 small reservoirs linked to them by an intricate system of canals — a complex of irrigation works which Toynbee, in his panoramic survey of civilizations, describes as an "amazing system of waterworks".[28] The philosophy of "sustainable development", which is only now emerging in international law, was exemplified in the policies of that age, for that king did not neglect development in the interests of his people — he constructed and restored 165 dams, 3910 canals, 163 major and 2376 minor reservoirs, including the famous Sea of Parakrama — a reservoir with a bund eight and a half miles long and fifty feet high. This was Parakrama's famous edict:

> Not even a drop of water that comes from the rain is to flow into the ocean without being made useful to man.[29]

The irrigation technology used was also consciously designed to meet environmental needs. For example, there were elaborate arrangements to prevent the accumulation of silt, which often poses a serious problem in modern irrigation projects, for as early as the third century B.C., the ancient Sinhal-

[28] Arnold J. Toynbee, *A Study of History*, Somervell's Abridgement, Vol. I, Oxford University Press, London, 1960, p. 257.

[29] *Ibid.*, p. 81.

ese engineers devised a contrivance for this purpose, known as the valve-pit, which came into regular use in Europe only in the 19th century.[30]

The concern for the environment shown by this ancient irrigation system has attracted study in a recent survey of the Social and Environmental Effects of Large Dams,[31] which observes that among the environmentally related aspects of its irrigation systems were the "erosion control tank", which dealt with the problem of silting by being so designed as to collect deposits of silt before they entered the main water storage tanks. Several erosion control tanks were associated with each village irrigation system. The significance of such measures can well be appreciated in the context of present environmental problems relating to silting, which have even surfaced as legal issues before the International Court of Justice.[32]

Another such environmentally related measure consisted of the "forest tanks" which were built in the jungle above the village, not for the purpose of irrigating land, but to provide water to wild animals.[33]

Such works and pronouncements are rich examples of an environmental philosophy and practice stemming from the philosophical roots of Buddhism, a source from which modern environmental law can draw a rich fund of inspiration.

30 "Already in the first century, A.D. they [the Sinhalese engineers] understood the principle of the oblique weir ... But perhaps the most striking invention was the intake-towers or valve towers (*Bisokotuwa*) which were fitted in the reservoirs perhaps from the 2nd Century B.C. onwards, certainly from the 2nd Century A.D. ... In this way silt and scum-free water could be obtained and at the same time the pressure-head was so reduced as to make the outflow controllable." (Joseph Needham, *Science and Civilization in China, op. cit.*, Vol. 4, p. 372.)

31 Edward Goldsmith and Nicholas Hildyard, *The Social and Environmental Effects of Large Dams*, 1985, pp. 291–304.

32 See *Gabčíkovo-Nagymaros Project (Hungary/Slovakia), I.C.J. Reports 1997.*

33 For these details, see Goldsmith and Hildyard, *ibid.*, pp. 291 and 296. The same authors observe:

> "Sri Lanka is covered with a network of thousands of man-made lakes and ponds, known locally as *tanks* (after *tanque*, the Portuguese word for reservoir). Some are truly massive, many are thousands of years old, and almost all show a high degree of sophistication in their construction and design. Sir James Emerson Tennent, the nineteenth century historian, marvelled in particular at the numerous channels that were dug underneath the bed of each lake in order to ensure that the flow of water was 'constant and equal as long as any water remained in the tank'."

OTHER ANCIENT TRADITIONS

The cultures of China and Japan have also been influenced to a large extent by such philosophies. Chinese philosophy had deeply ingrained within it the idea of balance. There must be a harmony between man and the environment. Nothing was to be practised and pursued in excess. As Joseph Needham, the celebrated scholar of Chinese science, has pointed out, there was an aversion to going against the grain of things. One must be in harmony with nature, not in opposition to it. Taoism requires that you follow the natural order and do not clash with it. Lao Tse taught that when you pursue one value or another to its extremes, you end with its opposite. A parallel would be that if you press on further and further to the east, you will end in the west. Press exploitation of the earth's resources to its extreme in order to get rich, and you will find yourself ending poor.

The Chinese planned not for this decade or that, but for work which would serve future generations for centuries to come. An ancient stone inscription teaching the art of river control says that its teaching "holds good for a thousand autumns".[34] Such action was often inspired by the philosophy recorded in the *Tao Te Ching* which "with its usual gemlike brevity says 'Let there be no action [contrary to Nature] and there will be nothing that will not be well regulated'".[35] Here, from another ancient irrigation civilization, is yet another expression of the idea of the rights of future generations being served through the harmonization of human developmental work with respect for the natural environment.

Chinese philosophy wanted human beings to experience the wholeness of nature, to live with it in harmony — the theory of the *yin* and the *yang*, each balancing the other. Buddhism and Confucianism provided the background to such thought. The early Taoists attached so much importance to nature that they often withdrew into the wilderness to meditate amidst the beauty of the forests and the mountains on the order of nature. This tremendous love for nature is reflected in Japanese culture as well. We all know the love it manifests for the mountains, streams, trees and cherry blossoms. There is a central harmony in Japanese culture which must not be upset, and a fundamental part of that culture is respect for nature.

I have already referred to the basic wisdom of another great global tradition, the African tradition, regarding the three-fold nature of the human community — past, present and future. Against this central philosophy, Afri-

[34] *Ibid.*, p. 295.

[35] Needham, *Science and Civilization in China*, Vol. 2, *History of Scientific Thought*, 1969, p. 69.

can tradition ordained that land was not a subject of sale, and that the chief was only the trustee, not the owner, of the land. The land had to be nourished, it had to be respected, it had to be looked after. Various ceremonies of offering a libation to the land, especially at the commencement of harvesting, or at the time it was entrusted to another to be tended and cultivated, indicated this respect. The land is the great sustainer, and one pays due obeisance to it. No chief could sell land.

Some African cultures, e.g., those of the Sonjo and the Chagga in Tanzania, had a sophisticated irrigation system that was maintained over several centuries. Their complicated networks of irrigation furrows, collecting water from the mountain streams and transporting it over long distances to the fields below, have aroused the admiration of modern observers not merely for their technical sophistication, but also for the durability of the complex irrigation systems they fashioned. Among the Sonjo, it was considered to be the sacred duty of each generation to ensure that the system was kept in good repair and all able-bodied men in the villages were expected to take part.[36]

Another example is that of the *qanats*[37] of Iran, of which there were around 22,000, comprising more than 170,000 miles[38] of underground irrigation channels built thousands of years ago, and many of them still functioning.[39] Not only is the extent of this system remarkable, but also the fact that it has functioned for thousands of years and, until recently, supplied Iran with around 75 per cent of the water used for both irrigation and domestic purposes.

THE ISLAMIC TRADITION

Another important cultural tradition — Islam — accords high priority to the idea that all land belongs to God. There is no such thing as an individual's absolute ownership of land. He or she is only the trustee. As trustee, the so-called owner of land must look after it for the benefit of those who are to enjoy it in the future. This trusteeship concept is highly developed in Islamic jurisprudence, not only in the realm of property, but also in the realm of

[36] Goldsmith and Hildyard, *op. cit.*, pp. 284–285.

[37] *Qanats* comprise a series of vertical shafts dug down to the aquifer and joined by a horizontal canal — see Goldsmith and Hildyard, *ibid.*, p. 277.

[38] Some idea of the immensity of this work can be gathered from the fact that it would cost around one million dollars to build an eight kilometre *qanat* with an average tunnel depth of 15 metres (*ibid.*, p. 280).

[39] *Ibid.*, p. 277.

power. A ruler is trustee of the power that he holds for his people: he is not the owner of that power.

There is also the notion in Islam of bidding unto good. It is one's duty to go out of one's way to do that which is necessary for the welfare of others. This contrasts with the individualistic concept that one is entitled to think only of oneself and one's own advancement. The social orientation involved in these two cardinal concepts could be of vital importance to the environmental law of the future, which must necessarily base itself on the notions of trusteeship and communal welfare.

All of these, in their various ways, harmonized the work of development of the land with a concern for the environment.

MODERN EUROPEAN IDEALISTIC APPROACHES TO NATURE

Modern European culture also reflects something of these traditions. Wordsworth's almost spiritual approach to nature could be cited as one of the better known examples. At the turn of the century, Russian literature reveals evidence of a strong devotion to nature, which is a reflection of traditional attitudes. The writings of Chekhov and Tolstoy, for example, reflect a glowing admiration for people who devoted their attention to the conservation of resources (such as the protection of forests). Such people are heroes in the works of Chekhov and Tolstoy.

The love of nature, so powerfully reflected in the poetry of Wordsworth, was itself a recognition of a long-standing tradition in English literature of attaching an idyllic importance to the unspoilt beauty of the countryside — a beauty sadly disturbed by the industrial revolution and its attendant belching chimneys and slagpiles of factory waste. There was also the political resistance to enclosure movements which again interfered seriously with the natural order — an interference captured in the verse:

> The law locks up both man and woman
>   Who steal the goose from off the common
> But lets the greater felon loose
>   Who steals the common from the goose.

In America, Thoreau, likewise, gave expression to ideas of the importance of nature, which were sweeping through Europe around that time. Nature was in fact identified with peace — a desire to get away from the ravages caused by man, and a reversion to the primeval state of peace. The Western tradition of love of nature can in fact be traced back through the millennia to writers such as Virgil who, in the first century B.C., reflected in his *Georgics* his great love of the Italian countryside and his resistance to the drift towards the cities, which was affecting the traditional agricultural life of Italy.[40]

THE AMERINDIAN TRADITION

Let us now cross over to the ancient civilizations of America and take a look at the Inca civilization. Regarding the Inca civilization at its height, it has been observed that it continually brought new lands under cultivation by swamp drainage, expansion of irrigation works, terracing of hillsides and construction of irrigation works in dry zones, the goal being always the same — better utilization of all resources so as to maintain an equilibrium between production and consumption.[41] In the words of a noted writer on this civilization, "in this respect we can consider the Inca civilization triumphant, since it conquered the eternal problem of *maximum use* and *conservation of soil*."[42] Here, too, we note the harmonization of developmental and environmental considerations.

I want to conclude by referring you to some of the wisdom of the Native American people. This is captured for us in a document which is attributed to the Chief of an American tribe in his reply to President Franklin Pierce of the United States, when the President made an offer for the purchase of a large area of Native American land. The Chief wrote to the President in poetic terms, which I quote *in extenso* for the multitude of environmentally related notions it contains. Writing to "the Great Chief in Washington", the Cherokee Chief observed:

[40] See the *Georgics*, Book II, l. 36 ff.; l. 458 ff. Also *Encyclopaedia Britannica*, 1992, Vol. 29, pp. 499–500.

[41] Jorge E. Hardoy, *Pre-Columbian Cities*, 1973, p. 415.

[42] John Collier, *Los indios de las Americas*, 1960, cited in Hardoy, *op. cit.*, p. 415. See also Donald Collier, "Development of civilization on the Coast of Peru" in *Irrigation Civilizations: A Comparative Study*, Julian H. Steward (ed.), 1955.

> How can you buy or sell the sky, the warmth of the land? The idea is strange to us. If we do not own the freshness of the air and the sparkle of the water, how can you buy them? Every part of this earth is sacred to my people. Every shining pine needle, every sand shore, every mist in the dark woods, every clearing and humming insect is holy in the memory and experience of my people. The sap which courses through the trees carries the memories of the red man. ... Our dead never forget this beautiful earth, for it is the mother of the red man. We are part of the earth and it is part of us. The perfumed flowers are our sisters: the deer, the horse, the great eagle, these are our brothers. The rocky crests, the juices in the meadows, the body heat of the pony, and man all belong to the same family. So when the Great Chief in Washington sends word that he wishes to buy our land, he asks much of us. ... The shining water that moves in the streams and rivers is not just water, but the blood of our ancestors. ... The water's murmur is the voice of my father's father.
>
> The rivers carry our canoes, and feed our children. ... One portion of the land is the same to [the foreigner] as the next ... The earth is not his brother, but his enemy, and when he has conquered it, he moves on. ... He treats his mother, the earth, and his brother, the sky, as things to be bought, plundered, sold like sheep or bright beads. His appetite will devour the earth and leave behind only a desert.[43]

He says, in other words, that this idea of our selling our land to you is absolutely contrary to our traditions, and if you treat land like this, you will end with a desert, because you will ruin all that is beautiful and all that is kin to man which is encapsulated in that land. If you destroy wildlife, if you destroy the land, you destroy man himself.

The fact that many of these traditions are not recorded, and are not the subject of precise analysis and definition, should not prevent us from attaching due value to all of this, and using it to fertilize our own thinking. If we do so, I believe the international law of the future will be considerably enriched, and we can perhaps make it an immensely more useful and widely accepted weapon with which to deal with these great problems, on which the future of humanity depends.

[43] See Guruswamy, Palmer, and Weston (eds.), *International Environmental Law and World Order*, West Publishing Co., 1994, pp. 298–299. There is some doubt about the authenticity of the actual wording, but the document is often cited as representing the traditional American Indian attitude to nature. On American Indian attitudes, see further J. Callicott, "The Traditional American Indian and Western European Attitudes Towards Nature: An Overview", 4 *Environmental Ethics* 293 (1982); A. Wiggins, "Indian Rights and the Environment", 18 *Yale J. Int'l Law* 345 (1993); J. Hughes, *American Indian Ecology* (1983).

In all these traditions, there is such a wealth of material that I think we could with profit draw upon it in our modern development of international law. Here is a list of environmentally-related principles which can be extracted from a variety of world cultures:

1. The principle of trusteeship of earth resources
2. The principle of intergenerational rights
3. The principle of respect for all forms of life
4. The principle that development and environmental conservation must go hand in hand
5. The principle of respect for land
6. The view that land has a vitality of its own
7. The principle that the community's health depends on the health of the land
8. The principle that rights are not restricted to human beings
9. The principle that rights are not restricted to the living
10. The principle that flora and fauna have a right to share the planetary environment with humans
11. The principle that "development" of land must not impair the long-term stability of the community for short-term gain
12. The emphasis on social duties rather than individual rights
13. The concept of sanctuaries for bird and animal life
14. The concept of protected forests
15. The principle that the human community is three-fold, consisting of those who preceded us, those who are now living, and those who are yet unborn
16. The principle that even animals have a right to freedom from fear and wanton killing
17. The purpose of development is the betterment of all living creatures
18. The principle that natural resources are collectively, rather than individually, owned

19. The principle that there should be no wastage of natural resources, but that they should be used for the maximum service of man
20. The maximization of the uses of all natural species
21. Equity in the sharing of natural resources
22. The concept that just as man did not weave the web of life, so also man does not have the right to interfere with the interrelatedness of all living species
23. The principle of community service to maintain the integrity and purity of the environment
24. The concept of affirmative duty towards one's neighbours in protecting and conserving the environment

Each of them represents the wisdom resulting from millennia of co-existence between people and their environment. Why may not international law turn to them for nourishment in its search for the guidance it urgently requires in this crisis of survival which could even threaten the fate of humanity?

Grotius, the father of modern international law, looked at the prior wisdom of all the civilizations he could study to gather from them the guiding principles of the new international law. We can do no less in searching for the guiding principles of the new international law of the environment. Far from departing from the method or traditions of international law, such an approach would be a tribute to the legacy of Grotius who left for us an example *par excellence* of marshalling the experience of the past for the solution of the problems of the future.

9. Some Illustrative Global Case Studies*

After a few international resolutions and declarations on the subject in the 1960s, the idea that science could become a source of danger to human rights gradually attracted greater international interest. By Resolution 3384 of 10 November 1975, the General Assembly noted with concern that scientific and technological achievements can be used to intensify the arms race, suppress national liberation movements, and deprive individuals and peoples of their human rights and fundamental freedoms. It also noted with concern that scientific and technological achievements can entail dangers for the civil and political rights of the individual and the group, and for human dignity. In addition, it noted the urgent need to make full use of scientific and technological developments for the welfare of man, and to neutralize the present and possible future harmful consequences of certain scientific and technological achievements. All States were therefore called upon to co-operate in strengthening the capacity of science and technology to further human rights.

In other words, there was a realization by the United Nations in the mid-1970s that, while the benefits brought by science to humanity were remarkable, there were indeed two sides to the coin. In the 1980s, there was more literature on this. The Brandt Report[1] showed that, while 51% of the scientific skill of the world was being used for the manufacture of armaments, only 1% of the world's scientific skill was used for solving problems of the developing world. There was also the Presidential report on the year 2000

* Based on an address delivered by the author at the United Nations University, Tokyo, on 14 May 1993 on the occasion of the launch of the second of a set of two volumes on Technology and Human Rights edited by the author. The lecture was published in the United Nations University Lectures (Public Forum Series) under the title "The Impact of Technology on Human Rights". The two volumes, published by the United Nations University Press, are titled *Human Rights and Scientific and Technological Development* (1990) and *The Impact of Technology on Human Rights: Global Case-studies* (1993). The studies were undertaken pursuant to an invitation issued by the Commission on Human Rights to the United Nations University to conduct a study into the beneficial and harmful effects of scientific and technological developments.

1 *North-South: A Programme for Survival*, Pan Books, 1980, p. 197.

and the OECD report titled *Interfutures*. The problem of the destructiveness of modern science began to attract wider public recognition.

Such are some of the considerations that have led the Commission on Human Rights, by its resolution 9 of 1986 on the Use of Scientific and Technological Developments for the Promotion and Protection of Human Rights and Fundamental Freedoms, to invite the United Nations University to undertake the studies that have led to the publication of these two volumes. In that resolution, the Commission recognizes "that the effects of scientific and technological developments on human rights and fundamental freedoms have both beneficial and harmful aspects and therefore must be examined in their totality". That resolution also specially recognizes "the need to extend the benefits of science and technological developments to the developing countries".

The Human Rights Commission's resolution which led the United Nations University to undertake this study and to organize the research leading to these two books was a manifestation of growing concern on the part of the international community that the time was ripe for a study of this problem in depth. The volumes that have resulted therefore only serve to highlight the magnitude of the research that awaits attention in this vital field. The further we delved into this topic, the more we realized the paucity of attention it had received. It is hoped these volumes will serve as pointers in the direction of further research that needs to be undertaken, if greater harmony is to be achieved between the two burgeoning forces of technology and human rights.

Needless to say, it has been a great privilege for me to be commissioned by the University to be the Editor of these two books. In these volumes, we have been able to survey a wide panorama of the problems — social, legal, economic and ethical — which modern science has raised in practically every field of human endeavour. The first volume outlined the general contours of the subject, and the second dealt with specific problems drawn from each major geographical area. We have learned much during this project, and I hope some of the conclusions we have reached will be found useful in continuing research on the all-important topic of the impact of science and technology on human rights in the very sensitive decades ahead. Just as the universal consciousness of human rights is expanding rapidly, so also is the power of science and technology. Areas of conflict must be identified and resolved, just as areas of harmony must be identified and expanded.

* * *

THREE SCENARIOS

Since, in the twenty-first century, technology will play an increasingly important role in every facet of international and national life, we must anticipate some of the grave problems that advances in technology will pose for the disciplines of law and human rights. The law moves very slowly, while technology moves with lightening rapidity.

Perhaps these influences could be compartmentalized in three great sectors. They concern the impact of technology on:

1. the human body;
2. the human environment;
3. human society.

To give you a somewhat graphic presentation of the dangers that probably threaten us in these fields, I will commence by asking you to imagine three scenarios, one from each of these different areas.

In the first scenario, let us imagine a poor man in a third world society. He has no job, no social welfare, four or five children to maintain, a wife, and an aged mother. The average job in that society brings about one thousand dollars per annum, but even that sort of job is beyond his reach. He does not know where the family's next meal is coming from. He lives in squalor in an urban slum. One day he goes to the market and there he meets somebody who tells him, "Have you heard of that agent who arranges organ transplants? He is there in the market place, trying to make arrangements for people to donate organs". Just out of interest, he meets and speaks with that man. The man tells him, "Well, you are a healthy person, and if you are prepared to donate a kidney for somebody who needs it desperately — it's a matter of life and death for that person — we will give you twenty thousand dollars. You can have three thousand dollars as a down-payment if you agree, and we will send you to one of the affluent capitals where the organ transplant will take place, and before you return, the balance will be paid to you".

The man spends a few sleepless nights thinking over this proposition. He thinks, "My children are growing up in malnutrition, I don't know what sort of permanent damage is being done to them by not having the basic nutrition they require. My aged mother doesn't have the nutrition she requires, and she may die prematurely. Am I not being selfish? The man assures me that I can live quite healthily with one kidney, and I will lead a normal life".

He deliberates over the matter and finally reaches a decision. "Well, I should not be selfish, I will take this offer". He goes to the man, he gets his three thousand dollar down-payment and gives it to the family. This keeps them affluent for some time, for they have three years' wages in one lump sum. He donates his kidney, and comes back with seventeen thousand dollars more, but without a kidney. There are many questions of human rights involved in that one scenario alone, and, from that man's point of view, that sum of twenty thousand dollars is a nest egg he could never have saved in his entire lifetime, even assuming he had a job.

The second scenario. Picture a few hundred million robots or mechanical men, each of whom gobbles up every day 30 kilograms of raw steel. Each robot drinks a barrel of oil a week. Steel is his staple diet, but he also varies it with sundry accompaniments of a few kilograms of copper, aluminium, lead, tin, zinc and plastics. He breathes out noxious fumes and he produces at least 2 kilograms of garbage every day. Professor Charles Birch, the Australian scientist, portrays that robot[2] as an image of what each and every one of us are, if we live in the developed world, because that is the amount of earth resources that each individual consumes. In consequence of this, millions of tons of garbage and refuse are accumulated in the big cities. The atmosphere is polluted and earth resources are drained. That is the second scenario, which pertains to the human environment.

The third scenario relates to human society. An ambitious politician has become a dictator in a small country. He is determined to have a tight grip over the people of his country. So he streamlines the administration. He has careful records kept in schools and detailed scholastic records in universities. He has access to insurance companies' records of health and has a complete medical history of everyone. Criminal records are all preserved and, unlike other societies where there are laws that prevent the pooling of all this data in a single data bank, the dictator we are describing wants it all pooled and there is nobody to prevent him. He can even make this control more sophisticated because technology is now available by which everybody's movements can be monitored. He offers his people a "travel card". They present that travel card on the buses and the trains and, of course, pay for it later, but every trip is documented. There are cards that open the doors to public buildings and shops, there is a library card which records all the books that they borrow and there is even a TV monitoring system which keeps a record of the programs they watch. Now, if our dictator presses a button in his office, the full data bank or dossier of information regarding any particular person of that country will appear on the screen in an instant. Information is what such people would like to have, because information is power. If you think back on English history, William the Conqueror launched the project of

[2] See Charles Birch, *Confronting the Future*, Penguin Books, 1975, p. 130.

the Domesday Book, which recorded every farm in England, the number of cattle on the farm, its extent and value and debts, who owned it, and how many people there were on each farm. If he could have done this in 1086, imagine what he would have done if he had lived in the computer age nine centuries later. In fact, there is further material available to our dictator because transmitting devices can be wallpapered into public buildings to capture and record the conversation that goes on within them. With all those devices available, imagine the life of people in that society.

I have placed before you three scenarios, one relating to the human body, one relating to the human environment, and one relating to human society. They are intended to show the immediacy of these problems, which are often treated in an abstract and academic manner. Examples can, of course, be multiplied as much as we wish, to include almost every area of scientific development. What should we do about it? I think it is clear that human rights are affected. Is there adequate protection available in our current structures of law and human rights to give some kind of protection against these invasions of basic rights?

* * *

SOME GENERAL OBSERVATIONS

All of these are worrying scenarios, all of them are with us already, all of them raise very specific human rights issues. These volumes address certain specific problems selected from each of the continents, as representative instances of the sorts of issues which confront us. However, there are certain general considerations which form the essential background to a study of those particular problems. I shall outline some of them briefly as a prelude to the consideration of those specific problems.

1. Any invention is a new source of power. The radio gives the power to influence opinion, a giant irrigation scheme gives control over vast agricultural areas, the steam engine gives power over communication between different parts of a country, nuclear science gives military and industrial power. While those who are at the commanding end of technology increase their power, those at the receiving end enter upon a new variety of subjection. Just as science opens up new power to the scientist and to those who command that technology, it opens up new ways of dominating others. While science creates power and strengthens humanity in one sense, it also becomes a new form of subjugation, for whoever controls that technology, has additional

power over people. If that power is used in a manner which runs contrary to our basic moral principles, that becomes power abused.

2. Very often the scientist who is pursuing some research feels absolved from liability because, after all, the activity engaged in is the pursuit of pure truth. It may be that someone else may misuse that knowledge and, if so, the blame lies on that someone else and not upon the scientist. That argument does not really take account of the responsibility of the scientist to inquire about what he or she is doing and for what purpose. So my second observation of a general nature is that all science gives power over natural phenomena, but, at the same time, it gives power over people, and hence generates responsibility.

3. The two great movements we are considering — the growth of science and the growth of human rights — are two of the most powerful forces making their impact on the global scene today. The human rights movement is pushing forward individual freedom as no legal movement has ever done in the history of humanity. It is one of the most significant movements we have ever had, of a universal nature, to push forward the rights of the individual. On the other hand, we have science and technology which are pushing forward the powers of control over the individual. This too is done to a greater extent than has ever occurred in the history of humanity. Unfortunately these two forces often push in different directions and, when they clash, it is a titanic clash at the conceptual level. At the practical level, we find that invariably it is science and technology that has the upper hand. The human rights movement does not have the power, even through law, to control it.

4. The scientific enterprise, after some time, develops a momentum of its own. It is not pure science operating in a neutral way with some researcher trying to discover some new rule of nature. Rather, there is an establishment that grows up around that piece of research. That establishment is very powerful. It is an establishment comprising not only the scientists concerned but, behind that, there may be an industrial establishment, a military establishment, or there may be the state itself. This becomes a sort of embodiment of power which has a life and vitality of its own and this pushes forward, irrespective of the individuals who are in it. It becomes a movement. The great pieces of research that have been done in recent times, especially in the field of weapons research, have a momentum of their own, and it is very difficult to resist the phalanx of power which that movement represents.

5. There is a widely-shared feeling that science, being the pursuit of truth, follows an inexorable course of its own. According to this view, science

takes its own direction, and there is very little that we can do to stop it because, after all, it is the pursuit of truth and this cannot be halted. There is therefore a feeling of resignation to the power of science and to the direction which it takes. In the literature on the subject, this is sometimes described as the deterministic theory, or the deterministic view. But we have to shake ourselves free of such resignation because modern science has grown so complex that choices have to be made constantly between numerous alternative areas of research. There are insufficient resources in the world to handle all the research projects that are possible. Two or three hundred years ago, only a few directions of scientific research were contemplated. Today the number of directions of scientific research has proliferated. So a conscious decision has to be taken at some point in time between alternative pieces of research. Which is the one that we choose? Which is the one to which we commit public funds? Which is the one to which we commit corporate funds? The result is that the deterministic theory is outmoded. There is room, and indeed a need, for a determinism of our own.

We have the ability, if we give our minds to it, to contribute something to the direction of scientific progress. This is a power many people do not realize they have. This is especially so in the developing world, where the need to direct it is even greater than in the developed world. It is very important that there should be a greater realization that this deterministic approach is no longer a valid approach. We have the power of determination and, to exercise that power of determination, we must exercise our right of participation.

6. When a scientist is engaged in research — I mean this with no disrespect to scientists — he or she tends to be caught up in the intellectual thrill of the chase. In pursuing research from one step to another, the researcher is thrilled to find a further fresh step which nobody has discovered before. The thrill of the chase is heightened because the scientist is engrossed in the particular scientific field under examination. But, while the scientist's vision may sometimes be bounded within the confines of a particular search, the world outside can see it in a wider perspective and they can see that particular piece of endeavour in its overall context. So there is room for a scientist to be reminded by the outside world that there are certain ethical considerations involved in what is being done, which may perhaps have escaped attention. That is why most universities now accept the importance of multidisciplinary ethics committees. In major hospitals, there are ethics committees which determine such fundamental matters as whether a life-support system is to be withdrawn, or whether a particular kind of research, involving experimentation on human subjects should be permitted. These sorts of

matters cannot be decided by doctors alone. They need the input of other disciplines as well. Hence, feeding ethics into the scientific enterprise is very important.

7. While, in theory, all scientific knowledge is open, yet, in practice, scientific knowledge is often confined — confined by the interests of the establishment that finances the research, whether corporate or governmental. A corporate establishment may be researching some aspect leading to a new product that will take it ahead of its rivals. But that is kept under wraps because, although it is science, and science belongs to everybody, that particular piece of science is kept guarded because it is in the corporate interest to keep it guarded. It is even more so in the military establishment. When the military establishment indulges in research, it often becomes classified information, and classified information is in files for only a very privileged few to look at, while the rest of the world is kept completely in the dark as to what sort of research is going on.

A major problem attendant on the use of scientific knowledge for the public benefit is that a large volume of scientific knowledge is owned by major corporations. They treat that knowledge as their private preserve and try to keep it secret as far as possible. Corporate science is targeted towards corporate profit. After all, why does a corporation indulge in scientific research? It indulges in scientific research to make a new or better product in order to increase its profitability. Thus, it is driven by the desire to make profit, not the desire to better the condition of the people. Of course, the corporation would probably say that what they are inventing is for the general good. Yet, the driving force is profit, not human welfare, and where the two interests clash, the profit motive would generally prevail.

If, again, you take defence science, you will find even greater secrecy, and you will find the driving force is again not human welfare, but military strategy. Indeed, in defence science, very often scientists are kept under an oath of secrecy that they will not talk about what they are doing. That is why what is truly knowledge, which truly belongs to all humanity, becomes information which is classified and made available only to a select few.

One of the human rights that we may need to discuss, subject of course to common sense requirements of safety and security, is the question of the openness of scientific knowledge. The openness of scientific knowledge is something that has come to us from shortly after the time of Galileo, and it is a principle so important that every effort must be made to preserve it.

I shall take the opportunity the occasion presents to outline some of the major themes we have dealt with.

8. We should also look at the object of the introduction of the technology. The object should not be development *per se*. Development is not an end in itself. Development is only a means to an end. The end is a better life for all. It is a qualitative end, improving the quality of life for the people of that country, and not merely the pursuit of development for the sake of development. So, we have to determine to what extent the technology in question promotes actual improvement of the quality of life in that country.

9. Modern technology creates inequality for the reason that it is capital intensive. Technological progress requires intensive research, and research is increasingly expensive. This requires vast resources. It consequently concentrates technological power in the hands of the powerful, and leaves out those who do not have the assets to participate in these cost-intensive procedures. Technology thus creates a centre of control and a periphery of those who will enjoy or not enjoy whatever the centre gives to them. It hence becomes a powerful economic force, as well as a powerful political force.

10. The last general observation I wish to make is that the developing world, which desperately needs development, is almost invariably the passive receiver of technology, and not the active originator of the technology that it uses. How does that technology come into the developing world? It comes sometimes through the country's own decision, sometimes through the pressure of external factors, and sometimes through a combination of the internal decision and the external pressure. What are these external pressures? There may be some technology that is tied to an aid package. A donor country gives an aid package to a needy country and there is some technology wrapped into that package which the recipient country must receive as part of that package if it wants that aid. Alternatively, the technology may be introduced into that country by a multinational corporation which is so influential and generates so many jobs that those who are in political control of that state cannot resist it. They have to agree because, if they do not, there will be many thousands of jobs lost. Again, there may be a prescription given to that country that it should adopt an open-door economic policy. Once it adopts an open-door economic policy, it is committed also to an open-door technological policy. Or, it may be told by its most powerful trading partner, "Well, there is this technology which we consider important to you, and it is a pre-condition for doing business with you that this technology should be accepted." There are many ways in which technology comes into a developing country, other than through its own volition.

One of the themes of some chapters in these books is that efforts should be made to examine ways in which developing countries can assume a greater role in determining the technology that they will receive. One of the methods advocated is to stimulate people in that country to a greater awareness of the ways in which technology affects them, because, after all, technology requires an input from the people themselves and, once it is achieved, it must be enjoyed by all. But many of these technologies are enjoyed by only a select few in the developing world. They are not spread around for the benefit of everyone. Therefore, great importance attaches to more participation in determining what technology will be accepted.

There is much discussion in these volumes on what constitutes appropriate technology, what are the yardsticks of appropriateness, and in what way third world countries can make themselves better equipped to determine what kind of technology they will receive.

* * *

I am glad the two volumes whose publication we celebrate today have been able to study in depth some of the major problems involving the impact of science and technology upon society. The first explores some general themes and the second addresses practical problems illustrative of those faced in all parts of the world.

In the first volume, we have looked at the theoretical aspects bearing on these matters, from the standpoint of legal philosophy, ethics, history, sociology, and economics. That volume looked at the history of the approaches by the United Nations to the problems of Human Rights and Scientific and Technological Developments. It examined global perspectives in the light of this problem, from the standpoints of the industrialized and the developing worlds, and studied the response of the international community to the problems of the impact of science and technology on human rights.

It then looked at some specific issues — the structure of the scientific enterprise, problems of development, and problems of the environment. In this respect, it was examining the two facets of the concept which later came to be called sustainable development — the need for attention to development and at the same time, the need to protect the environment.

It ended with a series of recommendations in regard to the training of personnel, new conceptual approaches, new surveillance mechanisms, and new research and educational projects. In particular, it stressed the need for education in attitudes of self-reliance and activism in order to overcome traditional attitudes of passivity and resignation to the power and inevitability of technology.

The second volume, which is being launched today, makes a series of practical studies consequent on that preliminary theoretical exploration. We have chosen five technologies, representing a spread of scientific activity, but these are only illustrative examples showing what a vast spectrum of topics awaits examination. We have chosen five countries from five different geographical areas — Thailand from Asia, Venezuela from Latin America, Poland from Eastern Europe, Holland from Western Europe, and Ethiopia from Africa — and conducted case studies in each of those countries on the practical impact in those countries of a given technology. The results are most interesting.

Some of these studies are not written merely by an individual, but by teams of researchers. This extensive research has yielded many practical suggestions, especially for developing countries, in relation to the choice of technology. Mistakes made in the past are also analysed so as to afford guidance towards a more appropriate choice for the future.

The Thai study examines agricultural technology; the Ethiopian examines the effect of weapons technology on the social and political life of that country; the Venezuelan examines the impact on the economy of oil and the technologies and projects associated with it. In Holland, our researchers have looked at modern medical technology, and the Polish study views the effects on human rights of modern industrial technology in the form of a steel mill. This spectrum of topics will give you some idea of the range and magnitude of the problems involved, seeing that we have taken only one country from each area and, in that one country, we have only looked at one kind of technology. This offers an index to the vast number of projects that are still waiting to be researched on the impact of so many other technologies that have been introduced into those and other countries.

The Thai study, conducted by Professor Vitit Muntarbhorn, deals with the ancient agricultural technology of Thailand, which has been in existence for seven to nine thousand years. It deals at length with the question of appropriate technology. The international transfer of technology is a matter of great importance to Thailand, as to all countries. Technology transfer is a very difficult operation to work out because, when technology is transferred from one country to another, all kinds of questions arise with regard to the right to that technology. What profits may be made from that technology? Should there be a code of conduct for the international transfer of technology?

There are ways in which a country can internally gear its legal system to handle these new technologies, for example, by revamping its patent laws, creating legal incentives, or sponsoring indigenous research. There can be tax benefits for inventors and the profits from their inventions; a reduction on tariffs for machinery that is brought in for industrial development; incentives for energy-saving devices such as solar heating; sliding scales on import duty for foreign components of machines locally assembled, so as to stimulate the production of components locally. There are many constructive ideas that emerge from indigenous sources in various developing countries which are often not proceeded with, for lack of encouragement and incentives.

In addition, the Thai experience is of great significance because it gives 32 indicators that have been worked out by the government of Thailand on the basic minimum needs to improve the quality of life, so that all technologies must be matched against those indicators. These indicators will be useful for all developing nations, especially those whose economy is strongly dependent upon agriculture. The 32 indicators are grouped under different topics such as food, shelter and environment, access to basic social services, security of life and property, and participation in the development process. Some of those indicators show that the introduction of foreign technology sometimes produces a negative effect. For example, pesticide technology produces many problems for the Thai farmer. There are many detailed studies on what the farmer can do in stimulating research on rice cultivars, new strains of rice useful for that country, on fertilizers, on pesticides, and on farm machinery, and what financial aids can be set in place.

Toxic wastes resulting from pesticides and attempts of foreign industry to transport toxic wastes to Thailand raise problems of the contrast between the advanced technology that produces these problems and the lack of technology at the level of prevention.

Environmental impact assessment is a notion that is gaining ground and has, in fact, received official recognition in certain areas, but here again the study points out (p. 127) that on intricate matters of pollution, where complicated measurements need to be conducted, the lack of appropriate equipment can produce difficulties. Environmental impact assessment is thus itself dependent on sophisticated technology.

An interesting aspect of this study, pertinent to all countries who are seeking to develop local and appropriate technology, is the fact that research and development (R&D) carried out by private firms in Thailand is at a minuscule level. R&D budgets of 105 companies surveyed were only 0.1% of sales. Personnel employed in R&D were only 0.21% of the total workforce (p. 136).

Thus, while appropriate technology is a well accepted concept, with a wide range of human rights benefits to be gained from it, there are many difficulties in the way of its adoption. These can be overcome only if they are systematically addressed. Agricultural economies in particular need to give these their systematic attention.

The Venezuelan study, conducted by Professor Edgardo Lander, emphasizes the fact that the march of science ought not to be viewed as inexorable, and that there is ample room for a choice to be exercised. It discusses a very special situation that arose in Venezuela as a result of the oil economy. Venezuela's oil reserves gave it a surplus budget. In the expectation of continuing oil revenues, a large number of new technologies of a very sophisticated and expensive nature were introduced and, once launched, depended on a continuing flow of that revenue for their continuation. Unfortunately, when oil revenues declined, the country found that it had all these highly sophisticated technologies in place, but did not have the wherewithal to keep them going. This raised a number of ecological problems, medical problems, etc., which are reviewed. In that context, the point is made that many developing countries, under the pressure of having to prove themselves, sometimes decide to launch a showpiece technology or project such as a huge engineering dam, or major industrial project, or even a nuclear reactor, which they feel will give them prestige in the eyes of the world. All goes well initially but, after some time, various problems surface, including ecological problems and problems of altered lifestyles and cultural patterns which create enormous problems for the future. It is said in the chapter that, at one stage, Mexico planned to have twenty nuclear reactors and Brazil planned to have eight. There were mega-development plans in the Amazon basin. All of this has been pruned in the light of later experience, but there is a very strong warning note in that chapter in relation to showpiece technologies and high profile projects.

The Venezuelan study makes the point (p. 47) that:

> As long as the Western model of science and technology is seen as equal to human progress and as necessarily positive in its impact on living conditions and human rights, there will be little public concern over these issues.

It cites as two instances which have raised awareness of these problems in Venezuela, the importation of 11,000 barrels of Italian toxic wastes which were left outdoors in Puerto Cabello by a company that wanted to dispose of them in Venezuelan territory. The incident led to a speech by the President of Venezuela in the General Assembly of the United Nations, condemning the deposit of toxic wastes by the industrialized world in the countries of the periphery (p. 71).

The second was the importation from the European Economic Community of 6,000 tons of meat contaminated by radioactivity from the Chernobyl nuclear accident. The importers used pressures to place the meat on the market, but public opinion did not give in (p. 71).

With such reawakened public consciousness comes a scrutiny of the adequacy of legal methods of control. The law's inadequacies are exposed here.

> The Venezuelan legal system, in spite of the number of norms that makes it up, presents empty areas and antagonisms. In effect, a large part of the laws allows transcendental elements of decision-making to escape their purview or, in many cases, permits a discretionary interpretation that favours the possibility of evading it or that legitimates and perpetuates situations contrary to those that have been announced for the environmental policy. The fact that there is no precision in the competence of each law, and the interference or superposition of attributions, further aggravate the problem. In many cases, neither the citizen nor the functionary can define, exactly, which law they must turn to, to determine the most convenient legal action or procedure.
>
> There are 80 laws and regulations and more than 400 resolutions, provisions, and specific decrees that, in one way or another, are related to environmental problems. In the face of each specific problem there practically arises a new norm which, in the majority of cases, adds to the tangle of those that already exist and function with the same old structure.[3]

The study warns against the tendency to resort to large-scale enterprises implying great investments, over modest proposals more in harmony with the needs of the country. One of the major conclusions of the Latin American study is stated by Professor Lander (p. 60) in the following terms:

> Given the cardinal and growing impact of scientific and technological decisions in shaping multiple spheres of contemporary life, and their powerful positive and negative impacts in terms of human rights, a genuine democratic control of the main scientific and technological decisions can be considered as a condition without which it is hardly possible to speak of a democratic society. Fundamental liberties and basic human rights are denied, and cultural freedom and self-reliance made impossible, if basic scientific and technological decisions are imposed in an authoritarian manner with little or no participation by those who are affected by these decisions.

The Venezuelan study of the making of technologically related decisions is thus of great practical importance to the planning of national economies, however prosperous they may appear to be at the time.

[3] Julio González Aguirre, "Definición, implicaciones y aspectos legales de la política ambiental en Venezuela" (Definition, Implications and Legal Aspects of Environmental Policy in Venezuela), in José Malavé, ed., *La gestión ambiental, impulso o freno al desarrollo?* (Environmental Management, Promotor or Retarder of Development?) (Ediciones IESA, Caracas, 1988), pp. 36–37.

From the problems of one species of over-commitment of a seemingly strong economy to technology, we pass now to another — the introduction of vast industrial and engineering schemes in order to hasten the transition of a comparatively weak economy into the technological age. Well-intentioned at the time of their introduction, they have turned into heavy liabilities whose maintenance drains the economies they were meant to uplift. They have become in this way a prolific source of human rights deprivations.

An illustrative example is the Nowa Huta Steel Project of Poland. The Polish study gives a very interesting case history of a great new project that was launched, known as the "Nowa Huta Steel Project". This project was launched in April and was conceived just prior to 1950. Construction work began in the early 1950s and the scheme went into operation in 1954. It was a huge manufacturing combine, which was to produce 5.5 million tons of steel per year. It generated 30,000 jobs by direct employment, and many tens of thousands more by indirect employment. To give you an idea of the magnitude of the project, to service the people employed in that factory, there were 50 nursery schools, 40 primary schools, 785 shops, 74 bars and restaurants. All that sprang up from the Nowa Huta project, and it looked as if it was the very answer to the problems of a country that needed development.

After some time, it was found that the effluent from the factory was polluting the Vistula river at the rate of 3 cubic metres per second. There were 200 million cubic metres of sewage per year; fifty thousand tons of particulate matter were emitted into the atmosphere every year; and four million tons of solid waste. The factory and the town covered some of the most fertile land which had been orchards and beautiful vegetable-producing areas, and the historic buildings of Cracow were deteriorating at an accelerating rate because of all this pollution.

Thus, this great new project created vast new problems. On the one hand, it seemed a magnificent achievement, but, on the other hand, after a few years, it began to show the other side of the coin. After about fifteen or twenty years of operation, the machinery became outmoded. Competitors in other parts of the world had raced ahead, and there wasn't the wherewithal in Poland to modernize the machinery. The result was that it was seriously contemplated as to whether the entire venture should be scrapped. To scrap the venture was a setback that the economy of Poland could not afford. This is an excellent case-study of a particular project, which may be of value to other planners.

The Polish study, which was conducted by Professor Pawel Bozyk, was worked on by seven research groups consisting of lawyers, economists and sociologists, both theorists and practitioners. It concludes that, although the restructuring process in the field of human rights can be short and radical, the restructuring process in the field of technological development requires time and planning and encounters many economic, cultural and social barriers. The Polish case-study is full of practical lessons on the dangers attending the adoption of enormous technological ventures, without adequate attention to the environmental, social and economic background in which they are to operate.

The African study, conducted by Professor T.B.G. Egziabher, deals with the entry of firearms into Africa, Ethiopia in particular, and shows how the whole social structure of Ethiopian society was shaken by the entry of firearms. It discusses thereafter the resulting instability in the country, how feudal leaders began to acquire firearms while the central state authority declined, how at some time it became almost a status symbol where every male's aspiration was to own a rifle, and every father would buy a rifle for his baby, even before clothing. Ultimately, there were many disturbances of social patterns and disturbances of peace and stability, and cottage industries were killed along with traditional skills. At a certain time traditional skills were adapted to make firearms, and they were also making bullets and gunpowder in Ethiopia. But, as modern technology became more and more sophisticated, the Ethiopian product could not hold its own, and that industry too died out.

The Ethiopian study shows a long-standing desire on the part of Ethiopian rulers, dating back as far as the sixteenth century, to acquire European technology. In that century, the reigning Emperor, realizing the power of European weapons technology, had written to the King of Spain requesting artisans who could make canons and gunpowder. In the nineteenth century, Emperor Theodros tried to establish a firearms industry. This preoccupation with weapons technology, combined with an uncritical importation of technological hardware of all descriptions, had the dual result of increasing the power of the feudal establishment, and smothering cottage industries. In the result, the development of science and industry in Ethiopia has been very unsatisfactory.

The study concludes that of all the European technologies introduced into Ethiopia, firearms have had the longest sustained impact, and have changed the country demographically, socially, politically, and economically.

This study is of importance in highlighting an aspect of Western technology which ran a similar course in many colonial territories, destroying traditional lifestyles, social protections, and indigenous industries in much the same manner.

The vast range of human rights considerations and problems that arise from modern medical advances is dealt with in the context of advanced methods of medical treatment in the Netherlands. This study, by Drs. Aart

Hendriks and Manfred Nowak, raises various questions such as the right to life, the right to equality, the right to health care, the right to privacy, and the right to found a family. All these are affected by *in vitro* fertilization, egg donation, artificial insemination, and sex selection. The Dutch study discusses the human rights aspects of all these. The screening of people for genetic defects, the screening of people for other defects that might be transmissible, the question of compulsory medical examinations, whether by the state or the employer, the question of informed consent where there is to be medical treatment — all of these issues are dealt with at a very sophisticated level in the Dutch study.

In discussing the effects of advanced medical genetics on human rights, the authors discuss the many benefits to human health resulting from these techniques and weigh against them the numerous risks and threats to human rights that result — including threats to the right to privacy, the right to mental and physical integrity, the right to freedom of movement and economic and social rights, and the right to found a family. To weigh the conflicting interests involved, precise knowledge is required of the effects, both positive and negative, on social life and psychological well-being. Each state's discretionary powers of interpreting legal provisions relative to such rights thus calls for more knowledge, for each right has to be separately considered. The increased possibilities for the human race to influence its own development cause concern; and amongst large sectors of Western European society, Nazi practices during the Second World War with gypsy twins, homosexuals, and Slavs account for a resistance against genetics (p. 268).

A carefully considered series of recommendations is evolved by the authors (pp. 273 *et seq.*), which include international co-operation, co-ordination, and exchange of information. It is stressed that the general public should be brought into the discussions and that democratic bodies should be set up to evaluate and monitor genetic research.

This is only a brief sampling of the rich range of human rights issues arising in this field.

* * *

Such are the results of this global research project which reveals that on every continent and in every country a variety of specific new issues is surfacing, each of which needs separate and individual study. We need the data to make the decisions, and the data will not emerge without concerted study. That study needs to take account of the historical, social and cultural nuances of each region and each country.

To conclude, I would say that there are many problems that arise from these studies. Problems of environmental concerns are a particularly important issue for the Third World. Especially, when it launches a new industry, it does not have the capital resources to equip that new industry with the environmental protections that are required today. In the developed world, there is the wherewithal to supply the environmental protections required by the product that is being manufactured. Where one is trying to introduce a new product from the drawing board stage, one has to build in the environmental safeguards from the commencement. This adds to the cost of the product and makes it less competitive, thus creating a practical problem that must be addressed. Environmental protections are vitally important. Development is also vitally important. Neither can be sacrificed. Where does one turn?

Other problems relate to the need for funds to stimulate research projects, the role of international monetary agencies which stipulate the adoption of certain technologies, and the role and codes of conduct of the multinational corporations. What restraints are necessary in relation to the technologies introduced by multinational agri-business which cause increased dependence on them? How may the dumping of shoddy goods and of industrial wastes be controlled?

Then, there is the question of urbanization which results from industrialization. We have a vicious circle, with the poor living in squalor in the cities. Governments, with the best of intentions, introduce industrialization to improve the lot of the poor. Some people are immediately benefited, but people in the villages, seeing that the townsfolk are prospering, drift into the town again and, just as a certain proportion of the townsfolk are provided with some employment, twice or thrice that number enter the city and add to the problems of the urban poor. So, it is a vicious circle. The more you industrialize, the more you attract population, and the more you attract population, the more you need to industrialize, and the more you industrialize, the more you attract. Another vicious circle arises in the context of the right to health and well-being, and the fundamental right to maintain a decent standard of living. This necessitates industrialization. Industrialization leads to pollution. Pollution damages health, as in certain towns of Brazil where the pollution is so extreme that people suffer permanent health damage for every day that they work or stay in the industrialized centre.

One other aspect that needs to be looked at is the armaments industry. Fortunately, it seems to be winding down in the world, but there was a time that it was estimated as consuming three trillion dollars a year. Three trillion dollars a year in a world of shortage and scarcity, where a hundred dollars can rescue a person from death through starvation! We claim not to have the wherewithal to feed the poor of the world, and yet we spend three trillion dollars on armaments. It could not be said that the earth does not have resources to feed its people. It is merely that its resources are not properly channelled. What can be done about that? Elsewhere, I have argued at some length the thesis that the armaments industry constitutes a blind spot in human rights and international law.[4] The small drug smuggler, who brings drugs into a city, is promptly arrested, charged and sent to jail, maybe for life. The arms manufacturer, on the other hand, holds arms fairs, with all the publicity of the marketplace, and the rich and powerful from all over the world come there as honoured guests. He is an honoured person selling weapons of death publicly, with the full backing and approval of the law. There must be something wrong with the law and human rights if the one activity is forbidden, and the other is openly permitted. There is a lacuna somewhere which we have to try to locate. Of course, arms are essential for certain purposes. They are necessary for defence and there are limited purposes for which arms are wanted. But there is a blind spot in the structure of human rights and international law when it comes to armaments.

Another area that needs to be considered is disaster relief technology. The world has been hit by cyclones in Bangladesh, famine in Africa, earthquakes in Georgia, volcanic eruptions in the Pacific, industrial accidents in India, nuclear meltdowns in Russia. These are all calamities that need some kind of disaster relief technology of an urgent nature that can swing into immediate action, on the basis of proved scientific research. We do not need to wait for the catastrophic event, to generate the means of giving the relief that might be demanded.

We find, as a result of these studies, that there are numerous areas that can be looked at. Perhaps, Mr. Rector, it may be that the UNU can take the lead. It commands high prestige as a centre of excellence for world-wide studies in the furtherance of peace. Peace is, after all, the prime object of the Charter of the United Nations. The University might be able to take up some of these issues by gathering together scientists, lawyers, theologians, philosophers, social workers and others, to give their combined wisdom to the evolution of guidelines that may be universally useful. If we do not attend to the problem, science and technology, unbridled and at large, can cause great damage to the human future.

If the swelling tide of human rights consciousness can function in step with the vigorous force of innovative technology to servc the human future, we would have harnessed two of the most potent intellectual movements

[4] "Traffic in Armaments: A Blind Spot in Human Rights and International Law", *Development Dialogue*, a Journal of the Dag Hammarskjöld Foundation, Sweden, 1987, Vol. 2, pp. 68 ff. See Chapter 11 of Volume 1.

ever seen, rather than watch in frustration while these two are on a collision course which negates them both. Wisdom in the choice of technology is essential to achieve this harmony. The studies in these volumes are intended to shed some light on this process. If these two forces — human rights and technology — can be harnessed to move in unison for the betterment of humanity, a radiant future could await humanity in the next century.

PART B

SPECIFIC PROBLEM AREAS

10. Computers*

INTRODUCTORY

Norbert Wiener, the father of cybernetics, once described the power of the computer through the analogy of a highly educated Greek slave in the service of a Roman slave owner. The slave owner required two qualities of his slave — intelligence and subservience. The two qualities are however in frequent tension, for each tends to negate the other. The more intelligent the slave, the less his tendency to subservience. The more sophisticated the computer, the less it may be amenable to control. It could eventually dominate society — if not by actually taking control, at least by inducing such total dependence on it as to compel society, its supposed master, to shape its lifestyle according to its dictates.

Lawyers have often used a well-known metaphor to describe concepts which lead in a direction we know not where. In the language of this metaphor, cybernetics is "a wild and unruly horse". When we are astride of it there is no knowing whither it will lead us. It is a horse that can run away from democracy if we give it free rein. But it is also a horse which can be harnessed in the cause of democracy, if we only knew how. Taming and harnessing this horse is one of the most difficult problems confronting our age. The hour is already well advanced, and even as the law tarries, the technology grows exponentially.

The computer is rapidly increasing society's dependence upon it, with the result that society becomes progressively more vulnerable to computer malfunction, whether accidental or deliberately induced, and to computer manipulation and white-collar crime. Computer monopolies of various forms can grant their holders informational and organizational power undreamed of

* Based upon a paper delivered at the Australian National Computer Conference, May, 1977 at Monash University, and published in *Law: The Threatened Peripheries*, *op. cit.*, pp. 239–262. It visualized dangers which could be perceived according to the state of computer development in the late 1970s. The explosive growth in computer power and technology since then only underlines the need for increased watchfulness as the computer steadily intrudes into areas of personal autonomy and democratic equality.

before, and the availability of computer technology to the affluent sector of global society can give it a dominance over the less affluent which can negate the concept of equality.

All this does not take account of developments in the realm of artificial intelligence which is a universe of discussion in itself. The ensuing discussion is premised on the assumption that, though the computer is taking over an increased volume of decision-making, it will not rule out a place for the human mind. For example, the computer can never substitute itself completely for the human judge, who must be the eventual decision-maker here as in other spheres of decision-making. Yet, within the limitations of this circumscribing assumption, the dangers are great. If, on the other hand, this assumption proves wrong and the computer acquires a complete decision-making capacity, and a self-preservation capacity of its own, the position would be infinitely more perilous. With the advent of true artificial intelligence, if it should ever come, we will have enormous problems, but those are not dealt with in this paper.

There has recently been much discussion regarding the impact of computers on privacy. This is but natural, as the integrity of the citizen's personality is one of the cornerstones of democracy, and the computer, almost more than any prior invention in history, has the power to marshal dossiers of information on every individual more complete than any that could have been compiled by the most powerful potentates of the past.

Yet, with all this, we can perhaps only foreshadow a fraction of the power of the computer, for its advance is such as to confound every forecast regarding its rate of growth.

At the same time, the computer's potential for assisting society is likewise enormous. The problem of the future will be to extract from it the maximum benefit it can confer, while at the same time minimizing its potential for harm. This task devolves heavily upon law and lawyers and is one of the principal challenges awaiting them in the decades ahead when the computer's grip upon society would have tightened beyond anything now thought possible.

THE COMPUTER IN LEGAL THEORY

Computers are such a powerful phenomenon on the legal and governmental scene today that legal theory must find a place for them in its scheme. How should legal theory view the advent of the computer age?

Society was once concerned primarily with biological survival. It organized itself on the basis of tribalism to meet this need, and tribalism contained within itself its own principles of social domination. When biological survival was sufficiently assured, people could turn their minds to other things — to wealth and industry and empire. These were the new imperatives. Each of them ordained a new way of life, and a new pattern of social organization. Each of them contained within itself a new principle of domination, and the instruments of that domination were wealth, the machine and the sword.

These were used to such good effect that they dominated all social organization. They were powerful instruments, and those who commanded them commanded society.

A new tool of domination is now emerging — information. Knowledge was always recognized as a source of power. The computer has now magnified the strength of informational power in much the same way as the gun and the cannon magnified physical power and gave their possessors dominion over the world. The world is perhaps on the way to giving those in command of the most sophisticated computer technology, the most extensive networks of communication and the most comprehensive data banks a position of dominance in the world. If down the centuries knowledge has been recognized as power, the tools for multiplying that knowledge several hundred fold, and marshalling it with several hundred times the speed and efficiency available before, must increase that power by many orders of magnitude.

In short, are we moving into an age dominated by information, which demands an adaptation of the law to meet this new challenge?

Moreover, just when wealth has been achieved in many societies, and the concept of empire is dead, other imperatives have come to the fore. Threats to human survival press in on every side — ecological, military, economic, technological. We must now come to terms with our environment or perish. Nothing will help us more along this road than the computer — the most powerful tool yet devised for the collation, classification, analysis and storage of information, wherewith alone we can face the challenge of the total environment. Are we passing from the age of biological survival through the stages of wealth and industry and empire into a new era in human history — an era where global survival has become our prime need, an era in which the computer has become our prime tool? This is another factor which greatly heightens the power of the computer, and our dependence upon it.

A COMMUNICATIONS-BASED SOCIETY

I shall start with the proposition that communication is one of the major activities of modern society. The centre needs to communicate with the peripheries, the peripheries with the centre, citizenry with bureaucracies, and bureaucracies with citizenry, interest groups with their membership and with the bureaucracy, candidates with their electorates, the electorates with their candidates. The more we "advance", the greater the volume of messages criss-crossing the fabric of a society, the greater the number of stimuli to be received, stored and assessed, the greater the number of action programs that need to be evolved and communicated. I need scarcely labour this point. It stands self-evident in its clarity.

Its implication for our topic is that a society based upon such an interlocking web of informational stimuli must grow towards increasing dependence on the computer for every step in the decision-making process. This immense mass of information cannot possibly be handled by the human memory and the human hand. No longer can it be manually stored and retrieved, presented as best it could be to a human mind, assessed, decided upon and disposed of.

At every stage we now meet the computer, handling with confident ease a million stimuli, classifying, assembling, storing and pointing to decisions for the humans who hold authority in any society. Without it the decision-maker is lost. A shifting and nebulous frontier marks off the province of the human decision-maker from the technological. That frontier is being constantly pushed back by an ever-expanding technology. Philosophers such as Jacques Ellul[1] carry this point much further and contend that, with the increasing complexity of technical problems, the decision which way the choice will fall among a multiplicity of alternatives, becomes very nearly automatic and the human decision-maker very nearly drops out of the picture.

We are thus caught up in a spiral. Cybernetics keeps multiplying the information available and the means for communicating it. With the multiplication of the information comes greater dependence on the computer for processing and retrieving it. As each new generation of computers emerges with greatly increased powers of communication and retrieval, we ascend into another loop of the spiral. The communications-based and computer-dependent society is trapped in its vortex.

THE COMPUTER AS DECISION-MAKER

Whoever has the ability to command and marshal this new plethora of information thus finds his or her power immeasurably increased. This must be so under any form of government, however democratic be its philosophy.

[1] Jacques Ellul, *The Technological Society*, Alfred A. Knopf, New York, 1964, p. 279. For an earlier study on this theme, see Siegfried Giedion's *Mechanization Takes Command*, Oxford, 1948.

Although computers can never be a total substitute for the human mind, they are already used as decision-making machines in the fields of industry and government. Co-ordinating a myriad pieces of information, they pour out decisions which regulate the movements of trains and assembly lines and aeroplanes. Political, economic and military decisions, depending on the co-ordination of a vast complex of facts, can likewise come out of the computer. We are told that a machine decision advised the Government of the United States against the use of atomic bombs in the Korean war and caused the retirement of General MacArthur.[2]

The "governing machine" of science fiction is not incapable of furnishing political decisions slanted in favour of those controlling it. Not without reason did Norbert Wiener warn that the new machine would "give new and potentially dangerous powers to the already powerful" and express a fear that a new fascism might seize the *machine à gouverner*.[3] Not without reason did the Communist Party in the U.S.S.R., as early as 1961, elevate cybernetics to a prominent position in its party programme and resolve that "Cybernetics, computers and control systems must assume an important position in industry, research, planning, accountancy, statistics and management".[4] When a computer, primed with information collected from a myriad sources, gives a decision based on its assessment of these factors, who is to contradict it except another which is similarly equipped? But as data become more concentrated in the data banks, there are fewer rivals and, indeed, there can be a monopoly situation in regard to certain types of data. That monopolist is then in growing control of the decision-making process.

COMPUTER MANIPULATION

Today's technology enables even a small group of technologists to hold an entire nation to ransom. On November 9, 1965 there was a total blackout arising from a power failure in the Eastern grid of the United States. This "illustrated the vulnerability of modern society to a breakdown of a single interlinking component in a complex electrical network".[5] Richard Falk has used this illustration to show the vulnerability of modern States to international disruption, which can easily be engineered owing to the inter-

[2] Karl Bednarik, *The Programmers, Elite of Automation*, Macdonald, London, 1967, p. 19.

[3] N. Wiener, *The Human Use of Human Beings*, Eyre & Spottiswoode, 1950, p. 214.

[4] Bednarik, *op. cit.*, p. 94.

[5] Richard A. Falk, *This Endangered Planet: Prospects and Proposals for Human Survival*, Vintage Books, 1971, p. 94.

connectedness of the networks of control and organization today. If that malfunctioning can be engineered, it can be engineered by a small group and can produce the same results. At every point, we encounter the growing power of those who control information and the need to control the controllers, as well as to protect them.

Such manipulations can occur whenever there is a vast network of information and control. Just as there are terrorists in the physical sense who, for reasons best known to themselves, are prepared to disrupt society, however great the suffering they may cause, there could well be similarly minded people in the field of computers who could hold the whole of society to ransom.[6]

Likewise, the manipulators could operate in the sphere of finance, upsetting markets, disrupting banking systems, breaking into private accounts, and transferring funds across the world. The law needs to be extremely watchful of such possibilities of white-collar crime.

In short, the tools could be available to break into a bank without touching its doors, to cripple a government without an army of saboteurs, or to ground a military system without lifting a weapon.

Hence it is to be remembered that groups of computer technologists, however small, are the repositories of very real power which can totally negate the functioning of democracy. A handful of computer personnel — or even a lone individual — will, if so minded, be able in that foreseeable future to hold a whole community to ransom.[7] The self-discipline, ethical codes and regulatory practices of the computer profession are one of our major safeguards against this threat of the future, and I would suggest that these aspects be viewed as problems of urgency right now.[8]

[6] For a variety of such possibilities, as anticipated in 1973, see Gerald McKnight, *Computer Crime*, Michael Joseph Ltd., 1973. The possibilities contemplated and illustrated include the hijacking of computers and holding them to ransom, the breaking of computer codes, the deliberate disruption of computer systems, the physical disruption of key data bases, organized slanting of information, and conspiracies of silence.

[7] The power of the computer professional in the 1990s has been summarized in the following terms: "As computers become more and more a part of our society, and as we become more and more dependent upon computer systems, we become more and more dependent upon computer *professionals*. Within organizations, computer professionals exercise power in how and for whom they design systems. As computing becomes an integral part of an organization, organizations become more dependent on the computer professional who maintains the computers. As our society becomes more dependent on computers, we all come to rely on computer professionals to ensure the smooth functioning of our social institutions." (Deborah C. Johnson, *Computer Ethics*, 2nd ed., 1994, p. 162.)

[8] Since 1976 computer expertise has progressed far beyond a group of professional specialists and, especially with the younger generation, is widely diffused through the entire

CONSOLIDATION OF THE *STATUS QUO*

Computers have played an important political role in another way to which our attention has recently been drawn by Joseph Weiszenbaum in his seminal work, *Computer Power and Human Reason.*[9] Weiszenbaum there observes that, in the earlier years after the war, the American military, commercial and bureaucratic machine had grown to such proportions that the clerical work involved in servicing these enormous structures would have required armies of civilians far beyond the resources of the American nation to supply. The natural consequence of this would have been the winding down of the enormous processes of expansion characteristic of the American system. Inevitably this would have led to a similar style of managing the American scene, a style more in consonance with availability of human and earth resources. Ways of life dependent upon continual growth and expansion would thus have been thwarted.

However, precisely at this stage, when further expansion was about to be constrained by limitations of available human resources, the computer descended on the scene. With all its wizardry in handling clerical and calculating functions, it made short shrift of work which contingents of human workers could not handle. Far from the processes of growth being arrested, the computer now produced a situation where more and more growth was called for. It made child's play of existing work and continually demanded more.

Viewed politically, this had the result of consolidating for the foreseeable future established life styles based upon growth and expansion. The one opportunity thrown up by the historical process of striking a mean between available resources and development was thus lost. Existing patterns of continuing expansion of the military establishment, the bureaucracy, the commercial sector and all else became entrenched and consolidated. The computer has thus played a significant role in increasing the power of the establishment, leading capitalism into an expansionist phase unthinkable before its advent, and eliminating competition from all that was small and consequently "inefficient".

community. Where nearly everyone in society dabbles in computers, the problems envisaged in this section have grown enormously more acute, and become even more difficult to control.

9 Joseph Weiszenbaum, *Computer Power and Human Reason: From Judgment to Calculation*, Penguin, 1984.

A NEW DIMENSION IN POLITICS

As already observed, the computer marks the commencement of a new age — an age ruled not by physical power but by information. Hitherto the power of technology has been measured in terms of force. The thinkers of this century have often drawn attention to the manner in which the force available to humanity has kept growing exponentially. Henry Adams, the philosopher historian, warned the world in 1905 that "it is quite sure according to my score of ratios and curves that, at the accelerated rate of progression since 1600, it will not need another century or half century to turn thought upside down. *Law in that case would disappear as theory or* a priori *principle and give place to force.*"[10]

But with the advent of the computer we face a new factor — information and the ability to manipulate it rather than naked power. It can be many times more dangerous than naked power, because this sort of power is much easier to manoeuvre and needs no deployment of armaments or personnel. It is a new dimension in politics — a mechanization of the means for the storage and dissemination of information on such a scale that it can mould our society and fashion our thinking. Here is a new sort of power, for which the truest analogy is possibly the power that religion once enjoyed, of moulding attitudes and habits. Such power the computer has now increased beyond the fondest dreams of the opinion moulders of the past.

The impact of such power, if uncontrolled, upon the basic principles of democracy is self-evident.

No one likes to argue with a computer. Indeed, as a detailed study points out,[11] it is possible for a hoax to be perpetrated on 99.99% of the population, at least temporarily. The surest way to silence opposition is to invoke the argument that the computer has pronounced in favour of a certain course of action. It will be all too easy for those in favour of a scheme to put out computer readings in its support and thereby put a practical end to debate. No doubt the reply to this is a reply in kind with an equal marshalling of facts and figures — but this may not be practically possible. The basic policy debate can itself be slanted by the computer unless we know how its programme has been prepared. One of the eternal questions of politics is whether the process of deception can be practised on a large scale in order to

[10] See, for a discussion of Adams' letter, Lewis Mumford, *The Pentagon of Power*, Secker & Warburg, London, 1964, p. 230 *et seq.*

[11] Richard R. Fagen, *Politics and Communication*, Little Brown, 1966, p. 44. If this observation could be made thirty years ago, the phenomenal growth of the computer in the interim must render it worthy of the closest examination.

induce a general acceptance of the policies of a government. The computer makes this immeasurably easier than ever before.

Marshall McLuhan[12] and others have plotted for us their prognoses of the direction in which this power will take society. Though everyone may not agree with their analyses of the mass media, such writers have given us new insights into the communication technologies. They have shown us how these technologies can create an environment of thought and opinion which becomes so all-pervading as to numb the senses. Humanity, after the electronic technologies, has moulded for itself a new environment and thereby remoulded itself.

If we are concerned with the problem "whither democracy?", we must concern ourselves with this new power to mould and condition both the social environment and human beings themselves. It is necessary to ask who exercises this power and by what authority.

THE NECESSARY INFRASTRUCTURE FOR COMPUTERIZATION

A grave problem arises in regard to the distribution of computer power, for computer power requires a certain infrastructure — education, the hardware, the software, data banks, electricity, telephone services, and the like. These are taken for granted in the industrialized world. They are as yet non-existent for vast sectors of the global community.

A potent new factor thus rears its head in the distribution of global power. It can operate so as to entrench the economic advantages enjoyed by the industrialized world in a manner which the developing world will find itself increasingly unable to redress. Likewise, it can entrench media power and this means the power to influence the formation of opinion on global issues. The balance of economic, media, and indeed other forms of power could thus be permanently enthroned unless a concerted effort is made now to spread the distribution of computer expertise and the infrastructure which makes widespread use of computers possible.

The question of the free flow of technological information is discussed in Chapter 7 of this book, and that is yet another aspect of the informational imbalance which the reign of computerization can produce. Technological knowledge is the key to new technology, and those who have access to such knowledge — already at an advantage over others — can increase and consolidate that knowledge to an extent that renders competition impossible.

[12] *Understanding Media: The Extensions of Man,* McGraw Hill, 1967; with Quentin Fiore: *The Medium is the Massage,* Bantam Books, N. Y., 1968.

COMPUTERS AND FREE SPEECH

The corollary of what has just been observed is that there could be serious infringements of the right of free speech and communication. This follows from the fact that those who have the computer power and the necessary linkages, data banks and infrastructure would be able to propagate their news and views to such an extent as to drown out the voices of those who do not have this advantage. In the name of their own right to freedom of expression, they would in effect be smothering the freedom of expression of others who are not so advantaged.

This becomes doubly so because the great media organizations will, as indeed they already have, establish a linkage with computer power. With their great resources, they will have computer power in its most sophisticated form. This means they will have both an unrivalled access to information and an unrivalled power to disseminate that information. With this greatly heightened power, the greater entities will swallow up the less and, where they are not so swallowed up, can push them to the wall through the informational imbalance.

With the enhancement of computer power, the right to freedom of expression will need to be closely watched.

AN INFORMATION TYRANNY

We hear from time to time of the latest advances in electronic systems of recording information of practically every known description. We know already that every international air trip we have undertaken in the last few years is recorded in a data bank with capabilities of retrieval at an instant's notice. Computerized cards are already in common use as a modern form of "open sesame" for entry into protected premises. The user's identification data on the card can be simply stored for retrieval whenever desired in the form of a complete record of all the times and dates of his or her entries and departures from those premises. Extend this operation but one step further by making such cards available to every citizen, and the decreasing cost of computerization, referred to elsewhere, will make it possible in a not too distant future to record on trams and trains and buses the comings and goings of every individual in a society. Put in for good measure a few check points at some important street junctions, and surveillance is complete. "1984" is upon us.[13]

But for legal safeguards, it is now possible for many government departments and bureaux to maintain a central data bank into which they feed all the information concerning a person, which may have been recorded in revenue files, health files, educational files, police files, taxation files, insurance files, and the like. In the result, a complete dossier of information can be built up to an extent unknown before. This information, if available on tap, means of course that every detail of a person's life as so recorded, whether pertaining to a matter which attracts confidentiality or not, will be instantly available, especially in a state where safeguards against the use of this kind of information are poor or do not exist. Based upon this information, it will be possible to dictate lifestyles and mould the habits of entire populations by reason of the ease with which deviations from the norms of behaviour are spotted, and by reason of the excellence of the surveillance systems that modern sophisticated technology will make available.

We read also of new devices as fine as a hair or as thin as a sheet of paper which can transmit conversations for recording. These can be wallpapered into any living room and will from there transmit for recording, storage and surveillance any conversation that needs to be monitored. Likewise, technology enables us to bounce a laser beam off a window-pane from a considerable distance and record conversations that occur within the room. The computer's seemingly unlimited power of storage and analysis of information makes possible a permanent record of all this data for immediate retrieval.

In these various ways modern technology may grow upon society unobserved and insidiously, to result in a concealed tyranny more difficult to guard against than the open tyrannies of the past.

All this, it is to be remembered, is set in an era of growing executive and bureaucratic interference with citizen activity — an interference which was occurring even without the assistance of such technological aids. Grant these same authorities the near-magical powers of computerization and you pave the way to an information tyranny that cripples individuality — unless through awareness and fore-planning we interpose some basic safeguards.

[13] *1984* is the title of the well known work by George Orwell in which he predicted many of the technological advances made today, especially in the field of information technology. "Big Brother is watching you!"

COMPUTER MONOPOLIES

This is a virtually unknown field, but one can only anticipate that the present rate of progress will lead to ever greater sophistication in every aspect of the new technology. This means more sophisticated machines and more sophisticated programmes for operating them. All these new ideas will carry with them the protections of intellectual property. Does this mean that there can be a consolidation of computer technology in the hands of a few who would be able to lay down their terms and dictate to others how this power is to be used? It is in this fashion that various forms of monopolies have arisen in the past and conferred untold power on those who possess them. With computers a whole new area of possible monopolistic territory opens up for increased watchfulness in the cause of democratic principles of equality and freedom.

The costs of research and development in the computer industry are particularly high, with research spending running to thousands of millions of dollars.[14] Few can compete in such a field, thus rendering the entrance fee into this specialized area of manufacture prohibitive. Whether in the hardware industry that makes the computers, or the software industry that enables them to run, a select preserve of near-monopolists is created. To what extent available options for processing and programming information will thus be foreclosed none can foretell. What effort this will have on liberty is an even more crucial subject for speculation.

THE RIGHT OF ASSOCIATIONAL PRIVACY

The computer opens up another field of scrutiny available to governmental agencies which was unavailable before.

Through computer scanning of widely scattered data, it is possible for a computer to detect linkages and associations between persons and/or organizations which it might otherwise have been impossible to notice. For example, the scanning of bank accounts, or the computerized scanning of mail, or a computerized register of telephone calls can show up links and patterns of association between individuals among each other or between individuals and organizations.

Arthur Miller refers[15] to a New Jersey case where the state attorney general sent to local officials a memorandum on "Civil Disorders" calling for the creation of a police intelligence system that would enable law enforce-

[14] These were estimates in the 1970s — see Adriani Buzzati-Traverso, *The Scientific Enterprise Today and Tomorrow*, UNESCO, 1977, p. 361.

[15] *The Assault on Privacy*, Signet Books, 1971, p. 215.

ment authorities to keep a tab on individuals and organizations considered to be potential trouble makers. The information to be recorded was to cover not merely numerous details such as physical description and credit background, but also "membership, affiliation and/or status with organizations and groups".[16]

The New Jersey branch of a national civil rights organization sought to have this intelligence system declared unconstitutional, and the trial court viewed such a centralized information system as having a "chilling effect" on the free expression of political views and on the freedom of association. The trial court prohibited the state from compiling this information. But what Miller describes as judicial myopia resulted in a reversal of this judgment by the New Jersey Supreme Court on the ground that it would be folly to deprive the government of its power to deal with the tyranny of lawlessness.[17]

The computer's power to classify fingerprints and handwriting has already made it a valuable tool for police departments. In Canada a new technique has already grown up of classifying the "scents" of people, for each individual has a "scent" peculiar to that individual, as distinctive as handwriting.

When all this information is stored and there is, even in limited circumstances, a transfer of information among governmental agencies, we are indeed in deep waters, for we shall not know whether or when we are being watched by unseen eyes. We will need to be on continuous guard not only against the governmental snooper, but also against our associates, for suspicion is contagious and inhibitive of free association.

THE PSYCHOLOGY OF CONTINUOUS SURVEILLANCE

Continuous surveillance, one of the standard instruments of totalitarian rule, breeds a psychology of its own. This is a prime factor to be watched with the growth of computer power.

The uncertainty as to whether one's conduct and conversation are the subject of investigation can have the effect of anaesthetizing public opinion against the natural and instinctive feeling of protest which would have been aroused had it been definitely known that one was under such surveillance. By degrees the public resistance to this phenomenon becomes undermined and a greater degree of interference tolerated than might earlier have been

16 *Anderson* v. *Sills* 106 N. J. Super. 545, 256 A. 2d. 298 (1969).

17 *Anderson* v. *Sills rev'd* 56 N. J. 210, 265 A.2d. 678 (1970).

countenanced. And as resistance decreases, so the practice grows, until it soon reaches proportions earlier thought unthinkable.

We have a graphic illustration of this from Dr. Jerome B. Wiesner, President of the Massachusetts Institute of Technology, and formerly Science Adviser to President Kennedy, who tells us that he participated in anti-Vietnam War demonstrations and marched in them.[18] He wondered thereafter whether he was being watched as a threat to, or as a dangerous enemy of, the State, asking himself the question whether he was under continuous surveillance. His frank answer was "I don't know", for he doubted that anyone was aware of the full extent of the surveillance and information collection activities that go on in the United States.

A consequence of this is that many persons operate on the assumption that it may be that they are being monitored. Dr. Wiesner has stated that he himself has not permitted this possibility to make him feel inhibited in his movements or conduct, as he has great confidence in the basic integrity of the safeguards built into the administrative and judicial system of the country. However, the average citizen, not steeled by the knowledge and confidence enjoyed by Dr. Wiesner, may well suffer much uneasiness in consequence of an uncertainty as to whether he or she is being watched. Indeed many students could quite reasonably feel themselves inhibited from participating in political activities of various kinds, as Dr. Wiesner observes, for fear that at some future date it might possibly cost them a job or make job clearance difficult to obtain. Such a fear may attach not merely to participation in movements involving open protest or violence, but also to participation in seminars and study groups that might indulge in a serious questioning of governmental policies.

SYSTEMS PLANNING

The computer brings within the range of possibility the totally controlled environment. Systems planners are no longer content to plan within the existing environment. They plan the environment itself. The concept of the engineered environment is already with us and is seen in plans for designing entire urban areas, master plans of traffic control, and massive irrigation schemes. The environment itself can be altered to suit the design, where formerly the design had necessarily to be tailored to suit the environment. The computer assists the systems designer to keep a finger on the multiple control factors which must all be syncromeshed into a smoothly working overall system — a concept inconceivable before the computer.

[18] *Law and Computer Technology*, March-April 1972, p. 44.

When such a system is set in motion, dependence on the computer is nearly total. Without the computer monitoring every move, the entire system breaks down. As William Kuhns observes, the systems engineer is like a juggler attempting to keep six balls in the air at the same time.[19] Should any one of them fall down, the whole scheme falls to pieces.

There is in this a twin danger.

The first is a near total dependence on computer technology — the *sine qua non* for the continued working of such a system. Once committed to it, one is committed also in increasing measure to dependence on the computer and those who work it.

The other is that, once such a systems plan has been accepted and is in the process of implementation, the scope for individual freewill is naturally circumscribed within the four corners of that system. Such overall schemes often call for rigorous conformities, for the master plan requires co-ordination, if nothing else. It will not brook individual divergences. It is dictatorial. It will regiment its society in a straitjacket of iron.

Authority will invoke, in support of this regimentation, the immense public expenditure already committed to the scheme. All deviance becomes and will be treated as anti-social. As technology progresses, the number and the scope of systems thus planned will increase, and the area of operation of individual free will must correspondingly decline.

Today, more than ever, there is therefore the need for the full implications of a systems plan to be discussed before a given society is committed to it. Such discussion may often involve some basics of computer technology.

It is for such reasons that the Secretary General of the United Nations in his report to the Commission on Human Rights of January 9, 1974[20] has referred to the need to give the ordinary citizen an understanding of computer methods — at least the elements of information about programming — so that he or she will not be at the mercy of the expert.

ASSISTING THE "FRAME-UP"

One of the weapons of political assassination which has been honed to a fine perfection in this century is the "frame-up". It is a great aid to demolishing one's opponents, to demonstrate to the public that they have been engaged in anti-social or unpatriotic activity, or in socially deviant conduct. A prime means of doing so is through surveillance and the misuse of private information. This has already been dealt with elsewhere in our discussion.

[19] William Kuhns, *The Post Industrial Prophets*, Harper & Row, 1971, p. 209.

[20] E/CN/4/1142/Add. 1. of 9.1.74.

Another is the use of technology to fabricate incriminating conversations or speeches in the very voice of the person sought to be attacked. Technological re-editing has opened up strange new possibilities of using prior recorded speeches and conversations as sources of words which, when strung together in a different order, produce an altogether different speech. Experiments in the United States have shown how speeches professing the deepest loyalty to the United States can thereby be transformed into the most treasonable, with no apparent loss of authenticity. Computerization will greatly facilitate the joining together of the pieces in the optimum combinations, whereas the human juggler with words would require many experiments and still not be able to reach the desired result.

With such methods at their disposal, who is to stay the hand of a dictator anxious to make mincemeat of his political opponents? Nor do we need a dictator for this purpose. A well-organized democratic political party can do likewise. In an age which has seen Watergate with all its misuse of technology, who is to say that the ethics of political parties and leaders in democracies will halt at such abuses?

Whether the technology will emerge which will check the authenticity of each tape before it is put out for public consumption, we do not know. But whatever be the position in this regard, it is clear that it can well produce a lack of credence concerning public utterances over the electronic media. The credibility gap receives a new dimension, the business of government an added impediment, the manipulators of power a potent weapon.

THE INTERLOCKING OF BUREAUCRATIC AND CORPORATE POWER

Today we face in all democracies an interlocking complex of bureaucratic-cum-corporate authority. This presents a solid phalanx of "establishment" power standing four-square against the forces that might assail it. Each of these empires — the bureaucratic and the corporate — is powerful enough in its own right to keep most challengers at bay. But when they combine they are nearly irresistible. The reality — that the combination is daily growing and being cemented — is largely concealed from a public who would else see in it a threat to the basic principle of democratic rule. In an age when information is stored and transferable in vast quantities this is portentous.

The American political scientist, C. Wright Mills, put this rather strikingly when he percipiently observed many years ago: "Across the bargaining tables of power the bureaucracies of business and government face one another and under the table their myriad feet are interlocked in wonderfully complex ways".[21] Throughout Britain, the U.S.A., France, Germany, in fact, through all the developed countries, this phenomenon is growing. It can seriously affect the right of the ordinary citizen if it grows much further. The principle of equal competition in trade can become a total myth. The democratic principle of responsibility for one's decisions can also be impaired, for the true decision-maker, not infrequently, is completely concealed from view.

Apart from this interlocking, there is also a constant drift from the public service into the ranks of corporate business. This drift not only carries into the ranks of corporate business the secrecy and expertise which the departing bureaucrats have acquired in the course of their official duties. It also stands them in good stead when it comes to questions of bargaining with government. The actual practical process of bargaining with government is in effect bargaining between corporate officialdom and bureaucratic officialdom and, if the personnel manning the two hierarchies tends to be interchangeable, the apparent bargaining can turn out to be a mutual accommodation between friends.[22]

Where this danger was formerly great enough, it will in the future be immensely facilitated by the computer. A briefcase can now remove to the corporate world the information that formerly needed dozens of cabinets to accommodate. Moreover, those who move across will also know the computer personnel who guard this information, and the computer reels wherein it is stored. It is the simplest of operations to tap these resources when one has these contacts and this knowledge. It will require the highest standards of integrity to resist the temptation to use this knowledge.[23]

Not all the movement has been at these high levels. It is important also to notice that many an aspirant to a position in the corporate world begins his career in the service of a government department and spends his time acquiring information and expertise before he receives the call from the private sector. When the call comes, he answers it armed with an informational repertoire which is invaluable to his future employer. Thus begins another bridge-building activity, unseen, insidious and undemocratic.

[21] C. Wright Mills, *White Collar: The American Middle Classes*, Oxford University Press, New York, 1950–51, p. 71.

[22] See, also, Sol Ensell, "The Top Men", *Outlook*, Vol. 4, No. 6, December 1960, p. 6 — "everywhere there are footbridges joining the spheres of politics, the civil service, banking, industry, the financial press and so forth".

[23] In regard to the Australian scene, see John Playford, *Neo-Capitalism in Australia*, Monograph Series No. 1, Arena Publications, 1969. The numerous crossings from the ranks of high bureaucracy to the ranks of the corporate boardroom are there documented in detail.

The fundamental incompatibility between this state of affairs and liberal democratic theory is self-evident. If, in the future, the giant corporation grows to new dimensions of power, annexing to itself information which is confidential to the public sector, the gulf between democratic theory and social reality will widen correspondingly.

THE IMPACT OF COMPUTER CRIME ON DEMOCRATIC GOVERNMENT

We are all aware of the growing importance of computer crime — the latest category of white collar crime, difficult to track down, immeasurably expensive, and surpassing most other categories of crime in its potential for social damage.

The notion of larceny of computer information is today gaining prominence and, in the context of democratic government, this is portentous. When classified information is the subject of larceny, not only private safety but also public security is in peril. The purloining of information in this way is already occurring in the commercial world, and we have no assurance that it will stop in the commercial world and confine itself to commercial secrets.[24] It must naturally extend to official secrets and classified information.

There are no doubt security devices in existence today by which it is possible for certain information to be placed beyond the reach of computers connected with a central data bank containing them. The computers so connected, as for example the computers of stockbrokers connected to the data bank of the Stock Exchange, can each be fitted with certain restrictive devices which prevent information of a classified nature from being accessible to such computer users. It would appear, however, that it is not impossible for a "patch" to be placed upon the connection which such a computer user has with the data bank so that the barrier to certain classes of information which are denied to him can be lifted. I gather that such a "patch" can be placed by the simple expedient of enlisting the co-operation of a worker employed within the data bank who for a consideration — perhaps running to several thousands of dollars, or perhaps of a more trifling nature, or perhaps for social or personal reasons — may be prepared to put in such a "patch" at some time when he is programming the machine or when he has access to it. It will be immensely difficult to detect later and the particular subscriber who has this patch upon his connection with the central computer

[24] For an impressive documentation of the cases that had already arisen by 1973, see Gerald McKnight, *Computer Crime*, *supra*.

would then be receiving classified information without any of his competitors or the operators of the data bank being any the wiser.[25]

CODES OF CONDUCT FOR COMPUTER PROFESSIONALS

A code of conduct for computer programmers has indeed been carefully worked out with a deep sense of responsibility on the part of the computer profession. This is a substantial protective factor, and the computer profession is to be greatly commended for the concern it has shown for its ethical duties — a concern exceeding that of many other groups of technologists.[26] Yet, the profession has grown very considerably, and numerous persons working in the computer field are not necessarily members of the governing professional bodies. There are today in Australia alone thousands of computer operators and programmers, and in countries like the United States, those who have access to computers and computer technology may well number half a million. It will be extremely difficult in such a vast group of people to preserve and enforce high standards of ethical conduct, despite the dedication of the professional bodies as such. Moreover sanctions can only be applied after the offender is found, but the process of tracking down the offender would itself involve a lengthy inquiry, and much damage will have been done by then.

In an age which has seen such phenomena as Watergate, it is not difficult to conceive of governments themselves using their powers or their influence to extract, from computers and data banks, information of a classified and personal nature, which they consider would be valuable to them for their purposes. Already we have reports that government agencies in some countries have surveillance tabs on several millions of citizens. The extent to which privacy will be preserved in regard to this information is a matter which must urgently call for attention in an age when computer crime is so

[25] This paragraph refers to technology that was known in the 1970s. Since then, protective devices have been enormously developed, but so, likewise, has been the technology enabling perforations of these screens of protection.

[26] Since the date of this lecture, considerable progress has been made in elaborating and refining these codes. For example, the Association for Computing Machinery (ACM) in the U.S. has formulated a Code consisting of 24 imperatives, including general moral imperatives such as contributing to society and human well-being, and avoiding harm to others; specific professional responsibilities such as improving public understanding and accessing computer resources only when authorized to do so; and leadership imperatives such as ensuring that users and others affected by a system have their needs clearly articulated during the assessment and design of their requirements. (See Deborah G. Johnson, *Computer Ethics*, *supra*, Appendix: "Codes of Computer Ethics".)

much on the increase that it is in fact marching ahead of the means for its detection.

AN AID TO GIANTISM

One of the phenomena of this age which threatens to swamp individual liberty and convert us all into cyphers is the phenomenon of giantism.[27] Increasingly, we are realizing how the cost of an operation is reduced per unit, the larger its scale. In the pursuit of "efficiency", we thus chase after bigness in our conglomerates, our bureaucracies and our cities.

Never did giantism have such an ally as the computer. It solves the organizational problems that bedevilled the early entrepreneurs and enables the captains of industry and government to keep the minutest tabs on operations upon a global scale. In the vastness of organization, in the conformity to rule and formula and programme, the individual finds that his personality as a human being — which mattered much in the small business or village — counts for nothing. Massive surveillance apart, the mere fact of massive organization reduces the individual to a faceless cypher and smothers human rights. In a hire-and-fire society, dominated by the concept of bigness, the individual is expendable from an organizational point of view.[28]

What is more, the expendability grows as the computer shows ways of reducing employment. The employer holds the whip hand and in a vast organization the threat of discontinuance must loom ever larger as a deterrent to employees who know that if they fail to please, even in the most minor regard, they will be the first to go. There is in this an inevitable denigration of human personality.

It may be said that a sense of fair play will prevent these abuses of power. Legal experience has shown, however, that power tends generally to be exercised, and unrestrained power to be abused. For generations the law has seen how bureaucratic power needs to be restrained lest bureaucrats, swollen with authority, trample on human rights. In all spheres of human activity this principle holds sway. The computer increases the scope for its operation.

With the growth of the welfare state and the billions of payments to be made or withheld annually, and with the computer to aid them, bureaucracies have grown phenomenally in power. In the social security field alone, tens of millions of cheques are made out every month in the United States. Medicare

[27] See the author's, *The Law in Crisis: Bridges of Understanding*, Capemoss, London, 1975, pp. 43–44.

[28] Laski, *Reflections on the Revolutions of our Time*, George Allen & Unwin, 1943, p. 343.

payments, agricultural subsidies, education allowances — all these bring the annual total to billions. Australia, proportionately, cannot be far different. The borderline cases invite and involve an adjudication. The bureaucracy are the judges. They decide quantitatively many thousands more of justiciable issues than the judiciary. With increased computerization this power will grow.

In a nation-wide radio broadcast in 1974,[29] President Nixon drew attention to the awesome potential of the computer for harm as well as good, and pointed out how government bureaucracies, though well intentioned, seem to thrive on collecting additional information. The citizen, he said, was in many cases not even aware what information was held on record and if he wanted to find out, he had nowhere to turn. Computer banks held information on 150 million American citizens, and in these circumstances he launched a high-powered inquiry into the way in which the Federal Government collected information on people and how that information was protected. "Adequate safeguards must always stand watch," he said, "so that man remains the master and never becomes the victim of the computer".

THE PROBLEM OF LIMITS

Here, as in so many other fields of computer activity, we face the problem which all technology — and indeed commerce — presents to the modern world. That which is intrinsically useful and good in moderation can become, when carried to excess, a millstone around our necks, a bane which we would like to wish away. Modern technology has pushed us from the simple genetic experiment to the structuring of microbial genes whose ultimate effect on humanity no person can predict; from the chemistry of poisons to the stage where poisons potent enough to decimate humanity can be contained within a teaspoon; from the handy internal combustion engine to the atmospheric polluter of all the great cities of the globe. So it can be with computers. On the one hand, they can be extremely beneficial to society and to their users but, on the other, too large a proliferation of computer technology and its application to every detail of life can produce a situation wherein the damage caused is more extensive than the resulting benefits.

For these reasons, American writers such as Dr. Wiesner, advocate a rigorous recommendation to Congress to take whatever steps are necessary to bring the Bill of Rights up-to-date. The Bill of Rights was drafted, they point out, in a simpler age when the concepts enshrined therein were adequate to protect the citizen in his or her relation to the modern state. There was no

[29] Presidential Documents, Richard Nixon, February 23, 1974.

need for protection against the sophisticated devices that have now proved to be available in restriction of individual privacy. The law is outmoded if it relies on two hundred year-old concepts and formulas to meet the futuristic problems of today.

COMPUTER ANALYSES AND THE ELECTORATE

Computer analyses of electorates have now become commonplace in regard to the more important elections. The opinion polls tell us and the candidates how they are faring in the public esteem. Those under observation must naturally adjust their stance accordingly.

This kind of direct feedback from electorate to candidate is both more comprehensive and more immediate than was considered feasible before the computer age. This has desirable features and is in a sense an advance.

But here too lurks danger, for if one can tailor one's policy to meet the opinion polls, the candidate with resources sufficient to buy more of this service has the edge over his or her opponents. Millions of dollars are today being spent on computer analyses of electorates. Here is another opening for the utilization of wealth for the purchase of political power, and this needs to be watched.

* * *

From a survey of the negative aspects, let us pass now to the brighter side and view the great potential of the computer as an aid to democratic government.

SPLINTERING THE MASS

There has been considerable discussion in political theory of the "mass mind" notion propagated by Marshall McLuhan. Debate has waxed hot on the extent to which the stamp of uniformity will be impressed upon us all by the mass media with their undoubted power to influence — if not to shape — our attitudes, our reactions and our habits.

Now, into that debate, there enters increasingly the universality and the potency of the computer.

Might there not be great uses for the computer in splintering the fused mass? The great social movements of the past — the Enlightenment, the French Revolution and the Industrial Revolution — rubbed out the social and occupational groupings of pre-eighteenth century society and flattened out the "estates" to a level of rigid uniformity. In the language of Burke, the zeal for equality in the abstract had the result of wiping the slate clean of feudal, guild, church and other groupings, thereby leaving the individual defenceless and alone when confronted by the power of an all-encompassing state.

The fuller exchange of information, likely to result in the future from the cheapening of computer technology, can produce an opposite tendency by enabling those with similar interests to group together. Large numbers of people with common interests have hitherto been prevented from pooling their resources and knowledge by lack of the means of communication. Instant communication, which will soon be brought within the reach of even the average pocket, will promote the cohesion of these people into interest groups, much more "together" in a sense not possible before. Across the length and breadth of a nation, if not of the world, those with common interests can "hook up" with each other, pooling their knowledge and experience for immediate use in their common sphere of interest.

This can result in a proliferation of groups, splintering up the fused mass into a new series of a myriad "estates of the realm". There is a great contribution the computer can make to this end and the new technology must be harnessed to the needs of the small-scale operator and not merely those of the giant user.

Much hope in this direction comes from the dramatic drop in computer cost over the last 15 years. In 1977, a microcomputer costing less than $1,000 is claimed to have performance capabilities comparable to those of computer systems which in the early 1960s cost in the vicinity of a quarter of a million dollars. Here is a cost drop of two orders of magnitude in two decades. If a similar drop should occur in the next decade, we may conceivably have such computers at a price range well within almost anybody's budget — making co-ordination of interest groups possible on a scale never possible before.

ENDING ISOLATIONISM

Lack of communication between similarly-minded persons has been one of the greatest obstacles in the path of democracy in the past. Physical isolationism imposed by distance, combined with informational isolationism imposed by ignorance, and political isolationism imposed by governmental systems and rulers, meant that individuals lacked the force which could come from a combination of their wills.

The computer could be the most powerful means available in history for breaking down such isolation. The declining cost of computers brings this ever closer to possibility. Just as radio transmission broke down some of the isolation of resistance movements during World War I, computer intercommunication may defeat the autocracies of the future.

Moreover, intercommunication between persons of similar interests, however far apart they may be physically, will be further strengthened by the ability to pierce through the screens in regard to large masses of information that were previously available only to particular élite groups that dominated certain fields of activity. Information that would hardly have trickled through to the outside world may in the future be available much more easily to those interested and, once so available, would be rapidly spread among a whole network of persons similarly interested.

This could also apply on the international scene, to render information on a diversity of matters more easily accessible to countries of the developing world, which might otherwise never have reached such countries.

This is another major democratizing influence of the computer.

This breakdown of isolationism will operate not merely on the political plane. It will also be a powerful means of intercultural understanding, thus breaking down the monocultural self-centredness that has been one of the prime causes of global problems.

A SHARPENING OF ISSUES

The computer holds promise also of removing the fuzziness that often surrounds the debate on public issues. Bell, in his work on post-industrial society,[30] has argued that technology will assist in making the whole range of available choices clearer. What had earlier been the subject of disputation can be brought into the realm of precise statistics. For example, if the question is what loss of business income will ensue owing to the diversion of a highway from the centre of a town, the computer may give us a specific background picture which was lacking earlier. Many basic decisions facing a community admit of such clarification and quantification of the competing considerations lying on either side of the argument. Indeed, this process might, on many an occasion, make the correct decision self-evident and remove it from the realm of controversy. Conceivably, even issues such as inflation, wage indexation, the benefits and detriments of a satellite scheme, and the proportionate costs and benefits of secondary versus tertiary education can all be presented with far greater clarity than they are now.

In other words, we could have a situation where the basic work is done and the broad policy issues are laid bare for society to pronounce upon them.

[30] Daniel Bell, *The Coming of the Post-Industrial Society*, Basic Books, 1973, p. 103.

Ranged against this view is the view of Herman Khan, Robert E. Lane and others that the average citizen would tend, with increasing technology, to regard political decisions as too complicated to understand and would hence lapse into further apathy.

It is perhaps too early to form conclusions, but it is necessary to generate the widest possible awareness of the potential for good as well as for harm. That way it may be possible to steer the technology now emerging in the direction of its maximum serviceability to the democratic ideal.

THE INCREASE OF LEISURE

Ever since the fall away from the ideals of Athenian democracy the business of government has been in the hands of a select few. The basis of selection may have varied from age to age — aristocracy, wealth, meritocracy or what you will — but the principle of exclusion has been in constant operation — in practice if not in theory.

In theory, of course, every citizen in a democracy has an equal right of participation, but in practice we know that, except for a minority of very small proportions, real active political power is not exercised by the populace — except perhaps when the community quickens into a burst of political activity at election time or in Watergate conditions, to subside thereafter into its customary quiescence.

The computer is now altering that situation by maximizing leisure. As we progress into the computer age, the time required for any act of manufacture or information-recording or retrieval will shrink dramatically, thereby releasing large sections of the workforce from the drudgery of their current long hours of work. A recent paper on the social implications of computers in Australia[31] shows that, even in 1973, a total of 3,266 full-time employees were displaced from their jobs by reason of the introduction, continued operation or extension of certain computer facilities. It is reasonable to assume that the exponential increase in the use of computers since then is at least partly responsible for increasing job losses in all industrialized countries. The computer industry itself may absorb some and the expansion of economies resulting from computers will absorb others, but basically, the clerical workforce may well be drastically affected.

Eventually, unless there is a massive lay-off of workers — which the political system cannot permit — the working hours of the average worker may decline and leisure time will correspondingly increase.

[31] Ashley Goldsworthy, "Computers and their Social Implications", *Australian Computer Journal*, Vol. 9, No. 1, March 1977.

An increase of leisure can have positive and negative effects upon society, depending on how this new phenomenon is handled. The creative use of leisure is an important and serious subject for study in the future.[32] We need to address it now.

It is said of the Roman empire that it collapsed from an increase of luxury. Modern society could be adversely affected if governments and social organizations do not make plans now for the time when millions of workers will be unchained from their workplaces without some planning in advance for alternative socially useful ways of absorbing their attention. There is a danger that a vast amount of unaccustomed leisure may encourage some people to turn it to socially damaging activities, whereas this is in fact an unprecedented opportunity for an increase in socially-oriented activity.

Indeed, this may well be history's unique opportunity for participatory democracy in the real sense of that term. The schools *as of now* need to train our future citizens for this participatory role which will be their inheritance above that of all other generations in history. We need to turn their thoughts to participation by practical schemes in the classroom and outside, which will make them active participants in the governance of their communities, and contributors to the amelioration of the human condition throughout the world.

INSTANT ELECTRONIC REFERENDA

In another sense too the computer brings us closer to the Athenian participatory democracy model than any other voting device or procedure we have seen thus far.

The technology is now available for instant response from homes on any issue of moment, on which the government is canvassing public opinion. There is the additional advantage that false votes can, for all practical purposes, be eliminated, as each home and voter would have an instantly recognizable code or signal. Once the initial expense is overcome of hooking up the home to the central computer, voting on any matter thereafter becomes completely inexpensive. The millions now spent on referenda will be drastically reduced.

If instant voting is thus available, there will also be a greater tendency to submit issues to a direct vote rather than to resort, as is currently the case, to all manner of representative or collegiate voting devices. Electoral procedures will be streamlined and there could be a move towards electoral sys-

[32] See Donald Scott, *The Psychology of Work*, Duckworth, 1970, pp. 185 *et seq.* on "Leisure".

tems based on the one-person-one-vote principle. Indeed, a system has already been attempted in West Germany which combines electronic opinion polls with TV discussions — the system known as ORAKEL. A panel of thirty representative members of the general public, all on telephone lines, can join in the discussion at any time. A group of experts in the studio supplies information whenever necessary on any factual matters raised. After the debate, arrangements are made for viewers to send in their responses. When the wired city of the future brings each home in direct contact with the central receiving station, there will be an instant recording of question and response.

Participation can then look forward to a new and important phase involving a methodology unknown before — but this is a possibility that cannot be translated into reality without much planning. It is a welcome sign that this aspect is already engaging the attention of scholars, as is evidenced by such works as Brian Groombridge's *Television and the People*[33] — a work stressing the importance of planning for participation.

A REFASHIONING OF CONSTITUTIONAL PRINCIPLES

The instant electronic vote has many other repercussions.

The election of governments for a period of years is a device that has been resorted to, largely owing to the immense expense and difficulty of general elections. Consequently, a government is voted into office and given the power to remain in office, despite the fact that opinion in the electorate may move dramatically away from it at various periods during its tenure of power.

With the possibility of instant electronic polls at practically no expense to the state, this whole picture changes. Indeed there could be a demand, if a definite and sustained swing is registered away from the government, for a change of power well ahead of the period set for the life of a government. Owing to the inconvenience of too frequent a change, some working rule will no doubt be evolved to meet this situation. What this means is that every government, conscious that what hitherto were surmises of unpopularity are now matters of fact, will be on its toes to keep its popularity level as high as it can. It will explain, inform and educate the public on every decision of consequence it needs to take.

The whole method of government can thereby be revolutionized.

[33] Brian Groombridge, *Television and the People: A Programme for Democratic Participation*, Penguin, 1972.

There may also be little or no time lag between dissolutions and elections, no delaying of issues until the will of the people becomes known, no smokescreens thrown over the true state of government popularity. New constitutional principles may emerge requiring governments, defeated on three successive national votes, to resign, or requiring that at the request of a stipulated percentage of the population a popularity poll of the government should be compulsorily taken.

There can also be a whittling down of the authority of ministers and heads of state to take fundamental decisions on behalf of the people. There may no longer be the need to rest such decisions on the fiction of representation when the reality of public opinion is available on tap.

All this can engender a feeling of immediacy in the affairs of government by taking away the feeling of remoteness and helplessness which now keeps the bulk of the people away from affairs of government.

THE WIRED CITY[34]

It has been estimated that the wired city is perhaps but twenty years away.

Once this is achieved we shall have not merely more participation and instant referenda. We may also witness the final breakaway from our present state of total dependence on the media for our news.

The media are free to a large extent to choose the news items we receive. They exercise their choice from a vast number of possible alternatives and present to the public their own mix of sport and foreign affairs and gossip and weather. Moreover, the rejected news stories are thereafter dead.

With the coaxial cable we shall all be able to choose our news, selecting the news we want. We shall be able to choose weather reports, foreign affairs, advertisements or what we will at the flick of a switch on a handy home terminal. Such a multiplicity of channels is, we are told, becoming a distinct possibility with glass fibre transmission media enabling a complete television picture to be transmitted on a fibre as thin as a human hair. Teletext enables viewers to have at their fingertips all the information given by their daily newspapers presented in written form on the screen and constantly updated.

There will under this technology be available also a ready machinery for a feedback into the system on issues one considers important enough to warrant the registering of one's opinion.

Not this alone. The rejected news items can be held in a news bank ready for instant retrieval should one desire to pursue an issue. Legislation can

[34] This section is based on such technology as was known and anticipated in 1977.

render them available to the public. The researcher who desires, for example, to investigate what happened in regard to a particular question in Angola on 10th June, 1975 will be able at the press of a button to obtain not merely the news despatches the media chose to publish but, more importantly, those which they thought fit to withhold. These will in an instant be flashed on a home screen.

Vast masses of information now denied to the researcher, the interest group or the interested individual will thus come alive, resurrected from the dust heap to which present media practice permanently relegates it.

The effects of all this upon the subject of participation need to be studied now. The changes are too fundamental to be taken as and when they come.

TOWARDS INTERNATIONALISM

The computer is also forcing us into a situation wherein we must necessarily move towards an international regulation of our affairs. By enlarging the scale of commercial, technological, and environmental operations so as to make their impact global, it is forcing the nations of the world to think globally and to regulate some at least of their affairs by global agreements.

Such global regulation is what the futurist, Buckminster Fuller, has described as "making the world work" — reorganizing the distribution of resources, the protection of the environment, the enterprise of food production, the guaranteeing of individuality, on a global scale. The computer is the tool by which we can achieve this.

Indeed the computer can force the recognition of new human rights which can add new dimensions to the protection of individuality thus far evolved by the law. This can be illustrated through many examples, and perhaps the transborder flow of data may be used as an illustration.

We are today in a situation wherein it is possible, and by no means particularly expensive, to collect data in one country, store it in a second, process it in a third, and print or display the output in a fourth.[35] Keypunching of some Canadian social security data is done in Taiwan. Significant volumes of Australian credit data are entered on computer readable media in Singapore. A consultant associated with the OECD computer privacy studies unit tells us how the fire hazards in every household in the Swedish town of Malmö can in an emergency be flashed immediately upon a screen from a computer in Cleveland, Ohio.[36] We do not want a situation where the credit-

[35] Paul Sieghart, *Privacy and Computers*, Latimer, 1976.

[36] *New Scientist*, 13 January 1977, p. 86.

worthiness or health records of each of us can be flashed immediately on a screen in Singapore, Tokyo or New York.

OECD (The Organization for Economic Co-operation and Development) has since 1974, been considering the question of harmonizing national approaches to data protection among its 23 member countries. The Directorate of Legal Affairs of the Council of Europe has launched studies upon this problem. The countries of the Third World are intensely concerned that their vital data is already stored in affluent countries largely through the transnational activities of the big corporations and can be flashed instantly on screens in the major capitals of the affluent world. They fear indeed that such availability of data about their own affairs may already be more comprehensive and more easily retrievable abroad than at home — and with such knowledge comes power, both economic and political, which interferes with their national sovereignty.[37]

The world cannot much longer tolerate this state of affairs and we must inevitably progress towards the recognition of a new human right — the right of every person, without regard to nationality or domicile, to data protection.

Laws are already overdue in most countries on the lines of the Swedish Data Act of 1973 which provides that items will be released for data processing abroad only after special permission has been granted by the Swedish Data Inspectorate. An interesting footnote to this provision is that some years ago the Inspectorate stopped data being sent to Britain because United Kingdom privacy laws are so weak.[38]

It is to be hoped that the threats thus posed to individual privacy and national sovereignty will soon provoke the necessary international response, and that from this there will ensue other avenues of international co-operation, in matters of global planning, wherein the computer has such a vital part to play.

[37] Although there has been, since the 1970s, a considerable development of the principles regarding transborder data flow, the danger here visualized has only grown with the years. The vast majority of the data concerning the developing world in every department of its activity — economic, industrial, demographic, medical, statistical, political — is held in the data banks of the developed world. This gives the latter the edge in practically every sphere of activity in its dealings with the developing world. To quote a study in the 1990s, "One of the concerns that has been expressed about the social effects of computers is that they have widened (and will continue to widen) the gaps between the haves and have-nots, in our society and in the whole world." (Deborah G. Johnson, *op. cit.*, p. 158.)

[38] *Ibid.*, p. 87.

THE ROLE OF THE LEGAL PROFESSION

Some of the aspects we have outlined show the challenge that today faces the legal profession. Law as taught in the pre-computer age will, not in the 1980s or thereafter, be capable of meeting the numerous onslaughts on established principles which will result from the impact of the computer.[39]

We need to realize that the computer will take over many of our mechanical tasks in the same way as it has taken over the mechanical tasks of mathematics. The mathematics student of today is permitted even at school leaving level to take a computer into the examination room. The law student of tomorrow will have an equal facility with the retrieval of legal knowledge. He or she will probably be able to feed into a pocket computer all the principles, cases and statutes that need to be known and to take these into the examination room.

What follows is that the student's mind is released for thinking upon the principles underlying the principles — the "laws of laws", to use an old academic expression. In other words, jurisprudential and sociological thinking will be released from the cabinet of wooden rules in which they are now confined. The legal mind, freed of much of its drudgery, will be able to roam about the precincts of the law in a way never possible before. It can thereby come more in contact with societal problems from whence the law should derive so much of its substance and inspiration — but which so far have been pushed aside because of the pressures of discovery and retrieval of the law itself.

There can then result also a true flowering of the interdisciplinary aspects which explore the relationships between law, science, linguistics, history, economics and technology — all sadly neglected areas today. The exploration of the law's interface with all other disciplines cannot but result in an enrichment of the law and an increase of its utility as an instrument of social welfare.

The lawyer will also be liberated for fundamental thinking on the ways in which the human inheritance of freedom under the law can be preserved. Here the computer, while furnishing him or her with inter-disciplinary aids, will also offer an unprecedented challenge, for the lawyer must devise procedures whereby the computer is kept in check as a servant and not become a master of legal procedures and legal administration.

The process of judgment too will be sharpened by the removal of unnecessary work-loads from the judicial arena, so that the judges can concentrate

[39] For an overall survey of law and computers, see Colin Tapper, *Computers and the Law*, Weidenfeld and Nicholson, 1973.

on the social and practical realities that lie behind the law. Even the greatest computer enthusiasts do not claim that the computer will replace the judge. "Even in my most manic fits of enthusiasm about the utilisation of computers, I am not ready to replace my lawyer with a machine" wrote Eldridge Adams, Research Consultant for the American Judicature Society,[40] and this is doubly true of the judge.

It is one of the most exciting periods in all legal history that lies ahead of us, and we must reorientate our thinking, our concepts and our legal education to fit the lawyer of tomorrow to be the master and not the abject dependent of the machine. If we so do, the law can be taken to fresh new possibilities of service which will transcend all that has ever been possible in its long and chequered history.

THE PROSPECT

In the result, then, we see tremendous potential for good, as for harm, arising from the computer science of today. Most of the traditional values of democracy and of human rights are capable of being undermined — and of being undermined without public awareness. Likewise, most of these values are capable of being immeasurably strengthened.

The choice is ours and the responsibility for the decision falls uniquely upon us. The way we fashion our answer to these challenges will set the pattern irreversibly for many generations to come. The harm that comes of a wrong decision or a wrong attitude can create patterns of individual, corporate and national domination which will negate much that the laws of many centuries have achieved. The good that comes of informed decision is greater than mankind ever before in its long annals had the power to achieve.

A greater awareness of the issues is the key, and that is why conferences of this nature are so vital and so greatly to be welcomed. It is fervently to be hoped that we, who have the privilege of living at this watershed in history, will not let it be said of us that we failed in our trust through want of concern amidst a plethora of problems, want of vision amidst a multitude of portents, or want of awareness amidst a deluge of information.

[40] Eldridge Adams, "A Lawyer's Introduction to Computers", *Judicature*, October 1968, 99 at p. 103.

11. Armaments*

The evolution of a vast body of human rights norms and doctrine in the post-war years is an unparalleled achievement in the transmutation of idealism into principles of practical applicability. This achievement has pierced the walls of sovereignty which in the pre-war years appeared impenetrable, with the result that today the human rights problems of people anywhere are everybody's concern everywhere. Consequently any major factor that militates against human rights anywhere in the world is a legitimate concern of the global citizen.

Over three centuries ago, Thomas Hobbes, a pioneer of modern political philosophy and one of the most searching analysts of human society, observed that, "Force and Fraud are in warre the two Cardinal virtues".[1] The same appears to apply today as truly as when Hobbes wrote, and the same appears to apply as truly to the ancillaries of warlike activity as to war. One of the principal ancillaries of war is the arms trade. It would not be wrong to assert that its vice-like grip over national and international society in our age depends to a large degree on the elements identified by Hobbes. Can modern human rights doctrine pierce the walls of protection of the arms trade as it has so successfully pierced the walls of sovereignty? If it can, this will be a fitting corollary to its general achievement in regard to human rights. If it cannot, that achievement can yet ring hollow for a large section of global society.

INCOMPLETENESS OF CURRENT CORPUS OF HUMAN RIGHTS AND INTERNATIONAL LAW

A gaping void in the midst of modern human rights achievement is that weapons of death, which negate every known human right, are freely manu-

* Based on a paper presented at the 14th Conference on The Law of the World, held by World Peace through Law at Beijing 22–27 April 1990. This paper pursues further the theme outlined in Chapter 11 of Volume I: "Traffic in Armaments: A Blind Spot in Human Rights and International Law".

[1] Thomas Hobbes, *The Leviathan*, Ch. XIII.

factured, freely sold and freely relied upon as legitimate sources of national revenue. What the immense body of human rights norms achieves is thus undermined at its very foundation.

International committees on disarmament talk wearily through months of interminable discussions every year. Despite this high powered activity, the armaments trade flourishes and relentlessly increases its revenue. Ironically, countries of the Third World, who most desperately need the income spent on armaments, have turned out to be among the best customers of the armaments industry. It is the theme of this paper that discussions on disarmament should make greater use of universally accepted human rights norms. The nations of the world are committed to implementation of these norms and ought not to be able to slip out of these obligations as easily as they seem able to do.

For the purposes of this paper, a broad view is taken of the meaning of the expression "arms trade". The arms trade ranges from the provision of sophisticated aircraft, submarines and radar equipment to the provision of skills and services intended for end-use by military or paramilitary personnel.

There is not a provision of the Universal Declaration of Human Rights or of the International Covenant on Civil and Political Rights or of the International Covenant on Economic, Social and Cultural Rights which is not violated and undermined by the arms trade. One could commence with the right to life, the right to health, the right to motherhood, the right to a healthful environment, and proceed all the way through to such rights as the right to self-determination, the right to development, and the right to sovereignty over natural resources. A detailed volume could be written on the ways in which each of the human rights which is universally accepted is set at naught by the armaments trade. There is neither the space nor the necessity to enter into such a discussion in this paper. This paper will rather query the completeness of our dedication to human rights when we leave it unattended at its heart, so that the whole structure rather resembles a giant doughnut through whose hollow centre this major trafficking in death passes with impunity.[2]

It is not unnatural, in a world where weapons flow freely, that more than a quarter of the world's population now alive has experienced the horrors of

[2] The author has in other articles examined the lacuna in international law and human rights doctrine in relation to the arms trade. See, Vol. I, Ch. 11, and "Traffic in Armaments: The Human Rights Dimension" in 27 *Indian Journal of International Law* (1987), p. 456. The present paper pursues some other aspects pertinent to the relationship between the arms trade and human rights and international law doctrine.

direct military rule. More national armies are used for internal repression than to fight external foes. Armies, whose sole theoretical justification is self-defence against external enemies, do not damage each other in combat, but rather damage the earth and consume its resources in their drive for more and better weaponry. Military forces, armed to the teeth, often split up within a country and fight internecine wars among themselves, ravaging their own land and causing untold human rights denials to their populations. Even where the forms of democracy are maintained, the need to placate the armed forces and pander to their weapons demands compels compromises with basic rights of free information, free thought and free movement. Military hardware and surveillance devices keep populations within a straitjacket of internal repression. Proscribed chemical and germ weapons become available and are, in fact, used against opposing armies. Refugee camps around the world burst at the seams with 15 million refugees, displaced from their homes by the bloody territorial and political conflicts which have escalated with the easy availability of arms. Terrorism feels encouraged and, along with arms, becomes an international export, thus threatening the life of every citizen.

Despite all these consequences, the major powers continue, with no apparent restraining influences either from human rights or international law, not merely to supply arms, but also to supply aid for military purposes. Such aid ties the recipient country to purchases from the donor. A triple human rights denigration ensues simultaneously, for the economic stranglehold on the recipient is tightened, the arms machine of the donor is lubricated, and the recipient's foreign policy is hitched to that of the donor.

Must the human rights lawyer and the international lawyer stand by helplessly, resigned to the inevitability of this scenario, or are there more effective preventive measures these disciplines can offer?

URGENCY OF THE PROBLEM

The rapid changes in the patterns of international politics in the past few years make this an even more urgent problem than before. With the growing rapprochement between East and West, it may be true that the prospect of a clash of Titans, armed to the teeth with nuclear weaponry, is growing more remote. But simultaneously with this movement we see the sprouting of numerous conflicts of a more limited nature — conflicts which in a sense are the arms manufacturers' delight because they are comparatively small wars conducted at a distance, involving the killing of distant peoples, and posing no real threat to their own security. Studies of arms transfers to the Third World reveal that since the early to the mid-1970s the arms trade with the

Third World has expanded rapidly, and formerly minor suppliers of arms have now become major providers. For example, prior to this period the USA and USSR were the dominant suppliers, while today the shares of West European suppliers and new exporters from the Third World itself have risen. Even more alarmingly, Third World arms procurement during this period has extended to the import of major weapons systems.

The restraints that operate in relation to global confrontations between two super powers do not operate at this very different level, and with the multiplication of leaders having the power to unleash a torrent of destruction, the chance of an irresponsible finger on the trigger multiplies correspondingly. It does not take long for a small war to be set off or for a nuclear or chemical or biological weapon to be used, which can immediately raise the danger of spreading into a major conflagration.

All this increases the urgency of attention to the problem, for the arms race feeds on global resources and as it progresses, the poor become more impoverished still. Social and political tensions, national and international, are brought dangerously closer to flash point. Associated with these problems is the problem of national debt, now weighing so heavily on many debtor nations that it has been described as a slowly ticking political time bomb, even more dangerous than the nuclear bomb itself. Countries already unable to provide their citizens with services essential to human rights such as health, maternity care, and education are compelled to divert from these areas scarce resources which instead of promoting human rights are thus diverted to destroying them. If a country is committed through its adherence to the international Bill of Rights[3] to the promotion of human rights, it cannot do this consistently with the obligations it has assumed under those documents. Diverting money to the purchase of arms when children are starving to death, mothers and infants perishing through a lack of maternity care, and children deprived of schooling to the point of illiteracy, is a basic denial of human rights which flies in the face of the many affirmative obligations specifically assumed under these documents. Internal tensions within that country soon reach explosive potential and in many a country today the clock of doom for human rights stands at five minutes to midnight.

[3] Meaning the Universal Declaration, the two Covenants on Civil and Political Rights and on Economic, Social and Cultural Rights, and the optional protocol to the Civil and Political Rights Covenant.

A SURVEY FROM THREE STANDPOINTS

The human rights denials involved in the arms race need to be seen against at least three different backgrounds — those of a specimen major supplier, a specimen purchaser, and a specimen minor supplier.

(a) *In relation to major suppliers*

The following features emerge which produce a damaging impact upon human rights.[4]

1. Arms production for export provides employment in the supplier country and helps its balance of trade. Successive governments have been anxious to play down this aspect, but this is an important factor in the cost-benefit analysis. Where the buyers are from the developing world, this channels scarce monetary resources from the developing world to the developed world.
2. As governments themselves have acknowledged, the economic advantage from arms exports helps them to lower the costs of their own weapons. The poorer countries thus help to subsidize and lubricate the military establishments of the affluent world.
3. The enterprise of manufacturing weapons for export not only reduces the cost of weapons to the exporter, but also broadens its own arms industrial base. To achieve this unaided by arms sales would throw a heavier burden on the taxpayer, who is thus a beneficiary of the arms trade.
4. The importance of the factors mentioned above is proved conclusively by the great effort spent in expanding the sale of foreign arms through the holding of various arms exhibitions, the publication of glossy catalogues of arms and equipment and, indeed, the maintenance of floating arms exhibitions which in accordance with deliberate state policy are sent around the world to attract customers.
5. The open peddling of weapons of death in the same manner as a department store peddles toys, with a carnival atmosphere surrounding it, has a depressing effect on human rights morale, for it creates a general atmosphere of acquiescence in major violations of basic human rights

[4] See, generally, Michael Brzoska and Thomas Ohlson, *Arms Transfers to the Third World 1971–84*, Oxford University Press, 1987.

principles. A structure of human rights norms looks ineffective if it polices the minor violations, while the major violations are encouraged. The drug trafficker in city streets is hauled before the law for his callous disregard of the life and health of others. The arms merchant moves with honour among the princes, potentates and generals who flock to his fair. His disregard of life and health dwarfs that of the drug trafficker, but his business is too important to be similarly restrained.

6. There is the added advantage to the supplier that it can co-ordinate its pattern of arms sales with the needs of its foreign policy. For example, the exporter could use its arms sales within the framework of its foreign policy and the need to help its friends and deny weapons to those who are thought to be unfriendly.

7. Supplying governments are naturally anxious to deny that the export of weapons is used as an instrument of foreign policy, but the realities are that there is some element of political support or lack of it which is a determining factors in arms sales. For example, an embargo may be imposed on arms exports to one country because of an anxiety to maintain good relations with its opponent. So also, when two countries were at war, as for example Iran and Iraq, arms could be supplied to one but not to the other. It is difficult to maintain that this selectiveness is totally unrelated to patterns of foreign policy.

8. Although governments are anxious to justify the sale of arms on some legal basis found within the framework of the UN Charter, the reality is that the arms, once supplied, cannot be regulated in their use. Thus, although the British government, for example, announced that its

   > stated attitude towards requests for exports of defence equipment is based on respect for the rights of other countries, as sovereign states, to protect their independence and to exercise their right of self-defence[5]

   it is clear that the supplier cannot supervise the actual use of these weapons and ensure that they are for self-defence only. Weapons supplied can, and no doubt often are, used for internal repression. It is true that governments have been reluctant to sell weapons that could be used for internal repression and have refused licences in the cases of some particular countries. In any event, continued supervision is

[5] R. Ellis, "Defence Sales", *Journal of the Royal United Services Institute for Defence Studies*, June 1979, p. 3.

impossible and, if this principle is strictly applied, the majority of buyers would be disqualified.

(b) *In relation to purchasers*

The following human rights aspects become relevant from the buyer's point of view:

1. Weapons are sometimes bought in such large quantities that the armed forces cannot absorb them and they are stored for future use. By the time they can be used, they could be outmoded or superseded by better models. The waste of resources is obvious.

2. Developing countries can become involved in an arms race among themselves. The process of escalation is reproduced among them in the same way as among the super powers. Each country thus creates for itself an artificial need of matching its opponent, who then raises its level of armaments, which its rival in turn tends to outdo. In the result, artificial needs and stockpiling ensue far beyond the original needs of self-defence.

3. Temporarily high incomes, as from oil, are mopped up by armaments purchases, with the result that money which should have been channelled into one's own development or the developmental needs of the Third World is pumped back into the developed countries who are the suppliers of the armaments. The arms industry is thus an important recycler of petro-dollars back to the industrialized world.

4. A large proportion of arms imports takes the form of military aid which ties the recipient country to certain alliances and economic dependencies which are a violation of its own sovereign rights to be the determiner of its own foreign policy. The concept of sovereignty is denuded of one of its most important components if free determination of foreign policy is excluded from it. Both sovereignty and the right to self-determination are thus considerably impaired.

5. It has been fashionable in developing countries whose weapons are outdated to launch ambitious programmes of modernization. Once launched, a modernization programme tends to proceed under its own momentum, heedless of the surrounding economic framework, and greedily absorbing resources the country cannot spare. Weapons manufacturers are adept at alerting these potential buyers to the outmoded nature of their weaponry.

6. External powers, by championing governments or their opponents and by giving them military aid, spur their rivals into an arms race whether they have foreign sponsors or not.
7. Where there are no foreign sponsors, the result is often national bankruptcy and social instability.
8. Weapons supplied to an unscrupulous regime are used for internal repression. A government once thought to be benevolent may turn repressive and use for its repressive activities the arms it collected earlier. This is particularly significant in the light of the fact that many armies in the Third World are used at some stage for domestic purposes in the suppression of dissent or political opposition or for plain police and investigation purposes.
9. Indiscriminate weapon supply foments civil wars with all the associated human rights deprivations and resulting internal chaos.
10. The circumvention by the arms industry of prohibitions and embargoes, e.g., in the case of South Africa, forces their neighbours to import substantial quantities of arms which they can ill afford and which consequently erode basic services essential to human rights, such as health and education. The front line states bordering South Africa are examples — Angola, Mozambique and Zimbabwe have suffered heavily as a result.
11. The flouting or circumvention of embargoes prevent international law and human rights from being maintained. The flouting of the arms embargo on South Africa by the arms dealers of several developed countries is the best known example, but a large number of other major arms transactions represent clever attempts to foil detection. Not only the arms themselves, but the payments are often camouflaged by routing them circuitously with the help of multiple electronic banking transfers. The international banking system has much to answer for in this regard.
12. The arms purchases of the Middle East which collectively accounted for around 46% of all major weapon transfers to the Third World between 1971 and 1985 gave new hope and strength to the arms industry. The Iran/Iraq war in particular provided new levels of profitability to the armaments industry. Iraq's enormous oil income, for example, was insufficient to cover the 6–8 billion dollar annual US weapons bill in the 1980s. If such a flourishing economy could be so severely dented, it is not difficult to visualize the economic impact of the arms trade on countries struggling for economic survival.

13. The import of sophisticated weaponry, as when Iran imported sophisticated defence systems, necessitated the presence of several thousands of foreign advisers to help in the repair and maintenance of this equipment during the days of the Shah. One of the first actions of the post-Shah government was to put an end to the enormous arms import programmes then current.
14. ASEAN countries, modest arms importers until the 1970s, enormously expanded their arms purchases from the 70s onwards. These went far beyond the needs of counter insurgency operations against guerrillas, which were the original justification for those imports. ASEAN countries purchase mainly from the West — USA, the UK, Germany, France and Italy. This represents a considerable flow of funds from Third World countries to the developed world.

(c) *In relation to minor suppliers*

A survey of major arms producers and buyers is inadequate to give us the whole picture. Across the world there are dozens of countries which are comparatively minor suppliers. Yet cumulatively their contribution to the arms trade produces a significant impact on human rights globally. Indeed, their contribution is an even greater danger in some respects, for they often lack the guidelines and supervisory mechanisms which the major suppliers have evolved.

Australia, for example, with arms exports estimated at around a quarter of a billion dollars in 1986–7, is a comparatively minor supplier. Its regulations and practices on vital aspects of the trade are hence not as comprehensive as those of some of the great arms suppliers.[6] Thus, according to research studies, the following human rights related consequences follow from Australia's modest programme of arms exports.[7]

1. There is no arms embargo upon the supply of arms to repressive governments. Rather, exports will be favoured "where there is no reasonable risk of using the equipment against the citizens of a country with a dubious civil rights record". The Defence Minister announced in June 1988 that the Government "aims to promote our defence exports

[6] The matters discussed here are in the light of situation as it prevailed at the time of this paper.

[7] *Australia's Arms Exports: Keeping them out of Repressive Hands*, Peace Research Centre, ANU, 1989, and *Australia's Arms Exports*, Peace Dossier No. 21 of the Victorian Association of Peace Studies.

without prejudice to important defence, international and human rights concerns". On the contrary, it may well be argued that the Government export drive is making it easier for Australian arms to find their way into repressive hands and into areas of tension.

2. Subject to vague constraints, like that mentioned above, there will be a presumption that if friends and allies of Australia export certain military equipment to country X, Australia may likewise export comparable equipment to country X. This is more than disturbing, given the known record of some countries in supplying arms to repressive governments.

3. There are no controls on equipment which is neither lethal nor of major military significance. This implies that there will be no control whatever upon intangible exports like maintenance and overhaul services, nor upon combat support equipment like small arms training aids and transport aircraft.

4. Instead of the onus lying upon the supplier to justify the need for an export, the onus of proof has been shifted to those opposing an export proposal. They must make a *specific* case against it — and do so within 21 days. Clearly the boot is here on the wrong foot and there is an avoidance of government responsibility to satisfy itself of the permissibility of the export. Human rights lawyers could well ask the question whether there is not here an abdication of state responsibility in regard to ensuring global peace and safeguarding human rights.

5. The Foreign Affairs Department, which was the human rights watchdog within the old control process, now has only consultative status. Routine administration has been assigned to the Defence Department, whose orientation is very different. Its concerns are primarily not with human rights, but with the military aspect and with keeping arms out of the hands of Australia's enemies.

6. There are no controls upon the retransfer of Australian-made components incorporated into foreign-built equipment.

7. There are no controls upon the supply of arms to First World countries. Thus even countries with a record of repressive intervention in the Third World can use these arms for such purposes, free of any restrictions imposed by the producer.

This brief survey sets the problem in context. From whichever angle one views it, the grave implications for human rights are clear. At each level, there are principles of human rights and international law that can be brought into the discussion, but the two disciplines have been relatively silent, largely perhaps for the reason that practising lawyers do not have the time, the opportunity or indeed the required information to move into action, even granted the required degree of sensitivity and concern with the problem.

WORLD PEACE THROUGH WORLD LAW

At these important Congresses held by World Peace through Law our central concern has always been how we can as lawyers contribute to world peace through the application of law rather than force. The armaments trade is one of those activities which foments *war* and cannot be restrained by *force*. We are engaged here in a *peace*-promoting activity which believes in restraints through *law*. Armaments is a field *par excellence* where law can act as a restraint on force, not parochially, but globally, not temporarily, but for the foreseeable future. There can indeed be few more appropriate forums for this than an organization dedicated from its inception to the achievement of *world peace* through *world law*.

World law means in this context international law and human rights. There are many rules of these two disciplines which can be used within domestic jurisdictions for the purpose of challenging the arms trade, but these have not thus far been adequately used.

Take, for example, the evolution of new weapons of increasingly destructive capability. They cause suffering which goes beyond the purposes of war and have indiscriminate effects. This offends several well-established principles of international humanitarian law, such as the principle against the causation of indiscriminate harm to combatants and non-combatants, the principle of proportionality, the principle against the aggravation of pain and suffering beyond the needs of war, and the prohibition of asphyxiating gases and analogous materials. What is more, new principles are emerging preventing destruction of the ecosystem, the decimation of mankind, and the causing of intergenerational damage. These principles are derived from customary international law and, if customary international law is part of the common law, as indeed it is considered to be in many common law countries, there is here a violation of norms already found within those legal systems. It may not be possible to invoke criminal sanctions in the absence of legislation, but injunctions, restraints and declaratory decrees can surely be sought.

Problems can perhaps arise on the question of standing, especially where one is seeking to restrain the supply of arms to a foreign country, but a citizen can maintain that he or she is entitled as a matter of right to the observance by his or her government of the laws of the land, including international law. Moreover, the individual petitioner's particular rights can be linked with the particular arms supply through such factors as environmental rights (especially where uranium or ancillaries of nuclear weapons are supplied, for any ensuing damage will be global), unlawfulness of the export in question under international law (at the point of export), unlawfulness of the act of manufacture under the Nuremberg principles and the citizen's interest in freedom from global terrorism which can harm him or her directly. It is important that these arguments be considered so as to attune legal thinking to the fact that in an increasingly interdependent world the disturbance of peace, even in a distant country, can have very quick practical repercussions on the life of every citizen in the supplier country. What is at issue is human dignity and to every human being this is a central matter of immediate concern.

When by such actions the legal system is sensitized to these issues, parliamentarians and governments themselves will begin to heed them and to take account of them when planning their activities.

Recent juristic work[8] shows many ways in which domestic legal systems can be used as a vehicle for enforcing domestically the principles of human rights and international law. Thus, in the US for example, principles drawn from the Nuremberg trial, the US case *Application of Yamashita*,[9] the Geneva Protocol of 1925, and the US Army Field Manual can be used within domestic tribunals to sustain principles of personal responsibility of those who lend assistance to plans for devastating cities and killing large numbers of people, as opposed to genuine military targets. From this state of the law, it is possible to work towards a principle of the right (and duty) to prevent the commission of international crimes.[10] For other jurisdictions, similar arguments can no doubt be mounted.

As yet we are at a very incipient stage in the use of human rights norms domestically for the purpose of checking violations of international law, but the consciousness of the need to do so and the availability of the machinery for this purpose seems to be growing. Lawyers can invoke these norms and judges can use them much more extensively than is currently the case; and

[8] For example, F.A. Boyle, *Defending Civil Resistance under International Law*, Transnational Publishers Inc., 1987.

[9] 327 US 1 (1946).

[10] See Boyle, *op. cit.*, pp. 138–139.

armaments are a very suitable field for resort to these norms.[11] This is a most fertile source for augmenting the domestic law in every jurisdiction.

As an illustrative instance, on 24 March 1990, the international press carried news that Czechoslovakia's President Havel had announced in London that the previous regime had exported enough Semtex explosive to supply the world's terrorists for 150 years.[12] Six ounces are said to be sufficient to blow up an aircraft, while 1,000 tons of the explosive had been exported. This is only part of an extensive arms trade which had earned, from countries outside the Warsaw Pact, an average of £850 million annually, amounting to a quarter or a half of the country's foreign exchange earnings.[13] Similar exports may well be taking place in many other countries and an alert public should be able to restrain such exports under law.

Facts relating to such a matter can in many jurisdictions be ferreted out now under Freedom of Information legislation or, in the absence of legislation, under the well-developed right to information as worked out in human rights doctrine. Should such an export be contemplated by any entity, including the State itself, there are enough international law and human rights norms currently available to seek to prevent such an export.

The same news reports revealed that in Bonn the State Prosecutor had announced the previous day that formal charges had been lodged against the chemical company suspected of designing an overseas chemical plant for producing poison gas. In this particular case, the prosecution was launched by the office of the State Prosecutor for Economic Crimes. Even apart from such prosecutions by the State, there are sufficient principles available within the body of international law and human rights norms for concerned citizens to seek the intervention of the legal system in such an internationally illegal activity.

In numerous countries we have today the situation we did not enjoy a generation ago of various human rights norms being built into their constitutions in the form of constitutional guarantees. This makes the work of the human rights lawyer easier, in drawing attention to the violations of human rights norms which governments and arms merchants are committing daily. Furthermore, in some countries, international treaty obligations assume the force of paramount law, equal in weight to constitutional provisions themselves, while in others the degree of recognition of international law varies

[11] For the countries of the British Commonwealth, see the volume titled *Developing Human Rights Jurisprudence: The Domestic Application of International Human Rights Norms*, published by the Commonwealth Secretariat, 1968.

[12] See *Time Magazine*, April 2, 1990, p. 31.

[13] *Ibid.*

from full incorporation into their legal systems to various degrees of more limited recognition.

The European Court of Human Rights and the European Commission of Human Rights have built up a significant body of human rights jurisprudence which offers a readily available reservoir of human rights decisions for consultation by the courts of any country. The European Convention itself offers a universally respected set of norms which is increasingly consulted. Likewise, across the world, the Supreme Courts of various countries are building up, through constitutional and other decisions, a vast body of human rights principles, many of which are relevant to the matters here under discussion.

With all this material available to it, the judiciary in all countries has available to it a body of human rights materials such as has never in history been available for incorporation into their legal systems. The universal body of human rights norms can fertilize national legal systems and there are numerous norms pertinent to the arms trade that can be called in aid — such as those relating to the environment, torture practices, surveillance devices, freedom of information on arms transactions, the elimination of racial discrimination, and the right to food, clothing and an adequate standard of living. All of these in one form or another are affected by the arms trade.

Moreover, current trends in international law render it possible to apply basic standards of international law to those who are physically present within a jurisdiction, despite the fact that the actual violation of human rights is committed by them in a foreign country.[14]

There are several heads of international law under which States which violate their basic human rights obligations can be held to their obligations, even by actions in their own courts — as, for example, where State actions in regard to the armaments trade violate solemn state responsibilities undertaken by that State under multilateral human rights covenants. Among them are the following:

(a) The principle of *ius cogens*. Peremptory norms in international law are binding on all States and no State can claim the right to violate a principle of *ius cogens*. Many human rights norms have now acquired the status of *ius cogens*, especially those relating to war crimes, crimes against humanity, indiscriminate killing, and environmental devastation. Where a State's sale of armaments can have these results, it may be argued that principles of *ius cogens* binding on all States are being violated. In any country which has an independent judiciary and a respect

[14] See the well-known case of *Filartiga* v. *Pena Irala*, (1980) 630 F 2d 876.

for international law and human rights, such a challenge to its actions can be mounted in its own courts.

It may be that such challenges may not meet with immediate success, but a climate of such actions can force judges and lawyers to give more thought to what is an incontrovertible principle of law.

(b) Binding obligations created by adherence to human rights treaties, e.g., the Convention on the Prevention and Punishment of the Crime of Genocide, the International Covenant on Civil and Political Rights, the International Covenant on Economic, Social and Cultural Rights, and the Convention relating to the Status of Refugees. Parties to these treaties have *bound* themselves to take the necessary affirmative steps to give effect to the rights recognized by the Covenant (e.g., Art. 2 of the International Covenant on Civil and Political Rights), even to the extent of enacting legislation for this purpose. If States are under a duty to go so far as to enact legislation, they are surely under a duty also to take affirmative steps to halt actions which can denigrate the rights they undertake to protect.

(c) The commitment to the United Nations Charter and its fundamental principle of the maintenance of international peace and security. The supply of weapons to belligerent states, or to states assuming a belligerent attitude to each other, or to states where internal dissension prevails is a clear violation of this basic obligation to maintain international peace and security to which all member states are pledged.[15] This is a solemn treaty obligation which in some countries has the force of paramount law and in others commands recognition by all authorities in the State, including the judicial.

(d) The Genocide Convention requires all contracting parties to prevent and punish the crime of genocide. Genocide includes the killing of members of a national, ethnical, racial, or religious group. Conspiracy to commit genocide as well as complicity in genocide are punishable crimes. It is difficult to argue that the supply of weapons to a country engaged in attacking another national, ethnical, racial or religious group is not complicity in genocide. A State cannot indulge in such conduct without violating its most basic international undertakings.

[15] See Art. 1 of the United Nations Charter. "The Purposes of the United Nations are: 1. To maintain international peace and security ...".

Indeed, not only public officials but private individuals are expressly caught up by Article IV of the Convention, which declares that they *shall* be punished for complicity in the offence. This clearly brings within the net such groups as private arms suppliers and indeed manufacturers who manufacture expressly for such exports. States have expressly undertaken to punish genocide, whether committed in time of peace or war. It does not matter that the actual act of genocide occurs outside its boundaries. The offenders not only *can* be tried, but *should* be tried wherever they are, if parties to the treaty are loyal to their obligations under it.

(e) As early as 1949, the International Law Commission, in Article 14 of its "Draft Articles on Rights and Duties of States", stipulated that:

> Every State has a duty to conduct its relations with other States in accordance with the principle that the sovereignty of each State is subject to the supremacy of international law.

This is an incontrovertible principle if we are to live under world law. Each State is thus under a clear duty to subordinate its sovereign power or interests where a proposed action constitutes a violation of international law.

(f) The Nuremberg principles are regarded as an authoritative statement of the rules of customary international law concerning individual criminal responsibility for crimes against peace, crimes against humanity, and war crimes. Under these principles, individuals who participate in the planning, preparation, initiation or waging of a war of aggression, or a war in violation of international treaties, commit a "crime against peace".[16] The supply of weapons for such a war, knowing that the weapons are to be used in it, is clearly caught up within the Nuremberg principles. States have a duty to prevent individuals from so acting, and individuals who so act can and should be restrained by national courts in accordance with the principles of international law. Defences such as superior orders of the State, state necessity, or state interest are clearly unavailable.

[16] See Boyle, *op. cit.*, p. 109.

SOME CONSIDERATIONS REGARDING WEAPONS AND MILITARY ACTION

Against this background of possible legal and human rights action, it would be helpful to consider some aspects that cause considerable concern.

(a) *Attacks on Nuclear Facilities*

In 1987, Iraq, introducing Resolution 42/38F on the development, production, stockpiling and use of radiological weapons, drew attention to a serious problem resulting from the proliferation of peaceful nuclear installations. There is the ever-present danger of a military attack on such nuclear facilities, which could cause radioactive contamination not only in the immediate area of the attack, but in adjacent regions. Chernobyl is a constant reminder to us of the extent of basic human rights denigrations that can follow from the malfunctioning of such a facility. The denigrations that can follow in the event of a bombing attack are too horrendous to visualize.

It is therefore essential to a proper concern with disarmament that the inviolability of nuclear installations be guaranteed by international law and agreements. In the words of Jordan, in discussing this resolution, "attacks against peaceful nuclear facilities constituted an unprecedented threat to international peace and security".[17] Israel voted against the draft but it is important to note that "Israel stressed, however, that its vote did not indicate a change in its long held view that all States must refrain from attacking or threatening to attack nuclear facilities devoted to peaceful purposes". The draft resolution was adopted by the General Assembly on 30 November 1987 with a recorded vote of 119 to 2, with 32 abstentions. It affirmed that armed attacks of any kind against nuclear facilities are tantamount to the use of radiological weapons owing to the dangerous radioactive forces that such attacks cause to be released.

The immense danger to humanity that can be caused by the simple rocketry needed to attack a nuclear station must surely be a warning to us of how lethal even an apparently simple weapons system can be. The duty of stringency in weapons control becomes all thc more apparent.

(b) *The Use of Outer Space*

Weapons systems that allow the deployment of weapons in outer space are so expensive and sophisticated that they represent a bonanza for the weapons

[17] *Ibid.*, p. 126.

trade. Under its pressure the militarization of space presents a more than ordinary danger.

The common heritage of mankind includes outer space. All future generations, irrespective of whether they belong to the developed or developing worlds, are entitled to use this resource which future technology may possibly prove to be richer than all the traditional resources we have inherited.

Here is a human rights problem on the grandest scale. Pollute this environment and the damage caused will be many multiples of any damage we can cause on earth. The arms race more than any other human activity imperils this inheritance and negates the rights involved. Fortunately we have been conscious of this danger and protected ourselves against it. By Resolution 2222(XXI) of 19 December 1966 — Treaty on Principles Governing the Activities of States in the Exploration and Use of Outer Space, including the Moon and Other Celestial Bodies — the subscribing parties undertook "not to place in orbit around the Earth any objects carrying nuclear weapons or any other kinds of weapons of mass destruction" (Art. IV), and not to install such weapons on celestial bodies. Yet so strong was the pressure of the arms lobby that the Star Wars programme, with its inevitable consequence of the militarization of space, was launched at a potential cost of trillions of dollars, on the basis that the programme was purely defensive rather than offensive.

The General Assembly's Resolution 42/33 for the Prevention of an Arms Race in Outer Space, passed by a recorded vote of 154 to 1 on 30 November 1987, called upon States, and in particular those with major space capabilities, to prevent an arms race in outer space in the interest of maintaining international peace and security and promoting international cooperation and understanding. This was not merely a negative undertaking, but imposed duties of affirmative action to prevent an arms race in space.

From the standpoint of the international lawyer, this Resolution is significant in its express recognition, in preambular clause 5, "that the lêgal régime applicable to outer space, as such, is not sufficient to guarantee the prevention of an arms race in outer space". It stressed "the need to consolidate and reinforce that régime and to enhance its effectiveness, and the importance of strict compliance with existing agreements, both bilateral and multilateral". One recalls President Kennedy's warning in 1960 that whichever nation controlled space could control the earth "as in past centuries the nation that controlled the seas dominated the continents". That still rings true. Through the control of space, new dominations could emerge unless international law places effective curbs now on the abuse of space power.

The peaceful use of outer space can be of environmental benefit to developed countries and indeed some of the technology achieved through weapons systems can be turned to these purposes. For example, a recent UN paper points out that the International Satellite Land Surface Climatology Project (ISLSCP) of the Committee on Space Research (COSR) would be particularly appropriate for developing improved techniques to study the effects of land surfaces on climate. Such a project would also have the advantage that scientists from developing countries could participate.[18]

Other applications of space research include satellite remote sensing communications and meteorology. In the words of the UN paper just cited, there is "a great potential for using space technology for economic and social development that is not yet being realized, particularly in developing countries".

Space science has progressed so far that the USSR plans eventually to send people to Mars, and advanced studies for manned missions early in the next century are being undertaken.[19] Man's journeys into outer space are perhaps closer than is commonly believed and with these will commence a new dawn for human rights too, provided of course that space is kept free of the weapons race. President Gorbachev has made it official policy to develop plans for a co-operative flight to Mars.[20] The resulting opportunities for international collaboration which would divert attention from the arms race are quite extraordinary.[21]

International attention, and particularly that of international and human rights lawyers, needs to be focused more intensively on space as an area of peaceful growth. The General Assembly struck the right note when it began the Resolution under consideration with the words "Inspired by the great prospects opening up before mankind as a result of man's entry into outer space". The cornucopia of plenty which can open up in this region has the potential to alleviate many of our human rights problems, for some forecasts visualize a several-fold rise in the standard of living of all people on earth as a result of space activity. If so, the human rights implications are enormous and it is doubly important that space should not be polluted by weaponry or its use pre-empted by a few powers.

[18] See information document presented by the United Nations to the Interparliamentary Union Centenary Conference, London, 4–9 September 1989, on *Peaceful Access to Space and Its Use for the Benefit of Mankind*.

[19] See B.I. Edelson and J.L. McLucas, "US-Soviet Planetary Exploration: The Next Step is Mars, Together", in *Space Policy*, November 1988, p. 337, at 343.

[20] *Ibid*., p. 345.

[21] The Mars landing in July 1997 riveted world attention, as did the stream of information relating to that planet which was relayed back.

(c) *New Weapons of Mass Destruction*

Despite these fairly evident humanitarian considerations, research proceeds apace on the improvement of existing weapons of destruction and on the production of new ones. There is here an alliance between the scientist and technologist on the one hand, and the arms producers on the other. It is indeed a pity that an ethical code has not yet been worked out for scientists engaged in the lethal enterprise of making weapons of mass destruction.[22] Human rights and international lawyers should make more meaningful use of principles of international law such as the Nuremberg principles for this purpose.[23]

On 30 November 1987, the General Assembly adopted, by a recorded vote of 135 to 1, with 18 abstentions, Resolution 42/35 on the "Prohibition of the development and manufacture of new types of weapons of mass destruction and new systems of such weapons". Also, in 1987, seventeen States, including the USSR, France, Sweden, Australia and Vietnam, submitted a draft resolution (Resolution 42/30 of 1987) entitled "Convention on Prohibitions or Restrictions on the Use of Certain Conventional Weapons Which May Be Deemed to be Excessively Injurious or to Have Indiscriminate Effects". Some weapons, such as incendiary weapons, sea mines and battlefield laser weapons, designed for anti-personnel use, could well fall within the prohibitions following from accepted principles of humanitarian law. The General Assembly approved the draft resolution without a vote.

The Byelorussian SSR, in introducing the draft resolutions, submitted that the emergence of such weapons would sharply destabilize the strategic situation and lower the threshold at which war involving weapons of mass destruction might break out. The resolution called upon all States, immediately following the identification of any new type of weapon of mass destruction, to renounce practical development of such a weapon and to commence negotiations on its prohibition. Another clause embodied the hope, so important to world peace, that all States would make efforts to ensure that scientific and technological achievements may be used solely for peaceful purposes.

[22] For a possible step in this direction, see this author's suggested Declaration of Scientific Responsibility for Nuclear Scientists, in *Nuclear Weapons and Scientific Responsibility*, Longwood Academic, 1987, Appendix K, reproduced also in the *Encyclopaedia of Social Inventions*, Institute for Social Inventions, London, 1989, pp. 194–196. This appears as Appendix B of the present volume.

[23] See, in particular, in regard to nuclear weapons, the author's *Nuclear Weapons and Scientific Responsibility, supra.*, Ch. 9.

(d) *Deterrence and First Use*

One of the main bases on which the proliferation of nuclear arms has been sought to be justified in the past has been the doctrine of deterrence. This doctrine served the interests of the armaments industry well, for massive numbers of nuclear weapons were constructed on the basis that it was never intended to use them, save for purposes of deterrence, through the possibility of retaliation. Such retaliation can be demonstrated to be itself a violation of human rights norms, just as is the case with first use.[24]

The possibility of first use could trigger off a nuclear war, and thus provides the core justification for the arms build up. First use is clearly not merely a violation of human rights, but a crime against humanity, having regard to the ecological dangers now proved to be attendant on nuclear war, and having regard to the danger to the survival of humanity itself. First use must therefore be addressed in all its human rights and international law implications.

The General Assembly directed its attention to this in Resolution 42/42A, adopted by a recorded vote on 30 November 1987 of 125 to 17, with 12 abstentions. One of its important clauses (Art. 3) requested the Conference on Disarmament to consider, *inter alia*, "the elaboration of an international instrument of a legally binding character laying down the obligation not to be the first to use nuclear weapons".

(e) *Other Nuclear Weapons Aspects*

Although there is no international trade as such in completed nuclear weapons, the arms trade does handle important component elements of nuclear weapons. This is being highlighted in the international press, even as this paper nears completion, for on 29 March 1990 the world came to know that 40 sophisticated nuclear triggers known as krytrons, on their way from California to the Middle East, were intercepted at Heathrow Airport in London.[25] These triggers fire the detonators of nuclear weapons with a very high-speed pulse of electrical current in microseconds. Because the detonators must be fired in precisely the correct sequence, timing is critical and the krytrons are crucial for successful detonation. The sophisticated electronics and engineering embodied in them is beyond the capability of many countries aspiring to be possessors of nuclear arms. With the availability of krytrons such countries come so much closer to their goal.

[24] *Ibid.*, pp. 111–116.

[25] *Washington Post*, 29 March 1990.

It is significant that the Director of the Washington-based Wisconsin Project on Nuclear Arms Control observed, in relation to this incident, that it showed that a country which was party to the Nuclear Non-Proliferation Treaty had been "caught red-handed in violation of this Treaty". One wonders why reference needs to be made only to treaty obligations. Is this not also a fundamental violation by both exporter and consignee of basic human rights and of other accepted international standards such as the *ius cogens* in relation to genocide?

Other matters pertinent to the nuclear arms race are the Cessation of all nuclear-test explosions (Resolution 42/26A and B); the Urgent need for a comprehensive nuclear test-ban treaty (Resolution 42/27); the Notification of Nuclear Tests (Resolution 42/38C); the Prohibition of the Production of Fissionable Material for Weapons Purposes (Resolution 42/38L); and regional denuclearization — of Africa (Resolution 42/34A), of the Middle East (Resolution 42/28), of South Asia (Resolution 42/29), and of Latin America (Resolution 42/25).

Serious human rights violations, including particularly a violation of the right to self-determination, are involved in the *threat* of the use of nuclear weapons. Such threats are rarely direct and overt. They are often covert and implied, and herein lie many dangers — including a build-up of arms in the threatened country which may even be driven to seek the acquisition of crude nuclear capability.

The General Assembly in 1987 adopted a draft resolution introduced by Bulgaria (Res. 42/31), and another by Pakistan (Res. 42/32) stressing the urgent need for an agreement to assure non-nuclear States against the *threat* of use of nuclear weapons.

Another important aspect of the nuclear weapons industry that cries out for a human rights solution is the secrecy that surrounds it. It is now being revealed that secrecy has, over the 40 years of the nuclear weapons industry, taken priority over safety and individual rights. As information leaks out about the lack of precautions in factories, laboratories and waste dumps, it is beginning to be feared that, although not one nuclear weapon has been used after World War II, the scale of past and future deaths owing to radioactive contamination will be a matter of major public concern. Security has been the reason why the information that might have saved the victims was not made available to them.

Alarmed by such evidence, the Bush Administration has temporarily closed most of the important nuclear factories, including the key factory at Rocky Flats, the only source of the plutonium triggers necessary to detonate nuclear warheads. Hanford Nuclear Reservation, probably the most contaminated site in the world, has acute soil and groundwater contamination which is slowly carrying radioactivity to the Columbia River, a source of drinking water, food and recreation for millions of people. It has been estimated as having released into the atmosphere more than 500,000 curies of radioactive iodine which strikes hardest at the thyroid glands of children. Moreover, the 177 underground storage tanks at Hanford reportedly contained 446 million curies of radiation, as compared with the official estimate of 8 million curies that escaped at the Three Mile Island accident.[26] In other nuclear-weapons-producing countries such as Britain, France and the Soviet Union, the position can be little different.

The right to information is a head under which the current norms of human rights can greatly assist the attack on secrecy. The damage to environment and health offers more than a sufficient basis for domestic human rights action, for these vital rights of individuals are *directly* affected and the information they require to protect these rights is an integral part of the right itself. No wonder the Energy Secretary, Admiral James Watkins, has stressed the need for more openness as he addresses his monumental task of cleaning up, costed variously at figures extending to 150 billion dollars over 30 years.

(f) *Chemical and Bacteriological Weapons*

Not only is a new convention required,[27] but measures must be devised to uphold the authority of the 1925 Geneva Protocol. An interesting initiative in this regard was taken up in 1989 by Australia when it convened for the first time an international conference, attended not only by the weapons-producing States, but by representatives of the chemicals industry. This conference, the Government-Industry Conference against Chemical Weapons, held in Canberra in September 1989, is one of the first major initiatives in arranging discussions not merely between States, but between representatives of the industry itself, which in the last analysis is the actual producer of the weapons. Nearly 70 nations attended and, in the words of the Australian Prime Minister, it was "the first time that a major industrial group has been called on in its entirety to participate in the disarmament process". With the growing discipline of "conversion", by which weapons factories are being diverted to the manufacture of goods for peaceful uses, it may be possible to

[26] Gerald F. Hess, "Hanford: Cleaning up the Most Contaminated Place in the United States", 38 *Arizona Law Review*, p. 165 (1996), citing Michele S. Gerber, *On the Home Front: The Cold War Legacy of the Hanford Nuclear Site*, p. 3, 1992.

[27] Since the date of this paper, the Chemical Weapons Convention has been ratified and the office of the Organisation for the Prohibition of Chemical Weapons has been set up in The Hague.

bring the arms manufacturers themselves to the conference table. The Australian initiative may show that industry and governments can be brought together and that, when they do so, industry adopts a creative and co-operative stance.

Perhaps in the chemical weapons field, more than in any other, we encounter the problem that there is an ever-increasing number of products which can be used for both military and civilian purposes, thus making control and verification extremely complex. Little can be achieved, therefore, without the co-operation and goodwill of the experts.

To contain the chemical genie in its bottle, the United Nations Conference on Disarmament Issues, held in Kyoto in April 1989, recommended action on the lines set out below, pending the successful conclusion of the Chemical Weapons Convention:

(i) Tightest possible export controls with strict survey of dual purpose chemicals;

(ii) Sanctions against any State that violates the Geneva Protocol of 1925;

(iii) Secretary-General of the UN to be given full authority to investigate alleged violations of the Geneva Protocol.

Each of these recommendations can be helped on by human rights concepts and procedures such as the right to freedom of information and the procedures provided therefor.

THE RELATIONSHIP BETWEEN DISARMAMENT AND DEVELOPMENT

India, in introducing the draft of Resolution 42/45 of 1987, — "Relationship between disarmament and development" — commented on the fact that both armament and development competed for the world's finite and material resources. The arms race not only consumed resources, thus making them unavailable for development, but also distorted economic structures, undermined the economic system, and adversely affected the attitude of nations towards the important concepts of co-operation. Co-operation is of course one of the main pillars of the changed international order, now that all nations are conscious of the finite nature of the earth's resources, and the universal nature of the ecological perils faced by humanity. Indeed, co-operation rather than mere co-existence is one of the imperatives of the only structure of international law that can ensure the survival of humanity.

The Sudan, in expressing support for the draft, urged that serious consideration should be given to the establishment of an appropriate international instrument to distribute the resources released by disarmament.

The United States announced that it perceived disarmament and development as two distinct issues that could not be considered appropriately in terms of an inter-relationship.[28] The United Kingdom, on the other hand, joined in the consensus on the draft, but stressed that it did not adequately reflect the complex nature of the relationship between disarmament, development, and international security.

Lest the common justification of the arms trade be reiterated, namely, that its limitation would affect the sovereign rights of States to arm themselves for self-defence, we should refer also to Resolution 42/36 on the Reduction of military budgets, submitted by Bangladesh, Indonesia, Ireland, Nigeria, Peru, Romania, Senegal, Sweden and Uruguay. This Resolution stressed that it was possible to reduce military budgets without prejudice to the rights of all States to undiminished security, self-defence, and sovereignty. The Final Document of the International Conference on the Relationship between Disarmament and Development stressed the need for disarmament, development and security to be comprehensively studied in their relationship to one another. It pointed out the need for an improved and comprehensive database on a global scale.

The Brandt Report in 1980 pointed out that, "The cost of a ten-year programme to provide essential food and health needs in developing countries is less than half of one year's military spending".[29] It also pointed out that, while total military expenditures are approaching US$450 billion a year, annual spending on official development aid is only US$20 billion.[30] The World Health Organization's programme to abolish malaria is short of funds, it being estimated that it will eventually cost about US$450 million — which represents only one-thousandth of the world's annual military spending.[31] In the face of such statistics, it is difficult to argue that there is no connection between armaments and development. Add to that statistic the fact that, until the recent cutback in armed forces, each superpower was spending more on its armed forces than the combined national incomes of the 62 countries at

[28] *The United Nations General Assembly and Disarmament 1987*, United Nations, 1988, p. 42.

[29] *North-South: A Programme for Survival*, Pan Books, 1980, p. 118.

[30] *Ibid.*, p. 117.

[31] *Ibid.*, pp. 117–118.

the bottom of the table of GNP's, and one sees the obvious disproportion between the strength of the armaments industry and the strength of those who are most affected by the claims it makes upon earth resources.

THE ARMS RACE AND GLOBAL HEALTH

The arms race is often cited as directly denigrating human health through its adverse impact on the environment. Its indirect effect, by absorbing resources which could end several traditional scourges in the field of human health, has often been written about, but bears repetition. Abstract recitals of human rights sometimes carry less conviction than such significant statistics.

I quote from a paper by Dr. Thomas L. Perry, M.D., delivered at the 1986 Vancouver Centennial Peace and Disarmament Symposium.[32] All the figures quoted are in US dollars.

> Public Expenditures in Preparation for War, 1986
>
> - $800–900 billion per year = 1.5–1.7 million dollars per minute
>
> Cost of:
>
> *(a)* Smallpox
>
> 10-year WHO campaign to eradicate smallpox
>
> - $100 million, or <u>1 hour of arms expenditure</u>
>
> *(b)* Measles
>
> Measles causes 900,000 deaths annually in developing countries, with 10–20% fatality rate
>
> - Probable cost of global eradication — $400 million or <u>5 hours' spending</u>
>
> *(c)* Iodine deficiency disorders
>
> Over 400 million people affected due to iodine insufficiency in soil and diet
>
> Likely cost of prevention — $2 billion or <u>22 hours' expenditure</u>

[32] "What the Arms Race is Doing to People in the Third World", in T.L. Perry and J.G. Foulks (eds.), *End the Arms Race: Fund Human Needs*, Proceedings of the Vancouver Centennial Peace and Disarmament Symposium, 1986, p. 167.

(*d*) Acute infant respiratory infections

2.2 million infant deaths per year. Along with diarrhoeal infections, these are the world's most important preventable causes of death. Mortality rate ten times greater than in developed countries.

- Relatively easy to prevent

(*e*) *Famine*

Causing recurrent death rate of millions per year (e.g., Ethiopia, Sudan)

UN special session on starvation in Africa (June 1988) concluded that $80 billion (<u>six weeks' expenditure</u>) would stop desertification, construct necessary irrigation facilities and introduce suitable agricultural practices to prevent famine everywhere in Africa.

(*f*) *Schistosomiasis* (parasitic worm infection)

affecting 200–300 million people in Africa, Latin America and South East Asia.

- Can be eliminated at cost of $2 per person ($600 million = <u>7½ hours' spending</u>) in treatment and proper sewage systems

(*g*) *Disease contaminated water*

2 billion people drink disease-contaminated water, which causes 80% of all illnesses among them

- cost of safe water supply — <u>18 days' military spending</u>

Apart from WHO studies, the medical information on which these observations are based is contained in various articles in authoritative journals such as *The Lancet*, the *New England Journal of Medicine*, and *Pediatrics and Science*.[33]

[33] (*a*) V.W. Sidel, "Destruction Before Detonation: the Impact of the Arms Race on Health and Health Care", in *The Lancet*, 2 (1985), pp. 1287–1289.

(*b*) B.J. Schmidt, "Current Outlook for Children Around the World", in *Pediatrics*, 74 (1984), pp. 294–295.

(*c*) J. Chrétien, W. Holland, P. Mackem, J. Murray and A. Woolcock, "Acute Respiratory Infections in Children: A Global Public Health Problem", in *New England Journal of Medicine*, 310 (1984), pp. 982–984.

THE TYRANNY OF THE ARMS RACE

When dealing with the arms race, it is important to bear in mind that the armaments industry has become an institution in itself, with a drive and momentum of its own. However great its dependence on governments, it has a way of making governments fall in line with its wishes. It has the power of several multinational corporations rolled into one. It enjoys hidden alliances with the military, the bureaucracy and political parties. It is a living, breathing entity with a vitality of its own, a power centre in itself. When it speaks, governments must listen. In the United States alone, it has consumed $10 trillion dollars of the national wealth since 1947. It views with disfavour any de-escalation of tension, urges continuous modernization and intensification of armaments, and foments national and international tensions. It increases the level of public alarm concerning weaknesses in defence, supplies armaments sometimes to both adversaries in conflict situations, and views with satisfaction the emergence of international conflicts which absorb its products. It exerts considerable political pressure through providing vast amounts of employment in vital areas of the economy.

In other words, we have here a new source of tyranny which, though not a nation state in its own right, has more than the powers of many a nation state. It flourishes even in the best of democracies because, as an entity, it is unseen. In the words of a recent American writer, this tyranny causes a crisis

> every bit as acute as the tyranny that caused the American Independence movement of the 18th century; or the enslavement of African Americans that caused the Abolitionist movement of the 19th century; or the outrage of segregation that caused the Civil Rights movement of the 20th century.[34]

(d) D.R. Hopkins, J.P. Koplan, A.R. Hinman and J.M. Lane, "The Case for Global Measles Eradication", in *The Lancet*, 1 (1982), pp. 1396–1398.

(e) B.S. Hetzel, "Iodine Deficiency Disorders (IDD) and Their Eradication", in *The Lancet*, 2 (1983), pp. 1126–1129.

(f) Anonymous, "Control of Iodine Deficiency in Asia", in *The Lancet*, 2 (1983), p. 1244.

(g) G. Kolata, "Avoiding the Schistosome's Tricks", in *Science*, 227 (1985), pp. 285–287.

(h) G. Kolata, "The Search for a Malaria Vaccine", in *Science*, 226 (1984), pp. 679–682.

(i) B. Lown, "Nobel Peace Prize Lecture: A Prescription for Hope", in *New England Journal of Medicine*, 314 (1986), pp. 985–987.

[34] L. Agran, *Ending the Tyranny of the Arms Race: A Peace Conversion Program*, Nuclear Age Peace Foundation, 1990, p. 8.

As that author points out, it is not possible for us to compromise with colonialism, slavery, or segregation. In the same way, we cannot compromise with the arms race, which involves a negation of human rights no less than did colonialism, slavery and segregation. We are not yet able, because of our mental conditioning, to see it in that light.

This tyranny indeed operates in more insidious ways than the three tyrannies mentioned before. Apart from the diversion of resources from areas where it is vitally needed, such as education, health, and environmental protection, it has caused a run on earth resources which is permanently impoverishing the planet and has already secretly polluted the air, land and water resources of entire communities — sometimes for periods as long as 280,000 years. This cannot go on much longer, and it is indeed a tyranny whose reach in time and space is unmatched by any tyrannies of the past. No observer of human rights can fail to see its obvious human rights implications.

The consequence is that, though not commonly thus perceived, the processes of democracy are becoming unable to contain the power of the armaments industry. Kenneth Galbraith puts his finger on the illusions surrounding this matter in these terms:

> The first source of the American military power is belief — the faith — that any government instrument is subject to democratic process. This belief is strong in our rhetoric; it is what children are still taught in school; but it is in fact what no fully informed citizen can believe. The modern military establishment, in the organizations it dominates, the money it controls, the politicians it commands, the scientific community it subsidizes and, under the cloak of patriotism that protects it, has become a polar force in its own right. It embraces and controls the civilian authority that legally and constitutionally is presumed to be the source of its restraint. The President, the Secretary of Defence, and the civilian heads of the three armed services are now the articulate and influential advocates of the military's purpose.[35]

The same is no doubt true of most other countries.

CONVERSION

It is true that if the arms race is stopped tomorrow, the money being poured into it cannot be siphoned off into development. If the arms race is stopped, the sources that supply it with funds will withhold supply for other purposes unless we speedily prepare the arms machine for conversion to peaceful

[35] In T.L. Perry and J.G. Foulks, *op. cit.*, p. 105.

purposes. This is easier said than done, for the weapons industry, in league with the military, corporate capital and many elements in governments itself, will stand in the way.

If we are planning for conversion in the next decade, we must start our preparation *now*. Studies in this new discipline are already well advanced and it would appear that the main difficulty is not so much the retraining of personnel (except in specially skilled high technology occupations, this can be done fairly readily), but the refashioning of plants.

For the "retooling" of industries, the following steps are necessary:

1. The establishment in arms-producing countries of a Ministry of Conversion, charged with the task of enumeration of personnel and factories engaged in the weapons trade, and with the compilation of a list of civilian uses to which the existing military technology can be diverted.
2. Research on alternative technology for each plant can take place at three levels:

    (a) *Governmental level*
    A Department of Research should research at macro level the ways in which existing technology can be matched against national needs, especially in such matters as health and the environment.

    (b) *the Factory level*
    Workers in a factory are among the most fruitful sources of ideas of alternative uses for their skills and plants. For example, in the British Lucas Company, the Lucas Aerospace Combined Shop Stewards Committee generated proposals for 150 alternative products.

    (c) *the Union level*
    Unions as a whole can address this question at a national level.

3. The establishment of a conversion fund for the purpose of funding research and, where necessary, seeding pilot projects.
4. The establishment of conversion committees in every corporation and municipality.
5. Disarmament being a matter particularly pertinent to peace and goodwill, churches and religious organizations should consider making a serious input into stimulating public consciousness regarding the need for conversion.

6. From the financial angle, studies are required:
   (a) of costing involved in conversion of sources from which such costs could be met; and
   (b) market research regarding alternative products.

* * *

At the start of the 1980s, it looked as if the arms race was getting the better of civilization and about to destroy it. That decade was a decade described by Professor Richard Falk as a time of hazard, but also of great opportunity and hope.[36] At the dawn of the 1990s, with the next century not even a decade away from us, we are able to say that, though the hazard remains, the opportunity has been grasped, at least to some extent, and the hope is growing. The nineties can see the cementing of that hope, and the shrinking of that hazard if we use to their full potential the tools that international law and human rights give us. A recent United Nations Disarmament paper points out that the improved world political climate "provides favourable opportunities of making a quantum leap in international relations".[37] As that study points out, scholars can make a major contribution to that leap by undertaking research to provide new theoretical concepts and practical mechanisms. That is the pre-eminent task to set before ourselves at Congresses such as these.

From the beginnings of recorded history, humanity has been the victim of an arms race of one kind or another and, in nearly every instance, the arms race swallowed up the civilization which fuelled it. The disciplines of human rights and international law, if used to their full capacity, can help us rise triumphant over this ancient scourge.

[36] Essay "On the Further Decline of International Law", in A.R. Blackshield (ed.), *Legal Change: Essays in Honour of Julius Stone*, Butterworths, 1983, at pp. 272–273.

[37] Boris Krasoulin, "Problems of Disarmament and Researchers' Tasks", *UNIDIR Newsletter*, December 1989, p. 3.

12. Nuclear Weapons*

The topic on which I am addressing you goes to the very heart of the paradox which faces our generation. How is it that in this age when the world of knowledge has at its service more power for good than ever before in human history, the real world is closer to destroying itself and its environment than it has ever been?

One would have thought that knowledge was the road to an improvement of the human condition and that technology, which knowledge produced, was the prime tool for this purpose. The real world in which we live presents the opposite picture — that knowledge is showing the road to a slide towards destruction and that technology in the form of nuclear weapons is the prime tool that knowledge has fashioned for this purpose.

Where does the law come into this paradoxical relationship between the theory that knowledge is a bounteous provider and the reality that it has become the ultimate destroyer?

Law is the great reconciler, harnessing, to the service of justice and human welfare, power which might otherwise career uncontrolled. It polices the departures from such norms. It reaches all departments of human life, and no sector, however powerful, is above the law. Is nuclear power so powerful that it is above the law? Is there no law that regulates it, or if there is, are nuclear weapons too powerful for that law? If there is no law that regulates them, is it because this dimension of power is so awesome that the law in this instance recoils from its habitual role and admits its incapacity?

We have throughout the ages been familiar with the maxim that no person is above the law. Emperors and kings have been reminded from time to time by lawyers, religious teachers and the sheer force of historical events that those who seek to override the law do so at their peril. In the context of the nuclear problem, the proposition must be restated in the form that no power

* Based on a Paper delivered at The Hague in 1989 at a Congress of lawyers against nuclear arms, and published in (1990) *Denver Journal of International Law and Policy*, Vol. 19, pp. 11–36, under the title "The Law, Nuclear Weapons and the Real World". Although the Cold War has since terminated, many of the concerns expressed in the paper are with us still.

is above the law. It may be power so great as to be able to destroy our planet. Yet the law is more powerful than that power, and if it is not already, we must inquire why it is not and must make it so.

In the field of nuclear weapons more than in almost any other field, there is a powerful collision between theory and reality, and that is perhaps the reason why the organizers of this conference, in their wisdom, have drawn attention to the contradictions between the law and the real world that exist in the context of nuclear weapons.

Where then is the law that in this real world dominated by materialistic forces can surmount such power and tame it to the social purposes of humanity?

Unperceived by most citizens, that law is found everywhere, both within national legal systems and on the international plane. It is found in the realm of substantive law and in the realm of procedure. Its conceptual roots can be traced in the most ancient legal philosophies and its practical justifications in the most modern scientific researches.

The fault is not in the law but perhaps in ourselves that we are not sufficiently conscious of its presence or, indeed, of its power. If one were to pursue this question of fault even further, one would find the finger of accusation pointing in a special way to those who are the custodians of the law — lawyers and judges. They have perhaps immersed themselves so deeply in the real world of profits and power as to lose sight of the greater realities confronting our age. Indeed, the legality (or otherwise) of nuclear weapons is perhaps the greatest legal question confronting our age, and yet for a quarter century after the first use of nuclear weapons in war there was a singular dearth of legal discussion of this all-important question. There were notable exceptions such as Schwarzenberger's, *The Legality of Nuclear Weapons*,[1] and Nagendra Singh's, *Nuclear Weapons and International Law*,[2] but on the whole, there was a neglect of this problem.

1 G. Schwarzenberger, *The Legality of Nuclear Weapons* (1958).

2 N. Singh, *Nuclear Weapons and International Law* (1959).

A central theme of this paper will be that the law is already there, waiting to be acknowledged and to be applied. It is our task at this world symposium to exhibit it to view so that both the legal fraternity and others — scientists, politicians and ordinary citizens — can use it more purposefully, annexing nuclear power to its domain in the same way as great events of the past, such as the Magna Carta[3] and the Declaration on the Rights of Man,[4] have annexed the domains of kings within the law's empire.

My task of analysing law and nuclear weapons in the context of the real world requires me, preliminarily, to note in general terms a few of the varying dimensions of reality that become pertinent to the problem. We have realities at the level of the politician — the *political* realities, national and international, in the midst of which we live. We also have *physical* realities which condition our very existence on this planet — of which political realities sometimes lose sight. These are assuming dimensions in our age which were never known before. *Economic* realities, such as money spent on armaments which diverts wealth and resources from the problem of poverty, are also particularly pertinent to the nuclear problem. While poverty is in the process of destroying hundreds of millions of lives on this planet, we have spent and are preparing to spend trillions of dollars on nuclear arms. We need also to consider what may be described as *nuclear* reality (i.e., the contrast between the mundane realities driving the nuclear weapons enterprise today and the idealism which gave it birth). Finally, *social* realities — the driving forces of power, profit, and prestige — must be addressed.

At all these levels of reality, nuclear weapons make a very real impact. Our comprehension of each one of them would be vastly different depending on whether we contemplate them in the context of a nuclear or a non-nuclear world.

After some general observations in regard to each of these levels of reality, I shall observe some notable contrasts between the world of theory and the world of reality in some selected areas especially pertinent to nuclear weapons.

3 See generally A. Pallister, *Magna Carta: The Heritage of Liberty* (1971).

4 See generally G. Jellinek, *The Declaration of the Rights of Man and of Citizens: A Contribution to Modern Constitutional History* (1979).

I. A PRELIMINARY SURVEY

A. *Political Reality*

The world of realpolitik has always been concerned with the sheer pursuit of power. In the world of realpolitik people, the principal actors, lay aside their humanity and play the game of power as a chess player plays the game of chess. Victory is the only objective. Participants can be sacrificed, for they are no more than chessmen who can be given away if need be, *en masse*, if only one's opponent's king can be checkmated. Armies on the battlefield are not very different from inanimate weaponry such as cannons and tanks. They are all tallied up in a common ledger, the humans dehumanized, the weapons anthropomorphized into living realities which are the equivalent of thousands of humans.

Checkmating your opponent's king has enormous advantages. Your opponent is wiped off the map. Your own forces may be decimated, but you are left sovereign over the field of battle, free to order it thereafter without let or hindrance from the enemy. The model of the chessboard translates very easily into the model of the battlefield. Your legions may have been cut to pieces, but your enemy is at your feet, his possessions yours for the taking, his economy at your disposal.

Underlying all of this is the assumption that like the magic of the chessboard, a whole new army can be brought into commission for the next battle as though the decimation of the last one was irrelevant. Thus far in warfare, these illusions of the chessboard have to a large extent held true. The victor, with all the strengths and fruits of victory, could soon field another army and reasonably hope to vanquish another foe.

Nuclear weapons have changed political reality beyond recognition. They have made such games irrelevant to real life. There is no longer an endless supply of revitalized chessmen nor a succession of games. The chessmen are extinguished and a new law ordains that only one game can be played. What is left on the chessboard will be a theoretically victorious but decimated army and a vanquished king. The victorious army will have no spoils to enjoy and no new battles to fight except its own battle for survival in the harsh world of nuclear winter. The ruler who plays the game of nuclear chess would have played his last game, whether he "wins" or "loses."

The world of make believe which lay beneath the so-called world of reality is gone forever and the world of reality, shorn of make-believe, stands exposed in all its starkness. The world of realpolitik could play out its games only against a framework of potential replenishment. When that framework is gone, so is the game.

In the past the most massive destroyers of human life and the environment, such as Genghis Khan or Attila, could kill and destroy to the limit of their ability but the reservoirs of human life and earth resources would be refilled. Realpolitik had a meaning. The next game of chess could be played. That scenario is gone forever.

B. *Physical Reality*

As the "realities" of politics are stripped of their illusions, the realities of physics and chemistry take over. Increasingly, our political and geopolitical thinking reflects an awareness of the physical laws which circumscribe human activity — an awareness which could be kept at a distance so long as the scale of human activity did not approach those circumscribing boundaries.

Today we are face to face with those physical realities because we stand at the interface between humanity's expanding capabilities and nature's limiting constraints. Physical realities thus limit our thinking in a manner not known to the generations that preceded us. In fairness to those generations, however, we must observe that though they did not stand at the interface as we do, they still had the wisdom to foresee that if and when humanity arrived at that interface it would be almost too late to stand back. They advocated then, in a manner which would have stood us in good stead now, a harmony with the forces of nature rather than a confrontation with them. Had we heeded these voices of wisdom, we would not now be in the predicament in which we find ourselves.

The days of the boundless ocean and the boundless atmosphere, able to absorb all the toxins we could deposit in them, are gone. As we stand at this significant interface, we search around desperately for new principles by which to govern our international conduct. The paradox is that those principles have long been with us though we have refused to recognize or apply them.

When the concept of the nuclear winter emerged in 1982 with the pioneering researches of P.J. Crutzen and J.W. Birks, this reality was unveiled in all its starkness and in a form so powerful that even governments and armies dedicated to the nuclear weapons enterprise were compelled to take note, that a nuclear war could kill a billion humans at first blast, two billion in its after-effects, alter climatic conditions by blotting out the sunlight, destroy agriculture and reduce humanity to its most primitive level since the stone age.

C. *Economic Reality*

Economic realities can be as crippling as political realities, economic subjection as harsh as political subjection and economic aggression as vicious as armed attack.

The economic reality facing the world today is that more than 2.5 billion dollars a day are spent on fuelling the world's armaments establishment. A hundred million dollars an hour, or over a million dollars a minute flow down the drain of negativity so far as human welfare is concerned. A day's expenditure on armaments would eradicate malaria or lift ten million lives out of the trough of starvation, but this is not our chosen option. Visitors from outer space would no doubt marvel at our sense of priorities, but that is economic reality today.

It has now been universally accepted by scholars in the field of human rights and development that there is an intrinsic linkage between development and the arms race. This linkage rests upon the economic reality that in a world of scarce resources the absorption of trillions of dollars by the arms race is one of the principal factors inhibiting the right to development.

We need to remind ourselves of the landmark event which occurred on 4 December 1986 when the General Assembly adopted the Declaration on the Right to Development,[5] which viewed development as an "inalienable right". If this be so, the economic reality of the nuclear arms race is one of the most potent forces denying this basic human right to vast sections of the earth's population.

D. *Nuclear Reality*

Nuclear weapons research started as an idealistic venture in the minds of many scientists. Their memoirs reveal that the news that Germany was conducting research in this field provided several of them with a powerful impetus to produce the weapon before it could fall into the hands of one of the most monstrous tyrannies that had yet appeared. One of them wrote:

[5] Declaration on the Right to Development, G.A. Res. 41/128, 41 U.N. GAOR Supp. Annex (No. 53) at 186, U.N. Doc. A/41/53 (1986).

> [T]here was not for a long time in history any worse aberration of human conduct and human monstrosity than the Nazi regime in Germany. And the idea of an atomic bomb that could win the war against Germany was highly attractive to me. While nothing required me to work more than eight hours a day, I spent at least sixteen in the average day on the bomb project. I was highly motivated simply because I thought it was important to win the war against Germany.[6]

There were many more, like Leo Szilard, who wrote:

> During the war, while we worked on the bomb, we scientists thought for a while that we were in a neck and neck race against the Germans and that getting the bomb first might make a difference between winning and losing the war.[7]

But it soon became clear that Germany was not in the race to produce the bomb. The capitulation of Germany made the defeat of Nazi tyranny no longer an issue. The bomb continued, however, to be the subject of research despite the disappearance of the earlier idealism which fuelled the nuclear effort. Its use against Japan was a significant fall away from the initial idealism. Continued research after the capitulation of Japan meant that the objective of defeating a particularly monstrous tyranny had now been superseded by the much more mundane motive of providing a weapon for the U.S. to use against its enemies. It also gave the U.S. a nuclear monopoly over the rest of the world.

Finally, when the bomb ceased to be a monopoly, the ideology behind its production changed dramatically again, and the nuclear arms race began. There was no longer the pursuit of ideals in the production of the bomb. In the real world of the post-war era that initial idealism had disappeared. In the nuclear weapons field as elsewhere the reality was that the powers were pursuing interests and not ideals. The scientists, on whose expertise the entire enterprise depended, had forgotten their idealism and were lending their expertise to the pursuit of national interests rather than universal ideals. The Nuremberg Principles,[8] which all nations accepted at the end of the war, dictated that crimes against humanity were prohibited, however much they promoted national interests. In such matters, universalism prevailed over

6 L. Freeman, *Nuclear Witnesses: Insiders Speak Out* (1981), p. 83.

7 L. Szilard, *A Personal History of the Bomb*, University of Chicago Roundtable, Sep. 15, 1949, at 14.

8 Principles of International Law Recognized in the Charter of the Nuremberg Tribunal and in the Judgment of the Tribunal (International Law Commission), 5 U.N. GAOR Supp. (No. 12), at 11, U.N. Doc. A/1316, (1950) [hereinafter the Nuremberg Principles].

nationalism. In the nuclear weapons enterprise, the real world of politicians, officials, soldiers and scientists has forgotten the Nuremberg Principles, which are an integral part of international law.

E. *Social Reality*

We need to face the fact that there is a solid wall of opposition to the abolition of nuclear weapons coming from various interested sources — those who derive profit, power or prestige from the nuclear weapons establishment.

Who are those who derive profit, power or prestige from these weapons that can fling all living systems and cultures into oblivion? They can be analysed under the three headings I have mentioned.

1. Profit

The profit motive has throughout history proved to be so powerful that even the certain knowledge that millions of deaths will result has not deterred those who pursue it. This statement is best illustrated through the armaments industry which, in all ages of modern history, richly documents the fact that where there is profit to be made, the fact that such profit is achieved at the cost of human lives seems irrelevant.

Great commercial houses that made the lethal weapons through which the killing of humans has been reduced to a fine art have flourished since the industrial revolution. They are indeed among the most respected businesses in their respective countries, and their clients are their own and foreign governments, not to mention terrorist movements and protagonists in civil wars. The whole world flocks to the arms fairs they stage like great carnivals of death, while the petty drug trafficker is hunted down in the side-streets of the city.

The nuclear weapons industry is but a sophisticated extension of the traditional armaments industry, multiplying several fold the scale of profit resulting from its operations. It is true that this industry does not have foreign customers in an open marketplace of weapons, but the scale of profit to be derived from a nuclear weapons contract is such as to take it almost beyond the dreams of avarice. Nuclear weapons manufacturers talk in billions rather than millions of dollars, and they seek to convince both rulers and the military that the level of expenditure must constantly be stepped up in the interest of national security.

Nearly a quarter century ago, President Kennedy addressed himself to the question of the alleged megaton gap between the U.S. and the Soviet Union in a radio and television interview. He was asked for his reaction to a newspaper advertisement of a weapons-manufacturing company urging a 2.5 billion dollar program for a nuclear delivery system. The President detailed the existing missile systems and said:

> There is just a limit to how much we need, as well as how much we can afford, to have a successful deterrent. I would say when we start to talk about the megatonnage we could bring into a nuclear war, we are talking about annihilation. How many times do you have to hit a target with nuclear weapons? That is why when we are talking about spending the 2.5 billion dollars, we don't think we are going to get 2.5 billion dollars worth of security.[9]

The possible destruction of the ecosystem and the prospects of a nuclear winter are no more a deterrent than the millions of deaths resulting from the use of conventional weapons. Indeed, in the nuclear weapons enterprise, there are many salves to the conscience apart from patriotism and self-defence, which are the traditional defences of the arms manufacturer. In the case of nuclear weaponry, we have the ever attractive argument of deterrence — the makers of the weapon, far from perfecting the means of exterminating populations, are in fact said to be saving billions of lives and lifting the scourge of war from suffering humanity. The enterprise is therefore said to be so laudable that constraints upon it would indeed be counterproductive so far as national welfare is concerned.

There is also another species of profit associated with the nuclear weapons enterprise. Nuclear weapons are the livelihood of many who have been trained specifically for their production. Ask any scientist in the nuclear weapons enterprise whether he or she would not rather devote his or her talents to something more humane, and you will often receive the answer that society has trained them expressly for this purpose, guided them towards a Ph.D. in nuclear physics, and thence into the weapons establishment. Society shaped their training in such a way that they are unsuited for any other occupation. If any blame is to be attached to their means of earning a livelihood, it is society that must be blamed and not themselves. The author has often received this response from scientists he has questioned on the moral aspects of their work. The trained nuclear weapons scientist thus has a vested interest in the continuance of the enterprise and he or she will not easily be persuaded to look elsewhere or to lower his or her living standards through devotion to moral imperatives.

The same applies to the thousands who depend for their livelihood on the nuclear weapons establishment. No doubt there exists in many of these cases

9 J. Wiley, *Environmental Consequences of Nuclear War* (1985), p. 490.

a lack of specialization that the nuclear scientist enjoys, but for them it is a livelihood. One would often prefer to continue in a secure occupation, salving one's conscience by convincing oneself of the moral rectitude of the enterprise, rather than taking the uncomfortable decision to opt out.

The military establishment is another sharer in the profits of the nuclear enterprise. Here too, is a considerable addition of privileges to the ordinary rewards of a military career. Among these are specialized employment and a high level of influence with the government and with the multi-billion dollar enterprises that produce the weapons. A specialized cadre of officers and enlisted personnel, trained particularly for the enterprise, also represent an additional nucleus of full time servants of the weapons enterprise, dedicated to its service and its success.

2. Power

Nuclear weapons are of course a source of power. Governments seek them as a multiplier of the powers they wield through conventional arms. Indeed, nuclear capability by itself can theoretically even displace the need for conventional weapons, so great is the power these weapons bring to their holders.

The power in question is primarily military power, but with military power comes an expansion of political power. The known possessor of nuclear weaponry commands many multiples of bargaining power as compared with the position of one that holds only conventional weapons. The nuclear weapons do not have to be used. They lie in the background but give stentorian tones to the voices of their owners at the bargaining table.

Enough said in relation to the power of governments; this is a point too obvious to need elaboration. However, nuclear weapons also give power to those who have anything to do with them — defence contractors, the military establishment, and research workers included. They proceed about their daily business with an aura of special importance that no other weaponry can match. They have access to the corridors of political power and are privy to the secrets of governments. The finances involved in their activities are also at such a level that association with these weapons in any way adds another dimension of power to the world in which they live.

There is also domestic political power in the nuclear weapons enterprise, for the enterprise means tens of thousands of jobs and every job represents a vote. The political systems (and the economic systems) of many states in the U.S. are heavily dependent on the weapons establishment, and the same can be said of power realities in other countries.

The nuclear weapons lobby is immensely powerful, and in Washington, as in other centres of power, the weapons enterprise, with vast funds at its disposal, has the ear of senators and representatives in a manner which the anti-nuclear movement cannot match. As for the military leaders themselves, their power keeps expanding as the nuclear weapons enterprise expands. With nuclear weapons, a static state is a lack-lustre situation. New contingencies must be envisaged and new plans made, for these mean glamour and expansion of power. Helen Caldicott in her book *Missile Envy*[10] suggests that such attitudes are a result of both the commitment to nuclear weapons and the fascination of building and experimenting with more and more complicated technology and weapons systems. New weapons systems are new sources of power. These are some of the psychological factors which operate in the real world.

3. Prestige

The nuclear weapons business is a business of high prestige. Everything associated with it is prestigious — position, privilege, finances, secrecy, all go with it. All sharers in the enterprise are partakers in this bounty of benefits.

In the socialist world, where private profit is not to be made out of the weapons enterprise, the element of prestige no doubt provides a substitute for the profit motive for all of those in the establishment, military as well as non-military, who are linked with the nuclear weapons enterprise. Through it, they enjoy a special aura of prestige.

Vested interests thus stand at every point in support of the nuclear weapons enterprise. Their combination of industrial-military-financial-bureaucratic strength presents too solid a phalanx for easy penetration. Do we have the weaponry with which to pierce this wall of protection?

My answer is in the affirmative. We have that weapon, and that weapon is the law. Strong enough by itself, it has been reinforced in recent years by scientific research which spells the end of civilization, of life-styles, and of life itself if the nuclear enterprise proceeds unabated. That reality combines with the law to spell the doom of nuclear weapons. This is the single central theme of this paper, and it rests on a principle so powerful that it must prevail in the face of even the most concerted opposition that vested interests can mount.

[10] Helen Caldicott, *Missile Envy: The Arms Race and Nuclear War*, Bantam Books, 1985.

II. SOME SPECIFIC CONTRASTS

A. *Contrasts Between the Real World and Nuclear Weapons Treaties*

We have not thus far been able to procure a treaty which bans nuclear weapons outright but we have had a series of partial successes. Each of these is, no doubt, a great achievement and is cause for congratulation, but we must not be so carried away by these treaties as to lose sight of the real world of nuclear danger that exists despite them.

In this paper, we shall not be able to cover the field of nuclear treaties completely but will use two of them as illustrations.

1. The INF Treaty of 8 December 1987[11]

This is no doubt a landmark event, as it represents the first significant move towards de-escalation and the cessation of the arms race. It is also significant as the first effective reduction of a whole category of existing nuclear weapons rather than an effort at merely controlling their numbers.

Yet these great achievements must not cause us to lose sight of reality. Let us not be carried away by the treaty, for without more steps in that direction it means very little. The elimination of 859 U.S. and 1,752 Soviet missiles over three years represents no more than four percent (4%) of the nuclear arsenals of the powers in question. Unless more significant reductions follow, this will remain in reality no more than merely a token gesture. Indeed, unless we keep these proportions in perspective, we could lull ourselves into a false sense of security that the nuclear weapons threat is on the way out. Such attitudes are already visible among lawyers and the general public and provide a formidable obstacle to the work of organizations working towards the elimination of nuclear weapons.

We have yet to see how this treaty works. For too long we have witnessed the sad reality that even the most well-intentioned treaties can be defeated and in fact circumvented or evaded through a lack of willingness to abide by their spirit. Perhaps the best illustration of this is offered by the celebrated Nuclear Non-Proliferation Treaty.

[11] Treaty between the United States and the Union of Soviet Socialist Republics on the Elimination of Their Intermediate-Range and Shorter-Range Missiles, Dec. 8, 1987, 88 DEPT. STATE BULL. 24 (Feb. 1988), *reprinted in* 27 I.L.M. 84 (1988) [hereinafter INF Treaty].

2. The Nuclear Non-Proliferation Treaty of 1 July 1968[12]

The Nuclear Non-Proliferation Treaty (NPT) was aimed at ending both the vertical proliferation of nuclear weapons among the nuclear powers and the horizontal proliferation of nuclear weapons among non-nuclear powers. It was a momentous step forward and should have spelled the beginning of the end of the arms race.

Yet the reality was that in the first decade of its existence the total number of nuclear warheads in the superpowers' arsenals tripled, rising from 5,800 to 16,000. By 1988, they had perhaps increased an additional fifty percent (50%), to 24,000. The reality was far from the undertaking contained in Article 6 of the Treaty which intended to negotiate an early end to the arms race.

Not only was the number of weapons increased, but also their quality and capacity for geographical deployment. So also was the ability increased to use the oceans as launching grounds, for of the combined U.S./USSR total of around 4,000 strategic ballistic missiles, at least one-third are deployed at sea.

The world of hope surrounding the NPT expected a reduction in nuclear weaponry as its outcome. The real world in which the treaty has functioned has seen no commitment to an ending of the arms race, but instead both a vertical and horizontal proliferation of nuclear weapons. The INF treaty made a dent in this world of reality but only a minor dent, easily reversible if its momentum is not sustained.

We have fears that more countries are on the verge of nuclear weaponry, and the fear has even been expressed that terrorist groups, who evidently have enormous funds at their disposal, are also potential possessors of crude nuclear weapons. This is the world of reality which contrasts so strongly with the principles on which the NPT is based.

B. *Contrasts Between the Real World And The Theory That Oceans Are a Common Resource of Humanity*

Legal and human rights theory teaches us that the high seas are a common resource of humanity. The vast maritime reaches of our planet which lie beyond coastal waters and exclusive economic zones are the common property of the whole human family, for all to enjoy and use. That use must presumably be for peaceful purposes and not for the destruction of the human

[12] The Nuclear Non-Proliferation Treaty, Jul. 1, 1968, 21 U.S.T. 483, T.I.A.S. No. 6839, 729 U.N.T.S. 161, *reprinted in* 7 I.L.M. 809 (1968) [hereinafter NPT].

species — least of all for the destruction of the vast majority of humankind who are not party to the quarrels of the nuclear powers.

Yet what is the reality? There are some 5,900 tactical nuclear warheads available for use by the naval forces of the nuclear powers to strike ships, submarines, planes and land targets.[13] Submarine-launched ballistic missiles (SLBMs) of the Soviet Union and the U.S. have the potential to destroy the major cities of both countries several times over. In destroying these cities, they would launch a nuclear winter upon the entire population of the globe — the very owners of the common resource, namely the high seas, from which their destruction was launched.

A Trident submarine carrying 24 Trident missiles, each of which has eight 100 kiloton warheads, would have a grand total of 192 warheads. Each of these could be separately targeted, thus making a Trident commander "the third most powerful man in the world" according to Robert C. Aldridge, a former Lockheed engineer.[14]

Another problem in this regard is the deliberate refusal of nuclear weapons-states to reveal whether their battleships carry or do not carry nuclear weapons. It is, for example, a deliberate U.S. policy to refuse to confirm or deny the presence of nuclear weapons on board their vessels, thus rendering it difficult for non-nuclear states to decide on an appropriate course of action in relation to them.

The oceans then are put to the most lethal purpose which humankind has devised. This is an abuse of basic principles so strong that it needs to be violently condemned on the basis of legal principle, and international lawyers could perhaps address this issue. The use of the oceans for nuclear weapons launching is no different in principle from the use of outer space for this purpose. Yet we condone it with scarcely a protest, save for comparatively feeble attempts to establish nuclear-free zones and zones of peace.

C. *Contrasts Between the Real World and the Theory That Only Heads of State Can Launch a Nuclear War*

We have seen in our discussion of Trident submarines how a single Trident commander has at his fingertips the power to launch nuclear weapons in such quantity as to amount to a major nuclear war. This will no doubt provoke a major nuclear response from the power attacked, with all the potential of triggering a nuclear winter.

[13] See Study on the Naval Arms Race, U.N. Doc. A/40/535 at 28 (1985).

[14] Aldridge, *First Strike Breakout in 1988*, Ground Zero, Dec. 1983-Jan. 1984, p. 1.

According to an authority on nuclear armaments,[15] there is a growing number of officers in the military chains of command among the nuclear weapons powers who are empowered to decide on the use of nuclear weapons in case of attack. These are officers at the operational tactical level — a level far removed from the head of state who theoretically alone enjoys the right to decide on the use of nuclear weapons.

Indeed, the time scale available for this decision keeps decreasing with improvements in the sophistication of nuclear weaponry; decisions would have to be taken in minutes — far less time than would be needed to awaken either President if he should happen to be in bed at the crucial moment. The decision not to use weapons and to stay passive and suffer the risk of losing one's whole arsenal of nuclear weaponry, or to strike back, is a crucial one and can in no circumstances be delayed.

To this must be added the Launch on Warning Capability (LOWC) which in many cases means that this decision is taken by a computer without human intervention at the moment of decision. The possibility of grave error resulting from malfunctioning machines is ever-present, and the record of near accidents in the past is so serious as to merit careful consideration.

As one United Nations Institute for Disarmament Research (UNIDIR) Study entitled *Risks of Unintentional Nuclear War*[16] tells us, the crucial factor affecting the propensity of a system to produce unintentional nuclear war is the urgency with which the decision must be made. If the forces enabling retaliation are vulnerable to sudden destruction, the deterrent threat can be removed by a pre-emptive attack. This can only be prevented by an immediate and urgent decision during the vital minutes when the attacking missiles are on their way. Where, in reality, is the time for a Presidential decision?

D. *Contrasts Between The Real World And The Theory That Nuclear Weapons Or Know-How Must Not Be Exchanged Between States*

There is a theory, enshrined in Articles I and II of the NPT,[17] that there should be no transfer between states of nuclear weapons or assistance in weapons technology. However, the phraseology of the two articles, read in the context of the general tenor of the Treaty, seems to concentrate on the prohibition of transfer between nuclear states and non-nuclear states rather

[15] Subrahmanyam, "The Link Between Horizontal and Vertical Proliferation", in S. Aga Kahn (ed.), *Nuclear War, Nuclear Proliferation and their Consequences*, Clarendon Press, Oxford, 1986, p. 136.

[16] D. Frei, *Risks of Unintentional Nuclear War* (1982), p. 5.

[17] NPT, *supra* note 12.

than among nuclear states *inter se*. Consequently, transfer of nuclear weapons or know-how as between two nuclear states (e.g., the U.S. and Britain), does not seem in reality to attract the same level of prohibition (notwithstanding the use in Article I of the expression "to *any* recipient *whatsoever*").[18] Thus a primary purpose of the treaty, namely the prevention of such transfer, is defeated.

An important reason for the geographical proliferation of nuclear weapons is the apparent freedom of the nuclear weapons-states to position nuclear weapons in the territory of non-nuclear states. It is possible to argue that this too is contrary to the spirit if not the letter of Articles I and II, but the real world of NATO and the Warsaw Pact flies in the face of such a principle.

In addition, the Treaty does not stand in the way of non-nuclear states such as Australia extending their active co-operation to nuclear states in technological co-operation (for example, by providing tracking stations which assist in the nuclear weapons enterprise). Such assistance is a real, indeed an indispensable, aid to the maintenance of the nuclear weapons enterprise and without it the enterprise would need to be conducted on a truncated scale. Yet this is what the real world offers the nuclear weapons enterprise despite principles and protestations to the contrary.

E. *Contrasts Between The Real World And The Theoretical Freedom Of Non-Nuclear Powers To Desist From Participation In The Nuclear Weapons Enterprise*

Non-nuclear powers may perhaps be divided into three categories. There are those, on the one hand, who are part of the two military alliances that are underpinned by nuclear power — NATO and the Warsaw Pact. Secondly, there are countries which are thought to be on the verge of achieving nuclear capability. The third category comprises countries which have no interest at all in the nuclear weapons enterprise and wish to distance themselves as far as possible from nuclear weapons, their manufacture, testing and tracking.

The majority of the world's nation states are in this third category. They are, in the real world, the passive victims of the nuclear weapons enterprise. However, whether they desire it or not, they provide the testing grounds for nuclear explosions and often the harbours for nuclear vessels. The Pacific Islands and New Zealand provide examples respectively of the two categories. The devastation caused to the natural environment of the former and the economic sanctions applied to the latter when it decided to ban the entry of

[18] NPT, *supra*, note 12; emphasis added.

nuclear vessels into its ports, illustrate how in reality there is often no true option to keep one's hands off the nuclear weapons enterprise.

F. *Contrasts Between the Real World and the Theory of Deterrence*

The theory of nuclear deterrence is the theory most often propounded as a justification for the manufacture of nuclear weapons. The manufacture of these weapons, we are led to understand, is almost a benign enterprise, for it has kept the world away from nuclear war for forty-five years. Nuclear weapons manufacture, far from being a means of destroying the planet, is indeed, from this point of view, a project that helps to keep the peace.

At any rate, such is the theory. But is it matched by conditions in the real world? In the real world, in which nuclear weapons will or will not be used, the reality is that weapons produced for deterrence are used as bargaining counters with no intention of using them in the last resort.

If there is no intention to use them in the last resort, one is only playing a game of bluff with one's opponent. Such a bluff cannot be maintained for all ensuing time. Sooner or later one's opponent will call one's bluff. One cannot persuade one's opponent that nuclear weapons will be used in deterrence unless one really means to use them.

The manufacture of nuclear weapons with a view to deterrence is nothing less than using them as a weapon of last resort. They are not manufactured with a view to their being locked away for all time in a closet. Thus, the real world intends, in the last resort, to use nuclear weapons that are manufactured supposedly for deterrence. Such use will annihilate both those who use them and those against whom they are used. It is mutually assumed destruction (MAD) — no more and no less. To think otherwise is to pull the wool over our eyes and to be blind to reality.

Lest all that I have said thus far should present reality in a dim and foreboding light, I hasten to brighten up the presentation of reality by reference to some truly hopeful features of the real world.

III. SOME HOPEFUL FEATURES OF REALITY

Having dealt at some length with the obstacles presented by the real world, let us now see what factors in the real world operate to bring closer the prospect that the international community will hold itself bound by international law in relation to nuclear weapons.

A. *Soviet Initiatives*

Truth is sometimes stranger than fiction, and the change that has come over the foreign policy of the Soviet Union[19] in the past few years must be a good illustration of this adage. In fact, this is one of the nicest aspects of reality we have seen manifested in our generation.

We now have in office a Soviet leader whose attitudes on a number of matters bearing upon our subject are significantly different from those of his predecessors. Among these are the following:

1. A recognition of the practical unsuitability of nuclear weapons for military purposes;
2. a proclaimed resolve to end the regime of nuclear weapons by the turn of the century;
3. an increasing recognition of and respect for international law and its binding nature;
4. a recognition that with the proliferation of nuclear weapons there is an ever-present danger of accidental war;
5. the idea of open discussion at all levels and on all topics concerning Soviet society and government, including necessarily, the question of the nuclear danger and the possibility of nuclear holocaust;
6. an acknowledgement that science and technology must be the servants of society, guiding it towards a richer future, rather than a dominant influence holding society in its grip;
7. a consciousness of the need to pay attention to the diversion caused by the arms race of scarce resources from much needed social welfare projects;
8. a support for the concept that security comes from mutual understanding rather than unilateral superiority;
9. an acceptance that reasonable sufficiency of military forces is the ideal to be arrived at, rather than military superiority;
10. the unprecedented notion that unilateral disarmament can be resorted to by a major power without detriment to its security or prestige;

[19] This address was delivered in 1989 and published in 1990.

11. a vision of a mutually supportive and inter-related world order of the future in which all sections of global society play an interlocking role;
12. an emphasis upon the vital need for humanity as a whole to address the problem of environmental protection of planet Earth rather than for each nation to pursue selfishly the policies that are in its best interests regardless of environmental repercussions; and
13. the recognition that imbalances in conventional forces such as Soviet tank superiority must be rectified as a prelude to more effective nuclear disarmament.

These factors in combination help considerably in transforming political reality from the life-consuming and soulless concept it once was, into a reality of hopefulness. For the first time in the post-war years, we are perhaps able to say that hopefulness has entered the real world and become part of it rather than being cloistered away in the wishful thinking of philosophers and idealists. When we speak of political reality, therefore, we are no longer talking of a concept that we view with helplessness, but we are talking of a concept vibrant with possibilities for bettering the human condition.

Early products of that new spirit are the INF Treaty,[20] the concept of Nuclear Risk Reduction Centers, the unilateral moratorium on nuclear testing, and the many speeches in which the Soviet leader has proclaimed his antagonism to nuclear weapons and his abiding faith in the strength of international law.

The declining priority given to such programs as "Star Wars" and the growing awareness of legislators and the public that it can at best deliver only a minute fraction of the protection it promised to offer, are other hopeful factors. Altered attitudes in the U.S. towards the Soviet Union and a softening of the attitude of distrust which once prevailed are also a very helpful feature of current realities.

Writers on nuclear weapons, including the present writer, have continually stressed the need to break the spiral of escalation which has kept the nuclear weapons enterprise growing from stage to stage to reach a situation where its very consumption of resources becomes a sort of cancer on the face of the planet. Escalation begets escalation, and so the spiral ascends until a magic formula can be found to break the escalation. It may be that the developments outlined above have provided that magic formula, and that the ascending spiral has been broken. Unilateral action can do this, for just as tension begets tension, relaxation of tension begets relaxation.

[20] INF Treaty, *supra* note 11.

When we speak of political realities we must not permit these hopeful aspects to pass unnoticed.

B. *Erosions of Sovereignty*

There is another aspect to reality that inures to our benefit. That is the erosion currently taking place in traditional attitudes towards the concept of sovereignty. Many forces combine to bring about this result, not the least of which is the reach of modern technology. Technology knows no national barriers and requires concerted international action for its handling.

As a consequence of this enormously expanded reach of modern technology, areas of sovereign power which the nation state would not have dreamt of letting out of its grasp, are now willingly handed over in an increasing number of fields to the regulation of an international controlling authority. Indeed, it is not merely in technical fields such as telecommunications or the prevention of atmospheric pollution that such international co-operation is becoming increasingly visible. The foremost evidence of this comes from the member States of the European Union who are progressively abandoning, to the supranational control of the Union, topics drawn from such fields as currency, trade and customs regulation.

This is a new internationalism — the internationalism of co-operation rather than mere co-existence. We are realizing increasingly that the age is past when different nations looked upon each other as necessary evils with whom they had to co-exist whether they liked it or not. Under the pressures of our age we are forced into a spirit of positive co-operation rather than negative tolerance — and co-operation means a willing acceptance of others as co-participants in a common enterprise — the enterprise of managing spaceship earth which is the common home of all. Co-existence is compatible with inimical states of mind towards each other. Co-operation is not.

An attitude of co-operation immensely strengthens the arm of international law by strengthening the willingness of all to abide by its spirit and its letter, whereas the age of co-existence meant only unwilling acceptance out of sheer self-interest.

As international law grows stronger in this new climate, its ability to curb the abuse of power — nuclear or otherwise — is likewise immeasurably strengthened.

C. *The Growing Authority of International Law*

Against that background as well, the authority of international law becomes all the stronger. Moreover, in the past decade in particular, international law in relation to nuclear weapons has exhibited a dramatic resurgence of interest among lawyers from all countries who have joined their voices in a common call for the outlawing of nuclear weapons. This development is occurring against a backdrop of a general revitalization of international law as a discipline.

In the aftermath of World War II there was a remarkable reluctance on the part of international law and international lawyers to address the question of the illegality of nuclear weapons. The U.S. was the one power that had thus far used the nuclear weapon in war and, in the immediate aftermath of war and the ensuing Cold War period, when the weapon was added to the arsenals of both sides, there was a reluctance to scrutinize its legality. Such considerations combined with other fortuitous events, such as the Korean War, to divert attention from this important problem of international law. Today those inhibitions no longer exist. Time enough has passed since Hiroshima and Nagasaki for the world to engage in a dispassionate appraisal of the legality or illegality of nuclear weapons. The world order is not likely to be thrown into turmoil by a consideration of this matter. Indeed, the time is propitious for doing so. Reality thus favours, rather than obstructs, the consideration of this matter.

D. *The Confluence of Global Perils*

Other global dangers drive us into each other's arms. Environmental dangers resulting from depletion of the ozone layer, deforestation of tropical rain forests and industrial pollution causing acid rain are some of these. New phenomena such as AIDS, which can be likened to mediaeval pestilences which swept through continents. require concerted international effort. Drug trafficking and terrorism cannot be tackled by countries singly. The fact that the globe is inhabited by one interlocking society is being emphasized and underlined in this age as never before.

United action calls for united regulation and universal norms. The climate of respect for these is growing. Borne on this tide of necessity towards a regime of universal norms, humanity in this age finds that reality is more on the side of international law than against it.

Students of international law have been taught in the past that but for international law the pirates would rule the seas, aeroplanes would collide in mid-air, letters would not be delivered beyond national boundaries, and telecommunication would be impossible. To those realities of the past have now been added a set of new realities, some of them grim and some of them benign, but all of them so compelling that they cannot be ignored.

We are not moving towards a world sovereign state. Our thinking has become clearer on this issue. But we are inexorably moving towards a world governed by international norms; and the epitome of those norms is the system of international law.

E. *Universal Popular Movements*

The past decade has witnessed the emergence, world wide, of a number of popular movements which aim at the preservation of our planet without further injury to it and its life support systems.

Popular movements such as Greenpeace have demonstrated their strength and a level of dedication to this cause which will not be deterred by physical danger. Green movements throughout the world are becoming a political force so significant that even hardened politicians who know only the world of realpolitik are beginning to recognize their force. They sway elections, make and unmake governments, stir the conscience of their generation, and perform a valuable educational role whose full potential has yet to be seen.

An important aspect of these popular movements is that they are now beginning to make use of national and international law in the ordinary judicial processes of their countries to assert the proposition that nuclear weapons are illegal and a crime against humanity.

IV. THE ILLEGALITY OF NUCLEAR WEAPONS

It is not the purpose of this paper to examine at length the question of the illegality of nuclear weapons. Sufficient literature has already appeared on this aspect to make such information readily available.

A. *Domestic Legal Systems*

There are numerous possibilities within each legal system to urge the question of illegality, whether on the basis of violation of international law *simpliciter*, the violation of human rights to which the country's legal system is committed, on the basis of constitutional provisions, or on the basis of principles embedded in the legal system. The variety of ways in which this can be done will come as a surprise to most lawyers practising in domestic forums, and one of the vital purposes this congress can serve is to alert the international legal community to the variety of procedures and forums available for taking up these issues. Professor Francis Boyle's *Defending Civil*

Resistance Under International Law,[21] explores these possibilities in detail. It shows the relevance of international law to the paradox of nuclear deterrence and sets out a range of trial materials on nuclear weapons and international law. The case of *20,000 Plaintiffs Against the Government of the Netherlands* is another notable source of a wide range of arguments that can be urged in domestic forums.

It was a sense of frustration induced by the failure of lawyers to take up these issues that urged George Delf to write his incisive book, *Humanizing Hell!: The Law v. Nuclear Weapons*,[22] in which he castigates the profession for failing to translate into domestic legal systems the principles of the Nuremberg trials which, if properly applied in ordinary domestic forums, could well have obstructed the preparations for nuclear war by countries with a commitment to the observance of principles of international law.

It is important to sensitize professionals all over the world and show the way. The materials to be used are those showing in what way international law forms part of each domestic legal system — the Nuremberg Principles,[23] the defence of superior orders, the Hague Regulations,[24] the Geneva Protocol of 1925,[25] the Genocide Convention,[26] military manuals setting out the recognized duties of the armed forces,[27] and issues of personal criminal responsibility, among others.

[21] F.A. Boyle, *Defending Civil Resistance under International Law*, Transnational Publishers, 1987.

[22] G. Delf, *Humanizing Hell!: The Law v. Nuclear Weapons*, Hamilton, London, 1985.

[23] The Nuremberg Principles, *supra* note 8.

[24] See Convention (No. IV) Respecting the Laws and Customs of War on Land, The Hague, Oct. 18, 1907, 36 Stat. 2277, T.S. No. 539, 1 Bevans 631.

[25] Protocol for the Prohibition of the Use in War of Asphyxiating, Poisonous or Other Gases, and of Bacteriological Methods of Warfare, June 17, 1925, 26 U.S.T. 571, T.I.A.S. No. 8061, 94 L.N.T.S. 65.

[26] Convention on the Prevention and Punishment of the Crime of Genocide, 78 U.N.T.S. 277 (1948).

[27] See, e.g., Dept. of the Army, FM 27–10, *The Law of Land Warfare* (1956); Dept. of the Air Force, AEP 110–31, *International Law: The Conduct of Armed Conflict and Air Operations* (1976).

B. *International Law*

It will suffice to observe that a strong argument can be set up under each of the various sources of international law as enumerated in Article 38(1) of the Statute of the International Court of Justice,[28] namely:

1. international conventions;
2. international customs;
3. general principles of law recognized by civilized nations;
4. judicial decisions; and
5. the teachings of the most highly qualified publicists.

These have been sufficiently dealt with elsewhere and it is not proposed to elaborate on them here.[29]

The contention set out earlier in this paper — that there are sufficient principles of international law already in existence pointing to illegality — can be amply sustained. It is time now to bring those principles into operation rather than permit them to continue to lie dormant. With their assistance it can reasonably be expected that the obstacles presented by the real world to the outlawing of nuclear weapons can be overcome. We must not be browbeaten any longer by "realities", for many of them can indeed be changed under pressure of the congruence of anti-nuclear forces and factors at this time in history. The law has achieved dramatic results in past eras of human history, upsetting apparently changeless structures and attitudes that have prevailed from the beginning of time. It can do so again in the greatest challenge humanity has ever faced.

It seems clear that the next round in the battle against nuclear weapons must be fought by lawyers. They have weapons at their disposal which other groups cannot match. It is for us at this convention to urge the legal professions of the world to rise to their responsibilities and to use these weapons which at present lie rusting in their legal armouries.

[28] Statute of the International Court of Justice, June 26, 1945, art. 38(1), 59 Stat. 1055, T.S. No. 993, 3 Bevans 1179.

[29] See *infra* Ch. 24. See also the author's *Nuclear Weapons and Scientific Responsibility*, Longwood Academic, N.J., 1987.

13. Nuclear Energy

This Chapter consists of two short pieces written and published in 1979 and 1985 respectively. The first was written before Chernobyl and foreshadowed the dangers that manifested themselves in that disaster. It was published in Habitat, Australia, Volume 7, Number 5(p.3) of 5 October 1979, and is reproduced as published. It deals with the impact of nuclear energy projects viewed from the angle of domestic law.

The second item, written after Chernobyl, is a book review dealing with the problems raised by nuclear energy in the arena of international law, and contains observations by the author on these matters, as perceived in 1986. It was published in 12 Monash University Law Review (1986), Book Supplement, p. 5.

A. THE LEGAL IMPLICATIONS OF NUCLEAR TECHNOLOGY

Nuclear energy raises a wide spectrum of possible issues touching on human rights and civil liberties. Among these are the erosion of parliamentary and judicial authority, the breakdown of protections of person and property, the lack of mechanisms of legal compensation, the entrenching of monopolies, curbs on trade union freedom, burgeoning powers for bureaucracies and nuclear inspectorates and the irreversible pollution of the global environment. I shall be able here to outline only some of these problems.

Some relevant provisions of the Universal Declaration of Human Rights are Article 3 which provides that everyone has a right to life, liberty and security of person; Article 25 (2) guaranteeing special care and assistance to motherhood and childhood, and Article 30 forbidding any group, state or person from engaging in any activity aimed at the destruction of the rights and freedoms set forth in the Declaration.

The right to life presupposes a right to the preconditions for a healthful life. The proliferation of nuclear reactors around the globe, the proved leakages form a number of them and the possibilities of major accidents, all impinge upon this basic human right. So also does the problem of waste disposal which, according to the best scientific opinion, remains still unsolved.

We face here a further human rights issue — the extent to which this generation can leave to its successors an unsafe environment through the dumping of wastes — be they in salt beds or in the depths of the oceans or in deep trenches dug in the ground. With a half life of tens of thousands of years, these wastes cannot be policed for a time span in which earthquakes and natural disturbances must be expected as virtual certainties.

It is said that safe means of disposal will be found, or alternatively that we are on the verge of a breakthrough which will give us clean nuclear energy. If and when such new circumstances emerge we shall need to review the situation in the light of those circumstances. Till such time however, the impossibility of safe disposal must provide the factual basis for discussion.

If we speak of human rights for ourselves, we are being selfish if we deny a similar right to the many generations yet to come. No lawyer could as counsel for the beneficiary of a trust agree to the dumping on trust property of radioactive waste. Can an international lawyer agree to the dumping on the earth — the sole trust property which all generations of mankind will inherit — of nuclear waste? There cannot be one legal standard for one's private client whose property interests are involved, and another legal standard for the rest of mankind.

The human right to special care for motherhood and childhood also stands violated, for scientists tell us that radiation causes genetic mutations and a heightened proneness to the production of defective offspring. Moreover, even a child who seems normal may inherit a damaged gene and transmit this to the next generation. Radiation can also result in seriously deformed offspring through chromosomal breakage in a sperm or egg cell. Children in the womb can be damaged in the first three months of pregnancy through radiation injury to specific cells which will then develop defectively into deformed limbs or internal organs.

Scientific opinion is also agreed that the possibility of such damage increases with the intensity of the exposure. Furthermore, radioactivity in the environment tends to collect in such foods as milk, with resulting damage to children. No entity, however powerful, has a right to create these perils and thereby endanger the rights of motherhood and childhood.

The right to health means also the right to procreate, free of artificially induced mutations. If the residents of an entire city should be exposed to radioactive contamination through a serious nuclear accident, they run the risk of producing defective offspring. This can well give rise to other problems, for it may then be argued that the national interest demands their compulsory sterilisation, or that a large crop of defective children ought not to be permitted to strain community resources through their continued survival. These are frightening legal problems but they are only a single nuclear accident away from us.

The Universal Declaration's guarantee of the right to work — Article 23(1) — must mean the right to work in safety. Workers in the nuclear industry, whether in the mines or in the reactors or in the transport of wastes, are exposed to a level of radiation which constitutes a serious danger. The extent of possible damage was demonstrated by the recent Karen Silkwood case where radioactive contamination was the basis of an award of over ten million dollars.

In England the heirs of two nuclear power workers at Windscale were awarded compensation earlier this year for injuries — a brain tumour and a mycloma type cancer — resulting from their work. This was the first admission in court in England that radiation exposure among plutonium workers had led to injury. A serious evidentiary difficulty in these cases is the establishment of the linkage between a particular cancer and the worker's service at a nuclear power plant, for the injury can manifest itself even 20 or 30 years later. The relatively short time limits imposed by the law of limitation raise yet another legal difficulty here, for a traditional principle of the law is that the institution of actions ought not to be delayed indefinitely.

Another legal problem concerns the uninsurability of nuclear risk. No insurance mechanisms in the world today can adequately compensate the citizens of even one city in the event of reactor accident. Legislation such as the Price Anderson Act in the US has sought to limit compensation to the inadequate sum of 560 million dollars per reactor. The class actions already filed over Harrisburg run to over a billion dollars and cover a wide variety of claims including damage to health and property, loss of employment, and damages for evacuation — and that, despite the Harrisburg trouble having been nipped in the bud.

Harrisburg has demonstrated how close we could be to nuclear accident, even in one of the best-policed systems of nuclear reactors in the world. Nuclear reactors are proliferating all over the globe, including countries with unstable governments. The legal powers of supervision of the International Atomic Agency within national boundaries are inadequate, for problems arise of infringement of national sovereignty. In these circumstances the risks of such an accident over the next 10 years somewhere in the world are serious. In such an event, wherever in the world it should occur, the same human rights questions we have been considering will surface, and will affect us all.

The same inadequacies of supervision increase the possibilities of theft and terrorism. The British Royal Commission on Environment Pollution drew attention in 1976 to their possible impact on personal liberty. The Commission thought it remarkable that none of the official documents thus far had conveyed any unease on this score and that nowhere was there any suggestion of apprehension about the possible long-term dangers to the fabric of freedom.

This is perhaps the most crucial of the law and order issues arising from nuclear proliferation. We must take note in this context of the fact that thousands of persons around the world today have the basic knowledge for constructing a crude nuclear device. The media have for some time been carrying descriptions of the preparation by a third year physics student at Princeton, of a blueprint for this purpose. He achieved this within three months, with information publicly available in physics libraries. As nuclear stations proliferate in dozens of countries, the circle of persons possessing this knowledge grows correspondingly.

The following legal consequences can ensue as part of a governmental response: intensified surveillance of the nuclear workforce; suspension of *habeas corpus* and of all provisions relating to freedom from arrest and freedom from search; a grant to the police and the military of the widest powers of interrogation; subjection of the entire population to complete surveillance; the tapping of all telephone calls and the scrutinising of all mail; the prohibition of free movement; wholesale evacuations of populations from target areas; suspension of international travel; suspension of press and broadcasting freedom to check panic; the calling out of the military; the freezing of food stocks; and the enactment of draconian anti-hoarding laws. Bureaucratic take-overs and policies of secrecy will be the order of the day. Should this unhappy state of affairs ever occur, it will leave a lasting scar on freedom.

Nor is this all. The extreme risk involved in atomic power has resulted in legislation which confers in time of peace, power which has hitherto been justified only under conditions of war or emergency. The British Atomic Energy Authority's Special Constabulary is an armed constabulary with power to arrest on suspicion. In Australia, the Atomic Energy Act of 1953 — a piece of defence legislation dating from the cold war — renders a person liable to a heavy fine or a prison sentence in the event of hindering or obstructing uranium mining. Search and arrest are permissible without warrant: and the government and the Atomic Energy Commission are immune from proceedings arising from wrongful arrest, detention and search.

The Act is not a dead letter. In fact it was the subject of careful amendment in 1978 in matters not affecting the generality of these powers. Such legislation is an index to the way in which nuclear energy can introduce a drastic note into peacetime legislative enactments.

The requirements of extreme security can also result in a withdrawal of matters from parliamentary discussion. In the United Kingdom for example, none of the following topics may be discussed in Parliament: the movement of plutonium around the country, the activities of the Atomic Energy Authority's Special Constabulary, the Security Service surveillance of individuals.

The US Office of Technology Assessment has noted three basic public attitudes on this question: The first is that a plutonium economy would require such extensive curtailments of civil liberties that its creation would jeopardise free society. This view accords with realities, for current dangers can only be effectively negatived by the most drastic countermeasures.

The second view is that safeguards can be adopted for a plutonium industry that would be both effective against terrorists and acceptable in terms of civil liberties. This view is unacceptable, for it turns a blind eye to the many legal dangers we have discussed.

The third view is that a program of plutonium safeguards keeping civil liberties risks at a low level is possible, but only if society is willing to run some permanent risk of theft and terrorism. This view involves a value judgment — for the sake of the benefits of nuclear power are we prepared to imperil our inheritance of freedom under the law?

The lawyer's traditional answer to any suggested limitation on liberty, as for example in war or emergency, has been — is it compellingly necessary? I leave that question with you, for the legal perils we run — we and our descendants — are great, and they will continue to increase. We still have time for decision. In a few years mankind will have passed the point of no return.

B. THE UTILIZATION OF NUCLEAR ENERGY AND INTERNATIONAL LAW[1]

The Chernobyl disaster has focused world attention on the inadequacies of current international regulatory mechanisms and norms in the field of nuclear energy. Ms. Vanda Lamm's book, published in 1984, is an imaginative and detailed analysis of many aspects which have become of intense general interest in the aftermath of Chernobyl.

The book provides the legal groundwork for these discussions. The opening chapter provides the reader with an overview of the Legal Status of International Norms regulating the use of nuclear energy. This is followed, in Chapter 2, by a historical review, from the years immediately preceding the

[1] Review of Vanda Lamm *The Utilization of Nuclear Energy and International Law*, Akademiai Kiado, Budapest, 1984, 156 pp.

Baruch Plan, of attempts to settle international problems concerning the utilization of nuclear energy.

The Baruch Plan, named after its author, was a proposal submitted to the United Nations Atomic Energy Commission by the United States in June 1946 for the control of atomic energy through the creation of an independent organisation, the International Atomic Development Authority. This body was to have been entrusted not only with control of all atomic energy activities but also with all questions concerning research and utilization of nuclear energy. The Baruch plan was a clear indication that in the 1940s the dangers were realized of a spread of nuclear facilities without international control. It is indeed depressing to contemplate how far international thinking has moved away from these common-sense perspectives which were widely shared at the dawn of the nuclear age.

The history and structure of the International Atomic Energy Agency are dealt with in the next chapter, followed by two chapters dealing with the Agency's safeguards. Further measures for the peaceful uses of nuclear energy are examined in Chapter 6. The concluding chapter of the book is devoted to various problems of international law relating to peaceful nuclear explosions.

Chernobyl has shown how what has been traditionally described as the "peaceful uses" of nuclear energy can trigger off a remarkable range of international problems in such fields as arms control, military research, early warning systems and international terrorism, in addition to problems relating to nuclear emergency plans, release of information, international environmental problems, international inspection, the rights and duties of States and the protection of third party interests. Ms. Vanda Lamm has anticipated and dealt with many of these possibilities. She has highlighted the rudimentary state of the principles and mechanisms dealing with these problems.

These are all problems which must be of more than passing concern to Australia as a major exporter of uranium. Australia's concern is reflected in Prime Minister Hawke's letter to the Soviet leader, Mr. Gorbachev, in May, which sought support for plans to initiate notification procedures and emergency assistance in nuclear accidents. Australia has also called for an international conference on this matter. There is much in this book that will be of relevance to students of Australia's policies regarding uranium export.

The book highlights the difference in approach of the nuclear weapons states, the threshold nuclear states and other states. Each of these groups sees nuclear energy in a different light.

As with the question of control of atomic energy and the growing divergence of positions on this matter among the nuclear powers since the late

1940s, so also on the question of nuclear exports the position of the nuclear powers diverged form the near consensus that existed in the early 1970s.

Examining the resulting problems in Chapter 6, the author draws attention to the consensus that existed among the nuclear weapon states at the time of their acceptance of the Zangger Memorandum in 1974 on the question of nuclear exports to non-nuclear weapon states not parties to the Nuclear Non-Proliferation Treaty (NPT). The Zangger memorandum was the result of a meeting in 1974 of nuclear supplier States who sought to negotiate the acceptance of a common set of principles on nuclear exports. The memorandum made a list of material, equipment and installations that could be supplied to non-nuclear weapon States and specified the conditions under which they could be supplied. However, when the "London Club" of the largest nuclear exporter countries met from 1975 onwards, major differences surfaced, with maximalist control proposals presented by the U.K. and Canada, strict control proposals by the U.S. and the USSR and a third position, represented by France, the F.R.G. and Japan. The essence of the maximalist position was that potentially dangerous nuclear materials, installations and plants may be supplied only to States which undertake to submit their entire nuclear industry to IAEA safeguards. Australia was among the States supporting the maximalist position. The clear danger of not having control over the entire cycle is that an importing State not party to the NPT could easily develop its peaceful nuclear industry under safeguards and at the same time direct its resources and expertise to the production of nuclear explosive capability in unsafeguarded installations.

The London guidelines could not embody the maximalist position owing to these differences and hence only the supplied installations came under the safeguards. Large loopholes were thus left for precisely the sort of danger visualised by the maximalists. Adding to the ensuing tensions were commercial rivalries between the US nuclear industry, and those of the F.R.G. and France. The US industry was subject to stricter domestic controls in relation to exports than either of the latter.

The cracks in the wall of protection soon appeared. In 1975 the Bonn Government undertook to supply ten nuclear installations to Brazil in fifteen years, with facilities covering the complete nuclear fuel cycle. France planned to conclude nuclear export contracts with South Korea and Pakistan. Even more controversial was France's sale of two nuclear power plants to the Republic of South Africa. South Africa, not a party to the NPT, undertook to submit certain — but not all — of its facilities to IAEA safeguards. This led to the assertion by many African states in the General Assembly that South Africa, in spite of the agreement concluded with IAEA, used its nuclear industry for military purposes.

Vanda Lamm's book skilfully assembles all this information and the supporting materials within a comparatively short compass. The presentation is scholarly and objective. Whoever is researching the hazards presented by nuclear proliferation will be richly rewarded by a perusal of this book.

The book also presents the standpoints of developing countries, to some of whom the peaceful application of nuclear energy is vitally important in the context of growing energy needs and the application of isotopes in the fields of agriculture, food and therapeutics. Non-aligned countries at the Havana Conference in 1979 stressed the right of all States to develop nuclear industries for peaceful purposes in accordance with their needs. Indeed the controls exercised by the nuclear exporters are often seen by many non-aligned countries as a manifestation of the inequalities embodied in the NPT.

"Peaceful" nuclear explosions are another source of worry. The NPT provides for such possibilities under appropriate safeguards, but where do we draw the line? The suggestion was made a few years ago of a nuclear explosion for the construction of the new Panama Canal. Other such proposals could emerge in the future. As Ms. Lamm points out, there are many gaps in the relevant provisions of the NPT, and non-nuclear weapon states who are not parties to the NPT are in many respects in a favoured position.

Inadequate controls, departing from the maximalist position favoured by some members of the London Club, have in the succeeding years led to major international tensions. Even as I write this review, on 16 July 1986, the international press reports that "tough talk" has taken place between the US and the USSR amidst growing indications that Pakistan's nuclear program has moved far along the path towards the production of an atomic bomb. Moscow has reportedly indicated to Pakistan (*The Age* 16/7/86) that it would not "tolerate" the construction of a nuclear bomb by Pakistan, to which the Reagan administration has responded with an "extremely grave" message to the Soviets asking Moscow to keep its "hands off" Pakistan. Another complication is that the Reagan administration's five billion dollar aid program to Pakistan depends on an annual certificate to Congress that Pakistan does not "possess" an atomic bomb. The French nuclear export to Pakistan over a decade ago has no doubt been an important factor triggering off this current cause of international tension.

International tensions in their acutest form could thus be sparked off by "peaceful" uses of nuclear energy. For other examples one need look no further than South Africa, now in ferment in what may well be a last-ditch stand, embroiling neighbouring and other countries.

Ms. Lamm's book is thus of great interest. For the non-lawyer it provides, in easily understood form, the international law background to the vexed question of the proliferation of nuclear weapons and expertise. For the lawyer it is a useful survey of the relevant material, pinpointing the flaws in present systems of protection and drawing attention to possible improvements. With around 25 countries well within reach of nuclear weapons before the turn of the century, this is a problem that must concern us all, especially as Australia is a source of the raw material from which this whole dangerous cycle commences.

This is not to say that the reviewer agrees with Ms. Lamm at every point. For example, her treatment of criticisms of the nuclear powers' conduct under the NPT seems to be too protective of them. It is difficult to agree with the author's defence of the nuclear weapon States in relation to their treaty obligations under the NPT. They have agreed "to pursue negotiations in good faith on effective measures relating to the cessation of the nuclear arms race at an early date ... and on a treaty on general and complete disarmament under strict and effective international control". Many would disagree with her view that

> The nuclear-weapon States parties to the Non-Proliferation Treaty have more or less kept this promise, in so far as since the adoption of this instrument disarmament talks have been held in different forums, and a number of agreements of a disarmament character, on reduction of armaments, have been arrived at. (p. 97)

It is this reviewer's view that unless attention is constantly drawn to the nuclear weapon States' gross failure to keep their treaty commitments on working towards the cessation of the arms race, the non-nuclear signatories will feel a lesser commitment towards their obligations under it, and the Treaty could weaken, with considerable damage to prospects of world peace. Not only the nuclear powers but all signatories should be kept reminded of their obligations under a Treaty which was after all, a bargain struck between the nuclear powers and the non-nuclears.

It is easier to accept, however, the author's defence of the NPT against many of its critics on the basis that unlike the Treaty of Tlatelolco, too much cannot be expected of a treaty intended to prevent the *spread* of nuclear weapons, rather than to *prohibit* their presence in a given region.

The difference of opinion mentioned earlier, does not detract in any way from the reviewer's view of the high quality of this book as an exposition of the principles of international law essential to an understanding of current problems of nuclear proliferation. Even more importantly, the book will contribute to more informed general debate on this important question, through a style of presentation well within the grasp of the non-legal reader.

14. Genetic Engineering*

This paper seeks to present an overview of the concerns felt at the commencement of the 1980s when the breakthroughs in genetic engineering achieved in the 1970s were still new. Few solutions have yet been found to the vast ranges of moral and legal problems that suddenly unfolded, and have developed in the 1980s and 1990s. This "snap shot" of the position at the commencement of the 1980s will perhaps be useful for enabling us to take our bearings on such progress as has been made over the past two decades in finding legal solutions to these problems.

The international press constantly highlights new clusters of legal problems thrown up by current genetic research. Many of these are problems that have moved in recent years from the pages of science fiction into the precincts of the courts. A complete catalogue would be beyond the competence of any researcher, but three cases which attracted world attention in July 1978 may be cited by way of illustration.

The first of these was the birth in England of the world's first *in vitro* (in glass) conceived baby to Mrs. Lesley Brown. Gynaecologist Steptoe and Physiologist Edwards, both highly respected scientists, had collaborated in removing a ripe egg from Mrs. Brown's ovary, placing it in a laboratory dish, adding sperm from her husband, causing penetration of the ovum wall by the sperm and planting the developing embryo in the uterus. The world knew in advance of the impending birth and it was hailed in the international press as a massive breakthrough, bringing 1984 six years nearer than anticipated.

The legal and ethical issues involved provoked unending discussion. The Catholic Church, relying on pronouncements of Pope Pius XII, found the procedure contrary to the law of nature which had ordained that procreation should take place only in the manner nature had intended, namely sexual intercourse. The end, namely Mr. and Mrs. Brown's desire for a child, was commendable, but the means was condemned and it was said to be another

* Paper delivered at the Symposium of the Australian and New Zealand Association for the Advancement of Science (ANZAAS) Congress, Adelaide, May 1980.

instance of an unjustifiable means being used for the achievement of a desirable end. Rabbi Siegel, professor of ethics at Manhattan's Jewish Theological Seminary argued on the other hand that the Browns were in fact trying to obey the commandment to have children.[1] When nature did not permit conception, it was desirable to attempt to assist nature, for the Talmud teaches that God desires man's co-operation. Other arguments advanced were — man attempting to play God; not converting the home into a laboratory; the failure to consider the rights of the child-to-be, who was undergoing a grave risk of deformity; the lack of informed consent owing to the total lack of information concerning likely effects upon the child; the daring nature of the experimentation; and the need for clearance with legal or semi-legal mechanisms before such a project is undertaken.

The second event which attracted attention to this field of science was the case instituted by a married couple against a doctor who had allegedly destroyed an egg said to have been fertilized externally by the husband's sperm. The doctor was stated to have acted in this manner because he had not been satisfied that the doctor responsible for the earlier procedures possessed the necessary skills, and also because the experiment had not received the approval of the hospital's committee on human experimentation.

The third event was the filing of fifty lawsuits against a San Francisco sperm bank for allowing its sperm deposits to thaw out. Men who had had vasectomies, or who feared they might become sterile, had banked their sperm in the sperm bank. They alleged that the frozen sperm was spoiled when a container of liquid nitrogen tipped over it, some of the damages claims running to over a million dollars.

I shall in this paper direct my attention to some of the legal problems arising from genetic engineering in three categories — the immediate problems, the problems likely to arise in the medium term, and the problems that may arise in the distant future but need legal planning now in view of their fundamental nature. In doing this I shall use the expression genetic engineering not in the narrow sense of recombinant DNA experimentation, but in the wider sense of any activity artificially interfering with the processes of nature in the reproduction of living organisms. All the items considered will have relevance directly or obliquely to problems of human genetics.

I should at the outset observe that many of the problems in this area arise from the inability of traditional legal principles to furnish satisfactory answers to many of these problems, owing to the inadequacy of traditional legal conceptualization and methodology for dealing with anything quite so unforeseen on the stage of human affairs.

1 *TIME Magazine*, July 31, 1978, p. 68.

Among the legal problems arising from the immediate state of scientific achievement are the following:

1. Family law problems arising from *in vitro* fertilization (IVF), embryo transplantation (ET), and artificial insemination by donor (AID) procedures.
2. The registration and regulation of sperm and ova banks.
3. The privacy of genetic information.
4. Problems of negligence towards the unborn child.
5. Legal actions for "wrongful birth".
6. Protections of foetal material in its use for scientific experimentation.
7. Curtailment of the right to procreate, where defective (and/or "inferior") genotypes are detected.
8. The scope of state regulation in the sphere of human reproduction.
9. The enforceability of national guidelines issued for the governance of genetic research.
10. Recombinant DNA research problems.
11. Conscience clauses for the protection of medical workers in research institutions which violate their principles.
12. The exploitation, to human detriment, of genetic engineering technologies.

All these require attention immediately.

Not already upon us, but likely to be with us shortly, are the following:

1. The transplant of reproductive organs — testes and ovaries.
2. Problems arising from the ectogenetic development of the foetus.
3. The introduction into human genetic material of new molecules aimed at inducing pre-selected characteristics.
4. The legal problems which will flow from the ability to identify genotypes of superior qualities.
5. International trade in human organs
6. The preservation of sperm by freezing

The last category, raising some of the most major issues, still distant from us according to the best scientific opinion, but not too distant to need conceptual planning now, are

a) Cloning

b) Parthenogenesis

c) Genetic mapping

d) Cryonic suspension

There are probably many more areas which a person competent in the sciences can now visualize. There will undoubtedly be many more which no one, scientist or lawyer, can now visualize, but which will undoubtedly reveal themselves as research progresses.

I shall proceed to deal with a few of the issues that arise in the areas I have enumerated.

A. *Immediate Problems*

1. Family Law Problems. We have already referred to some of the ethical and religious considerations involved in *in vitro* fertilization (IVF) and embryo transplantation (ET) procedures, in the context of the case of Mrs. Brown. Now that the procedure is known, it is certain there will be applications of it outside the marital relationship and that fertilization will not be confined to cases where the husband's sperm is used. The legal issues involved in such procedures include the privacy issue in regard to genetic data of the sperm donor, the regulation of sperm banks, conditions of sperm donation, legislation preventing donations to donees unfitted for medical reasons to receive particular categories of sperm, the prevention of sperm storage and donation by those with defective genotypes, the prevention of trafficking in sperm, the question whether private enterprise should be permitted to operate and commercialize sperm banks or whether they should be exclusively government controlled, and safeguards against the misuse of governmental power. Another possibility opened up by *in vitro* fertilization is that a woman wanting to avoid the rigours of pregnancy may be able to hire a foster-womb for the duration of the pregnancy with a promise of later delivery of the matured child to the true parent. In the Brown case the fertilized embryo could well have been implanted in a womb other than that of

Mrs. Brown. It is easy to imagine the width of the regulations this possibility calls for, when the procedure becomes more well-known and resorted to.

Even before science reaches the stage of being able to grow the *in vitro* fertilized ovum to full maturity outside the human womb, we have thus already opened out a Pandora's box of legal problems. These problems have perhaps not yet reached the intensity they will achieve in the years ahead when longer term *in vitro* growth is possible, but they have already achieved a greater penetration of society than many citizens realize. This penetration has been achieved already through techniques of artificial insemination. One estimate, over a decade ago, placed at a million the number of citizens of the United States who owed their existence to artificial insemination.[2] Even discounting this figure, which some describe as a gross overestimate, the number must run to several tens of thousands and is growing exponentially. In Australia the figure is probably around the five hundred mark already.

America is already encountering the problem of lack of proper records regarding the source of the sperm, for artificial insemination procedures are largely resorted to *ad hoc* by individual doctors, with no need for a recording of information regarding the source of the donation (or purchase). Indeed, the problem has recently been encountered of the marriage of persons who, unknown to each other, are half brother and sister. The effect on the validity of the marriage, as well as on the psychology of the parties is damaging. The probability of this event in a large community is perhaps too low to warrant serious concern, but in a small community it can be significant. In Australia the general practice is never to use the sperm of the same donor more than twice, thus reducing the risk.

2. It is essential that sperm and ova banks should be registered, their materials recorded, their donations indexed, their data safeguarded. Although the commercialization of sperm banks seems to have occurred in America, this seems so contrary to the Australian ethos that it is unlikely to occur here on any appreciable scale. They will therefore probably continue to be a government activity. As such, there is a danger of bureaucratization of the procedures, which needs to be guarded against — a result which can only be achieved by an informed vigilance on the part of the public and the medical profession. In any event there seems to be a need for guidelines (or regulations) regarding selection, storage, distribution, indexing and privacy. Value judgments will in many cases be necessary — Is particular sperm worthy of

[2] Goulder, "Children of the Laboratory", 4 Trans-Action 13 (1967) cited by Roderic Gorney in "The New Biology and the Future of Man" (1968) 15 *UCLA* 273 at 278.

storage? Is a particular recipient worthy of donation? The evolution of guidelines is a difficult but essential task.

In Australia there are at present six sperm banks in operation. Half of these operate on public funds and half are private, though not profit making. They are all run professionally according to the highest ethical standards, controlled as they are by responsible medical personnel.

However there is nothing to prevent the commercialization of sperm banks, and if a private organisation should want to commence operations, there will be no legal impediment in its way. Professional guidelines may be insufficient to meet such a situation and legislation may be called for.

At present the sperm banks function on the basis of complete privacy in regard to donor and donee. The donee will not know the source from which the sperm has been obtained, though elaborate information regarding the donor's physical data and medical history would be available to the bank. If this activity should fall into private hands the greatest vigilance and regulation might be necessary to achieve the standards that now depend on medical and scientific integrity.

Workers at the Monash AID centre are embodying the results of their experience and research in a book to be published shortly on AID Practice in Australia. This will contain the most up-to-date information upon this subject.

3. The issue of privacy of genetic information is important. Privacy is an important issue in Australia, and the Australian Law Reform Commission has done much to heighten public consciousness in this area. The genetic and personal information recorded in the data banks will no doubt be computerized and many of the issues relating to protection of computerized information will be relevant here. It is essential that both donor and donee be protected but that the relevant information should be available when required for medical purposes — that too under conditions safeguarding dissemination. Privacy law must take this within its ken.

The Australian Law Reform Commission, in its 1977 Working Paper on tissue transplants, draws attention to the need for privacy in a national register of donors (Arts.113–5). Different legal systems have different rules on this matter. The Canadian Uniform Act on Transplantation provides that no information revealing identity of possible donors and recipients may be released. The South African Act forbids disclosure of identity without the party's consent. The Australian Law Reform Commission recommended that disclosure of personal information should be forbidden except with the consent of the person himself.

4. Negligence towards the Unborn Child. The Victorian case of *Watt* v. *Rama*[3] was a trail-blazing authority on duties towards the unborn child. In that case the court held that damages could be awarded to a child for brain damage caused through an injury, before its birth, to its pregnant mother in a road accident. The child on birth became vested with this right.

The courts have been leaning increasingly in recent years towards recognizing such rights in the unborn child, which come to maturity upon birth. This is an interesting trend when viewed against the background of an increasing denial of rights to the unborn foetus, in relation to abortion. There is not sufficient opportunity here to consider this interesting ambivalence of the law towards the problem of foetal status, but something more of this is discussed in the section on foetal experimentation.

5. The concept of wrongful birth is new to all legal systems but has gained acceptance in the U.S.A. and will doubtless become increasingly important in most other legal systems in the years immediately ahead. The concept was originally formulated in 1964 in a case which had no connection with genetic experimentation — *Zepeda* v. *Zepeda*[4] where an illegitimate child sued his putative father for fraudulently inducing his mother to have sexual relations with him upon promise of marriage. The father was already married and the child claimed damages for deprivation of ordinary home life and for the stigma of being born a bastard. While refusing relief in the case before it, the court foreshadowed such later happenings as genetic malformation resulting from radiation, sperm banks, cloning, and chemical interference with foetal formation and suggested that in such instances an action for wrongful life could lie.

The idea underlying this concept is that a person did not choose to be born but, if born, has a right to be born without basic defects. If born with basic defects which were preventable by the exercise of due care on the part of those responsible for the birth, or which were directly caused by their negligence, there would be a cause of action for wrongful birth — for being born into a life of misery which could have been avoided if the persons concerned had not been negligent. A child born deaf and dumb or deformed owing to rubella would be an obvious illustration, if the mother's rubella was not diagnosed correctly and the child not aborted. Pre-natal negligence in the care of the mother by doctors and others responsible for her safety will also ground an action. Where a girl who had received the wrong Rh-type of blood transfusion gave birth some years later to a child with permanent brain dam-

[3] [1972] V.R. 353.

[4] 41 Ill. App. 2d. 240, 190 N.E. 2d. 849 (1963) cert. denied 379 U.S. 945 (1964).

age, the Illinois Supreme Court awarded damages for pre-conception negligence against the physician and the hospital.

These new types of tort are probably a judicial reflection of the growing recognition of the right to health as a human right — a concept recently elaborated in the human rights field at many international conferences. Although the tort of pre-natal negligence is now recognized in Australia, the tort of wrongful birth has yet to be established.

The right of parents to sue physicians and others for unwanted births where operations for sterilization have been unsuccessful are also other aspects of the new torts that are arising.

It is useful also, in the context of wrongful birth, for States to give some consideration to their obligations towards children born seriously defective. Whether through scientific negligence or otherwise, such persons carry a load of suffering which it is the duty of the community to mitigate. At present they are flotsam and jetsam on the waters of life — tossed around aimlessly and dependent largely on the good fortune of a concerned parent being alive. Scientific development in the areas of genetic engineering will help focus attention on this great social issue which is not a product of genetic engineering alone.

6. Protections of foetal material. An important substance used for experiments involving genetic research is foetal material. This comes both from aborted foetuses and from foetuses destined for abortion.

The issues involved are of immense importance from the humanitarian point of view. It may be that the unborn foetus does not yet have a legal personality, but modern scientific research shows unequivocally that the foetus has many characteristics of the human.

We are still far perhaps from having a complete picture of the extent of the foetus' susceptibility to emotions or to pain. Scientific evidence is however piling up regarding a number of abilities and reactions of the foetus and we can no longer feel as confident as the ancient Greeks or the mediaevalists in fixing an arbitrary period after conception as the period when sensation begins.

Among the facts now available to us are that the absolutely unique genetic pattern of each individual is set at conception, that the process of development is continuous from that stage onwards, that contractions of the heart have been observed as early as two weeks after conception, that the classical elements of the adult electrocardiogram can be observed at five weeks, that the primitive skeletal system is completely developed by the end of the sixth week, that the electroencephalogram can detect brain waves at forty-three days, that by the seventh week the child's shape and form is unmistakably human, that by the end of the third month the unborn child has become very active, kicking its legs, turning its feet, squinting and frowning.[5]

The question assumes great importance in the light of inflammatory reports of foetal abuse by scientists. It has been reported for example that living embryos have been sold by abortion clinics for research purposes,[6] that abortuses have had their chest wall cut to observe the living heartbeat,[7] and that scientists have cut off foetuses heads and kept blood circulating through them.[8] In the British Parliament there was even once a discussion of rumours regarding the sale of abortuses for the manufacture of soap and cosmetics.[9] One may discount all or any of these rumours, but they raise depressing questions which lawyers cannot shirk.

In Britain, and in Australia, foetal experimentation is governed by the medical profession which has formulated Advisory Group Guidelines, whereas in the United States there is governmental regulation in the form of HEW Guidelines.[10] These latter guidelines prevent experimentation on the pre-natal foetus unless the father and mother are legally competent and give their consent, the father's consent not being required if his identity or whereabouts cannot be ascertained. By contrast, there are no such prerequisites under the English guidelines. Another contrast between the two approaches is that where a foetus is scheduled for abortion, *in utero* experimentation is not banned outright by the HEW Guidelines but is prohibited by the English Guidelines.

Australian surgeons are governed by the Royal Australian College of Surgeons, which is associated with the Royal College of Surgeons in the U.K. Australian surgeons would no doubt be greatly influenced by the English guidelines. The English practice means that decision-making in this sphere is exclusively in the hands of the medical profession, whereas the American practice brings into the monitoring committees lawyers, clergymen, ethicists and laymen. In matters of ethics-related science it is not always the best course — however dedicated the scientist may be — to leave

[5] For all these details and more, and the medical references in support, see (1977) 22 *Villanova Law Review* at 343–7.

[6] Editorial, (1972) 40 *Med. Legal Journal* 75.

[7] (1974) 26 *Stan.L.Rev.* 1191.

[8] Culliton, "Fetal Research, The Case History of a Massachusetts Law" (1975) 187 *Science* 237.

[9] (1974) 4 *Brit. Med. J.* 775.

[10] (1974) 39 *Fed. Reg.* 30648.

decision-making entirely in his or her hands, and this is a matter the Australian public and legislators might desire to consider.

Indeed, even such techniques as the use of amniocentesis (a probe through the uterine wall into the tissues of the foetus to spot defects) as a genetic counselling tool have been the subject of debate, for they involve the risk of harm to the foetus to allay the parents' fears of a defective child. The issues involved are difficult indeed.

7. Curtailment of the Right to Procreate. Advances in genetic science have brought us a more precise knowledge of the situations in which it can be predicted that the children of a particular person will or are likely to be born defective. Genital damage caused by radiation exposure is a common illustration.

The view will be urged that persons whose physical condition is such that the chances of their procreating defective children are extremely high, impose a burden upon community resources should they choose to procreate. It will also be urged that they will be impairing the quality of the genetic pool when they do so because their children will in turn raise the same problem when they reach child-bearing age. Can such persons be prohibited in the public interest from having children?

Article 16(l) of the Universal Declaration of Human Rights states that men and women of full age have the right to marry and found a family, thus declaring the right to procreate to be a right of every human being. If and when society should attempt to curtail this right, the most serious legal and human rights issues will arise. Experience of the past has been that voluntary controls do not work effectively in this area, even if reinforced by legal incentives, and compulsion will no doubt be discussed as a serious alternative — especially in the context of the new tools for genetic analysis which research will evolve. Questions that will arise will include the categorization of the defects which make procreation a drag on society and the definition of the borderline of undesirability. The larger question will be the right of society to impose fetters upon an individuals right to procreate, which has hitherto been linked with the integrity of the human personality. These questions cannot be decided by lawyers or scientists alone but call for a considered community response. Awareness of the issues involved needs to be spread through society.

This is an issue that has engaged the attention of thinkers from the time of Plato. We will be called upon to reach an affirmative decision on what was once an academic question, and we shall have to come to grips with it.

8. The scope of state regulation. This is a question closely related to that just discussed. What has been discussed so far is the negative aspect —

should there be a prohibition on procreation by specified persons. The positive aspect is likely to loom large in the future, when the scientific means become possible to launch out on a programme of reproducing selected genotypes. The issue is a momentous one, on which strong emotions are aroused. It is perhaps a little more remote from us than the previous issue, but it needs consideration very early if we are to be ready for it when we should.

9. The enforceability of guidelines laid down by professional bodies in various areas of genetic engineering is a problem of great importance. The issue was highlighted in the context of recombinant DNA research. That branch of research, in view of the many potential dangers feared from it through the creation of microbes of unknown potency, provoked debates on the need for controls and safeguards. From this debate, which was prominently featured in the international news media, there emerged a set of guidelines issued by the National Institute of Health in America. That set of guidelines, running to two hundred pages of tightly framed rules, included a blanket prohibition on certain experiments. In the United Kingdom the Williams Committee did not impose blanket prohibitions but provided for *ad hoc* judgments in each individual case involving very high risk. In the United Kingdom the recommendations of the Williams Committee have been enacted into legislation. There is no such legislation as yet in Australia.

The question whether guidelines should be enforced by law raises questions of freedom of scientific research. At the 1975 Asilomar Conference on Recombinant DNA research, a powerful team of lawyers addressed the scientists on their legal responsibilities. Two of the points made were that absolute responsibility attaches in law to those who handle extremely dangerous materials, irrespective of the presence or absence of negligence. Another was that all persons are responsible to anyone who might foreseeably be injured by that person's act. Neither of these principles respects the principle of freedom of academic research. If, therefore, a scientist engaged in recombinant DNA research should manufacture a bacterium which has damaging effects on the human community, the pure pursuit of knowledge in the exercise of academic freedom of inquiry would be no excuse. The scientist would be personally liable for the harm caused. "Scientific freedom" or "academic freedom" would have no recognized status in law and could confer no immunity from the normal processes of courts.[11]

[11] On the Asilomar Conference, see, generally, June Goodfield, *Playing God: Genetic Engineering and the Manipulation of Life,* Hutchinson, 1977. On this aspect, see pp. 141 *et seq.*

Indeed, the lawyers of Asilomar drew attention to another important legal issue — the question of the experimenter's responsibility to show that the dangers were not trivial, to specify those dangers, and to show also that the benefits to society were so substantial as to justify the continuance of a risk-laden procedure. The burden of proof rested on the lawyers and not on society.[12]

Even in the United Kingdom, where legislation has taken the place of voluntary regulation, numerous legal problems have arisen of claims to secrecy and of the inability to police the regulations without co-operation from the scientists themselves.

The issue of the NIH guidelines provoked an interesting reaction in the United States. Pharmaceutical companies that desired to pursue their own research made a public declaration that NIH guidelines might be valid for those who functioned on public funds but could be disregarded by those who were funded independently. They consequently announced their intention to proceed with their own research and indeed to seek patents for the new life forms they would create.

It seems today to be the opinion among microbiologists that the NIH guidelines were too tightly framed and that the conditions of close security they required inhibited considerable useful research.

That is not, however, the issue. The issue is a much broader one — can such regulations be imposed upon the scientific profession by external authority and is it possible for such external authority to police such regulations? Self-regulation by the scientific fraternity is perhaps an unattainable ideal in many spheres of research. Where ethical and social issues are involved, as in genetic engineering, lay participation becomes vitally important and some provision needs to be made for this. But still, the presence of a commercial interest in scientific research, as in the case of the pharmaceutical industry, may on occasion call for external regulation and, so long as science is used in the service of commerce, scientists will need to be prepared for such external regulation in the future.

10. Recombinant DNA problems. The legal problems spawned by DNA research include the following:

(a) patents in new life forms;

(b) compensation for health damage to the public, in the event of the release of some newly created and dangerous virus;

[12] *Ibid.*, p. 147.

(c) environmental problems and property depreciation in the neighbourhood of recombinant DNA research;

(d) psychological damage and neurosis, resulting from anxieties regarding such research, especially after an accident causing damage;

(e) damage to the unborn.

Some of these are speculative. Some of them are real legal problems that are with us now.

(a) Patent rights. Pharmaceutical companies, as we have seen, announced quite early their intention to seek patents for new life forms. This has now become reality with two applications to the United States Courts and one application in Australia. The problem posed is momentous in that for the first time a legal right of property is sought by the creator of a new life form that has never existed before. The award may appear harmless in the context of bacteria, but raises a very serious issue for the future, for experimentation will surely progress up the scale of life and, in turn, there will be claims for the application of this principle to the higher forms of life. Cloning has already taken place with toads and, if some genetic variation or mutation can be induced, it may well be that such an animal with pre-selected characteristics or mutations might be produced. Whether property in such living creatures is a desirable principle for the law to accept is a momentous question.

In the United States the matter came before the courts in the cases of Chakrabarty and Bergy. The first of these scientists had assigned his interests to the General Electric Company in a specimen of Pseudomonas bacteria which he had produced, containing two or more different energy-generating plasmids which did not occur in nature. The second scientist claimed patent rights in a micro-organism which he asserted did not exist as a biologically pure culture in nature, and was therefore "a product of a microbiologist". This organism was capable of producing a desired antibiotic lincomycin under controlled fermentation conditions.

In the first case, the Patents Board held that Congress could not have intended the Patent Act to include any living thing and that it was for this reason that a special Plant Patent Act had to be passed in 1930 to provide protection for plants. In the second case, the Board reached a similar conclusion.

These decisions were reversed in March 1979 by the Court of Customs and Patent Appeals,[13] the court holding: "Microorganisms have long been

[13] (1979) 201 *U.S. Patents Quarterly* 352.

important tools in chemical industry, especially the pharmaceutical branch, and when such useful, industrial tool is invented which is new and unobvious, so that it complies with those conditions for patentability, there is no reason to deprive it or its creator or owner of protection and advantages of patent system by arbitrarily excluding it, on sole ground that it is alive, from categories of inventions patentable under 35 U.S.C. 101."

There has been an appeal to the U.S. Supreme Court from that decision and the latest information at the time of writing is that the matter has been sent back for rehearing to the Patent Court. The matter is thus still inconclusive in the United States. Present information is that hundreds of similar applications are awaiting the determination in that case.[14] In Australia the Commissioner of Patents, in the case of *In re Ranks Hovis McDougall Ltd.* in 1976, had occasion to consider quite early the patentability of living organisms, in particular micro-organisms. The 'invention' there was a new strain of micro-organism (Fusarium graminearum Schwabe) which had been isolated from a soil sample, and could be employed in the production of a substance containing an edible protein. The application failed on the ground of want of novelty, for the micro-organism was of a known species naturally occurring in a culture medium suitable for the cultivation of such species.

(b) It would seem that in the last three years scientific opinion has leant strongly to the view that many of the hazards feared earlier are not likely to eventuate. Still, the legal principles applicable in the event of damage thus caused need to be stated. One of these is that where a specially dangerous substance is brought upon property, there is a strict duty upon those in charge of it to prevent its escape. Where such escape does occur, and harm follows, those in control of the property whence the deleterious substance ensued will be under strict liability for damage. That they were not negligent may not be sufficient to save them from liability under the principle of *Rylands* v. *Fletcher*.[15] In any event there is a strong possibility that courts would, in relation to such new hazards, not be guided by traditional principles of liability based upon fault. However there will be many difficulties in the way of obtaining relief, not the least of which are difficulties of proof and the widespread nature of damage, if it is caused.

(c) (d) and (e) These are too remote to call for detailed discussion here, but are problems that could conceivably arise.

[14] Needless to say, there has been considerable development in this area and the patenting of living organisms is no longer the novelty it was at the time of this lecture. See Addendum A.

[15] [1868] LR 3 HL 330.

The fullest discussion of these aspects in Australia is contained in the Report on Genetic Engineering issued by the University Assembly of the University of Melbourne. There is a general insufficiency of principles of common law to meet these situations, and legislative intervention will perhaps be called for in the event of dangers manifesting themselves to an extent greater than has thus far appeared. Mr. Justice Samuels of the New South Wales Court adverted to this in an address in 1978[16] on the Legal and Moral Aspects of Genetic Engineering.

11. Conscience Clauses. Persons working in fields where interference occurs with normal processes of reproduction may suffer from qualms of conscience when called upon to participate in such research. Examples of this situation which are already with us are abortions of foetuses likely to be born defective, as well as abortions on request.

Institutions that offer facilities for abortion may well make it a precondition to their employment of doctors and nurses that such employees be prepared to assist in abortions. Moral and religious scruples may stand in the way, and a person obviously qualified for the position may well be unfairly disadvantaged. This may apply equally to state and privately funded institutions.

Conscience clauses safeguarding employees from such disadvantages are measures which call for active consideration by lawyers. In the United States this issue has been actively discussed in the context of personal liberty; medical malpractice in refusing to participate in abortions which the law permits; damages for refusal to abort; rights of defective children who might have been aborted to sue doctors who refused to participate and employment discrimination. Many states have passed legislation dealing with conscience clauses.

The issue of conscience clauses was examined in some detail by the New Zealand Royal Commission on Contraception, Sterilization and Abortion. The Commission drew heavily on the English provision contained in the Abortion Act of 1967, section 4 of which provided expressly for conscientious objection by a party to legal abortions. By subsection 1 this section provided that no person shall be under any duty, whether by contract or by any statutory or other legal requirement, to participate in any treatment authorized by the Act to which he or she had a conscientious objection.

In 1975, despite this provision, the Chief Medical Officer of the Department of Health and Social Security in England issued a memorandum, the effect of which was that doctors who objected to performing operations on

[16] *The Age*, 11 May 1978. Melbourne Assembly Report, p. 59.

grounds of conscience should not be appointed to certain posts. There was a protest by Cardinal Heenan, representing the Roman Catholic viewpoint, to which the Prime Minister replied that candidates would be questioned on their preparedness to assist in abortions solely on professional as opposed to religious grounds — a reply which did not satisfy the Cardinal.

The New Zealand Commission recommended that no medical, surgical or paramedical personnel should be under an obligation to assist at, or participate in, any abortion or sterilisation device ... if that person had a conscientious objection based on religious, ethical or other grounds.

South Australia has provided a conscience clause by legislation to the same effect by section 82(a)(5) of the Criminal Law Consolidation Amendment Act 1969.

12. Commercial Exploitation of the New Technologies. Some of the substances created by DNA experimentation are of undoubted value in the treatment or prevention of disease. The interferons which are being produced by these processes are powerful immunizers and their commercial value will be enormous.

When produced on a commercial scale there will be a danger of their misuse, for, used indiscriminately, they can create resistance on the part of the micro-organisms they are meant to control.

There is a very real danger that, unless their use is legally regulated, they may be indiscriminately sold, as penicillin tended to be included in all manner of products intended for general consumption, such as throat lozenges. Strict regulations will be necessary to guard against this and policing mechanisms will need to be evolved. This aspect of the dangers of recombinant DNA research has been considered to be a cause of much anxiety by scientists working in these fields.

There are serious portents for the future that can be drawn from another field of genetic research. The evolution of new strains of grain which produce miracle yields has led many poorer countries to substitute this seed material for their traditional seed stock. These miracle strains yield several times the crop of the traditional strains but are weak in propagating themselves and keep losing their productivity unless the seed stock is constantly replenished from the source of supply — invariably a multinational corporation. The pattern of dependence on these corporations for new seed stock then becomes established, the old seed stock is diminished, and the countries concerned become dependent for their cereals upon these great corporations. The price of new stock is constantly rising and with genetic manipulation the productivity of these new strains will increase. The result is a problem of international proportions, for many third world governments fear that in the near future the giant chemical and agricultural corporations will have the power to starve or feed populations by deciding whether to withhold or grant seed stock. Readers of international economic and political journals will be familiar with the concern which this problem is causing in the international field. In the national field, the lawyers of each country will need to step in, to work out guidelines or restraints that will keep this enormous new power within acceptable limits.

Though this last issue is only peripheral to this paper, it raises questions which go to the heart of the genetic engineering issue. It illustrates the high commercial value attaching to the field of genetic research and the fact that much of this research is conducted at the behest of large industrial corporations which provide the funds. Such corporations are likely to appropriate to themselves the commercial advantages flowing to them from their research and are likely to defy the guidelines which public authority may issue. The pharmaceutical companies defied NIH guidelines and it is interesting to note that the first application for a patent for a new life form — by a scientist, Chakrabarty — was in fact conducted by the General Electric Company which had taken an assignment of Chakrabarty's rights to his new invention.

New legal mechanisms will be required to deal with this problem so far as genetic engineering is concerned. One hesitates to think of the possibilities opened up by human genetic engineering know-how, if it should be in the hands of commercial operators.[17]

B) Medium Term Possibilities

1. Transplant of reproductive organs. The transplant of human tissue of all kinds — kidneys, corneas, hearts, skin, bone marrow, semen, testes, ovaries — raise many problems irrespective of the nature of the tissue transplanted. Among these are problems connected with the determination of death of the donor, questions of consent, commerce in human parts and State powers. I shall here deal only with the problems of transplant of reproductive tissue.

The Australian Law Reform Commission in its Working Paper No. 5 of 1977 referred to a paper received by it from Dr. Kevin Lafferty of the John Curtin School of Medical Research of the ACT, pointing out that when the "immune response" (*i.e.* the rejection of foreign tissue by the human body) can be overcome, hormone-producing glands — the pituitary, thyroid, parathyroid, adrenal, testes and ovary — will be capable of successful transplantation. Immunological research is progressing rapidly and within ten years improvements in the success rate will be seen, particularly in the hormone-producing tissues.

[17] See Addendum B.

If and when the testes and the ovary can be transplanted, it is not difficult to foreshadow the complex legal problems that will result. Quite apart from the problems associated with obtaining them (certification of death, consent, etc.), there could well be problems of inheritance, claims for maintenance, actions for wrongful birth and personality and psychological problems associated with the birth of a child from a reproductive organ 'belonging' to the apparent parent but transmitting the personality of another. It may be that the problems are no greater than one encounters in the field of adoption. It may be otherwise. Only time can tell.

It may be added that the Royal College of Obstetricians and Gynaecologists Australian Council, in a submission to the Australian Law Reform Commission, stated that the transplants of Fallopian tubes and ovaries, though not yet successfully made, are regarded as definite future possibilities and that they will be in demand because of the needs of infertile women whose infertility may be cured by such transplants.

The College's submission also refers to the possibilities of successfully treating a woman who may (or may not) be infertile, married to a man who may (or may not) be infertile by techniques which current medical research makes it feasible to contemplate in the future — the obtaining of eggs from a woman by surgery, the fertilization of those eggs in laboratory conditions by sperm obtained from a donor (the husband or another), and the transplant of the resulting embryo into that woman or another woman (the surrogate mother). The Law Reform Commission considered this future development as being within its terms of reference but thought it appropriate that the large social and legislative problems involved required separate attention, and did not therefore consider them in detail.

However the legal implications are far-reaching and are bound up with major ethical and theological issues. For example, is the reproduction of humans without normal heterosexual intercourse objectionable to principles of religion? Does the effective separation of procreation and love water down the latter of much of its traditional content, and to that extent impair the institution of the family? Is man usurping a function of God without the knowledge or wisdom that should accompany that function? We do not know what answers theology and morality will come up with when these projected developments become realities. These are not our concerns in this paper, but will influence community thinking and therefore the legal regulations of the future.

The law will need to face the practical problems these situations will raise — among which will be the regulation of the conditions for taking such a reproductive organ from a donor's body, the regulation of organ banks, the settlement of questions of parental responsibility for the maintenance of the child thus produced, the demarcation of areas of state responsibility, and the limits of state interference. Some of the discussions under earlier sub-heads will be relevant to these problems as well.

2. Ectogenetic development of the foetus to full term. We have already referred to the present state of ectogenetic development of the embryo. Australia is one of the leading countries in IVF research, and Monash University one of its leading centres. The best scientific opinion seems to be that it is scarcely possible to keep such an *in vitro* fertilized embryo alive outside the human body for more than forty-eight hours. However, longer periods have been reported in the United States and by researchers in Italy. Little is known about the United States claim, but it is believed that they achieved success for a few days in keeping the embryo alive. When their experiment eventually failed and they "washed the foetus down the laboratory sink" there was an outcry in Italy, and the Pope, reinforced by a strong public opinion, called for a halt to such experimentation.

Although the full-term test-tube baby, i.e. one grown to full term in laboratory conditions, seems still at least half a century away from us according to scientists working in this field, there can be no doubt that in the years immediately ahead many scientists in different countries will be attempting to keep embryos alive in the laboratory and will have varying degrees of success. Some will undoubtedly achieve longer terms than at present. If there should be success in keeping the embryo alive for close on three months, very grave issues will arise, for unsuccessful experiments will need to be terminated and "washed down the drain". Especially if this occurs on a large scale, with several dozen fertilized embryos being grown simultaneously, it may become necessary for the community to express its views on the question of creation and destruction of foetuses and the issue will cause grave concern to the law.

3. Preselection of characteristics. If and when it becomes possible, by interference with the DNA molecule, to induce pre-selected characteristics in the human, all the problems of Huxley's *Brave New World* will really be on us. Some of these issues have been foreshadowed in the earlier discussions. State power, principles of selection, mass production of pre-selected types, the balance between different categories of skills and aptitudes and many other frightening possibilities open up. We can do no more than make bare mention of them.

4. The ability to identify genotypes of superior qualities. In July 1978 it was reported that a single gene in the three to four million in a human cell

had been isolated and identified for the purpose of diagnosing a foetal defect.[18]

In the same way it will be possible to identify genes with superior qualities. The tools for analysis of the genes will certainly be refined in the years to come, although the ability to manipulate the genes by introduction or removal of component molecules may be longer delayed.

Once we have achieved greater scientific precision in identifying the superior genes, the move for eugenic selection will achieve greater momentum. There will be a clamour both from individuals and from the community for the selected propagation of the known superior genotypes. Arguments will then arise concerning the desirability of particular qualities and the extent to which they should be reproduced. The greater prevalence of sperm banks with an infinite variety of samples in them may provoke requests by prospective parents for particular genotypes. Present strict rules of selection, largely in the hands of doctors operating these banks, may tend to be watered down and, especially where the banks are commercially operated, there may be a tendency to please customers by granting them a desired sperm type — perhaps a highly intellectual one. At that stage legislation might be necessary to deal with the resulting problems.

5. International Trade in Human Organs. The suggestion was seriously made last month — that organ banks should engage in a trade with poorer countries, for human organs. It was suggested that a kidney, for example, could be purchased from a poor donor in a third world country, who would be quite happy to part with his kidney for a sum of four thousand dollars which would give him affluence in his country. Many a donor in the rich world would, according to this suggestion, be quite willing to pay four thousand dollars for this purchase.

The poor countries were, according to this proposal, looked upon as rich reservoirs of human organs which could meet the medical needs of the rich world.

Although this suggestion aroused a great deal of revulsion all over the world, such adverse opinion is not sufficient by itself to prevent it. Such a traffic in organs could be set up and might be difficult to detect. Commerce being what it is, it might be only too ready to pick up this new line of business, illicitly, if need be. International legal regulation will need to combine with the national to prevent this.

18 N.Y. Times, July 30, 1978.

When the technology becomes available for the transplant of reproductive organs such as testes and ovaries, and of ancillaries such as Fallopian tubes, this possibility will have serious implications for genetic engineering.

6. Cryonic Suspension. The freezing of sperm, a technique now available, makes possible the continuance, even for generations, of the reproductive abilities of an individual. People wishing to perpetuate themselves in the indefinite future thus already have the power to do so. Should this power be regulated and, if so, on what principles? Can a person by written instrument offer his sperm to a willing donee fifty years later for certain advantages to the latter — say an attractive payment — on condition the child is to bear his name and be considered his issue? Can a person be permitted to require or provide for his propagation in this fashion from generation to generation? Is there, as in the law against perpetuities, some principle ingrained in the law that the dead ought not to be able to bind future generations in this manner?

C) LONG-TERM POSSIBILITIES

The best scientific opinion is that the three possibilities discussed here are many years away from us, although in popular literature there are often treated of as very short-term possibilities.

The issues they raise are, however, so momentous that it would not be premature for lawyers and the public to give some thought to their legal implications. The possibilities they open up call for long-term planning, and the earlier we address ourselves to them, the more satisfactory will be their eventual solution.

1. *Cloning.*

This raises the most serious issues. They are discussed in Chapter 17 below, dealing with "Some Orwellian Scenarios".

2. *Parthenogenesis.*

This is the process of fatherless reproduction caused by stimulation of cell division. As with cloning, it eliminates the need for sexual union and permits multiple copies of a given individual. The issues discussed in the context of cloning have relevance here and many of the same legal considerations arise.

3. *Genetic Mapping.*

If and when we reach the stage when biological engineers are able to identify and locate each gene and molecule among the billions that make up the 46 human chromosomes, the urge will arise for making the first genetic blueprint. The structuring of humans in accordance with that blueprint may follow.

We are still so far away from this that we need to mention it only as a possibility — though a frightening one at that — which may become reality somewhere in the next century.[19]

4. *Cryonic suspension.*

This is the freezing of the human body itself for reactivation at a future point of time — maybe fifty years or a century later. This procedure, which is foreshadowed as a means of forestalling death and projecting oneself into a future age, raises legal problems regarding the preservation of property for an indefinite term, rights of succession and numerous others resulting from the sudden injection of a person into a futuristic environment. It is in a sense a reproduction of a current person in a future age and to that extent on the peripheries of genetic engineering. Cryobanks are already in existence for the freezing of human tissue and organs. This avenue will be explored for commercial purposes and needs legal regulation reflecting community wishes.

* * *

These then are some of the issues we must face. Immediate, short term or distant, they all raise not merely medical issues but issues which are ethical, theological, moral, legal and social. There is much contribution that other disciplines than science and medicine can make, which the technicality of the subject-matter is restraining them from making. Interdisciplinary seminars and discussion can clarify the issues and the areas of possible contribution. The lay public must participate and do so with the requisite knowledge and information.

It is hoped this cause will be greatly furthered by such seminars as these, for which there is so great a public need. One looks forward with hope for an

[19] See, further, Addendum C.

ongoing process of interdisciplinary discussion and lay participation in a field which is of such great importance to the human future.

ADDENDUM A (Patents in Living Organisms)

The *Chakrabarty* case went up to the U.S. Supreme Court and resulted in a landmark decision[1] in which the Court declared that man-made micro organisms were patentable subject-matter. The Court reasoned that the presence of man-made characteristics in the new bacteria made the invention patentable. The Court observed that the subject-matter of a patent includes "anything under the sun that is made by man" (at p. 307), and observed that Chakrabarty had created "a new bacterium with markedly different characteristics from any found in nature". Consequently his discovery was "not nature's handiwork but his own" (at p. 310). The Court also stated that an invention must have an industrial application if it is to be the subject of a patent.

It is to be noted that in the U.S., patent protection goes back to the Constitution, which provides that "Congress shall have the Power ... to Promote the Progress of Science and useful Arts, by securing for limited times to Authors and Inventors the exclusive Right in their Writings and Discoveries".[2] The first patent act was passed in 1790.

For long the prevailing patent doctrine was that laws and products of nature are not patentable.[3] In a case in the early post-war years the U.S. Supreme Court refused a patent to an inventor who made a claim for a patent on bacterial strains used to aid plants in fixing nitrogen. The Court held that this was precisely what each strain did in its natural state.[4] A distinction must here be drawn between genetic engineering and chemical plant breeding techniques.

1 *Diamond* v. *Chakrabarty* 447 US 303 (1980).

2 Art 1 s. 8(8)

3 See Dan L. Burk "Biotech & Patent Law: Fitting Innovation to the Procrustean Bed" 18 *Rutgers Computer & Tech Jn'l*, 1 at 26 (1991)

4 *Funk Bros. Seed Co.* v. *Kalo Inoculant Co.*, 333 US 127 (1948).

> Gene engineering allows nature to be cut into parts and recombined by transferring some parts across the boundaries of species and even genera. In contrast, classical breeding remains within those boundaries and may produce varieties of the species but — except for non-reproducing hybrid forms — not new species as such.[5]

It is this "cross-cutting capacity of genetic engineering"[6] that distinguishes it from plant patents which had received recognition as early as the Plant Patent Act (PPA) 1930, in the U.S.A.

Plant patenting "extended the incentives of the patent system to persons who cultivate asexually reproducing plants"[7] and applicants for a plant patent had to meet the criteria of subject-matter, utility, novelty and non-obviousness.[8] Thus while patents for plant varieties were recognized, and extended the patent system to living subject-matter, they did not constitute a precedent for inventions which chopped up and restructured the building blocks of life.

This was the innovation made by the *Chakrabarty* decision which held genetically engineered bacteria to be patentable.

After *Chakrabarty*, patentability moved higher up the scale of living organisms. For example in 1987 the US Board of Patent Appeals and Interferences determined that higher life forms such as oysters were patentable.[9]

In 1988 the focus shifted from genetically engineered plants to genetically engineered animals when, with the aid of recombinant DNA techniques, a mouse (known as the Onco-Mouse) was genetically engineered to be susceptible to human cancer.[10] This patent, by its novelty, generated a volume of academic literature world-wide,[11] and gave rise to a public controversy, with legislation being proposed in Congress for an outright prohibition of animal patents.[12]

[5] Gerd Winter, "Patent Law Policy in Biotechnology" 4 *Journal Env. Law* 168 at 172 (1992).

[6] *Ibid.*

[7] Dan L. Burk, *op. cit.*, p. 84.

[8] *Ibid.*; 35 USC s. 101–103 (1988).

[9] *Ex parte Allen* 2 USPQ 2d. 1425 (PTO Bd. Pat App. & Int. 1987).

[10] US Patent No 4,736,866 Off. Gaz Pat. Off 703 (April 12, 1988).

[11] See William H. Lesser, ed., *Animal Patents: The Legal, Economic & Social Issues*, 1989; Cynthia M. Ho "Building a Better Mousetrap: Patenting Biotechnology in the European Community" 3 *Duke Jnl of Comp. & Int Law* (1992–93) pp. 173–201.

[12] See *e.g.* S. 2111, 100th Congress 2d. Sess. (1988); Robert L. Baechtold *et al.*, "Property Rights in Living Matter: Is New Law Required?" 68 *Denv. V.L. Rev.* 141 (1991); Ho, *op. cit.* pp. 183–5.

In Germany, prior to the development of genetic engineering, the Supreme Court had in 1970 allowed a living organism to be patented in the *Red Dove* case[13] without much public controversy, but the *Chakrabarty* decision generated a public debate over the morality of patenting living matter,[14] and in Germany there is in place a special Commission of Inquiry on the Opportunities and Risks of Genetic Technology.[15]

This prompts an observation, from another angle, on biotechnology patents. The area is heavily commercialized (see Addendum B) and there is intense competition especially between the U.S., Japan and Western Europe for this burgeoning market. Patent Law, while it must take account of ethical concerns, has an impact also on the loss of business to competitors if it is more rigorous in one country as opposed to another. Industrialized countries, whose nationals file the largest number of patent applications each year, realize the importance of an internationally recognized intellectual property system, and have been pressing for its discussion in the General Agreement on Tariffs and Trade (GATT). The developing countries have resisted this, arguing, *inter alia*, that it affects national sovereignty, as intellectual property laws are properly contained within national legal systems, and should be discussed in the World Intellectual Property Organisation (WIPO), an organization set up to assist countries in regard to their intellectual property régime. The developing countries also fear that with such standardization they would lose a great deal of their control over the new technologies and their access to them. There is also a fear of an erosion of the world's biodiversity, with control over the whole process being centred in the industrialized countries. This is another momentous issue that arises from the new technology.[16] As one writer puts it,

13 *Rote Taube (Red Dove)*, *Int'l R. of Indus. Prop. & Copyright* L (IIC) 136 (1970).

14 Ho, *op. cit.*, pp. 196–7.

15 The European Patent Convention (EPC) controls the EC patent system. All members of the EC have signed the Convention. Under Act 53 the inventor may patent microbiological innovations but "essentially biological processes" are excepted from the patent procedures. The expression 'essentially biological' has not been defined, thus leading to much uncertainty.

16 See Rohini Acharya, "Patenting of Biotechnology: GATT & the Erosion of the World's Biodiversity" 25 *Journal of World Trade* 71 (1991); Rebecca L. Margulies, "Protecting Biodiversity: Recognising Intl. Intellectual Property Rights in Plant Genetic Resources" 14 *Michigan Jnl. of Intl. Law* 322 (1992).

> the system of incentives that has traditionally been used to encourage investment and innovation shows signs of strain in accommodating biotechnology. Almost from its inception biotechnology challenges the flexibility of patent doctrines that were never designed to address inventions fashioned from the very fabric of life. Biotechnology ought not to be forced to fit the measures of patent law, but neither should the patent law be butchered to meet the new demands of biotechnology.[17]

The issues are momentous, the risks are great and the rewards are attractive. This is an area of the law to be closely watched.

[17] Dan L. Burk, *op. cit.* p. 85

ADDENDUM B (Commercial Exploitation)

The biotechnology industry, while being one of the most research-intensive industries in the field of science, is also one of the most lucrative. Sales in the industry totalled four billion dollars in 1991 and are expected to reach fifty billion dollars by 2000.[18] Its importance can be gauged from the fact that in 1981 the government of Japan officially designated biotechnology as a key industrial technology,[19] and its spread is so wide as to include agricultural products, e.g., genetically-engineered corn, tomatoes, potatoes and grain which are more plentiful, tasty and attractive; solutions to environmental problems (e.g. genetically-engineered micro-organisms which literally eat up oil spills); and pharmaceutical products (drugs which treat heart disease, cancer, AIDS, anaemia, diabetes and facilitate bone marrow and organ transplants).[20]

Currently billions of dollars are invested by private industry annually on biotechnology research.

As genetic engineering of plants and micro-organisms proceeds apace, with major agrichemical, pharmaceutical and petrochemical transnationals vying with each other to organize patent rights, and as great transnational seed corporations increase their monopolistic grip over new varieties of food producing plant species, the human rights related problems call urgently for closer attention from the international community.

Indeed, as this book goes to press, the news media report that "terminator" seeds which are deliberately disabled from germinating when replanted could force farmers into the seed shop for a fresh supply every year, thereby rendering them totally dependent on international agribusiness and putting at risk 1.4 billion farming families world-wide.[21]

[18] See Akim F. Czmus "Biotechnology Protection in Japan, the European Community and the United States" 8 *Temple Intl. and Comp. LJ* (1994) p. 435.

[19] Brian C. Cunningham and Jou C Chow: "The Biotechnology Industry in Japan: A Framework for Entry", 7 *J Proprietary Rts* 13 (1992).

[20] Czmus, *op. cit.*, pp. 435, 436.

[21] *The Independent*, 22 March 1998.

ADDENDUM C (Mapping the Human Genome)

The Human Genome Project raises many issues of a nature which resemble those attending the patenting of living organisms. The Federal Government in the US has extensively funded research for mapping and "sequencing" the human genome.

The human genome resides in every cell of every human being. The Human Genome Initiative is the effort to map and identify each of the approximately three billion base pairs of nucleotides that make up the twenty-three different human chromosomes that compose the human genome.[22] The US Congress, in 1989, initiated a fifteen-year research project — the Human Genome Initiative.

The Genome Initiative raises a multitude of legal and ethical issues at the international level, at the family level and at the broader level of general society. Should applicants for military service and government service, immigrants, employees in security services, applicants for insurance policies, be screened? Should the new genetic knowledge be used to eliminate specific genetic diseases or improve the racial stock? Another problem that arises is the issue of ownership and control of the information generated. Once this knowledge passes from the realm of pure research to its practical applications, all these practical issues can conceivably arise when it is almost too late to prevent the subversion of this knowledge for private gain.

The enormous levels of research necessary for so vast a project have elevated it to the category of "big science", like space and nuclear projects.

Patent rights in bits and pieces of the human genome will probably be sought on the basis that the patent applicant has made a particular sequence available in a purified form that does not exist in nature.[23]This procedure carries heavy and macabre overtones, for patent law is here looking at bits and pieces of the human body as possible subjects for annexation into its

[22] See George J. Annas, "Mapping the Human Genome and the Meaning of Monster Mythology", 39 *Emory LJ* 629 (1990) esp. at 635 *et seq*.

[23] See Robert S. Eisenberg, "Patenting the Human Genome", *ibid.* 721 at 727.

territory. Particular sequences with particular characteristics, isolated, identified, and refined, could possibly become somebody's property. How will the law deal with this new species of proprietorial rights? Have we already taken a few steps down the slippery slope leading to such a result?

The contrary point of view is represented by the *Funk Brothers* case[24] where a patent was held on a mixed culture of different strains of bacteria, which helped plants to fix nitrogen from the air. The patent claims were held to be invalid. Justice Douglas in writing for the majority formulated the argument in memorable terms: "patents cannot issue for the discovery of the phenomena of nature... The qualities of these bacteria, like the heat of the sun, electricity or the qualities of metals, are part of the storehouse of knowledge of all men. They are manifestations of laws of nature, free to all men and reserved exclusively to none" (at p. 131).

There can be a wide range of arguments across the whole spectrum of variations separating these two views, but it seems likely, especially after the *Chakrabarty* decision, that the balance will swing away from the view articulated by Justice Douglas. The vast research interests involved will press for patentability of many of these genetic sequences, thus raising issues of vast importance not only to individuals and societies but also of a global nature, as these issues could cut across the North-South economic divide, giving economic rights even in the field of human genetic sequences. These will be held largely in the developed world, whatever the source of the genetic material that may be used.

There is a huge cluster of human rights issues here, to which the thoughtful lawyer will need to give attention. In a work of this nature it is only possible to alert the reader to this Pandora's box of future problems.

[24] *Funk Brothers Seed Co.* v *Kalo Inoculant Co.* 33 US 127 (1948).

15. Medicine: A Case Study*

INTRODUCTION

Many new advances in medical treatment raise new problems of their own. This examination of dramatic new advances in the treatment of the blood disorder known as thalassaemia is offered as an illustrative example of the variety of problems which can arise in the treatment of just one medical condition.

The subject is of such world-wide importance that there is now an International Thalassaemia Day which is observed on May 8 each year.[1]

The thalassaemic condition is one for which as yet no cure is known. Yet modern medical advances have evolved means of extending life expectancy to a level undreamed of before, thus raising a variety of significant human rights problems regarding such questions as the cost to the community; the quality of life; the assumption of the inevitability of death; the rights of patients; genetic counselling and religio-social attitudes, which make it a very appropriate illustrative study for a number of significant human rights issues. Some issues it raises, such as the progressive deterioration of the genetic stock of humanity, take one to the far frontiers of juristic theory.

If one medical advance can raise so many issues, the vast range of new ethical and legal issues which are constantly thrown up by modern medicine as a whole calls for special vigilance.

* This chapter is based upon a paper delivered at the Australian National Conference on Thalassaemia, Melbourne, May 1981.

[1] On International Thalassaemia Day on 8 May 1997, in India, it was observed that more than 10,000 thalassaemia major children are known to be born in India every year. Several others die even before they can be diagnosed as thalassaemia major. The thalassaemia trait (thalassaemia minor) is very common in many Indian communities like the Kutchis, Sikhs, Kumbis, Jains, Bengalis, Punjabis, Sindhis, Mahars, Kolis and Gaur Saraswatis (*Times of India*, 10 May 1997).

1. THE NATURE OF THALASSAEMIA

Thalassaemia is a blood disorder affecting persons of certain geographical regions of the Mediterranean and Asia who have lived for generations in areas exposed to malarial infection. The body's defence mechanism against this threat to life was a variation of the molecular structure of the red blood corpuscle.[2] Persons with such an extra molecule fall within the conditions known as *thalassaemia minor* and are able to live perfectly normal lives.

However, problems arise with the offspring of parents who are both affected by thalassaemia minor. In their case the probability that their offspring will fall within the category of *thalassaemia major* is of the order of one in four. *Thalassaemia major* is a serious condition with little life expectancy beyond the age of 5, prior to expensive modern medical advances in handling the disease.

Children suffering from thalassaemia major cannot produce red blood cells and are totally dependent on blood transfusions. These transfusions increase the iron content in their bodies to toxic levels and unless the iron is regularly removed it can prove fatal. Their spleens become enlarged due to the iron overload. Most countries cannot provide adequate medical facilities for the treatment of thalassaemic children.[3]

The treatment is painful and involves pumping a medicine through a syringe into the patient's stomach for over six hours each day. The side effects of the known forms of treatment are joint pains, nausea and weakness due to the lowering of the blood count. Hence many patients do not desire treatment. This raises grave questions regarding the quality of life, even if life is thereby prolonged. In any event, treatment is so expensive as to be beyond the reach of the average patient unless it is provided at the public expense, thus raising the further human rights problem of balancing resources and human rights.[4]

[2] *Cf.* sickle cell anaemia, caused by a variation of the blood corpuscle to combat malaria on the African continent. For a recent description of both types of variation, see C.D. Forbes and W.F. Jackson, *A Colour Atlas and Text of Clinical Medicine*, Mosby-Wolfe, 1993, pp. 437–439.

[3] An Indian mother of a thalassaemic child is reported to have said on Thalassaemia Day 1997: "Public hospitals do not even provide basic facilities for the treatment of thalassaemia. They assume that the child's death is inevitable. So they tend to neglect the patients." (*Times of India*, 10 May 1997.)

[4] In India the cost of iron chelation treatment, estimated at around Rs. 12,000 per month, is beyond the reach of even the middle class (*Times of India, ibid.*)

2. BASIC ASSUMPTIONS UNDERLYING THIS PAPER

It is necessary at this stage to deal with some practical statistics underlying the reasoning in this paper. They may perhaps need some modifications in the light of later research, but the basic reasoning would still hold good.

(i) The modern procedure of prenatal examinations known as foetoscopy does entail a risk which is almost negligible in the case of the mother, but there is thought to be up to a 5% chance of an injury to the foetus, which will result in abortion.

(ii) There is also the possibility of diagnostic error in foetoscopy. For example out of 30 cases where diagnosis was attempted on this basis, we have been told that we may expect one false positive and one false negative, thus resulting in an *error ratio* of around 6%.

(iii) The cost to the Australian community of keeping a child with thalassaemia major alive till the age of 30 is approximately $ 210,000.

(iv) Further treatment will cost the community approximately $ 10,000. per annum, thus bringing to half a million dollars the medical costs till the age of 60.

(v) In Victoria there are approximately 150 thalassaemia majors, in N.S.W. 90 to 100, and we can expect to have 6 or 7 thalassaemia majors, appearing every year. The cost in dollar terms is then several tens of millions of dollars, but spread over a number of years.

(vi) The incidence of the disease in its minor form among some communities of Mediterranean origin in Victoria is around 7.5%–8%.

(vii) As far as observation goes, and to judge from their responses to questions, thalassaemia majors seem happy to be alive, but their lifestyle is such that apart from constant blood transfusions they also need to have a regular injection every day of their lives. Such factors impinge on our assessment of what constitutes a reasonable quality of life.

I shall now proceed to outline a few of the human rights-related areas that call for attention in the context of medical advances in the treatment of thalassaemia.

3. THE CONCEPT OF GENETIC COUNSELLING

The impact of such new technologies upon basic rights has stimulated much thought relating to the appropriate legal responses to these dramatic advances.

In the first place there has been a considerable growth of the concept of genetic counselling.

Genetic counselling is now generally available in many countries and has grown almost into a discipline in its own right. It is heavily interlaced with human rights considerations.

Secondly, diagnosis of diseases of the foetus and the prognosis following therefrom was formerly a hit and miss kind of affair. There were broad Mendelian prophecies that one could make. New diagnostic tools are making it much easier for us to be more precise in our assessment of the situation. Amniocentesis and foetoscopy, to mention just two, are some of the ways in which doctors are able today to present to people with much greater clarity than ever before, the facts on the basis of which they must make their choice.

Thirdly, there is a consequent growth in the scope of the duty that is expected of doctors and those advising patients on the various options before them and the various possibilities attendant on these different courses of conduct. Human rights considerations come into this process today, as never before.

In the fourth place there has been much development of the concept of negligence in genetic counselling, because of the availability of this new range of devices for obtaining information.[5] This increases the duty and the responsibility of those charged with the function of giving advice. New advisory structures are developing for this purpose. The principal participants in these advisory structures are the medical advisors, the genetic counsellors, who might be attached to a hospital and members of the community. Since deep moral issues are involved, it is important that there be adequate representation of different groups with different kinds of religious persuasions and traditional backgrounds, on these advisory groups.

There are already cases where damages have been awarded, especially in the United States, for negligence in genetic counselling. The counselling takes the form of informing the patient what consequences will follow from the medical position as diagnosed, and on that basis, of advising the patient accurately as to what options are available and what would be the likely consequences of each of these options.

[5] See *infra*, Ch. 23.

It is also necessary to note that decisions are now emerging where the judges have held that amniocentesis is a procedure which is available, which is proved to be reasonably safe and which has become standard procedure. If therefore the adviser does not give advice about the availability of amniocentesis, the advisers would be guilty of negligence. These are developments in the law which have to be very closely watched and I have no doubt that, with the growth of new diagnostic tools in the next ten or fifteen years, we will have a whole crop of cases exploring such possibilities and perhaps constructing new causes of action on this basis.

4. THE CONCEPTS OF WRONGFUL BIRTH AND WRONGFUL LIFE

The concept of wrongful birth is now beginning to gain recognition, under which parents who might not have desired a particular birth can sue their doctor or genetic counsellor for lack of proper information or preventive action where a defective child is born.[6]

An even more controversial area is the wrongful life concept under which a child who has been born defective institutes an action on the basis that it did not desire to be born into an existence of suffering, but was brought into it through negligence on the part of those who were in a position to avert this tragedy.[7] There have been few types of action which run so counter to all our traditional concepts of causes of action. Though they have not been very favourably received thus far in the United States, more actions of this sort are in the process of institution and there has been a peripheral measure of success at least in advancing this concept. There is a growing body of case law on this subject based on the principle that a right under the law carries also a duty so to exercise that right as not to cause harm to others. Some exponents of this theory present the argument that while every woman undoubtedly has the right to procreate as she pleases, she must do so in such a manner as not to cause damage knowingly to the community interest.

There was a time when the general judicial attitude might be described as the "blessing" or "boon" attitude, implying that having a child is in all events a blessing. It is a blessing provided by providence. It is God's blessing and who are we to complain, whatever the defects of the child might be? There was then a movement to the theory that even if it might not be a blessing it certainly is an advantage to have a child. A child is an advantage in so many ways and it is not for us to complain if there has been the birth of an unwanted child. But now there is a trend emerging under which the courts are

6 On this concept, see further Ch. 23 below.

7 See further, Ch. 23 below.

showing increasing readiness to recognize that a child is not necessarily an unquestionable blessing, or boon, and is not necessarily an advantage upon a balance of favourable and unfavourable factors. This is an incipient judicial recognition that it can in fact be a positive disadvantage. Once we have judicial thinking recognizing that the birth of a child can be a positive disadvantage in that way, we are not very far from the construction of some altogether different causes of legal action in the future. These are new trends perhaps partially inspired by these new genetic tools. Old standards of discharge of advisory duty, where for example the doctor merely tells the patient that there is a chance that a child might be Mongoloid, are no longer adequate for the time when a parent can be told with near certainty that a child will be Mongoloid, or suffer from Down's Syndrome or thalassaemia major.

There are a few American cases, where some of these matters were discussed. The case of *Zepeta* v. *Zepeta*,[8] of 1963, was the beginning of this wrongful life concept. In that case, an illegitimate son sued his natural father for inducing his mother to have sexual relations with him upon promise of marriage, and he sought damages for deprivation of a normal home life, the stigma of being born a bastard, and the deprivation of rights of inheritance. That case aroused a great deal of interest because a person was alleging that he had been born into circumstances that were distasteful to him. The Court dismissed the case, but foreshadowed that cases of that sort could arise in regard to deformities produced by such causes as drugs, radiation, negligence on the part of sperm banks, and in cloning, and foreshadowed the possibility that in such cases there might be an action for wrongful life. There have been other cases thereafter. For example, an illegitimate daughter filed an action for deprivation of property rights, deprivation of normal childhood and proper care and support alleging that she was born to a mother who was a patient in a state mental institution and had been raped by another inmate and that she did not want to be born into that kind of life. The action was dismissed, the court holding that being born to one pair of persons or to another, or in one set of circumstances rather than another, is not an actionable wrong.

In another case, a man was found, upon a routine check-up, to have thalassaemia minor. The hospital subsequently found, incorrectly, that his wife was not a thalassaemia minor. In fact she was, and the offspring turned out to be a thalassaemia major. There was an action for wrongful birth against the hospital. The case was dismissed but the decision has been criticized on various grounds, one being that the hospital could have tested the child *in utero* and ascertained that it was a thalassaemia major, and also that there

[8] 41 Ill. App. 2d, 190 N.E. 2d 849 (1963) cert. denied 379 U.S. 945 (1964).

was negligence in testing the mother. In *Berman* v. *Allan*,[9] 1979, an action for wrongful birth of a child suffering from Down's Syndrome, the Court accepted that there was negligence in failing to inform the mother of the risk entailed, since the mother was 38 years old and therefore more than ordinarily prone to give birth to a child with such a defect. No amniocentesis was carried out. The New Jersey Supreme Court recognized the action for wrongful birth and held that amniocentesis was now standard procedure and should have been followed.[10]

5. THE STRAIN ON COMMUNITY RESOURCES — IS THIS A LEGITIMATE CONCERN?

If a woman insists, despite being advised that the child will be a thalassaemia major, on continuing her pregnancy, it would greatly strain community financial resources to keep such a child alive for the normal life span. It is argued by some that there is a duty lying upon the mother not to inflict that kind of commitment upon the community with full knowledge of that commitment in advance of the event. These are the vague outlines of new legal considerations that are likely to emerge in the future. The argument is that a right which a person is accorded by the legal system ought to be qualified by the principle that the right carries a duty not to cause injury or liability to the community in the exercise of that right.

In an age of dwindling *per capita* resources, this problem of cost must necessarily assume increasing importance. Thalassaemia is a case *par excellence* which raises this question in a very acute form. A woman desirous of going through her full pregnancy with the knowledge that the child she is carrying will suffer from thalassaemia major could, according to one point of view, be seen as deliberately imposing on the community a cost of half a million dollars. It may be that medical technologies in the future might be able to reduce that cost, but we can only act on the basis of factual information which we now have. An argument posed by those opposing the right of the woman is this:

9 80 N.J. 421, 404 A.2d 8 (N.J. 1979)

10 At the time of going to press, the High Court in London awarded a sum of £300,000 to a mother who gave birth to a boy with Down's syndrome after a military doctor advised her against taking an amniocentesis test, although she was nearly 36 years old and although women over the age of 35 have a risk factor up to three and a half times greater than women of 25, of giving birth to a Down's syndrome child. (*The Times*, May 2, 1997, p. 1.)

> With population pressures increasing and available resources remaining finite, can we pursue the luxury of continuing this human right of having a child despite the consequences?

The answer of those who view the sanctity of life as inviolable would be an unequivocal "yes", but we may be moving into an age where this question of shortage of resources becomes more acutely felt and the issues are crystallized in a manner that has not so far occurred.

Another way of viewing the question is to consider that every Government, in taking an important decision involving a major expenditure of public funds, is making a choice between alternatives, which may even involve questions of life and death. For example, if a Minister decides that he or she will build a concert hall at a cost of a few million dollars, that money comes out of the community coffers, and so much the less is available, shall we say, for kidney machines or life-saving devices. Each decision to embark upon expenditure of that sort is inferentially a decision curtailing to that extent the availability of life-saving services. Traditionally all governments have been taking those decisions, because there are scales of priorities in regard to public needs, with some needs taking priority even over matters of life and death. New medical technologies are facing this issue, and presenting it in a much more clear-cut form. It might be that in the future the community may have to take a hard decision as to how much it is prepared to pay to uphold the principle of the sanctity of life. It may in certain cases involve a greater price than the community can afford or is prepared to pay.

Certainly if you compare this community with another community such as one in a developing country, the luxury may be of such an order that the developing community may instinctively say "we can't afford it", and in that case there might be a qualification to that basic human rights principle. Issues such as these, which have been swept under the carpet in the past, may be thrust into the foreground by new medical technologies.

We have here an instance of an extreme clash between two conflicting rights — the right of procreation and the right to community support for one's children. The latter is maintained at a level which the community can afford. Claims based on this right may run to a level which the community deems unreasonable, according to standards of fairness and justice in the allocation of community resources. If each right is claimed or protected absolutely, there is no answer to the problem, but human rights have limitations when their expansion without limit impinges upon other human rights. Where extreme conflicts occur, as here, the problem will perhaps be resolved, in a world of shortage, on a case-by-case basis. A poor community may reject as unjust the infliction upon it of an expenditure which a rich community may deem affordable. In short, we are faced here with a problem which defies a principled solution.

6. THE RIGHTS OF THE MOTHER

Certainly the mother would have an overarching right to decide what is eventually to happen. If she says, "Despite all your advice to me, despite the fact that it is to be a thalassaemia major, I want this child", the mother's views are to be respected. She would be entitled to take this position, even where there is a substantial risk of severe abnormality such as would entitle her, in many jurisdictions, to a legal abortion. But whether this right is to prevail over those of the unborn child known for a certainty to be thalassaemia major or spina bifida will be a question for the jurisprudence of the future.

Of course, all women would not be so adamant in their choice. Given all the facts and figures some might be prepared to terminate the pregnancy and to attempt to have a normal child in another pregnancy.

Clearly, the mother cannot be called upon to give an undertaking, before the test, that if the foetus is found to be a thalassaemia major she will consent to the termination of pregnancy. The mother cannot be the subject of arm twisting in that way under the law.

7. CONFLICTING RELIGIO-SOCIAL ATTITUDES OF PATIENT AND ADVISER

An important factor relevant to this discussion is the cultural conflict that might arise between the value systems of people of various cultural groups within the same population. It arises with particular acuteness in the case of thalassaemia. This problem is dealt with in the context of genetic counselling in Chapter 23 below.

8. THE DUTY OF DISCLOSURE WHEN ROUTINE BLOOD SAMPLES ARE BEING TESTED FOR THALASSAEMIA

Another human rights-related question is whether, when a routine blood sample is taken from a patient, she should be informed also that she is being tested for thalassaemia. The answer is in the affirmative, because a person is entitled to know what particular test is being conducted and this really reflects, I think, on the duties of doctors. I understand this does not always happen but an important ground rule is that the patient is entitled to full consultation and full information of the nature and implications of any test carried out on her. Of course, there is an exception where the patient, not being of sufficient mental faculties, is unable to order her own affairs, in which case other arrangements would need to be made to secure the requisite consent.

Communication with the patient is sometimes difficult, especially if there is an obligation to inform her of all the purposes of a routine blood test. I would feel, however, that since this information is within her legal entitlement, every effort needs to be made to communicate this information to the patient at her level of understanding.

9. THE DOCTOR-PATIENT RELATIONSHIP

This leads naturally to another point which is becoming increasingly important in the context of the sophistication of modern medical treatment. The information which is relevant to the patient has grown enormously in the light of the vast medical advances of recent times. Some of this information is at a high level of technical detail and may well be beyond a patient's level of understanding. This has led medical professions world-wide to take another look at their techniques of communication with their patients. The old view that the doctor knew what was best for the patient and, in the light of his or her special knowledge and experience, took the decision that was best for the patient, is now superseded. The patient is at least an equal partner in the relationship, and every effort must, within limits, be made to explain procedures and consequences to the patient at the patient's level of understanding.

The era of subordination of the patient to the doctor is past. Lawyers have long recognized that there are in life many relationships such as lawyer-client, teacher-pupil, spiritual confessor-penitent, guardian-ward, in which one person is almost automatically in a position of subordination and another person in a position of dominance, without any adverse reflection on either. The doctor-patient relationship was eminently one of these and we have to bear this in mind throughout our discussions of these matters. The patient can well tend to be overawed by the fact that he or she is dealing with a person in a position of superiority both as regards knowledge, and as regards the power over himself or herself, for there is a relationship of complete dependency.

Very often we talk of free consent that is given to a particular medical procedure, but I would submit that those consents in many cases, if examined by the ordinary standards that we bring to bear on these special relationships, may not be really consents. I would submit that many of the numerous tests to which patients are subjected, are performed by doctors in situations where the doctor's decisions or advice are virtually law for the patient — not because the doctor is overbearing, but by reason of the very special position of ascendancy enjoyed by the doctor in the relationship. Especially in countries or in situations where the social gulf between the affluent class (to which the doctor belongs) and the deprived is vast, it is a bold patient who would say, "I am not prepared to go through this test or abide by this advice, even if that is what the doctor indicates".

That may be conduct on the part of the patient which one may in some cases disapprove of, but that is her right. The consent of the patient must be obtained in a manner which eliminates the possibility that the ascendancy of one party over the other was the determining factor in the decision.

10. NEW DIAGNOSTIC PROCEDURES: THE LEVEL OF ACCEPTABLE RISK TO THE FOETUS

Human rights-related medical problems also arise from the data I have outlined. One question is whether the dangers to the foetus arising from foetoscopy render it an unacceptable procedure? This arises consequent on the 5% death rate that may be imposed upon foetuses by this procedure. The answer depends, I would expect, on the value system of the person who is asked the question. If you should ask the question of a person who believes that all human life is so sacrosanct from conception onwards, that any interference with it for any cause whatsoever is unacceptable, the answer is likely to be negative, because a 5% death rate imposed on foetuses, some of which may be perfectly normal, may to this manner of thinking be unacceptable. This may not however be the result if one uses more objective standards not anchored in such special background attitudes. The mother would have the right to decide this question and she needs counselling in all its implications. She cannot however be compelled to a consent desired by her advisers but not by her.

11. THE RISK OF DIAGNOSTIC ERROR

Especially pending the perfection of new procedures, there can be a substantial risk of diagnostic error. Does the risk of diagnostic error stand in the way of the decision to abort? On the material presented to us today, the risk of diagnostic error at present seems to be as high as one in 30. This is not an overall figure, and no doubt, with improvements in technique, the risk will be brought to a lower level in the future. There can be real tragedy where a decision is taken to abort a perfectly healthy foetus on the basis of pre-natal diagnostic error.

The legal consequences of such a situation are as yet untried. If there was no negligence in the use of the procedures, and the decision itself was taken with due care and skill, possible claims would perhaps be defeated on the ground that the patient had consented. This raises again the question of adequate communication to the patient of the procedure, and of the degree of risk of error.

12. THE QUALITY OF LIFE

How is the right to life of the foetus evaluated against the quality of life? There are two aspects to this — the quality of life of the child and the quality of life of the family. As for the child there is some evidence that, despite their suffering, thalassaemia majors desire to be alive, or do not seek accelerated or natural termination of their lives. I would say that a counsellor is entitled to, and indeed obliged to, tell a woman of the dangers to the child of thalassaemia major, once it is discovered that she is carrying such a foetus, and to offer advice that such a child would have an existence that would be a burden to itself and to the community.

I said earlier that one of the factual bases that I proceeded upon was that thalassaemia majors seem happy to be alive, even despite their handicap. But I do not know whether that is a factor that is as decisive as it might seem, because they are making the best of a bad bargain, so to speak. They are born into this difficult situation and naturally making the best out of the life that they have, but whether, if they had had the option, they would have opted for that kind of life is a question that I think has to be answered slightly differently. The mere fact that the person is glad to be alive may not be a strong argument in favour of the quality of life of that person. I do not know what the answer to this is and the speakers who will follow me and deal more specifically with the quality of life will be able to give a more informed answer. I do not know whether the material before us is by itself sufficient to enable us to decide whether a particular child would have liked to live, even in this condition.

Legal philosophy may provide us here with some insights, and I would mention in particular the theory propounded by the British jurist, John Rawls, relating to the justice or injustice of a given social situation. If, behind a veil of ignorance as to the situation into which a person would be born, he or she were to be asked whether that situation is socially just, what would he or she answer? If the answer is in the affirmative, that situation, despite its inequalities, would not be one of injustice. Could we adapt this question to one where we ask a similar hypothetical question regarding the thalassaemic condition?

I do not know the answers, but it is time these questions became the subject of active discussion in the community.

13. THE RIGHTS OF THE CHILD

Here we come across a clash of value systems and, tracing the matter historically, one can go back to the ancient Greeks, who took the view where a new-born child was concerned, that there was a right on the part of the community, if the child was defective, to discard that child. The clash between individualist and communal values is highlighted in decisions of this sort. Human rights doctrine, with its emphasis on the rights of the individual and the sanctity of life, would reject the Greek approach.

Another Greek approach, very influential for many centuries in European law, was Aristotle's idea that a foetus did not have the attributes of a human until ensoulment, that is, until the soul took over or occupied the body that was in the process of formation. He fixed ensoulment, in the case of males, at 40 days after conception, and in the case of females at 80 days after conception.

By way of contrast, Buddhist philosophers take the view that, for a life to commence, three things must coincide in time: that is, the male element, the female element and the spirit. All three get together and form one entity at one precise moment of time, namely, the time of conception.

The early Church drew no distinction between stages of foetal development, prohibiting abortion absolutely, but later, under the influence of St. Augustine who was much influenced by Aristotelian biology, adopted the doctrine of "ensoulment". Thomas Aquinas, the twelfth century theologian, thought that sensation and movement were the only practical tests of "ensoulment". In 1621, Paolo Zacchia, who wrote on medico-legal questions from the standpoint of the Catholic Church, attacked the doctrine of ensoulment as an "imaginary thing" and, in the nineteenth century, Pope Pius XII removed the distinction under a Bull prohibiting every direct taking of human life after fertilization. The new Code of Canon Law, 1917, draws no distinction between various stages of formation of the foetus, and Vatican Council II endorsed this position in 1965.

Depending on the value system of the patient, vastly different results can follow as to how we view the rights of the child.

14. PROTECTION OF THE INTERESTS OF THE FOETUS

There is another important aspect to this sort of discussion. We are taking decisions on behalf of a foetus that is obviously unable to take a decision on its own, just as much as, very often, a court of law takes a decision on behalf of a child who is unable to make decisions for itself. In that kind of situation, where a person entitled to human rights is unable to make up his or her mind, we have a structure provided by the legal system for another decision to be substituted for the child's own, in the best interests of that child. That is a decision which requires a great input of all the skills that the community commands. We have to evolve some kind of structure for making that decision on behalf of the child and this is where counselling comes in, but of course with, in my view, a preponderant say on the part of the mother. Who are the persons entitled to make this decision? I have already outlined some of the structures that are available for this purpose. Ideally the doctors and third parties representing the community would provide counselling services for the mother.

When one is deciding such an important matter from the standpoint of the unborn child, there are perhaps other circumstances as well that require careful consideration. For example, is the hope of future advances in medicine relevant to the determination of these questions? Medicine is always progressing and it may well be said that there is a reasonable hope of better times ahead. Here again we can only act on the basis of our present knowledge, and our present knowledge is that thalassaemia is incurable, but that it is possible to sustain life by expensive means. That is the factual framework against which we must consider the problems posed to us.

15. THE ARGUMENT OF PROGRESSIVE DETERIORATION OF GENETIC STOCK

There is a major problem for the future here. We are for the first time in history creating a situation where a thalassaemia major can procreate and therefore bring into the genetic stock an infusion of thalassaemia major genes. The medical consequences of these must be studied. I am not equipped to deal with the medical nuances of this situation, but can see that it raises starkly some of the most dreaded issues regarding a curtailment of the right to procreate. With the methods of natural selection that have operated from the commencement of the human race, there was a natural elimination of those with defective genes. Modern medicine keeps them alive well beyond the age when nature would have brought about a termination of life. The situation is not peculiar to thalassaemia. It operates in many other areas of medical advance as well.

There are two periods of time relevant to this problem which raise particular difficulties — the period before procreation and the period after birth. The first raises the question of sterilization, and the second the withholding of life support. Totalitarian regimes had their answer to the first question and the ancient Greeks had their answer to the second, in abandoning defective children after birth.

Neither of these solutions would be acceptable in our day and age. Compulsion in the first case and abandonment in the second would violate the basic tenets of human rights doctrine. Could the solution lie in an airing of these issues in public, in the light of specific medical evidence, after which a climate of opinion may grow in the community to the extent that sufferers will impose voluntary restraints upon themselves? They would know better than any others the extent of their suffering and would not want to impose it upon their offspring. Counselling services could help considerably in the matter, and such persons would be exposed to all the pros and cons of the debate from their earliest years.

One can only hope that with greater general awareness of these problems they will resolve themselves. We will need to leave the problems to the wisdom and greater knowledge of future generations, while handing them the torch of a grave concern for the human rights issues involved.

16. GENETIC SCREENING

Should the entire community be screened or does one screen only pregnant women? This raises important issues relating to privacy. It is a comparatively simple procedure. It may be argued that general screening can avert quite a number of the problems that are posed later on. Some would argue that it can even be done on a compulsory basis, just as many other kinds of screening have been done in regard to tuberculosis and other diseases. One of the real advantages of that is that people would know ahead that they were thalassaemia carriers and could therefore plan their lives on a better basis of information. However, there are many groups of people in the community who are statistically so negligibly exposed to the risk of thalassaemia that it might be unjustifiable to impose this requirement upon them. Such a compulsory duty of disclosure cannot be imposed under the present state of the law. It is still a matter for individual discretion and, while I would expect that an ethic of disclosure will be built up, I do not believe one can, by law, compel disclosure.

* * *

I have attempted in a general way to draw attention to a few of the legal and moral issues that arise in the field of thalassaemia, in the context of recent medical advances. This is perhaps only the tip of the iceberg, with a vast body of problems lying below the surface and as yet concealed from our view. However, we cannot avoid addressing such problems, and the longer we delay, the more difficult they will be to resolve. We must hope that the insights resulting from such discussions will guide us towards the solution of such other problems as may arise from time to time. We do ill by ourselves and by society if we fail to face these problems now, on the basis that our intellectual or factual equipment is as yet unequal to the task. Least of all can we afford to sweep them under the carpet and treat them as if they do not exist.

Thalassaemia is only one illustrative example of the constellations of human rights problems attending the dramatic advances in medical science which have been achieved in our age. As medical science progresses, and confers its undoubted benefits upon us, we must not lose sight of the fact that these problems will multiply. With that inevitable multiplication of problems, there will be an inevitable increase in our level of unpreparedness, unless we brace ourselves now to face the comparatively few problems that are already with us.

16. Mining Technology: A Case Study

The industrial technology which is dominant in a community tends often to subjugate that community's lifestyles to its needs. This Chapter offers a case-study of the impact of modern mining technology on a small island and its people. It looks at the impact of mining on the land, the flora and fauna, the customs, the lifestyle, the health, and the culture of the people. Any assessment of the impact of a particular technology on a people would not be complete without a consideration of all these aspects.

The main principles of international law relating to responsibility for rehabilitation are briefly noted.

* * *

Nauru is a little island in the Central Pacific, 19 kilometres in circumference, and situated 3,000 kilometres to the north-east of Australia.

Nauru's phosphate deposits are, in quality, among the richest in the world. The island was covered by a massive blanket of phosphate rock, the value of which was assessed at hundreds of millions of pounds sterling, at the time of the commencement of the League of Nations Mandate after World War I.

The island, known to nineteenth century European traders in the Pacific as Pleasant Island, owing to its lush greenery, was reduced to an arid and crater-ridden condition by phosphate mining over a period of more than 50 years. The pock-marked surface of the central portion of the island presents a gaunter version of desolation than the lunar landscapes that have become familiar to us from space exploration. The craters, some of them 50 feet deep, are ragged-edged holes left over after the extraction of phosphate in which Nauru was exceptionally rich. Topsoil is non-existent and a verdant landscape, which boasted many indigenous plant species and was a refuge for teeming bird life, is now desolate, useless to humans, fauna and flora.

The mining of phosphate in Nauru has raised a major environmental problem which could well be duplicated in numerous other mining situations throughout the world.

Nauru was a German colony before World War I. After World War I, it became mandated territory under the League of Nations, and a joint mandate was issued to Australia, the United Kingdom and New Zealand. This joint mandate later became a joint trusteeship under the United Nations.

Using modern industrial methods, the British Phosphate Commissioners, during the periods of mandate and trusteeship, mined out large sections of the central portion of Nauru, reducing the land to its present condition.

The Government of Nauru, which attained independence in 1968, appointed a three-man Commission of Inquiry to investigate and report on international responsibility for the mining of Nauru during the periods of mandate and trusteeship. The author was the Chairman of this Commission which made its Report in 10 volumes, short extracts from which are reproduced below.

Consequent on this Report, the Government of Nauru instituted proceedings against the Government of Australia in the International Court of Justice, claiming compensation for the mining out of its phosphate lands. When the case came before the Court, the author, who had in the meantime been appointed a judge of the Court, recused himself from hearing the case, in view of his Chairmanship of the Commission. A series of preliminary objections taken by Australia were overruled by the Court[1], after which the matter was settled out of Court.

A summary of the Report was published in the author's volume, *Nauru: Environmental Damage under International Trusteeship*, Oxford University Press, 1992.

The ensuing documents deal with the nature, scope and legal implications of the environmental problem that has resulted. The legal implications of this case are rendered somewhat more complex by the fact that the territory mined out was trust territory, but the environmental principles applicable apply nevertheless to all mining situations.

The ensuing extracts from the Report and the book are reproduced by kind permission of the Government of Nauru and Oxford University Press.

* * *

[1] *Certain Phosphate Lands in Nauru (Nauru* v. *Australia), Preliminary Objections, I.C.J. Reports 1992*, p. 240. For the Order noting the settlement and the discontinuance of proceedings, and ordering the removal of the case from the list, see *I.C.J. Reports 1993*, p. 322.

(A) THE DEMAND FOR SUPERPHOSPHATES[2]

The value of phosphatic fertilizers was becoming increasingly known in Europe in the nineteenth century. Bone-meal, a source of phosphate, came to be extracted in bone grinding mills in England and elsewhere. Indeed, bone-meal had become so vital to agriculture that large quantities were imported to England in the 1850s. The German chemist, Justus von Liebig, who played an important part in building the modern fertilizer industry, complained that the battlefields of Waterloo, the Crimea and elsewhere were being turned up for bones to be carried away to England for this purpose.[3]

In 1840, in his great work *Organic Chemistry in its Applications to Agriculture and Physiology*, Liebig proposed that bone-meal could be greatly enhanced in its effectiveness if treated with sulphuric acid. This would increase the availability of phosphate to plant roots by converting it from an insoluble to a soluble form. This procedure had great value for rock phosphates as well, for in its natural form it is insoluble, but when so treated becomes soluble and hence easily accessible. Phosphate thus treated is known as superphosphate. Two years later, Sir John Lawes in England set up the first factory for the production of superphosphate from rock phosphate, using this method. By the end of the nineteenth century, there was a rapid increase in Europe of the demand for superphosphate, resulting in an increased search throughout the world, and especially in the unexplored islands of the Pacific, for sources of phosphate.

Nauru and its phosphate deposits were a rich prize whose value was discerned by the merchant adventurers scouring the Pacific.

(B) MINING METHODS[4]

When mining first commenced in 1906, the excavation and collection of phosphate rock was all done by hand. Initially, loose surface phosphate pieces were collected and bagged. This bagged material was manually handled and transported to the coast for shipment.

[2] From *Nauru: Environmental Damage under International Trusteeship*, Oxford University Press, 1992 (hereinafter referred to as *Nauru*), pp. 3–4.

[3] A. F. Blakey, *The Florida Phosphate Industry*, 1973, p. 7; Walter Pierce and A. G. Norman (eds.), *Soil and Fertilizer Phosphorus in Crop Nutrition*, Academic Press, N.Y., 1953, pp. ix–x.

[4] From *Report of the Commission of Inquiry into the Rehabilitation of the Worked Out Phosphate Lands of Nauru*, 1988 (hereinafter referred to as *Nauru Report*), pp. 1028–1029.

After loose surface phosphate pebbles had been removed, it became necessary to work deeper and, as this deeper phosphate had a higher moisture content, it became necessary to sun dry it before shipment. The technique adopted was to pick over an extensive area and leave the loosened material to dry out before collection and trucking. Later, to enable work to proceed during rainy periods, shelters were erected over the working areas. At about the same period, storage sheds were erected on the coast to keep dry the phosphate ready for shipment. Phosphate was transported to the coast by a small gauge railway.

A loading jetty had been constructed and phosphate was conveyed to the head of the jetty by hand-pushed rail trucks. This jetty was later replaced by two cantilevered jetties which overhung the reef by about 24 metres. Lighters being loaded from these jetties were clear of the surf which was a considerable advantage.

Hand raising was still the method used in the early years of the British Phosphate Commissioners (B.P.C.). Mechanical driers, installed in the early 1920s at the coastal treatment plant, ensured that the phosphate was shipped at the required moisture content. Since then, there was the progressive introduction of modern mining technology, which resulted in a vastly increased output.

In 1908, the first of the overhead cableways was installed. These varied in span from 500ft. to 1,000ft. and carried six cubic yard skips. The skips could be lowered anywhere along the cable for filling, and they were discharged into hoppers from which the rail trucks were loaded. In the early 1950s, the six cubic yard skips were replaced by one cubic yard grabs which were self-loading. This reduced the labour requirements for loading.

Cableway raising continued until 1956.

About 1951, Ruston Bucyrus RB19 machines, fitted with jibs and 5/8 cubic yard Blaw Knox clamshell buckets were introduced. These machines loaded directly into motor trucks which transported the phosphate to a central rail loading point on Topside.[5]

The RB19 machines were later replaced by RB30 machines fitted with one cubic yard round-nosed clamshell buckets. 22-ton trucks were introduced to transport the mined phosphate to a station in the centre of Topside, where unwanted limestone pieces were removed, the phosphate screened, the lumps passed through a primary 48"x30" jaw crusher and a secondary gyrator crusher, and the resultant fines loaded on a train for transport to the coastal processing plant. At the processing plant, the phosphate was either dried in a kiln and stored under cover ready for shipment, or was passed

[5] The central plateau of Nauru.

through a calcining plant (to prepare it for phosphoric acid manufacture) before being stored under cover.

The mining system has remained generally the same to the present day.

The introduction of the Ruston Bucyrus excavators and, subsequently, D7 Caterpillar bulldozers enabled production rates to be considerably improved.

(C) TOPOGRAPHICAL EFFECTS OF MINING[6]

Unmined areas still present on Topside enable the observer to gain a realistic impression of what the plateau was like, prior to mining on Nauru.

The plateau was well covered with a mature forest of tomano, wild almond, native hibiscus, and other indigenous trees, with a somewhat sparse understorey of shrubs and grasses. Ferns prospered in hollows. Coconut palms and pandanus grew on the plateau — generally where planted by the people. Coconut palms thrived in the lower levels of the Buada Lagoon, as also did mango and breadfruit trees. Noddy birds, terns and frigate birds utilized the trees for nesting, roosting and food and were there in considerable numbers.

The land was easily accessible and pleasant to walk over. The Nauruans, who lived on the coastal plain, used the plateau as a source of many of their essential supplies: timber for canoes; timber, palm fronds and pandanus leaves for hut building; timber to make tools, weapons and furniture; materials for clothing, fishing lines, etc. Nuts from the tomano trees were collected and crushed for oil to burn for light, almond nuts were collected for food. Other berries, nuts, etc. were collected for food or medicine. The Nauruans prize the noddy as a great delicacy and hunting parties sought them in the tomano forests.

Of particular significance were the pandanus groves. Pandanus were, and still are, highly esteemed as a source of food. The leaves were used for many purposes, including clothing, ground mats, and roof thatching. Woven into wall sheets, they provided wind and rain protection in their huts. When the fruit was ripe, the Nauruans moved up to the plateau in large parties and lived there for long periods, picking the fruit, extracting and cooking the edible jelly, and preserving food for the coming lean season. These pandanus expeditions involved many people. They were essentially clan or community undertakings. There was much work to be done and many hands were needed. It was also a time of rejoicing and the Nauruan community of today recall such events of the past with nostalgia.

6 *Nauru Report*, pp. 1032–1033.

In addition to pandanus, earlier generations of Nauruans had planted coconut trees and breadfruit trees, and these abounded on the plateau.

Mining changed the face of the land.

After a site had been mined, the area appeared barren, stark and grotesque. Nauruans have described it as being like freshly dug graves with white headstones showing conspicuously above. Removal of the phosphate left a densely packed mass of gaunt, white, towering, dolomitic limestone pinnacles which gradually darkened after long exposure to the sun and weather. The pinnacles varied in height to a maximum of over 23 metres. The close spacing of the pinnacles made walking between them difficult, if not impossible. For years after mining, the area was barren; completely devoid of any vegetation. Although ferns, plants and trees did ultimately grow on the site, this revegetation was almost entirely limited to the small pockets of residual phosphate left in the crevices of the pinnacles or in the hollows between the pinnacles. The land was useless and inaccessible.

(D) EFFECT ON FAUNA AND FLORA[7]

An early German writer, H. Meyer, writing in 1920, describes Nauru as deserving the name of Pleasant Island "because it offers a pleasant aspect with its pointed ridges and its rich greenery". He goes on to say that "the rocky shore is covered with lush foliage".[8] Going on to describe the vegetation, he describes coconut palms as being the most dominant. Apart from coconut and pandanus, there are cultivations of papaya and watermelon.

Meyer says that of the birds, most numerous is the frigate bird which is often kept in cages by the people. He notes that, apart from these, there are snipe on the shore and pigeons and songbirds in the interior.

Phosphate mining has had a very damaging impact upon the pleasant aspect that Meyer describes. The natural surroundings in which generations of Nauruans lived out their lives have been irretrievably damaged and, with it, the lifestyles that were dependent on it.

Drs. Harley Manner, Randolph Thaman and David Hassall, in a paper titled "Phosphate Mining Induced Vegetation Changes on Nauru Island",[9] have described how centuries will be needed for the forest to re-establish

7 *Nauru Report*, pp. 188–196.

8 H. Meyer, *Das Deutsche Kolonial Reich*, Leipzig, 1910.

9 65 *Ecology (Journal of the Ecological Society of America)*, (1984), 1454–1465.

itself naturally, even in a modified form, and how numerous plant species are scattered and stunted as compared with their growth in the unmined forest.[10]

They point out that the uniqueness and fragility of Pacific Island ecosystems and their natural vegetation have long attracted the attention of scientists.[11] These scientists have "stressed the disastrous effects and almost total disruption of island ecosystems that resulted from inappropriate development projects and land use".[12] Natural forest microclimates have been transformed into new microclimates with increased sunlight and lower humidity, resulting in greatly altered patterns of vegetation.

Such a transformation of a pleasant natural environment also has many human rights implications.

One of the conclusions in the paper referred to is that the only alternative to the process of natural reafforestation which will certainly take centuries is for the Nauruans to artificially alter and accelerate the revegetation of the central plateau. If a planned programme is not resorted to for rehabilitating the central plateau "Nauru could end up like Banaba (where phosphate deposits were depleted in 1979) an almost deserted island", to use the words of Manner, Thaman and Hassall.

On 21 July 1987, Dr. Thaman of the University of the South Pacific, one of the authors referred to, gave evidence before the Commission in relation to vegetation on the island, and also took the Commission on a field trip showing the Commission various points of interest on the island in relation to vegetation. Dr Thaman pointed out to the Commission some of the impacts of phosphate mining upon the vegetation of Nauru.

Of the limited indigenous plant species of Nauru, Dr. Thaman lists a number as endangered. Some of them are of great importance to the traditional Nauruan way of life. Among these are:

1. Pandanus tectorius — epo, epuh (pandanus) — some cultivars endangered or extinct.
2. Bruguiera gymnorhiza — etum, etam (mangrove) — scarce and endangered.
3. Hernandia nyphaeaefolia — yetiu (lantern tree) — rare and endangered.

10 For the processes of natural revegetation. see Manner, Thaman and Hassall, "Plant Succession after Phosphate Mining on Nauru", 17 *Australian Geographer* (1985) 185.

11 Fosberg (1965), Mangenot (1965), Dorst (1971), Mueller-Dombois (1975), Carlquist (1980) and Dasmann (1973).

12 Manner, *et al*, *Ecology, op. cit.*, at p. 1454.

4. Erythrina variegata — yoreh, yora (dadap) — rare and endangered.
5. Sida fallax — ekaura, idibinkaura (ilma) — endangered and almost extinct.
6. Triumfetta procumbens — ikiau, igiau (beach burr) — endangered and rare.

Dr. Thaman's evidence was that in conversation with Nauruans he had heard from them that they did not know where they could find these plants. According to Dr. Thaman, these plants are rare. They are not necessarily on the way to extinction but they are becoming increasingly scarce and endangered in Nauru.

There can be no doubt that the gradual disappearance of these species has been the result of mining. When we examine their importance to Nauruan life and culture the impact becomes quite serious.

As Dr. Thaman pointed out, Nauru had a wide range of vegetation and in early times whalers and others used to come to Nauru for food supplies. All the Pacific Islands, Nauru included, were basically self-sufficient until their traditional food systems were basically destroyed by the introduction of a cash economy.

Dr. Thaman sees it as vitally important to Nauru and its people that the vegetation on which their lifestyle and their culture was built should not be destroyed. It was vital, having regard to the fact that so much of their inheritance of flora was in the process of being destroyed, that every effort should be made to conserve what was left, as well as to get back what had already been lost. For this purpose, it is necessary to examine preliminarily the importance of these various plants to Nauru, then to look at the ways in which some of this inheritance of indigenous flora has been destroyed and, thirdly, to look at ways in which some planning can be done for the future so as to make good the losses and stabilize the existing inheritance.

(E) THE SOCIAL EFFECT OF PHOSPHATE MINING

(i) *Nauruan Reactions to the Loss of their Land*[13]

It is difficult for non-Nauruans, as indeed it is difficult for those who are not personally involved in such deeply emotional situations, to appreciate the full depths of Nauruan feeling regarding the damage inflicted upon their land. This feeling is intensified by the close bond that has always existed

[13] *Nauru Report*, pp. 177–179.

between Nauruans and their land, which has made the land an integral part of their lives rather than an article of commerce to be bought and sold as it is in many Western societies.[14] The emotional and sentimental trauma associated with the loss of the use of the land is one of the human costs which must be reckoned when considering the destructive effect of modern mining technology.

The Hon. Kinza Clodumar, Finance Minister, placed before the Commission three songs of Nauru, going back as far as the 1910s, which throw some light on the emotional overtones associated with this question. The first of these songs, which he places in the late 1910s or the early 1920s, expresses the sadness of the Nauruans at what was going on in their country. The song title, "My Dear Home Nauru" commences "My dear Nauru, one and only home I love", and speaks of the presence of foreign faces everywhere. It states with great lamentation that "these days Nauru isn't the home I used to know". There is a reference to the German telegraph station, the Jaluit Gesellschaft and their retail store with all sorts of "pretty things dangling here, there and everywhere", and to the dresses and perfumes which attracted the people and no doubt initiated important changes of lifestyle. The song paints an idyllic picture of how life was lived in old Nauru with pandanus and coconut, canaries, and frolicking young children, all forming part of a picture of life lived without the worries that came about with the advent of phosphate.

> By chance they discovered the heart of my home
>   and gave it the name phosphate.
> If they were to ship all phosphate from my home
>   there will be no place for me to go.
> Should this be the plan of the British Commission
>   I shall never see my home on the hill.

The reader will notice the reference to "my home on the hill" which expresses the Nauruans' deep sense of affinity with Topside. It was not a place apart from their home, as the partner governments often implied, but an integral part of it.

The second song repeats this theme that there would be nowhere to live if the lands were taken over in this fashion for phosphate mining, and underlying it all there is a tone of frustration and helplessness. The title of the song is, "I don't know what to do". It states that Nauru, your dear homeland, has changed, and laments that "your home is slipping away from you".

14 See further Chapter 3 of *Nauru*.

The plaintive chorus repeats:

> All would find nowhere to live,
> Oh there, there, I don't know what to do.

The third song, "My Tears Are For You", echoes the Nauruans' love for their native land and the charm of places like Moure, Buada, Anabar, Aneiyubwe and Ataro and the pleasant days spent there in the midst of their foliage and natural beauties.

The picture one is left with is one of disappearance of the traditional lifestyle based on harmony with a beautiful and bountiful environment. There is sadness and resentment at what is happening and a feeling of helplessness in the midst of overpowering forces — economic, political and technological. The old lifestyles are disappearing forever as is the very substance on which they were built, and there is nothing the Nauruans can do about it. The change was not the result of their own volition, but of circumstances they were powerless to control.

All of these songs are alive with the Nauruan love for their environment and their homeland and show how essential it is that Nauru be put back in a condition where its people can enjoy it.

Mr. Clodumar told us that he remembers that these songs were sung by schoolchildren, and were known by most Nauruans.

The date of the first of these songs is fixed by Mr Clodumar from the fact that the young girls at Oroo School for Girls had been singing this song in the late 1920s and early 1930s. There is also the internal evidence in the songs themselves which dates at least the first of them back to the German period.

The human aspect of the impact of mining technology on a small community is an important factor not to be ignored.

(ii) *Dilution of Nauruan Culture*[15]

The extensive scale of modern mining brings in its wake a number of cultural problems as well.

The mining industry brought with it a number of other peoples — the European, the Chinese, and the Gilbertese, among others. They brought their different lifestyles to the island and, among these, the European exercised the greatest influence upon the Nauruans.

The Europeans, who were the most affluent of the expatriate population, pursued a lifestyle which appeared to be the most attractive; and European

[15] *Nauru Report*, pp. 179–181.

values, modes of dress and styles of living, provided a pattern which tended slowly to displace many of the traditional Nauruan ways.

Among these European influences was the cash economy they introduced, which replaced the traditional subsistence economy of Nauru. No longer was it sufficient for Nauruans to have land and its produce but they needed also to have sufficient cash in hand with which to purchase the range of attractive merchandise which was displayed in the shops — commencing from the days of the Jaluit Gesellschaft store described in the song already referred to.

The habit of purchase of the manufactured goods of the West, which was introduced both deliberately and as an automatic consequence of the cash economy, meant that there was a growing demand for articles ranging from clothing and jewellery to imported foods. The latter ranked high on the list of Nauruan preferences, displacing the traditional foods.

All this meant also a decreasing emphasis on ancient Nauruan arts, chants and games. The games of the West displaced traditional Nauruan sports such as wrestling, stick games and the catching of frigate birds. There seems indeed to have been a rich variety of Nauruan games and sports, for the German author Hambruch, writing in 1914, describes them under the heads of combative games, games of capture, country games, games of patience, invitation games and social games and sports. Foreign music displaced Nauruan chants. Nauruan skill in art forms such as the weaving of patterns in thread tended to suffer. Games with threads must also have been sophisticated, for Hambruch describes twenty-seven varieties of them under such intriguing titles as "flying fish", "the blossom of the calophyllum", "the girl in the moon" and "a proud woman".

The enjoyment of Topside as a place of recreation and as a place for trapping of noddy birds was no longer available and the ancient lifestyles of Nauru had to be altered so as to accommodate them within the restricted land area of the coastal strip.

As with the games, so also with the myths and legends, comparatively little survives. Hambruch classifies the numerous myths prevalent at the time of his research under the heads of cosmic and cultural myths, astrological myths, cultural myths, and fairy tales of fauna and flora.

Traditional Nauruan skills have also gone the way of games, myths and legends. Thus in regard to fishing where, in the past, young boys were taught a variety of methods for use both on the edge of the reef and in the open sea, the easy availability of foreign fish has rendered these skills superfluous. An important area of self-reliance in the Nauruan lifestyle has thus been eroded.

No doubt a certain amount of Westernization would in any event have overtaken Nauru, even if there had been no phosphate mining. Yet the scale of the phosphate industry in comparison with the minuscule size of the island and the strength of the phosphate economy wielded an overpowering influence over this small island people, and substituted patterns of dependence on the phosphate economy for the habits of self-reliance of the past.

(iii) *Housing Construction and Land Shortage*

We have already referred to the uses of Topside for timber. Before phosphate mining on Nauru started, there was no shortage of housing. Each family had its own house.

Nauruan houses were not difficult to build, provided the necessary tools were available. All materials for a complete house were always available in abundance because the timber and other wooden parts which might be required were obtained from the tomano tree which grew prolifically on the plateau. Coconut and pandanus trees, both of which were also important in the construction of Nauruan houses, abounded on the plateau as well.

The construction of a house was a communal or joint family enterprise which was also an important social activity. It often involved camping on Topside and the gathering of timber would take several days.

The contrast presented by today's housing patterns is remarkable and goes far towards explaining how a totally different lifestyle and set of expectations has supplanted these ancient practices.

Prefabricated houses are imported from Australia. The roofs are corrugated asbestos sheets and the walls are of flat asbestos sheets (fibrolite). They are certainly not as well adapted for coolness in the tropical heat as were the traditional houses. There is no participation in the construction of the house, but, rather, an expectation that the materials as well as the labour will be provided.

From being the owners of their houses, the occupants have moved to a rental situation. A house reflects and complements lifestyles, and houses built to an alien model provide the backdrop against which Nauruans pursue a lifestyle which in many respects is alien to their traditions.

It should have been perceived that when the little land available on the coastal strip was exhausted as population grew, there would naturally be pressure for use of land on Topside for residential purposes. It was quite evident to the mining authorities that Nauruans had nowhere to go and, unless there was a firm commitment by the British Phosphate Commissioners to some other scheme of resettlement, or to rehabilitation, it should have been clear to them that the land which they were leaving in this unusable condition was land that was vitally important to the people of Nauru.

Land shortage resulting from mining has thus given Nauru one of the most important social problems which the country now faces.

(iv) *Nauruan Diet*[16]

The food of the Nauruans was simple, yet required much work and preparation.

Fish and coconut were basic to the diet of the Nauruans. There were other items too, such as pawpaw, breadfruit, beach almond, brown mangrove, and the fruit of the native banyan tree. Noddy birds caught on Topside were an important supplementation of the Nauruan diet.

Fish was, and still is, a favourite of the Nauruans. Nauruans went out in canoes for deep sea fishing and also fished with rods at the edge of the reef. When the tide was low, the reef fishing was done with net and spear. There is also the milk fish which is collected on the reef and reared in Buada lagoon.

Fish was dried and preserved in times of excess supply and so also was the paste extracted from the pandanus fruit. The customs attendant on the gathering and preparation of pandanus formed an important focal point of customary Nauruan life.

Such were the staple foods of old Nauru. Under the impact of the phosphate industry the basic Nauruan diet has substantially changed. Almost all food is now imported.[17]

Fish is still plentiful, but many Nauruans go in for canned fish. Canned food of all sorts has become extremely popular. Noddy birds have decreased in number with the destruction of the tomano trees.

The effect of this dramatically transformed dietary pattern has been damaging to Nauruan health.

As Thaman observes:

> every opportunity to industrialise or exploit the various mineral deposits in the Pacific has been pursued with enthusiasm ... with the hopes of 'development and modernisation'. In both cases, the major impact has been the relocation or migration of people to job sites, increasing monetisation of the economy and increasing consumption of imported goods at the job sites. In some cases like Nauru, with the onset of affluence there has been an almost complete disregard for agriculture and traditional food systems and a collapse of even the copra industry.

16 *Nauru Report*, pp. 192–193.

17 See generally R. R. Thaman, "Deterioration of Traditional Food Systems, increasing Malnutrition and Food Dependency in the Pacific Islands", (1982) *Journal of Food and Nutrition* 109 (FFD 13).

In short, the advent of the mining industry has not only altered the dietary patterns that prevailed in the Nauruan community for untold generations, but has also deprived them of their self-sufficiency in food and made them a totally dependent people in this regard. The damaging impact of this on Nauruan health is examined in the next section.

(v) *Nauruan Health*[18]

The change from subsistence to cash economies, which accompanies the advent of industrial activity into traditional societies, has resulted, in many developing countries, in drastic changes in the health of those societies, according to a paper in the *British Medical Journal*[19] by Doctors Zimmet, Whitehouse, Jackson and Thoma. This paper deals with the high prevalence of hyperuricaemia and gout in Nauru and concludes that 64% of men and 60% of women aged 20 years and over in Nauru had hyperuricaemia. The hyperuricaemia in men was accompanied by a high prevalence (6.9%) of clinical gout.

The increase in the rate of diabetes among the Nauruan population has been sudden.[20] In 1933 a medical survey made no mention of diabetes as a health problem and in fact no cases were reported. In 1962 the figures showed a prevalence of 2%. There has thus been a more than 17-fold increase over a period of 15 years.[21]

In Nauru nearly all food consumed by the population is imported in the form of canned meats, fruit and vegetables, flour, sugar, cordials and soft drinks. This has meant a drastic change from a traditional diet to a low-fibre refined carbohydrate Western diet. The medical literature suggests this as a possible inducing factor, for diabetes is rare in non-urbanized Micronesian and Polynesian populations.[22]

The researches of Dr. Zimmet have revealed that diseases such as diabetes are unknown on Pacific islands where Western contact is minimal and lifestyle is traditional, but that diabetes is reaching almost epidemic propor-

18 *Nauru Report*, pp. 193–194.

19 (1978) 1 pp. 1237–1239.

20 "The Effect of Westernization on Native Populations", (1978) *Australia New Zealand Jnl. of Medicine*, pp. 141–146.

21 *Ibid.*, p. 145.

22 *Ibid.*

tions in Westernized centres in Hawaii, Cook Islands, Tahiti, Guam, Nauru, Western Samoa, and in the New Zealand Maori population.[23]

The change from a traditional to a Western lifestyle has of course many components, as the researches of Zimmet and others point out. Among these are the stresses of a cash economy, new work patterns and reduced physical activity.[24]

On the basis of such information, Dr. Zimmet had predicted in 1975 that there would be an escalation of eye disease and blindness in Nauru, as well as kidney failure from diabetes. He foresees also the danger of a major problem of heart disease and heart attacks.[25]

(F) SOME RELEVANT ASPECTS OF ENVIRONMENTAL LAW[26]

(i) *The Stockholm Declaration*

The Stockholm Declaration on the Human Environment, passed at a United Nations Conference held in Stockholm from 5 to 16 June 1972, is a convenient point of commencement for the consideration of environmental law principles. It proclaimed, *inter alia*, that both the natural and the man-made aspects of the environment are essential to the enjoyment of human rights, and that the protection and improvement of the human environment is a major issue which affects the wellbeing of peoples and economic development throughout the world.

We shall consider the applicability of such of its principles as are relevant to the Nauruan situation.

> Principle 1
>
> Man has the fundamental right to freedom, equality and adequate conditions of life, an environment of a quality that permits a life of dignity and well-being, and he bears a solemn responsibility to protect and improve the environment for present and future generations

[23] Zimmet, "The Fatal Impact: The Medical Effects of Social Progress in the Pacific Populations", *Development with a Human Face*, (ed.) S. Hill et al, Australian Government Publishing Service, Canberra, 1981.

[24] Ringrose and Zimmet, "Nutrient Intakes in an Urbanised Micronesian Population with a High Diabetes Prevalence", June 1979, *American Journal of Clinical Nutrition*, pp. 1334–1341.

[25] Evidence before the Commission, p. 711.

[26] *Nauru*, pp. 337–353.

No one who has seen the landscape of the coral pinnacles in the mined-out areas of Nauru can view them as providing the Nauruans with an environment that engenders a life of dignity and wellbeing. The rehabilitation of that landscape is a solemn responsibility if the environment is to be developed and preserved for future generations. Leaving Nauru's environment in this condition is a clear violation of Principle 1 of the Stockholm Declaration.

The damage done to Nauru is such as defeats not merely the right to the use of the land vested in the current generation of Nauruans. Even more important than the rights of present Nauruans are the rights of future Nauruans. Any use of land which leaves it devastated and unfit for use is a violation of basic environmental principles. The problem is more serious where the damage is not of a self-repairing nature over a period of time, but will be permanent unless effective action is taken to restore the land to a condition of usability.

Even apart from environmental law, international law in general is more conscious now than ever before of the need to recognize and conserve the rights of future generations.[27] The First Principle of the Stockholm Declaration on the Human Environment, 1972, expressly mentions "a solemn duty to protect and improve the environment for present and future generations", and this concept has been explicitly incorporated in the language of numerous treaties.[28] Recent writings point out that diverse cultures have recognized that each generation is a trustee or steward of the natural environment for the benefit of generations yet unborn.[29] The concept of intergenerational fairness can, *inter alia*, be addressed under principles of equity in accordance with a long tradition in international law of using equitable principles to achieve a just result.[30]

The International Court of Justice has recognized the applicability of equity in terms that, "Equity as a legal concept is a direct emanation of the idea of justice. The Court whose task is by definition to administer justice is

[27] On the rights of future generations, see L. Prott, Future Generations: Can the Rights of the Unborn be Asserted Now?" in Alice Tay (ed.), *Teaching Human Rights*, AGPS, Canberra, 1981, p. 173.

[28] For example, the 1972 London Ocean Dumping Convention, the 1973 Convention on International Trade in Endangered Species, the 1972 Convention Concerning the Protection of the World Cultural and Natural Heritage.

[29] See, in particular, E. Brown Weiss, *In Fairness to Future Generations: International Law, Common Patrimony and Intergenerational Equity*, UNU, 1989, Transnational Publishers, Tokyo, pp. 18–20, where the author refers to civil law, Judaeo-Christian tradition, Islamic law, the socialist legal tradition, African customary law, and the non-theistic traditions of Asia and South Asia.

[30] *Ibid.*, pp. 36–38.

bound to apply it."[31] Friedmann, after a comprehensive survey of the authorities, concluded, "There is thus overwhelming justification for the view developed by Lauterpacht, Manley Hudson, De Visscher and Dahm that equity is part and parcel of any modern system of administration of justice".[32]

Having regard to these writings, if the environmental damage done to Nauru is left unrestored, it could be said of those who mined out the areas in question that they showed a disregard for the rights not only of those who were in their charge, but of the rights of their posterity. Succeeding generations of Nauruans would be able then to point a finger at the period of administration under the partner governments as a period when the rights of generations of Nauruans were jeopardized for the sake of the immediate advantage of the trustees. This is a situation which international law is well equipped to handle, having regard to the writings cited.[33]

The Australian government in the *Nuclear Tests* case asserted the rights of unborn Australians to be born into an undamaged environment. The rights of unborn Nauruans cannot be any different:

> Principle 2
>
> The natural resources of the earth including air, water, land, flora and fauna and especially representative samples of natural ecosystems must be safeguarded for the benefit of present and future generations through careful planning and management, as appropriate.

As detailed in the Commission's Report, the mining out of the phosphate lands has damaged land, flora and fauna and the natural ecosystems. Leaving the land in this mined-out condition has therefore violated another basic environmental principle.

> Principle 21

[31] *Continental Shelf (Tunisia/Libyan Arab Jamahiriya), I.C.J. Reports 1982*, p. 18, at p. 60.

[32] W. Friedmann, *The Changing Structure of International Law*, Columbia University Press, N.Y., 1964, p. 197.

[33] For other writings on equity in the context of environmental law, see Edward McWhinney, "Equity in International Law", in Ralph A. Newman (ed.), *Equity in the World's Legal Systems: A Comparative Study*, Etablissements Emile Bruylant, Brussels, 1973, p. 582.

> States have in accordance with the Charter of the United Nations and the principles of international law, the sovereign right to exploit their own resources pursuant to their own environmental policies, and the responsibility to ensure that activities within their jurisdiction or control do not cause damage to the environment of other states or of areas beyond the limits of national jurisdiction.

This principle it will be observed relates back to the Charter and the general principles of international law. Principle 21 rests upon classical legal conceptions[34] and as such was applicable even at the time of the mandate.

Of course, these concepts related to damage by one State to another. Nauru was not yet a State in existence but was being led towards this status which undoubtedly it would attain in due time. It was manifest throughout the period of preparation that it would as a future sovereign state be entitled to have its territory without environmental damage done to it which would, as discussed elsewhere in this Chapter, pre-empt its choices as a sovereign nation for the use of its property.

The principles embedded in the Charter and in international law against one State doing environmental damage to another would thus apply *a fortiori* to a State under the tutelage of another.

> Principle 22
>
> States shall co-operate to develop further the international law regarding liability and compensation for the victims of pollution and other environmental damage caused by activities within the jurisdiction or control of such States to areas beyond their jurisdiction.

Some of the principles of international law regarding liability and compensation for the victims of environmental damage are discussed in this chapter. These principles rest upon traditional legal notions of liability for wrongful damage and of state responsibility. By those principles the Commission concluded that a liability rests upon the partner governments to make good the environmental damage they caused to Nauru.

Principle 22 calls upon all States to co-operate to develop the international law relating to these matters. Development depends not merely on the theoretical and academic study of concepts but also on the study of their practical application.

The Nauruan situation offers a singular opportunity for the States that caused this environmental damage, all of them states with much technologi-

[34] Ian Brownlie, "A survey of international customary rules of environmental protection", (1973) 13 *Natural Resources Journal*, 179 at 188.

cal expertise at their command, to put this principle into effect by rehabilitating the mined out land. Principle 22 requires them to co-operate in doing this and it is to be hoped that the States concerned will assist in the development of international practice in this regard.[35]

(ii) *The trust doctrine*

Environmental law is based upon the principle that natural resources are treasures held in trust not only for this generation but for generations yet unborn. We quote, in regard to US environmental law, from a leading American text on the subject.

> The cornerstone of Environmental Law is the assertion that all of our national natural treasures are held in trust for the full benefit, use and enjoyment of all the people of the United States, not only of this generation but of those generations yet unborn, subject only to wise use by the current nominal titleholder.[36]

The duty to conserve these resources in the case of Nauru thus involves a trust superimposed upon a trust.[37]

Doctrines of private property in the Western world relied heavily on John Locke's reasoning that resources would be so plentiful that consumption even to the limit of what an individual could consume would not prejudice the rest of mankind.[38] Locke did not of course have any inkling of the scale on which consumption would take place or of the notion of exhaustion of non-renewable resources. Such thinking obscured the notion of the preservation of the beauty of nature which had been recognized in the Western tradition as early as Virgil.[39]

[35] See, in relation to the need for active co-operation as opposed to passive co-existence, W. Paul Gormley, *Human Rights and the Environment: The Need for International Cooperation*, A.W. Sijthoff, Leyden, 1976, esp. pp. 32–48.

[36] V. J. Yannacone, Jr., Bernard S. Cohen and Steven G. Davison, *Environmental Rights and Remedies*, Lawyers Co-Op Publishing Soc., Rochester, N.Y., 1972, Vol. 1, p. 11.

[37] Note however that the doctrine of public trust has not been developed in Australia. The argument of public trust was rejected in *Karl* v. *Johnson* (1973) 21 FLR 177, in relation to the declaration of Black Mountain reserve as a public trust, imposing upon the government the duty to maintain the environmental quality of the reserve by preventing the erection of a telecommunication tower.

[38] John Locke, "Essay concerning the true original extent and end of civil government", in *Of Property*, Ch. 5.

[39] The *Georgics*, Book II, l. 36 ff.; l. 458 ff. Also *Encyclopaedia Britannica*, 1992, Vol. 29, pp. 499–500. See also Ch. 8 above.

Since the beginning of this century the importance of conservation for the benefit of future generations and the realization that non-renewable resources could be endangered at present rates of consumption began to receive recognition. The revival of this line of thinking was almost coincidental in time with the beginning of the exploitation of Nauruan resources.

An early expression of such concerns from a most influential Western source was made by President Roosevelt's National Conservation Commission in 1909:

> The resources which have required ages for their accumulation, to the intrinsic value and quality of which human agency has not contributed, and for which there are no known substitutes, must serve as the welfare of the Nations. In the highest sense, therefore, they should be regarded as property held in trust for the use of the race rather than the single generation and for the use of the Nation, rather than for the benefit of a few individuals who may hold them by right of discovery or by purchase.[40]

Yannacone *et al*, in their treatise on environmental rights and remedies, draw attention to the duties of trustees and to the reversal of burdens of proof that result from the trust situation:

> The duty of the trustee to preserve the resource and protect it against loss, dissipation or diminution, and to act with diligence, fairness and faithfulness in doing so, is well-established in trust law. These presumptions result in shifting the burden to the despoilers of the environment to come forward with the evidence to prove the necessity for despoiling the trust corpus.[41]

This principle of environmental law when applied to Nauru means that the partner governments would be under the burden of proving the necessity for despoiling the phosphate resources of Nauru. Consistent with trust principles such necessity must be a necessity viewed from the standpoint of the people of Nauru and not the partner governments. Applying this principle the partner governments would fail entirely in establishing the justification for their actions. In relation to the rehabilitation claim this would mean that in the absence of sufficient justification, the responsibility for rehabilitation must rest with the partner governments on the basis of either trust obligations, or the trust notion in regard to the environment, and the trust notion in regard to

40 Report to the National Conservation Commission, 1909, Vol. 1, p. 110.

41 Yannacone, *et al*, *supra*, p. 14.

the international trust. When both trust notions are superimposed one upon the other there is no room for any doubt as to this legal result

(iii) *Strict Liability*

Moral obligation apart, an important aspect of the evolving regime of international environmental law is that it does not make liability necessarily dependent on fault.

In the *Trail Smelter* case, emissions of sulphur dioxide fumes from a smelter works in Canada resulted in the chemical contamination of the soil, streams and air, which in turn resulted in the poisoning of trees and crops on the United States' side of the border. No issue of fault was tried in that case. It is significant for our purposes that the Tribunal was prepared to apply stricter standards of liability than those reflected in traditional common law writings and decisions[42] and the Tribunal, rather than focusing its attention on the levels of emission, proceeded on the basis of a stricter standard of liability. What emerged was a principle of strict liability which Canada owed to the United States.[43]

Other cases reflecting such a stricter standard of liability in international law are the *Corfu Channel* case and the *Lac Lanoux* arbitration. To quote Professor Goldie:

> Since the *Trail Smelter* case should be viewed as an application of public international law the irreducible minimum of the relevant general principles of law contained therein is the strict liability which Canada owed to the United States. This interpretation is strengthened, further, by pointing out that no issue of fault was tried in that case. Again, in the *Corfu Channel* case, Albania's liability stemmed from the presence of the mines in her territorial waters, not from any malevolence or neglect which would have had to have been proved by the applicant State. Indeed, the question of Albania's liability did not even turn on whether Albania had laid the mines or had consented to their being laid. In the *Lac Lanoux* arbitration, finally, the Tribunal clearly considered strict liability to govern in the event of a finding for Spain.[44]

42 L.F.E. Goldie, "A general view of international environmental law: a survey of capabilities, trends and limits", (1973) *Colloquium: Académie de Droit International de La Haye*, 25, at 70.

43 *Ibid.*, p. 71.

44 *Ibid.*

Even if, therefore, the partner governments did not commit a "fault" such as would attract legal liability on such grounds as intention or negligence, they are still directly or indirectly the doers of the acts which have resulted in the environmental destruction of those portions of Nauru mined out during the periods of mandate and trust.

The strictness of this emerging doctrine in international environmental law transcends and overcomes many of the limitations attending strict liability doctrines in the common law. A number of exonerating factors recognized by traditional common law doctrines of strict liability are not considered to be exonerations under these principles of international environmental law.

Thus the large catalogue of exceptions available for example to the *Rylands* v. *Fletcher* principle, which caused Professor Winfield to argue that the expression "absolute liability" was a misnomer,[45] do not according to writers on the emerging international environmental law[46] afford grounds of exoneration for environmental damage. Modern international environmental law ignores many of these and traces liability back to the doer of the act who causes environmental harm, however long the chain of causation, with exculpation being recognized only in a very limited set of specified circumstances such as armed conflict and grave natural disasters of a catastrophic character which are completely unforeseeable.

The argument, even if it be available, that the partner governments were acting under their legal rights and entitlements would not thus be an exoneration in international environmental law, such as it would tend to be under municipal law, for there is no doubt that they caused or permitted to be caused, the acts which have resulted in the altogether foreseeable environmental disaster that has befallen Nauru. The chain of causation would lead direct to them and they would be the entities looked upon as accountable.

True, these are principles yet in a formative stage — *lex ferenda* rather than *lex lata* — but, as Professor Goldie points out, some of the concepts evolving are "totally dissimilar from the concepts of liability found in the Anglo-American common law".[47]

(iv) *The conflict between cost factors and environmental factors*

Where environmental damage is caused by industry, one of the most important conflicts that arises in the environmental field is the conflict between the

45 P.H. Winfield, "The myth of absolute liability", (1926) 42 LQR 37.

46 Goldie, *supra*, p. 75.

47 *Ibid.*, p. 79.

producer's interest in producing his product at the cheapest possible price and the environmental interest in prevention of environmental harm and rehabilitation. The more one spends on the latter items, the higher becomes the final cost of the article. Both considerations seem compelling — the one in the short term and the other in the long term. Usually the resulting environmental problem surfaces after the damage has been done and the article has been sold at the lower price, with corresponding advantages to the producer.

In the case of Nauru the British Phosphate Commissioners were anxious to produce phosphate at as cheap a price to the producer countries as was possible. The British Phosphate Commissioners were no doubt aware of the need to rehabilitate and were in fact putting aside a small sum of money for this purpose. They may have thought it was adequate but especially after the Davey Report[48] it was realized how inadequate this was. Yet they continued to mine and did in fact continue to obtain the costing benefit resulting from this saving on rehabilitation. To quote Goldie:

> the more such an enterprise is permitted to expose third parties to harm, or the environment to devastation, the more it will be in a position to reduce its operating costs. The costs of protection, however, still remain. They become 'social' or 'external' costs and are merely transferred from the enterprise to the environment, or to society — or some sectors of it. Enterprises which enjoy the privileges of externalising, of passing on, their costs clearly increase the risk of harm to other users. In doing this they pre-empt the privilege of deliberately creating risks, and thus expropriate from members of the public expectations of continued enjoyment of the environmental amenities of living — the emerging 'amenities rights'.[49]

The parallels to the Nauruan situation are clear. Whether one is dealing with the emission of dangerous effusions or pollutants, or the devastation of a landscape through mining, the principle is the same. One is cutting one's

[48] The Report of a Committee appointed in 1965 to investigate and report on rehabilitation. The Davey Committee placed the cost at over $100 million — *Nauru*, p. 303.

[49] Goldie, *supra*, pp. 65–66. On liability for damage, see Goldie, "Liability for damage and the progressive development of international law", (1965) 14 *International and Comparative L.Q.*, 1189, and Goldie, "International principles of responsibility for pollution", (1970) 9 *Columbia Journal for Transnational Law*, 283. On amenities rights, see Goldie, "Amenities rights — parallels to pollution taxes", (1971) 11 *Natural Resources Journal*, 274. On liability for transnational environmental damage, see Standford E. Gaines, "Transnational environmental liability: can developments in municipal law help break the impasse?", *Harvard Inst. L.J.*, Vol. 30, No. 2, Spring 1989, 311, at pp. 340–344.

cost and passing the burden on to the environment and the people who have the right to enjoy that environment.

As far as Nauru was concerned, the British Phosphate Commissioners (and the partner governments) were cutting the cost to themselves and passing it on to the island of Nauru and its people.

It needs little elaboration to establish on whom lies the legal burden of restoration. A developing environmental law principle is the PPP principle or the "Polluter Pays Principle", which was used in Japan to meet claims arising from Minamata sickness. This sickness was caused by mercury poisoning as a result of eating shellfish caught in Minamata Bay where the Minamata Company had discharged methyl mercury compounds. The pollution-related health-damage compensation law was passed in 1974, providing for various types of compensation benefits, all based on the polluter pays principle. This principle is equally applicable to all forms of environmental damage.

(v) *The Principle of Good Neighbourliness*

This is another principle of international environmental law. It is a broad standard of respect of States for each other and recognition of the rights of their peoples to the enjoyment of the environment and the basic human rights that go with it. "It obligates States, enterprises and individuals to respect the rights of others to participate in the enjoyment of community rights and in the social process."[50]

The good neighbourliness principle is not a merely moralistic or aspirational formulation. It has been built already into international case law, as in the *Trail Smelter* case or the *Oder* case. The good neighbourliness principle generally comes into play where there are States enjoying a common river, or States which are contiguous to each other. However it can equally apply to States which are far away from each other physically if the acts in question cause demonstrable damage, as in the case of Nauru.

In Nauru there is the further circumstance that Nauru was administered "as an integral part of Australia". In that view of the matter, Australia was causing damage either to an integral part of her own territory or to people dependent upon her — which is as close a connection as one can get.[51]

[50] Goldie, "A general view of international environmental law: A survey of capabilities, trends and limits", *op. cit.*, p. 68.

[51] For a fuller discussion of the good neighbourliness principle, see F. J. Berber, *Rivers in International Law*, 1959, pp. 211–213; and L. F. E. Goldie, "Special regimes and pre-emptive activities in international law", (1962) 11 *International and Comparative L.Q.*, 678.

(vi) *The human rights dimensions*

The claim to a liveable and usable environment can also be expressed in basic human rights terms. Among the rights involved are the right to life, the right to health, and what is now increasingly recognized as the right to a clean and decent environment. The Nauruan landscape (in the mined-out areas) is such that it cannot in its present condition be used to sustain life. It is not one on which either food may be grown or residences constructed. It is plainly one which cannot support life with dignity. This aspect is dealt with also in Principle 1 of the Stockholm Declaration. It is not necessary to expand on any of these. They are self-evident.

The right to a decent environment and the emerging category of "amenities" rights are other human rights that have been violated. To use the phraseology of the New Zealand memorial to the World Court in the *Nuclear Test* case, the rights affected are such that "their violation may fairly be said to affront the conscience of mankind".[52]

(vii) *Principles of co-operation*

The principle of co-operation underlies the Stockholm Declaration. The notion is growing that all countries with the expertise and the opportunity to do so should help in the solution of environmental problems. The notion stems from the increasing realization that an environmental problem anywhere is a global and not merely a national problem. The obligation is particularly pressing if the country whose environment has been damaged lacks the technology or the ability to repair the devastation by itself. This principle serves to underline the responsibility of the States which actually contributed to the problem — and benefited in the process. It would be contrary to all currently accepted international environmental norms for them to turn a blind eye to this problem.

The principle of co-operation to solve environmental problems is set out at the very forefront of the Stockholm Declaration. Clause 2 of the Preamble states that the protection and improvement of the human environment is the *duty of all governments*. Paragraph 6 of the Preamble asserts that:

[52] N.Z. Memorial, at pp. 69–70.

> To defend and improve the human environment for present and future generations has become an imperative goal for mankind — a goal to be pursued together with, and in harmony with, the established and fundamental goals of peace and of worldwide economic and social development.

This leads on to the appeal in paragraph 7 for international co-operation, calling upon governments and peoples to exert common efforts for the preservation and improvement of the human environment.

Principle 15 of the Declaration deals with the importance of planning for the protection of the environment, and Principle 20 with the importance of transfer of experience and expertise. Principle 18 deals specifically with the use of science and technology for the identification, avoidance and control of environmental risks and the solution of environmental problems and the common good of mankind.

At the Working Group of the Preparatory Committee which considered an earlier draft of this provision, Australia presented a very advanced version of the original proposal. Professor Louis B. Sohn has described the Australian proposal as "a more general and noble variation of this proposal, which contained references to development and to the needs of all mankind".[53] The Australian proposal read:

> Science and technology must be called upon to provide the solution of planning the development necessary for the adequate provision for the material needs of all mankind in such a way as to avoid a destructive impact on the environment, which could defeat the aim of development.[54]

Principle 20 stresses the importance of the free flow of up-to-date scientific information and transfer of experience which needs to be supported and assisted to facilitate the solution of environmental problems. It also states that "environmental technologies should be made available to developing countries on terms which would encourage their wide dissemination without constituting an economic burden on developing countries".

The consensus view that international co-operation is required for solving environmental problems is one of which all participating States should take note. It represents an emerging principle of international practice in this rapidly developing area of the law. In particular the call for scientific and technological co-operation is too important to be ignored.

53 "The Stockholm Declaration on the Human Environment" (1973) 14 *Harvard Journal of International Law*, 423, at 479.

54 U.N. Doc. A/CONF.48/PC/WG 1 (11)/CRP.9 at 2 (1972).

Nauru provides a textbook example of a situation of possible co-operation in the solution of environmental problems. It is serious enough to warrant international concern, while being yet small enough to be capable of significant contributions by all developed countries. The countries most concerned, as the doers of the acts producing the present situation, can least afford to ignore it if they are to make any claims to discharging adequately the responsibilities they assumed at Stockholm. Australia as a particularly idealistic contributor at the Stockholm Conference has a specially important role to play.

ADDENDUM TO CHAPTER 16

Commission of Inquiry into Rehabilitation of the Worked-Out Phosphate Lands in Nauru

OPENING ADDRESS OF THE CHAIRMAN, PROFESSOR C.G. WEERAMANTRY, ON 23RD FEBRUARY 1987 AT 10.00 A.M.

Mr. Speaker, Honourable Ministers, Your Excellencies, Distinguished Guests, Ladies and Gentlemen:

On behalf of the Commission, let me extend to you a cordial welcome to our inaugural sittings. We much appreciate your attendance here and the interest you are showing in this important event.

This is indeed a momentous occasion in the history of Nauru — an Island with an ancient culture and traditions that reach back into the mists of antiquity.

That long history took a new turn when at the close of the last century it became known that immense wealth in the form of phosphates lay buried beneath its topsoil. From that time on, the attractions of this wealth drew to these shores explorers and entrepreneurs, imperial powers and corporate establishments, in a steady succession of visits which, from small beginnings, grew to levels of commercial activity surpassing the most optimistic dreams of the pioneers.

In the eyes of many who came here, phosphate extraction and phosphate marketing overshadowed all else that the Island contained. Indeed to some at least of those in the phosphate industry, phosphate came first while the Island and its people were important only as a means to reach that phosphate.

Fortunes were made and major agricultural nations came to look upon this resource as vital to their economic future. In the result, a little Island acquired great importance to great nations and great economies.

It is not unnatural that in the resulting interaction, there were often conflicts of interest between the Islanders and those who came here for phosphates. How these conflicts were resolved, upon what terms and with what consequences, it will be one of our tasks to inquire.

We do know however that while the phosphates were being extracted, ancient lifestyles were eroded and the face of the Island scarred beyond recognition. The problem of rehabilitation thus assumed importance — an importance that became evident long before the day when Nauru became an independent nation.

Long before this day, it was known also that phosphate wealth was not inexhaustible. Plans required to be made, in the interests of the Island, against the day when the phosphates would run out. It was known also that those plans needed to be of a most comprehensive nature for they involved economic, social and ecological considerations of the first magnitude.

Yet although there were some investigations, the necessary comprehensive and interdisciplinary surveys in requisite depth were not undertaken. Those that were, were not implemented. The task of such a complete and comprehensive survey remained for independent Nauru to undertake.

Today we launch out on such a venture and that is what makes this occasion both unique and historic. Today, for the first time, we shall be commencing an exhaustive inquiry into the problem in the minutest detail, in the light of all the assistance we can derive for a multitude of disciplines historical, economic, sociological, ecological, technological, and legal. There is also an important human rights dimension to our inquiry. There is a vast amount of knowledge available from all these disciplines which we propose to harness as best we can in addressing the question how the problems caused by phosphate extraction in the past and by the cessation of such extraction in the future can best be handled.

We shall be calling in aid the goodwill and the expertise of all those who can, through their knowledge and experience, make a contribution to the solution of these problems. To this end, we have made public advertisement of the fact that the Commission will be pleased to receive information and evidence from such persons or organizations, and we shall be making further public announcements and invitations.

We are an independent Commission. Our terms of reference are wide and our responsibilities are onerous. The people of Nauru at long last are entitled to expect the most comprehensive answers which modern knowledge can offer to the serious problems that modern commerce and technology have created for them. We shall spare no pains to make as detailed, as conscientious and as independent an inquiry as lies within our power.

We are acutely conscious of the fact that the main resource of this Island consists of its people, not its phosphates. The people of this Island and their posterity, for countless generations to come must live on, and live happily on, this Island long after the last shipment of phosphate has left its shores. They must be able to lead an existence without their quality of life being in any way impaired by barren landscapes or uncultivable land. The enjoyment of their natural environment is a basic human right of all people everywhere. The people of Nauru and their posterity no less than any other people are entitled to this basic right.

If in any way any liability attaches to those who were responsible for the denudation of the Island, it will be the responsibility of this Commission to explore those principles of liability fairly and in accordance with basic principles of municipal and international law. If it is possible to seek through modern technology the means of rehabilitating this damaged land, it will be the business of the Commission to explore such ways and means. If alternative ideas can be sought on the improvement of the condition of the land and its people, it will be the business of the Commission to seek out those alternative ideas.

In this task we look forward to the co-operation of all the powers who at one time or another have had a share in the administration of the Island. Their co-operation is vital if comprehensive and just answers are to be obtained to the several questions we shall have to consider. We trust this co-operation will be forthcoming in full measure from these powers and we have invited their participation in our proceedings.

Every nation has the right to permanent sovereignty over its natural resources. This is an inalienable right and one which is integral to the concept of sovereignty. A large part of the natural resources of Nauru have been taken away from it. We shall have to consider with what degree of free and voluntary consent of the people these resources were thus extracted. This will necessitate an historical examination of the various agreements entered into from time to time, the conditions under which consent was given to those agreements and the fairness of the conditions embodied or involved in those agreements.

It is also a principle of international environmental law that the natural resources of the earth including land must be safeguarded for the benefit of present and future generations. We shall be examining this principle in all its ramifications and implications. This is particularly important as it is an essential principle that environmental quality should be such as permits a life of dignity and well-being to every citizen.

It is another well established principle that science and technology must be applied to the solution of environmental problems. Principle 18 of the Stockholm Declaration of the United Nations Conference on the Human Environment states that science and technology, as part of their contribution to economic and social development, must be applied to the identification, avoidance and control of environmental risks and the solution of environmental problems for the common good of mankind. We intend to explore to its fullest the ways in which this principle can be used for the relief of the Nauruan situation.

The same Declaration states that international matters concerning the protection and improvement of the environment should be handled in a co-operative spirit by all countries, big and small, on an equal footing. In the words of the Declaration, such co-operation is essential for the effective control, prevention, reduction and elimination of adverse environmental effects resulting from activities conducted in all spheres, in such a way that account is taken of the sovereignty and interests of all States.

Any major environmental problem is a human problem and as such a problem not limited to any one place or people. It is a problem affecting all people wherever they may be and calling for the co-operation of all. We trust and hope that we shall receive the co-operation of all people wherever they may be in the solution of this great environmental problem. We hope that not only governments of countries that have participated in the administration of this country, but all governments, will interest themselves in the subject of our inquiries, for what happened to Nauru could happen elsewhere and the necessary principles of international co-operation must be built up for the benefit of humanity. We hope also that environmental groups and concerned individuals throughout the world will take an interest in the problems we are addressing and offer us the benefit of their experience and advice.

Indeed this principle of co-operation is already well-developed and fifteen years have passed since the Stockholm Declaration laid down as Principle 22 that "States shall co-operate to develop further the international law regarding liability and compensation for the victims of pollution and other environmental damage caused by activities within the jurisdiction or control of such States to areas beyond their jurisdiction".

We believe that much development of this principle has occurred in international law in the intervening years. Our terms of reference require us among other things to inquire particularly into developments before and after independence with respect to municipal and international law relating to environmental harm and we hope we shall be able to do this in a manner which will be of lasting benefit, not only to the people of Nauru, but to all who may be affected by environmental problems.

Today, more than ever in the history of mankind, we are conscious that the resources of our planet are meant for the benefit of not just one or two or three generations but of all posterity and that environmental damage is one of the most severe species of harm that can be done to our children and our children's children. We also realize more than ever before that an environmental problem anywhere is an environmental problem everywhere, for disturbances in the environmental order are so full of intricate interactions that we cannot isolate environmental harm and say it affects this region or country and not that. In short, it is a global problem we are addressing and we look for global co-operation and global interest in our endeavours. We believe in fact that no country can stand aside from our problem and say that it does not concern them.

I have said sufficient to indicate that what we have to accomplish is beyond the competence of any one or two or three individuals. We approach our task with the confidence that we will receive in ample measure the co-operation of concerned individuals and institutions, and of environmental organizations and governments.

We approach our task with humility at the great trust that has been reposed in us and with the hope that we shall be able to make a contribution of enduring value. We hope that we shall be able to clarify the legal and factual position in regard to a number of issues which are of great importance not only to Nauru but internationally.

We are honoured and privileged that we have been called to this task and look forward with pleasurable anticipation to an inquiry fraught with such far-reaching consequences.

We thank you again for your attendance and interest, which are a great encouragement to us as we commence the work of this unique and arduous inquiry.

17. Some Orwellian Scenarios*

For humanitarian achievement, medical science stands high among all fields of intellectual endeavour. Inveterate scourges of mankind, such as smallpox, leprosy and polio, have been conquered or brought under control. The healing scalpel works its miracles from the macro-organ transplant to the delicate field of micro-surgery. Pain is suppressed and controlled. Longevity has been significantly increased. Presiding over all these activities is a humane medical profession, as skilled as it is dedicated.

In September 1978, the World Health Organization held a conference, from which emerged the Declaration of Alma Ata which began as follows:

> The conference strongly reaffirms that health, which is a state of complete physical, mental and social well-being and not merely the absence of disease or infirmity, is a fundamental human right.

But there is an attendant gloom. The ability to heal the body brings with it an ability to tinker, to fabricate, to mould, and even to interfere with the processes of creation and termination of life. Powers of healing grow into powers of control.

In this development there lies more than an ordinary share of peril to liberty, for it is to the human body that most basic legal and human rights protections are anchored.

From an inexhaustible list, only some of the danger areas can be singled out for illustration.

(A) CLONING[1]

The word "clone" (derived from the Greek word, *klon*, meaning a twig or slip) is used to describe the creation of an identical replica by the process of asexual reproduction. The technique is called cloning from the botanical

* The scenarios on cloning, psychosurgery, mind manipulation, selective breeding, chimeras, and neomort farms are reproduced from the author's *The Slumbering Sentinels: Law and Human Rights in the Wake of Technology*, Penguin Books (1983).

1 From *The Slumbering Sentinels*, pp. 91–95.

analogy of a cutting or slip from the parent tree. In 1952, frogs were successfully cloned, raising some possibilities for humans.

Very simply stated, cloning involves the removal of the nucleus of a female sex cell and the substitution in its place of the nucleus of an adult body cell of the individual sought to be duplicated. The egg thus enucleated and renucleated will, when it develops, yield an identical copy of the donor of the nucleus, for it would contain only the genetic pattern of that single parent, rather than the combined attributes of two parents, as occurs in normal bisexual reproduction. Cell multiplication occurs when the egg thus renucleated starts to develop as though it were stimulated by the natural process of fertilization. The experiment in which frogs were cloned yielded exact duplicates of the parent frog in about half of the renucleated eggs, but also resulted in frog monstrosities,[2] owing to insufficient knowledge of the factors necessary to produce total success.

The technique is capable of being practised on a massive scale, for the donor can yield a practically unlimited number of body cells for renucleation of enucleated eggs. Skin and intestinal cells provide favoured and unlimited sources.

The progression from the frog to the human requires some breakthroughs, none of them thought to be insurmountable,[3] although they will probably take several decades. The mammalian eggs which will need to be enucleated and renucleated for the cloning of humans are considerably smaller and hence more difficult to manipulate and more susceptible to damage than the amphibian eggs of the frog. New methods involving chemical techniques, however, are being developed for this purpose. Moreover, the interests of animal husbandry in breeding prize cattle and racehorses will carry these techniques forward to the point where, some decades hence, they may be sufficiently improved for the next step of experimentation with the human cell.

Well before the turn of the century,[4] we will need to make up our minds whether this new technology is to be given unbridled rein, whether it is to be

[2] R. Briggs and T. J. King, "Transplantation of Living Nuclei from Blastula Cells into Enucleated Eggs", 38 *Proceedings of the National Academy of Sciences of the USA* (1952), p. 455.

[3] J. Lederberg, "Experimental Genetics and Human Evolution", *American Naturalist*, Vol. 100, No. 915, 1966, p. 527; P. D. Turner, "Love's Labor Lost: Legal and Ethical Implications of Artificial Human Procreation", *University of Detroit Journal of Urban Law*, Vol. 58, 1981, p. 459; *Reform*, No. 26, 1982, p. 68.

[4] As forecast here, in 1984, the debate on cloning has gone public in 1997, with the cloning of a sheep. The President of the United States has carried the issue to the public and there is heavy discussion of the issue by the media. See, also, *supra* Chapter 2, footnote 29.

controlled and directed, or whether it is to be banned until we feel more competent to handle its problems.

The uniqueness of humans, their freedom to develop their own personalities untrammelled by the need or the desire to imitate or differ from a prototype, and the knowledge of the most intimate personal details and propensities which give substance to the concepts of privacy, will be under threat by cloning.

Among the issues we will need to resolve are the right to survival of subhuman experimental mishaps, the accountability to society of those desiring to use the new techniques for reproduction, problems of over-specialization, the possible imbalance in the proportion of males to females, an increase in genetic homogeneity, and the increasing state controls which may result. If there is a genetic material for the cloning of an Einstein or a Beethoven, will a thousand families compete to install exact replicas of the genius within their family? And if public authority decrees that not more than a certain number of identical replicas be produced, will an embryo genius be produced and marketed surreptitiously with false genetic tags?

Given the secrecy with which much scientific research is now conducted, there is every possibility that the technique of cloning, once perfected, can be carried on in secret. Secrecy need only be maintained for nine months before a series of full-term babies are produced. Who then is to decide that they shall not have all the rights of humans, receiving full and equal protection under the law?

The uranium debate in recent years has produced a consensus in many countries that the decision on its use is for the community to make, after informed debate at all levels. The difficulties of communicating scientific information have not stood in the way of such a debate. Likewise, in this field, the decision belongs to the community. In the field of genetic engineering, cloning is one of the aspects that requires most public discussion.

The arguments in favour of cloning are these:

- It will allow the reproduction of the genetically superior.
- Sex will be able to be predetermined, producing benefits in certain cases by avoiding some of the fifty or so sex-linked genetic diseases. It can also, though on a less important plane, help in assuring the continuance of a family.
- Eugenic distribution of biotechnical resources, without dependence on the lottery of sexual reproduction, will be possible. It may even be possible to preserve for posterity replicas of all-time greats — the

Newtons and the Mozarts of the future — rather than to rely for the reproduction of greatness on haphazard genetic chance.

- Sets of identical humans for the performance of a desired function would be created, e.g., artistic, mathematical, mechanical, manual.
- It will be possible to produce embryonic replicas, to be frozen or put away as sources of organs for members of the identical set. Such organs would not provoke a rejection on the part of the body cells of the recipient.
- It would reduce "genetic loading", the process by which increasing medical skill assists the weak and defective to survive and propagate themselves and their defects, to the progressive deterioration of the human stock.
- It would be one means of enabling infertile couples to have children.
- With the growing radiation hazards to our genetic stock, it will help to stow away undisturbed genetic material for developments in the future.
- Cell banks could also store for replication certain racial types of endangered humans.[5]

Those who argue in favour of continued and unrestricted experimentation point also to the fact that when artificial insemination first came within the bounds of possibility, warning voices were heard similar to those now raised against genetic experimentation. Despite the fears then expressed, the new knowledge has not thus far been used for purposes which can be described as wicked, power-oriented, or frivolous. So also, with the new technique of cloning, it is argued that current fears will considerably exceed the reality.

Although some of these advantages are undoubtedly real, some are of only distant value (as with the reduction of the genetic load), and some (such as the creation of sets of spare part banks) are not likely to commend themselves to liberal democrats.

On the other hand, there are many genuine areas of concern:

- Cloning will break down the family concept and established notions of fatherhood, motherhood, and parental rights.

[5] See Joseph Fletcher, "Ethical Aspects of Genetic Controls", 14 *New England Journal of Medicine* (1971), p. 779, mentioning such disappearing racial types as the hairy Ainu of Japan and certain strains of the Romany gypsies.

- There will inevitably be an increase in state control over matters of reproduction, and the breakdown of the concept of the right to raise a family.
- The new techniques will be used to mass-create selected types for predetermined purposes. In its most extreme form, this will enable a dominant group to perpetuate its dominance and cause all groups in opposition to reduce and disappear. The creation of clonal groups with a community of self-interest could result in a desire for self-perpetuation more intense than with the group orderings of the past.
- It will break down concepts of individuality.
- It will be an invasion of the concepts of privacy.
- A blurring of principles of personal responsibility will occur, because the clonant, being made to a pre-set pattern, is in a sense triggered to react in a predetermined way.
- It will be impossible to "uncreate" the humans created by such experiments, including the defective and the grossly deformed. The deliberate creating of defectives such as dumb-mutes on a large scale in order to provide an unprotesting workforce is not beyond the bounds of possibility.
- It will impair religious values and concepts.

(B) PSYCHOSURGERY[6]

In 1972, Dr. Jose Delgado, a pioneer in psychosurgical research, went into a bullring in the path of a charging bull. Using remote control to activate electrodes implanted by him in the bull's brain, he calmed the animal's rage and halted it in its tracks. This raised speculation about the possible application of such techniques to humans.

Delgado was illustrating only one of a multitude of techniques science has made available for influencing the workings of the mammalian brain. Psychosurgery, electroconvulsive therapy, drug therapy, psychotherapy, and behaviour therapy are others. They all raise ethical and human rights issues which penetrate the Universal Declaration of Human Rights' pronouncements on the dignity of human beings (Art. 1), their freedom from degrading treatment (Art. 5), their recognition as people (Art. 6), their rights to privacy (Art. 12), their right to freedom of thought and opinion (Art. 18), their right

6 From *The Slumbering Sentinels*, pp. 37–42.

to health (Art. 25(1)), and their right to the full development of their personalities (Art. 29(1)).

Noting the possibilities of these techniques, Albert Rosenfeld observed:

> One can easily imagine people in the future wearing self-stimulating electrodes (it might even become the "in" thing to do) which might render the wearer sexually potent at any time; that might put him to sleep or keep him awake, according to his need; that might curb his appetite if he wanted to lose weight; that might relieve him of pain; that might give him courage when he was fearful or render him tranquil when he was enraged.[7]

Electric stimulation of the brain can induce motor movements such as walking, although not as yet with sufficient sophistication to create a scenario of "men with intra-cerebral electrodes engaged in all kinds of mischief under the perverse guidance of radio waves sent by some evil scientist".[8]

External intrusions into the human brain raise questions about human identity. A split-brain operation, by which the principal connections between the two brain hemispheres are severed to prevent the spread of epileptic seizures from one side of the brain to the other, reveals some peculiar phenomena. If a picture is shown to a patient on the left side of his visual field, that information is transmitted to the right side of the brain, and since the speech centre is in the left half of the brain which sensed nothing, he or she will be unable to describe the picture verbally. Yet his or her left hand, which is controlled by the right half of the brain, can pick up the object. Indeed, it is possible to teach the two halves different things, with no transmission between them of the information they have received. In 1969, experiments on a chimpanzee showed that automatic learning is possible by directly feeding signals into specific parts of the brain.

Chemical techniques are other instruments for mind control. Minutely controlled doses of chemicals can induce foreseeable reactions. Such interference is even more dangerous than psychosurgery, because it needs neither direct surgical invasion nor destruction of tissue, and can be given without the recipient's knowledge.

In the 1950s, drugs such as chlorpromazine, isoniazid and imipramine, which were effective in dealing with mood phases, began to be used. These drugs enabled patients, once so utterly depressed or deluded that they had to

[7] Albert Rosenfeld, *The Second Genesis: The Coming Control of Life*, Prentice Hall (1970).

[8] Jose M. R. Delgado, *Physical Control of the Mind: Toward a Psycho-civilized Society*, Harper and Row (1970).

be confined in hospitals, to return to active lives in the community. Various new major tranquillizers — Melleril, Stelazine, Serenace and others — made their appearance in quick succession, and have provided relief for patients with severe psychiatric conditions. Unfortunately, these drugs may also be used for non-therapeutic purposes, for example, in interrogation.

In 1948, Phineas P. Gage, twenty-five years old and vigorous in mind and body, was preparing a hole for blasting, in the course of railway construction. When he was tamping it with an iron, the powder exploded, driving the iron through his left cheek and out at the top of his head. Gage survived the accident, regaining consciousness in a few minutes. But it altered his character, and he became more capricious and childish. This shrewd, energetic man was so transformed that in the eyes of his friends he was "no longer Gage".[9] This incident, reported in the *Boston Medical and Surgical Journal*, was followed by studies of the effects on behaviour of lesions of the cerebral cortex in dogs and by pioneering human brain surgery by Sir Victor Horsley at University College Hospital, London.

At a 1935 Neurological Congress in London, two American scientists reported details of behaviour modification in chimpanzees as a result of destruction of prefrontal areas of the brain. A Portuguese neurologist, Dr. Egas Moniz, asked the congress why, if frustration could be eliminated in animals, it was not possible to relieve anxiety in people by surgery. In Portugal, he put this idea into practice by operating on psychiatric patients who had failed to respond to other forms of treatment. He devised a technique of cutting brain fibres with a special knife, which was inserted through an opening drilled in the skull, thus initiating lobotomies.

Since Moniz's operations, which won him a Nobel Prize, psychosurgery has gone through many phases. Walter Freeman and James Watts, Moniz's enthusiastic followers, pioneered new techniques and, before the procedure fell into disfavour, an estimated 50,000 pre-frontal lobotomies were carried out in North America and 10,000 in Great Britain[10].

Following these developments in psychosurgery, it was possible for scientists to locate the bundles of nerve centres or neurons which controlled particular kinds of conduct. And later it was possible, without massive surgery, to burn or destroy selected groups of neurons by introducing delicate electrical devices into the brain.

Psychosurgery began to look ominous when possibilities appeared of using it to quieten violent people. Vernon Mark and Frank Ervin, two neuro-

9 Paul K. Bridges, "A Contemporary View of Psychosurgery" in R.N. Gaind and B. L. Hudson (eds.), 1 *Current Themes in Psychiatry*, Macmillan (1978), p. 307.

10 *Ibid.*, pp. 311–12.

surgeons, described in *Violence and the Brain* the surgical procedures by which they had controlled violent behaviour. The implications of brain surgery as an aid to law and order were not lost in the context of the urban violence of the 1960s.

The spread of psychosurgery caused alarm. Some states, such as Oregon, banned it in 1973 as a threat to public health. The Oregon statute defined psychosurgery as any procedure that destroys brain tissue for the primary purpose of modifying behaviour. This description included operations, which are now referred to as lobotomies, and behavioural surgery, but excluded surgery for the removal of tumours and abscesses, and the treatment of brain damage caused by accidents. The cutting of a portion of the frontal lobe is still a valid procedure for killing pain, and even in its most "barbarous" days up to 1955, psychosurgery was the last therapeutic resort for many psychiatric patients.[11]

With increasing improvements in psychosurgery, the type of control possible will be progressively refined, and it may be possible for the margin between therapeutic use and use for social control to be deliberately obscured. "Deviant" conduct may include violence, alcoholism, homosexuality, drug addiction, argumentativeness and political dissent.

The question who will determine whether a person is to be subjected to psychosurgery is more complex than in traditional medical or surgical treatment. By the very nature of the conditions for which the treatment is used, patients are often incapable of giving their consent.

Who then consents on behalf of the patient? What mandate does such a person have? What assurance of impartiality can there be when the "patient" is already an inmate of a state institution: a prison, an infirmary or a mental home? How can the law protect a person from being subjected to "treatment" in order to produce a particular behavioural pattern? Free will, the cornerstone of all concepts of freedom under the law, stands undermined.

The question of bringing psychosurgery and all forms of brain manipulation under greater control is a difficult one. The critics of brain surgery have been attacked as being uninformed; the enthusiasts for continued research are under fire for their insufficient humanitarian concern. These modern surgical techniques give a new dimension to the ability to manipulate human behaviour.

As a result of the protest sparked off in the early days of psychosurgery, there have been several detailed studies of the manner in which controls can be applied. Among the better known are the report of the New South Wales

[11] G. C. Tooth and M. P. Newton, *Reports on Public Health No. 104*, Ministry of Health, HMSO (1961).

Committee of Inquiry into Psychosurgery (1977), and the Report on Psychosurgery of the US National Commission for the Protection of Human Subjects of Biomedical and Behavioural Research (1977).

The New South Wales report suggests that all cases should be assessed by a psychosurgery review board comprising seven members, including a lawyer, a psychologist, two psychiatrists, a neurosurgeon, and a representative of the public. Where there is doubt about the competence of a patient to give consent, there should be a reference to a Justice of the Supreme Court for a ruling.

The US Report stresses that psychosurgery should not be used for any purpose other than to give treatment to individual patients. In particular, there is a prohibition on psychosurgery being performed on a prisoner, a patient involuntarily committed to a mental hospital, and a patient believed to be incapable of giving informed consent, subject to certain exceptions. Psychosurgery should, according to the report, be performed only at an institution, with an approved review board and by a competent surgeon, on a properly assessed, informed and consenting patient.

Particularly difficult questions arise where a patient in need of psychosurgery is in a prison and the medical officer in charge of the patient is a prison employee. To deal with a conflict of loyalties, he or she needs guidelines form the medical profession. Guidelines issued by the World Medical Association and by the United Nations Congress on the Prevention of Crime and the Treatment of Offenders (1958), however, have not worked with much success.[12]

Some doctors believe that attempts at setting up external machinery for surveillance and control are a slur on the medical profession. The New South Wales recommendations, for example, were attacked by a contributor to the *Medical Journal of Australia* as a "near-libellous slur upon the medical profession".[13]

No such slur is intended by the proponents of machinery for the safeguard of individual rights, just as no slur is intended on scientists when it is argued that the public should participate in scientific decision-making.

Article 6 of the World Psychiatric Association's Declaration of Hawaii suggests that whenever there is compulsory treatment or detention, there must be an independent and neutral body of appeal for regular inquiry into these cases and that every patient must be informed of its existence.

[12] A. Clare, "Ethics in Psychiatry", in R. N. Gaind and B. L. Hudson (eds.), 2 *Current Themes in Psychiatry*, Macmillan (1979), pp. 76–77.

[13] L. G. Kiloh, "Commentary on the Report of Inquiry into Psychosurgery", 2 *Medical Journal of Australia* (1977), pp. 296–301.

In this area, it is difficult to accommodate the human rights of the patient, the needs of society and its institutions of confinement, the professional autonomy of the medical profession, and the concepts and procedures of the law.

Blanket condemnations are not the answer. We need a skilled and careful delineation of indications and methods. The current unregulated situation, however, denigrates people's rights. Only carefully thought out regulatory guidelines, based on adequate expertise, offer a solution. Now is the time to take stock.

(C) MIND MANIPULATION[14]

If the humanist sets out with an absolute proposition that interference with the mind is not permitted in any circumstances, he or she meets the argument that this has always occurred and that the early training of children seeks to inculcate in them the values and thought patterns of the community — a matter in which the child has no choice. There is no such entity, therefore, as a mind that has always been its own master. The behavioural regulators argue that it is better that regulation be done by those with an expertise in the field rather than by haphazard processes.[15]

One basis for such reasoning is that many centuries of human development have left human beings as they were when civilization started, and that many millennia of human evolution have not succeeded in transmitting altruism genetically. Hence, since technology has raced ahead while human conduct remains largely the same, it is our duty, if we have the technology, to use it for structuring a better human body and a better human mind. Another argument is that if, in the past, we interfered with the processes of nature in regard to our bodily process — witness our dependence on cooked food, or clothes — might we not do so in the future with the sharpened tools now available for producing a better mind.

Apart from these general theoretical observations, there is little room for debate that surgical techniques can, with caution, be put into service for such humane purposes as curing acute depression and curbing violent behaviour. But further legal and philosophical work needs to be done on defining the justifiable boundaries of such interference.

The concept of autonomous people, whatever their limitations, cannot be abandoned. If people can be given thought and personality by means other than influence and persuasion, and if the brain can be tampered with (other-

14 From *The Slumbering Sentinels*, pp. 88–91.

15 Editorial, 40 *Medical Legal Journal* (1972), p. 75.

wise than for "treatment"), we allow a process of dehumanization. People become things; their mind becomes a manipulator's toy; their personalities reflections of other presences rather than lamps lit from within. An independent, free-willing person — the theoretical basis and fundamental value of legal systems and human rights — is cut away.

As brain science encroaches on the concept of autonomy, we need to face the problem of the control of control. If other people mould a person's thoughts and reactions, how can such controllers be guided?

A procedure as fundamental as physical interference with the brain requires the community's accumulated wisdom. A conference of physicians deciding on a course of treatment for a patient with a bodily ailment does not generally need community participation. Where the brain is involved, however, no community can afford to leave the scientists to arbitrate.

(D) SELECTIVE BREEDING[16]

The attempts by the Nazi regime to breed a master race were translated into several programmes. Among these were the compulsory sterilization of epileptics, the feeble minded, victims of hereditary blindness and deafness, manic depressives, and severe alcoholics. Dangerous and habitual criminals were castrated, and marriage was forbidden in cases where one of the parties suffered from a dangerous physical or mental condition. The world greeted information about these Nazi programmes with abhorrence, and any suggestions of using genetic techniques to breed a superior race of people have been strongly opposed.

Some writers have pointed out, however, that with selective breeding, it is possible to eliminate or reduce some of the afflictions which have lowered the quality of life for many.

This debate is not likely to occur in the context of breeding a "master race", but to be viewed rather in terms of progressive steps to be taken to reduce the incidence of inherited disease. It will be argued that those who wish to free their offspring from the possibility of genetic disease should not be denied the right to do so.

It is already possible to increase the possibility of reproducing desired characteristics by resorting to artificial insemination. Sperm banks offer this facility, and a greater range of desired qualities is likely to be offered in the future. Such selective breeding on the part of individuals is likely to grow, with the greater realization of the resources and techniques that are available. There is probably little the law can do to arrest such a drift which, even if it

[16] From *The Slumbering Sentinels*, pp. 86–88.

grows dramatically, is unlikely to affect more than a small section of the population.

What will be more at issue, however, is not individual breeding or "gene shopping" programmes, but selective breeding. If the incidence of a particular gene-borne disease, such as sickle cell anaemia, reached through alarmingly high proportions in a group, it could become a matter of public policy whether compulsory action should be taken to limit the transmission of this defect. As available resources become the subject of increasing competition, the right to procreate, of a person transmitting a genetic defect, may well be determined by public policy. With more effective screening programmes and improved technology, these people will be readily identifiable, and it will become increasingly difficult to resist the argument that their procreation rights should be curtailed.

Once this stage is reached, there is a danger that the border between preventing the transmission of genetic disease and preventing the transmission of undesired qualities, such as laziness, stupidity, proneness to alcoholism or criminal conduct, will become blurred.

As we approach the stage where genes can be tampered with (happily still remote), the issue will become more momentous, for if genes can be mixed according to a desired prescription, many fundamental assumptions relating to responsibility and humanness will fall away. The danger will be multiplied several-fold when the state enters the field.

When the benefits of selective breeding are already used for various animal species, why, some argue, should the benefits of selective breeding among humans be withheld?

This is an issue on which it will be necessary for populations to make choices. Concepts of the dignity and integrity of the human personality and religious concepts deeply ingrained in various cultures and traditions will range themselves in opposition to such propositions.

So far, the generation of life outside the body has not been significant enough to require state intervention. Mass cloning, once achieved, cannot be left in private hands and will demand state control. Indeed, it would be essential that cloning be the subject of international rather than national control.[17]

The greatest danger to be guarded against is that the state will not only be the controller, but also the initiator of these processes. Considerations of eugenics will no doubt be advanced as initial justifications, but considera-

[17] See Susan R. Izenstark, "Genetic Manipulation: Research Regulation and Legal Liability Under International Law", 7 *California Western International Law Journal* (1977), p. 203.

tions of power, state organization, and self-perpetuation will then emerge. Dominant groups will have the technology and the legal apparatus to perpetuate themselves and obliterate others. Selected racial or physical types could preponderate.

Once state intervention becomes a reality, it becomes difficult to define and impossible to police which person or what quality is to be reproduced.

The basic legal issues become evident in the light of judicial pronouncements on family life and the importance of preserving a person's right to control his or her marital privacy and the right to procreation. In the language of the US Supreme Court:

> The entire fabric of the Constitution and the purposes that clearly underlie its specific guarantees demonstrate that the rights to marital privacy and to marry and raise a family are of similar order and magnitude as the fundamental rights specifically protected.[18]

So also: "Of this whole 'private realm of family life' it is difficult to imagine what is more private or more intimate than a husband and wife's marital relations".[19]

We have already faced some of these problems with artificial insemination by donors and with techniques of IVF and ET. But what we are about to witness are these problems posed on an infinitely larger scale. In a detailed legal investigation into the implications for individual liberty of state power over human fertility, an eminent researcher observed:

> In coming decades the right of the individual to live, love and procreate will be put in issue as never before in human history. The pressure of supposed necessity will create a great temptation to sacrifice the individual and his family and sexual freedoms. As has been shown, the biological revolution will create new powers for man, but these powers may also be used to limit individual freedom. We may some day accept or even demand the use of these powers to control human fertility, but we must give serious consideration to the possibility that freedom may not survive the loss of individual choice over the roots of human existence.[20]

[18] *Poe* v. *Ullman*, 367 US 497, 552 (1961), Harlan J. dissenting, cited with approval in Griswold *v.* Connecticut 381 US 479 (1965).

[19] Justice Goldberg in *Griswold* v. *Connecticut* 381 US 479 (1965).

[20] Charles P. Kindregan, "State Power over Human Fertility and Individual Liberty", 23 *Hastings Law Journal* (1972), pp. 1425–6.

(E) CHIMERAS[21]

On 15 October 1982, *The Age* reported that a doctor at the Queen Elizabeth Hospital in Adelaide had been experimenting with the use of human sperm to fertilize rat ova. The research, conducted at the University of Newcastle, was intended to enable scientists to observe the constituents of human sperm after it had penetrated the ova. Such information, it was said, would make possible the detection of chromosomal abnormalities and the screening of men for suspected infertility. Fears were expressed immediately that human sexuality was denigrated and that scientists might be on the way to creating hybrids. The assurance that there was no possibility for a hybrid to develop because the human and the rat were so different did not stifle the criticism, and the Principal of the Jesuit Theological College in Parkville condemned the research as "*in vitro* bestiality". Scientists might condemn such reactions as over-emotional, while laymen might condemn such experiments as extremely dangerous. More interaction is needed between both groups.

More significant, because closer to possibility and even more disturbing in its implications, was the report in December 1980[22] that Chinese scientists were working on producing a man/animal symbiont by attempting to cross a human being with a chimpanzee. The object of the experiment, reportedly, was to produce a breed of low-IQ, muscular workers, who would be pliant tools in labour-intensive projects.

The scientific world described the suggestion as fanciful, but responsible researchers in the field of IVF have called on governments to legislate against such abuses.[23] IVF, a distant dream only a decade ago, has been achieved. Hybrids of different species have also been produced. We already have announcements of the successful transfer of a gene from rabbits to mice, and of the production of "three-parent cattle" through the introduction of added genes. We cannot shut our minds to the possibility that chimeras can and will be produced.

[21] From *The Slumbering Sentinels*, p. 95.

[22] *Australian*, 30 December 1980.

[23] Professor Carl Wood, leader of the *in-vitro* fertilization team at the Queen Victoria Hospital in Melbourne, as reported in the *West Australian*, 25 September 1980, in an address to the Melbourne Rotary Club.

(F) NEOMORT FARMS[24]

Postponing death raises its share of legal issues, but these are dwarfed by macabre techniques for making medical use of the legally dead. On 13 May 1976, the *Listener* announced a new series of documentaries that would look at important issues with which science was confronting society. An outline of one of the forthcoming features read:

> Rows of legally dead neomorts in bioemporia, still warm, breathing and pulsating, could revolutionize medical research. Instead of pulling out the plug, doctors could, with the aid of sophisticated medical equipment, keep a person's body alive, even when he is considered dead. The cadaver, or neomort, would be an ideal test-bed for new drugs, cancer research, tissue culture, and as a natural organ bank for transplant surgery. What are the moral, ethical and legal questions that arise from this potential for recycling human bodies?

The obvious practical medical value of such farms will be a potent factor in the pressure for their adoption.

The possibilities of such technological erosions are limitless. The human body stands assailed as never before. Will we rise to its defence now, or for ever more be silent?

[24] From *The Slumbering Sentinels*, p. 96.

PART C

PROFESSIONAL ETHICS AND HUMANISTIC PERSPECTIVES

18. Future Technology and the Scientific Ethic*

> "Life is short and Art is long; the Crisis is fleeting. Experiment risky. Decision difficult. The physician must be ready to do his duty ..."

Thus runs an extract from the *Aphorisms*, one of the most famous books of the medical writings known as the Hippocratic collection — a set of studies named after the father of medicine and permeated with a deep appreciation of the social responsibilities of the medical practitioner. The Hippocratic oath, one of the best known passages of this collection, reminds physicians specifically of a number of guiding ethical principles — treatment shall be for the benefit of patients, no deadly drugs shall be given even if requested, the physician shall refrain from wrongdoing and corruption, especially from acts of seduction, medical secrecy shall be preserved.

Hippocrates was an elder contemporary of Plato. These writings were brought together in the fourth century B.C. The medical ethics reflected in these writings are thought to hark back to ethical principles known and practised in Egypt two thousand years before.

This is concrete evidence that four thousand years ago the practitioners of a certain department of science — medicine — were acutely conscious that while knowledge was universal and abstract, its application was particular and practical. The pure stream of abstract universals did not run separate from the stream of practical realities but there was a constant intermingling of their waters.

In the realm of medicine the points of confluence were clear. The Platonic and Aristotelian ideal of a pure realm of universal abstract thought was however still a widely held vision in many other departments of knowledge. The ivory tower philosopher, divorced from the realities of the world and believing that the knowledge pursued was still an abstract realm, self-contained within itself, has continued to be very much of a reality for four thousand years and more.

* Paper delivered at a Symposium on "The Law and the Future: The Impact of Scientific and Technological Changes", held by the Australian Commission for the Future, March 1986, Melbourne.

Other departments of science — astronomy, chemistry, physics — did not display to the casual observer such obvious interrelationships with human and social issues as to direct the attention of their votaries to their ethical duties. The alchemist seeking to produce the elixir of life or to transmute base metals into gold, the astronomer making a chart of the heavens, the physicist investigating the principles of optics did not to give their attention to hypothetical ethical problems which, if seen at all, were far distant from their work. They were pursuing knowledge and knowledge was a good in itself.

Indeed for the first thousand years after the advent of Christianity, when the emphasis was on revealed rather than discovered knowledge, free inquiry was discouraged if not suppressed to such an extent that the freedom of pursuit of knowledge as an end in itself needed to be hard fought for. It was indeed won with such a struggle that it was prized thereafter as an end in itself.

Freedom of inquiry, having thus become a right won only after a hard struggle, was entrenched in the academic world, as well as in popular consciousness, as a value that needed preservation. Any attempt by authority to interfere with freedom of inquiry and research tended to be resisted as curtailment of liberty. In the academic world the notion that research was an intrinsic good inasmuch as it was the pursuit of pure knowledge, came to be accepted as one of the basic pillars on which academic liberty rested.

With this concept thus entrenched, it became difficult for those interested in the social responsibilities of scientists to attempt any curtailment, in the social interest, of scientists' absolute freedom to research as they willed. In the nineteenth century, while concepts of social responsibility were indeed receiving increasing attention in the social and political sphere, the area of social responsibility in science remained largely untouched. While many privileges were eroded under the influence of Benthamite philosophy and legislation, academic privilege remained intact. Indeed, it became even more jealously guarded. Antagonisms between the social interest and scientific and technological progress, despite such occasional assertions as in the Luddite riots, were rarely perceived and the widely accepted belief was that science in all its facets was the friend of freedom and the tyrant's foe.

The circumstances of the twentieth century, and in particular of the past half century, have however revealed five trends so self-evident as to compel attention to their impact upon traditional attitudes towards science.

1. The horrors of the concentration camps had shown how scientists — even medical scientists — could be compelled to use their expertise to bolster tyranny as its naked worst and how the pursuit of scientific

research through human experimentation could become a ghastly and macabre enterprise.

2. Where in the past, science and scientific research were comparatively inexpensive, science was now growing into one of the most expensive areas of state activity. No longer was the individual scientist able to lock himself away in his study pursuing his research in the realm of pure thought or, where experimentation was needed, with apparatus which was within the means of himself or a private patron. The cost of scientific research was rising exponentially even as the sophistication of the research increased. Research necessarily required funding from the public purse to the tune of hundreds of millions of dollars and began to compete with other claims upon the same source. Consequently scientific research, being dependent upon public funds, necessarily required that some account be taken of public needs. Those who paid for the research naturally had a right to some participation in the decision relating to the direction of such research and in relation to the choice among alternatives, all of which could not be simultaneously funded.

3. The power of science has increased to the point where we can well be described as living in a science dominated society. Science and technology make their impact on every aspect of our daily lives. They force us to alter our habits, lifestyles and methods of work to an extent not known before. The manner in which the average citizen attends to his business affairs, what he eats, the purity of the water he drinks, the transport he uses daily and the clothes he wears are all being fashioned for tomorrow in the laboratories of today. Science and technology dominate every moment of our waking lives. A citizen who is thus subject to the power and influence of science and technology cannot much longer be kept out of the decision-making process in relation to the directions which science should take. For example, should scientists devise means of manipulating the processes of the human brain, create life artificially in laboratory conditions, effect mutations in living creatures, assemble dangerous concentrations of nuclear waste, pollute the oceans or poison the land with chemicals? Should they devise increasingly finer methods for the surveillance and control of society? All of these cannot be considered solely on the principle of academic freedom and the pure pursuit of knowledge. The public interest is an integral part of the input into the decision whether such research should go ahead.

4. A fourth factor is the undoubted circumstance that science has grown into an interest in itself. There are empires of power within the scientific community and there are powerful alliances between science and industry, and between science and the military. Scientists and technologists who have to take decisions regarding the future directions of science thus become interested parties and do not have the detachment necessary for a decision where a choice must be made between alternatives. The old legal principle that there must not be a clash between interest and duty is profoundly infringed if some of the most important decisions concerning society are to be taken by the scientific community in such circumstances.

5. The areas in which scientific progress involves ethical issues have proliferated beyond the vision of even a decade ago. The scientist studying the processes of osmosis in the root system of a plant does not have to face the conscience problems arising from genetic engineering or improving nuclear weaponry. Value-laden decisions involving the interests of society, the *mores* of the community, or the rights of future generations did not often arise in traditional science. Modern science throws them up in basketfuls.

These are some of the factors which militate against a continuance in pristine form of the outworn principle that the scientist is free to pursue whatever course he or she wills, free of ethical constraints.

Numerous factors in the world situation lend emphasis to this view. The role played by scientists in the preparation and perfection of weapons of war, their duties when called upon as medical men to be present at interrogations or torture sessions, their role in relation to the economic exploitation by rich corporations of countries in the poor world, their work in relation to nuclear power — all these are a few illustrations of global problems which force a search for the social obligations of the scientist and for ethical codes embodying these obligations. It should be pointed out that most of these obligations lie in an area totally or largely neglected by the law.

It is true that the scientist, like everyone else, is liable in the law of tort for damage caused through negligence to those within the foreseeable circle of persons likely to be affected by his or her conduct. But there are various rules of remoteness and provable causal connection, in addition to numerous other procedural formalities, which lie between the victim and his or her legal relief. For example a radiation injury or a carcinoma caused by noxious chemicals entering the lung might ensue twenty years after the act in question. Proof is difficult and only individual cases might surface in the courts although a whole class is affected. Again, there are total legal lacunae in regard to certain areas of scientific activity because the law in the course of its centuries of development did not visualize either such activity or its damaging effects on basic legal rights and protections. Privacy, on which the common law was totally undeveloped, is an excellent example. Researchers in the field of computers and data banks still work unfettered in many areas where their work impinges on society but where the law is as yet totally undeveloped. Numerous surveillance devices such as those based on heat detection or laser reflection of sound waves off a distant window-pane are examples.

Recent developments in biochemistry open up a field of social importance so novel to the law that the scientist is at least a generation ahead of the ability of legal systems even to attune themselves to his or her activities. The processes of life creation, mutation of living species, embryo transplantation, *in vitro* fertilization, freeze preservation of sperm, cryosurgery and mind manipulation were till recently virgin fields so far as the law is concerned. Australia is particularly fortunate in this regard as a far-seeing Law Reform Commission has moved into these areas, generated public awareness and commenced the processes leading to urgently needed legislation. But scientists will need to work out their ethical attitudes to these developments long before the law gets to grip with them.

It is unnecessary at this stage to catalogue the numerous fields of modern scientific activity where the law is in this fashion unable, in view of its present concepts, procedures and structures, to cope with the phenomenon of the social impact of science. It is sufficient to observe that they are so numerous that vast legal resources, beyond the current capabilities of society, must be poured into this field before the law is equal to the problems confronting it.

We are left, then, with a heavy responsibility on the shoulders of the scientist and the scientific profession as a whole. They have several options in the matter, some of which are:

- to pursue their researches unconcerned, arguing that the task of regulating the social impact of their work is a task for other agencies and other minds.
- to draw a distinction between pure science and technology, arguing that the pursuit of pure science must always be free and that it is the technical application of science that needs social control.
- to hold regular conventions in every department of science, specially studying the ethical and social obligations attendant upon those special fields of activity, and formulating ethical guidelines or recommendations for workers in those fields.

- to formulate not only ethical guidelines but codes of conduct with an in-built enforcing mechanism.
- to work towards the acceptance of international codes of conduct endorsed by the relevant world organizations or associations — e.g. a World Council of Scientists, the World Health Organization — on the basis of a realization that in many areas of science purely national regulations will be futile.
- to accept a principle that in certain departments of science which might have dangerous impacts on society, moratoria be imposed on pure research until the issues are clear — as was done in relation to recombinant DNA experimentation.
- to liaise with the non-scientific world by setting up interdisciplinary ethical committees such as has already been done in the medical world in relation to such problems as the withdrawal of life support systems or experimentation on human subjects.
- to set up futures committees in all departments of science probing into likely future developments and their social impact and advising society on the various alternatives available.
- to form in every jurisdiction societies for social responsibility in science which will pursue ethical responsibilities in all departments of science.

Which course or courses the scientific fraternity chooses from among the many options open to it is a matter of great importance to itself and to society.

If it chooses to do nothing there is no doubt that society will intervene in one form or another and the scientific profession will find a great extraneous intrusion upon their freedom of activity. This is undesirable, not only because it will be an external imposition, but also because the lay world does not have the expertise to regulate these areas with the degree of refinement which is required.

Internal attention to the problem from within the ranks of the scientific profession is therefore required. This must, optimally, be in consultation with representatives of the lay public and of other disciplines, for scientists would be unable to perceive all the implications and perspectives by themselves. If there is to be regulation or a moratorium this comes best from the scientists themselves.

However there are many problems here and these need to be addressed.

Scientific research is expensive. Funds for it come in from the external world — e.g., the military or the corporate world. These entities are interested only in certain types of research. If scientists have qualms about such types of research, the money will not be forthcoming.

This is an important practical consideration which brings into clear relief some of the principal issues involved. Among these are the ethical responsibilities of universities and of the scientific bodies which may be the recipients of research grants. The military and the armaments industry offer the most prominent modern example of this ethical problem. There may be scientists in universities who approve of research into nuclear or other weapons such as chemical weapons. There are others who do not.

What is the ethical duty of a University when it is offered millions of dollars for research into some project of the military, which involves the construction of some new offensive weapon or the perfection of an existing one or the devising through computer science of an improved launching? The increased military spending on the Star Wars programme in the US is currently highlighting these problems. Current shortages of money for academic research contrast strongly with the apparently limitless sums available for such military oriented research — sums so large that an increasing proportion of the totality of US scientific spending now comes from military sources.

The Star Wars programme only emphasizes a special aspect of a larger problem — the problem of the heavy involvement of the scientific profession in the arms trade.

It has been estimated that more than 50 per cent of the skilled scientific manpower of the world is currently devoting itself to military research and development.

I admit that there may well be a diversity of view among scientists on this question. Some may be persuaded of the need for fresh and more weapons on grounds of defence or deterrence. But in a world which spends more than a billion dollars a day on armaments the ethical dimensions of the scientist's contribution need a general discussion in the community of scientists. The issues cannot be glossed over or avoided. The comment is not without substance that the scientific community by and large has preferred to shut its eyes to the problem, leaving it to individual scientists to grapple with it and make their own private decisions as best they may.

I know scientists in this country and overseas who are profoundly concerned with this problem and who are troubled that they have not as a profession paid more attention to it. The omission to do so is all the more significant when we consider that it is the scientific fraternity that has the greatest expertise in this area.

The point must also be made that many of the ideas that come to the generals and the statesmen in relation to new species of even more destructive weaponry are not ideas which those persons have thought up for themselves but ideas which have come up to them from the scientists in their laboratories.

I have had the privilege especially over the past two years to speak to numerous bodies of scientists on this very question, in the US, in Europe and in Japan. The reaction has been most encouraging for, once the question is raised, they realize their obligation to give it some further thought.

I was told by a group of young scientists working in the field of weapons science that they had been conscious of the ethical problem involved in their work but, being unable to come to grips with it, had relegated it to the "too-hard-basket" at the back of their minds. However, they later felt they had no alternative but to give it some deeper thought.

One of the matters raised by them gives food for thought. They were bright young men and women whose excellence in science had brought them awards and scholarships which, in the context of current research, had led them into fields such as nuclear physics in which they had specialized. Society had, in other words, guided their footsteps in this direction, induced them to specialize at PhD level in these areas of research and, in effect, rendered them unsuited for any other kind of activity. The reaction of one such person was "If there is an ethical or moral question mark over what we are doing, we blame society that has trained us for this, but not ourselves."

Undoubtedly there is here a great social issue and if there has been a lapse, a large part of the blame must be taken by society. Yet the duty of ethical scrutiny does not pass over the heads of the scientists concerned. If they are devoting to a particular activity a lifetime of special skill — indeed their entire intellectual and working lives — that is an inquiry they cannot avoid by shifting the responsibilities elsewhere.

The difficulties involved in the eventual decision are again no justification for shirking the inquiry. The problems involved are no less than would occur in the case of any person who finds himself in a situation where his work or his employer's demands do not accord with his conscience.

Suppose for example a person has trained himself for service in the tobacco industry. He feels at a certain point that scientific evidence is mounting to the level where he is convinced that the work he is engaged in is causing cancer and death to a large number of consumers of his product. He cannot avoid the conscience question of whether he is prepared to spend the rest of his life earning his livelihood, educating his children and providing for his retirement out of an activity which he is convinced is bringing death in its wake.

Of course the result is inconvenient but, if he is to heed his conscience, he cannot avoid the issue. No less can a person deeply committed to the fighting of apartheid, who finds that his employer insists on supplying to the South African regime materials which assist the latter in keeping in place the apparatus of apartheid. If his employment necessitates his participation in such activity, he must face the problem squarely. The same applies to service under a manufacturer who is releasing dangerous or defective goods to the public and requires his employee, out of loyalty to his employer, to assist in hiding the danger or defect from the public.

This brings me to a proposal I have been advocating for some time — an ombudsman for science — an idea which in my view should be built into the structure of the scientists' ethical code.

I refer here to the fact that there are, in numerous fields of scientific or technological activity, situations in which scientists or technologists have conscience problems in relation to the work they are called upon by their employer to perform. Should they speak out openly about them, they run the risk of dismissal or some lesser sign of disfavour. Persons with such conscience problems ought to be able to approach an ombudsman for science, who can look into their problem, give them guidance and offer them a mediation procedure, without the employee being in fear of adverse action by the employer. A statutory provision needs to be built into the legislation creating this office, precluding the employer from victimizing an employee who takes a conscience problem to the ombudsman.

The ombudsman should preferably be a person with a scientific and sociological or philosophical background who would have some familiarity with the basic disciplines involved.

The problem is an urgent one in all industrialized societies. Far too much activity which individual employees disapprove of goes on behind the corporate veil which screens from the public much that the public is entitled to know. This concerns not merely the industrialized society in the context of which the work is done but also the target society at which the goods are intended. A sensitive international question today, which has strong political overtones in regard to the relationship between the affluent and developing worlds, is the dumping of shoddy goods on Third World markets. Others are the exploitation of the mineral resources of the seabed, the dumping of radioactive waste in the oceans and the induced dependence of Third World agriculture on the "miracle" seeds and agricultural products put out by multinational agricultural business.

In all of these, ethical problems arise in which current legal barriers, combined with the lack of an open discussion of a scientific ethic, are causing much injustice and a stifling of issues of the conscience.

Indeed, though this is outside the scope of this paper, it is relevant to a Symposium on Futures to draw attention to the urgent need for more attention to the conscience problems which lie buried under several layers of protection created by the present structure of our corporate law. Our corporate law has not yet made up its mind whose interests a corporation serves or what values it should pursue.

Is the sole criterion of a company director's duties the pursuit of profit? Is he serving only the interests of his shareholders whose basic concern is naturally a maximum return upon their investment? Or does he have duties also to the general public — a duty to serve society in the field in which the corporation has developed special expertise? Should not a social service component be built into the structure of our company law? Should not companies of more than a certain size have also certain social service components in relation to which there is a social service audit, just as there is a financial audit in the sphere of finance? In the course of a company's activities is it the duty of directors merely to keep on the right side of the law however unethical their practices may be, or is there also a duty on the ethical side which our company law has in its current state neglected? This latter is precisely the sphere in which the scientist serving such a corporate entity could find his conscience problems swept under the carpet. If we are planning for an ethical future for our society the ethical problems which in so many departments are permitted to be concealed must be brought out into the open.

Against this background, the need for attention to the ethical problems confronting every department of science becomes clear.

It is true that rudimentary codes of various sorts have been worked out by certain groups of scientists and technologists. Engineers and computer scientists are two examples.

Some associations of engineers, for example, require their members to pledge themselves to the service of society. Computer technologists attempt to safeguard the confidentiality of their databases. Yet an examination of such codes shows that they are of a rudimentary nature, not proceeding beyond the level of generalization of the Hippocratic oath.

Now that modern science and technology have unfolded their powers to the extent they have, we are in possession of far more specific information regarding areas of possible danger to the ethical and social postulates which today receive global recognition as well as those which, within the context of a nation, receive national recognition.

Lest it be said that there are no such postulates let me refer straight away to the universally-agreed set of norms contained in the Universal Declaration of Human Rights, the International Covenant on Civil and Political Rights and the International Covenant on Economic, Social, and Cultural Rights.

Many scientific developments threaten these rights and it is rather surprising that the responsible governing or professional bodies of scientists have not to this day launched upon a systematic study of the ways in which new thrusts in science are undermining these rights, and of ways in which scientists can assist in preventing their erosion. There have been piecemeal attempts to nibble at specific areas but not, as far as I am aware, any overall surveys. This is in spite of the fact that as long ago as 10 November 1975 the General Assembly of the United Nations called upon all states to prevent the use of scientific or technological developments to limit or interfere with human rights and basic freedoms.

In its Declaration on the Use of Scientific and Technological Progress in the Interests of Peace and for the Benefit of Mankind the General Assembly placed all states under a duty

> to ensure that the results of scientific and technological developments are used in the interests of strengthening international peace and security, freedom and independence and also for the economic and social development of peoples and the realisation of human rights and freedoms in accordance with the Charter of the UN.

The next year there followed a Resolution on the implementation of this resolution and in 1982 the General Assembly issued a call

> to all states, specialised agencies and intergovernmental and non-governmental organisations to take necessary measures to ensure that the results of scientific and technological progress are used exclusively in the interests of international peace, for the benefit of mankind and for promoting and encouraging respect for human rights.

The emerging international ethical norms are clear but they need specificity in the context of modern scientific progress, and they need formulation and acceptance by the appropriate scientific bodies. But we must not rest there, for these documents only formulate a minimum standard. It may therefore be appropriate for concerned scientists to go beyond the norms which have received acceptance from the international community. We need, in Australia, as in the other countries with similar value systems, to address ourselves specifically to this task.

All this is activity by bodies of scientists. I go further than this in my submission. In an age of internationalism, with so many agencies of the UN concerning themselves with scientific matters, and with the General Assembly itself as a forum where these matters can be discussed, I look forward to the day when a detailed code of scientific ethics, agreed upon by the main scientific bodies in the world, can be subject of a Declaration by the General

Assembly, with a series of other Declarations to follow in specific areas. It is true such Declarations would not have the force of law but, once accepted by the General Assembly, their persuasive value as norm-setting documents would be immense. As only states can bring such matters before the General Assembly it needs activity on the part of the Australian Government itself to initiate such a move.

In a specific department of scientific activity which I have been researching, namely the manufacture of nuclear weaponry, I have been working towards such a Declaration. I have drafted a proposed Declaration which I have circulated among scientific bodies and among member states of the United Nations.[1] As is to be expected in such a controversial field I have received very encouraging as well as very discouraging responses. It may be that the proposal is too ambitious but its time will come.

However, on a lesser scale, in areas which are not so highly charged politically and in areas on which there is general agreement amongst the world community, there is no substantial reason why a start cannot be made by concerned scientists, through the process of interesting their respective governments.

It is to be remembered especially that there are certain areas where we may later regret that we had not attempted to close the stable door before the horse had bolted. Nuclear weaponry, which at one stage, in the era of Niels Bohr, could have been brought under international control, and could possibly have been brought under such control again at the time of the Baruch plan, is one such example of our living to rue the day when we lost these opportunities. But there are numerous others. Tampering with the processes of creation of human life is today in its infancy. The techniques of *in vitro* fertilization and embryo transplantation are as nothing to what will be evolved in the foreseeable future when scientists will attempt to prolong the period during which a foetus fertilized *in vitro* can be grown in laboratory conditions. I appreciate that the difficulties, as we currently perceive them, are immense, but seemingly immense difficulties have in the history of science been overcome time and again. The time will come when we will hear that the process of gestation *in vitro* has been extended — gradually, to begin with, but by leaps and bounds as the various hurdles are overcome. We do not have to wait until we awaken one day to the realization that a human embryo has been grown to full maturity by scientists in a laboratory. We need to address ourselves to this problem, bringing in the collective wisdom of the world's scientific community before it occurs, for once it does, a reign of total anarchy could be unleashed in the world of law. We would be asking

1 See Appendix B to this volume.

ourselves how we can control the number of babies so produced, how we can destroy those who are defective, who gives certificates of full "humanhood", whether we can breed for special characteristics, who has the right to specify such characteristics and so on, in an unending list of mind-boggling questions.

Universal data banks, a problem already out of the stable door, is an area in the social sphere which needs urgent attention. In the environmental sphere the problems are legion. When and in what forums will world bodies address them and what input can the scientific community conscientiously claim to be making to them?

We have indeed some angry international declarations on scientific responsibility such as the Cocoyoc Declaration of 1974, passed by participants in the UN Environmental Programme, and the Poona Indictment of 1978, adopted by the participants in the fourteenth meeting of the World Order Models Project.

The former document concluded, *inter alia*, that:

> Science and technology must be responsive to the goals we are pursuing. ... We call on universities, other institutions of higher learning, research organizations, and scientific associations all over the world to reconsider their priorities. Mindful of the benefits deriving from free and basic research, we underline the fact that ... it should be more focussed on research for the satisfaction of fundamental needs.

It called for the evolution of ways of life that are "more just, less arrogant in their material demands, more respectful of the whole planetary environment".

The document stressed the need for scientists to turn their attention to development — to basic needs of food, shelter, clothing, health and education. They should not permit themselves to be carried along on the current wave of devotion to materialistic concepts of progress but to other goals and values — in a word that scientists should reorientate their attitudes and use their skill in the development not of things but of man.

The ethical perspectives involved in such an approach are essential if technology is to lead us to a world of plenty and fulfilment, such as Bacon foresaw in *The New Atlantis*, and which it has the power to bestow on us all. If those perspectives are not kept before the scientific fraternity there is the danger of a perversion of science and technology — the very title of the Poona Indictment which specifically labelled itself *The Perversion of Science and Technology: An Indictment.*

Among the matters set out at the commencement of the document as ways in which science and technology have become "instruments of a global structure of inequity, exploitation and oppression" are "biological farming" in the Third World by pharmaceutical transnationals, drug testing among poor populations, export of blood from poor to rich societies, and the large proportion of scientific talent devoted to the technology of mass destruction and repression.

There will be more of such angry declarations in the future if science and technology do not soon come to grips with the problem of their ethical obligations. Such declarations are couched in such terms only because the general bodies of scientists have not addressed themselves to these problems.

An important beginning must be the introduction of compulsory courses for the scientists of the future on the social responsibilities of scientists. Our university and other tertiary curricula are lacking in this area and insufficient attention is paid to the problem in all science faculties. The solemn words of the Russell-Einstein manifesto are a constant reminder of the need for the body of scientists to pay heed to these ethical obligations.

> Remember your humanity and forget the rest. If you can do so, the way lies open to a new Paradise; if you cannot, there lies before you the risk of universal death.

Lest it be thought that this was only a reminder of their obligations to the politicians of the world it is worth remembering that this was an appeal specifically addressed also to the scientists of the world.

When we are marshalling what resources we can to take a glimpse at the human future it is essential that we do not neglect the vital area of the ethical problems posed by science. We should not be so dazzled by its undoubted achievements or so enthralled by its power as to cease to exert our influence on its direction.

19. Doctors*

THE TWIN PROFESSIONAL EMPIRES

If one reflects on the past relationships between the professions of law and medicine, they seemed to resemble two powerful empires, surveying each other at a respectful distance, each regarding with deference the expertise of the other, but each being jealous of the slightest intrusions upon its territory. The autonomy of each profession was all-important and any interference was resented. There was an early exceptional area of inter-relationship — the area of forensic medicine. This was a necessity of life as medical matters occasionally came before the courts. But it functioned within tight constraints of relevance and obedience to the letter of the law. With this minor exception, the twin empires remained unchallenged — unchallenged in their exclusiveness and unchallenged in their autonomy.

Today, however, they have come closer together under the pressure of modern intellectual attitudes and modern medical advances. Whether they like it or not, they are compelled to function together in a great many areas, rather like the great empires of power on the global scene. Those great powers once claimed complete autonomy in their internal affairs, but now realize that the world is so interlinked that they cannot be completely independent of other countries, even in the management of their internal affairs.

These two professional empires also sought a high degree of respect from the general public, who viewed them from a respectful distance. They spoke to the public from a pedestal and believed that their professional expertise gave them authority to prescribe for the public what was good for them. Their word passed largely unquestioned. Yet, today, the height of their pedestal has diminished considerably and they are forced to face an unprecedented level of public scrutiny and criticism.

No profession is an island unto itself and, when they are forced to venture outside their specialist territory, they find themselves treading uneasily on

* Based upon the Inaugural Medico-Legal Society Oration, delivered by the author, on 4 September 1992 at the Medico-Legal Society, Colombo, Sri Lanka.

common ethical ground. Moreover, that ethical ground is shared also by members of the "lay" public, who increasingly claim the right and the ability to contribute to the formation of professional standards.

It also happens that both professions have been somewhat untrained for functioning on this rather new terrain which traditionally has not been taught in either of their training schools. The change is all the more remarkable because each profession strongly believed that it had all the answers to any moral questions that might arise within its own territory, and claimed to be the sole arbiters on these questions. The area of interdependence is growing exponentially, and is of great importance to the future of both professions. It would therefore be useful to consider the implications of modern developments in these fields.

POSITIVISM IN LAW AND MEDICINE

I propose to address this topic at two levels, first at the philosophical level and, second, at the practical level. I will of course not be able even to make bare mention of the myriad instances where these issues become practically relevant, but I will choose a few illustrative examples to show the way in which moral problems have become the shared domain of both lawyer and doctor.

I commence with a few words at the philosophical level. Both professions at one stage were wedded to the view that they were in command of a very specialized and exact discipline, of which those outside their fold knew nothing worthwhile. Lawyers liked to think of their discipline as an exact science and very often wrote of it in that way. When one thinks of one's discipline as being scientific and logical, one begins to think that the objective application of this body of knowledge to a specific set of facts yields an objectively correct answer. Indeed, one begins to think of that discipline as containing the key to all the answers — the definite, logical and only answers to the numerous problems that arise. And why is this? Because there are fixed and certain principles. You apply those principles logically to a given set of facts, you then obtain a logical result and that result is the correct result.

Lawyers were for generations under the misapprehension that this was the process that they were in fact following, and this was heavily influenced by the jurisprudential works of the nineteenth century, in particular, the works of the positivist school of jurisprudence, typified by John Austin. The Austinian school, the epitome of the positivistic approach to law, taught that law is an exact science. It contained definite rules. The logical application of those definite rules to the facts produced a logical and correct result.

The American realists at the beginning of this century were the first to explode this myth. They pointed out that the process of legal decision-making is not an exact scientific process such as the lawyers had imagined it to be, and such as they had informed their clients they were engaged in. It was rather a process into which value judgments entered at every stage. When a value judgment comes in, that value judgment tends to be made on the basis of one's own set of moral standards. These are often the result of one's own moral background. That background tells the individual what values should be regarded as primary values.

The American realists at the beginning of this century drew attention to this truth in what was thought by many traditionalists to be a somewhat disrespectful manner. The name of Justice O.W. Holmes (Jr.) ranks high among those who first drew attention to the real nature of the judicial process — a view which discarded "childish fictions" and earned him the reputation of being the completely "adult" lawyer. Closer to our time, outstanding jurists, like Cardozo and Julius Stone, spent considerable effort in pointing out to lawyers and to judges that the process which they thought was a scientific and definite process was really laden with value judgments at every stage of decision-making. They showed that many results were possible upon an application of logical principles in a logical way to the same set of specific facts. Therefore the judge's personal preference, among a number of alternative choices, was what very often determined the result of a case. That was the position in law, accepted by a few lawyers and judges, grudgingly recognized by others and still denied by many.

In medicine, there was likewise a belief that here was a definite body of scientific knowledge that showed the correct course of conduct in a medical situation. The medical people, who had been trained for years in this body of scientific knowledge, knew how to apply that scientific knowledge to a given set of facts and, by applying that set of principles to a given set of facts, they obtained a definite scientific result. The doctor was in command of the medical case, the doctor was the authority on the relevant medical knowledge, and who knew better how it should be handled? So you found a matching philosophy in the medical profession.

There was the Hippocratic oath, of course, and you therefore had to do everything in the best interests of the patient. But it was *you* who decided what was in the best interest of the patient and how *you* would apply that very special body of expertise of which *you* were in command. The patient was not an equal partner in the relationship. He took from you your verdict on what should be done, just as the lawyer knew what was best for his client. Just as the judges of a previous generation saw themselves as oracles of the law, so also the doctors of the past were the oracles whose unquestionable opinions were sought by their patients.

There was thus a high degree of parallelism between the two professions in their attitude to matters within their jurisdiction. But in medicine, as in law, that belief in the internal moral adequacy of the discipline has been exploded. In the 1960s and the 1970s, a number of situations arose which made world headlines and forced these issues out of the purely medical domain. Among these were the organ transplants and cases like the Karen Quinlan case, which made doctors begin to have second thoughts about the adequacy of the guidance afforded by their discipline in these areas.

THE RUDIMENTARY NATURE OF PROFESSIONAL CODES

It is certainly true that there were ethical codes in both professions. Yet an examination of the ethical codes of both professions shows that they dealt largely with intra-professional matters. How did one lawyer or doctor treat another lawyer or doctor? How did he or she maintain the high ideals and standards of the profession? How did they prevent lay people from encroaching on their sacred ground? How did the profession prevent one doctor or lawyer from drawing upon another's clientele? There were rules against advertising, rules against touting and rules of professional conduct which were all ethical rules, no doubt, but confined very largely to the intra-professional relationships among lawyers or among doctors, with a view to maintaining the prestige and the profile of the profession. What has happened now is that that little compartmentalized box of rules, centred on intra-professional relationships, has been shown to be totally inadequate to handle the moral problems that surge into professional practice. There is precious little in that traditional box that helps us to answer some of the fundamental issues that now arise. Both professions alike are feeling their inadequacies in this regard.

This situation forces upon both professions a realization of the importance of some exposure of their students to philosophical thought. I have always maintained that legal studies without some exposure to the main currents of philosophical thought can be quite inadequate.[1] I venture to think that medical studies, which also involve future practitioners in great issues of life and death, and the quality of life, likewise require some exposure of the future practitioner to the rich perspectives that can be gained from a study of

[1] See this author's "The Importance of Philosophical Perspectives to the Judicial Process", (1991) 6 *Connecticut Journal of International Law*, No. 2, pp. 599–620.

philosophy. Let me illustrate what I mean by specific reference to the process of judgment.

THE DECISION-MAKING PROCESS IN LAW AND MEDICINE

Traditionally, it is thought that the judgmental process consists of three stages. One is the findings on primary fact, that is, the whole gamut of facts and circumstances which are placed before the judge. Each one of those must be decided by the judge, who has to determine whether he will accept or reject the version presented by each party. There is then a base of accepted facts upon which the judge can work. From that base of accepted facts, the judge will draw his conclusions. He will have facts, for example in a testamentary case, that there was an old lady or gentleman living with a relative who had great influence over that person. Eventually a last will has been drawn up leaving the old person's entire estate to that relative. Was undue influence used? There will be many witnesses who will testify to a range of matters, such as the lack of freewill enjoyed by the testator. These are matters of primary fact. From those primary facts the judge must draw his conclusions — the secondary facts. Was pressure used on the old lady or gentleman to write that will in favour of that party? These are the conclusions of secondary fact that are drawn from the earlier findings of primary fact.

The third stage is the stage of applying the law to the secondary facts as thus found. Traditional analyses of the judgmental process have ended there. But there is in fact a fourth stage. The fourth stage is reached when, after the findings of primary and secondary fact, and after the ascertainment of principles of law applicable to the matter, there will be the need to make a choice among the principles of law that will be applicable to the facts thus found. In this fourth stage, the judge must make a choice, from a variety of alternative legal principles, of that principle or principles which he or she will apply to the case. And that depends on the judge's own personal preferences. It is not dictated to the judge, but comes from the judge's own personal background. It comes from the judge's value system. Does the judge believe that the terms of a contract must be literally adhered to, however unfair they may be, or does he or she pay attention also to principles of fairness of contract? Is a statute to be applied strictly according to its letter, or according to the spirit and purpose behind it? Is the judge a person who attaches great value to individual rights such as rights of ownership or free expression, or one who believes that those rights should be circumscribed by the interests of society? Depending on these factors, there may be different results on the self-same facts as, for example, on the extent of a doctor's duty to divulge all the details of a medical procedure to the patient. So the fourth stage of judgment — of choosing from a number of available alternatives that which suits the personal preferences of the judge — is a value-laden process. It is not a process of scientific application of logical rules to a certain given set of facts.

With the necessary adaptations, let us take the parallel situation in the medical world. I would expect that a doctor first of all asks himself or herself what are the symptoms. Second, what is the conclusion to be drawn from those symptoms? Third, what remedies are available upon those conclusions? Fourth, how does one make a choice from among the available range of remedies? So that fourth stage seems to me to be present likewise in the medical profession as well. And, there again, the process that the doctor — or medical administrator — goes through is somewhat like the process that the judge goes through. Which is best in the circumstances? Which is best according to my understanding of the needs of society or the needs of the patient? Which is best having regard to social resources? Which is best in the long term rather than the short term? Which is best as indicating a principle of choice that may be useful to the whole community? This last question can assume great importance where resources are scarce and conflicting needs, e.g., of the young and the elderly, compete for those scarce resources. There are lots of questions of this nature, all of which are dependent upon values that the person who makes the decision may entertain. The range of such issues increases dramatically with the progress of technology and the ability of modern medical science to achieve the seemingly miraculous — which raises more than ever before grave questions such as the cost to the community and the desirability of an indefinite prolongation of life when the quality of such life may be so poor as to raise questions regarding its desirability.

So the value-laden decision is found in medicine as in law. And that is a replacement of old traditions such as that a definite result was arrived at by a scientific process through the application of scientific method, or that the object of a doctor's care was the prolongation of life to whatever extent was possible.

EPOCHAL EVENTS OF THE 1960S AND 1970S

How did the choices facing medicine change? How did the importance of value judgments and philosophical considerations assume such a high profile?

In the late 1960s, early 1970s, there was a series of dramatic achievements which compelled consideration of their ethical implications. The heart transplant technique sent a chill down the spine of thinkers in the field of law, philosophy, theology, and needless to say, of medicine. Man was getting so close to tinkering with life, diluting the integrity of the human personality and revealing possibilities for the indefinite prolongation of life, as to throw up a cascade of ethical issues.

In the late 1970s, *in vitro* fertilization procedures focused public attention on the ethics of embryo research and surrogate motherhood, and opened the door to distant possibilities of breeding children in laboratory conditions.[2]

In the early 1970s the case of Karen Quinlan brought ethical issues to the forefront once more, involving the public in them as never before.

These are just three examples of matters which attracted very great popular interest. Different value systems would have led to different judgments as to what should be done. The doctor found himself or herself not only in the glare of publicity, but charged individually with ethical responsibilities for which the traditions of the medical profession offered no guidance. Moreover, in cases such as organ transplants very often an instant decision was requested. If organs were to be transplanted, what procedures needed to be devised to ensure that the donor was truly dead? If one major organ could be transplanted, why not another? What possibilities existed for the transplantation of the brain or sections of it? What safeguards existed against the commercialization of a traffic in human organs such as kidneys, which could be procured from the poorer parts of the world? Could transplants be made from animals? Did this violate religious sensitivities? A Pandora's box of problems was opened.

With the indefinite prolongation of life, problems relating to the quality of life came into the spotlight. What was the minimum quality of life which rendered it worthwhile to prolong a given human life? Was this a subjective or an objective judgment? If the patient could not make the decision for himself or herself, who should do so on behalf of the patient? What were the interests of the community in this matter? Did economic considerations come into the picture? If human life was of infinite value, how could one weigh economic considerations against it?

More than ever before, the problem of the withdrawal of life-support systems raised issues for decision which depended on one's own personal background. Depending on that background and one's personal philosophy, there could be different judgments as to what might be done, although the medical science to be applied was the same. So the value-free idea was gone.

[2] This stimulated the Warnock Report of 1984 in the United Kingdom, and a huge political, ethical and academic debate. A Bill was introduced by Mr. Enoch Powell in the British Parliament outlawing embryo research, which was bitterly attacked by those favouring this line of research — See *The Times*, May 30, 1985 and June 6, 1985 for extensive discussions of the opposing points of view.

MEDICAL ADVANCES BEGET NEW HUMAN RIGHTS PROBLEMS

The development of modern medicine also brought problems of resource allocation into the arena of the medical decision. There is very sophisticated medicine available. Community resources are not large enough to make those remedies available to all and sundry. Sometimes a choice has to be made. Cost-benefit analyses entered the process of decision in various shapes and forms. To take a simple example, let us take the case where one kidney machine is available, but there are three claimants for it. There may have to be a judgment as to which of the three competing patients should be awarded the use of the machine. That situation could arise in practice quite especially in poor, rural communities, and the doctor who is in charge of that particular community resource may have to make a decision on the spot. He or she would literally be dispensing life to A and death to B and C, even more powerfully than any judge in a case of capital crime, and there would be no one to sit in review of his or her judgment. How shall he or she exercise this awesome power of judgment?

To complicate the situation further, let us assume that the three candidates for the one kidney machine are a brilliant young university graduate, a mentally retarded boy, and a social worker whose lifelong record of dedicated service has won national acclaim. How does he or she choose? Is age the criterion, or potential to serve the community, or community service already rendered? On what scales can one weigh one human life against another? I shall have more to say about this later.

There may again be some kinds of treatment that are very expensive to the community. With the sophistication of modern medicine, yesterday's visions become today's possibilities, but the required treatment could be very expensive. I addressed a conference some years ago in Australia on the human rights problems of sufferers from thalassaemia. This raised in an interesting manner a whole spectrum of human rights issues, ranging from privacy issues through problems of cultural conflict, to issues relating to the use of community resources.[3] Nearly every major medical advance spawns its own crop of human rights issues.

NON-MEDICAL COMPONENTS OF MEDICAL DECISIONS

Value judgments, ethical considerations, financial priorities, community standards, cultural traditions, religious concerns — all these come into the making of what was once thought to be a purely medical decision.

[3] See *supra* Chapter 15, for a fuller discussion.

Let me refer to two areas which have in recent times provided much food for thought regarding basic ethical principles applicable to medical practice. The first relates to the sharing of community resources. The second relates to the growing power to influence and control the human mind.

With special reference to developing countries, with shortages of hospital resources, the problems are even more acute. How much time will you allocate in a hospital bed to a person who is suffering from some disease when numerous other claimants for that bed are in desperate need of it? Is one life more valuable than another or do you treat them all on the footing of absolute equality? Maintenance of life support systems becomes all the more critical when community resources are scarce.

In the economic conditions that prevail in large sectors of the world today, the demand for medical technology grows, even as its cost keeps increasing. State insurance schemes are totally unable to absorb the expense. Decisions have to be made constantly on questions of resource allocation for which current patterns of medical training have provided the doctor with no guidance.

Mental health raises a range of problems all of its own. Our knowledge of the human brain — how it works and how it can be controlled — has grown several-fold in the past quarter century. Psychiatric techniques, psychosurgery, chemical manipulation of the human brain have raised the doctor's power over the patient's mind to levels never known before. There is no body of ethical principles coming down from ancient practice that is sufficient to regulate this new-found power. New guidelines must be found.

There can be varying philosophies regarding possible approaches to the problems of the mentally ill — and, depending on one's philosophical background, the range of responses can vary widely. For example, should there be attempts at pharmaceutical or surgical interference with the brains of those who have criminal tendencies? The value judgment that determines one's answers takes one deep into moral territory, and far afield from the pure science of medical knowledge such as is taught in schools.

Care of the aged and the terminally ill raises other fine ethical issues which the medical profession must consider most seriously. To what extent can the quality of life be improved, even in the case of the terminally ill, so that psychologically they can be conditioned to an attitude of enjoyment of life, even in the shadow of the certainty of impending death? I believe the medical profession, in facing such issues, has a great deal to learn from other disciplines, just as in numerous new legal areas touching the quality of life — such as the right to development — the legal profession has much to learn from other disciplines. I refer, in relation to the terminally ill, to wonderful new insights made available to us by the hospice movement which has negatived the old expectation — "Abandon hope all ye who enter here" — which characterized approaches to the problems of the terminally ill. We have been taught by the vibrant ethicism of the hospice movement that new enjoyment of that which remains of life can be built up in the minds of the terminally ill — and that imports new dimensions to medical treatment through greater emphasis on these ethical ideas. Studies of what constitutes the quality of life in ethics-related disciplines can greatly enrich the medical practice of the future.

At all these points there is the possibility that more and more medical decision-making will depend upon the personal ethical background of the decision-maker.

A PARALLEL SCIENTIFIC PROFESSION: ENGINEERING

Doctors are not alone among the science-based professions for whom modern technology has raised a whole crop of new ethical issues. Chemists, physicists, and engineers are all facing this impact, and must give fresh thought to their responsibilities in the light of these ethical imperatives. The honest pursuit of truth is not the only ethic to which they are bound.

Take, for example, the profession of engineers. Engineers, even more than doctors, were of the view that theirs was an exact science and it was for them to decide how they would apply it and they would apply it according to principles which they alone knew. It is my contention that the engineer cannot shut his or her eyes to the purposes to which his or her scientific skill is put. When an engineer is called upon to undertake a given project, there is a duty lying upon the engineer to scrutinize the ethical purpose or the objectives of that particular piece of work, and to see whether it squares with his or her own ethical standards. In relation to the ethical responsibilities of weapons scientists,[4] I believe that under international law there is a duty on scientists, in accordance with the Nuremberg principles, to have regard to the purposes of their work. Such considerations have in recent years made engineering faculties more conscious of the need to introduce into their curricula a growing ethical component.

On an academic visit to the Kirby Hall of Civil Rights at Lafayette College, Pennsylvania, I held a series of seminars for engineers in the Le High Valley, in Pennsylvania, where there are many major engineering projects. The subject was the social responsibilities of engineers.[5] One impression that came through to me very strongly when I was talking to these engineers was

4 See *Nuclear Weapons and Scientific Responsibility*, Longwood Academic, 1987.

5 See Ch. 21 below.

that in recent years they were becoming increasingly alive to the fact that their work, however precise and scientific, was also laden with value judgments, laden with questions of personal preference. As between a variety of alternatives in a given engineering situation, the individual engineer's sense of values assisted in determining the choice. Their response depended on their moral standards, their sense of social needs, and their judgments as to what was in the social interest. In the last analysis, this came down to their sense of basic and comparative values. Engineers are not uncommonly asked to use their skills on a sophisticated project such as a nuclear reactor or a chemical engineering project which could cause considerable damage to the public interest. Their codes of professional ethics were beginning to enter into the area of social responsibility.

If these ethical considerations can be of growing importance in other professions, this is doubly so in the legal profession and in the medical profession.

IMPORTANT RECENT CHANGES

I come now to some important changes that have occurred recently in both our professions.

(i) *The Growth in the Power of the Medical and Legal Professions*

The first is that when one examines the way in which the professions function, one sees that the power of both professions — law and medicine — has grown, again, exponentially. They are both expanding outward. In the old days, the traditional lawyer's hunting ground was largely contract and tort and property and crime. But, today, the law has extended into the spheres of constitutional law, human rights, economics, technology, social welfare, planning law, income tax, administrative law, and international trade law, to name a few. There is counselling to be done at many levels — for example, corporate planning, tax planning, informal dispute resolution, social welfare entitlements, not to speak of counselling in the medico-legal area. Arbitration, international law, indeed, even space law, with its importance for satellite communications — all this has vastly increased the empire of the law. All of this was virtually unknown in the past.

Just as the empire of the law is expanding, so also is the empire of medicine. With the growth of modern technology, there is a vastly increased range of power over the body and the mind of the patient, with a vastly increased range of options available to the doctor. Life can be prolonged beyond anything that was possible in the past. Genes can be tampered with.

Sex can be predetermined, medical infirmities predicted even before birth, personality can be changed. People long deceased can beget children, and new techniques such as microsurgery are constantly pushing back the frontiers of medicine's ability to cope with disease.

(ii) *Increased responsibility resulting from increased power*

Secondly, with increased power comes increased responsibility and a greater obligation to be a custodian of the ethical values of the community. Should individual contractual rights be pushed to the point where they clash with the social interest? Should property rights be pushed to the point where the environment is damaged? Should life be prolonged to the extent of absorbing valuable community resources while the individual in question remains virtually a vegetable? Should the community bear the responsibility that comes with new citizens being born of a parent long deceased? Should sex be preselected? Should the mind be conditioned medically to more responsible social behaviour? When one is close to playing God, what ethical codes should one follow? Should these be left to the discretion of the individual doctor or should not the medical profession take the responsibility of laying down the rules? Or is this the responsibility of society?

(iii) *Clashes of value systems*

Thirdly, both professions are increasingly faced with the problems of the clash of value systems within a community. How does one advise, whether in law or medicine, a future parent who has been advised of a serious defect in a child to be born? Different ethnic or religious groups have different value systems on such matters, and does one advise in such cases according to the traditions of a minority group to which such a person may belong, or of the majority group in the midst of which that person lives? In Australia, for example, in such matters as abortion for foetal defects, it has been recognized that counselling — and indeed the choice of counsellor — should take into account the traditions of the subject's ethnic group.

Does the lawyer or the doctor advise clients or patients according to his or her own set of values, or according to *their* set of values? And, if you are a doctor trained in one set of values, are you competent to advise patients where their thinking is based on a different set of values, or should there be an intermediate adviser, a competent counsellor, who is aware of their set of values and can advise them in that way? Similar problems can arise in every society because, after all, the world is seeing the mixing of people from many different cultural backgrounds and doctors can often encounter this problem of treating a patient from an altogether different cultural background from their own. What set of values do you adopt in deciding how you will give counsel to the person who comes under your influence?

(iv) *Increasing autonomy of client and patient*

Patients served by the medical profession and clients served by the legal profession are now much more questioning than they used to be in the past. Under the influence of modern human rights doctrine there is an emphasis on individualism, so that patients are anxious to be involved. They want to be equal partners. Consultation is not a situation of a doctor talking down to a patient, but an equal relationship between doctor and patient. Respect for the patient's autonomy means that the decision to be made, such as submission to a course of treatment, belongs to the patient and not to the doctor. Case law recognizes this right of the patient "to make his own decision", and elevates this to "a basic human right protected by the common law".[6] As we have just seen, when a matter goes to court today, questions of patients' rights are linked with modern human rights doctrine, thus giving it a firmer conceptual base than was available in the common law alone. The greater importance given to the individual as a result of human rights doctrine reflects itself in the doctor-patient relationship.

The same applies in the field of the law and today's client does not humbly accept a lawyer's or a judge's verdict on his problems in the same way as the clients of a previous generation.

(v) *Increased legislative intrusion*

Fifthly, both professions are alike feeling the intrusion of parliament and other public authorities into areas which were formerly thought to be their professional preserves. For example, in the law, large areas of the law of contract have been the subject of legislation, even to the extent of specifying what constitutes a fair contract — a domain which the law of contract, as administered by the judges, had considered to be sacrosanct. Likewise, if you look at the statute book you will find that there are acts of parliament on many matters which were formerly thought to be purely medical preserves. There are acts of parliament on human tissue, on abortion, on organ transplants, on mental health, on *in vitro* fertilization, on living wills, a whole series of areas which formerly were left untouched by parliament. We thus

[6] *per* Lord Scarman in *Sidaway* v. *Governors of the Bethlem Royal Hospital*, [1985] A.C. 871, at 897.

have, in the United Kingdom for example, an Abortion Act (1967), a Human Tissue Act (1961), and a Mental Health Act (1983). So, as a result of all this, you will find that the whole situation is something far more than the restricted, court room medical jurisprudence we studied in our days as law students or medical students. The narrow little subject which represented the interaction of law and medicine has truly exploded under the influence of new medical issues of great public concern.

(vi) *Growing impact of international law on both professions*

A sixth phenomenon is the growing impact on both professions of international law. I do not think that when we devise courses on professional ethics, or indeed on the core content of the respective disciplines for lawyers or doctors, we can lose sight of the important international developments in these fields.

In the legal field, questions relating to the rights of an accused person in custody, the right to fair trial, the right to freedom from cruel and unusual punishments, protection against arbitrary arrest and detention, the right to freedom of association, the rights of minorities, the rights of the child — all these and a myriad others are constantly influenced by the standards prescribed by international law.

In the medical field, international law, which never entered into the medical curricula, now assumes a role of vital importance. We all know that after World War II in particular, and the violation of medical ethics in occupied territories, and, more particularly, in concentration camps, there was a worldwide demand for laying down international guidelines with a view to stepping up the level of medical ethics. The Nuremberg Trials laid down that doctors who participated in mutilation, torture or human experimentation were committing a crime against humanity, and that superior orders were no defence. The duties of medical personnel in time of war were laid down in international conventions with a degree of precision never known before. This is vitally important in today's world where, despite a so-called global peace, savage wars are raging in dozens of places across the world.

Numerous articles of the Geneva Conventions — and these are applicable to all persons including medical personnel — result in the principle that medical personnel who commit abuses or breaches of international law are subject to punishment.[7] For example, donations of blood for transfusion are allowed only if the donor's agreement is obtained without coercion and then only for therapeutic purposes.

Medical personnel who provide their services in armed conflicts must respect the principles of medical ethics in the same manner as in peacetime.[8] Doctors are required to give care to injured personnel without any distinction based on other than medical criteria.[9] It is prohibited to subject protected persons such as prisoners, whether in time of war or peace, to any medical procedure which is not indicated by their state of health, and to carry out on them any medical, biological, or scientific experiments.[10]

Likewise, all doctors should know their rights under these Conventions, such as that they cannot be compelled to act in a manner contrary to medical ethics.[11]

Other international instruments which should be mentioned are the Declaration of Tokyo of the World Medical Association in 1975 laying down guidelines regarding the role of the doctor when he or she came in contact with a situation where torture or cruel or unusual punishments were being inflicted; the 1982 Resolution of the General Assembly of the United Nations on the Role of Health Personnel in the Protection of Prisoners and Detainees under Torture; and the 1983 World Medical Association Rules Governing the Sick and the Wounded. Indeed, there is a whole plethora of international medical documentation which one has to look at.

Apart from international law applicable to medical personnel in wartime, there is a large body of material pertinent also in time of peace. In 1948 the World Medical Association (WMA), with an impressive membership of around 700,000 doctors, adopted a modern version of the Hippocratic Oath which it called the "Geneva Oath", along with a supplementary "International Code of Medical Ethics". The World Health Organization (WHO) also developed a draft code of medical ethics. Among the rules in the "Geneva

[7] See the *Manual of the International Committee of the Red Cross on the Rights and Duties of Medical Personnel in Armed Conflicts*, ICRC, Geneva, 1982. Among the relevant articles are 3, 44, 49–54 of G I; 3, 44, 45, 50–53 of G II; 3, 13, 129–132 of G III; 3, 146–149 of G IV; 11, 18, 85, 86 of P I; and 4 & 5 of P II.

[8] Art. 16, P I; Art. 10, P II.

[9] *Manual*, *op. cit.*, pp. 39–40.

[10] *Ibid.*, pp. 40–42.

[11] Articles 15 & 16, P I; Articles 9 & 10, P II.

Oath" which may be noted here are the duty of the doctor to abstain from any religious, national, racial, political, or social discrimination in the performance of his or her duty, and not to use his or her medical knowledge against the laws of humanity, even under threat.

Thus no medical society within a domestic jurisdiction can afford to lose sight of the fact that great developments are taking place internationally in the medical ethics field.[12]

The most blatant example of conflict between superior orders and ethical duty emerged in the Nuremberg Trials, where it was revealed that scientists were compelled to perform the most unethical acts under superior orders. The manuals prepared by various countries for the guidance of their armed forces embody the Nuremberg principles, and you will find that many of them recognize the importance, the supreme importance, of the doctor's conscience. For example, the United States Manual for Courts Martial, in paragraph 14, says that "the physician's supreme guide is his conscience". So, there can be a situation where the physician would be able to say, "My commanding officer orders this, but my professional ethical code and my conscience would guide me in the opposite direction", and that would be a good defence. But if you want to pursue this further, I would refer you to the *Levy* case,[13] where a doctor in the United States Armed Forces refused to obey a lawful order which he thought was against his professional ethics. That case has provoked much discussion, and many articles have been written upon it. So, all these are areas which I think we need to look into with greater care and which in our traditional medical and legal curricula just passed us by.

Lawyers, likewise, although they may have neglected international law studies in the past, just cannot afford to do so today because whatever their field, be it criminal law, constitutional law, environmental law, family law, labour law or welfare law, the standards of international law increasingly tend to become the governing standards.

[12] On this topic see, generally, N. Rodley, *The Treatment of Prisoners under International Law*, Clarendon Press, Oxford, 1987; L.C. Green, "War Law and the Medical Profession", in L.C. Green (ed.), *Essays on the Modern Law of War*, Transnational Publishers, 1985; and Françoise J. Hampson, "Conscience in Conflict: The Doctor's Dilemma", (1989) *Canadian Yearbook of International Law*, 203.

[13] *Parker* v. *Levy*, 417 US 733 (1974).

SOME AREAS OF INTERACTION BETWEEN LEGAL PRINCIPLES AND MEDICAL PRACTICE

So far I have spoken in somewhat general terms. I shall now take a few specific examples of problems where law and medicine interact. I shall select just a few, as representative of the sort of problems that might arise.

(i) *The Right to Know*

The development of the patient's right to know is a consequence of the development of the concept of patient autonomy. The patient has a right to be told what's wrong with him or her, what the treatment is, what the treatment proposes to achieve, and what alternatives are available, especially to surgical procedures. But how much is the patient to be told? Is the doctor under an obligation to give the patient a whole medical lecture on the treatment and its possible effects, the dangers, the possible benefits and so on? And, of course, if he or she were talking to a medical student he or she would need hours to explain it at that level. Is that the sort of explanation that is required for a patient? Quite obviously that is not feasible. Do you draw a distinction between the patient who inquires and the patient who does not inquire? There are inquiring patients who want to know. They'll ask the doctor, "Why are you doing this, what will be the effect of this, what are the possible side effects of this?" And there are others who will just take that treatment without inquiring. Are you to give more to the inquiring patient than to the patient who does not inquire? And if the inquiring patient goes too far, and asks you questions the answers to which may demoralize the patient, are you going to answer those as well?

I know of an instance where an inquiring patient who was to have a heart operation asked his doctor for details of the operation. The doctor described these in some detail and the process proceeded smoothly until the doctor said, "And then, of course, we will be taking out your heart and keeping it outside the body for a while. And we will stop your heart for a very short period until we put everything else right." And then the patient said, "And would you be sure you can restart the heart?" And the doctor said, "There's no guarantee", whereupon the patient withdrew from the operation.[14]

Problems of that sort can arise which involve a sense of judgment as to how far one should go, and I notice that the medical traditions of different countries differ on the extent of information which is considered proper and

[14] After some days of reflection, he submitted to an operation, which was performed with great success.

appropriate. Are you entitled to tell the traditional "white lie" to the patient? All these are areas where the good sense of both professions, in association with ethicists and psychologists, must work out some sort of guidelines.

The House of Lords gave its considered attention to this matter in *Sidaway* v. *Governors of Bethlem Royal Hospital*[15] where the plaintiff, who had a spinal operation to relieve pain in her shoulder, suffered severe injuries due to interference with her spinal cord. She had been warned of the risks, but not of the risk of this specific injury. Although her action was dismissed, there were various important pronouncements by the Law Lords. Significant among them was Lord Scarman's observation that the legal standard of disclosure was not to be measured by the standards of the medical profession, but rather by the risks a "prudent patient" would wish to know in the patient's circumstances. Lord Bridge stated that the doctor's duty was "to answer both truthfully and as fully as the questioner requires".[16] Thus the inquiring patient would be entitled to more information than one who does not bother to inquire and, in the words of one commentator, "Accordingly if the doctor is satisfied that the questioner is seeking out information and not simply reassurance, he is required to tell the truth — the whole truth and nothing but the truth".[17]

On this sort of problem the autonomy-oriented judge may reach a different conclusion from the socially-oriented judge on the same set of facts as to what is the duty or the extent of disclosure. The autonomy-oriented judge may desire to enlarge the rights of the patient, while the socially-oriented judge may try to preserve the discretion of the doctor because, otherwise, there would be too much defensive medicine, with resulting damage to the social interest. So, depending on the judge's background thinking, you can have different results, even on the identical facts. What is important is that, whatever his or her basic background, few judges today would proceed on the basis that the doctor knows best. That old theory that the doctor knew best and the patient must take it from the doctor no longer holds good. But within the application of that theory, of course different results can follow.

(ii) *Standards of proof*

Lawyers have various formulae in regard to the burden of proof and the way in which a matter is proved. In a criminal case, there is a certain standard of proof, while in a civil case there is another standard of proof — proof be-

15 [1985] A.C., 871.

16 *Ibid.*, p. 899.

17 Andrew Grubb, (1987) 50 *Modern Law Review*, 241 and 249.

yond reasonable doubt in a criminal case, proof by a balance of probabilities in a civil case. Of course if we are asked to define or quantify what we mean by proof beyond reasonable doubt we find ourselves in difficulties. If somebody were to inquire, "Do you mean 85% proof, or 93% proof, or 78% proof?", no lawyer or judge would be able to answer him. Likewise, when you speak of proof by a balance of probability, do you mean 51%? Of course, if you go strictly on the meaning of words, it could be argued to be 51%, or even 50.01%.

What is the standard of proof of diagnosis that a doctor requires before deciding to act? Can it be quantified? At what level of conviction can a *bona fide* decision to recommend an operation be described as negligent? Here, again, quantification is impossible. These are unanswerable questions, but the experienced professional in both professions has his instinctive and intuitive answer.

Questions of medical proof also raise problems of legal proof. Let us take the case of a medical problem which could be the result of medical negligence, e.g., a clearly wrong diagnosis of an abdominal pain which was treatable had it been correctly diagnosed. In its untreated state, the ailment could cause the death of the patient. Later, under the additional effect of food poisoning, the patient dies. The immediate cause of death was the food poisoning. Had the ailment been properly treated, the medical evidence is that the patient may well have survived. Did the patient die of the food poisoning or the misdiagnosis? Can one assess this in terms of percentages of probability? Since the medical negligence is proved, should not some damages be awarded for it?

(iii) *The principle that the human body or parts thereof are not to be the subject of commerce*

The first kidney transplant took place in the USA in 1954; the first heart transplant in South Africa in 1967. Earlier, the attitude of traditional law to meddling with dead bodies and taking parts from them was that it constituted an act of desecration or of mutilation. But we are past that stage. Nobody any longer argues in that traditional way, so long as the bodily parts are taken with due regard to the principle of consent and the dignity of the dead.

Yet, a whole crop of fresh problems has emerged — the problems of buying and selling organs. You might recently have read of the enormous concern they feel in India at the multi-million dollar trade that has grown up in the buying and selling of organs. The ability of modern medicine to keep the heart and lungs functioning, though the brain is dead, raises questions also as to whether one can take organs from people who are brain-dead. Is it legitimate to keep their bodies pulsating so that the organ can be there for use when required? Or is that repulsive to our moral sensibilities and should we reject this possibility?

Quite recently the international newspapers referred to an interesting Italian case of a man aged about 30 years, who was accused of murder and in need of a good lawyer. Of course, the good lawyers whom he could retain were quite expensive. So he had worked out a novel way of his own. He advertised in the newspaper that he was prepared to sell one of his kidneys in order to raise the money to pay the expensive fees of a good lawyer. Can the law permit even the owner of a bodily organ to attach commercial value to it in that way? Law, as traditionally taught, would feel quite repelled at this possibility. But, then, I have encountered articles in the law journals as early as the 1970s seeking to argue that it is after all not a bad thing to permit a person to gift his organs for a fee because both parties benefit. The poor man gets $10,000 which is a fortune for him. He can live in comfort for the rest of his life and the rich man gets a new lease of life. Argument has been swaying to and fro on this issue, but the fundamental legal principle has been and should be that bodily organs are not for sale.

Then there is the vexed question of foetal tissue. The use of tissue of aborted foetuses is occurring on a very great scale. Foetal brain tissue, I understand, has been found useful in the treatment of Parkinson's disease and foetal pancreatic tissue in the treatment of diabetes. There are probably many other potential uses. Yet, however great its usefulness, the trade in foetuses presents both law and medicine with one of the most poignant problems. Of course the foetus is dead, but are we prepared to permit the foetuses that are discarded to be used for medical or pharmaceutical purposes without regard to parental consent or human dignity? Will not a slackness in this regard encourage a trade in foetuses? And trade can be very unscrupulous where large profits are involved.

(iv) *Questions of consent and autonomy*

Likewise, difficult legal questions arise regarding the taking of organs from children, from the disabled and from the mentally incompetent. Who is empowered to consent on their behalf, if indeed a competent consent can be given? The best interests of the donor would be the legal criterion in such cases, and how can that standard be satisfied? One could mount persuasive arguments the other way in extreme cases. For example, there was a case in the US recently where a feeble-minded person in his twenties gave his consent to a kidney donation for a brother whom he loved dearly. There could be an argument supporting such consent on the grounds that the donor would be distressed if his brother died for lack of a kidney donation, leading to a later feeling of guilt and a feeling of anger if the guardian had refused to confirm the consent. Both law and medicine are helpless in the face of such problems and perhaps need ethical guidance and community support in reaching the correct decision.

Suppose somebody wants, for financial reasons, to donate an organ and the doctor tells him, "No, it is too dangerous". Can he still insist on the procedure? If the doctor tells him, "You shall not do it", is the doctor infringing on his autonomy? Is it for the doctor to dictate to him if, with all the information that is available to him, he makes up his mind that he will take that risk? Some writers argue that the case is no different in principle from the case of the stuntman who risks his entire life to earn some money, or from the case of the professional boxer who risks his life in order to earn a living out of his profession. Is there a difference in quality between the two? How do you differentiate? These are very difficult problems.

In relation to the use of human tissue, here, again, there is a constellation of problems. Human tissue can of course be used *post mortem* with due respect for the dead. The question arises — to what extent can you use tissue that is discarded after an operation? There was an interesting Australian case of a woman who had a hysterectomy and, normally, after that, I suppose that part would be discarded. And it could be used for research or other medical purposes. But in this particular case, the woman said she wanted her uterus which the doctors wanted for research. She insisted on having her uterus back and she went to court over it. The court ruled that if she wanted it, she must have it, and it was returned to her. This illustrates the variety of values and attitudes that people bring to bear on matters of this sort.

(v) *The principle that every human life is equal and of infinite value*

Here's another example — value judgements regarding priorities. A traditional illustration given to us in our law school days was that there are three people on a raft — yourself and two others. You are the only one who knows how to navigate the raft, so, if anyone at all is to survive, your presence is essential. The raft can carry only two, and is certain to capsize with three on board, in which event all three lives will be lost. The two other people are a prince and a penniless young man whose background nobody knows about. If one person is tossed overboard, two will survive. If not, all three will perish. What does one do? Is one entitled to make a choice or must all three perish? And if a choice is to be made, how does one choose between the prince and the pauper? The problems are much more complex now. Similar situations arise every day in relation to the allocation of medical resources.

The scarce resources in a hospital may throw up a problem regarding the allocation of the last remaining bed in its intensive care unit. What is the criterion that you would apply? Do you allocate it on the "first come, first served" principle? Is it given, irrespective of other considerations, to the person who is foremost in the queue? Or do you give it to the person who is most sick? Or do you give it to the person who has the greatest chance of recovery? Do you give it to the most valuable person? We have referred to a similar problem earlier.

Then again, are you to be guided by the length of time during which that person may enjoy the benefit? You have an old person and a young person. Do you discard the old person because he has only a few years of life left, in favour of the young person because he prospectively has more? But the old person may be the Rembrandt of his generation and the young person may be one whose potential is yet untried. And if you save the life of the Rembrandt he might not produce any tremendous works of art in his remaining five years. So are those factors that you are entitled to take into account? Current legal literature contains many reflections on such matters and so, I am sure, does the medical literature. But all of these are issues of ethics and all of these cannot be answered purely from the principles you find in the books on law and medicine. In fact, they give us no guidance whatsoever.

(vi) *The question of the right to die*

Euthanasia is the subject of great debate. It has attracted immense national and international attention.[18] People talk of the right to die. I don't know whether there is such a thing as a right to die, because if you have a right to die, an unqualified right to die, that means that you ought to be able to decide that you will commit suicide, but the law does not permit that. If the right to die were an unqualified right of the individual, there could be a suicide machine in the corner drugstore, or suicide pills in the supermarket! So there isn't an unqualified right to die. Even the most extreme proponents of euthanasia would concede that there is no unqualified right to die.

But they would say that a person who is *in extremis*, a person who is in terrible physical condition and feels that life is not worth living, should be given a right to die. That might be one way of arguing it but, once you propound a limitation of that sort, the question is where do you draw the line? Once you stipulate the standard of life being *in extremis*, or life being totally

[18] A country that has now gone very far along this path is The Netherlands. See I.J. Keown, "The Law and Practice of Euthanasia in The Netherlands", 108 *LQR*, p. 51 (1992).

not worth living, might not that margin start shifting as the community gets accustomed to the idea that there is such a right? Might not doctors themselves start shifting the line? This of course would be a heavily unpoliced area where everything would depend on the patient and the doctor. Would that be socially desirable?

Who decides? And according to what standards? And whose standards? Do you decide according to the standards of the patient or according to the ethical values of the doctor? What if there are relatives waiting in the wings who might benefit from the inheritance? What ethical standards do you adopt? It is a gigantic problem.

In high medical decision-making, as in legal, there is no decision you can take which does not have a ripple effect upon society. We need to be intensely conscious of this.

If you start by permitting a doctor to terminate the life of one who is extremely sick, the dividing line between the permissible and the impermissible starts shifting and the climate of opinion changes. This could be extremely dangerous.

Indeed, it could have an effect upon the old and the sick themselves, who may begin to think that if they are a burden to the community, they have a duty to stop making a burden of themselves.

(vii) *The "living will"*

The problem under discussion has sometimes been thought to be partially solved by the device of the 'living will". The living will is a device by which you can make a declaration which you might carry on your person, which says that if you are reduced unfortunately to a situation where you would lead only a vegetable existence, you do not want to be kept alive. That raises another awesome problem because it is very difficult for us in our state of knowledge to know how a person who is extremely ill feels about the continuance of life. We may guess how a vigorous 30-year old would think, in the fullness and vigour of youth. He would not perhaps value a life which is decrepit and spent in a wheelchair. From his 30-year old, vigorous, physical standard, he might think that, "If I am ever reduced to that situation, well, let me go". But when he comes to that situation, 50 years later by a series of gradual declines, he may still value at 80 the lifestyle which he had hypothetically rejected at 30. We do know, and doctors know better than we do, that there are lots of people who cling to life despite being desperately ill. That is because they value life. And because they value life, it is for those who attend to them to give them the means of continuing to enjoy that which they value. However hard it may be for them, it is their choice. So the living will has got that great logical flaw that you are applying to the standards of a person who is terribly ill the standards which he used for himself when he might have been exceedingly well. And I don't know whether that would be quite correct.

The Karen Quinlan case raised a whole lot of these issues concerning the situation where patients and families sought to have life-support systems — and indeed further treatment — stopped on grounds of futility of treatment and unnecessary suffering at a time when the medical ethic was seen as requiring treatment until the very end.[19] Today, in the 1990s, there has been a swing towards giving a pre-eminent place to the principle of patient autonomy.

But there are also converse situations of the Quinlan case. There have been recent cases, for example, where a seventy-four year old patient, who was in end-case renal failure, refused blood transfusion and yet insisted on resuscitation in the event of another cardiac arrest (which the physician thought futile), and where a thirty-six year old man suffering from AIDS was placed on a ventilator and had become mentally incompetent, but his partner intervened, saying they had discussed the matter and the patient had stated, "Don't let them give up on me".[20] Such situations are the opposite of the Karen Quinlan case. Suppose, in such situations, the physician, in his or her medical wisdom, feels this is a medically futile case, there is nothing the physician can do. Is it the doctor's assessment or is it the patient's wish that must prevail? And if that is communicated to the doctor who says that this is a hopeless case and that it is nothing but a waste of community resources to keep this person alive, is the doctor entitled to take that point of view or, in consequence of the doctrine of individual autonomy, must greater weight be given to what that patient desires? So, even though it may look medically hopeless, even though they may be suffering visibly for all to see, if they want to cling on to life, that is their decision and has to be honoured.

(viii) *Growing foetuses* in vitro

Monash University, where I taught for many years, was one of the pioneers in *in vitro* fertilization research. Once *in vitro* fertilization takes place, the question arises, "How long can you keep the foetus alive *in vitro*, how long

[19] For a recent discussion, see Robert M. Veatch, "Medically Futile Care: The Role of the Physician in Setting Limits", XVIII *American Journal of Law and Medicine* (1992), p. 15; Lawrence J. Schneiderman, *et al*, "Medical Futility: Its Ethic and Implications", 112 *Annals of Internal Medicine* (1990), 949.

[20] Veatch, *supra.*, p. 17.

can you keep it alive in laboratory conditions?" Of course, we do not know of cases where a foetus has been kept alive for a significant period of time in those conditions, but one does not know where such research is being conducted, and when some researcher, somewhere, may burst upon the world the news that a foetus has been kept alive in laboratory conditions for the full gestation term. What if some day there should be a possibility of keeping the foetus alive until five or six months? What happens then? It has been rightly said in this context that all hell would then break loose in the world of the law because, once you can do that, there is a potential human being, for such a foetus could well be viable. Grave legal questions arise as to the particular point of time at which it becomes a human being, vested with all the rights of a human being. In short, we do not know when this new human being comes into its own. Since, under our legal systems, all assertible rights enure only to human beings, there is a virtual *carte blanche* given to the controllers of the laboratory where the foetus is growing to terminate that potential human life.

To determine questions of entry into the human community, all races have, from the beginning of time, used the traditional landmark event of birth. None other has ever been dreamt of in the wildest flights of poetic fancy — certainly not decantation from a bottle. Yet that could certainly be upon us and find both law and medicine totally unable to grapple with the problem.

Under such a dispensation, a new human life begins not when it issues forth from the womb, but when, at the discretion of the controller of the laboratory, it issues forth from the bottle! If he wants to keep it there for the rest of time, he may. If he wants to deep freeze it, he may. If he wants to destroy it before releasing it from the bottle, he may. By what laws is he bound? Are there enforceable criteria? All this is shrouded in the mists of uncertainty.

(ix) *The Integrity of the Human Personality*

Profound questions arise regarding the integrity of the human personality in consequence of modern surgical and medical techniques of interfering with the thought processes of people. Much of this is done with the most commendable intentions, but here, as elsewhere, the potential for abuse raises grave questions.

Psychosurgery, which treats people by surgical invasions of the human brain, can of course be a valuable form of treatment for certain mental conditions. Yet it opens up possibilities of deliberate conditioning of the brain which can be resorted to, particularly in instances of complete confinement.

This has been known to be done by law enforcement authorities so as to bring a person who is usually given to rough behaviour to a more docile condition. Apart from prison officials, an unscrupulous government or dictatorship could also do this. Who takes the decision? What of the requirement of consent? Who consents on their behalf? Can this procedure, apart from being used to curb violence, be used to modify personality? To what extent can drugs be permitted to achieve the same ends? Indeed, it shocked the legal and medical professions a great deal recently when it was known that tens of thousands of unnecessary psychosurgical operations had been performed in the early days of psychosurgery.[21]

(x) *Surrogate motherhood*

Another meeting point of law and medicine is in regard to surrogate motherhood.

Vast legal questions are involved here — the surrender of rights of motherhood, commercial disposal of the fruits of pregnancy, the commercialization of the human body, the sale of children.

Contrariwise, one can speak of individual autonomy, the happiness of the recipient, the altruistic desire to help people who cannot have children on their own.

We in Sri Lanka have not faced this problem yet, but doubtless it will surface in one form or another and may even be commercialized on a substantial scale. The professions must pool their wisdom on this matter and reach a solution, seeking for that purpose the assistance of other sections of the community as well.

* * *

There is a range of problems of this sort which law and medicine have to grapple with, without the necessary legal or medical guidelines, but only with ethical tools to help them. The professions are in the common situation that their traditional disciplines have been so wholly overtaken by scientific advances that they are in much confusion as to how they should respond. It is in the field of ethics, rather than in their traditional repositories of learning, that the two professions will find the necessary answers.

These are some of the prospects we all face in the future. What can we do by way of helping the community through this jungle of ethical problems?

21 Psychosurgery is somewhat more fully dealt with in Chapter 17*(b)* of this book.

May I just toss out a few suggestions because this is a joint meeting of the two professions.

(i) *Multidisciplinary Committees*

An outstanding instance of a body that was set up to look into this sort of matter was President Carter's President's Commission for the Study of Ethical Problems in Medicine and Bio-Medical and Behavioural Research. It has some very distinguished reports to its credit. In Sri Lanka, there is room for a highly qualified Committee of that sort, comprising both professions, and also theologians, sociologists, community workers, and ethicists. Moreover, we have in our country an infinite richness of varied ethical backgrounds — Buddhist, Hindu, Christian, and Islamic — and we can draw copiously from these sources. Community workers, sociologists and others can keep track of the way in which these numerous developments in medical science are raising a whole spectrum of ethical problems which are of great importance to the community, and refer them to the Committee. Parliament, likewise, could refer questions to them for informed study and report.

(ii) *Statistical Surveys*

There are many areas where statistical surveys may be necessary as a prelude to the reference of such matters to the Committee. Take, for example, the case of traffic in organs. In India, and I am sure in Sri Lanka too, it would be a problem which sooner or later would require some sort of fairly detailed study. We do not know to what extent this traffic is in fact already in progress, and in what way and by whom it is conducted. In India, they have described it as a multi-million dollar business. Should there not be a committee investigating this trade and compiling information? Likewise, we need statistics of the number of patients who may require modern medical apparatus such as kidney machines, and how many such machines are available. As medical facilities grow, we shall need statistics regarding the numbers of people requiring sophisticated medical treatment of various kinds, the number of persons *in extremis* who are on life-support systems, the quantities of substandard drugs unloaded here by pharmaceutical companies, the number of terminal tobacco-induced lung cancers languishing in hospitals. The problems are numerous and we are not paying adequate attention to them for lack of statistical information.

(iii) *References to the Law Reform Commission*

Law Reform Commissions are too busy usually for this kind of venture, though if sufficiently interested, they can prove extremely useful in this area. An outstanding example was the Australian Law Reform Commission under Mr. Justice Kirby. This Law Reform Commission concerned itself very much with this sort of issue, and produced a number of pioneering studies on this topic which have proved useful, not merely in Australia, but throughout the world. The problems of a developing society like ours can be quite different from those of more economically developed societies, and, with the advanced medical and legal skills available in this country, we could make studies which could be of great use throughout the developing world.

(iv) *Interdisciplinary education*

Interdisciplinary teaching has been vastly neglected in legal and medical education. There is room for a much heavier ethical component in schools of both Law and Medicine. Theologians, ethicists, judges, and community workers could be invited to deliver lectures to law students and medical students in these areas. Medical jurisprudence courses need to be widened. In law, we should not drop the philosophical content of the legal course. Jurisprudence or legal philosophy should still continue. Very often, we find lawyers and judges discussing some great question of principle as though they were discussing it for the first time, not aware that from the time of Aristotle this particular issue has been discussed in very great detail. That can happen if you do not have a component of philosophy in a law course, and I would suggest that our legal courses be weighted a little more with philosophy. The same applies to courses in medicine.

(v) *Ethics committees in universities and hospitals*

It is important to have ethics committees in every hospital and university. I understand the university has an ethics committee, but hospitals, too, could have an ethics committee which deals with such questions as medical experimentation and withdrawal of life support systems. Having been on the ethics committee of Monash University and of the Queen Victoria Hospital in Melbourne, I am aware of the range of problems that can surface, often quite unexpectedly. The range of ethical matters that need attention, but which would be swept under the carpet if there is no ethics committee, is quite astonishing. These problems require the concentrated wisdom of lawyers, doctors, theologians, community representatives, and others, and they build up an ethical climate as these decisions increase, and set trends in medical ethics. Especially in a developing country, there is the constant danger, for example, of medical experimentation being financed by some other agency, like a pharmaceutical company, which wants some new technique tried out in the developing world before they release it in the developed world. Rich rewards can be offered to those who conduct it — doctors included. Doctors or scientists undertaking such research should be required to place it before the Committee for clearance before they can undertake it. Such matters need to be carefully scrutinized.

* * *

These are some areas where it may be possible, with our combined experience and knowledge, to devise some means of assisting the community in medico-legal ethical matters. The problems are growing from day to day. Every advance in scientific knowledge opens up a whole new range of problems. These have to be addressed with vigour. We will not serve our people well unless we match the dynamism of this area with an intellectual dynamism of our own.

20. Microbiologists[*]

A VOYAGE INTO THE UNKNOWN

The microbiologist must today feel like Cortes when, lonely, upon a peak in Darien, he surveyed the vast Pacific and knew not what it held for humanity or himself. In its vast expanses might be immense wealth beyond the dreams of avarice, or whirlpools, tornadoes and sea monsters that might be the destruction of all who ventured there.

But there the analogy halts, for Cortes was not surveying an unbounded sea; and the supposed dangers were such as mankind had visualized for centuries. Microbiology, on the other hand, faces a vast and limitless expanse of knowledge, a new and unprecedented universe of concepts and experience.

I come to this topic as a layman, unversed in all the esoteric knowledge that underlies the current debate. I see, however, that amongst the undoubted experts there is a division of opinion — on fundamentals. Where long years ago lone voices were heard to warn us of impending dangers, we are today in a situation where those voices have been immeasurably strengthened by the voices of those who command the greatest and most up to date expertise. We are in a situation where Nobel prize-winners are divided and the public knows not to whom to turn.

This is not a debate such as one often encounters in the frequent differences of opinion among technical experts. As lawyers, we are well accustomed to seeing experts divided in their views.

This is not such a debate. It is a debate concerning matters vital to the future and, indeed, the survival of the human race. We are warned that an

[*] Address delivered at the Annual Conference of the Australian Society of Microbiology, May 1977. At the time of this paper, a considerable debate was in progress on the question of a moratorium on recombinant DNA experimentation, in view of the possibility of new microbes of unknown potential being released into the atmosphere. As humans would have no resistance to these new creations, it was feared that they might have the potential to decimate the human population. Some of these issues have been more specifically dealt with in Ch. 14 above.

issue exists as gravely fundamental as this and that the ranks of microbiology stand divided. Where can we, as laymen, turn except to appeal for caution? What course can we adopt but plead that if the issues are as yet unclear, we stay our hand until the mists dissolve? And, with all respect, are scientific experts our best guides?

In matters of this nature time is not of the essence. We have all time ahead of us and we are not in a race to meet an iron deadline. If, on the other hand, we hasten to a wrong and irreversible step; our entire future can be jeopardized — not merely because we lawyers and laymen have such fears, but also because, from those who know their science, sufficient has emerged to justify any judge in pronouncing that a debatable issue exists.

A BASIC DEMOCRATIC PRINCIPLE

We laymen have seen the current microbiology debate on TV and in the print magazines and we sometimes wonder at the heat displayed on the question of uninhibited research. We see strong language used and strong emotions roused.[1] As laymen we can only point out that emotion never settles an argument nor makes right that which was wrong before. We point out also that, on issues of this nature involving the whole community, the ultimate judge must be the layman, not the scientist, and if it takes time to educate the layman to an understanding of the issue, the layman is entitled to that time. It is a basic democratic principle that, whatever the interests involved — be they private property, or specialist knowledge, or privilege of any sort — the public interest stands paramount, and to that all these must yield. If, arguably, the future of the race is at stake, I submit there is no basis for a claim that the decision whether the risk is to be taken or not can be taken behind the closed doors of the scientific community — in this case not all the scientific community, but only the microbiological.

I argue that the first social responsibility of the microbiologist in these circumstances is to stay his or her hand on doubtful research and to support the principle of moratoria if a debatable issue exists concerning a matter fundamental to the human future. The problems we face in this field are of so unprecedented a nature that there is little that past human experience can offer us as guidelines.

When Plato expressed his views on eugenics and the way in which the human race should be improved by selective breeding, he was considering

[1] The reference is to the virulence of the debate then taking place among microbiologists. At the Asilomar conference, scientists attacked each other personally in the most vituperative terms.

the problem in the limited perspectives of the knowledge of his day. What he would say if the science of his time was capable of releasing into the biosphere a microbe of unknown and irreversible potential for good or evil we do not know. However, with his deep concern for humanity and its well being, I do not see even Plato, with all his ideas of regimentation for the public good, permitting haste to cloud decision. The matter would have been one for his philosopher kings — not for the technologists or technicians — to decide, and their mature deliberations would have required fuller information and more deliberation time. In matters of this moment we can ask for no less.

BRINK SITUATIONS COMPARED

Very special responsibilities now lie upon microbiologists by reason of current advances placing them in what has been described as a "brink situation" — a situation wherein a few further advances can well take mankind over the brink. We have met this situation in atomic physics and learnt to live with it for a generation. In that sphere we have had the good fortune to survive, despite all the odds, merely because the prospect of retaliation has held prospective contenders at bay.

In microbiology there is no such danger arising from a clash of opposing forces. Progress is all one-way and the only element of restraint is one that can emerge from the social consciousness of the microbiologist. Such a background, coupled with the fact that microbiological research is, like atomic research, one of the outstanding instances of the brink situation, must necessarily make for a greater consciousness of social responsibility among the fraternity of microbiologists.

The brink situation in the sphere of microbiology is in a sense more complex than the brink situation that arose in atomic physics. There it was only a question of unleashing dangerous physical power. Here there is no doubt an unleashing of forces fraught with great powers of destruction. But it is very much more, for, uniquely in human history, it brings within human reach the power of moulding to a pattern the physical, mental and emotional qualities of man. There immediately arises an ethical debate regarding the moral propriety of such activity, for such work directly assails the concept of the sanctity and inviolability of human personality. If technology brings this power within reach, it opens up with intense immediacy a problem which mankind from the time of the ancient Greeks has discussed rather academically but has never hitherto felt the need to get to grips with. We must resolve the questions whether such a power should be exercised and, if so, who is to have authority to exercise it. And we must ask ourselves who is to be the arbiter of the social interest and of the individual's welfare, when power is available which is large enough to create new species, to create tailor-made humans,[2] and even to interfere with the genes of unborn generations.

If legal principles are demonstrably inadequate, then all the more does moral responsibility lie on the microbiologist to exercise this power with responsibility, especially in the absence of a framework of legal constraints.

I proceed to an examination of some specific areas.

THE NEED FOR ETHICAL CODES

As knowledge grows, it may be possible to build in certain characteristics, remove others, shape aptitudes for pre-selected social roles, perhaps breed entire communities to a set pattern.[3]

The argument will no doubt be advanced that the interests of science and knowledge must not be thwarted by such possibilities, but that once we have the knowledge we must then turn it only to social and desirable uses. As already observed, human experience has however been the reverse, and history consistently demonstrates the stark fact that knowledge which can give power will always be used. The fields in which such knowledge has not been used are fields where its use has been held back not by ethics but by fear of retaliation — as in germ or nuclear warfare. No such restraints operate in this field. The only restraints will emerge from the heightened social consciousness of the scientist and that is where an especial onus lies upon the microbiologist.

The profession hence needs, I submit, to address itself urgently to these ethical aspects so as to provide its members with some basic guidelines, against the prevalent background of obscurity surrounding philosophical and social thinking on these issues. Science is marching ahead of philosophy and law, and cannot do so blindfolded. If adequate guidance does not filter through to it from other sources, it must itself be the trail blazer and lead the community in its thinking. But I would submit, with all respect, that this aspect of its responsibilities has thus far suffered from comparative neglect. Plato spoke eloquently of the need for philosopher kings. Our age urgently needs philosopher-scientists when it begins to tinker with individuality, with humanness and, indeed, with creation.

The creation of ethical codes for any profession involves the creation of rules and guidelines at different levels — binding rules of conduct, principles

2 See June Goodfield, *Playing God: Genetic Engineering and the Manipulation of Life*, Hutchinson, 1977, esp. CHs. 3 and 4.

3 Kass, "New Beginnings in Life", *New York Times*, Feb. 15, 1969.

of conduct, precedents of conduct, which gradually develop into the practice of the profession and, indeed, the creation of moral attitudes towards the activity in question. A recent writer in the field of genetic engineering describes these aspects under the intriguing titles of creating new commandments, creating new guidelines, creating new precedents, and creating new moralities.[4] One needs conscious activity at all these levels if the problem is to be adequately addressed.

ECTOGENETIC RESEARCH

The *New York Times* of February 15, 1969 quoted Dr. Donald Gould, editor of the *New Scientist*, in these terms: "What happens to the embryos which are discarded at the end of the day — washed down the sink? There would necessarily be many. Would this amount to abortion — or to murder? We have no law to cope with this kind of situation."[5]

The reference was to experimentation in the growing of human foetuses in artificial conditions. The background was the actuality that such experiments had already been in progress for at least a few years. The fact that the achievement of bringing such a baby to full maturity yet lay at least a generation ahead could not cloud the ethical and legal issues involved, for it is now they must be attended to rather than when success has already been achieved.

The present state of ectogenetic research shows us that it is possible to achieve a successful fertilization of a human egg and to nurture such an embryo in the laboratory for short periods, variously estimated from a few hours to even a few days.[6] Dr. Bentley Glass, a past president of the American Association for the Advancement of Science, is reported to have warned us that before the year 2000, human ectogenesis from conception to decantation will have been achieved.[7] Dr. John Rock at Harvard, Dr. Landrum Shettles at Columbia, and Dr. R. G. Edwards at Cambridge are all reported to have succeeded in human test-tube fertilization and growth of the embryo up to various stages of initial development.[8]

[4] June Goodfield, *op. cit.*, Chs. 6–9.

[5] See *TIME*, April 19, 1971, 36, 48. Dr. Daniele Petrucci of Bologna was reported to have kept alive an ectogenetic embryo for nearly two months as early as 1961.

[6] Kevin Abel, "The Legal Implications of Ectogenetic Research", 10 *Tulsa Law Journal*, 243 at 245.

[7] *Ibid.*

[8] Bernard Davis, *Trends in Biochemical Sciences (TIBS)*, August 1976, p. N178.

In the twenty years that have elapsed since this address was delivered, vast advances have no doubt been made. As this book goes to press in 1998, we are perilously near the forecast date of the year 2000. Could we wake up one day to the headline news that the breakthrough has been achieved? Twenty years of valuable time would then have been squandered for devising ways of putting the genie back in the bottle!

We know that such experimentation is undoubtedly in progress in many laboratories across the globe. There will surely be thousands of instances between today and the day when the complete process of gestation would have been successfully accomplished, in which individual experiments will be brought to an end in consequence of abnormalities. It is certainly conceivable that these experiments will be conducted on a massive scale, with a thousand test tubes taking the place of the single test tube with which early researchers began. Can the community look on with unconcern when these embryos are washed down the drain?

The thought is unpleasant but the reality needs to be faced and the community must make up its mind. It will not, unless it knows the facts and realizes the issues. The duty of alerting it lies clearly upon the scientists indulging in these experiments — not merely because they concern ethics and morals, but also because they open frightening possibilities of abuse by the powerful if so minded.

Concepts of parenthood and parental responsibility are already changing under the influence of *in vitro* fertilization and embryo transplantation. It is already routine procedure to remove the eggs of an infertile woman, fertilize them in the laboratory, and transplant the resultant embryo into the woman's uterus. It may, where the woman is incapable of carrying the child in her womb, be transplanted into the womb of another woman who acts as surrogate mother and bears the child, perhaps for a fee, or perhaps for other considerations, raising grave contractual and human rights considerations regarding motherhood. Likewise, semen banks, already a reality, are bringing concepts of paternity into the melting pot and the commercial exploitation of sperm sales, especially from talented donors such as Nobel prizewinners, is widely reported in the international press.

Cloning is already talked of — a process by which reproduction is possible from the cells of a single progenitor. Concepts of parentage, as mankind has understood them from the beginning of time, can disintegrate under the force of such biological "achievement" should it ever become reality.

Microbiologists will need to resort to philosophy to untangle these issues. They fail in their duty if they address themselves mechanically to their research, without giving thought to them. They need also to educate others in the benefits as well as the dangers, so that the community becomes alive to the issues when the time for decision comes.

It is often argued that acceptance of the commencement of a line of experimentation does not mean acceptance of all the undesirable consequences that ensue from it — an argument which, as I have submitted, must be viewed against the consistent record of history that knowledge which opens new paths to power will never pass unused. A decision which may be ethically right can be practically wrong if we know that, irrespective of its "rightness" at the time, it will be used to further the ends of "wrongness".

In law we are accustomed to speaking often of the "foreseeability test" in regard to accountability for the consequences of one's actions. Can we not invoke some assistance from this principle in relation to this debate? We speak in law of the "*novus actus interveniens*" as an exonerating factor when some unforeseen act intervenes between the cause and the eventual consequence. When we know that third parties are standing by, waiting to misuse any knowledge that comes within their reach, can we claim that such act is unforeseen and hence a *novus actus interveniens*? We all foresee it and know it will intervene. Can the scientist claim exoneration on the ground of unforeseeability?

One does not know the answers. One only knows that the issues are insufficiently realized, and even more insufficiently discussed. I would draw your attention to them and suggest certain ethical duties in this regard. While it is not given to us to have the prescience to solve these problems, we can still try, and avoid thereby the reproach that an age of so much achievement has been an age of too much apathy — conduct particularly culpable in a generation privileged to stand at a watershed in human history.

GENETIC ENGINEERING

The complexity of genetic manipulation is a subject beyond the layman's capacity to comprehend. What the layman does understand is that scientists are now able to stitch together blocs of DNA from different sources, producing combinations which even the strongest proponents of uninhibited research[9] have conceded could not have arisen in nature in one step. The incorporation of mammalian DNA into bacteria is, even they concede, a danger, though a danger which they submit can be avoided or contained.

When against this background we are warned by scientists of equal competence[10] that:

9 Bernard Davis, *op. cit.*

10 *Ibid.*

> in simple truth it is impossible from present knowledge to predict the consequence of the introduction of such organisms into our existent biosphere. Our present understanding of the principles and detailed process of biological evolution is simply inadequate.

We feel we are justified in adducing the argument that we must tread warily till the consequences become clearer. If, as Professor Sinsheimer tells us, "it is simply impossible to predict the past or present likelihood of such events in the intestines of man or other animals", we become strengthened in this view.

Joseph Califano, Health, Education and Welfare Secretary in the Carter administration, appeared before a Senate sub-committee to ask Congress to impose federal restrictions on recombinant DNA research. He was voicing precisely these fears and bewilderment. He described recombinant DNA as "a scientific tool of enormous potential", warned about possible though unknown hazards, and observed that there was no reasonable alternative to regulation under law.[11] The fear expressed by Sir MacFarlane Burnet, the eminent Australian scientist who had warned that bacteria of unknown potential might be created which could cut through the human population of the planet as myxomatosis once cut through the rabbit population of Australia, was at last being heeded.

Since these events, much water has flowed under the bridges. Scientists have met at a notable conference at Asilomar where all the issues were aired in great depth. They have taken the historic step of imposing a limited moratorium on this species of research. They have voluntarily subjected themselves to a series of very stringent guidelines in regard to the safety conditions under which these experiments are to be performed. With experience, some of the original fears have been proved groundless and some of the stringencies have been relaxed. Still, all portentous possibilities have not been eliminated and we still face many unknowns. All causes of lay fears have not been laid at rest.

While reiterating the layman's fears, it becomes legitimate to raise the question whether in these areas the scientist is not himself or herself a layman, with an altogether inadequate equipment to face the great unknown. Here is a breakthrough in science which parallels in sheer practical impact the extraction of energy from the atom. For the first time nature's processes of ordering genetic change cease to be nature's monopoly. For the first time we have the power to steer living organisms away from the genetic patterns with which millions of years of evolution have endowed them — not by

[11] *TIME*, April 18, 1977, p. 48.

mere processes of breeding, but by the process of chopping up the chains of molecules which are the building bricks of life. The barriers which nature had set up against the combination of genes have been breached and once we launch out on this activity of fashioning unprecedented genes, where will we end, considering the almost limitless repertoire of genes that are available to the scientist and the truly limitless number of possible combinations?

Dr. Robert Sinsheimer tells us: "Few people that I know would argue that one could not by these techniques *design* some quite fearsome micro-organisms."[12]

The argument seems then to centre not on the innocuousness of such organisms, but on the good sense that will prevent such organisms from being created. But good sense cannot be assured in all scientists and for all time, nor can one be assured either that such good sense will not be overpowered by demands from superior authority. Indeed, the picture has been painted of a possibility of rule through microbiology in the sense of immunizing one's supporters — or indeed an entire nation — against some particular microbe and then releasing it to do its deadliest against the rest of the world.[13]

In discussing problems of this nature we must allow ourselves a vision that is of longer range than one that takes in the work of just the next generation or two.

We are at a watershed in science and you microbiologists are privileged to belong to that department of science which enjoys uniquely the power to mould the human being and his or her environment in a real, physical, biological sense. What you are doing in your laboratories now has the potential to enrich civilization or to destroy it. We already see glimmerings of possibilities of pre-ordaining sex, of baby factories, of reproduction without males, of organ banks, of man-animal transplants, of cyborgs (hybrids of man and machine — from cybernetic organisms), of cryonic suspension ("deepfreezing" human beings), of arresting death, of raising a breed of hyper-intelligent individuals, of memory injection, and of brain-computer links. Biological engineers are reported to have begun the task of human genetic mapping — the identification and location of each gene along the forty-six human chromosomes.[14] Parthenogenesis, which will produce an individual of the same sex as its parents, but not a twin of its parent, and cloning which will produce an exact copy of the parent, are already the subjects of experimentation with non-human subjects; and the expertise which is being built up will slowly take the experimenter up the scale of life.

12 *TIBS*, August 1976, p. N179.

13 G. Rattray Taylor, *The Biological Time Bomb*, Mentor Books, 1969, pp. 185 *et seq.*

14 See, further, *supra*, Ch. 14.

Many of these researches may only achieve success in the distant future. Some of them are conceivably within the range of achievement before the century is out.

Any one of these can turn society upside down and call for a complete reassessment of all our traditional values and social systems. What is needed above all is to focus attention on these issues before they overtake us and to consider how microbiology proposes to address itself to its ethical responsibilities in this regard. I see it as an obligation of each body of microbiologists to set up immediately a futures committee, co-opting some element of lay and legal membership, to assist it in looking at these problems.

PRIVATELY SPONSORED RESEARCH

Another aspect of the microbiologist's social responsibilities arises from the financial interests of pharmaceutical companies in DNA research. The issue has surfaced recently in America of the extent to which the National Institute of Health (NIH) guidelines on DNA research ought to be observed by pharmaceutical companies engaged in this field.

These companies are already admittedly carrying out recombinant DNA research and expect that they will thereby be able to achieve many desirable objectives which are both beneficial to society and profitable to themselves, as for example producing insulin, breaking up oil globules or inducing in plants a greater protein content which will help to solve the world's food problems. They are anxious to get on to these breakthroughs ahead of their competitors and, indeed, they have sought and obtained patents for the new life forms they are creating.

There is here a situation of conflict between interest and duty. There is, on the one hand, their interest in profit and, on the other, their duty to the community. In the event of conflict between these opposing forces, where do they stand? The pharmaceutical firms claim that they are self-policing their activities, and that NIH guidelines should affect only projects financed by NIH grants. By this test they are immune from supervision.

This raises the issue of the ethical duties of scientists working on recombinant DNA projects for such firms. What is their duty if their employer requires research in some direction which the scientist considers dangerous? Do they have the right to refuse to proceed with the work required? Do they have the duty to pressurize their employer to abandon such plans? Do they have the right of whistle-blowing upon their employer?

These are difficult issues, and scientists placed in such positions will undoubtedly gather much strength in their attitudes if their professional bodies furnish them with ethical guidelines to assist them in this conflict. Such guidelines can also be of assistance in restraining the over-enthusiastic researcher who has fallen upon something exciting and desires to pursue it for the intellectual stimulation of the chase.

Those opposed to self-regulation contend that the government should know of such research, that the Attorney General should launch an enquiry into privately sponsored DNA research, and that there must be laws applicable to everyone, NIH sponsored or otherwise, who is dabbling in this field.

Even if one discounts fears regarding the creation by genetic manipulation of tailor-made people, there must be deep concern with the dangers of genetic manipulation in the field of viruses. Here, the remedy lies not in legislation but in the creation of a climate of opinion in laboratories that when a new and potentially dangerous development emerges it must be discussed at once. The researchers concerned must see it as their duty to inform the central committee of their professional body, or the international committee overseeing this area.

This leads to another ethical duty which lies upon the microbiologist — not only to pursue such standards in his or her personal conduct, but to engender such standards among professional associates.

In the context of the current debates in microbiology, is there not an ethical responsibility of the microbiologist, which needs to be formulated as a code or set of guidelines for governing the scientist's approach to his work? Should there not at least be a pledge to pursue microbiological knowledge for the good of humanity?

REACHING OUT TO THE PUBLIC

Decisions of this nature, involving legal, ethical and scientific issues, require impact assessment studies in which scientist and layman participate jointly. An excellent example was provided recently by the citizens committee at Cambridge, Massachusetts, which spent a vast amount of time to make a most competent study of the impact of recombinant DNA research. The machinery for such studies needs to be set up urgently in all countries where such technology is in progress. An interdisciplinary approach will be fundamental to its activities and I see it as a primary social obligation of the microbiologist to assist in the setting up of such bodies and to help them in their deliberations. It is wrong, I submit, for the microbiologist to confine these debates to the closed enclaves of science.

Associated with this approach is his or her social responsibility to carry into the community an awareness of the great debate that now rages. It is a hopeful sign that leading microbiologists have appeared over the media to bring these issues to the notice of the public.

On September 22, 1976, in an address to the Subcommittee on Health of the US Senate Committee on Labor and Public Welfare, Senator Edward Kennedy made this point very strongly. He observed that

> the implications of technological advances must be carefully considered early on, and must be considered in public processes with wide participation from as many diverse elements of society as possible ... I believe the debate over genetic engineering must go on. Scientists must tell us what they are capable of doing, but we as members of society must decide how it should be or whether it should be applied.[15]

The momentum for such activities must not come from the media alone. It must come from the microbiologists as well, in the form of active promotion of an awareness through seminars open to the public, through articles in popular journals, through an outward-reaching campaign towards popular education in the implications of current microbiology. Also implicit in this is an obligation to reach out to the other disciplines — law and philosophy and sociology, among others — for these have much to offer which will be of assistance. I do believe that many an expert scientist pursues his or her expertise in a degree of isolation from the other disciplines, and I have encountered scientists to whom such names as Jacques Ellul or Lewis Mumford or Buckminster Fuller — not to speak of Bentham, Berkeley or Locke — sound strange.

I urge, therefore, as another aspect of the social obligation of microbiologists, that you require in your students, who will be the microbiologists of the future, some awareness of philosophical and sociological perspectives which can only heighten their awareness of their social responsibilities. All too often in tertiary institutions — and law is no exception — we pursue an approach which misses the wood for the trees. We see the minutiae of our subject as indeed we must, but we fail to see it in its setting and thereby miss some of the most valuable insights into the direction in which our researches should take us.

A SHARING OF TECHNOLOGY

Social problems today are increasingly urgent and will admit of no delays in attention to them. The spread of technology into parts of the world where it is urgently needed is one of our pressing problems, rather than the pursuit of technology into areas of unknown peril. The latter can wait. The former will brook no delay, for a world of want is waiting impatiently for an ameliora-

[15] See the extracts from this speech in Goodfield, *op. cit.*, p. 153.

tion of its problems, and failure to solve them can result in a massive eruption of pent-up forces.

Microbiology has now become big business as it is a burgeoning multibillion-dollar industry. There will naturally be a tendency on the part of the large commercial concerns sponsoring this research to keep their knowledge to themselves to maximize their private profit. There comes a point in such matters at which private interest ends and public interest begins. The point at which one shades into the other must be fixed with equity to all concerned and with fair compensation to the rights of the discoverer. Yet the principle remains that such technology should be shared, for it belongs to all mankind.

There is also much microbiological knowledge which is of great practical utility to the Third World — in plant or livestock breeding in particular. Miracle strains of grain have resulted in the international marketing of seeds in a manner which has resulted in an increasing dependence of Third World farmers on great multinational corporations.

A social responsibility of microbiologists which I thus see as increasingly urgent is their social responsibility to the world community for the sharing of their technology.[16] The topic of the sharing of technology is one of the urgent problems engaging the attention of international bodies at every level and numerous complaints have recently surfaced regarding the manner in which technology, in regard to which all mankind has an equal stake, has confined itself to the privileged nations.

The indictment lies of course against all branches of technology, and microbiology is perhaps not one of the areas in which the strongest complaints have been registered. Nevertheless it is of profound importance to the developing nations. In all schemes for the advancement of microbiology there must necessarily be planning on the basis that this is among the technologies which must not be kept confined. In all developing nations there are institutions of tertiary education wherein the technologies of today can be taught. I believe it is an important responsibility of associations of microbiologists in the affluent countries to assist these centres of learning in equipping the personnel of developing nations to meet the particular problems arising in their own region.

I am conscious in making this observation that microbiologists have given much attention in their researches to the problems of the less privileged world, but I would submit that attention needs to be stepped up considerably in accordance with the altered pattern of the world's demands today. In an age when 80% of the world's technology concentrates on serv-

[16] See *supra*, Ch. 7.

icing the needs of 20% of the world's people, microbiologists, along with other scientists, have a deep social responsibility to assist in righting the balance.

INTERNATIONAL ACTION

The ethical and social responsibilities of microbiologists need endorsement, not merely at a national level. They also need international endorsement for the reason that it is idle for such research to be eschewed in one country while it is actively pursued in another.

An ethical obligation thus lies upon microbiologists to work through their professional bodies towards an international scientific arrangement or treaty among the microbiologists of the world. They need to press upon their governments the urgency of this matter and to require them to bring it before such forums as the World Health Organisation. We need international accord not merely on nuclear proliferation, but international accord too on "brink situation" microbiological research.

Professor Julius Stone has in a recent paper said:

> I admit, for example, that the techniques of *in vitro* human birth might lift great sorrows and burdens from some potential parents, and afford comfort and solace to others. I admit also that genetic surgery and engineering may be able to mitigate gene-borne disease and disability. I would not admit that relief afforded for such cases (admirable in itself though it might be) could even begin to tip the scales against the formidable dangers to a liberty-based society to which test-tube birth or any analogue of this would open the way.[17]

He points out therein that there is a baseline of freedom which is now coming increasingly under threat from dramatic work already proceeding in modern microbiology, genetics, neurophysiology, electronics and pharmacology, and he concludes with a motto drawn from ancient Rabbinic wisdom: "If mankind is not for itself, who then will be? And if not now, when?"

[17] Julius Stone, "Knowledge, Survival and the Duties of Science", (1973) 23 *Am. U.L.R.* 231.

21. Engineers*

The ancient Code of Hammurabi (1758 BC), one of the first and best known of the early codes, took a very stern view of the builder's responsibility for his constructions. If a house collapsed and killed the householder, the builder was to be put to death. If it killed the householder's son, the builder's son was to be put to death. If it killed the householder's slave, the builder should give a slave to the householder. A defective house was to be rebuilt, and a bulging wall made sound at the builder's own cost.

Both society and the art of engineering have travelled far since the time of Hammurabi, yet the central question of the engineer's responsibility for the effects of his or her work remains. That responsibility has both ethical and legal implications. It is the purpose of this paper to examine some of the ethical implications.

THE DUTY TO INQUIRE

People often question engineering ethics. They say "Well, we understand the need for ethics in medicine, but if a person is to construct a building how is ethics relevant to what he or she is about to do?" That attitude ignores the fact that every technological activity has some objective in view. The engineers are involved in the immediate process of putting the technology into operation. They cannot shut their eyes to the end result of their work. The same rules of engineering apply whether one is constructing a church or a torture chamber. It is not good enough for the engineer to say that all he or she has been called upon to do is to use his or her skill to construct a building. The engineer needs to know also what this building is being constructed for. The engineer may be happy to work upon a church or a school but not upon a torture chamber, and in the latter case it will not do to pass the blame on to others and claim that the object of the work is the responsibility of the employer, the politician, or the bureaucrat, who wanted it done.

* Developed from a lecture delivered at the Conference on Ethics and Engineering, University of Melbourne 1987. A summarized version of the lecture was published in *The Electrical Engineer*, Australia, April 1987, pp. 40–44.

The engineer's function is thus not limited to the mere input of engineering expertise into a particular job. At every point in the activity of engineers they come up against the implications of their work. A significant portion of the responsibility rests with them.

As observed in a recent work on engineering professionalism, "In engineering a moral issue may be raised with the next telephone call, letter or luncheon appointment. Thus the engineer must rely upon his or her value system to cope with ethical problems on a daily basis."[1]

The ways in which engineering talent can be misused and result in an essentially anti-social activity are numerous. Take for example the construction of nuclear reactors and the operation of huge chemical plants like that at Bhopal. If such installations malfunction they can produce disastrous effects upon society. The engineer cannot avoid the moral responsibility of ensuring that such work accords with the interests of society as far as he or she can discern them. This responsibility goes beyond the mere satisfaction of safety standards but concerns also the purpose of the work done and its impact upon society.

The first proposition I would wish to establish is, therefore, that there is a duty lying upon the engineer to inquire for what purpose his or her work is required.

A second principle follows from this, namely that the engineer has a right to make this inquiry and a right to receive an honest answer so far as is possible at that stage of the operation.

A third principle resulting from these propositions is that if the engineer has qualms of conscience regarding the work, in the light of the response, he or she should have the right to discuss it with management or the employer and to make his or her point of view known without fear of reprisals.

The employer may well tend to be dictatorial and to brook no opposition to its plan but this would give the engineer a right to take a conscience problem to an external arbiter such as an ombudsman for determining problems of conscience in the engineering profession.

A fourth consequence of the first principle is therefore that a public institution or an official from within the engineering profession should be appointed to inquire in ombudsman fashion into such complaints or inquiries and to give rulings thereon. In due time a body of rulings would evolve which would become the basis for more detailed codes of engineering ethics. I shall deal with this aspect more fully later.

[1] James H. Schaub & Karl Pavlovic (eds.) *Engineering Professionalism and Ethics*, John Wiley & Sons, 1983, p. 332.

THE POWER OF THE ENGINEER

This need for attention to ethical perspectives becomes all the more important when we consider the all-pervasive influence of the engineer in society today. We often tend to take the work of the engineer for granted without sufficiently appreciating its magnitude and power.

Look around you today, anywhere in the developing or the developed world and you are likely to see around you the power of the engineer and our dependence on that power. Apart from such dazzling achievements as the spacecraft, the satellite and the wizardry of electronics, at a more mundane level the automotive engineer dominates our roads, as the mechanical engineer dominates our factories. Without their particular skills all transport and industrial activity grinds to a halt. The construction engineer is transforming the skyline of our cities, the electrical engineer keeps the power lines throbbing without which those cities cannot function, and the irrigation engineer transforms entire landscapes in implementing some master plan. The computer engineer designs, builds and maintains the computers on which all society is so dependent, while the telecommunications engineer binds the world together in a network of instant information. Marine and aeronautical engineers ensure the smooth flow of international traffic and chemical engineers seem to be able to bend the elements to their will.

Our total dependence on the engineering profession every moment of our lives is a sign of its power; and the enjoyment of power brings with it a social responsibility proportionate to that power. What guidelines have been devised to guide the wielders of this enormous power in the exercise of that power?

Is each of them a skilled technician who hires his or her skill to the highest bidder and works to the dictates of that employer or is there a set of ethical principles and values lying beyond such immediate employment, to which the engineer is pledged? To what extent have the organizations of this learned profession worked out ethical codes and codes of social responsibility for the guidance of their members?

There is a problem here that needs to be addressed.

THE MILITARY/INDUSTRIAL/TECHNOLOGICAL COMPLEX

An added dimension is given to this power by the emergence of what may be called the military/industrial/technological complex.

President Eisenhower, in his farewell address to the American people regarding the military-industrial complex, referred to the very great power this combined organization had over the lives of nations and in fact over the human future. But it is what you might in a more extended phrase describe as the military/industrial/technological complex and that is a combination of very powerful forces which the average citizen of the world has very little power to contend against. The engineer, a person who is part of that complex, has the ability to make an impact and that power is not sufficiently realized by many engineers.

In the broad sense the word "engineer" refers to people who implement technology, and because of the technological age in which we live, they are clearly linked integrally to the political and economic process.

THE NEED FOR CROSS-FERTILIZATION WITH OTHER DISCIPLINES

Power so great can scarcely be addressed in terms of one discipline alone.

Not long ago, scientists and technologists tended to resent the attempt of exponents of other disciplines to intrude upon their sphere. Today we face a different scene. All the scientific disciplines recognize that in a complex technology, the combined wisdom of several disciplines is required if the social problems it raises are to be faced adequately. Most large hospitals have ethics committees combining such disciplines as law, philosophy, theology, social science and medicine. Universities have their human experimentation committees combining a similar mix of interdisciplinary expertise. The engineering profession too needs to review its existing procedures and codes to satisfy itself that its own discipline is in step with the movements that have occurred in other areas of science and technology.

There is another important reason why it is vital to society that scientists of all descriptions, and perhaps engineers in particular, should be specially conscious of the ethical and social implications of their work. This follows from the particular position of power and responsibility they enjoy in shaping the world order of the future.

A SOCIALLY RESPONSIBLE ENGINEER IS NOT A HIRED TECHNICIAN

The engineer is much more than a hired worker, just as a lawyer is not the hired mouthpiece of a client, but owes loyalties to higher concepts of justice and duty. Can the engineer be any different? If a government or a great corporation, for its own political or economic ends, should want to foist on the public some technological enterprise which is to the detriment of the public, engineers are not morally inert mechanical components of the overall plan. They are its human agency — in fact, they are often the only human agency with the power to make a meaningful impact upon the entire plan.

It would be appropriate at this point to draw a parallel with the law. In the last generation the accepted legal wisdom was that that the good lawyer's main concern was to be an expert, technical craftsman in the law. Its social impact was a matter for other hands and minds, but the lawyer should confine himself within the closed cabinet of legal rules and principles. Today, we teach our students that the responsibility of the lawyer goes far beyond the two covers of a law book. Indeed the lawyer would be ill-equipped if he or she did not know something about the impact of law on society and did not give of his or her expertise so as to improve the law in its service to society.

The analogy with engineering is quite clear. The engineer must of course be an expert in his or her job and must set that very high in the scale of priorities, but must not forget the social implications of the work in hand.

These are problems that are now surfacing internationally and the United Nations has drawn attention to this time and again in various declarations. In 1975 the General Assembly drew attention to the need to realize that technology was very often used as a means of undermining human rights, and a resolution resulted which stressed the need to prevent the use of science or technology to limit or interfere with basic human freedoms. Thereafter there has been a series of international conferences pursuing this objective.[2] It is important to work out international ethical codes that might assist scientists and technologists.[3]

AN ETHICAL CODE FOR ENGINEERS

I come now to the question of an ethical code for engineers. Rather lamentably engineering professions around the world, have been very slow in requiring a commitment by engineers to the observance of an ethical code in the same fashion as there is a commitment of doctors to the Hippocratic oath.[4] No doubt engineers bring their conscience to bear on their work, but

[2] For further details see Ch. 5 above.

[3] In treating engineers as a class of professionals, with corresponding high ethical duties, it is interesting to note that the American Society of Engineers defines "profession" as a pursuit of a learned art *in a spirit of public service*. This definition is amplified by the society in the following terms: "A profession is a calling in which special knowledge and skill are used in a distinctly intellectual plane *in the service of mankind*, and in which the successful expression of creative ability and application of professional knowledge are the primary rewards." — see James H. Schaub & Karl Pavlovic, *op. cit.*, p. 331.

[4] On this aspect see 9 *Social Inventions, Journal of the Institution for Social Inventions*, London, 1987 which is devoted to developing a Hippocratic-style oath for scientists, engineers and technologists.

the approaches of people of conscience to the same problem may well differ considerably, depending on the personal background and philosophy of the person concerned. A general engineering code of ethics adopted by the profession as a whole is thus essential as providing at least a basic core of ethical principles which will be the minimum from which each individual will start.

It is sometimes very difficult for the individual unaided by group ethics to make up his or her mind on questions involving ethics and social welfare. They need guidelines embodying the collective wisdom of the profession. In order to assist engineers in the ethical aspects of their work more information and more perspectives from the other disciplines are required.

An increasing number of engineering institutes across the world are now adopting ethical codes, however rudimentary they may be. The total absence of ethical codes for a profession so important as engineering, with so much power wielded by it over the lives and lifestyles of people, would indeed be quite unacceptable in this age of technology.

Some rather rudimentary codes have been suggested as a starting point. I could cite for example a Hippocratic oath suggested in 1966 for the engineer of the future which reads as follows "On becoming a Chartered Engineer, I vow to use my best endeavours to consider how my engineering skill may contribute towards the happiness of mankind".[5] This is at least a starting point, for it poses the moral issue to the engineer regarding the purpose of each of the works he or she is called upon to undertake. With the adoption of such a code as a starting point, finer tuned principles arising from specific situations can be engrafted upon the Code in the light of experience.

As the notion of an ethical code slowly gathered momentum since the 1960s, the formulations of the engineer's ethical responsibilities became progressively more comprehensive. The American Society of Civil Engineers, in a Code of Ethics effective January 1, 1977 and amended October 25, 1980, adopted a set of Fundamental Principles and Fundamental Canons. The first Fundamental Principle requires engineers to uphold and advance the integrity, honour and dignity of the engineering profession by using their knowledge and skill for the advancement of human welfare. The First Fundamental Canon states that engineers shall hold paramount the safety, health and welfare of the public in the performance of their professional duties. Many of the remaining provisions centre on the honour, integrity and dignity of the profession.

The Society's *Guidelines to Practice under the Canons* does go some way to meeting public concerns, as where they stipulate that "engineers

[5] *Journal of the Royal Society of Arts*, April 1966

should seek opportunities to be of constructive service in civic affairs and work for the advancement of the safety, health and well-being of their communities", and that "engineers should be committed to improving the environment to enhance the quality of life".

More far-reaching codes have of course been suggested, as for example "I vow to strive to apply my professional skills only to projects which, after conscientious examination, I believe to contribute to the co-existence of all human beings in peace, human dignity and self-fulfilment".[6] The note of idealism contained in such formulations will no doubt have an impact on the progressive development of ethical codes.

Since the date of these lectures there has been much progress. Thus the Code of Ethics, 1994 of the Institution of Engineers, Australia, as revised on 27 July 1997, contains two very significant socially-oriented Tenets among the 9 Tenets of its Code of Ethics:

1. Members shall at all times place their responsibility for the welfare, health and safety of the community before their responsibility to sectional or private interests, or to other members;

5. Members shall apply their skill and knowledge in the interest of their employer or client for whom they shall act as faithful agents or advisers, *without compromising the welfare, health or safety of the community*.

It is to be hoped that, throughout the world, engineering codes will progressively highlight the importance of the social interest and make provision for the conscience problems that beset the engineer when there is a clash between the work the engineer is called upon to do and the social interest.

ETHICS COMMITTEES

Ethics committees in various professions tend to be composed of members of those very professions. It is inevitable that there will be a protective attitude towards the profession, when a matter comes before it which involves a clash between the public and the professional interest. Every profession is of course entitled to its autonomy, but there are certain areas where the members of the professions by themselves are unable to see the full picture. Especially in socially-oriented matters they need an input from external sources. In the legal profession a limited role is now played by lay observers

[6] M.W. Thring, "Our Responsibility to Mankind", *The Chartered Mechanical Engineer*, 1970, p. 351.

who sit in on sessions involving such matters. There is scope for such in engineering as well.

Exclusively professional committees tend to confine their activities to fine points of professional etiquette but rarely face the broader social issues such as this article has addressed. What is the ethical duty, for example, of an engineer who is in a situation where his conscience dictates some kind of whistle-blowing activity upon his employer? What moral or ethical guidelines are offered to the individual engineer who, having worked in a particular sort of activity, then revises his attitude towards it, e.g., nuclear energy, and needs guidance on how he should react? What protective institutional mechanisms have such committees provided to shield the engineer against victimization for honest public interest concerns he genuinely feels regarding his work? What is the engineer's duty when he serves a powerful corporation in a third world country?

As persons with a conscience and with an ability to influence their employers, do they lie under a duty to register their views if they feel the technology they are engaged on might be damaging to the host country? Indeed the same problem arises even in the developed world where there could be various problems raising conscience issues — for example the production of shoddy goods, goods that damage the environment, goods that are not entirely safe. There is the recurring problem of built-in obsolescence. There is also the problem of wasteful use of energy in appliances which, with more care in their construction, can be more energy-effective. The employer would have an interest in producing goods as cheaply as possible so as to maximize his profits, but the engineer being the expert in the field would know that there is danger to the public interest in releasing these without adequate safety controls. Does the engineer have a duty to be a whistle-blower? To what extent or how does he balance the considerations of social conscience against the needs of the employer? The individual engineer is often at sea in facing these problems.

AN ENGINEERING OMBUDSMAN

This raises another issue. We live in a very practical world and an engineer who is too outspoken may of course run the risk of losing his position. This is another area where institutes of engineers can make a very substantial contribution, by giving their attention both to substantive questions of ethics and to procedural aspects. The substantive aspects require the construction of ethical codes more comprehensive than any we now have.

In regard to the procedural question, should there not be an official, of the nature of a scientific ombudsman, to whom people can go with a complaint that a conscience problem is involved in what they are being asked to do? The purpose of such an institution would be to ensure that if this is in reality a conscience problem, the person raising it would not be in jeopardy of losing his position. It is only right that no adverse consequences should ensue to persons who, out of pure moral concern regarding the impact of their work, begin to fear that they cannot give the entirety of their skill and dedication to the work their employer wants them to perform.

If technology dominates the lives of all of us and if those who actually supply the technology have their mouths closed for fear of adverse consequences in their workplace, we are deprived of the special knowledge of that very body of individuals who can do more to safeguard us than anyone else. It is essential for society therefore to protect itself by giving these people a voice.

Take the very practical case of a man who has worked for an employer for 20 years. He has loyally served him and he knows that his future is bound up with that particular employer — he is paying off his mortgage, he is educating his children through university and his superannuation depends on the proceeds from his workplace. His employer then launches upon some large scheme which is ethically unacceptable to the employee and calls upon the latter to give his engineering skills to that project. If the employee is to complain against his employer, he runs the risk of his entire life plan being upset and his children's education being prematurely ended. The practical dangers are too great to risk by being conscientious enough to complain against the employer.

The problem is one of immense importance as around 90% of engineers are salaried employees, serving some employer or organization.[7] "There are obvious benefits in terms of prudential self-interest and concern for one's family which make it easy to emphasize as primary the obligations to one's employer."[8] This circumstance should not of course blot out the vision of the engineer's social responsibility. The engineer's responsibility may in fact be stated in such high terms as to view engineers as "guardians of the public interest" regarding the matters with which they are charged.[9]

7 Mike W. Martin and Roland Schinzinger, *Ethics in Engineering*, McGraw Hill, 1983, p. 64.

8 *Ibid.*

9 *Ibid.*

WHISTLE-BLOWING

It is of the greatest importance that the ethical codes of engineers should give some special attention to this problem. It is most reassuring therefore to note, for example, that the 1994 Code of Ethics of the Australian Society of Engineers provides a fairly detailed scheme of guidance to its members on the subject of whistle-blowing:

It recognizes that a significant moral problem is involved, but observes that a decision to undertake an act of whistle-blowing is a serious matter. The information on the basis of which action is taken may well be privileged information which is not otherwise in the public domain. However, within these limitations members are advised to make any objections to unethical practices promptly, so as to avoid any misinterpretations of motives. Members are advised to proceed in a tactful, low-key manner to avoid unnecessary personal antagonism, to keep their supervisors informed of this action, to consult colleagues for advice and avoid isolation, consult with the Institution of Engineers on the ethical issues involved and seek legal advice concerning potential legal liabilities.

The issue has thus come into the open. The recognition of the problem by the Institute will no doubt strengthen the individual engineer, as well as keep employers on their guard against malpractice or damage to the public interest.

Other engineering societies would no doubt have comparable provisions on this matter. There is still a long way to go but a very significant beginning has been made.

ENGINEERING EDUCATION

Engineering education needs to give more attention to these social perspectives at every level.

It is essential that courses on engineering contain a component — at least one subject somewhere along the line — called the Engineer's Responsibility to Society, or Engineering in Context, or the Social Responsibilities of the Engineer. Such courses should, in my submission, have a legal component as well, for that would also be a means by which attention can be drawn to the human rights aspect of the engineer's duties towards society.

There is also the all-important field of environmental rights and duties. Engineers are often called upon to construct vast projects which may adversely affect the environment. They have a right to be alerted to the environmental duties they owe to the public and a duty to consider these in their work. They need also to have regard to social concerns and sensitivities. A textbook example would be that of a New Zealand engineer designing a gas pipeline which is required to go through a burial ground sacred to a Maori tribe. The 'efficiency' of this particular design may well be outweighed by the social cost of the dissatisfaction this would cause.[10]

Courses in such subjects as ethics, sociology, and economics will also assist the engineer in planning his or her work in its social context. As observed in a work on *Environmental Ethics for Engineers*:

> it is not possible to sensitise engineers to broader social values without an education which sensitises them to concepts of religion, sociology, political science, anthropology, history, and perhaps most importantly, ethics. It is imperative that engineers ask the proper questions about how their work will affect others, and the formulation of these questions is only possible through a broad engineering education.[11]

Evaluating the effect of major engineering projects of the past on the societies in which they were located can be a most fascinating study, with their varied impacts upon lifestyles, economies and the environment. Since these need to be ever present in the engineer's mind it is important to sensitize the mind of the future engineer to these issues. The tremendous possibilities available to the engineer for bettering the human condition can also be a source of inspiration to the young engineer at the commencement of his or her career.

Many an engineer may have to serve as a military engineer and he or she needs to know the rules of humanitarian conduct laid down for military activities by various international conventions such as the Geneva conventions. If such standards are prescribed even in time of war, they are pointers to the existence of a conscience problem in all engineering work. Moreover, international human rights conventions and declarations going all the way back to the Universal Declaration of Human Rights 1948 prescribe a set of basic human rights entitlements of every citizen which are now accepted by international law and by all domestic legal systems. An engineer called upon to be part of an operation which violates these human rights would be obliged not to lend his skill to such human rights violations.

I would advocate the holding of constant seminars at which groups of engineers consider among themselves and with others what guidelines they should lay down for their professional colleagues. This is a process of continuing education such as now occurs in all the professions. These seminars

10 For this example, see A.S. Gunn & P.A. Vesilind, *Environmental Ethics for Engineers*, Lewis Publishers, 1986 p. 38.

11 Gunn & Vesilind, *op. cit.*, p. 38.

should draw in the benefit of perspectives from lawyers, environmentalists, sociologists, historians and ethicists. On the matters which will face tomorrow's engineer, the engineer, left to his or her own discretion, without group support or guidance, would be powerless and ineffective.[12]

PROJECTS IN THE DEVELOPING WORLD

Engineers have a special responsibility in regard to projects concerning the developing world.

I believe there is an insufficient awareness on the part of scientists and technologists in general that in the developing world, which has, by and large, emerged from the legal status of colonies or dependencies, there is a feeling that the new instrument of domination by which power continues to be exercised over them is technology. This is for the reason that the vast bulk of the technology in the world today is in the hands of the developed world and is used by the developed world to its own advantage both at home and abroad.

Consequently much of this technology and the personnel who operate it, are exported to the developing world, where they are used to further the interests of those who possess it. It may be it is used for the construction of a chemicals factory or a nuclear station or a vast irrigation project. It may be exported in the form of finished products ranging from agricultural machinery and pesticides to the most sophisticated weapons.

Most of these are the works of engineers who very often do not see this distant dimension of their work.

All of these in one form or another impose a dependence on the developed world which can theoretically argue that the technology is freely accepted by the receiving country. It is ostensibly received by these countries on the basis of free contract. Yet that contract is in many cases far from free, for several reasons, among which are tied aid packages, financial inequality, lack of technological information and lack of alternatives. These are dealt with in other chapters of this book.

The engineer must be ever on guard not to be used as an instrument of domination or oppression — an aspect which, I believe, is not often perceived by engineers.

[12] See, to much the same effect, James H. Schaub & Karl Pavlovic (eds.) *op. cit.*, p. 336. An additional suggestion therein is that *every* engineering college or university should establish an ethics advisory committee consisting of educators, students, practitioners and philosophers.

THE ENGINEER AND THE ENVIRONMENT

It is becoming increasingly evident to all the world that development and environmental protection must go hand in hand. Development projects are essential to the welfare of populations all over the world but at the same time they must not significantly damage the environment. Development is effected through the work of the engineer and it is therefore vitally important that the engineer should be alerted to this principle and to its wide recognition throughout the international community today.

Major construction projects of all sorts — dams, roads, mines, multi-storeyed buildings, harbours, factories, nuclear and other power plants, industrial complexes — all of these are a feature of modern life and all of them make a significant impact on the environment. Natural vegetation is interfered with, fish life in lakes and rivers and in the sea is affected by interferences with the natural flow of water and by discharges of noxious wastes. The quality of the soil is affected by mining and by pesticides, fauna and flora are disturbed and their natural habitats reduced, dangerous chemicals are dumped whether into the sea or in the ground. The results are often disastrous. This is not to speak of the work of the engineers in the weapons industry — those who make land mines, nuclear weapons and the like, when the ethical issues are far more self-evident. To this day farmers in areas where wars were fought decades ago, are being injured by land mines and are thus inhibited from making full use of their land.

The environmental issues loom large both at the stage of planning and at the stage of construction and must in fact be kept in mind throughout the operation of the scheme. Environmental impact assessment has become a routine requirement in many countries and it is now internationally accepted as a pre-requisite to any major scheme. It must form part of the basic course content of the engineer's training.

Environmental law is now beginning to incorporate into its governing principles the concept of environmental impact assessment, which was first incorporated in a national legal system by the National Environmental Policy Act (NEPA) of 1970, in the United States. This principle will soon be universally recognized as imposing upon the engineers responsible for a scheme the duty of conducting a systematic impact assessment of that scheme in advance of its commencement. Failure to do so may well be regarded as negligence, and the engineer of the future needs to take note of this ethical duty, which will soon be a legal duty as well.

The engineer must be sensitized to the need to give attention to this aspect as a matter of course — how much waste will be discharged whether into the soil, the rivers, the sea or the atmosphere? How much of such waste can these elements take? What level is permissible? Is there any plan to dispose of this waste in other countries? Is it legitimate to plan an industrial project on the assumption that its noxious waste is to be deposited in the sea or in some other country where it will pollute the environment of those who are not benefited by the project?

It is significant that the Guidance for Members issued under the 1994 Code of Ethics of the Australian Institute of Engineers states that members shall give due weight to the need to achieve sustainable development and to conserve and restore the productive capacity of the earth.

The concept of the common heritage of mankind must be explained to the engineer from the moral, historical and legal angles. So also should the concept of inter-generational rights, which is fast gaining recognition throughout the world.

Catastrophes caused to populations as far afield as Bhopal and Chernobyl by lack of attention to these concerns must be placed before all engineers as constant warnings of the extent of the disasters and human sufferings that can result from their work.

The wisdom of ancient cultural tradition, which sought to harmonize the great works of man with the environment, needs to be looked on as sources of inspiration in this regard. The cultures of China and Japan, the Pacific, the peoples of Pacific and Africa — all of these contain rich traditions of respect for nature and harmony with nature. The world's religious traditions have much to teach on this, e.g. the Buddhist tradition of respect for all forms of life and the Islamic teaching that all land is held in trust for God.[13]

In fact the engineer of the future must be a multi-cultural and multi-disciplinary person, drawing his or her insights from many sources. Engineering expertise comes not only from special technical training but also from the ability to place that technical expertise in its overall social and historical context, for what the engineer does today will affect, for better or for worse, the lives of generations of people to come.

THE ARMAMENTS INDUSTRY

This paper would be incomplete if it did not refer to the fact that there is currently, as always, a tremendous input of engineering talent into the armaments industry.

I have spoken to groups of scientists engaged in weapons manufacture, and it would be wrong to say that they do not have a conscience problem. Many of them do, and are troubled by it.

13 On this aspect, see further Chapter 8 above.

It is a dismal fact that a large proportion of the world's technological skill is devoted to military R & D. A huge volume of the world's best scientific talent is thus emptied into totally non-productive channels, and drains away into the ocean of wasted resources, while hundreds of channels through which scientific talent can fertilize fields of productive activity which eagerly await it in the developing world are left bone dry.[14] There is a major ethical problem here of basic professional priorities, which ethics committees of engineering professions cannot neglect.

TRANSITION FROM GOVERNMENT EMPLOYEE TO CORPORATE ADVISER

Another important ethical problem for engineers arises in the case of people who are employees of a government department or commission and thereafter become consultants to a corporation in the private sector. These people, while they are in positions of authority in the government sector, absorb a great deal of information which comes to them in confidence or is given by private individuals or organizations to the appropriate government department, under statutory compulsion. When the public official becomes the director or servant of a private corporation, he or she carries into the private sector, often very unethically, a large amount of the information that was supplied in confidence to the government organization of which he or she was a member at one stage.

These are very deep ethical problems which are causing concern throughout the developed world and Australian examples are not difficult to find.

CORPORATE SERVICE

The corporate employers drive their technological people to produce the maximum profit for the corporation. But the engineers may find themselves asking: "Am I to push my corporation's interest to the limit, with the technical knowledge that I have, or is there also a social duty to the country in which I work in which the technology I am about to employ is likely to cause social damage?"

The corporate complexes bring in technology on their own terms. The host countries, dependent on the technology, are not in a position to bargain.

[14] 51% of scientific talent devoted to armaments as compared with 1% for the needs of the developing world, according to the Brandt Report (*North-South: A Programme for Survival*, Pan Books, London, 1980, pp. 197–198).

In the result the host countries very often have to take deals which are not entirely in their interests.

* * *

This paper has dealt with some of the vast spectrum of problems facing the engineer in this advanced stage of technology and industrialization. Codes of professional conduct, whether implied in the practice of the profession, or reduced to writing in the form of professional codes, have barely touched the fringe of the problem.

The observations made in this paper are intended to show that the engineers of the future have a grave obligation to themselves and to society to step up their levels of concern with the social impacts of their work. The services they render to society are so specialized that they cannot be duplicated by those without the necessary professional training. There is a total dependence by society on the skills and expertise of the medical profession.

If their work is so practically-oriented that its impact on society is profound, their responsibilities to society are correspondingly high. Their power over society is correspondingly great. With power comes responsibility. That responsibility cannot be properly discharged unless associations of engineers sensitize their membership to the ethical issues involved in their work, press for the inclusion of socially oriented instruction in engineering education and elaborate and develop their own codes of engineering ethics.

At stake are the rights and indeed the liberties of people, though these may not be readily perceived by engineers immersed in the intricacies of the day-to-day demands of an exacting, learned and highly esteemed profession.

22. Nuclear Weapons Scientists*

I INTRODUCTION

THIS TOPIC has deep and immediate significance to mankind in general and to a country that has seen the horrors of nuclear war in particular. The arms race takes on a legal and political complexion in the nuclear age, which separates it from the arms races of the past. Scientists who knowingly participate in this endeavour consciously assume the responsibility which marks them out from those who by compulsion or other pressures, find themselves engaging in war-related activities over which they have no control. There are principles involved here of responsibility to the community of mankind, on which international law and the United Nations cannot be without their message to the scientists involved.

This paper will not attempt to discuss the responsibility of scientists in general. That would involve many fine evaluations of the varying roles of scientists in the nuclear enterprise. It will rather examine the particular case of a scientist who, knowing that the object of his work is the manufacture or the improvement of nuclear weaponry, nevertheless deliberately participates in such activity. This paper will also not examine the legality of other dubious weapons, of which there are many, such as chemical and biological weapons. It will only concentrate on nuclear weaponry and thus confine itself to the limited situation of a scientist knowingly engaging himself at the heart of the enterprise of nuclear weapons production. Any principle established in relation to this clear-cut case will have implications for differing and peripheral situations which will need to be separately assessed and are beyond the scope of this paper.

* Paper presented at the International Symposium for the Prohibition and Elimination of Nuclear Weapons held at the United Nations University, Tokyo, in January 1985, and published in the *Journal of the Indian Law Institute* Vol. 27 (1985) p. 351. This theme has since been examined in greater detail in *Nuclear Weapons and Scientific Responsibility*, Longwood Academic, 1987.

The first proposition to be established is that the use of nuclear weaponry is illegal under prevailing principles of international law and constitutes a crime against humanity as well as an international delict or tort, *i.e.,* a civil wrong. The principles from which this conclusion follows and the inadequacies of the justifications commonly advanced will be examined briefly. Having thus established the illegality of *use*, what has to be argued is that this illegality attaches also to *production*.

From this basic position questions of responsibility will have to be examined. First, the questions of individual responsibility under international law and then the responsibility of statesmen and generals will be considered. Thereafter will be examined the responsibility of scientists who knowingly use their expertise for the construction of such weapons. It is hoped to outline some principles of personal responsibility of scientists which, it is submitted, would follow as an inescapable conclusion from the legal principles currently applicable in international law.

Although there is a fairly universal sentiment that the use of nuclear weaponry is clearly contrary to morality and that its production is probably so, this position does not go far enough. These activities are not only opposed to morality but also to law, and if the legal objection can be added to the moral, the argument against the use and manufacture of these weapons will be considerably reinforced.

In the concluding part of this paper reasons of policy which may militate against this proposition will be examined and their adequacy tested.

Before proceeding further, a few background details will be helpful. The 1983 report on the world social situation tells us that there are 50 million persons around the world, directly or indirectly earning their living from military activities, of whom 25 million are in the regular armed services. The report points out interestingly that the number of persons wearing military uniform exceeds all the physicians and teachers throughout the world. The nuclear stockpile now available is around 50,000 nuclear weapons, which is the equivalent of about one million Hiroshima-type bombs. Now, to set this in its proper context, in the 1970s there were, around the world, approximately 50 armed conflicts or wars, and there are today 20–25 countries capable of acquiring a nuclear force. Another interesting fact found by the Stockholm International Peace Research Institute[1] was that there were 1,564 major arms races throughout history. Of these all have ended in conflict, barring 13, and in these instances the economy of the countries engaged in the arms race has self-destructed. So, apart from the destruction of their own

[1] They have conducted a study of all the arms races that have taken place from the material available.

economies, the other logical consequence of an arms race seems to be, if one goes on the theory of probabilities, that it will end in a conflagration.

To all this must be added the fact that more than 50 per cent of the skilled scientific manpower in the world is now engaged in the armaments industry. How appropriate it is in a world of want that all this valuable skill should be devoted to the manufacture of weapons of death is a question that must touch the scientific conscience. It is not proposed to examine this in general terms in this paper but it will seek to address the specific question relating to the use of a significant portion of that body of expertise in the manufacture of nuclear weapons.

It is the objective of all peace-loving citizens of the world to explore every possible means of creating a consciousness for peace and reducing or delaying the threat of war of any sort. One means of doing so is to explore questions of responsibility, under international law, at all levels, of those who participate in the enterprise of nuclear weaponry.

It must be observed that the bombs now available in the armouries of the nuclear powers bear no relationship in their power of devastation to the Hiroshima bomb, although that bomb killed more people (80,000) than had died in all the bombing raids on Britain during World War II. That bomb was a 12.5 kiloton weapon, *i.e.*, the equivalent of 12,500 tons of TNT high explosive. Today's weapons are measured not in thousands of tons' equivalent of TNT but in millions — not in kilotons but in megatons.[2] The Hiroshima bomb was light weaponry in comparison.

A brief recapitulation of the consequences of nuclear war will help in demonstrating that the slaughter and suffering consequent on the use of nuclear weaponry is in no way comparable to anything mankind has known before. A forecast by the Office of Technology Assessment concludes that 77 per cent of the American population could die from a single large-scale attack.[3] This figure has been described as unrealistically optimistic for smaller countries like the United Kingdom because military and industrial activity is far more concentrated in towns and cities than in the United States.[4]

The casualties in a large-scale nuclear war have been estimated in recent studies at 750 million deaths from blast alone,[5] a total of about 1.1 billion

2 P. Goodwin, *Nuclear War: The Facts on Our Survival*, Ash & Grant, 1981, p. 14.

3 Office of Technology Assessment, *Effects of Nuclear War*, 1980, p. 8.

4 Goodwin, *supra* note 2 at 71.

5 Ambio II, 76 (1982) reprinted in J. Peterson (ed.), *The Aftermath: The Human and Ecological Consequences of Nuclear War*, Pantheon Books, 1983.

deaths from the combined effects of blast fire and radiation[6] and approximately 1.1 billion injuries requiring medical attention.[7]

A meeting of biologists on the Long-Term Worldwide Biological Consequences of Nuclear War held at Cambridge, Massachusetts, in April 1983, added frightening biological dimensions to those forecasts. Its report[8] suggested that the long-term biological effects resulting from climatic changes may at least be as serious as the immediate ones. To summarize:

> Subfreezing temperatures, low light levels, and high doses of ionizing and ultraviolet radiation extending for many months after a large-scale nuclear war could destroy the biological support systems of civilization, at least in the Northern Hemisphere. Productivity in natural and agricultural ecosystems could be severely restricted for a year or more. Postwar survivors would face starvation as well as freezing conditions in the dark and be exposed to near-lethal doses of radiation. If, as now seems possible, the Southern Hemisphere were affected also, global disruption of the biosphere could ensue. In any event, there would be severe consequences, even in the areas not affected directly, because of the interdependence of the world economy. In either case the extinction of a large fraction of the Earth's animals, plants, and micro-organisms seems possible. The population size of *Homo sapiens* conceivably could be reduced to prehistoric levels or below, and extinction of the human species itself cannot be excluded.[9]

This is the nuclear winter, the direct result of nuclear war.

President Eisenhower, in 1956, said: "One day both sides must meet at the conference table with the understanding that the era of armaments has ended and the human race must conform its actions to that truth or die." President Carter warned in his farewell address that "[t]he survivors if any, would live in despair amid the poisoned ruins of a civilisation that had committed suicide". The Soviet Union has officially pronounced that it views nuclear war as a universal disaster which would most probably mean the end of civilization and may lead to the destruction of all mankind. That realist view, though confirmed by the latest research, is being undermined by widely publicized concepts of a "limited" nuclear war and by attempts to equate nuclear weapons with conventional ones. These questions of fact

6 S. Bergstrom, *et al.*, *Effects of Nuclear War on Health and Health Services*, WHO, 1983.

7 *Ibid.*

8 22 *Science* 1283–1300 (1983).

9 *Id.* at 1283.

convert into questions of law, as will be shown in this paper because the rules of war applicable to conventional weaponry cease altogether to apply to situations such as those described by Presidents Eisenhower and Carter and the Soviet Union.

II PRINCIPLES OF INTERNATIONAL LAW RENDERING THE USE OF NUCLEAR WEAPONS ILLEGAL

The first proposition this paper seeks to establish is that the use of nuclear weapons is illegal and a crime against humanity. In addition, it argues that whether or not it be a crime under international law, it is an international delict or tort, *i.e.*, an act which is a wrong, whether or not it be criminal.

Article 38 of the Statute of the International Court of Justice enumerates the sources of international law and among them are international custom, the general principles of law recognized by civilized nations and the opinions of outstanding jurists. There is as yet no treaty banning the use or manufacture of nuclear weapons but there is certainly a large body of international custom, general principles of law recognized by civilized nations and juristic writings which have this effect. It will be shown that, contrary to much popular belief, this is a live part of international law and is binding upon all nations. It will also be demonstrated that, contrary to popular belief, the advent of the nuclear bomb and the manufacture of nuclear weaponry in several countries have not displaced this principle. There are international declarations as well, which, although they do not have the force of law in themselves, yet strongly indicate the sense of the international community on this issue and reinforce the contention that such a principle now forms part of customary international law.

Reasons which bring nuclear weaponry into the category of weapons forbidden by customary international law and the general principles of law recognized by civilized nations include the following:

(i) *Causation of indiscriminate harm to combatants and non-combatants*

This is an ancient principle recognized in several cultural traditions that have fused to make it a generally accepted rule of customary international law — Hindu, Chinese, Jewish and Islamic laws, and ancient European tradition regarding the law of war join in acknowledging this principle. In the nineteenth century and in the years preceding World War I, this principle received such a wide approval that it came to be embodied in the military and naval manuals of the Great Powers. There could be little doubt that by the end of the nineteenth century this principle could clearly be described as "a general principle of law recognized by civilized nations".

As the nineteenth century, sometimes described as the Clausewitzean century, reached its close, aggressive war gradually fell into disfavour as a normal instrument of state policy, and as aggressive war declined, the humanitarian aspects of the laws of war received increasing recognition. European attention came to focus on humanitarian law when Henri Dunant, a young Swiss banker, wrote a book *A Memory of Solferino* in 1862. Dunant had by chance been in Solferino in northern Italy when the famous battle was fought against Austria by France and Italy, resulting in over 40,000 dead and wounded. Dunant concerned himself mainly with lessening the suffering of the military personnel involved but his efforts helped to concentrate attention on the horrors of war in general. His work led to the foundation of the Red Cross and to the Geneva Convention of 1864, the precursor of many other conventions which did not limit themselves only to combatants.

With the progressive increase in destructiveness and cruelty of military weaponry, the European conscience, thus stimulated, moved on to the banning of certain categories of weapons,[10] and the formulation of the customary rules of warfare.[11] The two World Wars and the massive scale of death and devastation caused by them intensified the feeling that the laws of war needed more precise formulation, amplification and development to meet the new situations posed by modern conditions of warfare. With the formation of the United Nations and the proliferation of international committees and agencies the stage was set for a series of conventions, declarations and resolutions which gave more clarity and substance to the broad general principles formulated earlier.

The Nuremberg Charter, under which the Nuremberg trials took place, declared the extermination of a civilian population in whole or in part to be a crime against humanity. It is true that the Charter and the trial were the actions of the victors. It is also true that by the same standards there was much the victors themselves had to answer for, and for which they naturally could not be brought to trial. Yet the underlying principle of the trial was that the accused were being brought to justice not for new offences created by the Charter but for the violation of pre-existing principles which had formed part of customary international law long before World War II began. In 1946 the U.N. General Assembly unanimously adopted a resolution by which it subscribed to the norms laid down in the Charter of the Nuremberg Tribunal and also those embodied in the tribunal's judgment. Since then a large number of

[10] E.g., the Declaration of St. Petersburg, 1868.

[11] E.g., the Hague Rules of 1899.

other resolutions and draft conventions relating to war crimes and crimes against humanity have been adopted, such as the Convention on the Prevention and Punishment of the Crime of Genocide (1948), the four Red Cross Conventions (1949), the Convention on the Non-Applicability of Statutory Limitations to War Crimes and Crimes Against Humanity (1968), and the Convention on the Suppression and Punishment of the Crime of Apartheid (1973).

The prior existence of such principles can be demonstrated from pronouncements of nations which were ranged against each other in World War II. Thus, the United States protested against the Japanese bombing of Nanking in 1937 in these terms: "The Government holds the view that any general bombing of an extensive area wherein there resides a large population engaged in peaceful pursuit is unwarranted and contrary to the principles of law and humanity."[12] The Supreme Court of Japan in the *Shimoda* case likewise affirmed this principle in great detail, although the claim of the plaintiffs against the Japanese government resulting from injuries suffered from atomic bombs was dismissed for other reasons.[13]

References can be multiplied. For example the Proclamation of Teheran, adopted by the U.N. General Assembly in Resolution 2442 (XXIII) by 115 votes to none against and one abstention, affirmed that the right of the parties to the conflict to adopt means of injuring the enemy is not unlimited and that it is prohibited to attack civilian populations as such. This is one of many resolutions, each not having the force of law but which in their cumulative effect can be evidence of a generally accepted body of customary international law. They are certainly evidence that such rules which were undoubtedly once part of customary international law have not been abrogated in the post-war years. If further confirmation is required of this position it can be drawn from the Geneva Conventions. The 1977 Protocol I (Additional) affirms in article 48 that parties to the conflict shall at all times distinguish between the civilian populations and the combatants.

The next means of determining the rules of international law is the opinion of jurists. From this area as well there is confirmation of the existence of such a principle in the post-war years. The meeting of the Institute of International Law in Edinburgh in September 1969 declared that "[e]xisting international law prohibits, irrespective of the type of weapon used, any action whatsoever designed to terrorise the civilian population".[14] It likewise provided:

[12] See the *Report of the Fortieth Conference, International Law Association* (1939), 69.

[13] See *Japanese Annual of International Law*, vol. 8. pp. 212–52 (1964).

[14] Art. 6.

> Existing international law prohibits the use of all weapons which, by their nature, affect indiscriminately both military objectives and non-military objects, or both armed forces and civilian populations. In particular, it prohibits the use of weapons the destructive effect of which is so great that it cannot be limited to specific military objectives or is otherwise uncontrollable....[15]

It is thus sufficiently established that weapons which cause indiscriminate harm to combatants and non-combatants are contrary to international law, and that this principle has not been abrogated by contrary practices. A factor of special importance in this regard is that the civilians affected by nuclear war are not merely the civilians of one or other of the conflicting powers, but civilians of other countries which are not parties to the conflict. There is even less justification for their destruction — a destruction which will be inevitable in the context of nuclear war.

The position of civilians in occupied territories came to the forefront in the context of the German occupation of many countries such as Poland in World War II. Under the Fourth Geneva Convention such persons are regarded as "protected persons" and are entitled to humane treatment at all times. All forms of brutality towards them are forbidden. One of the most recent instances of recognition of the right to protection of civilians occurred during the Falkland Islands war in 1982 when neutral zones were established for their benefit. Such provisions are obviously impossible in a situation of nuclear war.

The proportion of civilians affected by war seems to be steadily rising owing to the destructiveness of modern weapons. Of those killed in World War I only about five per cent were civilians. In World War II it was about 50 per cent.[16] In World War III, if it should occur, the percentage will be the total percentage the non-combatant population bears to the combatant. Even in the Vietnam War, estimates of civilians injured ran to around 70 per cent.[17] If it is valid law that civilians are entitled to protection, the impossibility of doing this in nuclear war is by itself sufficient ground for the conclusion that such weapons are illegal.

15 *Ibid.*

16 G. Kewley, *Humanitarian Law in Armed Conflicts*, VCTA, 1984, p. 38.

17 *Ibid.*

(ii) *Aggravation of pain and suffering*

It is illegal to cause needless aggravation of pain and suffering. The first support for such a principle comes again from the ancient traditions of many cultures. The crossbow and siege machines were outlawed by the Second Lateran Council on this ground in 1139. In India the principles of Hindu law were used, according to the *Ramayana*, to counsel Rama to avoid the use of a hyper-destructive weapon available to him.[18]

The mainstream of nineteenth century European international law pursued this principle in the more specific instances of the increasingly cruel weapons of war which modern technology was making available. When the *dum-dum* or expanding bullet was invented, the Declaration of St. Petersburg 1868 affirmed that the right of a nation state to injure a belligerent was not unlimited. It also affirmed that *(i)* the only legitimate object of war was to weaken the military forces of the enemy; *(ii)* the object would be exceeded by the employment of arms which uselessly aggravated the sufferings of disabled men or render their death inevitable; and *(iii)* the use of such arms would be contrary to the laws of humanity.

The Hague Declaration of 1889 regarding Asphyxiating Gases declared that if a projectile has the sole object of diffusing asphyxiating gases it is so heinous and odious as to be unequivocally illegal. This declaration extends to *production, possession,* threat or use of *any* poisonous substances or *emissions* as weapons of war. *(Query*: Does this not extend to radioactivity?).

The Geneva Gas Protocol 1925 prohibited the use of gases and bacteriological means of warfare. The Protocol applies not only to gases but to "all analogous liquids, materials and devices" — whether solid, liquid or gas. The Convention on Prohibitions or Restrictions on the Use of Certain Conventional Weapons Which May Be Deemed to be Excessively Injurious or to Have Indiscriminate Effects, 1980 agreed, *inter alia, (a)* to ban fragmentary weapons which inflict wounds with particles which are not detectable by X-rays; and *(b)* to limit the use of air-delivered incendiary bombs.

It is to be remembered that while the laws of war admit of actions which further the aims and purposes of war, the infliction of suffering *per se* does not fall within these purposes. Hence the prohibition of "unnecessary suffering" and "superfluous injury". Nuclear weaponry by all accounts causes so much suffering to the survivors as to make them envy the dead.

18 Nagendra Singh, *Nuclear Weapons and International Law*, Stevens & Sons, 1959.

(iii) *Violation of the laws of humanity*

International law has always contradicted the proposition that "all is fair in (love and) war". One cannot massacre one's prisoners, or deliberately destroy hospitals or refuse treatment to one's enemy, sick or wounded. Such principles stem from considerations of humanity, which are part of the inheritance of civilization. Numerous historical documents such as the Declaration of St. Petersburg 1868, the 1925 Geneva Protocol prohibiting chemical weapons and the Draft Additional Protocol of 1973 of the International Committee of the Red Cross embody such principles.

Of particular significance is the "de Martens clause" in the preamble to Hague Convention IV on the laws of land warfare. It provides that in cases not covered by the regulations inhabitants of occupied territories and belligerents "remain under the protection and the rule of the principles of the law of nations, as they result from the usages established among civilised peoples, from the laws of humanity and the dictates of the public conscience". This was a specific recognition of the significance in international law of the laws of humanity. The parties to the Geneva Conventions of 1949 expressly recognized the clause as a living part of international law. The sufferings induced by nuclear weaponry clearly bring this weapon under the prohibitions rendered imperative by the laws of humanity.

(iv) *Contradiction of the principle of proportionality*

This principle becomes relevant both in attack and defence. In attack it prevents the causing of harm which is disproportionate to the military objective. It also prevents the causing of suffering to civilians which is disproportionate to the military objective sought.

In defence the principle means that retaliatory force must be proportionate to the nature of the attack. This principle has its analogue in the principle of self-defence in criminal law. One does not use a sledgehammer to kill a fly. The criminal law acknowledges, of course, that grades of force cannot be weighed on fine scales but there must be no obvious disproportion between the suffering inflicted in defence as compared with what is necessary for purposes of defence.

(v) *Nullification of a return to peace*

Once war has broken out, the objective of each party is the attainment of victory; once victory has been achieved the object of both parties is a return to peace. Indeed this is an interest which goes even beyond the contending parties. A return to peace cannot be achieved if all that is left of both victors and vanquished is a virtually dead mass of territory. Peaceful co-existence in such circumstances is only an empty concept. It is true that there have been wars in the past which have come close to decimating the population of the vanquished country but the magnitude of the destruction of persons, property and life-support systems in nuclear war bears no comparison.

Immanuel Kant wrote in 1797[19] that acts ought not to be resorted to in war which make difficult the return to peace. Perfidy and treachery have traditionally been examples brought within the operation of this principle for they obstruct the re-establishment of harmony. Nuclear war is an infinitely stronger example.

(vi) *Destruction of the ecosystem*

The laws of war, like the general rules of international law, cannot stand still. They must take account of fresh developments in weaponry and international affairs. The nuclear age set in forty years ago and it is more than time enough for international law to have adapted to the unprecedented change. In modern times rules of international law do not necessarily require the long periods necessary in previous ages for their principles to be settled, as the rate of change is so rapid. The consequences of nuclear war cannot possibly be handled adequately with the conceptual legal tools we have inherited. We need new concepts and principles. One of them is that destruction of the ecosystem, and with it the future of mankind, is an international crime.

Protocol I Additional to the Geneva Convention of 1949 provides as follows:

Article 55 — Protection of the natural environment

1. Care shall be taken in warfare to protect the natural environment against widespread, long-term and severe damage. This protection includes a prohibition of the use of methods or means of warfare which are intended or may be expected to cause such damage to the natural environment and thereby to prejudice the health or survival of the population.
2. Attacks against the natural environment by way of reprisals are prohibited.

The power of nuclear weapons to cause permanent destruction to the environment ought *per se* to be sufficient to outlaw a weapon, and if traditional

[19] Kant, *Die Metaphysik der Sitten,* para. 57 (1797).

international law does not embody such a principle, it needs to be created. This has in fact been foreshadowed already not only in the Geneva Conventions but also in international documents such as the Treaty of Tlatelolco 1967 spelling out that nuclear weapons, through the persistence of the radioactivity they release, constitute "an attack on the integrity of the human species and ultimately may render the whole earth uninhabitable". A potent case exists for arguing that this new principle has already, of necessity, engrafted itself upon the existing principles of customary international law.

It is interesting also to note that the U.N. General Assembly, by Resolution 3264 (XXIX) of 9 December 1974, emphasized the necessity "to adopt, through the conclusion of an appropriate international convention, effective measures to prohibit action to influence the environment and climate for military and hostile purposes".

(vii) *Decimation of mankind*

On the ground already mentioned the reasonable possibility of the decimation of mankind should provide another fresh principle of international law sufficient in itself to outlaw the use of nuclear weapons. Details on such possibilities have been set out in the summary of the nuclear winter. The survival of mankind is a value which prevails against any kind of national interest. All these reasons establish that the use of nuclear weaponry is illegal and a crime against humanity. They are reasons which, using the analogy of municipal law, would bring the case within the ambit of criminal law.

However the same act can, in municipal law, constitute at the same time both a crime and a civil wrong (which in different legal systems may be described as a tort or delict). Likewise, the same act may constitute in international law both an international crime and a delict. It is submitted that the act of use of nuclear weaponry falls into both categories through its proved potential to damage the human habitat. In municipal law it is a civil wrong to cause loss to one's neighbour by doing an act whose foreseeable consequence is to cause damage. For example, no one is entitled to release from his property a deleterious substance which can enter his neighbour's property and cause damage to him. In international law an example of such damage is provided by the *Trail Smelter* case[20] wherein Canada was held responsible for air pollution as a result of sulphur dioxide fumes emitted by a smelter plant at Trail, British Columbia, which caused damage in the State of Washington from 1925–1937. Canada was directed to pay an indemnity and halt the pollution. The tribunal observed:

[20] *U.S.* v. *Canada,* 3 *U.N. Rep. Int. Arb. Awards* 1911 (1941).

> Under the principles of international law, as well as of the law of the United States, no state has the right to use or permit the use of its territory in such a manner as to cause injury by fumes in or to the territory of another or the properties or persons therein, when the case is of serious consequence and the injury is established by clear and convincing evidence.

Nuclear pollution and devastation must attract the principle *a fortiori*. Likewise with the use of nuclear weaponry. The warring powers, whether or not they commit a crime, are also guilty of a delict when they poison the atmosphere or in other ways damage the environment of countries which are not party to the conflict.

A second head of liability, both cumulative and alternative to the first is, therefore, the liability for the commission of an international wrong or delict. The rest of this paper must be read in the light of this additional and alternative liability.

III ALLEGED JUSTIFICATIONS AND THEIR INADEQUACY

(i) *Abrogation of international law by contrary practice*

It is true that in the great wars that have been waged in this century the principle of indiscriminate slaughter of civilians and non-combatants has often been violated. It was violated also in the fire bombings and the aerial bombardments of World War II, not to speak of the devastation of Hiroshima and Nagasaki. These, it is submitted, do not contradict or abolish the rule which was once a settled rule of international customary law.

A cogent reason for so contending is that even if there has been a consistent violation of this rule in the manufacture and use of weapons that indiscriminately destroy civilian populations, that violation has been by a very small group of powerful nations who could be counted in single digits as opposed to a world community of nations now reaching the level of 150. Customary international law, once accepted by the world community, cannot be abrogated in this day and age by the wishes or the conduct of a less than 10 per cent minority of the world's nations. We are past the stage when a small body of powerful nations could dominate international law and dictate its rules. Thus, if it is correct that these rules were an established part of international law, and if it is true that these rules still command the unqualified support of the vast majority of the world's nations, those rules cannot be abrogated by the wishes or conduct of a small minority.

Moreover, as we have seen, despite contrary practice, the relevant principles have been reaffirmed time and again both by the international community and by eminent international jurists. Even great powers who have in practice violated these principles have reaffirmed them in the Nuremberg Charter and by their acceptance of the principles set out in the Nuremberg judgment.

(ii) *Necessities of war*

Necessities of war are, in the view of some jurists, a ground on which the rules of international law can be overridden. This is not however a generally accepted rule, for if it were to be accepted without limitation, most of the other rules of international law relating to war would be reduced to a cypher. The governments participating in the Declaration of St. Petersburg 1868, which was held in the context of the *dum-dum* bullet, foresaw that new technologies could heighten the conflict between necessities of war and laws of humanity. Such weapons (of which the nuclear bomb is the example *par excellence*) tend to promote the argument — as it did in Hiroshima and Nagasaki — that in one fell swoop one could terminate a war and thereby save thousands of lives, if only the laws of humanity could be temporarily overlooked.

They therefore reserved to themselves the right, in cases where new technology was leading towards new developments in armaments, "to come to an understanding ... in order to maintain the principles which they have established, and to conciliate the necessities of war with the laws of humanity". This decision of St. Petersburg was in fact approved by legal experts advising their governments at the 1973 International Committee of the Red Cross (I.C.R.C) Conference of Government Experts. They recommended restraint or prohibition in respect of new weapons that may be inhumane or indiscriminate such as incendiary and fragmentation weapons. The rule that even military necessity does not override international law was upheld in the judgment of the United States tribunal which tried Field Marshal List:[21] "The rules of international law must be followed even if it results in the loss of a battle or even a war."

It will be argued by some that such a sweeping pronouncement overstates the principle and that there are certain dire and immediate urgencies in the life of a nation in which a statesman or general is compelled to protect his country from destruction by whatever means available. One instance of this, sometimes cited in discussions of military necessity, was the position of Britain when Hitler stood poised for the attack in 1940. This was a supreme

[21] *Trials of War Criminals Before the Nuremberg Military Tribunals*, 759, No. 10, at 1277 (*U.S.* v. *List*) (1948).

emergency in which a statesman or general might have sought to argue that to save his country from destruction he had no alternative but to carry death and destruction indiscriminately to the enemy population, if that was a means of halting the attack. That indeed was the argument of Bomber Command.

An examination of such arguments shows however that two extreme factors must coincide if the argument is to carry any weight at all — the danger must be both imminent and supreme.[22] When by 1942 the bombing campaign, following Lord Cherwell's Minute of 1942, made working class residential areas in Germany the prime targets, the two factors of imminence and supreme danger no longer co-existed. Even if it had been at any stage legitimate to direct attacks at civilian targets or cities as such, the enormous injuries inflicted on Germany and its army by the Russians and the presence at Britain's side of the United States with all its resources had certainly removed the imminence of the danger.

A group of scientists objected to the calculations on which the Cherwell Minute was based but their objection was apparently not formulated in moral terms,[23] although there were moral objections from professional soldiers.[24] But the raids on German cities continued and this was certainly a situation for which 'supreme emergency' no longer provided an arguable justification. Bombs were dropped on the city of Dresden killing 100,000 people as late as 1945. The bombs were dropped on Hiroshima and Nagasaki when even less justification was available under the doctrine of "supreme emergency".

Is the situation in which nuclear bombs are used for first strike one of "supreme emergency"? Do imminence and supreme danger come together? Even if they do, can one then proceed in such a manner as to annihilate civilians by the million — far in excess of the Dresden or Hiroshima attacks — with the certain death of millions of one's own people as well? It is submitted that the defence of "supreme emergency" is insufficient justification for the deliberate act of killing millions of innocent people.

(iii) *Concept of a just war*

A word is necessary here for the non-legal reader in relation to the legality of the use of force under international law.

22 See, on this point, the excellent discussion in Michael Walzer, *Just and Unjust Wars*, Allen Lane, 1978, Ch. 16.

23 *Id.* at 257.

24 See also, C.P. Snow, *Science and Government*, New American Library, 1962, p. 48.

Article 2, paragraph 4, of the Charter of the United Nations contains the imperative provision that all members *shall* refrain in their international relations from threat or use of force against the territorial integrity or political independence of any state, or in any other manner inconsistent with the purposes of the United Nations. These purposes of the United Nations, as set out in article 1, include the maintenance of international peace and security to which end effective measures have to be taken by it "for the suppression of acts of aggression or other breaches of the peace". However, article 51 provides that nothing in the Charter "shall impair the inherent right of individual or collective self-defence if an armed attack occurs against a Member of the United Nations until the Security Council has taken measures necessary to maintain international peace and security". There is thus a recognized interim right of self-defence until the Security Council can move into action.

Although, as we have seen, the word "aggression" is used in the Charter, it is nowhere defined in it. The definition was not without difficulty but the U.N. General Assembly was able to arrive at an agreement in 1974 on a definition in the "Definition of Aggression" Resolution of December 14 1974. The definition adopted was that: "Aggression is the use of armed force by a State against the sovereignty, territorial integrity or political independence of another State, or in any other manner inconsistent with the Charter of the United Nations." Article 5 of the same resolution states that no consideration of whatever nature, whether political, economic, military or otherwise, may serve as a justification for aggression. It goes on to provide that a war of aggression is a crime against international peace.

It is possible to elaborate more upon these basic propositions. However it will suffice for the present to state that the general framework of international law regarding the use of armed force is to exclude its use for wars of aggression but to permit its use for self-defence. Other limited uses of force, as for purposes of humanitarian intervention, need not detain us here, as one cannot conceive of the use of nuclear weaponry for such purposes without totally defeating the object of the enterprise.

Another important concept coming from traditional international law is the concept of "just war". Wars to defend the faith or recover the holy places of one's religion, as in the Crusades, are historical examples. A war of self-defence or of humanitarian intervention would be modern examples.

Is the illegality of nuclear weaponry confined to those uses of force only which cannot be justified on one or other of the above principles? It is submitted that, for the reasons set out earlier, the principle of the illegality of nuclear weapons applies equally whether the war in which they are used is legal or illegal, just or unjust. Hence the use of such weapons even in a war of self-defence would be illegal, if the basic proposition of their illegality is correct. Reference may be made in this context to U.N. General Assembly Resolution 1653 (XVI) of 24 November 1961. This resolution condemned the use of nuclear weapons in any situation as being a crime against mankind and civilisation.

The general principles relating to violation of the laws and customs of war are not limited to illegal wars. This appears clearly from Protocol I Additional to the Geneva Conventions of 12 August 1949 containing the following provisions:

Article 35 — Basic rules

1. In *any* armed conflict, the right of the Parties to the conflict to choose methods or means of warfare is not unlimited.
2. It is prohibited to employ weapons, projectiles and material and methods of warfare of a nature to cause superfluous injury or unnecessary suffering.
3. It is prohibited to employ methods or means of warfare which are intended, or may be expected, to cause widespread, long-term and severe damage to the natural environment.

(iv) *Self-defence*

Mention has already been made of article 51 of the U.N. Charter and the reference therein to self-defence. Should not a nation be entitled, therefore, to use nuclear weapons in retaliation if it is attacked? The attack, however limited, will be delivered by nuclear weapons which, however small in today's terms, will exceed several times the firepower of the Hiroshima bomb. It will in all probability be a multiple attack and many Hiroshimas will be blasted out of existence.

Retaliation needs to have a logical justification, but once the first strike has arrived, all reasons for retaliation disappear, for the society of the country attacked would be destroyed and its survivors too severely injured and dazed to constitute anything like a civic society. It is not for national security then that the retaliatory button will be pushed from a bunker far removed from the real world. Not for victory. Not for a balance of advantage. All those pre-nuclear concepts would be meaningless. Revenge may be the reason. Panic, hysteria, terror may be the mood. Annihilation of the human race or of its life support system may be the result. Retaliation would be an emotional act of total futility. In addition, it would attract to itself again the illegalities of destruction of the environment and annihilation of non-combatants which we have already discussed.

The words of the President of the United States are quoted to illustrate this point. He states:

> The word comes that they're (the missiles) on their way. And you sit there, knowing that there is no way, at present, of stopping them. So they're going to blow up how much of this country we can only guess at, and your response can be to push the button before they get here so that even though you're all going to die, they are going to die too.[25]

The President went on to observe: "There is something so immoral about it." I would also add "illegal" to the word "immoral".

(v) *The preservation of one's way of life*

Democracy, free enterprise, communism or the socialist way of life are objectives which may be sincerely and deeply cherished by those desiring their preservation. How much is it legitimate to sacrifice for the preservation of such cherished ways of life? Clearly a great deal, but this reaches the point of irrationality when the means used for the protection or such lifestyles will assuredly be the means also of their destruction. Whatever else is unclear about nuclear war it is certainly beyond dispute that the survivors of the nuclear war will not be able to preserve the lifestyles of the period before. What then is the purpose of such an exercise?

(vi) *Preventing de-stabilization of areas of influence*

The reply to this argument is similar to that in the previous section. The nuclear winter already described will see post-war survivors struggling for survival in freezing conditions and in the midst of near lethal doses of radiation. The threshold for major climatic consequences may be very low. Only 100 megatons detonated over major urban centres can create sub-freezing land temperatures for months.[26] A 5000 megaton bomb can spread dust cloud and radioactivity from the northern to the southern hemisphere. A serious threat to other species and to human survival would be on the cards.[27] What value can there be in the justification that one of the protagonists is seeking to prevent the de-stabilization of its areas of influence?

25 *Time*, 28 Jan. 1985, p. 11.

26 *Supra* note 8 at 1283.

27 *Ibid.*

IV EXTENSION OF ILLEGALITY TO PRODUCTION

To extend the principle of illegality from *use* to *manufacture* requires a consideration of two possibilities — that weapons may be manufactured not for use but for deterrence and that manufacture does not need to be for a war of total destruction, but could be for a contained nuclear war. If either of these positions has validity, it would remove or reduce the culpability associated with manufacture.

(i) *Deterrence*

Assured destruction is the very essence of the deterrence doctrine. As McNamara observed in explaining the doctrine,[28] the potential aggressor must believe that this capability is actual and the will to use it is unswerving. This belief must be induced for the rest of time. It can only achieve success if the potential aggressor is permanently terrified into inaction. If there is a period of time in which one's opponent ceases to be terrified or calls one's bluff, deterrence has failed.

One might, if one does not really want to use these weapons, deceive the enemy for some of the time into the belief that one means to use them. One cannot expect to deceive him for *all* of the time from now to eternity. Hence deterrence strategists have sensed that deterrence cannot be achieved by an empty threat. We must really mean the threat clearly enough for the other side to be terrified by it. Deterrence then becomes not the storage of weapons with intent to terrify, but a stockpiling *with intent to use.* We straightaway come within the ambit of the prohibitions applicable to *use* of the weapon. We need to face squarely the reality that nuclear weapons are with us not only for deterrence but for use and not permit this smokescreen to cover up illegalities that sovereign states may wish to conceal.

(ii) *Contained nuclear war*

There has been much serious discussion in recent years of the possibility of a contained nuclear war. If this concept is a possibility, it is argued that the laws of war relative to such a conflict would approximate more nearly to those relating to a traditional war, for total or near total annihilation would not be the result. Wars can in that event be fought to produce specific political effects.

[28] Robert S. McNamara, *The Essence of Security: reflections in office*, Hodder & Stoughton, 1968.

Has mutually assured destruction (M.A.D.), as the inevitable consequence of a nuclear exchange, given way to the possibility of a limited war? This hypothesis must be seriously examined in the light of three scenarios — theatre nuclear war, nuclear war limited to specific tactical targets, and the new notion of 'star wars'.

(a) Theatre nuclear war

Possible theatres of tactical nuclear war are the European, the Sino-Soviet, the Middle Eastern, the South African and the Indo-Pakistan theatres. The concept here is that a nuclear exchange could take place without escalation to a level at which the superpowers are involved.

However possible such limitation may be in the context of some of these theatres, at least two of them directly involve the superpowers — the European and the Sino-Soviet theatres. The theatres that do not directly involve the superpowers have all the potential, however, to draw them in. Having regard to the power vacuum that will result from the annihilation of one or other of the participants, the superpowers are not likely to remain spectators on the sidelines once the bombs begin to fly.

In the theatres where the superpowers themselves are directly involved, the scale of devastation will be of such an order as to render the description of theatre nuclear war totally inappropriate. In the European theatre, for example, thousands of short-range tactical nuclear devices available on both sides would be brought into action, with resultant death and destruction on a scale too frightful to contemplate.

This theatre is in fact specially vulnerable in view of the serried ranks of nuclear missiles confronting each other at comparatively close range while opposing ground forces also stand poised against each other. What may begin as a conflict with conventional arms can create a tinder-box situation in which one side or the other could suddenly decide on escalation to the nuclear level. First nuclear strike has strategic value in such a situation. When this happens, a nuclear exchange on a scale sufficient to result in global devastation is very much on the cards. In the Sino-Soviet theatre, the conflict will be too important for the other superpower, the United States, to be a mere spectator.

(b) Limited nuclear war

It is argued by supporters of the limited war theory that nuclear weapons can now be targeted much more accurately. They can reach within a few feet of their targets and enemy nuclear delivery systems can thus be much more effectively hit to prevent their use in retaliation. Hence 'war-winning strategy' is replacing M.A.D. as a preferred scenario for nuclear war.[29] Confinement to military targets resembles the actions of conventional warfare and makes more relevant the legal principles applicable to the latter.

It needs little elaboration to point out the defects in such theorization. In the first place, however accurately a nuclear missile may be targeted, its massive range of destruction, as compared with any conventional weapon, destroys all life within an extensive area. All civilian life is thus destroyed on an unprecedented scale, seeing that it is not just one weapon's target that will be aimed at, but a series, spreading through the length and breadth of a country. The entire country receiving the attack can, therefore, be destroyed.

In the second place, the danger of the doctrine is the inducement it offers for a pre-emptive strike. The power that makes the first attack will, if the theory works, be the country to emerge the victor. This places nerves on edge on both sides, for every action needs to be interpreted so as to enable the forecasting of the 'enemy's' next move. Such forecasting is never error-proof and sooner or later a misreading of the evidence can precipitate an unwanted war.

It is to be noted, thirdly, that submarines can also now be targeted no less than weapons silos at home. An important value of the nuclear submarine is that it must be used for first strike, for they can be reached only by Very Low Frequency (V.L.F.) and Extremely Low Frequency (E.L.F.) broadcasts which require extremely large aerials. These may not be possible once nuclear war has broken out. The pre-emptive first strike thus assumes added importance and has all the potential for the destruction of the 'enemy' power. Moreover the 'enemy' in that situation is scarcely likely to remain totally prostrate and inactive. Even that 10 per cent of its weaponry which escapes destruction in the most successful of first strikes will indubitably be directed at its assailant. Even if some of these are intercepted, the damage caused by those that get through will be on a scale sufficient to destroy the attacker.

This leads naturally to the question of the 'star wars' and the suggested 'defence shield' aimed at throwing a blanket of protection over the air space of an entire country.

(c) Star wars

On 23 March 1983 President Ronald Reagan expressed the hope, in a dramatic speech, that the United States would be able (by virtue of new advances in such areas as kinetic-energy projectiles, particle beams and lasers) to construct for itself a defence shield against incoming nuclear weapons. This claim, if correct, gave a new complexion to the arms debate, for it

29 *SIPRI Yearbook* 1979, p. 419 referred to this.

meant that superpowers were now not necessarily bound to plan their strategy on the basis that M.A.D. was the inevitable consequence of nuclear war.

Earlier negotiations between the superpowers had proceeded on the basis that limiting the proliferation of missiles [30] made sense, because deterrence was made real by the undoubted capacity of each protagonist to destroy the other with weapons already in hand. If such capacity to destroy is removed, the basis of negotiation is altered. "Star wars", therefore, assumed a position of key importance in arms negotiations. There is strong scientific opinion that a complete shield is unattainable. To quote Nobel Laureate Hans Bethe, even being "as optimistic as you can be within the laws of physics and geometry, the system is unworkable".[31] To quote *Time:*

> Other experts maintain that even if a Star Wars system could be made operational, it would never be 100% effective. Thus a Star Wars capacity might well intensify the arms race, since the Soviets would build more and more ICBMs to ensure that at least some of their missiles penetrated U.S. defenses.[32]

Even a small proportion of missiles filtering through the shield would be sufficient to achieve total destruction. Moreover the cost, variously estimated at between 500 billion and a trillion dollars,[33] is well beyond the reach of even such an economy as that of the United States.

There are factors in the claim, however, which have relevance to the present thesis, for if it be theoretically possible to work towards a complete defence, scientific research directed at this objective alone may indeed be commended. There is however the possibility that the projectiles, particle beams or lasers developed for this purpose may be used to perfect offensive weapons and this must cause concern to a scientist genuinely examining all the implications of his work. It is for informed scientific opinion to inform the lay world whether such a "dream of total safety"[34] is realistic.

It will thus be seen that whichever of the three scenarios one observes, nuclear war becomes impossible to contain. Limited war expands once more into mutually assured destruction, and we are where we began.

[30] Such as was achieved in Strategic Arms Limitation Talks (SALT I) in 1972 and was attempted in SALT II in 1979.

[31] See *Time*, 26 Nov. 1984, p. 10.

[32] *Ibid.*

[33] *Time,* 21 Jan. 1984, pp. 10–11.

[34] *Ibid.*

V THE QUESTION OF RESPONSIBILITY

(i) *Individual responsibility in international law*

If it can be established that illegality attaches to production, the next question for inquiry must centre on the question of responsibility. Responsibility clearly attaches to the statesman who gives the order for manufacture, as it attaches to the general who might order its use. What of the responsibility of those who *knowingly* participate in the production of the weapon?

This necessitates an examination of the term *knowingly*. We may exclude straightaway those whose research is used for the production of a nuclear weapon without their knowledge. There can be many categories of such persons, such as, (i) those who pursue some research, *e.g.*, mathematical, and then find their work used for production of nuclear weapons; and (ii) those who are put to work even by the defence department on some limited piece of research which together with other similar pieces of work is welded together in some overall nuclear weapons project.

For the purpose of this argument we will concentrate on the clear-cut case of the scientist who is asked to work on nuclear weapons production or research and accepts the invitation knowing full well to what end his activity will be used. There are peripheral cases such as the case when a scientist who has done some academic research (*e.g.*, working out a new mathematical theorem or equation) which is later found to be useful in nuclear arms production, is invited to explain it to the manufacturer. Another is the scientist working on an isolated piece of research which is part of an overall nuclear weapons' operation, who is in a position by intelligent inquiry to find out for what purpose his research will be used, but deliberately refrains from making the inquiry because he fears that it may reveal some purpose not to his liking.

We will not deal with these peripheral cases which can be the subject of examination later if our basic thesis is accepted. We will concentrate on the clear case of the scientist working with full knowledge that his services are being used for the production of a nuclear weapon.

The term 'scientist' here could mean not merely the pure researcher engaged in pushing forward the frontiers of scientific knowledge, but also the technologist or technician who lends his or her scientific expertise to the process of construction in those intricate operations which can only be performed by one deeply versed in scientific knowledge.

The responsibility of such a scientist can be established, it is submitted, under both municipal and international law. In municipal law, the law of tort or delict imposes responsibility upon those whose dangerous activities cause foreseeable damage to those who are within the circle of persons likely to be affected by their act. This aspect is more fully discussed elsewhere in this paper, under the responsibility of scientists.

Passing on now to the question of international responsibility, we must commence with the question of responsibility of individuals in international law.

International law has traditionally operated at the level of states. States are bound by obligations, entitled to rights and may sue and be sued. The heads of states or other officials who might act in a manner contrary to international law are not ordinarily held accountable at international law. This, however, is not an absolute rule. Numerous instances can be cited in which individuals can be held accountable and punished for acts contrary to international law. For example a soldier violating the provisions of the Geneva Conventions on the treatment of prisoners of war can be tried by a belligerent state and punished. The Convention Relative to the Protection of Civilian Persons in Time of War authorises similar prosecutions for offences against civilian populations. Article 6 of the Nuremberg Charter, 1946 provides:

> The following acts, or any of them, are crimes coming within the jurisdiction of the Tribunal for which there shall be *individual responsibility*:
>
> (a) Crimes Against Peace: namely, planning, preparation, initiation or waging of a war of aggression, or a war *in violation of international treaties, agreements or assurances,...*
>
> (b) War Crimes: namely, violations of the laws or customs of war. Such violations shall include ... wanton destruction of cities, towns or villages, or devastation not justified by military necessity.
>
> (c) Crimes Against Humanity: namely ... extermination ... and other inhumane acts committed against ...civilian populations, before or during the war....

The continuing trend towards such personal responsibility for criminal acts under international law is well illustrated, in a manner very relevant to the subject of this thesis, in the Convention on the Prevention and Punishment of the Crime of Genocide adopted by the U.N. General Assembly on 9 December 1948 which entered into force on 12 January 1961.

Article I of that Convention provides that genocide, whether committed in time of peace or war, is a crime under international law which the parties undertook to prevent and punish.

Articles II and III are quoted below *in toto:*

> Article II. In the present Convention, genocide means any of the following acts committed with intent to destroy, in whole or in part, a national, ethnical, racial or religious group, as such:
> *(a)* Killing members of the group;
> *(b)* Causing serious bodily or mental harm to members of the group;
> *(c)* Deliberately inflicting on the group conditions of life calculated to bring about its physical destruction in whole or in part;
> *(d)* Imposing measures intended to prevent births within the group;
> *(e)* Forcibly transferring children of the group to another group.
>
> Article III. The following acts shall be punishable:
> *(a)* Genocide;
> *(b)* Conspiracy to commit genocide;
> *(c)* Direct and public incitement to commit genocide;
> *(d)* Attempt to commit genocide;
> *(e)* Complicity in genocide.

Article IV of the Convention provides that persons committing genocide or any of the acts enumerated in Article III shall be punished, whether they are constitutionally responsible rulers, public officials or private individuals. Prosecution is provided for in Article VI which renders prosecution obligatory on the state in the territory of which the act is committed "or by such international penal tribunal as may have jurisdiction with respect to those Contracting Parties which shall have accepted its jurisdiction".

These provisions give rise to many comments on the act of engaging in nuclear warfare and on complicity in such act. If nuclear warfare exterminates whole populations, then those who engage in it are guilty of the crime of genocide and punishable as such. Rulers, public officials and private individuals who are guilty of complicity in the act are culpable and punishable.

Secondly, the Convention, while giving jurisdiction to the state in which the act is committed, looks forward also to competent international criminal tribunals which may be established in the future for the trial of such offences. There can be little doubt that world opinion is moving in that direction and that after the next use of nuclear weaponry on however limited a scale, such a tribunal will be called into operation. It is submitted that scientists involved in the creation of such weaponry would clearly come within the jurisdiction of such a tribunal.

Thirdly, even apart from the creation of such a tribunal, the Convention of 1948 sufficiently conveys the spirit and climate of international law in regard to acts such as these. We do not have to await the creation of a competent tribunal to pronounce on questions of illegality if the illegality already exists under international law. The present illegality of the act, rather than the existence or non-existence of the tribunal is the criterion by which the scientist should guide his conduct.

Other illustrations of individual responsibility under international law come from many areas. Piracy has always been regarded as a crime against nations, for which individual states could punish offenders. The Vietnam war produced instances of private accountability for violation of international norms relating to protection of civilians in time of war, when Lt. Calley was prosecuted.[35]

Although there have been problems in defining the offence of terrorism and making it punishable, hijacking has been made an international offence and the Tokyo Convention of Offences and Certain Other Acts Committed on Board Aircraft (14 September 1963) and other conventions — Hague Convention for the Suppression of Unlawful Seizure of Aircraft, (16 December 1970) and the Montreal Convention for Suppression of Unlawful Acts Against the Safety of Civilian Aviation (23 September 1971) — require any State party either to extradite the offender or bring him to trial.

The *Eichmann* case showed the possibilities that exist for the trial of an individual for a crime against humanity by the courts of a country considering itself affected — and what country is not affected by genocide or crimes against humanity? The sentiment of international lawyers is moving towards the punishability of such offences and the creation of procedures and tribunals for this purpose. It will not be long before they come into existence — certainly within the lifetime of the younger scientists now working in this field.

Moreover the growth in authority of the human rights concept has broken through the barrier once posed by international law that individuals were not the subjects but only its objects. The growth of human rights doctrine has meant that individuals are vested with an ever-increasing circle of rights. Along with rights must come duties and if rights can be claimed in the international forum, duties can likewise be enforced. It would be a lopsided international order that gives the individual an ever-increasing circle of

[35] See *United States* v. *Calley*, 46 C.M.R. 1131 (A.C.M.R.) affirmed II C.M.A. 534, 48 C.M.R. 19 (1973); *Calley* v. *Callway*. 382 F. Supp. 650 (M.D. Ga. 1974) rev'd 519 F. 2d. 184 (5th Cir. 1975).

enforceable rights and leaves the duty not to commit a crime against humanity in a status of total unenforceability.

(ii) *Responsibility of statesmen and generals*

Article 7 of the Nuremberg Charter specifically provided: "The official position of the defendants, whether as Heads of State or responsible officials in Government Departments, shall not be considered as freeing them from responsibility or mitigating punishment." Similar principles of personal responsibility have been reaffirmed more recently by the Genocide Convention.

The question of superior orders was also the subject of express provision in Article 8 which provided: "The fact that the defendant acted pursuant to order of his Government or of a superior shall not free him from responsibility, but may be considered in mitigation of punishment." The defence that many of the defendants were acting under the direct orders of Hitler was held not to exonerate them. Of this provision the tribunal observed that it was in conformity with the law of nations. It held:

> That a soldier was ordered to kill or torture in violation of the international law of war has never been recognised as a defence to such acts of brutality.... The true test, which is found in varying degrees in the criminal law of most nations, is not the existence of the order but whether moral choice was in fact possible.[36]

If this reflects the state of international law — whatever the criticisms of the structure of the trials — the liability of the principal actors — (the statesman and the generals) — is clear.

The tribunal also observed:

> [I]ndividuals have international duties which transcend the national obligations of obedience imposed by the individual state. He who violates the laws of war cannot obtain immunity while acting in pursuance of the authority of the state if the state in authorising action moves outside its competence in international law.[37]

[36] International Military Tribunal, *Trial of the Major War Criminals* 141 (1947).

[37] *Ibid.*

(iii) *Responsibility of the scientist*

What then of the responsibility of the scientist? It is submitted that the general principles outlined in the preceding discussion have equal applicability to the case of the scientist. Far more than officials of the state or soldiers he has a freedom of choice, "a moral choice" as the Nuremberg judgment put it. In the case postulated in this article, of the scientist *knowingly* engaging in such operation, it is submitted that there is no legal principle distinguishing his guilt from that of the more prominent actors.

Even if in a particular country the scientist should be *ordered* by public authority to participate in weapons production, such order does not on the ordinary principles of international law exonerate him from liability. At best these are factors to be considered in mitigation.

Complicity in a crime against humanity is also a crime against humanity. Knowingly being party to the construction of weaponry without which the crime cannot be committed is equivalent to complicity in the crime. The swordsmith who is asked to produce the sharpest possible weapon for a person who desires to use it to kill unlawfully, and who knowingly produces the weapon for that purpose, cannot avoid culpability in ordinary criminal law. It does not avail him to plead that he did not know when or against whom the weapon would be used. He is, to use the language of criminal law, a *particeps criminis*, an accessory before the fact. If he recklessly failed to inform himself of the purpose of the research, his conduct may amount to criminality, through its reckless negligence.

There are also other principles of municipal and international law which will attach legal responsibility to the scientist. In civil law, clear foreseeability of probable damage, together with action despite such foreseeability will in most cases suffice to fix liability. For example leaving a car unattended on a slope without locking it, when one knows children are around who might enter it and release the brake, would suffice to attach liability to the owner if someone is injured as a result. The intervention of a third party was foreseeable. An explosive left unattended without warning in a public place would be another illustration. It is submitted further that responsibility and accountability in such instances would be both moral and legal, for there is always a duty of reasonable care to avoid injury to others who may foreseeably be damaged by one's actions. Julius Stone, one of the great jurists of our time, expressed this, in the context of nuclear weapons, when he observed:

> Unless then, we indulge a belief in such a miraculous transformation of the known world, we must attribute moral responsibility to those who, after they realised that their work would lead 'almost inevitably' to nuclear weapons, nevertheless continued on this path.[38]

Where scientists reach a point in their research when they can anticipate its use for dangerous and destructive purposes, it is naive for them to plead that they exercised their freedom of research, in the expectation that this knowledge, despite its great commercial or military value, would be left unused. They must be fixed with the responsibilities that would normally attach to any person who foresees the reasonable probability of damage from his or her action but nevertheless chooses to act in the manner productive of such probable harm.

The proposition is not without its difficulties. Situations can arise where the possible consequences of the most dangerous knowledge are not foreseen, as where Lord Rutherford's pioneering work on the atom was continued by him in the belief that "whoever talks of extracting power from the atom talks moonshine". Another dilemma arises where the knowledge unravelled can be used for both damaging and beneficial purposes. Nuclear irradiation for example can be used for nuclear weaponry as well as for peaceful purposes. Difficult ethical considerations arise here.

These are problem cases where the collective experience and wisdom of scientist, lawyer and layman must work out the solutions. They do not detract from the general principle which is all we are contending for at this stage, that a scientist who knowingly lends his skill to the active production of a nuclear weapon cannot avoid moral or legal blameworthiness for the consequences of its use.

Although international law did occasionally fix responsibility upon individuals, it did not in general deal with individuals as subjects of international law, invested with duties for breach of which they could be punished. The Nuremberg principles have changed all that and established the accountability of individuals for crimes against humanity. There are further developments such as the *Eichmann* trial, which show how national jurisdiction can be assumed by the courts of a country to punish individuals for crimes of this nature.

A growing sentiment in the field of international law is that international tribunals need to be established to adjudge and punish criminal acts. There is no doubt that in the unlikely event of mankind surviving a nuclear war or a

[38] Julius Stone, " Knowledge, Survival and the Duties of Science" 23 *American Univ. Law Review* 259 (1973).

limited nuclear war with its institutions intact, such an international criminal court will be set up. Even now various groups of jurists have set up the procedures for such trials and have actually enacted them.

If mankind is to survive without a nuclear war for the indefinite future it is inevitable that sooner or later there will be a change of heart in regard to nuclear weapons. In that changed climate of opinion those who have actively contributed to their manufacture will attract the opprobrium that they were knowing parties to the manufacture of weapons calculated to destroy mankind. Where their activities are today permitted to proceed uncondemned, they may well at that stage attract censure for their past actions, if not be actively branded as guilty of a crime against humanity.

Such changes of heart are not rare or unknown. A striking example from the last war was the post-war attitude towards Bomber Command's fire bombing of German cities. This was permitted and even applauded during the war but did not bring its commanders the same plaudits when peace arrived. When comparable commanders were decorated with peerages and loaded with honours, Air Marshal Harris received a marked lack of recognition. He retired finally without some of the honours he might otherwise have received.

That change of attitude was within the ranks of a victorious power. When, on the other hand, we move towards a peace where there are neither victors nor vanquished, but into an era where world opinion rather than national opinion is dominant, it may well be that a feeling of revulsion might set in against all who are actively associated with the manufacture of such weapons. Certainly, international law at that date will be adjusting its principles and attitudes in regard to this matter.

Thus, either scenario — that of nuclear war or of enduring peace — have adverse consequences for the scientist involved in this activity and international law will respond accordingly.

So far as concerns national law, principles of responsibility are also available. A scientist employed by an armaments manufacturer or the defence department would not be free of responsibility under ordinary principles of tort to those who are injured as a foreseeable consequence of his actions. The case of *Donoghue* v. *Stevenson*[39] extended the common law in regard to liability for manufactured products to the entire circle of those who could be foreseeably injured by negligence in manufacture. The case of *Rylands* v. *Fletcher*[40] recognized the principle of absolute liability to all those who might be foreseeably injured by the accumulation of a deleterious substance

39 [1932] A.C. 562.

40 L.R. 3 H.L. 330 (1868).

on one's premises. There is a growing circle of people to whom a duty is owed by those engaged in activities which might be dangerous. The same principles would certainly suffice according to ordinary principles of municipal law to fix responsibility upon a scientist for the consequences of his or her actions.

Academic freedom or freedom of research is not yet a defence and is not likely to be regarded as a defence when the freedoms they destroy are as weighty as those imperilled by the nuclear bomb.

(iv) *Levels of scientific involvement*

Thus far only the case of the scientist who is working actively on the frontiers of research regarding nuclear weaponry has been postulated. We are content to establish this principle initially, since from it various consequences will follow which will, no doubt, be the subject of specific analyses appropriate to the particular kind or level of scientific activity involved. It is important to note, however, that there are many levels of scientific participation in such activity. They can range from the level of high research mentioned earlier to the level of the humble technologist engaged in some comparatively low-level repetitive activity. Some of these levels may be enumerated as follows:

(*i*) Front line research, pure or applied; (*ii*) the high-level scientific expertise necessary for applying existing scientific knowledge to the processes of manufacture. At certain levels this can be done only by the highly trained expert scientist; (*iii*) the high-level scientific expertise necessary for maintaining in service order the weaponry and weapons systems that scientists and technologists have devised; (*iv*) middle-level scientific expertise involved in manufacture or servicing of weapons and weapons systems — this area will be progressively taken over by less trained technologists as the procedures become more stereotyped; and (*v*) low-level technology, mainly mechanical, though intricate.

At levels (*i*), (*ii*) and (*iii*), it is submitted that it is clear that the scientist's special expertise is involved. If an ethic such as has been outlined above results from this examination of the legal material it should be applicable at least to levels (*i*) to (*iii*). Whether it should apply further down the line is a matter for discussion and determination.

We are aware that the technology for the manufacture of crude nuclear devices is now said to be well within the range of the comparative amateur — the college level physics student to whom all the basic knowledge necessary for this purpose is available in published literature. Even granting this, and that this level of technological application does not attract to the actor the title of scientist, we would still submit that the process of nuclear weapons manufacture calls for a high level of scientific expertise. Without such expertise the highly sophisticated weapons manufacture which is now at the cutting edge of the nuclear armaments industry cannot proceed.

The argument will not thus be available that this is an attempt to close the stable door after the horse has bolted. There is still sufficient employment of true scientific expertise for the inhibitions resulting from the current thesis to be meaningful and productive of worthwhile results.

VI ALLEGED JUSTIFICATIONS FOR SCIENTIFIC INVOLVEMENT

(i) *Principle of freedom of scientific research*

There was a time when the right to uninhibited scientific inquiry was assumed. Pushing forward the frontiers of knowledge was an absolute right, because knowledge was beneficial to humanity and man had not yet reached the stage where the concept of "forbidden knowledge" had any relationship to reality. The voluntary moratorium by scientists in the field of recombinant DNA research in the 1970s provided an important practical illustration of the first recognition of the concept that there could be situations where the unravelling of knowledge may need to be halted in the public interest.

Knowledge now enables man to destroy his planet, alter his species and create new forms of life. The earlier assumptions are, therefore, being questioned, for however altruistic the scientist, he is opening up the possibility for those less altruistically motivated, to use this knowledge for questionable purposes. There is never a dearth of such persons acting in pursuit of political or personal power.

A theoretical answer to the claim to uninhibited research is that it is not the unravelling of knowledge that is at fault but its uncontrolled use. This is however not an adequate answer to the situation where manifestly the use cannot be controlled, and the scientist unravelling the new knowledge knows this well.

Academic freedom, like all other freedoms, is not an absolute right. The right of freedom of speech gives way to the right of others to preserve their reputations, and the law of defamation results. The right of freedom of trade gives way to the right of the citizen not to be the victim of artificially manipulated prices and the law of monopoly results. One must always recognize that there are limits beyond which one does not have the right to pursue one's individual freedom. In Kantian terms, one must act according to a rule of conduct which can be adopted as a governing rule of conduct by everyone else. In Christian terms, there is the golden rule — do as you would be done by.

There are always cases in the borderline area, in which one is in a sort of no man's land where A's freedom ends and B's begins. But there are clearly cases where A's freedom is so far exceeded that A is found trespassing well within the territory belonging to the like freedom of B. There are extreme cases, in other words, where one is left in no doubt of the encroachment upon another's rights. It seems clear that work on nuclear weapons is *par excellence* such an extreme case. To work knowingly in an activity that can contribute to the destruction of humanity and of life as we know it, is clearly an unwarranted extension of one's individual freedom and a deep intrusion into the similar freedom of every human being on this planet.

(ii) *Patriotic duty*

Patriotic duty is sometimes cited as a justification for placing one's talents at the disposal of one's country in situations of peril. The object of such devotion is no doubt to save one's country from peril, but even patriotism does not afford a justification for violating the rules of war. Patriotism could not be a defence to a charge of genocide, nor ought it to be a defence to a charge of ecocide, nor could it have saved the defendants at the Nuremberg trials, for if that were an answer, the laws of war would have no meaning. These issues have been sufficiently examined under the defence of "necessities of war".

(iii) *Defence of one's political beliefs or economic interests*

Neither political nor economic systems can survive the horrors of nuclear war, and this deprives such an argument of validity.

It is true that announcements have sometimes been made that powerful countries are prepared to resort even to nuclear war to defend their vital interests, as in the Gulf region. For either power bloc to resort to nuclear war to protect its oil supply or to keep its political influence in the region is to commit a crime against humanity just as much as if it were to resort to genocide for the same object. However vital such objective may be, it does not excuse the commission of a crime against humanity. The considerations discussed under 'necessities of war' have relevance here.

(iv) *Slippery slope argument*

Freedom of scientific research and inquiry is a principle of far-reaching importance. Even if it is conceded that it may be legitimately overridden in the extreme case of nuclear weaponry, will this argument be the beginning of a series of other measures aimed at curtailing academic and scientific freedom? One can see that this will be a substantial fear in the mind of the scientific community, which must be met.

Prohibitions of all sorts, whether in the moral, legal or merely administrative area, always involve questions of degree. There will inevitably be cases shading away in intensity from those where the rule clearly applies. A stage is soon reached where one is in an area where two views are possible and the rule may or may not be applicable. However there will be areas also where the prohibition or its lack is beyond question. How many hairs make a beard and how many books make a library? These are old scholastic questions where answers in certain situations are clear, but if one comes down to fifty hairs or twenty books one might be in difficulties.

With nuclear weaponry, it is submitted, the case falls too clearly into the area that does not admit of argument. One may encounter difficulty if one goes down the grade of research that involves massive danger to humanity, but nuclear weaponry is so clearly at the extreme end of the spectrum as to raise little doubt.

(v) *Belief in self-defence, deterrence or the concept of a contained nuclear war*

We have already explained the reasons for the untenability of these justifications of nuclear war. What then is the position of the scientist who works on nuclear weaponry, sincerely convinced that these justifications are valid?

To this the answer would be that the issues involved are too important for the scientist concerned to shuffle off his responsibility to pay due attention to these considerations. Many scientists would probably not have given them adequate examination. Such scientists do not qualify for exemption from responsibility. It is not adequate to desist from inquiry where the results of that inquiry may not support one's activity or to argue that the matters involved are too difficult.

We are left then with the case of the scientist who has carefully given his mind to these justifications and is convinced by them. This is an important group to whom this appeal is addressed. The various implications discussed in this paper may not have attracted their attention. It is submitted that if they had been aware of the matters discussed here they would arrive at a different conclusion.

There will still remain the case of scientists who, having heard the arguments, continue to be convinced that the justifications are valid. Their position will be no different from that of the persons who mistakenly believed that the fire bombing of Dresden or the nuclear bombing of Hiroshima were justified by the exigencies of national defence. The arguments considered under the head of 'necessities of war' cover this situation as well. It is submitted that, if ever the matter of their guilt under international law would come up for consideration, their *bona fide* but mistaken belief in the justifications for such action would not excuse them.

Especially at a time when the attention of all thinking persons has been directed at the problems of nuclear war, the scientist involved in the production of these very weapons will be expected to give very special attention to all their implications. Just two extracts from Anglican and Catholic viewpoints can be cited to illustrate that problems of deterrence and just war, among other legal concepts, have been well within the area of non-legal discussion.

The Archbishop of Canterbury, in his speech during the British Council of Churches debate on nuclear weapons in November 1980, said:

> It is impossible when talking of nuclear warfare to talk about the just war — the war prosecuted in a just cause in which gains can be judged to outweigh the inevitable injuries inflicted on individuals and societies. After the Second World War, even the defeated nations, Germany and Japan, were able to recover fairly rapidly. This would not be true after a Third World War.[41]

So also the National Conference of Roman Catholic Bishops of the United States 1976 resolved:

> With respect to nuclear weapons, at least those with massive destructive capability, the first imperative is to prevent their use. As possessors of a vast nuclear arsenal, we must also be aware that not only is it wrong to attack civilian populations but it is also wrong to threaten to attack them as part of a strategy of deterrence.[42]

These are all considerations well within the range of concern of the average layman and the scientist cannot keep away.

41 G. Goodwin (ed.), *Ethics and Nuclear Deterrence*, Croom Helm, 1983, p. 191.

42 *Id.* at 190.

(vi) *Belief that nuclear weapons control 'small wars' and prevent big ones*

One hears this argument often advanced, with the alleged supporting fact that it is the nuclear bomb that has held back the onset of World War III for a longer period than the interval of peace between World Wars I and II. The argument is fallacious. The nuclear powers play the role of policemen in this scenario, keeping the non-nuclear nations under control. The 'small war' between Iraq and Iran has not shown any amenability to control by the nuclear powers, nor have many of the other disputes ranging from international wars to internal liberation struggles.

When the nuclear nations fall out, there is no superior force to control them. They must play the game of brinkmanship, each attempting to stretch the other's restraint as far as they think it can be stretched. It is by a series of happy accidents and a run of good luck that a nuclear war between the big powers has been delayed. On realistic forecasts of probabilities, the chances are that serious disputes between them could occur within the next ten years. The Stockholm Institute of Peace Research has made even more pessimistic forecasts.

(vii) *Futility of individual protest*

There is a widely shared view that in matters decided at the summit level at which nuclear arms issues are decided, there is no scope for individual protest.

It is not the purpose of the present paper to indicate the ways in which individual opinion within a nation does make an impact upon those in control of the nation's affairs, although we believe that the impact is not inconsiderable.

This paper addresses the narrower question of what scientists can do. They are an indispensable link in the chain leading to the construction and improvement of nuclear weaponry. They are willing participants in the enterprise, not conscripted labour. They form an elite group within their respective nations, with an ethos and a conscience of their own. It is through their assistance in the first place that nuclear arms first emerged. It would be idle to contend that a body of persons in this key position can make no impact. If they choose to avoid the moral and legal issues involved they will indeed make no impact. If they do face these issues fairly and squarely, the consequences will be felt all the way up the chain of command.

(viii) *Culpability and responsibility lie with the decision-makers*

This has already been dealt with under the topic of individual responsibility.

(ix) *Superior orders*

The Nuremberg trials dealt specifically with the defence of superior orders. It has in military and international law never been sufficient to plead this excuse. Thus, even if a scientist is ordered by a government to engage in this kind of work, this will not exonerate him. In the case of most scientists, however, the difficulty is even greater, for the choice of employment is voluntary. If he opts to work in this particular field and remain in it even after knowing its objective, he cannot rely on this defence.

(x) *Economic necessity*

Scientists, like most others, need to earn their living and they may not always have a choice of employments. Once employed by a government or an arms producer, the possibility of a shift to alternative skilled employments can in many cases be practically difficult. The scientist may in effect be opting out of the only employment in which he can put his special skills to use.

The difficulty of the situation in which such scientists are placed is admitted. The crisis of conscience he must experience is however not peculiar to the nuclear weapons scientist. There are other walks of life as well in which economic necessity is not a strong enough answer. For example a skilled employee who has worked long years in a company which suddenly takes on a contract to supply South Africa with goods or expertise with which to bolster up the apparatus of apartheid may be faced with a similar option. A scientist in the nuclear industry, if convinced that it is dangerous to the human future, may opt out to his economic detriment, as many have done. A debt collector may be faced with this choice when he discovers that his employer is pursuing totally unprincipled business methods. The decision is uncomfortable but the choice is clear. As the climate of scientific opinion against nuclear weapons involvement grows, the choice will become still clearer.

VII CONCLUSION

Practical advantages of underlining scientific responsibility

(a) Clarification of the issues for scientists

The information contained in this paper could assist scientists seriously concerned with their role in nuclear arms production to debate and clarify the principal issues involved. Systematic discussions of these issues tend to be confined to the legal literature, which may not always be easily accessible to scientists. Once the legal principles are clear, the choices before scientists will also assume greater clarity. The view that such activity is immoral is perhaps already held by a large number of scientists. It will fortify them in their position if they are also aware that it is not merely immoral but illegal, criminal and tortious.

(b) Sharpening of the scientific conscience

Scientific studies and practice have concentrated on the pursuit and analysis of scientific knowledge. The scientific enterprise (save, principally, in the field of medicine) has not often had to grapple with matters of conscience, largely because the pursuit of knowledge has always been an elevated value in its own right and has not often produced high profile conflicts with moral considerations. There has also been a rather complacent confidence that questions of conscience would adequately be handled by each individual scientist as a person of conscience and integrity.

Recent developments in many branches of science have shaken this confidence in the adequacy of individual judgment. There has been in the past decade a marked increase in the scientist's concern with issues of conscience. There can be no area of sharper confrontation between freedom of research and issues of conscience than in regard to nuclear arms.

(c) Creation of a climate of scientific opinion

The individual scientist will be helped greatly in charting out his or her course of action by the growth of a climate of scientific opinion. If, in consequence of these discussions, a stronger general feeling develops regarding scientific responsibility, refusal to participate in the nuclear enterprise will become easier for the individual scientist. This climate of opinion will lead to a growing consciousness that the scientist cannot pass on responsibility to the decision-maker by way of exoneration.

(d) Evolution of codes of ethical conduct

Many branches of scientific activity have been able thus far to function without working out ethical codes. Physicists, chemists, botanists and zoologists do not thus far have even the rudimentary ethical code based on the Hippocratic oath, which doctors have adopted for their profession. Computer scientists, engineers and some other scientists are beginning to evolve codes for themselves. It is time that an ethical code emerged for nuclear scientists, and current discussions will no doubt help such a code to emerge.

(e) International declarations

International declarations, in relation to the duties of scientists engaged in nuclear weapons manufacture, are overdue. This paper is based upon propositions of international law. If those propositions are correct, the code of conduct consequent on them is a matter for the world community and for international law. This code needs to be worked out by international bodies at all levels. Councils of scientists must deliberate on these issues and formulate a code — possibly a code which has the approval of a body such as a World Council of Scientists. Appropriate organs of the United Nations and the United Nations itself could adopt such declarations in the light of international law. Once adopted such declarations could reinforce the current set of norms applicable to this matter under customary international law.

(f) Greater public awareness

Public awareness regarding the nuclear peril is growing and every additional means of increasing awareness is useful. There is no general awareness that a well-developed body of international law exists on this matter and there is a general feeling of futility.

(g) Reinforcing of anti-nuclear moral sentiment

Thus far the principal stimulus for anti-nuclear sentiment has been moral. Legal approaches have not been sufficiently used. It will considerably reinforce the strength of anti-nuclear sentiment if it is known that it can be rested on two bases — moral and legal — rather than on the moral basis alone.

One must not, in the midst of superpower politics and summit diplomacy, underestimate the strength and resolve of ordinary human beings at every level. Once their conscience is sufficiently awakened, once they realize how much is at stake and what they can do about it, they can move to a level of activity that can impinge upon state policy and international relations. The ordinary citizen has done this in the past. Scientists can do no less, placed as they are in a position in which the most powerful are but their clients. Scientists must be more conscious of the power they wield. They must also be more conscious of the responsibility that goes with that power.

23. Genetic Counsellors*

Genetic engineering, now advancing rapidly on many fronts, is showing a surprising potential for throwing up novel legal and human rights issues. The field of issues is indeed bewildering in both variety and complexity, so that a new range of professional skills is required in the field of genetic counselling.

In former times genetic counselling if it existed at all was a hit and miss kind of affair. There were broad Mendelian prophecies that one could make, but the new diagnostic tools are making it much more easy for us to be precise in our assessment of the situation. Amniocentesis and foetoscopy to mention just two, are some of the ways in which we are able today to present to people with much greater clarity than ever before, the facts on the basis of which they must make their choice. In consequence, there is also a growth in the scope of the duty that is expected of doctors and those advising patients on the various options before them and the various possibilities attendant on these different courses of conduct. The concept of negligence in genetic counselling has also grown dramatically, for the greater availability of information enlarges the duty and the responsibility of those charged with the function of giving advice.

It will be readily seen that genetic counselling involves a combination of many skills — medical, sociological, ethical and theological to mention a few. Moreover the legal ramifications run into several departments of the law — criminal law, tort, contract and human rights are all involved. New problems as yet unforeseen are likely to crop up in the next decade. The training of the genetic counsellor needs therefore to be multidisciplinary, multicultural and futuristic. It is a challenging new profession whose future is as yet uncharted. It is an exciting one and deeply involved also with human rights.

* Keynote address at World Congress on Law and Medicine, New Delhi, 24 February 1985.

The average citizen, who will feel the multiple impacts of genetic engineering in his or her private life, must feel increasingly inadequate to handle them and needs counselling on many issues.

Counselling cannot however be given on a set of general principles equally applicable to all individuals. Ethnic and cultural backgrounds can vary to such an extent that, in the same factual situation, differing advice may need to be given to different individuals.

The best example of this is in relation to the counselling of abortion.

It is not possible to visualize all the problem areas confronting the genetic counsellor but a few of the more important will be considered in this paper.

Genetic counselling has been defined by the American Ad Hoc Committee on Genetic Counselling[1] as a communication process which deals with human problems associated with the occurrence, or the risk of occurrence, of a genetic disorder in a family. Their report goes on to identify five areas in which an appropriately trained person may help an individual or family:

1. in comprehending the medical facts, including the diagnosis, probable cause of the disorder and the available management;
2. in appreciating the way heredity contributes to the disorder and the risk of recurrence in specified relations;
3. in understanding the alternatives for dealing with the risk of recurrence;
4. in choosing the course of action which seems to them appropriate in view of their risk, their family goals and their ethical and religious standards, and to act in accordance with that decision; and
5. in making the best possible adjustment to the disorder in an affected family member and/or to the risk of recurrence of that disorder.

It will be understood, of course, that counselling in all these areas has been carried on informally for generations by non-physicians and physician counsellors according to such knowledge as was available. The clergy, psychotherapists, lawyers and respected members of the group to which the patient belongs have all been giving this informal advice in the past. Such counselling has been aptly described by one writer as "a kind of folk genetic counselling" which existed long before its current medical framework in the West".[2] The level of scientific knowledge now involved has however ad-

[1] (1975) 27 *Am.J.Genetics* 240–41.

[2] T. Powledge, "Genetic Counsellors without Doctorates" in *Genetic Counselling: Facts, Values and Norms*, A. Capron (ed.), 1979, pp. 103–4.

vanced dramatically. With the application of new molecular techniques to medical genetics, the loose collection in the 1970s of isolated pieces of genetic information has now transformed this area into systematic new subdisciplines such as neurogenetics, immunogenetics, and behavioural genetics, each of them raising groups of human rights issues.

The skills involved in genetic counselling are so diverse that they may well be beyond the competence of an individual and may require a team effort. Indeed such a team effort is commonly used in genetic counselling in medical clinics. Yet the need for individuals to be trained in a proper approach to such issues is great, for it is not always or indeed often that such team services would be available to the average citizen. It is true that in the more economically advanced countries hundreds of specialized genetic clinics have grown up (estimated in the U.S. in 1971 at 440) and probably very many more today,[3] but the problem is equally important to the poorer countries and needs to be appropriately provided for.

The catalogue of situations in which counselling becomes relevant is constantly growing. At present the range of problems includes the following: *in vitro* fertilization, embryo transplantation, artificial insemination by donor, freeze preservation of sperm, sperm banks, surrogate motherhood, new techniques of contraception for males as well as females, new methods of overcoming child-bearing disabilities and techniques of foretelling the sex of an unborn child. Each of these produces new crops of complex problems. The law, correspondingly, has also to handle unprecedented concepts such as wrongful birth and wrongful life claims. All of these concern the duties, responsibilities and liabilities of genetic counsellors.

The legal issues involved in genetic counselling are the subject of a growing literature. I shall only attempt here to deal briefly with the general principles of legal liability and then examine some illustrative new advances in technology and law. I shall then use this material to discuss some important issues of policy relating to genetic counselling.

PRINCIPLES OF LEGAL LIABILITY

New advances in diagnostic procedure such as amniocentesis, foetoscopy and ultrasonography result in higher expectations of counselling regarding the likelihood of defects in the child to be born. Nearly a hundred metabolic defects — among them Tay-Sachs disease, anencephaly and spina bifida — can be detected by these procedures. Suits have been instituted regarding alleged defective genetic counselling in the birth of children with Down's

3 See H. Lynch and H. Guirgis, *International Directory of Genetic Services*.

syndrome (mongolism), "cri-der-chat" syndrome (a chromosomal abnormality leading to mental retardation) and polycystic kidney disease, to mention but a few.[4] Those at the receiving end of such suits have been not only medical personnel but also genetic counsellors.

What is the liability of persons who either fail to resort to available procedures and hence fail to advise that a defective child is on the way, or who fail to advise of the availability of these procedures, or use these procedures and reach incorrect conclusions, or use these procedures and thereby cause harm to the mother or the foetus?

We shall not consider here the duties of advisers who are consulted in the situation where the defective child has already been born and a decision has to be taken as to whether life support or sustenance is to be withdrawn. This is a larger question which cannot adequately be considered here, though some of the issues in genetic counselling bear an analogy to the issues arising in that field.

The general principles of negligence liability in the common law of tort were well enunciated by Lord Wilberforce in the House of Lords in *Anns* v. *Merton London Borough Council.*[5] Lord Wilberforce there formulated a two-stage approach.

> First one has to ask whether, as between the alleged wrongdoer and the person who has suffered damage there is a sufficient relationship of proximity or neighbourhood such that, in the reasonable contemplation of the former, carelessness on his part may be likely to cause damage to the latter, in which case a prima facie duty of care arises...
>
> Secondly, if the first question is answered affirmatively, it is necessary to consider whether there are any considerations which ought to negative or limit the scope of the duty or the class of person to whom it is owed or the damage to which a breach of it may give rise ...[6]

The legal liability of the genetic counsellor can be tested by these principles.

1. *Relationship of proximity*

By its very nature genetic counselling must contemplate at least three classes of persons as being within the area of those affected by the advice — namely

[4] See A.M. Capron, "Tort Liability in Genetic Counselling" (1979) 79 *Col. L.R.* 619.

[5] [1978] A.C. 728 at pp. 751–72; (1977) 2 All E.R. 492 at 498. For a reformulation and amplification of this test by the House of Lords, see *Caparo Industries plc* v. *Dickman and others*, [1990] 1 All E.R. 568; *Murphy* v. *Brentwood District Council*, [1990] 2 All E.R. 908.

[6] [1978] A.C. 752.

the person who is the immediate recipient of the advice, the members of the family (especially the spouse) of such person and the child (or children) born subsequent to action upon such advice.

The duty of care, in the light to modern medical techniques, will perhaps vary with the resources available in a given community. Techniques such as amniocentesis which may be considered routine in certain cases in some societies, may not be as commonly expected in others. Standards of care expected may consequently vary and failure to suggest amniocentesis in certain conditions may amount to negligence in some societies but not in others. Ordinary negligence principles will determine the standards of care expected.

As for the spouse, there are obvious situations in which a duty is owed to the spouse, as where matters concerning children or prospective children are the subject of the advice. The action for wrongful birth is increasingly resorted to where an unwanted child is born and damages are sought for failure to advise that the child was to be defective.

Some broad issues relating to this type of action are discussed later. More complex issues could be raised in the context of *in vitro* fertilization, embryo transplantation and surrogate motherhood, where the rights of a third party outside the matrimonial or *de facto* relationship are involved.

The third group of persons who have obvious rights in regard to negligence of the genetic counsellor are the children who are in a sense the subject matter of the advice. When a defective child is born, with its quality of life hopelessly impaired, the claim is being advanced with increasing frequency that the very life of suffering of the child — which the child did not elect to have — is a wrong. The child thus claims damages from the adviser for the wrong done to it. This is discussed later in this paper.

2. *Limiting Factors*

There are numerous circumstances, many of them considerations of policy, which will in the years ahead present problems to genetic advisers and the courts.. Among these are questions relating to the value of human life. Can one say in any circumstances that a child is a burden rather than a blessing? If a child can claim in certain circumstances that it ought never to have been born, are the floodgates being opened to an unlimited range of actions by dissatisfied children, including actions against their own parents? Are doctors and genetic advisers, faced with the prospect of numerous fresh kinds of claims, likely to practise defensively, always protecting themselves rather than giving their patients or clients the best possible disinterested advice? Where does one draw the line in relation to birth "defects", for slight departures from the ideal, whether mentally, physically or emotionally, can often be alleged? In admitting certain types of claims, should the courts have regard to the ability of the new principles they lay down, to handle future medical advances such as cloning or genetic selection? For purposes of damages, how can one place a value upon non-existence, as in claims for wrongful life?

Modern case law in the common law world is only beginning to grapple with some of these problems but it shows that the way ahead is very much like a legal minefield. Two newly developing types of action, negligence claims for wrongful birth and for wrongful life, illustrate the problems that can arise.

Wrongful Birth

The concept of wrongful birth comes into play when the patient, or the father, might not have desired a particular birth had all the facts been known, and for lack of proper service or preventive action there is a birth of a defective child. To what extent is there an action for negligence against the person who was in possession of the information or alternatively was in a position to find out the information and did not advise her or advised her wrongly? In consequence there can be an action for damages and there have been successful institutions of actions on that basis.

There was a time when the general judicial attitude might be described as the 'blessing' or 'boon' attitude, implying that having a child is in all events a blessing. It is a blessing provided by Providence, God's blessing, and it is not for us to complain, whatever the defects of the child might be. There was then a movement to the theory that even if it might not be a blessing, life was certainly an advantage to the child. The birth of an unwanted child was still not a matter for complaint. Today we find a trend emerging, under which the courts are being asked to recognize that a child is not necessarily an unmixed blessing, or boon, that life is not necessarily an advantage to it, but that it can in fact be a positive disadvantage, to both parent and child. Once we have judicial thinking recognizing that the birth of a child can be a positive disadvantage, we are not very far from the construction of some altogether different causes of legal action in the future. Old standards of discharge of advisory duty, where for example the doctor merely tells you that there is a chance a child might be defective, are no longer adequate for the time when a parent can be told with near certainty that a child will, for example, suffer from spina bifida.

Berman v. *Allen*,[7] a case in the New Jersey Supreme Court, overcame some of the initial barriers to a wrongful birth action. The parents of a Down's syndrome child were suing their doctors alleging negligence in informing them of the high risk of chromosomal abnormalities involved in the pregnancy of a thirty eight year old mother. They were not informed about the availability of amniocentesis and its potential for detecting abnormalities. This decision overruled the earlier landmark decision in *Gleitman* v. *Cosgrove*,[8] a case based on failure to advise of the harmful effects of rubella upon unborn children. One of the considerations on which the rubella decision was based was that it was against public policy to grant damages for denial of the opportunity to terminate the existence of a defective child in embryo.

That obstacle having now been overcome, a number of other successful actions followed the *Berman* decision. Assessment of damages is of course a difficult question but pecuniary loss as well as emotional damages will have to be considered. The way is wide open in common law jurisdictions for the development of this cause of action. In the words of one writer, "Torts law is a mechanism of social engineering. As such it should be utilised to encourage physicians to carry out their duty of disclosing genetic information to pregnant women thereby rendering more meaningful the constitutional right established in *Roe v. Wade*."[9] The reference is of course to the landmark American decision recognizing a woman's constitutional right to have an abortion.[10]

The availability of wrongful birth actions will thus depend on the law in each country in relation to abortion. The action will only be available within the strict confines of the legal permissibility of abortion in the relevant jurisdiction.

Wrongful Life

An even more controversial area is the wrongful life concept, where a child who has been born defective, brings an action on the basis that that child did not desire to be born into an existence of suffering and that this came about through negligence on the part of those who were in a position to avert this tragedy. There have been a few institutions of actions on this basis which run counter to all our traditional concepts of causes of action. Though they have not been very favourably received thus far in the U.S., more actions of this

7 80 NJ 421, 404 A 2d. 8 (1979).

8 49 NJ 22, 227 A 2d. 689 (1967).

9 T. Ryan Durkan. "Tort — Wrongful Birth.." (1980) 55 *Wash. L.R.* 701 at 713.

10 *Roe* v. *Wade* 410 US 113 (1973).

sort are in the process of institution and there has been a peripheral measure of success at least in one or two of these cases.

This is a concept which in fact gives a person an action, arising from an act which occurs even preconceptually. We have long been familiar in the common law with the idea of a cause of action based upon a prenatal wrong. For example, there is the well-known Victorian case of *Watt* v. *Rama*[11] where a child was able to recover damages for prenatal negligence which had caused her injury. What we are now considering is something even more dramatic, where the child is asking for damages for an act which preceded its very conception. The opinion of the judges in America seems to be against this but there have been fairly strong views that it is not quite so absurd as it might appear, and one basis on which it might be possible to construct such a right is this: If you have a right under our law, you also have a duty so to exercise that right that it will not cause harm to others who are, as Lord Wilberforce observed, within the reasonable contemplation of the doer as likely to be affected by his negligence. True, the child was not yet in existence, but the concept of the rights of the unborn child is gaining greater acceptance. Genetic engineering is forcing the law to come to grips with the rights of the child who is as yet unconceived. When these concepts were beyond the contemplation of the law, the law of earlier ages was prepared to give rights to the unborn child which the child could claim when it came into existence. Today legal thinking is being forced to cross another barrier — not the barrier of birth but the barrier of conception. With the new scientific possibilities now before us, this may well occur.

In *Curlender* v. *Bio-Science Laboratories*,[12] an infant born with a severely disabling hereditary disease — Tay Sachs disease (amaurotic familial idiocy) — was held to have a cause of action in relation to detectable genetic abnormalities against those under a duty to counsel its parents on their genetic health.

Once the principle is admitted, the question of its extension to mental, emotional and even economic and social damages is perhaps only a matter of time. The question is, where does one draw the line? We must remember in this context that the first action in which a wrongful life claim was made was one in which an illegitimate child claimed damages against his father for "causing him to be born an adulterine bastard".[13] Damages were claimed in respect of person, property and reputation.

[11] [1972] V.R. 353.

[12] 106 Cal. App. 3d. 811, 165 Cal. Rptr. 477 (1980).

[13] *Zepeda v. Zepeda* 41 [1].c App. 2d. 240, 190 N.E. 2d. 849;379 US 945 (1963).

Writers have analysed several actionable situations which would arise if the concept of wrongful life actions becomes established. These include the illegitimacy situation involved in the case just mentioned, actions for failure to diagnose a pregnancy within the time allowed for legal abortion, resulting in birth with deformities and actions for negligent genetic counselling.[14] American cases are increasing,[15] but there is a marked reluctance to give infants a cause of action.

In the *Curlender* case it was held that a legal obligation of care existed on the part of the genetic testing laboratory to both parents and the infant. They hence had a duty to use requisite care in administering tests aimed at advising the parents of potential genetic defects in their unborn children.

Of course an important barrier to such a cause of action is the difficulty of giving rights to one who has not yet been conceived. I would submit that one of the weaknesses of our current legal systems is that they do not look for enough into the future. In other spheres, as for example, the environmental, modern technology is forcing the law to think in terms of the rights of future generations. Legal attitudes outside the common law and the civil law (e.g. Chinese, African, Melanesian) are deeply concerned with the rights of children yet unborn.

The barrier is therefore not insurmountable. The law must come to grips with the problem and I submit will not fail to cross this barrier in the near future.

Especially in the field of genetic counselling, if we view genetic counsellors as professionals engaged in an area of specialization, I would submit that there is no conceptual obstacle to the conferment of a right of action upon those not yet conceived.[16]

A great conceptual difficulty will be the assessment of damages. How does one value existence or, to be more precise, non-existence? Is non-existence preferable to existence for anyone?

Extreme cases such as the Lesch-Nyhan Syndrome, where the subject of this hereditary disease can neither walk nor sit upright, and suffers muscle spasms which result in dislocation and even self-mutilation (such as biting and partial amputation of one's own fingers), may suggest that non-existence has a value in some instances. On the other hand even the sufferer from some very painful disability may still value life and desire to cling on to it.

14 See Kelly L. Frey, "Torts — Wrongful Life — Infant's Right to Sue for Negligent Counselling", (1981) 48 *Tenn. L. Rev.* 493 at 496.

15 An English case involving wrongful life is *McKay* v. *Essex Area Health Authority* (1982) 2 W.L.R. 890.

16 See on this K.L. Frey, *op. cit.*, at. 509.

Courts have very difficult conceptual tasks ahead of them in this area, but will no doubt evolve some principles in the foreseeable future.

In Vitro Fertilization and Embryo Transplantation

The process of fertilizing human egg cells by spermatozoa outside the human body, culturing the fertilized egg and then transferring it by artificial means to a uterus which has been hormonally prepared to receive it, has progressed to the point where numerous normal births have resulted from it. We have not of course reached the stage of full term gestation outside the human body. If and when that stage is reached a host of new legal and genetic problems will arise. However present developments have already raised sufficient problems to engage our attention for many years.

The genetic counsellor's services will become relevant in the following among other situations:

1. Fertile husband married to an infertile woman with normal ovaries and uterus but with a diseased Fallopian tube. Her eggs could be surgically removed, fertilized with her husband's sperm and the embryo transplanted into her uterus.
2. Fertile husband married to an infertile woman with normal ovaries but defective uterus. Use of uterus of another woman who acts as deputy or surrogate mother.
3. Infertile husband married to a fertile woman. Her eggs could be fertilized by donor sperm and the resulting embryo transplanted into her womb.
4. Infertile husband married to an infertile woman. Donated eggs fertilized with donated sperm and implanted in the woman.

Other situations are also possible. All of them point to the need for expert genetic counselling before the procedures are resorted to.

These procedures can also, by precise timing, increase the probability that a child of a particular sex will be produced. They admit also of freeze preservation of sperm for a practically indefinite duration and of sperm banks storing semen of men with particular characteristics., Each of these, as will be appreciated, produces a whole new range of genetic problems.

All this is of course in addition to procedures of artificial insemination which have long been practised.

What ethical and other problems confront the genetic counsellor in these areas?

The counsellor will need to have a clear view of his or her own stand on questions such as whether it is right to interfere with the processes of life creation and whether genetic material or assistance could be used from outside the bonds of matrimony. He or she will need a clear appreciation of the positions of various religious and ethnic groups on such questions and must have the necessary sensitivity to be able to communicate with such groups without imposing the counsellor's own point of view.

Various questions of professional negligence also arise in regard to all those who have counselled a particular procedure or participated in it, and those responsibilities will be not only to the immediate patient but to the husband and the child.

We are also moving to an age where gene manipulation and gene therapy will assume more practical importance and the counselling problems involved will then multiply.

Having thus outlined two or three specific problem areas, I proceed now to consider some general policy issues involved.

1. *The Problem of the Risk Involved in Diagnostic Procedures*

The genetic counsellor needs to be familiar with risk assessment and must have the skill and understanding necessary to communicate this information sympathetically.

An illustration of the ethical and counselling issues relating to probabilities is seen in the diagnosis of Down's syndrome by amniocentesis. The probability of a mother aged thirty-five having a child with Down's syndrome is one in 360. The risk of damage to the foetus by amniocentesis is one in hundred. A mother aged thirty-five who has amniocentesis exposes her foetus to a risk of death four times as great as the risk that the child has Down's syndrome. If an action for negligence could arise from not using modern diagnostic procedures to warn of the defect, an action should also be possibly maintained for negligent counselling services if there is no adequate warning of the risks attendant on the procedure. Clearly, expert counselling skills will be needed side by side with the new procedures.

There are indeed cases where the judges have now expressed the view that amniocentesis is a procedure which is available, which is proved to be reasonably safe and which has become standard procedure and if a medical adviser does not give advice about the use of amniocentesis to detect disease prenatally, he or she has been guilty of negligence. These are developments in the law which have to be very closely watched and I have no doubt that in the next ten or fifteen years, we will have a whole crop of cases exploring these possibilities and perhaps constructing new causes of action on this basis.

The procedure of foetoscopy entails a risk which is almost negligible in the case of the mother, but there is a 5% chance of an injury to the foetus which will result in abortion. There is also the possibility of diagnostic error in foetoscopy. For example, out of 30 cases where diagnosis was attempted on this basis, there is a possibility of one or two misdiagnoses. The element of risk involved to the foetus is one which the mother is entitled to know.

Thus while the duty to advise of the available procedures is growing on the one hand, the duty to advise of the dangers involved is also increasing. It is a rather difficult path that the adviser has to tread.

2. *The Problem of Cultural Conflict*

In multi-racial societies there is an important area of possible clash between the cultural values of one group and another. The genetic counsellor needs to be acutely aware of this, especially in countries like Australia, where many migrant groups function within the matrix of a largely Anglo-Saxon culture. Especially if the entire programme is maintained and operated by people of one cultural background — people of Anglo-Saxon values — and the community affected is another community, whether it is Greek or Italian or Indian or Lebanese, the problem of culture clash becomes acute. This raises problems about the principles one follows in giving advice as well as the class of people from whom the counsellors are to be drawn.

Where many sub-cultures function within a major culture one must also look at the problem against the human rights background of an evolving recognition of the rights of minorities — not merely as to their basic and economic rights but also as to their cultural rights.[17]

In the context of countries with a high rate of illiteracy, another danger to be avoided is the danger of speaking down to the patient or of laying down the law. Persons from such backgrounds will tend to be very much under the dominance of their social groups and will need to be counselled with special sensitivity to their backgrounds. The need for children, the value of children, the duty to procreate, the sanctity of life, the inviolability of processes of procreation — all these may be concepts deeply ingrained.

[17] This problem is examined at greater length in Chapter 15 above in the context of thalassaemia.

3. *The Problem of Disclosing the Sex of the Unborn Child*

Modern medical science can now predict the sex of the unborn baby. Many doctors act on the ethic that unless it is really necessary for therapeutic purposes, they will not divulge the baby's sex to the parents. Genetic counsellors presumably act upon the same ethical rule.

The reason is not difficult to see, having regard to the strong preferences prevalent in certain communities for children of a particular sex. If sex is known in advance, requests for abortion can result, as indeed has been the experience of some doctors and counsellors. The author has been told of a case where community pressures for a boy were so great that withholding of information on this matter was misconstrued by the mother as an indication that the child was a girl. On such information abortion was sought, only to discover too late that the aborted child was in fact a male.

Where, in the future, procedures become available for determining sex even prior to conception, the duty lying on genetic counsellors to advise on such matters will be very onerous. Free information and availability of such procedures could even alter the sex ratio in a given community and upset the balance of the sexes on which so much family law and other law and custom have been built.

This is a great issue of the future on which the genetic counselling profession needs to work out guiding principles now. There will need to be more specific discussions of the many cultural, social, ethical, and political issues involved.

4. *The Problem of Cost*

An important element in genetic counselling is the question of the cost to the community of permitting a defective child to be born. The mother who is advised of some grave defect may opt, as she is entitled to do, to have the child, despite contrary advice. She is within her legal rights in refusing an abortion.

There are two groups of persons who could be adversely affected by this decision. The first is the immediate family, who may be placed under severe emotional and economic strain by the necessity of caring for and living with a seriously defective child, who may not be able to fend for itself throughout its life. The mother may take the decision but the family bears the cost. The counsellor is on delicate ground in giving advice in this situation.

The second group involved is the community at large. The burden of supporting such a child will in most cases be thrown eventually upon the community. Expenses involved are not merely hospital beds or places in institutions. There is also the staffing of those institutions and the withdrawal or diminution of facilities which other members of the community may need. Sometimes, as is the case with thalassaemia major, the cost of medication for a normal lifetime may run to half a million dollars. The community must bear this cost. Can the counsellor legitimately take into account the question of cost to the community when advising an individual mother?

As noted jurists such as Roscoe Pound have constantly observed in relation to the distribution of community goods, we live in a world of shortage and we must evolve legal principles which will achieve the optimum distribution of community resources.

Guidelines for genetic counsellors will need to be urgently considered in relation to this particular problem. In Third World societies it assumes special importance.

5. *The Problem of Birth Control and Sterilization*

Where policies of birth control are officially adopted, this is a very sensitive political issue, especially in the poorer countries, where children may be looked upon as a form of social insurance. It is beyond the scope of this paper to examine the duties of counsellors in this field.

However the Bhopal tragedy draws attention to other situations where counselling not to have children or indeed counselling for sterilization may take on grave practical importance. I refer particularly to possibilities of nuclear contamination from nuclear accidents and to exposure to other deleterious substances, e.g., agricultural sprays which may lead to the tendency, the probability or even the certainty of defective children.

Should there be such an unfortunate event, the duty of genetic counselling would assume a new importance. The Three Mile Island Reactor accident resulted in massive evacuations of populations. So did the Bhopal tragedy. If industrial or nuclear contamination should occur on the Bhopal scale and if scientific information at some future date should be able to forecast with some assurance that the victims would probably produce defective children, a question of persuading large groups to adopt sterilization could arise. This is a new situation which the genetic counselling profession may need to foreshadow as a possible problem of the future.

On a lesser scale there is the problem of advising sterilization in other instances where the genetic history of the patient indicates proneness to procreate children with a particular defect. It is a human right of all persons to procreate and found a family. It is difficult to override this right by compulsion. It is for the counsellor to perfect the necessary skills in persuasion to achieve such a result without compulsion.

6. *The Problem of Reaching through to the Public*

Although genetic counselling has become an accepted profession in the affluent world, the poorer countries can ill afford this service. Interdisciplinary teams in the major urban centres can no doubt offer genetic counselling with the same level of expertise as in the affluent world, but to reach through to the hundreds of thousands of villages in the country is another problem. Moreover sociological research has shown how difficult it is to break through the screens of tradition by which women in such societies are hedged around.

This imposes special responsibilities upon the individual counsellor and on community service groups, to give thought to the methods of reaching through to the people who need their advice in such communities. Those who plan genetic counselling services for such societies need to be acutely conscious of the need for planning in this regard.

It will also be necessary to have teams of persons with the various requisite kinds of expertise at the nearest urban centres, for consultations by workers in the field.

It is important also that in hospitals there should be teams of persons with the requisite interdisciplinary skills to back up genetic counselling services. The idea of an ethics committee in hospitals is still new and many large hospitals still exist which lack such an ethics committee. Such committees need to be established as a matter of course in every major hospital.

7. *The Problem of Sharing the Burden of Defective Children*

Social organization is still such as to place the burden of maintaining the retarded child upon the parents. To most parents this is a burden beyond their capacity to bear, although they no doubt willingly assume this burden at least initially.

As the law develops there need to be mechanisms for spreading this burden throughout the community. The broad shoulders of the community can bear a burden which could break the back of an individual or a family. It is essential therefore that as part of genetic counselling services there should also be available a back up service of institutions for maintenance and care. In many communities this still depends on private charity and philanthropy. It is a social responsibility of the community, and genetic counselling services should be able to offer this facility as part of their overall service to the community. The appropriate state and local government instrumentalities must be persuaded that this is also an important aspect ancillary to genetic counselling. Merely to plan for genetic counselling services is insufficient.

8. *The Problem of "Defensive Counselling"*

As negligence liability for genetic counselling becomes an established concept, there will be a growth in what may be described as "defensive counselling". This phenomenon has been encountered in the context of growing damages awards against doctors, resulting in the phenomenon of "defensive medicine". Doctors, naturally concerned with their own liability, sometimes make this consideration rather than the interest of their patient their governing concern. Advice would therefore be given which would be safe for themselves rather than in the best interests of their patient.

Courts would need to bear this in mind as a policy consideration in the formative days of legal liability for genetic counselling. If the circle of damages is drawn too wide it can have a counter-productive effect upon the emergence of satisfactory genetic counselling services. It can also raise the cost of this service by increasing insurance expenses which will be borne by the patient.

These considerations are easier stated than given effect to, for the courts must also build new principles to protect those who receive or are entitled to receive such advice. It is a difficult problem and raises questions whether some general scheme of state insurance might provide at least a partial answer. It would indeed be a pity to see the infant genetic counselling profession stunted in its growth by fear of litigation.

9. *The Problem of Medical Experimentation*

Medical experimentation is necessary for the advancement of knowledge. It has often to be practised upon parents, including expectant mothers. The element of independent counselling assumes great importance in this situation, for the patient is under the influence of the doctor and the hospital. These latter are anxious to conduct their experimentation. Although they are conscious of the need to safeguard the interests of the patient, numerous conflict situations arise. So much is this the case that detailed guidelines have been evolved for medical experimentation, the main object of which is to safeguard the interests of the patient. Particularly when an expectant mother is involved the need for independent counselling is great.

It is vital that the subject be fully informed of the risks both to herself and to the foetus even of apparently routine experimental procedures. Rewards should not be offered for participation. The safety of the subject should always take priority over the needs of the experiment. Consent once given should at any time be capable of being withdrawn. The investigator should not be absolved from liability.

All of these, and the other safeguards internationally worked out should be known to the genetic counsellor who should be available to give independent advice to the patient.

An important problem here, with political overtones, is the alleged 'dumping' of untried drugs and foods in Third World countries by large pharmaceutical and other firms. Expectant mothers are often the victims of such attempts at developing products and extending sales. Genetic counsellors especially in Third World countries must be sufficiently apprised of this area of danger.

10. *Whom Does the Counsellor Counsel?*

There is an important question to be answered here. It is true the immediate subject of the advice given by a genetic counsellor, in cases where abortion and similar issues are involved, is the mother or both parents. But are these the only parties? There is also a third party, the unborn child, whose interests there is no one to protect. If a counsellor considers himself or herself to be the adviser only to the mother, the infant's rights go unheeded. If the counsellor considers that he or she is watching the interests of the child as well, the mother may have a feeling that her interests are not being adequately considered.

Genetic counsellors will need to bear in mind their responsibilities to the unborn. They must not lose sight of the fact that they are taking decisions on behalf of a foetus that is obviously unable to take a decision on its own, just as much as, very often, a court of law takes a decision on behalf of a child or an unborn child. In that kind of situation, where an entity entitled to human rights is unable to decide for itself, we have a structure provided by the legal system for a decision to be substituted for the child's own in the best interests of that child. I suggest that the process we are resorting to here, is in a sense analogous to that, because we are now substituting for a decision of that foetus unable to decide for itself, a decision influenced by the advice of the genetic counsellor. It is a decision as to whether that foetus is to be given life or not. We have to evolve some kind of principles for making that decision on behalf of the child. This is where counselling comes in, but of course with a preponderant emphasis on the interests of the mother. Ideally the doctors and third parties representing the community would provide counselling services for the mother, but it is most important that the interests of the child-to-be are not discounted. How the possible conflict of interest between mother and foetus is to be worked out is an important matter for discussion by the genetic counselling profession.

It will be seen then that apart from the technical specialities which are part of the genetic counsellor's training, there are also many broader perspectives which must be borne in mind by those who are responsible for the training of genetic counsellors. In Third World situations these social dimensions acquire even greater importance than in developed countries.

Genetic counselling is a challenge and an important new area of knowledge and responsibility. Its development in the years ahead will be anxiously watched.

24. Towards More Humanistic Science: The Profile of a National Effort*

(A) JAPANESE CONCERNS WITH HUMANISTIC SCIENCE

There is a substantial measure of concern in Japanese scientific and legal circles with the damaging impact on human rights of various branches of modern science. Environmental dangers are of course high on the list of Japanese concerns, but there have been added to this in recent years such types of activity as recombinant DNA research and mind manipulation. Unfortunately however, as in most countries, there is an insufficiency of interdisciplinary contact between the scientific training centres and the humanistic disciplines. The sociology of science, the history of science, science and ethics, the philosophy of science — these subjects are taught but are generally not compulsory, and the scientist moves out into the world of specialized research without the guiding influences such disciplines can give.

The Minister of Education has set up an advisory council known as the *Gakujutsu Shinjukai* (The Science and Research Council) which has a number of standing and special committees involving a cross-disciplinary membership. One of the committees set up this year is the Science and Society Committee, which is chaired by a lawyer — Professor Aomi of the Tokyo University Faculty of Law. It is expected to survey and evaluate the roles which the natural, social and human sciences play and need to play in contemporary society. This Committee has set up sub-committees to deal with such problems as research on recombinant DNA. .

Apart from governmental and university organizations, there are also private institutions that sponsor studies in the fields of Science and Society. Perhaps the outstanding institution in this field is the Mitsubishi-Kasei Institute of Life Sciences, funded by the Mitsubishi organization to the extent

* Extracted from a report on *Human Rights in Japan*, prepared by the author after a period of research at the Law Faculty of Tokyo University in 1979. The report was published as *Human Rights in Japan*, Lantana, Melbourne, 1979.

of five million dollars a year. One of its important divisions is the laboratory of social life science, headed by Dr. Keiko Nakamura, one of Japan's outstanding social scientists, whom I had the privilege to meet. The entire institution is devoted to research aimed at contributing to the welfare of human society.

Japanese scientific thought appears to have undergone a transformation around 1970 with an increasing emphasis on all aspects of science which have a bearing upon human happiness and respect for life. The concept of science for the sake of science has receded somewhat. It is significant that in a survey conducted in 1974 among scientists, 85% saw a potential danger in unrestricted research in life sciences, while only 4% contended that all research activities should be completely free without any restriction being placed on scientific research.[1] This has been partly the cause of the popularization of the expression "life sciences" between 1970 and 1972, the characteristics of life sciences being:

(1) the emphasis placed on people, and their happiness and welfare;

(2) the importance of participation of social and humanistic disciplines; and

(3) awareness of the importance of the scientific impact on daily life.

Three of the kinds of activity envisaged towards this end, but not yet nationally achieved, are:

(1) incorporation in natural sciences education of courses on the social significance of science and on science and society;

(2) systematic mass educational activities by leading scientists, for improving rapport between the scientific and the lay world; and

(3) interdisciplinary research activities, e.g., "Does Research Threaten Privacy or Does Privacy Threaten Research?", "Science and the Police", etc.

The Japanese public too has altered its attitude towards science significantly around 1970 with a realization of its close connections with their own lives and environment.[2]

[1] Annual Report, Mitsubishi-Kasei Institute of Life Sciences, 1974, p. 64. By way of contrast, the only accepted model of the scientist in pre-war Japan was the "scientist-as-truth-seeker" model, or the scientist as dweller in an ivory tower (Annual Report, 1976, p. 114).

[2] Annual Report, Mitsubishi-Kasei Institute of Life Sciences, 1976, p. 110.

Although there is this upsurge of interest in ethical and value problems, there is still no obvious move towards an academic and professional acceptance of this change of emphasis, as observed by the Social Life Science Research Centre:

> The professional societies of scientists and engineers in Japan are essentially passive organizations consisting of groups made up of individual scientists who share common formal organizations, institutions and methods or means of research, and the members within each group being bound to each other by strong mutually-dependent relationships. The relationships among the groups are rather loose and they often appear independent of each other ... In this relationship the principle of live-and-let-live is favoured over arguments, following a Japanese proverb saying "in a quarrel both groups are to blame".[3]

The individual's loyalty to his or her group is such that it is considered unlikely that any member of a particular group would ignore the common agreement of the group in regard to some socially or humanistically damaging line of research. This lack of independence of the individual scientist can be damaging to the ethical and human value implications of science, for a scientist who feels strongly on these issues may find himself compelled by group pressures to go along with the views of the group.[4]

In consequence of these attitudes, there is little fear of positive external restrictions on various types of research, nor will attempts at self-regulation be induced by fear of external regulation. Such regulation by external authority is not on the cards for Japanese science as may be with American science.

The growing interest in the ethical implications of science is reflected in an important bibliography of works on Ethical and Human Value Implications of Science and Technology in Japan, which has been compiled by the Laboratory of Social Life Sciences. This covers Intrinsic Problems of Science, Social Responsibility of Scientists, Science in Japanese Culture, the Philosophy of Science, the Religious Implications of Science, Medicine and Medical Law, Environmental Problems and Nuclear Power, and Peace Problems.[5] The spread of topics is impressive and so is the growing volume of literature upon the topic.

3 *Ibid.*, p. 113.

4 *Ibid.*, p. 114.

5 Among the works available in English are Nakayama, Shigeru, Swain and Yagi (eds.), *Science and Society in Modern Japan*, Tokyo University Press, 1974; Hideomi Toge, *Historical Development of Science and Technology in Japan*, Kokusai-Bunka-Shinkokai, 1961;

(B) GENETIC ENGINEERING

Outside the United States, recombinant DNA research is probably most advanced in Japan.

The Science and Society Committee's sub-committee on recombinant DNA has completed drafting a set of guidelines for industry in the same way as the National Institute of Health has done in the U.S. Like its U.S. counterpart, the guidelines contain no sanctions, but industry is expected to comply with them. The problems experienced with pharmaceutical companies in the U.S. which refused to follow the N.I.H. guidelines are not anticipated here.

The national and international importance of Japanese recombinant DNA research cannot be overemphasized. The statistics set out below will show the large scale on which this research is done. If, as many believe, there are dangers to humanity at large from such research — and indeed, dangers of interfering with the genes of humans themselves — unrestrained work in any one country can affect all humanity.

The Social Life Science Laboratory sent out a questionnaire to 1,205 institutions of higher education and universities asking whether they were engaged in recombinant DNA research. 485 responded and 70 indicated that they were engaging in such research. Of these 70, 23 were science faculties or divisions, 27 were medical, 7 pharmaceutical, 7 agricultural, 3 engineering, and 3 others. The private field is now being surveyed and there will probably be many more centres there.

In addition to centres where research is actually being conducted, there are 348 more that have indicated the possibility that they may venture into this kind of research in the near future. Of them, 92 are science divisions, 152 medical, 34 pharmaceutical, 45 agricultural, 16 engineering, and 9 others.

This brief survey will indicate the extent of Japanese activity in these fields — activity which almost without doubt places Japan second only to the United States in the volume and intensity of its research. All of this bears intensely upon the human future. The more sophisticated forms, including gene manipulation and cloning, can undermine the very bases on which our structures of the rule of law and human rights are built. Current work on microbes has, in the view of many, the potential to damage the global environment if handled carelessly. It is a great pity that all this extensive work is

Tetsuji Bunko Kobayashi, *General Education for Scientists and Engineers in the U.S.A. and Japan*, University of Michigan, 1965; Yujiro Hayashi, *Perspectives on Post Industrial Society*, University of Tokyo Press, 1970.

little known outside scientific circles in Japan for sheer lack of dialogue caused largely by language difficulties.

Both in the human rights field and in the scientific field, it is necessary that clearing houses for information should be set up between Japan and the rest of the world. There are occasional attempts to collate this information in English, as through the Annual Report of the Social Life Science Centre of the Mitsubishi Institute or the Bibliography of Japanese works on Science and Ethics prepared by the same Institute. Still this is grossly inadequate.

On a visit to an American University earlier this year, I was shown a PhD thesis on Recombinant DNA experimentation and its impact on human rights and society. There was not a single reference in this thesis to the Japanese experience, and I draw the attention of those concerned to this omission. This illustrates pointedly the communication gaps which need to be filled.

There is not in Japan the same level of concerned activity as there is in the U.S. regarding bio-hazards in recombinant DNA experimentation. In the U.S. there was the well known Asilomar International Conference on this topic in 1975 which received world-wide publicity. Apart from this, several symposia on bio-hazards are held regularly, detailed information is available for the design of physical containment facilities and for the selection of laboratory procedures, and courses are conducted periodically for the purpose of giving instruction in sufficient safety techniques in microbiology to technicians and graduate students. Japan has not yet reached this stage, but the impending issue of DNA research guidelines will be a great step forward. So, also, will be the appointment of the sub-committee on DNA research.

There is little doubt that Japan's efforts in connection with this all important environmental and human rights problem will be stepped up remarkably in the next few years. It would be of mutual benefit to Japan and the rest of the world if more should be known about these developments.

(C) BEHAVIOUR MANIPULATION

Behaviour manipulation by scientific means is the subject of very advanced research in Japan. It has recently aroused strong human rights concern from a Justice of the Supreme Court, Justice Dando, Professor Emeritus of the University of Tokyo.[6] Among the methods used are psychosurgery, of which

[6] Justice Dando's consideration of the matter is easily accessible to English readers in *Equality and Freedom*, Vol. 11, Papers of the World Congress on Philosophy of Law and Social Philosophy, St. Louis, 1975, Gray Dorsey (ed.), Oceana Publications, 1977, pp. 727 *et seq.*

many varieties are practised, cerebral biopsy, electroshock therapy, psychotropic drugs and narcoanalysis (interview under narcotics).

Psychosurgery has apparently produced strikingly successful results in individual cases. It is practised in many forms which only the initiated will understand — orbitoventromedial, undercutting, stereotaxic amygdalotomy, stereotaxic thalamotomy, thalamolaminotomy, and posterio-medial hypothalamotomy. The percentage of failure is thought to be small. The human rights angle is sought to be safeguarded in two ways:

(a) the surgeon gives a full explanation of the operation to his patient or his guardian in advance, and obtains his written consent; and

(b) the selection of cases for operation is based upon a case conference and is not the sole decision of the surgeon.

The operation irreversibly affects the patient's personality, in addition to involving, in many cases, a danger to life. The requirement of informed consent presents in every case of mental illness an almost insuperable legal problem, and even the guardian's consent is open to a variety of objections — for example, the guardian may have an interest in the patient's estate, or may desire to be rid of a burden to the family. One of the suggestions in this regard is that an appropriate person such as a lawyer should be required to join with the guardian in giving consent. The problem becomes acuter still in institutions of detention, such as prisons, for voluntariness is suspect under such conditions. Justice Dando has drawn pointed attention to the circumstance that prisons tend sometimes to be looked upon as laboratories for scientists,[7] and hence special diligence is needed in order to protect prisoners' human rights, so far as psychosurgery is concerned. Compulsory measures in the case of dangerous psychotics raise also the conflict between the interests of the individual and of society. There are no judicial determinations thus far upon the matter, but Justice Dando, writing extrajudicially, has, in what must be a most influential warning upon the subject, urged the need for the strictest possible caution in administering such compulsory measures.

Where experimentation is involved, the question also arises of limits upon the right of a person to consent to experimentation upon himself or herself — both from the aspect of public policy and from the viewpoint of human dignity. This question has arisen in Michigan,[8] but no such case has come to light thus far in Japan.

7 *Supra*, Note 6, p. 734.

8 *Doe* v. *Michigan Department of Mental Health*, Mich. Cir. Ct., July 10, 1973.

Psychotropic drugs, effective for psychotics, are used in prisons, being usually administered at the doctor's discretion without the patient's consent. A serious human rights problem arises which is not peculiar to Japan. Justice Dando warns of this in terms that:

> A problem of human rights is involved in using them, because some of them, when misused, will possibly reduce spontaneity of personality and cause repression in schizophrenic patients. Narcoanalysis involves the further question of confidentiality of the information thus acquired. Whether an expert witness can resort to narcoanalysis in order to determine an accused person's mental capacity has been the subject of some argument. No Supreme Court case has pronounced on this, but some inferior courts have ruled in the affirmative.[9]

In regard to the use of polygraphs — a practice fairly prevalent in criminal investigation in Japan — the Supreme Court has ruled that polygraph tests are admissible as evidence, if administered on a defendant with his consent.[10] This concerns the privilege against self-incrimination, and there is a division of learned opinion on this, as it is not the utterance of the subject that is given in evidence, but the reaction shown on the graph.

Various methods of control of behavioural manipulation have been suggested. One is that public awareness of the problems involved be stepped up, as it is the people themselves that must play an important role in controlling this potential threat to freedom. Public opinion needs not only to be created, but also to be organized. Agencies at local and national levels, international organizations, such as Amnesty International and the United Nations Commission on Human Rights, academic societies, and scientists are also urged to act. A sort of jury system involving laymen to be set up at appropriate places, e.g., prisons and boards of education, and a human rights review committee for checking on experimental projects have been suggested by Justice Dando.[11] All these remain, however, at the level of suggestion, and much work yet remains to be done. The bar will probably take up some of these, e.g., in regard to prisoners' rights, but there are few signs of an overall attack upon the problem by the scientific and legal worlds jointly.

[9] *Supra*, Note 6, p. 729.

[10] 22 Sup. Ct. 55, 1967, Dando, *supra*, Note 6, p. 729.

[11] *Ibid.*, p. 736.

(D) EUGENIC SURGERY

Eugenic surgery involves a serious question of individual rights, for however desirable it may be from society's point of view to incapacitate a person from reproducing, there is an invasion of his or her rights if surgery is performed for this purpose against the subject's will. In Japan, Article 4 of the Eugenic Protection Law (1948) permits a eugenic operation "for the sake of the public interest", even against the will of the person concerned. The phraseology "for the public interest" is, of course, fraught with danger because of its wide range and subjectivity. To counteract this, considerable safeguards have been built into the statute. The medical expert who performs the operation must first get the permission of a local eugenic commission. Upon the grant of such permission, the patient or the guardian, if dissatisfied with the decision, has the right to ask for a review of such permission by the Central Eugenic Commission. An appeal lies from the decision of this body to a court of law.

There thus appear to be many protections against abuse, and the number of cases in which such surgery has in fact been performed without consent has been small. No appeals have come up to the central commissions over the years.

The mode of operation legally permitted in Japan, within these safeguards, is a surgical operation to incapacitate a person from reproduction, without removal of the genital glands. Even in the case of aggressive sexual criminals, castration is not permitted either for eugenic or for security purposes.[12]

(E) ENVIRONMENTAL RIGHTS

The damage caused by industry to the quality of human life is a constant preoccupation in Japan. Japan is probably more environmentally conscious than any other nation on earth, both because of the density of its population and because of the magnitude of its industry. The pollution of the environment had proceeded almost unthinkingly in earlier years, with grave damage to the basic human right to a healthy environment.

An extended note on this aspect is appropriate in view of the increasing recognition of the right to health as a fundamental human right. This concept is fast developing, and a United Nations University seminar at The Hague earlier this year dealt in great detail with the right to health as a fundamental human right, developing the concept far beyond the duty of the state merely

12 See, generally, Dando, *supra*, Note 6, p. 730.

to provide health care. Protection of the environment is an integral part of this human right.

Pollution-related damage to health has been very considerable, and attention first became focused on the issue through the occurrence of Minamata disease in the Minamata Bay area. Since then the history of legislation, both to counter the occurrence of such tragedies in the future, as well as to compensate the victims is worthy of study by all industrial nations, as showing the magnitude of the legal and human problems that pollution can cause.

The Minamata episode commenced with a report to the Minamata Health Office from the hospital attached to the Chisso Corporation Minamata Factory regarding the occurrence of a strange disease. An interim report by a research team from Kumamoto University was to the effect that the disease was caused by poisoning resulting from the ingestion of fish and shellfish caught in Minamata Bay. It took some years before an announcement was made by government that Minamata disease was caused by the ingestion of fish and shellfish contaminated with methyl mercury compounds discharged from the Minamata factory of the Chisso Corporation. In March 1973 there was a court decision in favour of the plaintiffs awarding them damages against the Chisso Corporation.

As at the end of March 1977, 722 persons have been certified for Minamata disease in Kumamoto Prefecture, 44 died before a law came into force granting them relief, and 138 have died since then. In Kagoshima Prefecture, 138 persons have been certified and one died before the Relief Law, and 15 since then. Applications for certification still pending are 3,641 for Kumamoto Prefecture, and 467 for Kagoshima Prefecture. The number of pending applications is increasing and so are the patients who have not received due compensation.

The Pollution-Related Health Damage Compensation Law was passed to take effect on September 1, 1974. It provides for seven types of compensation benefits: (a) medical care benefits and expenses; (b) disability compensation; (c) survivors' compensation; (d) lump-sum survivors' compensation; (e) child compensation allowances; (f) medical care allowances; and (g) funeral expenses. Elaborate formulae have been worked out for the calculation of compensation in each category. Costs of the compensation system are collected from those responsible for the discharge of pollutants, on the "polluter pays" principle (PPP). Office expenses, however, are met out of public funds. Decisions regarding certification can be taken for review before the Pollution-Related Health Damage Compensation Grievance Board.

Minamata disease in Minamata Bay is only one episode. Since then, Minamata disease has been detected in the Agano River Basin (616 persons certified, 43 deaths, 462 pending applications); a new disease called Itai Itai disease has been found in Toyama Prefecture, traced to cadmium poisoning from the effluent of the Kamioka Refinery of the Mitsui Mining and Smelting Co. (57 certified, 62 deaths); chronic arsenic poisoning has been found in Miyasaki Prefecture involving the Sumitomo Metal Mining Co. (89 certified, 1 death). Air pollution, causing chronic bronchitis, bronchial asthma, pulmonary emphysema and related complications have caused numerous disabilities and deaths (53, 416 certified as at March 1977).

Soil pollution by agricultural chemicals is being investigated, and many areas have been detected with more than maximum permissible amounts of copper, arsenic, and cadmium — 78 areas in the cadmium survey, 34 areas in the copper survey, and 6 areas in the arsenic survey.[13]

Other environmental problems are noise pollution, vibration, offensive odour, and ground subsidence. In regard to each of these, an elaborate preventive apparatus is now in operation.

An important new development is environmental impact assessment by which the environmental impact of any new development is studied in advance. New chemicals are not released until they are screened under the October 1973 Law Concerning the Examination, Screening and Regulation of Manufacture of Chemical Substances.

Comprehensive environmental administration was inaugurated in Japan around 1971 and, within six years, a noticeable improvement has been registered in many areas of pollution. Standard-setting in every area — air pollution, water pollution, marine pollution, sound pollution — is controlled by the central government in the greatest detail. For example, standard values to protect human health have been set for cadmium, arsenic, cyanides, organic phosphorus, lead, chromium, mercury, polychlorinated biphenyls, among others, and controls are strictly administered. Where formerly the Factory Effluent Control Law covered 130 business categories, the new Water Pollution Control Law has expanded controls four-fold so as to subject 500 business categories to its regulations.[14] The sub-committee on Thermal Pollution of the Water Quality Committee in the Central Council for Control of Environmental Pollution has progressed far in its studies of the effect on the environment of the large-scale discharge of heated waste water. The Maritime Safety Agency has increased its staff for surveillance and enforcement with surveillance ships and reinforced patrol boats.

Oil pollution damage is the subject of much attention. For surveys and guidance on careless handling of fuel a "Period to Prevent Ships' Oil Leakage Accidents" was proclaimed. Regarding compensation for oil pollution

[13] *Quality of the Environment in Japan*, Environment Agency, 1977, p. 180.

[14] *Ibid.*, pp. 145–146.

damage, Japan has ratified the 1969 International Convention on Civil Liability for Oil Pollution Damage, and the 1971 International Treaty Relating to the Establishment of an International Fund for Compensation of Oil Pollution Damage.

Regulations relating to emission control for motor vehicles are probably the most stringent in the world. Most standard foreign cars fail to satisfy the requirements set. The new regulations (maximum permissible level for nitrogen oxides emission is set at 0.48 g/km) will cut down by 60 to 70 per cent the emission level under pre-1978 regulations, and by 92 per cent the emission level that prevailed when there were no regulations in force.[15]

In regard to conservation of the environment, the Nature Conservation Law was enacted in 1972 to provide the base principle for environmental conservation but, as the measures taken under it are of an "aftercare" nature, further measures were considered necessary. Hence, in 1973, the Nature Conservation Council formed a Special Committee for Formulating Long Range Nature Conservation Plans, and has published its study results in the form of a Basic Concrete Scheme for Nature Conservation Long Range Plans. The aim is not merely to prevent pollution, but to create a rich environment. Its plans are not merely for protecting nature, but also for restoring and fostering nature and are in four categories:

(a) primary nature, e.g., primary ecosystems, including wild animals and natural flora in marshlands, alpine and alpine zones;

(b) secondary nature, e.g., forests, parklands, landscapes;

(c) urban nature, e.g., grass lands, waterside areas, green areas; and

(d) sea-shore, lake and riverside areas.

An important human rights aspect of pollution control is the way in which the law has been seeking to place on the polluter the burden of preventing pollution, as well as of clearing up the pollution he has caused. This is, on the world stage, one of the great human rights grievances of Third World countries who complain that the nations responsible for giving the whole planet a polluted environment are under an obligation to pay for the clearing up of the pollution for which they are responsible. Else those who have made no profit from these activities must suffer to the same extent as those who have, with no redress in sight for themselves or their posterity.

Internally in Japan, this principle receives clear recognition in the Law Concerning Entrepreneurs' Bearing of the Cost of Public Pollution Control

[15] Environment Agency Report, *supra*, Note 13, p. 122.

Works. This law was enacted in December 1970 and has been in force since May 1971. By the end of February 1977, costs of pollution control projects undertaken by prefectural governments totalled about 84.1 billion yen, and business paid 43.7 billion yen out of this. Apart from prevention projects, there were 21 projects to clear up the bottom deposits of rivers and sea beds.[16]

* * *

These are a few illustrative examples of the ways in which national consciousness in Japan focuses more intensively than in almost any other country on the need for a humanistic approach to the vast industrial and technological component of the country's social scene. In addition to density of population and intensity of industry, a third factor that has contributed to Japan's preoccupation with the environment is that Japanese culture and tradition are deeply permeated with humanistic perspectives.

The contribution of these three factors — density of population, density of industry, and humanistic tradition — have forged a humanistic attitude towards science and technology which can be of great value to all countries. These perspectives are too valuable to be confined, as they presently are, within Japan, with little of its richness percolating through to other cultures. The Japanese experience is worthy of more attention than it has thus far received.

[16] Environment Agency Report, *supra*, Note 13, p. 230.

25. Agenda for Action*

The effect of technology on human rights must give concerned people cause for disquiet.

A number of suggestions are contained in this chapter, involving changes of structure, attitudes, and procedures. They will not be appropriate for every society and situation, but they deserve consideration if we are to face the future with confidence. Not all of them are intended to be adopted simultaneously. They offer a range of choices from which a selection needs to be made.

TECHNOLOGY CLASSIFICATION COMMITTEES

Only a small proportion of scientific research poses real dangers; most of it will prove to be innocuous. A classification committee could identify the projects that are potentially harmful and of doubtful value, and alert the public to the dangers.

TECHNOLOGY ASSESSMENT BOARDS

Technology assessment is the informed examination of the effect of a particular development in technology. Its purpose is to clarify policy and set out options so that intelligent choices can be made by responsible public and private decision-makers. It should provide early warning systems.

In 1967, in the US, a bill was introduced to establish a technology assessment board, which resulted in the passage of legislation in 1972, creating an Office of Technology Assessment which was to report to the US Congress.

The objectives of the Office of Technology Assessment[1] include identifying existing or probable effects of technology and alternative technological

* Reproduced from Ch. 11 of *The Slumbering Sentinels*.

[1] See Michael S. Baram, 'Technology Assessment and Social Control', *Science*, Vol. 180, 4 May 1973, p. 470.

methods and programmes, presenting findings to the appropriate legislative authorities, and identifying areas where additional research is needed.[2]

TECHNICAL HAZARDS BOARDS

Representatives from technical hazards boards will appear before the legislature as lobbyists against schemes which involve potential risks. Public servants with the requisite scientific background would be employed by the board as full-time researchers and legislation would guarantee the board's right to be heard by the legislature or its committees.

This machinery can in a sense be likened to the opposition in government which keeps Westminster-style democracy alive.

FUTURES SCANNING AGENCIES IN GOVERNMENT DEPARTMENTS

A futures scanning agency in every government department, as well as a government department exclusively devoted to the scanning of futures, should be set up. Any technological measure of social importance should need clearance from this department. Staff working for the futures department should be protected constitutionally from victimization lest their advice does not please the government. The department should have close contact with the public in a consulting and educating role.

An example of a measure designed on these lines is HR988, the 'foresight' provision in the US House of Representatives, which requires that standing committees engage in futures research and long-term analysis.

COMMITTEES FOR ALTERNATIVE FUTURES

Forecasting the future involves not only passive predictions about the direction in which technology is taking us, but also active choices between alternatives. Committees need to map out these alternatives in detail, and bring them before the public and the legislature to enable informed decisions to be taken.

Many other methods are possible for increasing 'anticipatory' democracy. Among them are citizens grouped together in '2000' organizations, community action programmes, discussion groups in schools, Lions, Apex, Rotary,

[2] See 'Readings in Technology Assessment', August 1975, a compendious collection of papers issued by the Program of Policy Studies in Science and Technology, George Washington University, Washington D.C.

YMCA, Red Cross and other service groups, futures resource centres, and futures-oriented primers for schoolchildren.[3]

CENTRES FOR THE STUDY OF SCIENTIFIC POLICY

Not all countries have a ministry that is responsible for scientific policy, and where they do exist, scientific policy tends to be confused with the political policies of the government in power. Any presentation to the public of the technology relevant to some governmental programme runs the risk of being slanted to fit into the government's plan. It is important that impartial committees, guaranteed independence by law, make it their business to research governmental scientific policy and point out possible alternatives and flaws.

This involves a constitutional question. The constitutional position of science may vary from country to country depending on the interpretation placed by its courts on questions of freedom of speech and thought and belief.[4] In the US, the constitutional position of science has been moulded by a series of decisions giving science an affirmative and protected status.

CENTRES FOR INTEGRATING TECHNOLOGY WITH NATIONAL GOALS

The short-term perspectives of traditional political structures make them unsuitable for formulating a country's national goals, and expert committees are needed, such as the National Goals Research Staff appointed by President Nixon or the high-powered commission appointed by President Eisenhower, which reported on goals for Americans. Once these committees put forward their proposals, studies must be launched to see in what way technology can be used to achieve them.[5]

PROFESSIONAL FUTURISTS

With the evolution of university courses on futures, expert futurists will be trained as professionals to advise on futures. A high ethical standard en-

[3] See for suggestions, Alvin Toffler, 'What is Anticipatory?', *Futurist*, Vol. IX, 1975, p. 224.

[4] A series of United States cases involving the conflict between the teaching of the Biblical account of creation and the evolutionary theory were resolved in favour of science in the United States. These could be answered differently in other jurisdictions. For references to the United States cases, see S. Goldberg, *The University of Illinois Law Forum*, Vol. 1, 1979, p. 1.

[5] See A. Toffler, *Future Shock*, Pan Books, 1970, p. 348.

forced among them should prevent them from reporting on projects in a manner calculated to please their clients. They need the same degree of detachment as is required of futures departments. It should be set down by statute that any major project involving technology should be accompanied by a report from a registered futurist. Years of experience in technology assessment should be a prerequisite for registration as a futures expert.

UNIVERSITY COMMITTEES

Universities should set up committees to study the future. More especially, science and law faculties need to set up futures committees to survey the direction in which their disciplines are going and their adequacy to meet the needs of the future. These committees would be specially effective as universities are both repositories of information and agencies of research.

Through the committees, universities need to guard against being lured by the funds, power, and prestige of powerful sponsors — whether military or commercial — into undertaking research which runs counter to their ideals. Provisions to this end may need to be built into university statutes and research contracts.

COMMITTEES OF THE BAR

The bar has been insufficiently used as a source of guidance and direction. Sub-committees of science-oriented members of the bar could be set up to keep an eye on the challenges posed by science. The impact on the law of each new scientific development must be kept under scrutiny and reported back to the bar for appropriate action.[6]

The establishment of the Standing Committee on Law and Technology of the American Bar Association is a step in this direction, as is its quarterly review, *The Jurimetrics Journal*.

SCIENCE COMMISSIONS

Like a law reform commission, a science commission is needed to issue annual reports on the state of science in a country, and compel scientists to acknowledge their responsibility to their society by acting as public watch-

[6] On the various roles that lawyers can play in technology assessment, see Joseph C. Goulden, *The Superlawyers*, Weybright and Talley, p. 15, and 'The Role of Law and Lawyers in Technology Assessment' in Marvin J. Cetron and Bodo Bartocha (eds.), *Technology Assessment in a Dynamic Environment*, Gordon & Breach, 1973, p. 629.

dogs. Its composition would ideally be interdisciplinary and non-political, with the inclusion of legal and scientific members being statutorily required. Its annual report would be one of the most important documents on public welfare.

STRUCTURES FOR ACCOUNTABILITY IN SCIENCE

Public safety, education, health, housing, freedom of expression, thought and belief, privacy, cultural pursuits, family security, and leisure are important factors in social welfare, often forgotten in the preoccupation with economic benefits. A true social accounting on any scientific development must take note of its effect in all these fields.

A structure to audit various scientific activities could be set up and a social auditor-general appointed, who would issue a regular report to the general public. In business and company law, progressive writers[7] have mooted the notion that every company should submit to an annual social audit in the same way that it submits to an annual financial audit.

REVIVING HIDDEN TECHNOLOGY

There are many technologies of potential value to society which are not developed — and indeed sometimes deliberately suppressed — because there is little or no private profit to be made from them, or because they affect the profits from existing technology. Not all socially useful inventions reach the market, just as not all socially useful technology benefits the public. These agencies could research such areas and rediscover such hidden technology. The motor industry, for example, has often shelved technologies that might prove useful to the public but damaging to its business interests.

INSURANCE MECHANISMS

Many of the technology-related public risks carry no adequate insurance cover. A general state insurance system is needed which will automatically compensate the victims of technology, for example, victims of pollution or exposure to dangerous chemicals. The polluter-pays principle used in Japan to meet claims such as those from Minamata sickness is useful here, but the resources of the polluter may be inadequate to meet the number and size of the claims. In the nuclear industry, for example, claims for damage from a

7 See G. Goyder, *The Responsible Company*, Basil Blackwell, 1961, pp. 62 *ff.*; note in particular the proposals and illustrations contained in Part B of this volume.

leaking reactor would run to thousands of millions of dollars; there are no private insurance schemes capable of dealing with claims of this size.

LEGISLATIVE RESTRUCTURING

An increasing amount of the legislation of the future will be science related. Legislatures do not have the time or the expertise to come to grips with the complicated technological issues which they need to consider before passing laws.

- A council could be formed from among the ranks of distinguished scientists to advise the legislature.
- A house of scientists could be established as an adjunct to the legislature, and a chamber of scientists elected from the ranks of scientists by scientists themselves.[8] This body could be given limited legislative status and have powers of discussion and debate. A scientific measure would have to pass through this legislative house.
- Legislative sub-committees could be formed of science-oriented legislators who would make it their special responsibility to look into science-oriented pieces of legislation and inform the house of their views.
- A certificate from the technology assessment board could be routinely required to accompany every bill involving science, which is placed before the house.
- When any major science-oriented bill is presented, there should be procedures to facilitate a public debate on the social consequences.
- A given number of members of the public or of the legislature should have the right to call for an open debate on the scientific implications of a measure before the legislature.
- Where there are competing claims for a share of the public funds allocated to science, the public should be kept informed of the reasons for the eventual allocation. For this purpose, a detailed statement of social objectives should accompany every major allocation.
- The recognized scientific bodies should have an automatic right of audience before the legislature on legislation that is in their field.

[8] This suggestion was made by J. Harvey Wheeler in 'Bringing Science Under Law', *Dialogue*, Vol. 4, 1971, pp. 104 *ff*.

JUDICIAL RESTRUCTURING

Along with legislative restructuring, there could be a restructuring of the judiciary. Judges untrained in science lack the expertise to decide scientific disputes. It may be necessary to set up a scientific division of the judiciary to which would be appointed only those judges who had combined a scientific background with their legal training. These tribunals would also have lay advisers to help them. The suggestion of establishing a science court manned by a panel of scientist/lawyer judges was made in 1967 in the US, and received strong, if qualified, support from the ranks of the judiciary.[9]

SCIENTIFIC RESEARCH ARM OF THE JUDICIARY

All divisions of the judiciary need the help of a scientific research arm to provide basic information and scientific expertise. The judicial research arm of the Japanese Supreme Court is a prototype, because it provides the judges, not themselves expert in all departments of law and law-related areas, with the necessary research back-up by specialists. In the same way, it will be possible for a scientific research arm of the judiciary to arm the judges with the necessary scientific data.

Such a judicial research arm could be set up as an ancillary organ of the court structure, to be drawn upon by judges of any section of the judiciary who may need this kind of technical information.

EXECUTIVE RESTRUCTURING

Many suggestions can be made in this field.

- A network of scientific research units could be attached to various ministries, which would be co-ordinated through a central bureau of scientific research.
- A pool of highly skilled bureaucrats with an inter-disciplinary science/administration background could be set up.
- Secrecy provisions which many governments impose upon their scientific staff should be removed. Requirements of defence and public safety will, of course, limit the scope of this principle.

[9] See J. N. Martin, 'The Science Court Proposal', *Harvard Journal on Legislation*, Vol. 16, 1979, p. 443.

- Barriers which compartmentalize scientific work in government departments should be broken down.
- Scientific research of all sorts conducted within various government departments should be reported to a central body.
- Futures sections should be set up in all scientific departments.

A NEW ADMINISTRATIVE JURISPRUDENCE

A new administrative jurisprudence for science will need to be evolved, containing attitudinal, conceptual, and procedural innovations.

The world shortage of raw materials may, by the close of the century, result in highly regimented forms of government strictly controlling the expenditure of natural resources.[10] There will be a plethora of administrative decisions involving the use of raw materials and the grant or refusal of permits, and it will be necessary for new structures to be evolved to survey these licensing procedures and ensure that individual rights are not subsumed in bureaucratic excesses.

Bodies such as environmental protection councils, technology assessment boards and science commissions must be given independence from political pressures.

INTERNATIONAL COVENANTS AND TREATIES

To lend effectiveness to the internal regulation of science-related activities, an increasing number of international covenants and treaties will need to be entered into in many fields, such as DNA experimentation, organ transplants, chemical testing, psychosurgery, data protection, and health regulations. It will also be necessary for an international organization to be set up to issue warning signals when crises are reached in scientific research. There will also be a need for a constitutional provision building such international agreements into national law.

The idea of a world council of scientists with powers of control over science, voted to it by the world community, may come about in a modified form such as an advisory body whose opinion the world community would treat with great regard.

[10] Arnold Toynbee, 'After the Age of Affluence', *The Observer*, 14 April 1974.

LINKS BETWEEN INTERNATIONAL AND NATIONAL BODIES

There is often lack of communication between international and national bodies working in the same field. An example is the case of the Human Rights Commission which for many years has been working intensively on the effect of science on human rights, but in comparative isolation from similarly oriented university and national bodies. The absence of any entity for establishing such liaison results in much duplication and waste.

In the human rights field, journals such as *Internet* bring to human rights workers news of similar activities in every country. A journal similar to *Internet* is required in the field of science and human rights.

INTERNATIONAL TECHNOLOGY ASSESSMENT BOARDS AND TECHNICAL HAZARDS BOARDS

These are the international counterparts of the national bodies that have been suggested earlier. The first of these bodies, the International Society for Technological Assessment, was set up in 1973.

AN INTERNATIONAL CODE OF CONDUCT ON THE TRANSFER OF TECHNOLOGY

An internationally recognized code of conduct on the transfer of technology needs to acknowledge that technology is a part of the human heritage. As such, it is a body of knowledge to which all countries should have the right of access. To withhold technology is to refuse to use the resources of the community to improve the living standards of its members.

The interests of all countries, developed and developing alike, demand a recognition that there can be no private empires in the realm of scientific knowledge. The code needs to embody a statement on the lines of the Declaration adopted at the sixth special session of the General Assembly on the establishment of a new international economic order. Paragraph 4P of this Declaration sets out a principle giving the developing countries access to the achievements of modern science and technology, promoting the transfer of technology, and creating an indigenous technology for the benefit of the developing countries in forms and procedures suited to their economies.

Restrictive business practices in transactions involving the transfer of technology need the most careful scrutiny and the technology supplier must likewise be protected.

The Brandt Report[11] points out that barely 1 per cent of spending on research and development in the developed countries is specifically concerned with the problems of the developing countries, while 51 per cent is devoted to defence; that the corporations involved in bringing technology to the developing countries have sales ($830 thousand million) which are equal to the gross national product of all the developing countries excluding oil-exporting developing countries; and that 97 per cent of the world's research takes place in the developed countries.

The report makes many suggestions for the transfer of more technology and shows how dangers threatening our children and grandchildren can be averted, among other things, by a sharing of technology. It also refers to possible revisions in the Paris Convention on intellectual property and patent rights, securing greater recognition by patent holders of the public interest in developing countries, for example, by limiting the duration of patents. The World Intellectual Property Organization and the United Nations Committee on Trade and Development are working on these aspects.

A SCIENTIFIC OMBUDSMAN

A high-ranking appointment is needed at a national level of a scientist-lawyer as science ombudsman. Sometimes scientists working for a corporation, university or a government department are required to participate in research which they consider morally objectionable. Such employees may be unable to register their protest without losing employment or promotion prospects. They may already have been victimized for doing so. They need a source of protection.

EXPANDING THE SCIENTIFIC ETHIC

The primary ethical responsibility of the scientist is his or her loyalty to truth. The greatest scientific crime is the distortion of results, and the greatest obligation is accurate reporting of results.

This ethic might have been sufficient in earlier ages, but as danger grew from scientific research, so did the ethical responsibility of the scientist. The scientific community must realize the inadequacies of its traditional ethic and work on developing a broader one.

11 *North-South: A Programme for Survival*, Pan Books, 1980, p. 197.

ETHICAL CODES FOR SCIENTISTS

Francis Bacon, despite his insistence on uninhibited scientific research, still visualized an ethical code for scientists. In his work *New Atlantis*, scientists took an oath of secrecy for concealing inventions and experiences which they thought fit to keep secret. Between Bacon's age and the post-war twentieth century, little has intervened to create an ethical code for science.

It was against this ethical void that Bertrand Russell and Albert Einstein outlined in 1955 the risks of thermonuclear war.[12]

The formulation of ethical codes which will say what is 'right' and 'wrong' from the standpoint of research will be difficult and will suffer in their initial stages from being too general and vague. Broad formulations, however, are a useful start, and they will be refined with experience and with each ruling. Doctors, engineers, and computer scientists have worked out brief ethical codes for themselves. These need to be expanded and refined. All scientists should be brought within the operation of ethical codes.

SOCIETIES FOR SOCIAL RESPONSIBILITY

Societies for social responsibility in science have been formed in many countries following the lead given by scientific groups in the US. An early sign of a developing sense of responsibility in scientists was the one-day strike in March 1969 by faculty members of the Massachusetts Institute of Technology and other US universities protesting against the abuses of science for purposes of war. Another sign is the proposal that practitioners of some branches of science should take oaths to be of service to the public and to place service above self.[13]

Under the impetus provided by such societies, scientists are beginning to see implications of their work to which they had been insensitive before.

OBLIGATORY CODES OF PRACTICE

Obligatory codes of practice should develop out of the social concern of the scientific community, but scientists have so far not shown any willingness to adopt such codes. In the field of recombinant DNA experimentation, when

[12] This led to the Pugwash movement, by which Cyrus Eaton, Cleveland industrialist, financed meetings of leading scientists at Pugwash, his birthplace, and afforded a forum and means of expression for scientists in the cause of peace.

[13] *Journal of the Royal Society of Arts*, April 1966. The suggested oath reads: 'On becoming a Chartered Engineer I vow to use my best endeavours to consider how my engineering skill may contribute towards the happiness of mankind.'

US scientists announced their intentions to set up a voluntary code of practice early in 1982, several city and state legislatures expressed unwillingness to accept procedures which were only voluntary, and threatened to impose stringent regulations unless the guidelines adopted were mandatory.[14] This lack of confidence was heightened by the ambitious plans of the genetic engineering industry which would not necessarily permit its scientists the freedom to observe the voluntary rules. Indeed, in California, the home of genetic engineering research, the state assembly's health committee threatened legislation if the guidelines were not made obligatory.

Clearly, the scientific community needs to build up public confidence, not merely by proposing voluntary codes when under pressure, but by resorting to them out of an ethical sense even in the absence of public pressures.

SELF-IMPOSED MORATORIUMS

In 1974, a group of leading molecular biologists in the US called for a world-wide moratorium on certain kinds of experiment in molecular genetics. In renouncing the experiments in their own laboratories, scientists had the support of the US National Academy of Sciences and of the vast and powerful National Institute of Health. In the UK, the Medical Research Council issued instructions to its laboratories to observe the ban. The president of the association, Sir John Kendrew, announced his support of the moratorium. A meeting of scientists at Asilomar, California, in 1977, considered and assessed the arguments on either side for restraints in recombinant DNA research, and produced an impressive set of safeguards.

But there are many obstacles to self-restraint. Narrow disciplinary backgrounds and self-interest combine with the lack of ethical values in existing professional training (apart from medicine) to prevent such trends.

COURT-IMPOSED MORATORIUMS

A legal principle needs to be worked out by which the public or a representative body of them is able to petition the court for a moratorium on scientific activity, where the scientists are unwilling to adopt one themselves. The procedural and conceptual aspects would need careful legal study.

[14] *Nature*, Vol. 295, 4 February 1982, pp. 358–9.

REFERENDUMS

From time to time, science-related issues, such as nuclear weapons and fluoridation, attract public attention. There are a number of other areas on which the opinion of the public needs to be sought by referendums in view of their profound impact on society. Experimentation with foetal material, *in vitro* fertilization, and the release of fluorocarbons are some of these.

A prerequisite to such referendums is the construction of machinery for involving the public in scientific debate. Lawyers, scientists, and administrators need to pool their expertise to plan this structure. One procedure, tried out in the Austrian nuclear debate in 1977–78, was to present panels of experts and lay people on television. Viewers joined in their discussions through a telephone network.

After the questioning of scientific experts, a referendum was held to obtain the views of the public on the policy questions involved. Constitutional provisions are needed to make a consideration of this view of the public obligatory upon the legislature.

PLEBISCITES ON THE FUTURE

Public participation in government should not be restricted to the short-term political issues of election time. This inherent weakness in the parliamentary process can be overcome by plebiscites on the sorts of alternative futures society might want.

PUBLIC RELATIONS COMMITTEES

The increasing inter-relationship between science and society makes it essential for scientific societies to set up public relations committees, both for communication of information and for better understanding. Scientists often still believe that their devotion to pure science is in some way diluted by involvement in issues of public interest. This will need to change.

SCIENCE-ORIENTED CIVIL LIBERTIES COMMITTEES

A number of civil liberties associations flourish in most democratic countries, but it is only incidentally, if at all, that they consider science issues. We need to have civil liberties organizations which are specially concerned with the impact of science on civil liberties.

SCIENTIFIC JOURNALISM

Science reporting, if taken more seriously, will become increasingly important. It will become a regular item of news coverage like foreign news, and special journalists will be trained for it.

CITIZENS' COMMITTEES

Citizens' committees have constantly demonstrated their value in stopping or modifying socially harmful technology. Such committees have been hampered in the past, however, by a lack of recognition, information and funds.

Traditional legal rules have required that a party to an action have a direct interest in its subject-matter. To prevent pollution from a river, for example, I must show that my paddock is irrigated by it and that I have suffered property damage. We need law reform which entitles a person to bring an action to protect an amenity in which he or she has no proprietary interest, such as, for example, a wildlife preserve or the beach. An extension of this principle will enable concerned groups to litigate to preserve the rights of posterity. At present, such groups are denied any sort of legal hearing.

Citizens' committees also need more information as a matter of right from governments and corporations, for which the law must provide through freedom of information acts. They also need guidance on the intricacies of piloting a case through the rules and regulations of statutory bodies. Ralph Nader's *Action for Change: A Student Manual of Public Interest Organising* is a step in this direction. Other jurisdictions need similar guidelines.

CLOSING THE COMMUNICATIONS GAP

Interesting studies have been conducted on the communication gap between law and science. One such, conducted by the Oak Ridge National Laboratory in the United States under the sponsorship of the National Science Foundation, sent out a circular to 2,300 lawyers working in the area of natural resources and environmental management law, of whom 575 responded.[15]

Although there was a tendency to fix less blame on lawyers, several respondents felt that the blame must be shared equally between the two disciplines. Some saw both professions as using too much jargon: lawyers writing for lawyers and scientists for scientists.

Some features of the scientific attitude and method which attracted criticism were the peer approval systems of science, the failure of scientists to be

[15] *American Bar Association Journal*, Vol. 59, 1973, p. 157.

sufficiently vocal in public debate, and the publication and distribution policies of scientific literature.

COMMITTEES OF INQUIRY INTO TECHNOLOGICAL CHANGE

The Myers Committee, which was appointed to inquire into the economic and social effect of technological change in Australia, published its report in 1980, and drew attention to the difficulties involved in the process of adjustment to technological change and to the necessity for the 'social partners' — government, unions and employers — to consult each other. Employment opportunities could also be anticipated and prepared for in this way.

A COMMISSION ON THE INTEGRITY OF THE HUMAN BODY

Whether and to what extent the human body can be tampered with are policy decisions for the community, and indeed for the international community, and are too serious to be left to scientists. Before the turn of the century, dramatic new developments will make far deeper inroads on bodily integrity.

A commission which reports on the areas of threat to bodily integrity could stimulate a more timely legislative response. According to some forecasts, developments such as cloning, pre-selection of sex, and full-term test-tube babies are possibilities by the turn of the century. An annual report by a commission outlining the occurrences of the previous year and the dangers which are imminent will remove much of the haziness of any public debate. This is a function that an agency of the UN, such as the World Health Organization, could best perform. Such reports should be required by statute to be tabled in every national legislature.

CENTRES FOR STUDYING LEGAL RESTRAINTS ON WEAPONS SCIENCE

There has been comparatively little research into the violations of basic legal rights by the arms trade. The smokescreen of defence and military emergencies inhibits lawyers from undertaking such enquiries despite the peacetime conditions in which the armaments industry conducts most of its operations. There is little doubt, however, that many civil liberties and human rights rules and principles can be invoked nationally and internationally to restrain some aspects of this activity. Study centres promoting such research are vital. Without any legal requirements of disclosure of information, peace-loving people are persuaded to invest their life-savings in companies specializing in the manufacture of weapons of death. The scientific resources of universities are extensively used for these lethal purposes. More than half the world's scientific manpower and more than a thousand million dollars a day are tunnelled into our most inhuman activity without any hindrance from the law.

DATA PROTECTION AUTHORITIES

The possible abuses of computerized information need far more surveillance than current legal structures afford. The infringements of privacy and of basic rights — even the right to employment — resulting from the abuse of data are so numerous that they require a special authority to oversee them. The courts are too busy and too formal for this purpose. Penal powers are not essential, for such a body can function very much along the lines of a press council, contenting itself with investigation and giving maximum publicity to its findings.

The same organization could be used to deal with computer crime. The police force often lacks the expertise to handle the very sophisticated investigations required, and data protection committees could be a valuable reservoir of expertise upon which the police could draw.

PRIVACY PROTECTION AUTHORITIES

Privacy protection authorities would perform the functions in the area of privacy that data protection committees could perform in the computer field. They would concern themselves with the investigation and control of surveillance of all sorts. The easy availability of surveillance devices will let the situation get out of control unless some authority keeps a continuous watch on it. Privacy committees are overdue in the common law jurisdictions and New South Wales was one of the pioneers in setting up such a committee.

The powers of the authority, like the powers of the data protection committee, or of the press council, could be investigatory rather than punitive. Indeed, in the case of all these authorities, it is important that they do not constitute encroachments upon the authority of the ordinary courts.

CYBERNETIC SURVEY COMMISSIONS

With the progress of cybernetic science (the study of systems of control through electronic devices) the frontiers of machine decision-making will push back the frontiers of human decision-making. There will be a natural tendency for the computer to be used for decisions involving even a humanistic element as, for example, in the imposition of routine fines or the determination of alimony in a matrimonial action. The progressive increase of such uses needs to be monitored.

There is also a fear that when a machine is invented which will teach itself, it will be a danger to us. We do not know when this machine will appear, but already supercomputers, such as the newly released Cray-2, are reported to be several hundred times faster than the largest IBM machines currently available.[16]

Cybernetic survey commissions would have jurisdiction to call for information on developments in this field, to study their implications on basic rights, and to publicize the information. Such a commission would be society's insurance against the possibility of mankind abdicating some basic and essential powers to machines.

WASTE-WATCH ORGANS

Modern society lacks bodies specially charged with the duty of noting and controlling areas in which modern technology wastefully uses scarce natural resources.[17] Waste will be one of the great political issues of the future and one of posterity's principal grievances against the present. Our age, increasingly conscious of its duties towards posterity, is ill equipped governmentally if it does not institutionalize its waste-watch operations.

Waste-watch will mean more controls. A rigidly administered permit system may determine when and by whom materials are to be used. But controls engender bureaucracy and bureaucratic excesses. How these are to be prevented are matters for attention now.

Waste-watch will also involve research, for many engineering undertakings, for example, make wasteful use of material. Similarly, miniaturization, a great material-saving idea of the future, will need to be more amply researched. The US engineer, Buckminster Fuller, has given brilliant leadership in this area, showing how a minimum of materials can be used to produce a maximum of results.

INDEPENDENT AUTHORITIES FOR PRODUCT RECALL

Technology and industry often combine to produce goods that are basically dangerous or unfit for the purpose for which they were bought. Proof that these goods are unfit or dangerous may depend on technology which is often in the exclusive command of the manufacturer. Pesticides, paints and indus-

16 *Newsweek*, 11 January 1982, p. 33.

17 See Vance Packard, *The Waste Makers*, David McKay Co., 1960.

trial chemicals, for example, often continue to be used despite the damage they cause to health and life. Ralph Nader has shown how some motor companies have failed, for reasons of cost, to build in specified safety features in their cars.[18] An independent authority could be vested with the power to recall these products.

RESTRUCTURING EDUCATION SYLLABUSES

When students are introduced to science in schools there is invariably no presentation of its social implications.

Science should be taught in such a way that it demonstrates the social problems posed by modern technology.

In addition, the sociology of science should be a compulsory component of every science course offered at tertiary level.

LAW SCHOOL CURRICULA

Law school curricula could be refashioned to equip lawyers with skills to deal with the demands of the scientific age.

Law schools could offer a variety of subjects dealing with the interrelationship of science and law, one of which should be compulsory.

A course in basic scientific literacy, which would equip the student with knowledge of basic chemistry, physics, and biology could be offered.

A course on science and social responsibility could be added to existing jurisprudence courses, especially those already based on sociology.

Research programmes which law students undertake at law school could include at least one piece of research and writing in the area of law, science and technology.

Law faculties could build up contacts with institutions which examine and disseminate scientific knowledge. The Scientists' Institute for Public Information was founded for this purpose in the US in 1963. Australia has the Scientific Policy Studies Section of the Department of Science and the Environment in the national capital.

Current courses in constitutional law, government and politics seem heavily anchored to the past. They will need to develop futuristic perspectives which will be of growing importance in all studies of law and government.

[18] *Unsafe at Any Speed*, Bantam Books, 1973.

INTERDISCIPLINARY EDUCATION

Interdisciplinary courses should be offered in tertiary education to provide staff for technology assessment, for future civil liberties movements, and for training future bureaucrats.

At Boston University Law School's Center for Law and Health Sciences, law students meet and work with graduate students from other disciplines, earning academic credits for this work. In a summer pilot programme, fifteen graduate students from Boston, Brandeis, Harvard and the Massachusetts Institute of Technology were divided into four interdisciplinary teams, each of which worked on a complex problem, such as genetic counselling. Monash University's graduate school of environmental science is an outstanding Australian example of interdisciplinary education and team work.

COURSES IN TECHNOLOGY ASSESSMENT AND FUTUROLOGY

Although all the consequences of a decision cannot possibly be foreseen, we are certainly now in a position to see a few further steps ahead than was possible earlier. Trained futurists, aided by computer models, are now in a position to see the possible consequences of a decision well ahead.

Courses in technology assessment and futurology were beginning to be offered at US universities in the early 1970s, starting with a course at the University of Maryland's Chemical Engineering department and at Harvard University's School of Engineering. Courses on futures are also being offered in law, although there are only a few of them.

WORKSHOPS OF LAWYERS AND SCIENTISTS

There is still a marked lack of enthusiasm on the part of lawyers and scientists for multi-disciplinary activities. Many attempts have been made. The National Conference of Lawyers and Scientists, for example, convened a workshop in Virginia in 1978 on cross-education of lawyers and scientists, including an equal number of representatives of the American Bar Association and the American Association for the Advancement of Science. The workshop considered such matters as the traditional barriers to law/science education, multi-disciplinary education in continuing education programmes, ways of encouraging education of lawyers about scientific methodology, and ways of encouraging education of scientists about legal process.[19]

SCIENCE REPORTING

The public should be given more reports on science, and scientific projects. Journalistic associations could contribute by funding courses at tertiary institutions to teach specialized scientific reporting.

One reason why scientists have been able to pursue their activities free of public scrutiny is that although 'political' politics is subjected to exposure in the press, the politics of science, though often just as political, has nearly altogether avoided scrutiny.

INSTITUTIONS FOR THE STUDY OF HUMANISTIC SCIENCE

In recent years, there has been an emphasis on those branches of science pertaining to life and the life sciences. An institution such as the Mitsubishi Kasei Institute of Life Sciences in Tokyo (financed by the Mitsubishi Corporation) emphasizes the humanistic aspects of science and promotes cross-disciplinary and public understanding of the inter-relationship between science and society. Other similar institutions could be set up under the aegis of governments, private enterprise, or other academic bodies.

RE-ORIENTATION OF PUBLIC ATTITUDES

A concerted educational effort is required on the part of governments, scientific establishments, educational authorities, and public interest organizations to reorientate public attitudes towards science. All or any of the organizations set out in this chapter can make their contribution to this effort.

RE-EXAMINATION OF THE LEARNING PROCESS

How does mankind learn the skills essential for survival in a world of unprecedented situations? Experiential learning processes, no longer adequate to meet this need, will yield to anticipatory processes. Law, experientially structured, will need anticipatory structuring. The learning process in many of its aspects will need to be overhauled. The Club of Rome has launched an

[19] For details regarding this workshop, see William A. Thomas, 'A Report From the Workshop on Cross-Education of Lawyers and Scientists', *Jurimetrics Journal*, Vol. 19, 1978, p. 92.

important study of the learning process. Governments and other organizations must follow.

EDUCATION IN THE USE OF LEISURE

Modern science and technology have greatly reduced the number of hours of labour needed from the average worker. With increasing computerization, the number of leisure hours available for most people will dramatically increase. By the end of the century, many of the industrialized countries will require workers to be at their desks for only an hour or two each day. Indeed, they may not even need to attend their places of work.

A large number of people will be unprepared for their increased leisure time. United Nations' studies have shown the need to formulate educational programmes for using leisure. There is urgent work to be done in this area, especially in the industrialized countries.

EDUCATION IN WAYS OF LIVING FOR THE FUTURE

A technological society depends on an ever-rising curve of production and its attendant waste. The elimination of waste cannot be achieved without an alteration of attitudes and ways of living. It is important, therefore, that students be shown how ways of living can be simplified without diminution and indeed with enrichment of the quality of life.

Such teaching should not involve an attempt to pressure schoolchildren into suggested alternative lifestyles, but try to make them aware of the alternatives that are not based on material possessions and consumer goods. Preparing students for tomorrow requires that the teacher teach *styles* of life as much as the facts of life.[20]

WHITHER LAW, SCIENCE AND SOCIETY?

Some of the principles discussed in this chapter may provide the basis for a new jurisprudence for science. Some jurists have envisaged that even as mankind has lived thus far under the regime of law, it may in the future be

[20] Donald N. Michael, *The Unprepared Society: Planning for a Precarious Future*, Basic Books, 1968. This book has been criticized as largely delegating the task to the educational establishment: see *American Sociological Review*, Vol. 34, 1969, p. 957. There is no gainsaying, however, that the preparation of educators is one of the important aspects needing attention. This is of course only one item on a many-point programme.

constrained to live under the rule of science.[21] If this is a possibility, new structures must evolve now.

As we move on to the close of this century and the beginning of the next, and as society's centre of gravity shifts inexorably towards technology, many areas will need to be rethought. The relative disparity which now exists between scientific and non-scientific skill will soon increase alarmingly, relegating non-scientific knowledge and skills to an ever-shrinking corner of human activity. If the law is to come to grips with science, it must do so now.

Arthur Clarke, in *The Children of Icarus*, has observed that we are now in a phase when 'history is holding its breath and the present is detaching itself from the past like an iceberg that has broken away from its icy moorings to sail across the boundless ocean'. We need the combined wisdom of scientist, lawyer and layman lest we drift to our destruction on these uncharted seas.

[21] W. Seagle, *The Quest for Law*, Alfred A. Knopf, 1941, p. 374.

APPENDIX A

New Legal Institutions for a Science-Dominated Age: A Blueprint from the 1970s*

A SUMMARY OF PROBLEMS AND CONCEPTS

This paper sets out in summarized form some of the principal problems and concepts that receive extended discussion in this collection of essays. They were the problems as perceived in 1975, and are presented here to show that these problems, though scarcely addressed on a systematic basis, have been with us for well over a quarter century.

I. CIRCUMSTANCES GIVING RISE TO THE DISCUSSION

A. Incapacity of existing legal institutions to handle complex scientific problems.

B. Erosions of human dignity and freedom caused by new scientific devices and techniques.

* This paper was presented as an inventory of topics for discussion for the session "New Legal Institutions for New Social Relations" at the World Congress on Philosophy of Law and Social Philosophy, St. Louis, Missouri, 24–29 August 1975, and is reproduced by kind permission of the International Association for Philosophy of Law and Social Philosophy.

C. "Brink situations" resulting from dangerous scientific experiments with potential to destroy or seriously damage humanity and its prospects of survival.

D. Abdication of decision-making to the scientific community, although such decisions affect daily living as much as political decisions.

E. Absence of built-in ethics regulating conduct of scientists.

F. Scientific potential, available to those who can command it, to produce a mass society stamping out individualism, with resulting debasement of the quality of life.

G. Undermining of democratic principles of government resulting from the above.

II. OUTMODED PRINCIPLES IMPEDING SOLUTIONS

A. That the pursuit of knowledge for the sake of knowledge is a sacrosanct activity.

B. That science and freedom naturally support and complement each other.

C. That a principle of *laissez faire* should operate in science and technology, leaving scientists free to pursue whatever activity they please.

D. That scientists are so expert in their area that it is beyond the competence of lay people to interfere in their activities and, hence, that the decision-making process in scientific affairs should be left to scientists.

E. That law as presently administered is competent to protect society against the dangers of science.

F. That science has a built-in ethic which automatically restrains scientists from engaging in work which is damaging to society.

G. That the enrichment of the quality of life is a natural corollary to the progress of science.

H. That the main drive actuating scientists is the pursuit of knowledge, and that mundane politics are absent from the world of science.

I. That free dissemination of knowledge is an attribute of scientific activity.

J. That dangerous scientific knowledge can be kept away by law from the hands of unscrupulous elements within the state.

K. That as science advances, the law increases its resources for controlling the increased power produced by such scientific advances.

III. POSSIBLE SOLUTIONS

A. From within the scientific community

(1) Increasing awareness of the social impact of scientific work, through:
- (a) interdisciplinary education at qualifying level;
- (b) postgraduate exposure to social implications;
- (c) international organizations of scientists, for laying down professional guidelines.

(2) A charter of scientific ethics voluntarily adopted.

(3) Legal endorsement of such codes or guidelines.

(4) Voluntary moratoria.

B. State Action

(1) *Legislative restructuring*
- (a) Restructuring of legislatures, providing for scientific participation in the legislative process, e.g., a committee of the scientific institute of a country, with authority to participate in legislative discussions and, in certain cases, with the right to vote;
- (b) Provisions excluding from such committees of scientists those with a special interest in the subject of discussion;
- (c) "Devil's Advocates" drawn from the ranks of scientists, vested with legal rights to present to the legislature the opposition to a proposed measure;
- (d) Requirements that the discussions be thrown open to the public and be carried over the media, so as to generate greater public awareness and interest;
- (e) A possible scientific chamber as an adjunct to the legislative chamber, whose approval is sought before a scientifically oriented measure passes into law;
- (f) Legislative provisions withdrawing privileges of secrecy from scientific data;

(g) Legislation insulating scientific bodies from political and economic pressures;

(h) Legislation freeing scientists employed in government departments from risks involving career considerations.

(2) *Executive restructuring*

(a) Cutting across existing patterns of departmentalization so as to be able to reach for the growth points of science, whatever the ministry under whose aegis they may be found;

(b) Employment of interdisciplinary, trained bureaucrats with ability to make overall assessments of patterns of current scientific research;

(c) Skilled bureaucratic groups insulated from governmental pressures by statutory protections, reporting to appropriate legislative sub-committees;

(d) Setting up offices of technology assessment with competence to advise and recommend courses of action, perhaps with a presumption that such recommendations be followed unless they can be displaced;

(e) Insulation of such technology assessment boards from executive and political interference;

(f) Inclusion, in all planning agencies, of technology assessment personnel and the imposition of an obligation to consult with technology assessment boards;

(g) Open lines of communication between technology assessment authorities and the public;

(h) Technical hazards boards with power to appear before the legislature as lobbyists against schemes involving potential risks;

(i) Freedom of Information Acts withdrawing from lists of protected matters all items of scientific research, except those where secrecy is deemed vital by *ad hoc* vote of the legislature;

(j) Departmental science reporting, requiring departments to report to the public on scientific activities in their field.

(3) *Judicial Restructuring*

(a) A possible Scientific Division of Supreme or High Courts, corresponding to Divisions such as Probate, Divorce and Admiralty, which have been set up in the past to deal with special classes of litigation.

(b) Requirements that Judges appointed to this Division should combine a scientific background with their legal training;

(c) Possible co-opting of lay advisers or assessors — scientific or otherwise — to assist them.

(d) Provision for Judges to be made aware, when reaching a decision involving scientific matter, of possible impacts of their decisions upon the public — analogous to the Brandeis Brief;

(e) Vesting courts with jurisdiction to issue injunctions staying research on wider grounds than are now recognized by injunction law.

(f) Increased court power to order disclosure of scientific or research information upon a suit filed by a member of the public;

(g) The jurisdiction to require conformity by scientists and others with provisions to be embodied in a Charter of Science, which is to have legislative sanction;

(h) A possible review jurisdiction over decisions of groups of scientists, wherever ethical and sociological considerations are involved;

(i) The vesting of courts with a jurisdiction to hear and determine complaints by scientific workers regarding the ethical aspects of the work they are called upon to perform.

(j) An ombudsman in the realm of science, geared and empowered to receive and review complaints against the wielders of scientific power;

(k) Judicial apparatus, perhaps along with public assessors, to hear and determine "whistle blowing" complaints from scientific workers;

(l) A review of the adequacy of the adversary system — its possible abolition or modification for the purposes of the Scientific Division of the Courts.

C. Action by the Legal Profession

(1) Sub-committees of science-oriented members to keep an eye on the continuing challenges posed by science;

(2) Attempts, through such reviews as the *Jurimetrics Journal* of the A.B.A., to keep such problems in constant focus and draw the attention of the profession to them;

(3) Lending support to technological assessment at national and international levels;

(4) Helping refashion injunction procedure to enable issue of stay orders until a proper impact assessment has been made;

(5) Developing new theories of risk, liability, impact investigation, devil's advocacy, regulatory mechanisms, and ombudsman functions;

(6) Stipulating a broader interdisciplinary background in new recruits, fitting them to function as effective lawyers in a scientific age.

D The Universities

(1) Acting as repositories of information concerning all scientific activity within the university. This information to be available on request by public authority or individual desiring to take up a matter on behalf of the public;

(2) Co-ordination of such knowledge with other repositories of information;

(3) Sponsoring further interdisciplinary training at all levels, particularly of future scientists and lawyers;

(4) Acting as controllers of research, with the co-operation of scientific personnel involved;

(5) Devising machinery ensuring that University resources are not available on tap merely because external sources, government or otherwise, are prepared to provide funds;

(6) Setting up the necessary environment for scientists, lawyers, sociologists, and others to meet and cross-fertilize each other's thinking.

E. The Media

(1) The democratization of science by laying before the public the politics of science in the same way as the politics of politics;

(2) Information to the public regarding competition among the scientific fraternity for public funds — in particular, the conflict between the claims of "big science" involving sophisticated and expensive equipment, e.g., nuclear accelerator, and "little science";

(3) The provision to the media of a legal right of access to scientific decision-making processes and scientific information;

(4) Entitling the scientific reporter to the right of attendance at deliberations of scientific committees in the same way as parliamentary reporters have access to proceedings of parliament;

(5) The assumption by the media of a duty to focus public attention on scientific questions affecting the life of the community, and to provide sufficient data for the formation of informed opinion;

(6) Acceptance by public bodies who are the repositories of scientific information, of the principle of voluntary disclosure to the media;

(7) The reinforcement of departmental scientific reporting, not merely to the legislature, but also to the public;

(8) Bringing to the public notice various aspects of technology assessment on which the public can make a contribution.

F. The Military

(1) Reduction of military secrecy and of classified items;

(2) Alteration of public attitudes which consider that military technology is too crucial or too complex to allow of challenge or discussion;

(3) Recognition of the principle that humane and ethical considerations can override even military considerations and entitle the public voice to prevail, e.g., germ warfare or atomic weapons;

(4) Increasing civilian control over military scientific technology.

G. International Activity

(1) Unesco to build up public awareness of the dangers to humanity posed by science;

(2) International organizations concerned with human rights to draw attention to the threats resulting from present and possible scientific developments;

(3) The passing of covenants embodying principles relating to public control of dangerous science;

(4) The setting up of effective international technology assessment agencies and the strengthening of existing mechanisms towards this end;

(5) Encouragement of the creation of a World Council of Scientists — a supra-national scientific body analogous to the World Health Organization;

(6) The adoption of fundamental principles of science-law doctrine, as above envisaged, leading to a new jurisprudence of science;

(7) Creation of international sanctions for ensuring compliance with ethical standards internationally adopted;

(8) Helping towards the incorporation into national law of science-law principles receiving international recognition.

IV. PRINCIPLES REQUIRING RECOGNITION

A. That interdisciplinary education is essential to suit the citizen for survival in a scientific age.

B. That there is no room for proprietary interests in science, and that scientific knowledge is public property.

C. That scientific decision-making vitally affects the public no less than political or commercial decision-making and cannot, therefore, be permitted in isolation from the public.

D. That scientific activity needs to be reported to the public and that exemptions from such publicity be limited to most exceptional circumstances.

E. That the principle that the pursuit of knowledge for its own sake is sacrosanct must yield in the face of the "brink situation".

F. That the era of *laissez-faire* in scientific activity is past.

G. That the scientist must accept the moral responsibility for his work and its foreseeable consequences.

H. That the scientific ethic must be broadened beyond loyalty to truth to take account of the objectives of a given piece of research.

I. That a body of scientific ethics is necessary to be worked out by the scientists themselves, and to be given legislative sanction and implementation.

J. That it may become necessary to encyst dangerous scientific knowledge to prevent further research upon it.

APPENDIX B

Proposed UN Declaration of Scientific Responsibility in Relation to Nuclear Weaponry

A central theme underlying this volume has been the need to step up the sensitivities of scientists to the social and human rights implications of their work. This can be achieved by stepping up the social awareness content in scientific education, by the evolution of internal ethical standards and a climate of opinion within the profession, by professional codes adopted voluntarily by the profession, by external guidelines, by externally imposed standards and, finally, by legal regulation. As one travels up the scale from internally induced self-awareness to externally imposed rules of conduct, there is a progressive erosion of the autonomy of the profession. Ideally, all regulation should come from within.

However, the story of modern human rights has illustrated the process by which externally adopted standards, if universally accepted, could gradually infuse themselves into the internal consciousness of vast numbers of people and, indeed, entire populations. The aspirational principles embodied in the Universal Declaration of Human Rights have now become internalised in the minds of the world population as acceptable and necessary minimum standards of conduct. So, also, have several Declarations of the General Assembly in the human rights field. They have no binding force, but their formulation in a Declaration helps forward the process of internalization of the norms they contain.

With this in view, the following Declaration on the responsibilities of scientists engaged in manufacturing nuclear weapons was formulated by the author in 1985, and had the advantage of being considered from a variety of angles.

It was looked upon by some as a welcome move to formulate international guidelines for nuclear weapons scientists, but was looked upon by others as amounting to a possible erosion of the autonomy of scientists. The *Encyclopaedia of Social Inventions*, London, 1989,* reproduced it among its selection of ideas for teaching social problems and improving the quality of life.

Olof Palme, Prime Minister of Sweden, in a letter to the author dated 6 December 1985, while welcoming certain aspects of it, drew attention to the need that the motive force for regulation should come from within the community of scientists. His letter emphasizes the importance of scientists self-regulating themselves. This is an important aspect which no study of this question can afford to lose sight of.

The proposed Declaration, as appearing in *The Encyclopaedia of Social Inventions*, is reproduced below, followed by the letter from Olof Palme, which is reproduced by kind permission of the Government of Sweden.

Possibly the optimum means to the desired end is a combination of internal restraints and a non-binding expression of external concern, which helps, without any attempts at compulsion, in focusing the attention of scientists on matters which are perceived internationally as encroaching upon human rights or humanitarian principles.

* *Encyclopaedia of Social Inventions: Over 500 of the best ideas from around the world — new and imaginative (non-technological) visions, systems, services and projects for teaching social problems and improving the quality of life*, Nicholas Albery and Valerie Yule (eds.), Institute for Social Inventions, London, 1989, pp. 194–196.

Proposed UN Declaration of Scientific Responsibility in Relation to Nuclear Weaponry

Preamble

THE GENERAL ASSEMBLY

Recognizing that in an age dominated by science and technology, it is essential that science and technology should be devoted to the service of humanity

Gravely concerned that the development and production of nuclear weapons and the nuclear arms race are endangering the future of humanity and indeed of life on this planet

Conscious that the most recent and meticulous scientific inquiries have established the probability of a nuclear winter with disastrous consequences to humanity and our planet in the event of a nuclear confrontation

Realizing that the nuclear arms race would be impossible to sustain without the active co-operation of scientists and technologists

Taking account of the fact that the general principles of international law as contained in

a. International custom

b. The general principles of law recognized by civilized nations

c. Judicial decisions and the teachings of jurists

d. International Covenants

place beyond doubt the illegality of the use of nuclear weaponry, having regard *inter alia* to its violation of the principles of proportionality, discrimination, aggravation of pain and suffering, nullification of a return to peace and inviolability of neutral states

Aware that the use of nuclear weaponry would undoubtedly result in ecocide, genocide and, if there are any survivors, in massive intergenerational damage

Convinced that the concept of a limited nuclear war is unrealistic and a nuclear war once started is totally unlikely to be contained

Persuaded that the concepts of self-defence and deterrence have become meaningless in the context of nuclear weaponry and thus afford no justification for their production, possession, testing or deployment

Mindful that the use, production, testing, possession and deployment of nuclear weapons thus constitute a violation of international law and a crime against humanity

Recalling that this Assembly by Resolution 3384(XXX) of 10 November 1975 proclaimed the Declaration on the Use of Scientific and Technological Progress in the Interests of Peace and for the Benefit of Mankind and has since taken numerous steps towards the implementation of this resolution, including the passing of Resolution 37/189A of 18 December 1982 calling upon all States, specialized agencies, intergovernmental and non-governmental organizations to take the necessary measures to ensure that the results of scientific and technological progress are used exclusively in the interests of international peace, for the benefit of humanity and for promoting and encouraging respect for human rights and fundamental freedoms

Noting that the Human Rights Committee of the United Nations at its 563rd meeting (23rd session) held on 2 November 1984 in its general comment 14(23)c/(article 6) declared that the production, testing, possession, deployment and use of nuclear weapons should be prohibited and recognized as a crime against humanity

Noting also that the said Committee in the said general comment called upon all States, whether Parties to the Covenant or not, to take urgent steps unilaterally and by agreement to rid the world of this menace

Persuaded that the legal and moral responsibility borne by scientists participating in such activities is today infinitely greater than at the time of the creation of the first nuclear weapons by reason *inter alia* of the greater knowledge now available of the disastrous atmospheric, agricultural, medical and social impacts of the use of nuclear weaponry, the possibility of nuclear retaliation, the enormously enhanced destructive power of current nuclear weaponry and the vast nuclear arsenals now available in the event of nuclear war

Deeply moved by the consideration that the power of science is such, in the words of the Russell-Einstein Manifesto, as to open the way to a new paradise or lead to the risk of universal death

Believing that the participation of scientists and technologists is crucial to the determination of the choice between these alternatives

Convinced that the principle of individual responsibility for crimes against humanity is well established in international law

Convinced also that superior orders do not constitute a defence in international law in regard to crimes against humanity and *Determined* that in the light of the above circumstances a consideration of the responsibility of scientists and technologists engaged in the nuclear weapons enterprise should no longer be further delayed by the international community,

This Assembly hereby *reaffirms* the principles that

(a) the use, production, possession, testing and deployment of nuclear weapons are contrary to international law and constitute a crime against humanity

(b) the participation in scientific or technological research in this area is contrary to international law and is a crime against humanity

(c) those who consciously participate in the manufacture of nuclear weapons and nuclear weapons research are personally guilty of a violation of international law and of a crime against humanity and/or of complicity in such acts

(d) such activity is incompatible with the dominant principle underlying all scientific activity, namely service to humanity, and is therefore unethical and contrary to the express Declarations of this Assembly

and *calls upon* all scientists and technologists throughout the world to abide by the legal and ethical obligations outlined in this document and to desist from any activity involving the development, production, testing, possession, deployment or use of nuclear weapons.

Prime Minister's office
Address Statsrådsberedningen
S–103 33 STOCKHOLM
Sweden

Dnr 6462/85 1985-12-06

C.G. Weeramantry, LL.D.
Professor of Law
Monash University
CLAYTON, Victoria 3168
Australia

Dear Professor Weeramantry,

Thank you for your letter of October 23 1985.

I share your conviction that there is no more urgent task for mankind than to try to reduce, and ultimately eliminate, the threat of nuclear war.

Negotiations have produced some concrete results, for example the Non-Proliferation Treaty (NPT), and they should not be underestimated. But by and large the nuclear arms race continues unabated. The main responsibility for halting and reversing this ominous process falls on the nuclear-weapon powers themselves.

For that reason it is my firm belief that efforts of the international community to halt the nuclear arms race should primarily be directed towards influencing the Governments of the nuclear-weapon states to take concrete measures aimed at real disarmament, such as concluding a comprehensive test ban treaty.

Your letter and the proposed UN Declaration of Scientific Responsibility in Relation to Nuclear Weaponry attached to it contains many elements of value for the further discussions on the issue of eliminating the nuclear threat. However, in the view of the Swedish Government, the General Assembly should not, as a matter of principle, take decisions with the purpose of restricting the activities of individual scientists. Rather it is up to the scientific community itself to, through its different organizations, consider the drafting of an ethical code concerning the involvement of scientists in programmes of research and development relating to .nuclear weapons. The General Assembly should, in my opinion, give priority to the task of inducing the Governments of the nuclear weapon states to reach agreements on concrete measures of disarmament.

In a statement I delivered on the occasion of the commemoration of the Fortieth Anniversary of the United Nations I presented the Swedish Government's view on, *inter alia*, the nuclear arms race. I enclose a copy of the statement in the hope that it will be of interest to you.

Yours sincerely,

Olof Palme

Index